Paths of Song

Trends in Classics – Supplementary Volumes

Edited by
Franco Montanari and Antonios Rengakos

Associate Editors
Evangelos Karakasis · Fausto Montana · Lara Pagani
Serena Perrone · Evina Sistakou · Christos Tsagalis

Scientific Committee
Alberto Bernabé · Margarethe Billerbeck
Claude Calame · Jonas Grethlein · Philip R. Hardie
Stephen J. Harrison · Richard Hunter · Christina Kraus
Giuseppe Mastromarco · Gregory Nagy
Theodore D. Papanghelis · Giusto Picone
Tim Whitmarsh · Bernhard Zimmermann

Volume 58

Paths of Song

The Lyric Dimension of Greek Tragedy

Edited by
Rosa Andújar, Thomas R. P. Coward and
Theodora A. Hadjimichael

DE GRUYTER

ISBN 978-3-11-068527-5
e-ISBN (PDF) 978-3-11-057591-0
e-ISBN (EPUB) 978-3-11-057399-2
ISSN 1868-4785

Library of Congress Cataloging-in-Publication Data
A CIP catalog record for this book has been applied for at the Library of Congress.

Bibliographic information published by the Deutsche Nationalbibliothek
The Deutsche Nationalbibliothek lists this publication in the Deutsche Nationalbibliografie;
detailed bibliographic data are available in the Internet at http://dnb.dnb.de.

© 2019 Walter de Gruyter GmbH, Berlin/Boston
This volume is text- and page-identical with the hardback published in 2018.
Editorial Office: Alessia Ferreccio and Katerina Zianna
Logo: Christopher Schneider, Laufen
Printing: CPI books GmbH, Leck
♾ Printed on acid-free paper
Printed in Germany

www.degruyter.com

Preface

This collective volume stems from an international conference with the title 'Paths of Song: Interactions Between Greek Lyric and Tragedy' that was held at University College London UK in April 2013. The conference was organised by Michael Carroll, Thomas Coward, and Theodora Hadjimichael and was sponsored by the A.G. Leventis Foundation (UCL Leventis Fund), KCL Classics, the Institute of Classical Studies, the Faculty Institute of Graduate Studies at UCL, and the Gilbert Murray Trust. The conference had a truly international and welcoming character, and the high quality and thought-provoking agenda provided the stimulus for enthusiastic discussions in a friendly and well-run atmosphere.

Of the twenty-one papers that were presented at the above event, thirteen appear in this volume in revised and reworked versions, while some of the other conference papers have already been published in other venues. We thank Andrew Ford for taking up the task of writing an Afterword to the volume and Enrico Emanuele Prodi who contributed to this volume with a new chapter different from the paper that he presented at the 'Paths of Song' conference. We would like to thank the contributors to this volume for their cooperation and patience during the peer-review process for publication, as well as the anonymous readers for their generous feedback and helpful comments which much improved the presentation of this volume.

The volume was prepared for publication while Rosa Andújar was the A. G. Leventis Research Fellow at University College London and while Theodora Hadjimichael held a post-doctoral research fellowship at Ludwig-Maximilians-Universität in Munich Germany that was funded by the DFG Exzellenzinitiative. The financial support of both of their research during this period is gratefully acknowledged.

Rosa Andújar
Thomas R.P. Coward
Theodora A. Hadjimichael

Table of Contents

Abbreviations —— IX

Rosa Andújar, Thomas R.P. Coward, and Theodora A. Hadjimichael
Introduction —— 1

I Tragic and Lyric Poets in Dialogue

P. J. Finglass
Stesichorus and Greek Tragedy —— 19

Thomas R.P. Coward
'Stesichorean' Footsteps in the *Parodos* of Aeschylus' *Agamemnon* —— 39

Pavlos Sfyroeras
Pindar at Colonus: A Sophoclean Response to *Olympians* 2 and 3 —— 65

Lucia Athanassaki
Talking Thalassocracy in Fifth-century Athens: From Bacchylides' 'Theseus Odes' (17 & 18) and Cimonian Monuments to Euripides' *Troades* —— 87

II Refiguring Lyric Genres in Tragedy

Laura Swift
Competing Generic Narratives in Aeschylus' *Oresteia* —— 119

Andrea Rodighiero
How Sophocles Begins: Reshaping Lyric Genres in Tragic Choruses —— 137

Anastasia Lazani
Constructing Chorality in *Prometheus Bound*: The Poetic Background of Divine Choruses in Tragedy —— 163

Alexandros Kampakoglou
Epinician Discourse in Euripides' Tragedies: The Case of *Alexandros* —— 187

III Performing the Chorus: Ritual, Song, and Dance

Richard Rawles
Theoric song and the Rhetoric of Ritual in Aeschylus' *Suppliant Women* —— 221

Giovanni Fanfani
What melos for Troy? Blending of Lyric Genres in the First *Stasimon* **of Euripides'** *Trojan Women* —— 239

Rosa Andújar
Hyporchematic Footprints in Euripides' *Electra* —— 265

Enrico Emanuele Prodi
Dancing in Delphi, Dancing in Thebes: The Lyric Chorus in Euripides' *Phoenician Women* —— 291

Naomi A. Weiss
Performing the Wedding Song in Euripides' *Iphigenia in Aulis* —— 315

Timothy Power
New Music in Sophocles' *Ichneutae* —— 343

Andrew Ford
Afterword: On the Nonexistence of Tragic Odes —— 367

Bibliography —— 381

Notes on Contributors —— 415

Index of Proper Names and Subjects —— 419

Index Locorum —— 433

Abbreviations

ABV	Beazley, J. D. (1956), *Attic Black-figure Vase-painters*, Oxford.
BNJ	Worthington, I. (ed.) (2006-present), *Brill's New Jacoby*, Brill Online.
CAH	*Cambridge Ancient History*, 2nd edn. (Cambridge 1961– ; 1st edn. 1923–39)
DAGM	Pöhlmann, E. / West, M. L. (2001), *Documents of Ancient Greek Music: The Extant Melodies and Fragments Edited and Transcribed with Commentary*, Oxford.
EGM	Fowler, R. L. (2000–2013), *Early Greek Mythography*, 2 vols., Oxford.
FGE	Page, D. L. (1981), *Further Greek Epigrams*, revised and prepared for publication by R. D. Dawe and J. Diggle, Cambridge.
FGrHist	Jacoby, F. et al. (1923–1958), *Die Fragmente der griechischen Historiker*, 15 vols., Leiden and Boston.
FHG	Müller, K. / Müller, Th. (1841–1873), *Fragmenta Historicorum Graecorum*, 5 vols., Paris.
GEF	West, M. L. (2003), *Greek Epic Fragments. From the Seventh to the Fifth Centuries B.C.*, London and Cambridge MA.
H–C	Hansen, P. A. / Cunningham, I. C. (2009), *Hesychii Alexandrini Lexicon. Volumen IV. T–Ω* (Sammlung griechischer und lateinischer Grammatiker 11/4) Berlin and Boston.
IEG	West, M. L. (1989–1992), *Iambi et Elegi ante Alexandrum cantati*, 2nd edn., Oxford.
IG	*Inscriptiones Graecae* (Berlin 1873-present day). [Roman numerals indicate the volume; index figures the edition, Arabic numerals the number of the inscription. Thus, IG II³ 558 is inscription no. 558 in the third edition of volume II.]
KPS	Krumeich, R. / Pechstein, N. / Seidensticker, B. (eds.) (1999), *Das griechische Satyrspiel*, Darmstadt.
LIMC	*Lexicon Iconographicum Mythologiae Classicae* (1981–1999), 8 vols. plus indexes, Zurich, Munich, and Düsseldorf.
M-W	Merkelbach, R. / West, M. L. (1967), *Fragmenta Hesiodea*, Oxford.
PCG	Austin, C. / Kassel, R. (eds.) (1983–1998) *Poetae Comici Graeci*, 8 vols., Berlin and Boston. Vol 1 *Comoedia Dorica Mimi Plyaces* (2001); vol. 2 *Agathenor-Aristonymus* (1991); vol. 3.2 *Aristophanes Testimonia et Fragmenta* (1984); vol. 4 *Aristophon – Crobulus* (1983); vol. 5 *Damoxenus – Magnes* (1986); vol. 6.2 *Menander* (1998).
PEG	Bernabé, A. (1996–2007), *Poetae Epici Graeci. Testimonia et Fragmenta*, 2nd edn., 2 vols., Stuttgart, Munich, Leipzig, Berlin, New York. [1st edn of vol. I 1987]
PMG	Page, D. L. (1967), *Poetae Melici Graeci*, Oxford.
PMGF	Davies, M. (1991), *Poetarum Melicorum Graecorum Fragmenta* Vol. 1, Oxford.
SH	Lloyd-Jones, H. / Parsons, P. (1983), *Supplementum Hellenisticum*, Texte und Kommentare 11; Berlin and Boston.
S-M	Snell, B., rev. Maehler, H. (1987–1989), *Pindari Carmina cum Fragmentis*, 8th edn., 2 vols., Leipzig.
TrGF	*Tragicorum Graecorum Fragmenta*, 5 vols., Göttingen. Vol. 1 *Didascaliae Tragicae, Catalogi Tragicorum et Tragoediarum, Testimonia et Fragmenta Tragicorum Minorum* (ed. B. Snell; 1971, 2nd edn. 1986); vol. 2 *Fragmenta*

	Adespota (eds. R. Kannicht / B. Snell; 1981); vol. 3 *Aeschylus* (ed. S. Radt; 1985); vol. 4 *Sophocles* (ed. S. Radt; 1977, 2nd edn. 1999); vol. 5 *Euripides* (ed. R. Kannicht; 2 parts 2004).
Voigt	Voigt, E. -M. (1971), *Sappho et Alcaeus*. Fragmenta, Amsterdam.
Wehrli	Wehrli, F. (1967–1969), *Die Schule des Aristoteles. Texte und Kommentar*, 2nd edn., 10 vols., Basel and Stuttgart.
	[Heft 1] *Dikaiarchos*. [Heft 2] *Aristoxenos*. [Heft 3] *Klearchos*. [Heft 4] *Demetrios von Phaleron*. [Heft 5] *Straton von Lampsakos*. [Heft 6] *Lykon und Ariston von Keos*. [Heft 7] *Herakleides Pontikos*. [Heft 8] *Eudemos von Rhodos*. [Heft 9] *Phainias von Eresos. Chamaileon. Praxiphanes*. [Heft 10] *Hieronymos von Rhodos. Kritolaos und seine Schüler. Rückblick: der Peripatos in Vorchristlicher Zeit. Register*.

Rosa Andújar, Thomas R.P. Coward, and Theodora A. Hadjimichael
Introduction

Choral performance was the communal mixing bowl of ancient Greek song-culture. Choruses performed at a multitude of festivals both inside and outside the *polis*, whether representing sacred delegations at cult centres or promoting the identity of the commissioning *polis* (*theōria*),[1] while songs performed by a chorus regularly featured alongside rituals and sacrifices (e.g. *paianes, dithyramboi, humnoi,* and *partheneia*). As performers and poets travelled to different venues or gathered at particular places on a regular basis, the features of a song or type of song became standardised. Festivals and associated musical competitions created the need for the performance of repeated tasks, such as cult songs and competitive musical and dramatic performances, all of which further fostered a repertoire of poetry.[2] Assuming that the Athenian dramatic viewing audience actively participated in this larger performance- and song-culture, either as members of *kuklioi khoroi*, of dithyrambic choruses, of *theōric* choruses sent to pan-Hellenic sanctuaries, or even as audiences to such lyric performances, we might expect that they would have been aware of myriad forms of non-dramatic lyric beyond the tragic stage.

The extant plays testify to the tragedians' alertness of the genre's complex lyric nature, which was indebted to this broader choral culture. Firstly, they use the term *melos* to identify the choral odes as lyric components, a term which not only distinguishes the sung from the recited parts of tragedy, but also further draws attention to the manner in which choral odes may be seen as foreign bodies that have been inserted into tragedy.[3] Tragedians also liberally make use of various traditions of the wider song-culture, both appropriating and misappropriating a number of features of non-dramatic lyric songs and performances. Specific non-dramatic lyric genres are named throughout the extant trag-

---

[1] See Rutherford 2013 on *theōria*.
[2] Cf. Pl. *Ion* fr. 530a; Timon. fr. 754 F1 *FGrHist*; Chamael. fr. 30 Martano = 28 Wehrli; Athen. 14.620c.
[3] E.g. *melos*, Aesch. *Suppl.* 1023; *Pers.* 1042; *Sept.* 835; *Suppl.* 1023; *Ag.* 706; *Eum.* 329; [Aesch.] *PV* 555. *Molpē* and *melpein* are similarly used, e.g. Aesch. *Ag.* 106, *Eum.* 1043 and 1046, and Eur. *Heracl.* 780. Both Aeschylus and Euripides situate their odes within the framework of a larger song-culture, alluding in sophisticated ways to the taxonomy of this culture; see Rutherford 2001, 118 and below on Euripides and New Music. Sophocles, in contrast, is relatively silent in this particular practice, although see the contributions of Sfyroeras and Power in this volume.

edies, which implies that the tragedians consciously incorporate particular lyric song-types into the poetics of the tragic genre. Such incorporation additionally reveals an awareness of the specific generic characteristics and functions of each lyric genre, as well as of the original context within which the integrated lyric song-type was performed. Individual characters likewise appear mindful of song traditions and of particular places associated with certain songs,[4] as does the tragic chorus in moments when they state that they will perform a particular type of song.[5] Moreover, the conscious labelling and naming of specific lyric songs in the tragic action would have functioned as special cues for the audience itself.[6]

Euripides' *Hercules Furens* offers an example of a wide-range of poetological imagery that a tragedian can employ. In the first *stasimon* (Eur. *HF* 348–450), Euripides demonstrates an intimate familiarity with the larger landscape of song-culture, as the chorus invoke different traditions of song. Prior to the ode, the family of Heracles is in despair: Amphitryon and Megara, ready to die and believing Heracles to have perished, have taken the children indoors in order to dress them for their funeral. The chorus, alone on stage and unable to help Heracles' family begin to sing a song of praise with threnodic and paeanic elements for Heracles, whom they believe to be dead. Their song opens with a striking programmatic statement:[7]

αἴλινον μὲν ἐπ' εὐτυχεῖ
μολπᾶι Φοῖβος ἰαχεῖ
τὰν καλλίφθογγον κιθάραν (350)
ἐλαύνων πλήκτρωι χρυσέωι·
ἐγὼ δὲ τὸν γᾶς ἐνέρων τ'
ἐς ὄρφναν μολόντα παῖδ',
εἴτε Διός νιν εἴπω
εἴτ' Ἀμφιτρύωνος ἶνιν,
ὑμνῆσαι στεφάνωμα μό- (355)
χθων δι' εὐλογίας θέλω.
γενναίων δ' ἀρεταὶ πόνων
τοῖς θανοῦσιν ἄγαλμα.

(Eur. *HF* 348–58)

---

4 E.g. Eur. *Alc.* 357 and 436–55, *El.* 112–66, *HF* 1346, *Hyp.* 752 h *TrGF*[5.2].
5 E.g. Aesch. *Ag.* 106; Eur. *HF* 676–9, *Erech.* 370.5–10 *TrGF*[5.1], Aesch. *Suppl.* 1023, *Sept.* 835, *Ag.* 979; *Eum.* 329, 342, 1043, 1047.
6 Roselli 2011, 19–20 emphasizes the collaborative role of the audience at a performance, whereby the audience's expectations and interests should be successfully negotiated through the performance.
7 The text is that of OCT and the translation is that of LCL, at points modified.

Phoebus sings a lament after a song of good fortune as he strikes his sweet-voiced lyre with a golden plectrum. In like fashion, I wish to hymn with praise, as a crown of his labours, the man gone into the dark of the earth, the realm of the dead, whether I am to call him the son of Zeus, or the offspring of Amphitryon. For high deeds of noble toil are a glory to the dead.

The chorus justify their choice of song, citing the divine precedent of Apollo playing the lyre, who shifts from singing about joy (ἐπ' εὐτυχεῖ / μολπᾶι) to singing about sorrow (αἴλινον).[8] It is unclear whether the chorus have a particular song in mind or are referring more generally to songs that are performed to the lyre. The *stasimon* is nevertheless presented as a mixture of poetic features and genres. The ode additionally contains a clustering of epinician motifs,[9] and the addition of this epinician language transforms the ode into a song of praise in honour of Heracles at the point where a lament (*thrēnos*) might have been expected.[10] The reference to Apollo also evokes the paean, and through his figure the chorus offer a divine precedent for their song.[11] Here, the chorus draw on several forms of genres using periphrasis (*eulogia*) rather than using specific label terms. This is supplemented by outlining the setting and purpose for their song, as well as by evoking a number of their performative features and *topoi* (e.g. *stephanōma*, a pervasive metaphor for song in epinician).

In the second *stasimon* (637–700) the chorus begin to refer generally to song traditions, singing activities, and precedents, while employing label terms of specific lyric genres. The chorus now assert their devotion to song and their lasting praise of the returning Heracles in a paean which praises his divine parentage and beneficence:[12]

---

8 Cf. Pind. *Ol.* 6; *Ol.* 7; *Nem.* 5; Bacch. 12.1–3.
9 Heracles is set up as a model of an athletic victor, and as in Pindaric victory odes the subsequent catalogue of labours (359–441), which notes their benefits to mankind, focuses on the places where the events occurred rather than the moment of victory. Ὑμνῆσαι στεφάνωμα μό-/χθων δι' εὐλογίας θέλω, has several epinician motifs: the chorus declare their status as performer of a praise-song and their ownership of the praise (e.g. Pind. *Ol.* 2.1–6, 3.1–9, 4.1–5, 7.1–10, 9.21–7, 10.1–6, 11.8–15, 13.11–2, *Pyth.* 2.1–6, 9.1–4, 10.4–7, *Nem.* 1.7, 3.9–17, 4.9–13, 5.1–5, 10.19–22, *Isth.* 1.1–12, 8.5–7. cf. also Bacch. 1.183–4, 5.16–33); praise of family and paternity and song is a reward for virtue (e.g. *Pyth.* 1.92–4; Bacch. 1.181–4), and the song is construed as a form of gift exchange, on which Kurke 1991, 97–107.
10 See Swift 2010, 124–9 for further discussion.
11 See Rutherford 2001, 120 on this oxymoronic use of paeans and dirges together.
12 Each of the four stanzas in this *stasimon* is a separate entity, leading up to the praise of Heracles. See Kranz 1933, 177 ff. and Barrett 1964, 186–7 for further discussion on the independence of stanzas in tragic choral odes.

οὐ παύσομαι τὰς Χάριτας
ταῖς Μούσαισιν συγκαταμει-
γνύς, ἡδίσταν συζυγίαν. (675)
μὴ ζώιην μετ' ἀμουσίας,
αἰεὶ δ' ἐν στεφάνοισιν εἴην·
ἔτι τοι γέρων ἀοιδὸς
κελαδῶ Μναμοσύναν,
ἔτι τὰν Ἡρακλέους (680)
καλλίνικον ἀείδω
παρά τε Βρόμιον οἰνοδόταν
παρά τε χέλυος ἑπτατόνου
μολπὰν καὶ Λίβυν αὐλόν.
οὔπω καταπαύσομεν (685)
Μούσας αἵ μ' ἐχόρευσαν.

παιᾶνα μὲν Δηλιάδες
<ναῶν> ὑμνοῦσ' ἀμφὶ πύλας
τὸν Λατοῦς εὔπαιδα γόνον,
εἱλίσσουσαι καλλίχοροι (690)
παιᾶνας δ' ἐπὶ σοῖς μελάθροις
κύκνος ὣς γέρων ἀοιδὸς
πολιᾶν ἐκ γενύων
κελαδήσω· τὸ γὰρ εὖ
τοῖς ὕμνοισιν ὑπάρχει. (695)
Διὸς ὁ παῖς· τᾶς δ' εὐγενίας
πλέον ὑπερβάλλων <ἀρετᾶι>
μοχθήσας τὸν ἄκυμον
θῆκεν βίοτον βροτοῖς
πέρσας δείματα θηρῶν. (700)

(Eur. *HF* 673–700)

I shall not stop mingling the Graces and the Muses, a union most sweet. May I never live a Muse-less life! Ever may I go garlanded! Old singer that I am, I still sing the praise of Mnemosyne, still hymn Heracles' glorious victory in company with Bacchus giver of wine, in company with the song of the seven-stringed tortoise shell and the Libyan pipe. Never shall I check the Muses who have made me dance!

A *paian* about their temple gates the maidens of Delos sing to the fair son of Leto, weaving their lovely dance steps. And *paianes* about your house, I, an aged singer, swan-like from my hoary throat shall pour forth. For the power of right is in my hymns. He is the son of Zeus. But surpassing even this high birth with his deeds of valour, he has made peaceful by his struggles the life of mortals and overcome dread monsters.

This excerpt combines features and themes from a *paian* (691–4), an *enkōmion* and a *kōmos* revel-song (Ἡρακλέους / καλλίνικον ἀείδω (680–1) in a passage in which both labels are clearly marked. The chorus praise Heracles to the accompaniment of music and wine, and the catalogue of merits (694–700) echoes those of the *laudandus* in a victory ode.¹³ In the first *stasimon*, the chorus drew a parallel between their own singing of praise songs for the living and dead and Apollo's singing of paeans, and here, in the third stanza, they compare themselves to Delian maidens (an example of choral projection),¹⁴ who perform a *paian* in honour of Apollo.¹⁵ In this passage, as the chorus evokes a lyric tradition of praising mortals and deities, they establish their credentials both as praise poets and as performers, and declare that their praise will have no end (οὐ παύσομαι), a declaration that touches on the promise made in lyric poems that its effect will last forever.¹⁶ Both these *stasima* showcase the diverse manner in which tragedy incorporates and evokes lyric genres: it refers to and frames its odes within other song traditions, ranging from evocations of features by means of marked labels to unmarked features perceptible in performance. It is therefore possible for a tragic poet to communicate an association with lyric through marked or unmarked references in performance, by the use of features of particular genres, and by repeating or reformulating themes, imagery, content, and vocabulary.

These lyric associations assume further significance when we consider the probable lyric expertise of the Athenian viewing audience in the fifth century BC, which no doubt witnessed many other non-dramatic performances as part of the annual cycle of competitions and festivals. The City Dionysia, held each year in early spring at fifth-century Athens, featured contests among three dramatists, each producing three tragedies and one satyr play, as well as a comic competition with three or five dramatists.¹⁷ The festival saw even larger numbers competing in dithyrambs, competitions which involved two choruses of fifty men and fifty boys for each Athenian tribe. With a thousand performers annually in the dithyrambic competition and another hundred or so in the dramatic productions, the state-sponsored dramatic competitions enjoyed an audience consisting of up to 7,000 spectators in the auditorium and many 'unofficial' spectators watching from the south slope of the Acropolis.¹⁸ Audiences would have

---

13 Parry 1965, 373.
14 Henrichs 1994–1995.
15 Rutherford 1994–1995, 124–5.
16 Cf. Ibyc. S151.48 *PMGF*; Bacch. 3.88–92; Pind. *Ol*. 10.91.
17 On the placement and performance of a satyr-play in a dramatic tetralogy, see Sansone 2015.
18 Recent excavations suggest that the capacity of the fifth-century theatre did not exceed 7,000 spectators, on which Csapo 2007, 97–100 with Goette's archaeological appendix to the chapter. See Cratinus fr. 372 *PCG*⁴, Eust. ε 64, and Photius α 505 with Roselli 2011, 72–5 on the space be-

been thus immersed as participants in an all-encompassing song-performance culture and would have been able to recognize, to differing degrees, many lyric and dramatic forms. Modern perceptions of tragedy need therefore to accommodate the likely fact that the viewing audience was well-versed in choral matters and as a result well poised to understand the associations, rhythms, and themes conjured up by the use of certain labels. An average Athenian might not have known particular texts, but he certainly might have known what a certain song-type or form tended to or ought to sound like in performance.[19]

Despite the fact that many of tragedy's odes are steeped in the language, imagery, and ritual elements of non-dramatic choruses, as demonstrated above, the genre's debts to particular lyric kinds of poetry have no place in Aristotle's conceptualization of a universal tragedy, which has had an unparalleled influence over modern understandings of the genre. For example, though the philosopher recognizes song (μελοποιία) as being one of the most important sources of pleasure (1450b15–16), he unusually makes little mention of types of lyric genres or songs in the *Poetics*.[20] His emphasis on a universal art that transcends the particularities of history produces a specific dehistoricised and depoliticised reading of tragedy, from which the chorus is crucially absent.[21] Aristotle's relative silence on the tragic chorus is not only remarkable, given its fundamental and structural significance to the whole genre, but it is also partly responsible for modern rigid understandings of the tragic chorus' role and potential on stage. The few times when he does address the tragic chorus, he either insinuates its increasing irrelevance in the development of the form (*Poet.* 1449a15–17), or offers an ambiguous value judgment on its dramatic function (*Poet.* 1456a25–27). Aristotle's disparaging remarks, coupled with his downplaying of the role of the chorus throughout the text of the *Poetics* and above all his relentless focus on

---

neath a poplar tree in the south slope of the Acropolis from which many spectators watched dramatic performances.
19 See Revermann 2006a, 102 on the theatrical competence of a fifth century audience.
20 This is with the exception of dithyramb (1447a14, 1454a30–1), hymns and encomia (1448b25–27), the nome (1448a.14–15). Μελοποιία is Aristotle's usual term for 'lyric song': cf. Ar. *Metaph.* 993b15; *Pol.* 1341b24; *Poet.* 1449b33, 1450b16; *De poet.* F21 Janko. Other works, however, show that Aristotle was well versed in lyric forms, e.g. *Rhet.* 1400b5–8, 1409a1–3. Ford 2011 also shows that Aristotle was himself a poet. On song in Aristotle see Janko 2001, 62–4.
21 The philosopher pays remarkable little attention to the chorus itself in the *Poetics*; cf. Halliwell 1986, 250: 'the fundamental premises of Aristotle's theory of poetry and tragedy virtually dictate the devaluation and neglect of choral lyric.' See also Peponi 2013b, esp. 23–6. On tragedy as an abstract and universal art that is the result of the philosopher's juxtaposition of poetry and history (*Poet.* 9.1451b), see Billings 2014.

plot (*muthos*) as the 'soul of tragedy', suggest that the choral and sung parts of Greek tragedy occupy secondary and subsidiary importance.

One of the great virtues of tragic scholarship of recent decades is the manner in which it has fought against these universal ideas of the genre that originated from Aristotle. In the past four decades we have seen an explosion of a historicizing movement concerned with situating tragedy in its original socio-political, historical, performative, and religious context.[22] Given the importance of dramatic performances and the centrality of theatre to classical Athenian society, Rush Rehm and Simon Goldhill have characterised classical Athens as a 'performance-culture' within which the theatre gained social, religious, educational, and communicative importance.[23] The study of Greek song forms has also profited from this shift from text to performance, as scholars have similarly located Greek lyric genres in their wider contexts.

We recognise the importance of dramatic performances in fifth-century Athens, but we take this acknowledgement a step further in this volume, which stresses that fifth-century Athens was undeniably also a song-culture, wherein *mousikē*, that is performances of song, music, and dance, was integral to its socio-political, cultural, and religious core. *Paths of Song* thus bridges the two cultures that are perceived by scholars to comprise the poetic world of fifth- and fourth-century Athens – song-culture and performance-culture – and demonstrates how through its dramatic performances, Athens' performance-culture absorbed and adapted to its own needs its own song-culture that was formed in choral competitions at Athenian festivals, as well as the song-culture that originated beyond Athens and before the fifth century BC. As a number of contributions to this volume show, lyric song that was absorbed by tragedy often retained its ritualistic and social function, its generic identity, at times also its performative nature, though inevitably tragedy also adapted these external and non-tragic features into its own poetic fabric and core.

Paths of Song aims to locate ancient tragic drama within this larger map of Greek lyric activity, stressing tragedy's vital participation in the wider Greek song-and-performance culture. In doing so, it builds upon path-breaking recent research on the nature of ancient Greek song and choral activity, which situates

---

22 E.g. Vernant/Vidal-Naquet 1981; Winker/Zeitlin 1990; Martin 2007; Revermann/Wilson 2008; Carter 2011; Rosenbloom/Davidson 2011; Wyles 2011; Harrison/Liapis 2013; Marshall 2014. All these performance approaches to tragedy are ultimately indebted to Taplin 1977 and subsequent publications.
23 Rehm 1992, 3–11; Goldhill 1999.

Greek lyric poetry more fully in its original cultural and performative contexts.[24] Similarly, it adds to current scholarship on Athenian song-culture and the choral nucleus of fifth-century tragedy: starting from John Herington's seminal work,[25] scholars have revealed not only that many lyric genres continued to be performed in Athens alongside drama, but also that, in their extant plays and fragments, Aeschylus, Sophocles, and Euripides evoke and blend a variety of non-dramatic poetic genres with a persistence that surpasses mere tradition or incidental interest.[26] Given these advancements in both ancient Greek song and Athenian tragedy, the aim of *Paths of Song* is to rethink the broader relationship between ancient Greek lyric and tragedy. The essays in this volume illustrate the dynamic and nuanced relationship between these two poetic forms within the larger frame of Athenian song- and performance-culture, and foreground various important aspects of the interaction between the two. *Paths of Song* presents case-studies that have to date not been discussed in scholarship and picks up old questions again in order to address and answer them by combining literary and historical evidence, thus offering a variety of approaches that illustrate the myriad forms through which lyric is present and can be presented in tragedy.

The volume is organised into three sections to demonstrate central aspects of the dynamic interface between Greek lyric and tragedy. The first section, 'Tragic and Lyric Poets in Dialogue', examines the interplay between lyric and tragedy by illustrating relationships between specific tragic plays and lyric poets. The first pair of chapters offers new considerations about the range and limits of Stesichorean and lyric-epic influences on tragedy. The second pair of chapters moves to Pindar and Bacchylides respectively, and examines their positioning in the political and socio-cultural realms of fifth century Athens. All the chapters in this section consider the legacy of lyric poets and of the features and ideas of their poetry. It highlights both similarities and differences between the works of lyric and tragedy, as lyric features are adapted for tragic settings.

Patrick Finglass questions the *communis opinio* that Stesichorus had a wholesale influence on Attic tragedy and identifies more precise lines of influence and excludes others. He first surveys the evidence for the early transmission of Stesichorus and the presence of his works in Athens, and then proceeds through the extant Stesichorean corpus for which titles have survived. Finglass takes a different approach from the prevalent analysis of verbal similarities,

---

24 We now possess a far more nuanced picture of a number of genres of choral lyric genres than ever before, e.g. *epinikia*: Hornblower/Morgan 2007, Agócs/Carey/Rawles 2012a; *partheneia*: G. Ferrari 2008; dithyrambs: Kowalzig/Wilson 2013.
25 Herrington 1985.
26 See, e.g., Swift 2010 and Nooter 2012.

and instead analyses the material from a mythological perspective. Stesichorus' *Nostoi* and *Boarhunters*, along with *Geryoneis*, *Iliou Persis*, and *Eriphyle*, could have influenced the extant tragedies of Aeschylus, Sophocles, and Euripides, but the material is too fragmentary and the passages too specific to discern any connections. He identifies the impact of Stesichorus' *Oresteia* on Aeschylus and the later tragedians with plot elements, such as the dream of Clytemnestra, the bow of Apollo given to Orestes, and the recognition of Orestes and Electra by means of a lock of hair; the relationship between the *Thebais* fragment (fr. 97 Finglass = fr. 222b *PMGF*) and Euripides' *Phoenissae* in their differing portrayals of the Theban Queen; and probable similarities in the overall plot between the *Palinode* and Euripides' *Helen*. Finglass argues that Stesichorus should not be seen as a poet who merely laid the seeds of the tragedians, but rather offered fully fledged versions that the tragedians took advantage of to adopt and adapt in their works.

Thomas Coward argues that the *parodos* of Aeschylus' *Agamemnon* shows the influence of Stesichorus and citharodic epic in terms of its metre, language, and style. As the ode progresses, it evolves to present an Aeschylean version of the story and Aeschylus' own refiguration of older choral lyric. Coward starts with a survey of evidence for the performative context and content of citharodic epic and Stesichorean lyric-epic poetry, and demonstrates that the narrative style of the *parodos* shows several features that are found in the Stesichorean corpus. Coward shows, for example, that the presentation of *Agamemnon* has a Stesichorean or lyric-epic flavour to it, whereas Aeschylus has in mythological terms distanced himself from the epic/lyric versions of the sacrifice of Iphigeneia. This choral ode sets the tone and mood for the play, but the content of the myth shifts from the Stesichorean *Oresteia* to the Aeschylean version. He also tentatively suggests the musical mode that may have accompanied the *parodos*, by taking into account a comment in Aristophanes' *Frogs* (*Ran.* 1281–2) on the opening choral songs of Aeschylus and another by the ancient critic Timachidas of Rhodian Lindos (Aesch. T155 *TrGF*[3]) that Aeschylus performed his choral songs to the *orthios nomos*. Coward proposes an argument, based on the *testimonia* in terms of metre, sound, and format for this particular *nomos* and its connections with citharodic and choral lyric epic that the *parodos* could have sounded like an old style chorus.

Pavlos Sfyroeras argues for Pindar's particular place in the dramatic and political culture of late fifth-century Athens and considers what Sophocles would expect his Athenian spectators to recognize. He first examines some aspects of *Olympian* 3 that tacitly engage with Athenian ideology and may thus continue to resonate in Athens decades later. Then, he offers a reading of the two Sophoclean odes (the first and third *stasima* of Sophocles' *Oedipus at Colonus*) that show how, in some important ways, they constitute a diptych. He proposes that the themes and content of these *stasima* are a unified response to *Olympians* 2 and 3. Finally, he examines a set of historical circumstances, not yet considered in conjunction with *Oedipus at Colonus*, in order to demonstrate that the 'horizon of expectations' of the Athenian audience that Sophocles could count on was broader than has been assumed and to outline a frame in which this return to Pindar can be meaningfully inscribed. He proposes that an intertextual dialogue with the celebration of a Sicilian tyrant's Olympic victory enables Sophocles and his audience to reflect on recent developments in Sicily that may affect Athens' fortunes, perhaps even on the poetics of tragedy as a receptacle for lyric genres.

Lucia Athanassaki focuses on the prologue of Euripides' *Trojan Women* and argues that it conjures up the Athenian thalassocracy of the late sixth century onwards. She draws attention to its rationale, its challenges, and its threats in both its immediate context and over the *longue durée* through events recorded in Herodotus, Thucydides, and art. Athanassaki explores the thalassocratic message of the play and discusses its points of contact and contrast with a dithyramb of Bacchylides (*Ode* 17), which, like the Euripidean play, addressed the Athenians and their allies some 60 years before the production of *Trojan Women*. The dithyramb offers an optimistic account of the sea-dominion of the league at the time of Cimon, whereas the *Trojan Women* depict a far more complex world. The Bacchylidean dithyramb shows the privileges of divine favour and action, whereas the *Trojan Women* depicts a world in which mortals are responsible not only for what they do, but for what they fail to do. The paper briefly presents some of the reasons why Euripides did not need to presuppose his audience's familiarity with the Bacchylidean dithyramb, but notes some intriguing points of contact between the Euripidean play and Bacchylides' Theseus songs.

Building more specifically on the enquiries of John Herington and Laura Swift concerning the manner in which tragedy evokes and refigures particular individual lyric genres,[27] the second section of this volume, 'Refiguring Lyric Genres in Tragedy', presents a nuanced examination of the way in which tragedians play with multiple generic interactions, either by selecting and reworking material from the broader lyric tradition or by contrasting that same tradition. Whereas the first two chapters present general patterns across several plays, the final two trace specific characteristics of lyric poetry and genres in various tragic plays. The section as a whole demonstrates that tragedy is aware of the specifics of types of melic songs, or of lyric genres, in terms of generic characteristics or

---

[27] Herington 1985; Swift 2010.

features rooted in their primary performance. These particulars are both explored and exploited on the tragic stage in ways that the tragedians see fit for their own dramatic purposes. An essential conclusion that one can draw from this section is the rich and varied reception of lyric forms in tragedies. The discussion in whole demonstrates the differences between formal definitions of a particular genre and the manner in which this genre is dramatized on the tragic stage.

Laura Swift updates her own work with an analysis of the *Oresteia* to show how multiple song-types are at play simultaneously within the trilogy. She explores in her contribution how the tragedians use multiple lyric genres within a play to problematise a genre's normal associations or to create competing generic narratives. Since lyric genres carry normative associations and social norms, cases where we find the blending of multiple lyric genres are particularly suggestive, as the interaction creates tension between competing interpretative and ethical possibilities. Swift thus expands upon her previous work in which she had traced the tragic path of individual lyric genres.[28] The discussion concentrates on the *Oresteia*, where one can find systematic use of language derived from both the *paian* and the *epinikion*. It shows that the evocation of the *paian* and the epinician in the play could operate as narratological techniques. The *Oresteia* promotes a specific ethical and cultural standpoint, and the two genres come to reflect competing ethical forces. Swift demonstrates that for the tragedian language from the paeanic genre is associated with the possibility of divine intervention, whereas epinician language becomes connected with human struggle and violence. A number of passages also show that tension is often created between the tragic and the lyric narrative when the lyric conventions and imagery of a specific genre are misapplied in a tragic passage. The chapter overall brings forward the issue of the audience's expectations and interpretation, and how these two map onto generic conventions and cultural expectations of a poetic genre.

Andrea Rodighiero considers Sophocles in conjunction with specific Pindaric stylistic features, and focuses particularly on the *incipits* of a number of choral songs in Sophocles. The discussion centres on style, imagery, diction, and syntax, and the analysis shows that one can identify in Sophocles stylistic features taken from the lyric tradition. The lyric poet mostly used as a model by Sophocles is Pindar. The chapter takes as case studies the *parodos* in the *Antigone*, a fragment from the lost *Laocoon* (fr. 371 *TrGF*⁴), and passages from the *Trachiniae* and *Ajax*, and the analysis shows that Sophocles incorporates in

---

28 Swift 2010.

his text typical features of hymns, especially from Pindar. This incorporation, however, does not take the form of plain duplication or quotation. Rodighiero demonstrates how Sophocles often challenges the lyric tradition by re-contextualising and applying the received feature to situations other than their original content, or by elaborating as well as deconstructing well-known generic components. It becomes evident therefore that Sophocles may be aware of contemporary lyric production, but he reworks and transforms the traditional lyric imagery and language into new forms of sung and danced poetry.

Anastasia Lazani traces the parthenaic resonances in the presentation of the chorus in *Prometheus Bound* to the divine chorus in Alcman's *partheneia*, and thus sheds light both on the reception of non-tragic lyric by tragedy and on the construction of choral identity in drama, especially as regards divine choruses. The chorus of Oceanids in the *parodos* of the *Prometheus Bound* are assimilated to the status of human *parthenoi*, as they identify themselves in the Alcmanic *partheneia* and in wedding songs. Through references to the physical appearance of maidens and to the paraphernalia of a performance by maidens, the poet specifically recalls in the *Prometheus Bound* the attractive, socially viable human *parthenoi* of choral lyric and transposes them out of their usual ritual and cultic context into the wilderness of Scythia. The associations of grace, beauty, and peacefulness that are inherent to the performances of *partheneia* by maidens are maintained and employed in the specific tragedy to create a familiar social and performative framework that is re-contextualised for the needs of the *Prometheus Bound*. At the same time the mythic divine choruses of pre-dramatic poetry are materialized on the dramatic stage through its association with the performative reality of choral lyric, and Lazani demonstrates how the *partheneion* becomes the model of female chorality in the play. The analysis in the particular chapter also presents a unique *testimonium* for the survival and reception of Alcman in Athens, which probably predates Aristophanes' *Birds* and *Lysistrata*.

Alexandros Kampakoglou traces and discusses Pindar's epinician discourse in Euripides' plays and in more detail in his *Alexandros*. He examines the use of epinician motifs in the surviving fragments, and their importance for the reconstruction of the lost tragedy and the articulation of the Trojan Trilogy (*Alexandros, Palamedes, Trojan Women*). After exploring epinician discourse in a number of Euripidean tragedies (*Heracles, Alcestis, Electra, Bacchae*, and *Andromache*) Kampakoglou focuses on the *Alexandros*. He surveys the evidence for the influence of epinician poetry on the development of the plot and the presentation of the characters in the *Alexandros*, and discusses in particular the aristocratic idea of inherent excellence, the dissemination of *kleos*, the *nostos*, and reintegration motif as those are elaborated in the Pindaric odes. The epinician discourse that is identified in the play is employed as a tool in order to recognise the ironic touch of the tensions in the plot (mainly before the recognition of Paris as Priam's exposed son). Paris is socially transformed from a slave to Priam's legitimate son and from an anonymous foreigner to an epinician *laudandus*, whose glory and *aretē* however are not celebrated by a true *laudator* in the play. The overall discussion shows how the epinician language is employed in the particular tragedy, and offers a testimony of the continuous social function of an epinician celebration, though in an altered narrative context and also in other means.

Section three, 'Performing the Chorus: Ritual, Song, and Dance', articulates the manner in which the Athenian playwrights evoked lyric genres in order to discuss chorality and the performance of *mousikē* on the dramatic stage. The chapters in this section trace the manner in which the tragedians – and crucially this also includes Sophocles as a playwright of satyr drama – invoke both conceptions of non-dramatic choral activity and evocations of lyric genres during moments of choral self-referentiality, in which dramatic choruses specifically draw attention to the conditions of its own or another chorus' song, music, or dance.[29] The chapters in the section showcase a continuing and evolving engagement with lyric genres, such as dithyramb, *hymenaios*, epinician, *citharodia*, and the *hyporchēma*, particularly in late Euripidean tragedies. As a result this section extends the discussion of the relationship between lyric and tragedy to the New Music movement, and thus to the increasing trends in professionalization and specialization that are associated with Athenian drama in the last quarter of the fifth century. These chapters also clarify various neglected aspects relating to the performance of tragic odes, such as the category of 'dithyrambic *stasimon*' that is frequently applied to Euripidean odes which have been deemed dramatically irrelevant, and even the manner in which dance might have been performed and self-consciously discussed in tragedy. By illustrating the manner in which tragedians invoke other lyric genres in self-reflective dramatic odes that are concerned with ritual and music, this section moves the discussion of the place of lyric genres in tragedy beyond the account of reception and refiguration of lyric genres that was advanced in the previous section.

The contribution of Richard Rawles examines the rich chorality of the *Suppliant Women* of Aeschylus, which is unique among surviving tragedies in its use of a chorus as the main character. His chapter studies the manner in which Aeschylus continually draws attention to the Danaids' status as a chorus that performs various non-dramatic choral activities and ritual, as a group which sings a

---

[29] This is a phenomenon illustrated by Henrichs 1994–1995.

processional song with characteristics of hymns and *hymenaioi*, and which also approaches Argos as theoric chorus. As Rawles concludes, attention to the chorus' own presentation of its excessive chorality reveals the manner in which the tragedian plays with audience expectations of ritual in general.

Giovanni Fanfani reflects on the performative implications suggested by the first *stasimon* of *Trojan Women*, which pits two New Musical genres against one another, the citharodic *nomos* and the dithyramb. Applying the results of the most recent scholarship on the dithyramb, the chapter reassesses both the meta-literary stance offered at the opening of the ode and the category itself of 'dithyrambic *stasimon*' that is frequently applied to it and other New Musical odes. The chapter also demonstrates how Euripides subsumes choral projection into the dithyrambic frame of the ode. After an analysis of similar pronouncements in Timotheus, who according to ancient sources was the first to bring the citharodic *nomos* into the structure of choral dithyramb, he situates Euripides' claims to poetic novelty in a New Musical context, and discusses the implications for the performance of this ode that is suggested by the generic rivalry between the citharodic *nomos* and the dithyramb.

Rosa Andújar proposes in her contribution that Euripides engages playfully with one conception of the *hyporchēma* involving a strategic disjunction between singers and dancers in *Electra* 859–79, an ode typically discussed in terms of its epinician evocations. The chapter reconsiders the ancient evidence for the notoriously elusive *hyporchēma*, revealing in particular one conception that might have involved a strategic disjunction between singers and dancers. The chapter then illustrates the manner in which both the genre and conceptions of dance more generally have been misunderstood in tragedy, due to a misapplication of the term by Byzantine scholars to exuberant choral odes. Andújar suggests that this elaborate, mimetic and rapid dance-form is more directly present in Euripides' *Electra* 859–79, an ode in which the chorus invite Electra to sing a song that will accompany the chorus' dance, and in which the song's addressee unusually interrupts this brief ode with her immediate response. The chapter concludes with a consideration of the self-reflexive way in which tragedians could allude to the performance of choral dance on the tragic stage.

The chapter of Enrico Prodi discusses the intimated characterisation of the chorus in Euripides' *Phoenissae* as a cultic chorus. The chapter first investigates the elements of choral characterisation that are woven into the chorus' self-presentation in the early part of the play, while analysing parallels from cultic (and para-cultic) lyric and dedicatory epigrams. It then explores the Phoenician women's status as a theoric chorus, examining in particular how such status is integral to the narratives they sing and to the role that they perform in the play.

Naomi Weiss demonstrates the dramatic relevance of the 'dithyrambic' third *stasimon* of *Iphigenia at Aulis*, in which the chorus re-enact the wedding celebrations of Peleus and Thetis. The chapter explores the similarities between the ode's depiction of hymenaeal choreia and the descriptions in archaic lyric of both this prototypical ceremony and other mythical marriages, as well as various visual representations. Noting these parallels, Weiss argues that the chorus in *Iphigenia in Aulis* seem not only to perform self-consciously the celebratory *mousikē* of the wedding of Peleus and Thetis, but also to enact the *hymenaios* of Iphigenia and Achilles, just at the moment when Clytemnestra and Achilles hope to persuade Agamemnon not to sacrifice his daughter. The chorus' performance of the *hymenaios* ultimately underscores the lack of any such music or dance for Iphigenia in the play.

The contribution of Timothy Power examines the presence of lyric and musical genres in the often overlooked 'appendage' to tragedy, satyr-play, and points to the manner in which the self-reflective odes there also provide powerful critical commentary on choral music trends in Athens. The chapter analyses the second-best preserved satyr play, Sophocles' *Ichneutae*, and its multiple depictions of *mousikē*. Power proposes that Sophocles' play demonstrates a similar awareness and complex evocation of various musical genres in self-reflective odes on the performance modes of drama, much like those found in the previous chapters. In particular it demonstrates that this satyr play engages with the New Music choral trends typically associated with Euripides. Throughout the chapter, Power urges us to reconsider the relevance and importance of satyr play as evidence for contemporaneous music and lyric trends in Athens, since its odes also abound in the meta-musical and meta-performative language linked to the Euripidean 'New Music' and 'dithyrambic' odes examined in this section. As these chapters make clear, Greek tragedy was not only the culmination of an evolutionary poetic process, but also a vital participant in a rich and broad culture of choral song and performance.

I Tragic and Lyric Poets in Dialogue

P. J. Finglass
Stesichorus and Greek Tragedy

In Athens of the fifth century [Stesichorus] was universally known ... There was scarcely a poet then living who was not influenced by [him], scarcely a poet who did not, consciously or unconsciously, represent his version of the great sagas. In tracing the historical development of any myth, research almost always finds in Stêsichorus the main bridge between the earliest remains of the story and the form it has in tragedy or in the late epos. In the Agamemnon legend, for instance, the concentration of the interest upon Clytaemnestra, which makes the story a true tragedy instead of an ordinary tale of blood-feud, is his; Clytaemnestra's dream of giving suck to a serpent is his; the conscience-mad Orestes is probably his; so are many of the details of the sack of Troy, among them, if the tradition is right, the flight of Aeneas to Italy. This is enough to show that Stêsichorus was a creative genius of a very high order.

Thus Gilbert Murray, writing more than half a century before the first papyri of Stesichorus were published.[1] He is not the only scholar to emphasise the importance of Stesichorus for Greek tragedy. Writing in 1888, Mayer asked 'how little of the plot of that most splendid trilogy, the *Oresteia*, would be left, if we took away what comes from Stesichorus?'[2] Wilamowitz made a more general point, saying 'I have myself long shared the belief that Stesichorus, alone of all the lyric poets, had a significant influence on the development of heroic myth'.[3] And that influence will have been mediated mainly through tragedy. Indeed, Wilamowitz elsewhere remarked that 'tragedy cast a shadow over all narrative lyric',[4] which is another way of asserting the close connexion between these two genres: so close (in his view) that the popularity of tragedy led to the relative neglect of the lyric poetry which had had such a powerful influence on it. Similar views about the impressive legacy of Stesichorus[5] have been expressed since the arrival

---

I am grateful to the organisers of the 'Paths of Song' conference for the invitation to speak there; this chapter is a lightly revised version of my text delivered on that occasion. I am grateful to the editors and to Dr Henry Spelman for helpful comments; and to the AHRC for the award of a Research Fellowship for the academic year 2012–13, during which this paper was written.

1 Murray 1897, 103–4.
2 Mayer 1883, 4: 'quantulum relinquitur de Orestiae nobilissimae trilogiae argumento, dempto exemplo Stesichoreo?'
3 Wilamowitz 1913, 241: 'Ich habe selbst den Glauben lange geteilt, dass Stesichoros, allein von allen Lyrikern, einen bedeutenden Einfluss auf die Ausbildung der Heldensage gehabt hatte.'
4 Wilamowitz 1900, 12: 'Die Tragödie überschattete alle erzählende Lyrik'.
5 By contrast, the importance for tragedy of Stesichorus' fellow-westerner and near-contemporary Ibycus has received less attention; see however Ucciardello 2005 25–7 for some possible links.

of the papyri, published between 1956 and 1990, that have yielded so many new fragments of his works.[6] Stephanopoulos refers to his 'great influence on tragedy';[7] Haslam remarks that 'his importance for tragedy, both in its nascent and in its developed stages, is great and multifarious'.[8] For Arrighetti, the very subject is somewhat passé, a commonplace of modern (and ancient) scholarship.[9] How true is all this?[10]

Stesichorus was certainly familiar to theatrical audiences in fifth-century Athens.[11] Aristophanes extensively interacts with his *Oresteia* in one of the lyrics in his *Peace* of 421. There Aristophanes' chorus sing

Μοῦcα, cὺ μὲν πολέμουc
ἀπωcαμένη μετ' ἐμοῦ
τοῦ φίλου χόρευcον,
κλείουcα θεῶν τε γάμουc
ἀνδρῶν τε δαῖταc
καὶ θαλίαc μακάρων.

(Ar. *Pax* 775–9)

Muse, reject wars and dance with me, your friend, celebrating the marriages of the gods, the feasts of men, and the banquets of the blessed.

The scholia on this passage tell us that this passage is 'Stesichorean', which has encouraged editors of Stesichorus to reconstruct a fragment of his poetry, as follows:

Μοῖcα cὺ μὲν πολέμουc ἀπωcαμένα πεδ' ἐμοῦ
κλείοιcα θεῶν τε γάμουc ἀνδρῶν τε δαῖταc
καὶ θαλίαc μακάρων

(Stes. fr. 172 F.[12])

---

[6] For a list and discussion of the papyri see Finglass 2014a, 73–6, Finglass/Kelly 2015b, 4–13.
[7] Stephanopoulos 1980, 18: 'was Stesichoros ferner eine besondere Stellung gibt, ist sein großer Einfluß auf die Tragödie'.
[8] Haslam 1978, 30.
[9] Arrighetti 1994, 15–6 n. 15: 'non torniamo a trattare della caratteristica di Stesicoro come anticipatore della poesia tragica, un tratto ben individuato da molta critica moderna e che un attento esame delle fonti rivela già percepito anche dagli antichi'.
[10] For another attempt to answer this question, which reaches similar conclusions via different paths, see Swift 2015.
[11] See Ercoles/Fiorentini 2011, 21–3.
[12] References to Stesichorus are taken from my edition, Finglass 2014b; for an account of that edition and its aims see Finglass/Kelly 2015b, Finglass forthcoming-a ≈ forthcoming-b.

Muse, rejecting wars with me, celebrating the weddings of gods, the feasts of men, and the banquets of the blessed ...

We encounter slightly later in *Peace* another passage, which corresponds metrically to the one cited above:

τοιάδε χρὴ Χαρίτων
δαμώματα καλλικόμων
τὸν σοφὸν ποιητὴν
ὑμνεῖν ὅταν ἠρινὰ μὲν
φωνῆι χελιδὼν
ἑζομένη[13] κελαδῆι

(Ar. *Pax* 796–800)

Such are the songs of the fair-tressed Graces that the good poet must sing, when in the spring the swallow sits and sings out with its voice.

This passage too has a scholion which cites the following fragment as its model, and specifies that the lines in question come from Stesichorus' *Oresteia*:

τοιάδε χρὴ Χαρίτων δαμώματα καλλικόμων
ὑμνεῖν Φρύγιον μέλος ἐξευρόντα‹c› ἀβρῶc
ἦροc ἐπερχομένου.

(Stes. fr. 173 F.)

Such are the songs of the fair-tressed Graces that we must sing, devising a Phrygian melody in refined comfort, at spring's approach.

These lines provide the metre for what would otherwise be an excessively confident reconstruction of Stesichorus' text in fr. 172. The scholia to Aristophanes go on to cite a further passage from Stesichorus on which Aristophanes is drawing:

ὄκα ἦροc
ὥραι κελαδῆι χελιδών.

(Stes. fr. 174 F.)

when the swallow sounds in spring-time

---

13 I print ἑζομένη, the reading of the mediaeval manuscripts, not ἡδομένη, the reading of the ancient manuscript and almost certainly what Aristophanes actually wrote, because ἑζομένη was probably the text known to the writer(s) of the scholia.

In the case of the latter two fragments, we can be sure, and in the case of the first, can reasonably infer, that Aristophanes' text is extremely close to that of Stesichorus. Not all Aristophanes' audience will have recognised the allusion; as Hadjimichael points out, Aristophanes in his citations generally requires his audience to recognise that lyric poetry is at issue, but not necessarily the name of the poet.[14] But Aristophanes would hardly have put in an allusion that no-one was going to appreciate. Some people would have recognised that it came from Stesichorus' *Oresteia*; others that it recalled to a piece of Stesichorus, forgetting the precise poem; others that it alluded to a piece of archaic lyric, without knowing the name of the author; and others would have missed everything and simply enjoyed the song. No doubt the last group was substantial, but the other groups would have been far from negligible. Some people who missed this particular lyric allusion will have picked up on others, and vice versa; we should not think of an intellectually segregated audience, some people getting everything, and the rest nothing at all. And the audience for comedy was the same as the audience for tragedy.

How would the audience members of fifth-century tragedy have encountered Stesichorus' poetry? Opportunities at Athens to perform Stesichorus in full, chorus and all, may have been limited or non-existent,[15] but the symposium was a potential locus for smaller-scale reperformance. Eupolis twice refers to Stesichorus as the subject of symposiastic song, and Stesichorus is associated with the symposium in two other later sources.[16] That institution afforded men the chance to sing extracts from his poems, which would have encouraged the circulation of written texts; men will have wanted to learn their contributions by heart, or to read more of a poet whose songs they first encountered in that convivial environment. These texts would have circulated mainly among the elite, which includes the tragedians, and perhaps some women too. Moreover, to argue for a moment from first principles, it feels intuitively probable that the tragic poets, once they had encountered the Stesichorean corpus, would have availed themselves of the great storehouse of myth that it contained, not least because it was composed in the lyric metres which were so important an antecedent to the tragedians' own verse.

---

14 Hadjimichael 2011, 92–6.
15 See however Bowie 2015a for some exciting, if currently unprovable, hypotheses about the possibility of full performances of Stesichorus' works at various points in Athenian history from the 560s to the 440s.
16 Eupolis frr. 148 (*Helots*, early 420s?), 395 *PCG*⁵, Σ Ar. *Vesp.* 122a (pp. 192.1–192.3 Koster), Hesych. τ 1343 (p. 71 H–C).

When we sift Stesichorus for these alleged tragic associations, the results are initially discouraging. In terms of verbal echoes, we do not find anything remotely comparable to the Aristophanean passage mentioned above. That may be mere chance – we only know about the allusion in Aristophanes because the scholia happen to tell us about it – but we now have quite a bit of Stesichorus, and a fair amount of tragedy, so we might have hoped, at least, for something.[17] Allusions have been alleged, of course. For example, Euripides' description of Helen as 'the father-leaver, the marriage-leaver' (τὰν λιποπάτορα λιπόγαμον)[18] is said to show the influence of Stesichorus; according to Willink, 'the λιπο- words ... reflect Stesichorus' description of Helen and Cl<ytemnestra> as λιπεcάνορεc'.[19] But Helen was most famous for leaving her husband (and daughter) when she sailed to Troy with Paris; words meaning 'leave' would come naturally to the mind of poets wishing to describe her, whether or not they knew their Stesichorus.[20] If the verbal echo were stronger, that objection might not be absolutely overwhelming, but in fact it is rather weak; Stesichorus uses λιπεc-, which is morphologically distinct from λιπο-.[21] If Euripides had wanted to make his audience think of the Stesichorean passage, or if he had been subconsciously influenced by it himself, it is hard to see why he should have failed to avail himself of the strikingly Stesichorean stem.

Ercoles and Fiorentini have made a fresh attempt to find verbal connexions between Stesichorus and Euripides, this time between the poem represented by the Lille papyrus[22] and *Phoenissae*.[23] When we consider the proposed instances, however, none seems particularly convincing. Their first example concerns the Euripidean Jocasta's prayer in her opening speech

---

17 Contrast the state of affairs for Stesichorus and epic, where a strong relationship between individual passages can easily be identified in many places; see Kelly 2015. As Peek 1958, 173 asked after the publication of *P.Oxy.* 2360, one of the first two papyri to be published, 'who would have suspected that the dependence [sc. of Stesichorus on Homer] could have gone so far in matters of content too? [sc. in addition to the imitation of words and phrases, something already evident from the quoted fragments]' ('wer hätte geahnt, daß die Abhängigkeit auch im Stofflichen so weit gehen könnte?').
18 Eur. *Or.* 1305. Thus the manuscripts; for the text see Renehan 1998, 257, who rejects West's λιπογάμ<ετ>ον.
19 Willink on Eur. *Or.* 1305–6, referring to Stes. fr. 85 F. ('husband-leavers').
20 Cf. Sappho fr. 16.6–9 Voigt, Alcaeus fr. 283.3–8 Voigt, Eur. *Andr.* 602–4, *Or.* 99, *Cycl.* 185–6.
21 For λιπ- compounds in general see Hummel 1997.
22 Stes. fr. 97 F. ('*Thebais*').
23 Ercoles and Fiorentini 2011, 25–9.

ἀλλ' ὦ φαεννὰς οὐρανοῦ ναίων πτυχάς
Ζεῦ, cῶcον ἡμᾶς, δὸς δὲ cύμβαcιν τέκνοιc

(Eur. Phoen. 84–5)

But you who dwell in the bright folds of the sky, Zeus, save us, and grant an agreement to my children

and the Stesichorean Queen's words

τοῦτο γὰρ ἄν, δοκέω, λυτήριον ὔμμι κακοῦ γένοιτο πότμο[υ,
μάντιος φραδαῖcι θείου,
αἴτε νέον Κρονίδας γένος τε καὶ ἄcτυ [◡ – –
Κάδμου ἄνακτος,
ἀμβάλλων κακότατα πολὺν χρόνον

(Stes. fr. 97.225–30)

This, I think, may prove a release from grim fate, as a result of the divine prophet's advice, depending on whether the son of Cronus [will save?][24] the latest offspring and city of lord Cadmus by long delaying the trouble

Both women look to Zeus as a potential saviour for their family; but that is not surprising, as appeals to Zeus are common in all kind of desperate situations. Moreover (as Ercoles and Fiorentini admit, p. 26), there is no verbal connexion. Nothing suggests that Euripides was influenced by the passage of Stesichorus, or that members of the audience of Euripides' *Phoenissae* would have thought of the Stesichorean lines when they heard Jocasta's speech.[25]

In their second example, Ercoles and Fiorentini cite *Phoen.* 951–2, where Tiresias tells Creon 'choose one or the other of two fates: save either your son or the city' (τοῖνδ' ἑλοῦ δυοῖν πότμοιν / τὸν ἕτερον· ἢ γὰρ παῖδα cῶcον ἢ πόλιν), and claim 'la formulazione dell'alternativa tra il figlio e la città ricorda [Stes. fr. 97.216–17 F.]', where the Queen prays to die before she sees 'her children dying in their halls, or the city captured' (παίδαc ἐνὶ μεγάροιc / θανόντας ἢ πόλιν ἁλοῖcαν). The Euripidean passage uses ἤ ... ἤ in the sense 'aut ... aut' (Creon can choose to save either his son or his city), whereas in Stesichorus the force of ἤ probably approximates to 'vel' (the Queen does not want to see either her sons die or the city destroyed, but there is no sense that one, and only one, of these things is going to happen). Even if we accept for the sake of argument that Ercoles and Fiorentini are correct to urge that ἤ in Stesichorus means

---

24 Reading cαώcει (*supp.* Barrett, Lloyd-Jones, West *ap.* Meillier 1976, 299).
25 The basic similarity of situation, which goes beyond any specific verbal reminiscence, will be discussed below.

'aut', that would still be insufficient to establish a connexion. The conflict of loyalties between family and city is familiar in all kinds of archaic and classical poetry; we would need a more substantial similarity to trigger an association in the minds of an audience. Moreover, Creon is being presented with a specific, dreadful choice by Tiresias; in Stesichorus, however, there is no question of the Queen selecting a particular fate. So this example, too, is less than cogent. The remainder that Ercoles and Fiorentini suggest are no more persuasive; they involve the sort of similarities that are inevitable when two poets are dealing with comparable situations.

A fragment of Aeschylus which refers to 'Himera on its high crag' (ὑψίκρημνον Ἱμέραν) has been taken to show the influence of Stesichorus, the famous poet from that city.[26] This is just a guess, however; there is no reference to Himera in what remains of Stesichorus' work. According to Himerius, Stesichorus celebrated Himera in his lyrics,[27] but no trace of encomiastic poetry can be observed in the fragments;[28] they contain mythological lyric, and Himera as a relatively recent settlement may not have featured there. Nor did Aeschylus need Stesichorus' poetry to alert himself to the existence of Himera, a substantial town with close ties to 'mainland' Greece.[29] Aeschylus may even have visited it on one of his trips to Sicily; he would certainly have heard of it.

The absence of verbal parallels is a pity, but might be the result of chance; a single new papyrus, of Stesichorus or of tragedy, could change the situation dramatically. Let us try a different approach, and look how the mythological range found in Stesichorus' poetry compares with what is on offer in tragedy. According to the *Suda*, Stesichorus' works were collected into twenty-six books.[30] We have the titles of thirteen poems. One of these, the *Scylla*, deals with a topic that unsurprisingly does not seem to have received a dedicated tragic treatment – it is hard to see how the moral complications that characterise Greek tragedy could have surfaced in an account of a six-headed monster feasting on Odysseus' crew.[31] The subject of Stesichorus' *Cycnus* was enormously popular in the archaic

---

26 Aesch. fr. 25a.2 *TrGF³*; thus Franco 2008, 20. Cf. Pearson 1975, 188: 'even if Aeschylus is following Stesichorus when he says Heracles took a bath in the hot springs of Himera, it still does not tell us how or why Heracles came to Himera'.
27 Stes. fr. 299 F.
28 Two apparently encomiastic fragments from *P.Oxy.* 3876 (Stes. frr. 214, 219 F.) may well not be by Stesichorus; more than one poem, and author, may be represented among the fragments of *P.Oxy.* 3876, which may even represent more than one papyrus (see Finglass 2014a, 75–7, 2014d, 531–2).
29 See Finglass 2014a, 6–12.
30 Stes. test. Tb2 Ercoles.
31 For the myth of Scylla and her appearances in literature see Hopman 2013.

period, in both poetry and the visual arts,³² but does not seem to have interested the tragedians. Stesichorus' *Nostoi* (*Returns*) again presents a theme familiar from epic, and in a format that epic favoured – a single work discussing the return of several Greek warriors from Troy.³³ A tragedy, by contrast, will tend to concentrate on an individual. Episodes connected with the return of the Greeks from Troy do occur in tragedy, but our fragments of Stesichorus' *Nostoi* are too exiguous for us to tell whether they influenced the tragedians. Stesichorus' *Cerberus* might have influenced Sophocles' play of that name, but since we have barely more than a title for either work, speculation on that matter is unfruitful; similarly, with Stesichorus' *Europa* and Aeschylus' *Carians* or *Europa*. We have a bit more information, on both sides, for the *Boarhunters*. The tragic relationship between Meleager and Atalanta in myths of the Calydonian boar hunt was handled by Euripides in his *Meleager*, and perhaps by Aeschylus in his *Atalanta* and Sophocles in his *Meleager*; but whether they were reacting against all earlier treatments, or picking up an element first made prominent by Stesichorus, is unknown. Stesichorus seems to have dealt extensively with the hunt for the animal, as we know from a fragment listing the various hunters and contingents, which seems preparatory to such a narrative.³⁴ This sets him apart not only from other archaic poets, who deal with the boar hunt in a few lines,³⁵ but also from the tragic poets, who could not have portrayed the hunt itself directly; it might nevertheless have been described in a messenger speech. The legend of Eriphyle offers considerable scope to both lyric and tragic poets, so it not surprising that alongside Stesichorus' poem of that name we find a tragedy *Eriphyle* by Sophocles, who also wrote at least one, and perhaps two, *Amphiaraus* plays, and an *Alcmeon*, which in turn was the name of two plays by Euripides. Yet here too we know little about any of these treatments.

We have rather more of Stesichorus' *Sack of Troy*, but this subject does not lend itself to dramatic portrayal. Tragedy is interested in the immediate aftermath of the sack – think of Euripides' *Hecuba* or *Trojan Women* – but it would exceed its technical capacity to depict the many events and extensive cast involved in the night of that city's destruction.³⁶ Stesichorus' poem begins,

---

32 See Zardini 2009.
33 For this poem see Carey 2015, 57–61.
34 Stes. fr. 183 F., on which see Finglass 2012; cf. fr. 184, a description of activity by the boar which presumably comes from a narrative of the hunt.
35 Hom. *Il.* 9.543–5; Bacchyl. 5.111–3.
36 According to Podlecki 1971, 318–9, 'some of the details of Troy's capture which the Messenger tells at *Agam.* 524ff. and Agamemnon's own recapitulation at 818ff. (especially the description of the horse, 824–6), may well come from the *Ilioupersis*, while the Messenger's account of

remarkably, with the menial figure Epeius, emphasising the glory that he won thanks to the building of the Horse;[37] Epeius is attested as the title-character of a Euripidean satyr-play, but not in tragedy. The *Games for Pelias* depicts another subject not easily represented in tragedy; Pelias does feature in fifth-century drama, but in connexion with either the rescue of his mother[38] or his death at the hands of his daughters.[39] A tragic representation of the myth of Geryon is conceivable, and a tragedy of that name by the third-century tragedian Nicomachus of Alexandria is known;[40] Diodorus Siculus remarks that 'three-bodied Geryon' was typical (together with centaurs) of monsters found in the theatre.[41] But there is no evidence for plays on this subject by the classical tragedians.[42]

For the above Stesichorean poems, then, we have no evidence for specific connexions between Stesichorus' treatment and any tragic account. Podlecki is right to claim that many titles of classical tragedy 'are based on the same legends as had been handled by Stesichorus',[43] but that is only to be expected given a finite body of myth; more than this is needed to establish a real relationship between Stesichorus and tragedy. After this process of elimination, we are left with only four works: *Helen*, *Palinode*, *Thebais*, and *Oresteia*. Let us look briefly at each of these.

---

the disastrous homeward journey at 649 ff. could be a summary of events told at length in the *Nostoi*; but this is speculation. Similarly, Podlecki's assertion (*ibid.*) that Euripides' handling of the sacrifice of Polyxena, and the death of Heracles' children, owes a debt to Stesichorus goes beyond present evidence.

37 Stes. fr. 100 F.; see Finglass 2013a, 2014e, 2015b, 2017.
38 Sophocles' *Tyro A* and *Tyro B*.
39 Euripides' *Daughters of Pelias* (so also plays of this name by Aphareus and Diphilus); perhaps Sophocles' *Rootcutters* (*Rizotomoi*).
40 Nicom. 127 F 3 *TrGF¹*; there was also a fourth-century comedy of that name by Ephippus (fr. 3–5 *PCG⁵*). See Finglass forthcoming-d.
41 Diod. Sic. 4.8.4.
42 Podlecki 1971, 319 justifies his claim that 'Euripides' debt to Stesichorus seems to have been equally heavy [*sc.* as was Aeschylus' debt]' by reference to a supposed link between Heracles' drinking bout with Pholus in the *Geryoneis* (frr. 22–4 F.) and the gluttonous Heracles of *Alcestis*. But Heracles' prodigious appetite was a standard enough characteristic of that mythological figure; there is no reason to think that a spectator of *Alcestis* in 438 BC would think of the Pholus episode in Stesichorus. An attempt by Musso 1967, to demonstrate that since Aesch. fr. 74 *TrGF³* depicts Geryon as three-bodied, and shows Heracles travelling to meet him in the Sun's golden bowl, it must be influenced by Stesichorus' *Geryoneis* and indeed could be considered a fragment of that poem, fails to take account of how such details would be found in many different poetic narratives of the myth.
43 Podlecki 1971, 320.

The *Helen*'s portrayal of Helen is too conventional for us to identify connexions with tragedy; but one aspect of the poem is perhaps worth highlighting. It is likely that in Stesichorus' poem, the young Helen was abducted by Theseus, and bore him Iphigenia; she transferred the baby to her sister Clytemnestra to bring up as her own child.[44] Iphigenia was probably sacrificed later in the poem by the Greeks on the way to recover Helen.[45] Both Sophocles and Euripides would later exploit the dreadful irony that one sister's crime led to the killing of the other sister's daughter, and that a father had to sacrifice his daughter to recover his brother's wife.[46] In Stesichorus we find another painful paradox: a daughter is sacrificed in order to put right the offence of her mother.[47] The parties to the sacrifice would not have known about this relationship – indeed, the chief sacrificer, Agamemnon, thought that she was his own daughter – but the mother would have known it only too well; the daughter is herself the product of the mother's chequered sexual past. The tragic paradox in Stesichorus is perhaps even greater than the one that we find in the tragedians. But we are a long way from being able to say that Stesichorus' treatment had an influence on tragedy here; this kind of ingenious paradox could have occurred independently to thoughtful people scrutinising the details of a myth. For the same reason, it is not clear that an audience, on hearing the tragic passages, would have connected them with Stesichorus.

The *Palinode* is our first evidence for a Helen who did not go to Troy at all, but was magically transported to Egypt and kept safe there until the end of the war; this was the version used by Euripides in his *Helen*, and mentioned at the end of his *Electra*.[48] It would be hypercritical to say that Euripides took this highly distinctive myth from anywhere other than Stesichorus: here, then, we at last have some tangible evidence of a connexion between Stesichorus and tragedy. Unfortunately, the almost total loss of the *Palinode* prevents us from saying for certain anything else of value about Euripides' use of the poem. What follows, then, is a hypothesis that falls well short of proof, but still perhaps worth venturing. Somewhere Stesichorus depicted a visit to Egypt by the Athenian warrior Demophon on his way home from Troy; it is quite likely that this visit took place in the *Palinode*, and that Demophon during his visit was accompanied by the seer

---

44 Stes. fr. 86 F.
45 See Finglass 2015b, 94; the attention evidently paid to Iphigenia's genealogy strongly suggests that she played some part in the poem beyond simply being born, and there is nothing else that Iphigenia could do except be sacrificed.
46 See Finglass 2007a on Soph. *El.* 539, citing Eur. *El.* 1041–5, *Or.* 658–9, *IA* 1201–2.
47 See Finglass 2015b, 96–7.
48 Eur. *El.* 1280–3.

Calchas.⁴⁹ If this is correct, Demophon might have played a role in the poem similar to that of Teucer in Euripides' Helen: a visitor who anticipates Menelaus' arrival and acts as a foil to him. And Calchas might have been put to use in a manner similar to that of Euripides' Theonoe: a prophetic individual able to bring some certainty to the confusion caused by Helen's remarkable tale. But this suggestion piles hypothesis on hypothesis, and is vulnerable to the charge of *petitio principii:* if we reconstruct Stesichorus' poem by using Euripides' play as a template, of course it will seem as if Euripides was engaging with Stesichorus. We cannot rely on this as anything like a certain, or even probable, instance of a tragedian putting Stesichorus to use.

Only one scene from the *Thebais* has survived: an attempt at reconciliation by Oedipus's wife between her sons.⁵⁰ This at first sight is remarkably similar to Euripides' *Phoenissae*, where Jocasta tries to mediate between Eteocles and Polynices.⁵¹ But there are many differences. In Stesichorus, one brother takes the kingdom, the other Oedipus' property, whereas in Euripides, the pair agree to rule in alternate years, and Eteocles refuses to give up the throne at the expiry of his first term.⁵² In Stesichorus it is almost certain that the Queen is not Oedipus' mother, and hence that Eteocles and Polynices are not Oedipus' half-brothers. Euripides might allow an incestuous wife to retain a position of moral and political authority within her family and the state, but it is hard to imagine an archaic poet making light of such a taboo.⁵³ Stesichorus' Oedipus is probably dead: that is the natural motivation for the situation, in which the division of his property is at stake.⁵⁴ In Euripides, however, he is still alive. And in Stesichorus, the Queen's intervention takes place shortly before Polynices' departure for Argos, so well before the expedition of the Seven. Euripides, by contrast, makes no reference to any intervention by Jocasta at that time; the brothers themselves,

---

49 See Stes. fr. 90.15–30 F. with Finglass 2013b, which argues tentatively for these points in detail; further discussion in D'Alessio 2013a, Mancuso 2013, Bowie 2015a.
50 Stes. fr. 97 F.
51 Eur. *Phoen.* 261–637.
52 Stes. fr. 97.218–24 F., Eur. *Phoen.* 69–76. We do not know how the settlement broke down in Stesichorus.
53 In the earliest accounts Oedipus' wife and mother kills herself shortly after her marriage, without producing offspring; that is implied by Hom. *Od.* 11.271–80 (on which see Finglass 2014c, 358) and is explicit in the *Oedipodea* (fr. 1 *GEF*) and the Pisander scholium (*PEG* I 17–19). The first author to give Oedipus children from his incestuous relationship is Pherecydes (fr. 95 *EGM*), where however these children do not include Polynices and Eteocles; Pherecydes makes that pair (with Antigone and Ismene) his offspring from a subsequent, non-incestuous marriage. See further the introduction to Finglass 2018.
54 See Finglass 2014c, 364–5.

as Jocasta tells us, arrange a mutual settlement out of fear for Oedipus' curses.[55] Jocasta intervenes once Polynices and his companions have launched their expedition and are about to attack Thebes. The curses from Oedipus just mentioned constitute yet another difference between the two poets. Included by Euripides, the curses seem to be absent from Stesichorus, who puts the focus on Tiresias' prophecy. If Oedipus' curses did feature in his poem, it is surprising that the Queen makes no mention of them in what is left of her speech, and instead concentrates throughout on negating Tiresias' predictions.[56] Finally, Jocasta in Euripides fails to achieve a reconciliation, even in the short term; the scene descends into angry stichomythia between her sons, who separate without reaching an agreement. Stesichorus' Queen is remarkably successful, at least for the present; her sons accept her division without further discussion.

This impressive array of differences does not mean that Stesichorus had no influence on Euripides here. We should not expect a tragic poet (and nor would an ancient audience) to have a single 'source' that he follows, or adapts, in the course of a scene or play. The very prominence of the Queen could be enough to connect the two versions: Euripides may have taken this idea from Stesichorus, and reapplied it in different circumstances in his own work. In terms of the audience's perspective, it is plausible that some spectators of *Phoenissae* were reminded of the Stesichorean scene, not least as that episode was prominently placed towards the beginning of its poem. Moreover, once the link had been established via the figure of the Queen mediating between her sons, members of the audience might have been encouraged to reflect on the differences between the two versions. This would have made the association all the more productive, since the audience would have had to consider why Euripides had diverged from Stesichorus' account. So Euripides gives the role of mediator to the brothers' mother, as had Stesichorus, but his intended peacemaker (unlike Stesichorus') was a participant in incest, someone whose actions, although unwitting, might have been thought to exclude her from any such role. This underlines the very different attitude towards this fundamental aspect of the myth that we find in Euripides. And whereas Stesichorus' Queen at least enjoys some short-term success in persuading her sons to compromise, this only highlights the failure of Jocasta to achieve any kind of reconciliation between the warring parties.

---

[55] Eur. *Phoen.* 66–74.
[56] So Burnett 1988, 111: 'it is plain that no curse is in question, for it is specifically Teiresias's prophecy ..., not some damaging word from Oedipus, that the queen hopes to render ineffective.'

Froma Zeitlin qualifies the suggestion that Euripides was influenced by Stesichorus here, arguing that 'while a fragment of the sixth-century poet Stesichorus indicates a likely precedent for Jocasta's active, mediating role between the brothers ..., Euripides' emphasis on the maternal qualities of Jocasta and the tragic consequences of her passionate devotion are surely his own elaboration'.[57] Zeitlin says 'surely', but unless she has got hold of a very exciting papyrus it is not clear how she can be so sure. Stesichorus' Queen dominates the action in the *Thebais* fragment with a speech that shows her passionate maternal concern: 'throughout she is direct and focussed; the speech has no digressions, despite its length, as if to emphasise the gravity of the situation, the intensity of her emotion, and the efficient manner in which she acts on that feeling.'[58] She in no way falls short of Euripides' Jocasta in terms of maternal qualities. Moreover, it seems most unlikely that such a commanding figure will not have appeared later in the work, when the agreement that she so carefully engineers at the start of the poem falls apart, and when the fratricidal conflict that she had hoped to avert leads to the deaths of both her sons, and perhaps to her own death too. She will not have merely stood by as the catastrophe approaches, and during her appearances, whatever form these took, her maternal role and tragic situation will surely – to use Zeitlin's word – have been paramount. We cannot prove that this inspired aspects of Euripides' portrayal of Jocasta, but it is an enticing hypothesis; if we had more of Stesichorus' work we would probably be able to posit further links.[59]

The tragic nature of Steschorus' *Thebais* is well brought out by Burnett's eloquent appreciation:

> In this poem ... the notion of the helplessness of all mortality in the face of destiny is coupled with another, that of the flawed nature of even the greatest of humankind ... This is not a poetic impulse typical of epic compositions; instead it is close to that of Attic tragedy. Here is a prototype of the tragic principal, a figure of august presumption, forewarned but blindly preparing the grief she would avoid. Here is a model for the tragic episode, a decision that provides the germ of an entire saga.[60]

---

57 Zeitlin 2008, 329.
58 Finglass 2015b, 91, citing in addition Burnett 1988, 113: 'the lines reflect the mental dynamism of a woman engaged in making a crucial decision while under the pressure of strongest emotion'.
59 See further Swift 2015, who notes similarities between the use of the lot as a means of dividing Oedipus' inheritance in Stesichorus (fr. 97.218–52, with Finglass 2013c) and in Aeschylus' *Seven against Thebes*.
60 Burnett 1988, 129.

Burnett is right to emphasise this tragic dimension; nevertheless, her language might lead us astray. Referring to Stesichorus' Queen as a 'prototype of the tragic principal' makes her seem a figure merely preparatory to characters drawn by poets not even born when Stesichorus' choruses were singing. Our admiration of the tragic elements in Stesichorus, and the links between Stesichorus and tragedy, should not cause us to think of Stesichorus merely as a forerunner to other people's work. If Euripides and other tragedians were inspired by aspects of his poetry, it does not follow that they improved on what they found.

We are left with Stesichorus' *Oresteia*, the very poem that Meyer and Murray focussed on all those years ago,[61] where the similarities with tragedy are unmistakable. Moreover, we have the advantage of a second-century papyrus unavailable to those earlier scholars – a papyrus not of Stesichorus' poem, but of an anonymous scholarly text composed between c. 150 BC and c. AD 100, which provides the earliest surviving discussion of Stesichorus' relationship to the tragedians.[62] The first passage that we will consider, however, comes from one of the quoted fragments. Stesichorus' Clytemnestra has a dream, from which the following two lines are preserved:

τᾶι δὲ δράκων ἐδόκηϲε μολεῖν κάρα βεβροτωμένοϲ ἄκρον,
ἐκ δ' ἄρα τοῦ βαϲιλεὺϲ Πλειϲθενίδαϲ ἐφάνη.

(Stes. fr. 180 F.)

A snake seemed to come to her, the crest of its head covered in gore, and then, out of it, appeared a prince of the line of Plisthenes.

The snake probably represents Agamemnon, the king Orestes. Plutarch, who quotes these lines and knew their context, took them as an example of how a criminal conscience which had been bold enough before the deed is subsequently overcome by fear:[63] this suggests interest in Clytemnestra's psychology and motivation. Similarly in Aeschylus, Clytemnestra dreams that she gave birth to a snake, put it in swaddling clothes, and offered it her breast; the snake bites the breast and draws forth a gout of blood; Orestes identifies himself with the snake, and interprets the dream to mean that he will kill his mother.[64] Sophocles' Clytemnestra also has a dream, though that play banishes the snake.[65] Both the

---

61 The most interesting account of this poem is still W. Ferrari 1938; see also Stephanopoulos 1980, 133–9.
62 *P.Oxy.* 2506, published by Page 1963; For the nature of this text see further Finglass 2014a, 81.
63 Plut. *De Sera Numinis Vindicta* 554f–5a.
64 Aesch. *Cho.* 523–53.
65 Soph. *El.* 410–27.

tragedians use the dream to motivate Clytemnestra sending her daughter to Agamemnon's tomb to placate his ghost;[66] this too is probably a Stesichorean device, since we know, thanks to the papyrus, that in his poem Orestes is recognised by means of a lock of hair (a motif used by Aeschylus and twisted in different ways by Euripides and Sophocles).[67] This implies an offering by Orestes at his father's tomb, as in the tragedians; it also implies recognition at the tomb by a family member friendly to him, possibly his sister (again, similarly in tragedy). Stesichorus included the Nurse, as did Aeschylus in his *Choephoroe*.[68] But she is also found in Pindar, Pherecydes, and mid-sixth century art, either saving the young Orestes or assisting him on his return;[69] and Stesichorus' Nurse, with her aristocratic name Laodamia, is likely to have been a rather different creation from the lowly character of Aeschylus' Cilissa. Stesichorus' Laodamia might have recognised Orestes; compare how Odysseus is recognised by his nurse Eurycleia.[70]

In Stesichorus Apollo gives Orestes his bow, as is discussed by the author of the papyrus:[71]

..]. Ε[ὐ]ριπίδης δὲ τὸ τ[όξον
τὸ Ὀρέςτου ὅτι ἐςτὶν δε[δο—   (15)
μέ]νον αὐτῶι δῶρον πα[ρὰ
τ]οῦ Ἀπόλλωνος· παρ' ὧι [μὲν
γ]ὰρ λέγεται· δὸς τόξα μ[οι
κ]ερουλκά, δῶρα Λοξίου, οἷς εἶ—
π'] Ἀπόλλων μ' ἐξαμύ[νας]θαι   (20)
θεάς (Eur. *Or.* 268–9)· παρὰ δὲ Cτηςιχ[όρω]ι· τό—
ξα .....] τάδε δώςω παλά—
μα]ιςιν ἐμαῖςι κεκαςμένα
..]..[ἐ]πικρατέως βάλλειν·

(Stes. fr. 181a.14–24 F.)

Euripides included the bow of Orestes that is given to him as a gift from Apollo, since in his work come the words 'Give me the horned bow, the gift of Loxias, with which Apollo said that he would ward the goddesses away from me'. And in Stesichorus: 'I will give you this bow, excellent in my hands, ... to shoot with power.'

---

66 See Finglass 2007a on Soph. *El.* 410.
67 Stes. fr. 181a.11–13 F., Aesch. *Cho.* 164–204, Soph. *El.* 899–915, Eur. *El.* 509–29.
68 Stes. fr. 179 F., Aesch. *Cho.* 730–82.
69 Pind. *P.* 11.17–8, Pher. fr. 134 *EGM*, and a metope from the temple of Hera at Foce del Sele; see Finglass 2007b on Pind. *P.* 11.17.
70 Hom. *Od.* 19.467–75.
71 Apollo's gift to Orestes of his bow was already known before the publication of the papyrus, however, thanks to a scholion on Euripides (= fr. 181 F.).

The anonymous scholar compares the gift of the bow in Stesichorus with the request of the maddened Orestes in Euripides' play for exactly that weapon; we may compare in addition Aeschylus' *Eumenides*, where Apollo himself brandishes his bow against the Erinyes.[72] The gift of the bow in Stesichorus implies the pursuit of the Erinyes; the bow is a defence against them in the two tragedians, and gods do not hand over their weapons to mortals for no reason. The presence of the Erinyes implies a morally problematic matricide,[73] and this too is characteristically tragic. The enticement of Iphigenia to Aulis and her subsequent sacrifice feature in Stesichorus, as they do in the *Cypria*, not to speak of later texts;[74] these events supply Clytemnestra with perhaps her most powerful justification for the killing of her husband. These isolated details do not just correspond to similar isolated details in tragedy; they build up a picture of a poem with a profound interest in the moral consequences of the matricide and Clytemnestra's character and motivation.[75] So when Ferrari writes 'if already in Stesichorus the matricide implies the persecution by the Erinyes, that leads us to believe that it must have appeared to the poet as a crime (even if this problem will acquire its decisive importance only in tragedy)', he is right only up until the beginning of the parenthesis.[76] Similar discrimination is required when we consider Ferrari's description of the characterisation of Stesichorus' Clytemnestra:

> Certainly an already complex figure, since we must remember that Stesichorus referred to the sacrifice of her daughter as a means of justifying her, even if she is not investigated to the core of her complicated psychology, as she is presented to us in the original creation of Aeschylus. A figure already potentially rich in fertile dramatic seeds, such as the motif of the dream which puts to the fore the author of the crime and the killing, even if we must consider that she is depicted in powerful and vigorous glimpses. A figure, finally, perhaps still characterised by a certain archaic rigidity, but capable of exerting a fascination on later poets.[77]

---

72 Aesch. *Eum.* 179–84.
73 Thus Garvie 1986, xxi.
74 Stes. fr. 181a.25–7 F. (the text refers only to Iphigenia's enticement in Euripides before it breaks off, but it is clear that it would have gone on to state that the same event featured in Stesichorus), *Cypria* Arg. §8 *GEF*, Soph. fr. 305 *TrGF*⁴, Eur. *El.* 1020–3, *Iphigenia at Aulis*.
75 Kurke 2013a, 124–5 misses the interest implied in Clytemnestra's motivation in these passages, although her point that later treatments, such as Pindar's and Aeschylus', should not be regarded as simple reflexes of Stesichorus', is well taken.
76 W. Ferrari 1938, 24: 'Se già presso Stesicoro il matricidio implicava la persecuzione delle Erinni, ciò ci induce a sopporre che esso doveva apparire al poeta come una colpa (anche se questo problema acquisterà solo con la tragedia la sua importanza decisiva)'.
77 W. Ferrari 1938, 21: 'Figura certamente già complessa, se dobbiamo ammettere che aducesse a sua discolpa il sacrificio della figlia, anche se non ancora scrutata al fondo della sua compli-

This deftly painted picture of Clytemnestra well brings out the tragic aspects of her character, and in particular the interest that Stesichorus takes in her motivation, which, although it does not necessarily excuse her actions, nevertheless encourages the audience to engage imaginatively with the question of what drove her to act as she did. But like Burnett as cited above, Ferrari uses unhelpfully developmental language, as if all that Stesichorus could do was to anticipate a later form of literature, and as if the mere fact that he was earlier than Greek tragedy meant that his characters could not show depths and subtleties mysteriously reserved for that later genre alone. Rather than see in the lyric Clytemnestra mere 'seeds' that would achieve fruition only decades later, we should recognise that Stesichorus was just as able as Aeschylus to delineate a passionate woman capable of a terrible response in the face of enormous provocation.[78] The fragments hint that Stesichorus' intention was indeed along these lines.[79]

Still, once we dispense with the developmental model, Ferrari's analysis of Clytemnestra and of the poem as a whole remains most penetrating and evocative. We may briefly contrast a more recent, and more often cited, piece by Neschke, who claims that 'the most important modification introduced by Stesichorus consists in the fact that the whole responsibility for the killing of Agamemnon is placed on Clytemnestra. Stesichorus' entire poem bears witness to the poet's intention to blame the queen and to excuse Agamemnon; the sacrifice of Iphigenia is presented as a pious act of the king obedient to the demand of the goddess Artemis, who compensates the king by saving his daughter'.[80] Yet we

---

cata psicologia, come ci si presenta nell'originale creazione di Eschilo. Figura già potenzialmente ricca di germi drammatici fecondi, come il motivo del sogno che pone a fronte l'autrice del delitto e l'ucciso, anche se dobbiamo ritenere che fosse delineata a scorci potenti e vigorosi. Figura, infine, forse ancora atteggiata a una certa rigidità arcaica, ma capace di esercitare suggestione sui poeti posteriori.'

[78] The prejudice that tragedy is superior to lyric in exploring this kind of psychological complexity lies behind the willingness of many scholars to claim that Aeschylus' *Oresteia* is earlier than Pindar's *Pythian Eleven*, on the ground that Pindar could not have shown such fascination with Clytemnestra's motivation if he had not been aware of Aeschylus' play; see Finglass 2007b, 11–17.

[79] Stesichorus' interest in the inner psychology and motivation of this apparently unappealing figure might be compared with his approach to Geryon, another 'monster' (albeit of a different kind) whose character is nevertheless explored by Stesichorus in such a way that the audience feels sympathy for him (see e.g. Finglass forthcoming-d). We cannot tell whether an audience would have gone as far as to show sympathy for Stesichorus' Clytemnestra, but they would at least have been confronted by her side of the story.

[80] Neschke 1986, 296: 'la modification la plus importante introduite par Stésichore, consiste dans le fait que toute la responsabilité du meutre d'Agamemnon se pose sur Clytemnestre. Le récit *entier* de Stésichore témoigne de l'intention du poète de culpabiliser la reine et de disculper

know that in Stesichorus Iphigenia was summoned to Aulis by deceit – hardly a sign that her sacrifice was morally uncomplicated. So too Neschke does not take account of the presence of the Erinyes, who would be otiose in a poem where the matricide was unproblematic.[81]

Caution is in order when we associate Stesichorus' poem with tragedy. The earlier presentation of the story in the *Odyssey*, which downplays the aspects of the story discussed above, reflects the particular aims of its author, who did not want to linger on the mechanics of Orestes' vengeance or its consequences; his intention was to make Orestes a suitable figure for Telemachus' emulation. We cannot conclude that such information was not already in circulation at the time of that poem's composition. And indeed, we are told by the fourth-century scholar Megaclides that Stesichorus' poem owed much to a work by the lyric poet Xanthus.[82] Xanthus' poem, as Aelian remarks (probably himself drawing on Megaclides), included Electra, who was given that name via a false etymology because she was growing old unwedded.[83] That fascinating detail implies a greater focus on the impact of Agamemnon's death on his family than we find in Homer. At the very least Xanthus' Electra is left distraught by her father's death, and thus presumably hostile to her mother; that mother might even have prevented her from marrying, to punish her or to avoid the prospect of a potential avenger, in the form of Electra's husband or son. The familial tensions familiar from tragedy, and probably present in Stesichorus, can thus be traced to an even earlier source. Xanthus did not make it into the canon of lyric poets, but his work was apparently known in the fourth century to Megaclides; we may guess that the tragedians knew it, too. This complicates any attempt to tease assess Stesichorus' distinctive impact on fifth-century tragedians.

A pessimist might conclude that aside from the *Oresteia*, the *Thebais*, and the *Palinode*, hard evidence that the tragedians interacted with Stesichorus is scarce, and that even in those three poems we cannot do much more than identify similarities without saying much of literary, as opposed to literary historical, significance. But such a view is excessively sceptical, and places too much emphasis on what we do not have as opposed to what we do. The explicit connexions are indeed few, so few that the kind of sweeping claims cited at the start of this piece cannot be justified. But there are connexions nonetheless: as well as

---

Agamemnon: le sacrifice d'Iphigénie se présente comme un acte pieux du roi obéissant à une demande de la déesse Artémis qui recompense le père en sauvant la fille.'
81 Nevertheless, the complete loss of the Stesichorean matricide is particularly grievous for our appreciation of the poem.
82 Stes. fr. 171 F.
83 Xanthus fr. 700 *PMG*.

the *Oresteia*'s impact on Aeschylus and the later tragedians, we have the relationship between the *Thebais* fragment and Euripides' *Phoenissae*, and between the *Palinode* and Euripides' *Helen*. In each case, members of the audience familiar with the Stesichorean version would probably have achieved a more profound appreciation of the tragedies that they were watching thanks to their knowledge of Stesichorus and consequent understanding of how the tragedian had interacted with his work. Moreover, it is intriguing to note that our discussion has time and again been dominated by tragic women: Clytemnestra in the *Oresteia*, the Queen in the *Thebais*, Helen in the *Helen* and *Palinode*. There were tragic women before Stesichorus, but the prominence that he gives to them, and to others such as Althaea, or to Geryon's mother Callirhoe, could have inspired the tragedians just as much as the portrayal of women in Homer did. In other words, we must be open to the fascinating possibility that Stesichorus was a crucial early antecedent for the representation of strong-minded women in Greek tragedy.

Thomas R.P. Coward
'Stesichorean' Footsteps in the *Parodos* of Aeschylus' *Agamemnon*

1 Introduction

The choral odes of Attic tragedy stand within the same traditions as non-dramatic lyric poems, with their use of mythological exempla, paradigms, and general reflections on the morals and rules of human life.[1] An audience member at the Theatre of Dionysus would have been familiar with how choral language sounds and works in different forms of ritualistic and mimetic performance, even if that person would not precisely know every composition by line and verse on each occasion.[2] While dramatic choral lyric is in the same family of song as other non-dramatic lyric, it is marked off by the involvement of the chorus within a dramatic performance involving actors, which creates a sense of distance from the genres it incorporates, and maintains its own 'tragic' lyric identity.[3] Therefore audience members at the performance of a Greek tragedy could pick up these references through marked statements to different songs, or recognise aural patterns and descriptive passages that evoke or nod towards epic, lyric and musico-poetic traditions.

The *parodos* of Aeschylus' *Agamemnon* (40–263) is the longest in extant Attic tragedy. It narrates the departure of the Greek army from Aulis, the portent of the two eagles and of the hare, and the sacrifice of Iphigeneia. Much has been said about its theology, morality and presentation.[4] Scholars have also acknowledged the influence of Stesichorus on Oresteia-based tragedies, and made statements in passing concerning Stesichorean narrative techniques and themes in

---

I am grateful to P. Agócs, R. Andújar, G.B. D'Alessio, P.J. Finglass, T.A. Hadjimichael, E.E. Prodi, and to the participants in the London conference for their helpful suggestions and comments on previous drafts and on the oral version of this paper.

1 Herington 1985, 21.
2 Schein 2009, 377. Aristophanes (*Pax* 775–800) clearly parodies a precise passage of Stesichorus (frr. 172–4 Finglass = 210–12 *PMGF*). There are a range of levels of understanding in which an audience would perceive this connection, from Stesichorus' *Oresteia* to mythological choral lyric/lyric epic, and Aristophanes would be aware of this. See Finglass in this volume on this passage of Aristophanes.
3 Swift 2010, 367.
4 See Gruber 2009, 270–310 and Raeburn and Thomas 2011, liii-vi for summaries.

the *parodos*, but they offer little clarification on the range or nature of Stesichorean influences.[5] I shall examine the truth and implications of these statements.

This chapter focuses on two questions: what are the lyric-epic and musical influences on the *parodos* and how does Aeschylus situate and distance himself from the traditions of the *Oresteia* story? Epic poems (*Oresteia* and *Nostoi* stories) and choral narrative poems are some of the several lines of influence on the *parodos*.[6] I shall argue that Aeschylus is adapting and adopting the extended narrative techniques found in the poems of Stesichorus and is evoking the sound and rhythm of a Stesichorean-like poem (i.e. lyric-epic), through lexical, metrical and mythical associations, at the beginning of his *Oresteia* trilogy to indicate a point of beginning and departure into his own treatment of the *Oresteia* mythology.[7]

Stesichorus was re-performed in Athens and his influence can already be detected in Aeschylus' *Septem contra Thebas* (467 BC).[8] I first look at the epic (rhapsodic and citharodic) and Stesichorean influences on the music and rhythm of the *parodos*, and then the mythical content.[9] I propose the musical *nomos* that

---

[5] E.g. Hutchinson 2001, 438 n.18 states that 'the parodos of the *Agamemnon* in some ways recalls Stesichorus' and Raeburn and Thomas 2011, lxiii note that 'the first odes in the *Agamemnon* might be compared with the fragments of Stesichorus in terms of extended choral narrative technique'. Cf. also Griffith 2008, 7 n.13. A papyrus commentary (Stes. fr. 181ab Finglass = fr. 217 *PMGF*) explicitly states that tragedians owed several motifs to Stesichorus' *Oresteia*. See Prag 1985, 73–6, Garvie 1986, xvii-xxiv, Sommerstein 2010a, 136–45, Swift 2015, 127–32, and Finglass in this volume for further analysis. Stesichorus' *Oresteia* consisted of at least two books in a Hellenistic edition, and it was supposedly influenced by one Xanthus (frr. 699–700 *PMG*); however, no fragments of his works survive and his performative context is unknown; see Finglass 2015b on this work.

[6] The Cyclic *Nostoi*, which based on Proclus's summary (*Nost.* Argumen. §§1–5 *GEF*), focused mainly on the return of Agamemnon and Menelaus. There are also parallels in the *parodos* with Homeric similes: Aesch. *Ag.* 40–54 ~ Hom. *Il.* 16.428–9; *Od.* 16.216–19; *Ag.* 56–62 ~ *Il.* 16.431; *Ag.* 60–7 ~ *Od.* 14.68–71, *Il.* 2.38–40; *Ag.* 108–24 ~ *Il.* 6.57–60; *Ag.* 357–61 ~ *Il.* 5.485–9. West 1979b = 2011–2013, II 215–22 and Janko 1980 have noted the use of Archilochean animal imagery (Archil. frr. 172–81 *IEG*) in the *parodos*.

[7] Both poets were also indebted to citharodic and rhapsodic epic.

[8] See Ercoles and Fiorentini 2011, with the reservations of Swift 2015, 132–43 and Finglass in this volume on Stesichorus' influence on tragedy, which can be recognised at the level of characterisation, theme, and imagery as well as narrative shaping. He was also a mythological innovator therefore providing source material to follow and diverge from. For the performance of Stesichorus in Athens, see Bowie 2015a, who acknowledges that some of his suggestions are speculative, and Finglass 2014a, 60–72 for the transmission of Stesichorus to Athens.

[9] During the archaic and classical periods, there were two distinct but interacting traditions of poetry: 'melic' and 'epic'. The former was a heptatonic system of tuning, the latter a recitative mode based on linguistic pitch, see Nagy 1990, 17–51; Wilson 2009, 58. Epic poetry consisted

may have accompanied the *parodos*, one indebted to the citharodic and Stesichorean traditions. The metre of the *parodos* shows resonances that indicate that Aeschylus was evoking the sound-effect of this *nomos* and the metres of narrative choral lyric (e.g. Stesichorus and Alcman) and *kitharōidia*. I finish with the narrative technique of the *parodos* – i.e. how events are told, characterisation, and the tone and style of the narrative. Aeschylus' aim was to set the *Agamemnon* within the ethos of Stesichorean poetry so as to familiarise his audience with the mood and setting of the story, and then to mark off his own version of the *Oresteia* myth as the *parodos* and play progressed. I show the influence of Stesichorus on the beginning of the *Oresteia* and how the study of interactions between lyric and tragedy involves the simultaneous study of content, metrical context, and stylistic register of choral odes.

2 Music and Rhythm

While there is plenty of *testimonia* on the music and (some on) the choreography of Greek poetry: very little actual music has survived. Nevertheless it must be acknowledged that the full development of the dramatic themes of a play was a combination of costume, words, meter, and music and dance.[10] According to the *testimonia* on Athenian drama and Aeschylus' literary biography, Aeschylus was deeply interested in scene design, choreography, costume design, and music.[11] Aeschylus' plays were also criticised by Aristophanes as being full of empty noise, which is a further *testimonium*, in spite of the satire, of Aeschylus' musical concerns.[12] 'Euripides' in Aristophanes' *Frogs* makes an interesting observation when he states that Aeschylus borrowed citharodic *nomoi* in his aulodic choral songs as part of his satire on Aeschylus' fondness for dactylic rhythms and refrains:

μὴ πρίν γ' ἀκούσῃς χἀτέραν στάσιν μελῶν
ἐκ τῶν κιθαρῳδικῶν νόμων εἰργασμένην.

---

of performance by recitation (rhapsodic) and performance with musical accompaniment (citharodic). There is an intersecting tradition of hymns, elegy and *iambos*.
10 Ancient testimony (e.g. Prat. fr. 708.6–7 *PMG*; Pl. *Resp.* 398c-d) also suggests that music was strictly subsidiary to the words themselves in archaic Greek poetry.
11 Aesch. T100–14 *TrGF*³.
12 Cf. Ar. *Nub.* 1367, perhaps also Phld. *De Poet.* 3 fr. 59 Janko. Aristotle says something similar about dithyrambic poets (*Rhet.* 3.1406b2, cf. *Poet.* 1459a9, cf. also Dion. Hal. *Dem.* 7.4, 7.6).

> No, not till you've heard the next set of choral lyrics, made from citharodic *nomoi*.
>
> (Ar. *Ran.* 1281–2)

'Euripides' then quotes the *parodos* of *Agamemnon* as an example.[13] Aristophanes cites this *parodos* and other passages; thereby indicating that Aeschylus' use of citharodic *nomoi* was a recognisable feature of the archaizing style of his choral odes.[14] According to the *scholia* to *Frogs*, Timachidas of Rhodian Lindos (*fl.* 100 BC) indicates that Aeschylus would seem to have borrowed the rhythms and melodies of citharodic *nomoi* into his own choral odes and used the *orthios nomos*.[15]

> "ἐκ τῶν κιθαρῳδικῶν νόμων": Τιμαχίδας γράφει, ὡς τῷ ὀρθίῳ νόμῳ κεχρημένου τοῦ Αἰσχύλου καὶ ἀνατεταμένως.[16] —ἀντὶ τοῦ ξένην τραγῳδίαν.
>
> (Tim. Rhod. fr. 11 Blinkenberg = Aesch. T155 *TrGF*³ ~ fr. 26 Matijašić)

'from citharodic *nomoi*': Timachidas writes that Aeschylus made use of the *Orthios nomos* and strained it to the highest pitch. In the sense of something which is unusual for tragedy.

The comments of Timachidas on this section of the *Frogs* concern Aeschylus (9–12 Blinkenberg ~ 24–28 Matijašić). The other fragments of Timachidas' com-

---

13 Ar. *Ran.* 1284–5 = Aesch. *Ag.* 108–9, cf. also 1276 = 104, 1289 = 111–2. There are citations from other Aeschylean *parodoi*, which are metrically similar to the *parodos* of *Agamemnon*: *Priestesses* (1273–4 = fr. 87 *TrGF*³), *Myrmidons* (Ar. *Ran.* 1264–5 = fr. 132 *TrGF*³), and *Psychagogoi* (Ar. *Ran.* 1266 = fr. 273 *TrGF*³). Other Aeschylean plays: Ar. *Ran.* 1269 = fr. 238 *TrGF*³; 1287 = fr. 236 *TrGF*³; 1291–2 = fr. 282 *TrGF*³; 1294 = fr. 84 *TrGF*³.
14 Cf. also Ar. *Ran.* 814–29. *Nomoi* are best understood as unchained 'melodies' akin to Indian *rāgas* i.e. there were prescriptive modal-melodic structures but a performer had some freedom to vary or interpret it with their own musical gestures or riffs of varying lengths, see Barker 1984, 249; West 1992, 216 n.66; Gostoli 1993, 172. Musical *nomoi* such as οἱ Ἅιδου νόμοι (Soph. fr. 861 *TrGF*⁴) or ὄρθιοι ἐν νόμοι (Aesch. *Ag.* 1153) are not precise terminologies, like references to genres, in archaic and classical Greek poetry; rather they evoke the wider theme and connotations of the reference.
15 Σ Ar. *Ran.* 1282 Chantry. Timachidas composed the *Lindian Chronicle* (*FGrHist* 532, cf. Higbie 2003), treatises on Aristophanes' *Frogs*, Euripides' *Medea*, and Menander's *The Flatterer*, a *Glossai*, and an epic poem of at least eleven books called *Deipnon* (769–73 *SH*). West 1986, 45 and Borthwick 1994, 21–2 remind us that the tragic chorus was performed to the *aulos* and emphasise the satiric edge of "Euripides'" words of how old-fashioned Aeschylus' lyrics are. They do not propose a mixing of instrumental *nomoi*.
16 Cf. also [Arist.] *Pr.* 19.37 (920b).

mentaries on drama indicate that he was aware of different editions of tragedies and comedies, of music, and engaged in scholarly debates on the literary and socio-historical contexts of dramatic texts.[17] While there are no extant examples of texts with musical notation until the middle of the third century BC (*DAGM* No. 3), and the Alexandrian scholars tended to produce text-only editions of the lyric poets; there were, however, musically annotated tragic texts during the lifetime of Timachidas (*DAGM* Nos. 2–4, 8–9, 17–8).[18] Therefore, while his *testimonium* cannot be completely proven, it cannot be ignored.

The *parodos* of *Agamemnon* may well have been performed to the *orthios nomos*, with some modification, based on Timachidas' *testimonium*, its dactylic, iambic and trochaic metres (see Section III for further analysis), the use of certain refrains, Aeschylus' perversion of Apolline motets, and the descriptions of synonymous *nomoi* that indicate the type of melody or rhythmical characteristics and so help to reconstruct the *orthios nomos*. *Testimonia* indicate several general characteristics. *Orthios* probably refers to its structure and rhythm.[19] It has high-pitched melodies,[20] was used in a wide variety of musical genres,[21] has martial connotations in later sources,[22] and had lyric dactylic rhythms with some iambo-trochaic elements.[23] The *orthios nomos* was also known as the Terpandrian

---

[17] Timachidas (fr. 25a Matijašić = fr. 10 Blinkenberg) attributed Aesch. fr. 238 *TrGF*³ to Aeschylus' *Telephos*, whereas Asclepiades assigned it to *Iphigeneia*, and Aristarchus and Apollonius were unable to assign a title. Nauck 1889, Radt in *TrGF*³, and Lucas de Dios 2008, 614–9 follow Timachidas. On line 1294, which is quotation from *Thracian Women* (84 *TrGF*³), Timachidas (fr. 27 Matijašić = fr. 12 Blinkenberg) states that this line was absent from some texts of the *Frogs*. Both are interesting and understudied *testimonia* on the pre- and post-Alexandrian transmission of drama.

[18] See Prauscello 2006 on the Hellenistic and post-Hellenistic examples with notation. Pöhlmann-West 2012, and West 2013b have published an early (*ca.* 430–420 BC) literary papyrus and wooden tablets, which were found in the tomb of a musician in Attica.

[19] Cf. Arist. Quint. 36.29.

[20] Aesch. *Ag.* 1153, [Arist.] *Pr.* 19.37 (920b), Σ Ar. *Ach.* 1042 Wilson, cf. e.g. Soph. *Ant.* 1206; Eur. *Tro.* 1266; Ar. *Ach.* 16, *Eq.* 1279; Hdt. 1.24. Aulus Gellius (16.19.14). notes *carmen, quid 'orthium' dicitur, voce sublatissima catavit.*

[21] The citharodic *orthios nomos* was traditionally ascribed to the Ur-citharodes Terpander (Heracl. Pont. fr. 109 Schütrumpf = fr. 157 Wehrli), and Thamyris (Gloss *ad* Hdt. 1.24 Latte and Erbse (p. 197), see Wilson 2009 on Thamyris), and the auletic version to the Ur-aulete Olympus or Polymnestus of Colophon (Ar. *Eq.* 8–10; Σ Ar. *Arch.* 16 Wilson; [Plut.] *De Mus.* 1134d; Poll. *On.* 4.71). The *nomos* was also played by Arion (Hdt. 1.24.5) and by Pindar (Him. *Or.* 60.4 Colonna).

[22] Max. Tyr. *Or.* 17.5.15–22; Eust. *ad Il.* 11.11, 13 van der Valk.

[23] Ps.-Plut. *De Mus.* 1133f. Pseudo-Plutarch (*De Mus.* 1140f) and Pollux (*On.* 4.65) pair the *orthios* and *trochaios* rhythms together, which may reflect the rhythm of song composed in this *nomos*

nomos and was synonymous with the *oxus nomos*.²⁴ The auletic version was vigorous (ἔντονος) and had a tense or violent tone (ἀνάτασις).²⁵ ἀνάτασις and ἀνατείνω denote the same tone of speaking that rises upwards in tension, either of a threat or of boasting.²⁶ Graf suggests that ἔντονος/εὔτονος could also be understood as σύντονος ('intense' or 'severe').²⁷ This indicates a *nomos* that is high pitched and had a stirring tone. The citharodic version was played at the Panathenaia (Ar. *Ach.* 16) and so would be recognisable to the audiences of Aeschylus and subsequently Aristophanes. An unidentified writer on rhythm (*P.Oxy.* 2687 col. iii.30-iv.1) notes the expanded beats of the *orthios* (⏔ ⏔ |⏔ ⏔ ⏔ ⏔ or – ⏑ – ⏑ | – ⏑ – ⏑ – ⏑ (– ⏑)) or *trochaios sēmantos* ('marked trochee', (⏔ ⏔ ⏔ ⏔|⏔ ⏔) rhythms, and indicate a slow beat, but a brisk tempo. The iambic rhythm can have the same measure as the dactylic.²⁸ Aristides Quintilianus (36.3, cf. 36.29, 83.4, cf. also Ps.-Plut. *De mus.* 1140f) indicates that these have a dignified manner and a slow tempo, but had a higher unity of syllables within a single beat. These could correspond to runs of dactylo-epitrites, which Stesichorus uses, and the lyric dactyls in the *parodos*.²⁹ Stesichorus and Aeschylus adapted the *orthios nomos* into their own works (see below), though the citharodic version would have been stichic, whereas Stesichorus and Aeschylus' versions are triadic and more metrically diverse, which opens the possibilities for adaptations and modifications.³⁰

There is some evidence regarding the music of Stesichorus.³¹ According to Glaucus of Rhegium, a contemporary of Democritus and Aristophanes (*c.* 425 – 375 BC), Stesichorus used the *Harmateios nomos* in dactylic rhythms (κατὰ δάκτυλον εἴδει),³² which was derived from Olympus' auletic *orthios nomos*, which also had dactylo-anapaestic rhythms.³³ The description of the rhythms

---

24 See Phot. α 1303 Theodoridis = *Suda* α 1701 Adler and Gostoli 1990, xviii-xix respectively.
25 Σ Ar. *Ach.* 16a Wilson with Hom. *Il.* 11.10–11; Poll. *On.* 4.71; *Suda* α 575 Adler.
26 ἀνάτασις is also used of the acute accent (Dion. Thrax 620.1).
27 Graf 1888, 518.
28 Ar. Quint. (p. 38.5) and *P.Oxy.* 2687 col.ii.3 δάκτυλος κατ' ἴαμβον.
29 West 1992, 157.
30 Cf. Danielewicz 1990, 141.
31 See Barker 2001 and Ercoles 2013, 546–60 on the music of Stesichorus.
32 Aristophanes, a contemporary of Glaucus, uses similar terminology (Ar. *Nub.* 649–51 with Σ Ar. *Nub.* 651c Holwerda).
33 Stes. Tb20 Ercoles = Glauc. Rheg. fr. 2 Gostoli/Lanata = fr. 3 *FHG*. Glaucus emphasises that Stesichorus' *nomos* is derived from auletic and not citharodic *nomoi*. The *Geryoneis* and *Games of Pelias* are in dactylo-anapaests. See Ar. *Eq.* 1278–9 and Phot. α 2835 Theodoridis on players of the *orthios nomos*, and Graf 1888, 514–15; West 1971, 309–11= 2011–2013, II 90–1; Power 2010, 238–40 on the *nomos*. Glaucus composed two known works on literary history: Περὶ τῶν

of this *nomos* suggests something like dactylo-epitrite.[34] It can be understood that the rhythms of Stesichorus' poems are in part derived from Olympus' *nomos*, but Stesichorus 'choralised' citharodic/auletic *nomoi* to triadic song-and-dance narratives, which included the use of auletic *nomoi* for citharodic ones.[35] Stesichorus is never explicitly identified as a citharode in ancient literature, rather as an analogous singing poet.[36] It is very likely Stesichorus was the first, or one of the first, to adapt this auletic *nomos* to his choral poems and that this was 'his only or at least his regular nome.'[37] As noted above, the names of musical *nomoi* are not fixed technical terms in the archaic and classical periods, but are related families with synonymous labels.[38] The Euripidean *scholia* say that the *Harmateios* was also called the νόμος Ἀθῆνας, and that it was high pitched (ὀξύφωνος).[39] The *orthios nomos* is also high-pitched. The νόμος Ἀθῆνας was also said to be in the Phrygian mode (or key) and was also attributed to Olympus.[40] West and Barker plausibly proposed to identify the *Harmateios nomos* with the Φρύγιον μέλος, which is referred to in the opening of Stesichorus' *Oresteia* (fr. 173.2 Finglass = fr. 212.2 *PMGF*), as the tune to which the poem

---

ἀρχαίων ποιητῶν καὶ μουσικῶν (fr. 1 Gostoli/Lanata = fr. 2 *FHG*) and Περὶ Αἰσχύλου μύθων (fr. 9 Gosotli = fr. 7 Lanata = Σ Aesch. *Pers. Hypoth.* 1 Dähnhardt, cf. also fr. 10 Gostoli). See Hiller 1886, esp. 428–31, Huxley 1968 and Gostoli 2015 on Glaucus.
34 West 1992, 217 n.65.
35 Cham. fr. 30 Martano = fr. 28 Wehrli; Power 2010, 236–7. Bowra 1961, 242 proposes that Ibycus may too have adopted a Stesichorean *Harmateios nomos* (ap. Him. *Or.* 22.5 Colonna). Philochorus (*FGrHist* 328 F 23) says that Lysander of Sicyon, a contemporary of Stesichorus, was the first to place *aulos*-like performances to the *kithara*.
36 Citharodes are identified as ἄνδρες ἀοιδοὶ καὶ κιθαρισταί; see Hes. *Theog.* 95, fr. 305.2 M-W, Hom. *Hymn Ap.* 3.188, Hom. *Hymn Mus. et Ap.* 25.3, Theocr. *Id.* 22.24, cf. also Hom. *Il.* 2.599–600, 13.731, *Od.* 1.159, 21.406. The hendiadys highlights the narrative content of a singer who tells lengthy tales to music. Timomachus (*FGrHist* 754 F 1) says that Iliadic and Odyssean episodes were performed to the kithara. The citharodes played poems, which were stichic, and possibly monostrophic (cf. Alcm. fr. 1 *PMGF* = fr. 3 Calame) or a form of *parakataloge* ('recitative', a 're-duced-melody vocal delivery to the accompaniment of the *aulos* (or less typically the lyre)' according to Budelmann and Power 2013, 11, in dactylic rhythms, see Moore 2008 for a thorough review of the scholarship on *parakatalogē*.
37 West 1971, 311 = 2011–2013, II 92.
38 Barker 1984, I 251.
39 Σ Eur. *Or.* 1384 Schwartz. Cf. also *Et. Magn.* 145.34–43 Gaisford. Pollux (*On.* 4.65) also notes that the *ethnoi* of the Terpandrian *nomoi* includes the 'Boeotian.' See Grandolini 2002 on the *Harmateios nomos*. The *Suda* (α 1122 Adler) refers to an auletic τῆς Ἀθηνᾶς τὸν ὄρθιον νόμον.
40 Pl. *Cr.* 417e; Ps.-Plut. *De Mus.* 1143a-c; Poll. *On.* 4.77; West 1992, 216–217. There was also a citharodic version (Poll. *On.* 4.66).

was performed.⁴¹ Stesichorus' *Oresteia* has trochaic and dactylic rhythms (related to dactylo-epitrites), which further underscores this proposed connexion.

The evidence above shows that Stesichorus was understood to have composed music that was high-pitched, an adaptation of an auletic *orthios nomos*, and was in dactylic metres with iambo-trochaic and anapaestic elements (~ dactylo-epitrite). Stesichorus' *Oresteia* (and other poems) were performed to a *nomos* that was derived from or imitated an *orthios nomos*, which, according to Glaucus, was a recognisable feature of his poetry, and was derived from instrumental music for the *aulos*, rather than the kithara. The *parodos* of *Agamemnon*, a tragic choral performance with *aulos* accompaniment, perhaps shows the influence of the citharodic *orthios nomos*, has rhythmical analogies and thematic connexions with this *nomos* and continues Stesichorus' practice of adapting instrumental *nomoi* into new settings. Fraenkel proposed that the *parodos* was a conscious attempt to evoke the metres of archaic citharodes.⁴² The attested titles of and comments on citharodic poems would indicate that the earliest lyric poets such as Thamyris, Terpander and Stesichorus set dactylic metres to music.⁴³ Aeschylus was exposed to *kitharōidia* at the various *mousikoi agōnes*, in his own education in Athens, and in his travels to Sicily, where he may have also heard reperformances of Stesichorus and similar poems.⁴⁴ There are representations of citharodic songs in Attic tragedy (Soph. 242 *TrGF*⁴; Eur. *Ant.* 6 Kambitsis) and songs in imitation of citharodic epic (Eur. *Alc.* 445–54, *Tro.* 511–15), which are in dactylic metres with some aeolic elements.⁴⁵

Timachidas notes that Aeschylus' version was at a very high pitch (τῷ ὀρθίῳ νόμῳ κεχρημένου) and the *nomos* was stretched to its limit (ἀνατεταμένως), i.e. the syllables were drawn out or contained long dactylic runs. This suggests that Aeschylus was experimenting with the *nomos* and using it in a way that subverted or played with the sound, tone and effects of the *orthios nomos*. This *nomos* is

---

41 West 1971, 310 = 2011–2013, II 91–2; Barker 2001, and West 1982, 125–6; Nagy 1990, 95 n. 64; esp. Cingano 1993, 253–7.
42 Fraenkel 1918, 321–3 = 1964, I 202–3.
43 Terp. T27 Gostoli = Heracl. Pont. fr. 157.10–20 Wehrli; Chaem. fr. 30 Martano = fr. 28 Wehrli (see D'Alfonso 1994, 129–31; Power 2010, 236 on this passage); Terp. T34, T50 Gostoli; Alexander Polyhistor *FGrHist* 273 F 77; Plut. *Quaest. Lac.* 17.238c. See West 1986, 46 and Gostoli 1990, xxxvii for general discussion.
44 Aesch. T1.8–12; T88–92b *TrGF*³. Vases show that there was a Panathenaic contest in Athens for *kitharistae/kitharistes* from 550/540 BC (BM London B 139 = *ABV* 139, 12; Power 2010, 425–7). Vases were awarded as prizes for *kitharodoi* from 500–480 BC onwards (Musee du Louvre, Paris, F282; Kotsidu 1991, 294, pl. 13–15).
45 Such patterns are also found in the lyric triad of the *parodos*, see below. See Athanassaki and Fanfani in this volume on Eur. *Tro.* 511–15.

associated with Apollo as a healer, and the *parodos* is filled with Apolline references.⁴⁶ Before her sacrifice, Iphigeneia entertains her father and his guests at a symposium with a *paian*.⁴⁷ Calchas calls upon Apollo Paionos (Aesch. *Ag.* 146) to amend the action of Zeus and restore order among the fleet, whereby Agamemnon carries out the sacrifice after some initial deliberation. The refrain (αἴλινον αἴλινον εἰπέ) followed by the paeanic τὸ δ' εὖ νικάτω, and Agamemnon's closing words (εὖ γὰρ εἴη, 217) are two generic and apotropaic references to the *linos* and *paian* song.⁴⁸ In Aeschylus, the apotropaic and celebratory functions of the *paian* and the power of Apollo are perverted with the foreshadowing of future events, again showing his deliberate distortion.⁴⁹

Aeschylus also connects the murder-sacrifice of Iphigeneia with the murder-sacrifice of Cassandra, as both Calchas' interpretation and the Chorus remark that their final actions are ἄνομον 'impious/unmusical' (Aesch. *Ag.* 150, 1142).⁵⁰ The Chorus compares Cassandra to Procne (1140–5) and Clytemnestra describes Cassandra's utterances as swallow-like and incomprehensible (1050–3).⁵¹ Aeschylus portrays Cassandra as a hyper-swallow and this depiction could (very tentatively) be seen as a distortion of the swallow at the beginning of Stesichorus' *Oresteia* (fr. 174 Finglass = fr. 211 *PMGF*) and to its performative context, and nod to the music accompanying her frantic speech. The Chorus then observe that her words are ὀρθίοις ἐν νόμοις (1153) in their strophic dialogue with Cassandra in iambo-dochmiac metres.⁵² The swallow is also associated with high-pitched (*orthios*) lamentation.⁵³ The Aeschylean *scholia* also note Cassandra's *nomos* is threnodic and citharodic.⁵⁴ So, later

---

46 Terp. fr. 2 Gostoli, cf. also Sapph. fr. 44.32–4 Voigt.
47 Aesch. *Ag.* 243–7. See Rutherford 1993, 77–9, 2001, 79–80 on the paean.
48 See Finglass 2011, 322 on the *linos* song. Repetition is common in ritual invocations, e.g. Pind. *Pae.* 2.35b, 71, 107 = D2.35b, 71, 107 Rutherford, *Pae.* 4.31, 62 = D4.31, 62 Rutherford; fr. 738.1 *PMG*; Eur. *HF* 772, *Andr.* 1031; Hesych. θ 300 Latte.
49 See Swift in this volume on the *paian* in Aeschylus' *Oresteia*.
50 'The implication here is 'song without order or bounds', an apt description of Cassandra's frenzied utterances' (Barker 1984, 70 n. 51).
51 The swallow was also a simile for foreign speech (Ar. *Ran.* 678–82). Cf. Gostoli 1993, 177.
52 Aeschylus uses *nomos* in a musical sense (Aesch. *Sept.* 951–4; *Supp.* 69; *Ag.* 418, 1141, 1472; fr. 43 *TrGF*³).
53 Hom. *Od.* 19.518; Hes. *Op.* 568; Sapph. fr. 135 Voigt; Aesch. *Pers.* 1038–77, *Supp.* 57–72; Eur. *Phaet.* 69; Ar. *Av.* 212, Apollod. *Bibl.* 3.14.8; Ov. *Met.* 6.424–674; Hyg. *Fab.* 45. Plato (*Phd.* 85a) thought the cries of the nightingale, swallow and hoopoe were not really laments, however they are in literary works.
54 Σ Aesch. *Ag.* 1142ab Smith. Fraenkel 1950, III 519 dismisses this piece of evidence, but has taken things literally. He correctly states that *nomos* is not a specific term, but perhaps we should understand the statement that Cassandra's song is *like* or *as if* citharodic.

in the play, Aeschylus may have used a *nomos*, perhaps the *orthios*, which was high-pitched and mournful sounding, but set it to a different metre to emphasise Cassandra's oracular, but frenzied, tone.

The music of Stesichorus was a choral emulation of *kitharōidia*, derived from an auletic *orthios nomos*, and it can be proposed that Aeschylus followed a similar practice. Aeschylus' adaptation of the *nomos* allowed a grand and expansive manner for a heroic narration and a general tone of stateliness and magnificence.[55] The *parodos* is a perverted heroic narrative set at the departure of the expedition to Troy. The *parodos* of the *Agamemnon*, then, was perhaps, either originally or in re-performance, a high-pitched, slow, solemn, and dignified sounding choral ode that sets the tone for this play as it transitions from a song steeped in a musico-poetic tradition to acclimatise its audience to the story and emphasise key points and sounds of that Aeschylus appropriates and subverts. It can be argued that Aeschylus is alluding musically to Stesichorean and citharodic poetry, based on descriptions of his music and auletic/citharodic music. The dactylo-anapaests and dactylo-trochaics of Stesichorus are also a convenient link between martial epic and tragic choral lyric. As already hinted at, there are indications of such a metrical link in the *parodos*.

3 Metre

There is surprisingly little resonance in the metres of tragic choral odes and the metres of lyric choral poems.[56] The *parodos* of *Agamemnon*, however, shows resonances that indicate that Aeschylus was evoking the sound-effect and *kola* of Stesichorus and *kitharōidia* (lyric dactyls) at the beginning of his *Oresteia* trilogy.[57] The effect of this would be to introduce the audience into the mythical arc of the trilogy and to establish a foreboding atmosphere.[58] The structure and combination of metres in the *parodos* are unusual for Attic tragedy. Tragic choral songs are usually structured in a stream of constantly modified strophic pairs (sometimes with an epode), often with radically different stanzas and metrical structures from one ode to another or within a single choral ode.[59] Instead in the *pa-*

---

55 Cf. [Arist.] *Pr.* 19.48 (922b), Procl. *Chrest. ap.* Phot. *Bibl.* 320b.17 (V.161 Henry) on the *nomos*.
56 Herington 1985, 114.
57 An anonymous metrician (Alcm. TXIII Calame (p. 227) = Sim. fr. 649 g *PMG*) noted that Aeschylus used a certain type of metre, which was used earlier by Simonides and Alcman. It is unknown what particular type or colon of metre the critic was referring to.
58 Easterling 1997b, 167 notes that the Watchman addressed the audience (Aesch. *Ag.* 39).
59 Griffith 2008, 18; Rutherford 2012, 217–36.

rodos, there is a juxtaposition of different kinds of meters in blocks within a single ode.⁶⁰ There are overlaps in the *kola* and the distribution of periods between the *parodos* of *Agamemnon*, especially in the opening lyric triad, with the poems of Stesichorus that recall epic, lyric and lyric-epic traditions.

The opening lyric triad (104–59) is a mixture of dactyls and iambo-trochaic and choriambic phrases, familiar since Alcman.⁶¹ This mixture of dactyls and iambics is rare in tragedy (Aesch. *Supp*. 40–93, *Ag*. 104–59), and it has analogies with dactylo-epitrites, which are found in Stesichorus.⁶² Dactylic sequences with iambic or trochaic clausula are quite common in Stesichorus.⁶³ The opening dactylic lines of the strophe/antistrophe have parallels in Stesichorus and tragedy:

6 *da*: 104 = 122, 118/9 = 136/7, 155 ~ Stes. fr. 97 stro. 1, 3 Finglass = 222(b) *PMGF*; Soph. fr. 242 *TrGF*⁴; Eur. *Ant*. fr. 6 Kambitsis.

5 *da*: 106 = 123, 121 = 139, 145/6, 159 ~ Stes. fr. 97 stro. 2 Finglass = 222(b) *PMGF*, Tb17 Ercoles.

---

60 Herington 1985, 122. My own summary of the metres of the *parodos* is drawn from Scott 1984, 33–8 and Sommerstein 2010a, 148–9.
61 Alcm. fr. 39 *PMGF* = fr. 91 Calame, fr. 241 Calame = formerly Pind. Dub. fr. 345 S-M. See Appendix for the metrical scheme. A similar mixture is seen in Bacchylides' *Ode* Three for Hieron (468 BC) and Pindar's *Olympian* Thirteen (464 BC) with their combination of aeolic/iambic strophes and an epode of dactylo-epitrites. The opposite is seen in Soph. *Aj*. 172–93. Notably the opening choral song of the *Agamemnon* and final processional hymn of the *Eumenides* frame the *Oresteia* trilogy with dactyls.
62 Westphal coined the term 'dactylo-epitrite', see Rossbach and Westphal 1868. For an explanation of the term see Martinelli 1995, 257; Battezzato 2009, 140–2. Maas 1962, §55 proposed the symbols *D*, *E*, *e*. Some, following the ancient metrical treatises, would prefer κατ' ἐνόπλιον, e.g. Gentili 1952, 105–29; Gentili and Giannini 1977, 11–12 n.8. Dale 1968, 157–94 uses both. Aeschylus has shorter and simpler examples of dactylic stanzas with some iambo-trochaic elements (*Pers*. 852–907; *Eum*. 347–53 ~ 360–7, 368–70 ~ 377–9, 1040–6, cf. also Soph. *Aj*. 174–93, *OT* 151–215 (both *parodoi*); Ar. *Pax* 775–800 (in imitation of Stesichorus, see Finglass in this volume), *Av*. 737–51. Purely dactylic stanzas are found only in Euripides (Eur. *Heracl*. 608–28, *Andr*. 1173–96, *Supp*. 271–85, *Tro*. 595–608, *Hel*. 375–85, *Phoen*. 784–817). There are no dactylo-epitrites in extant Aeschylus, except in the Aeschylean *Prometheus Bound* (526–60, 887–906).
63 Haslam 1974 and 1978 divided Stesichorean metres into dactylo-anapaestic (*Games for Pelias, Geryoneis, Boar-Hunters*, frr. 187–269, 270a, 301 Finglass = frr. 222(a), 233, 244 *PMGF*) and dactylo-epitrites (*Helen, Palinode, Eriphyle, Thebais, Iliou Persis, Nostoi?, Oresteia,* and probably 214, 271, 302 Finglass = 222(a) fr.35, 232, 245 *PMGF*). Haslam 1974, 10 divided Stesichorean metre into three categories: dactylo-trochaics (forerunners of the dactylo-epitrites of Pindar and Bacchylides); dactylo-anapaestic, largely dactylic runs of hemiepes (*D*), with opening and closing sequences of en(h)oplians, paroemiacs and prosodiacs; and an intermediate between the two in Stesichorus' *Iliou Persis*. West 1982, 49 divided the key features into two categories. In the first there are iambo-trochaic elements, mainly at period end (e.g. *Iliou Persis, Oresteia, Palinode, Thebais, Nostoi*); in the other, they are absent.

The tragic parallels are from imitations of citharodic epic/nomoi and these metres are found in the citharodic *prooimia* of Terpander (frr. 2–3 Gostoli = frr. 697–8 PMG), which were *prooimia* performed to the Terpandrian *orthios nomos*.[64] Servius (Stes. Tb17 Ercoles) states that the pentameters were also known as 'Stesichoreans.' D'Alessio has also shown that the metrical pattern of the opening two lines of the *parodos* are found in Eumelus' famous *prosodion* (fr. 696 PMG), a poem thought to date to the eighth century BC, but this dating is doubtful.[65] Eumelus composed both epic and lyric epic (Paus. 4.4.1, 4.33.2). This shows that the opening of the *parodos* conjures up the rhythms of a citharodic nome and Steschorean poems, and it creates an archaising and long, but stately, effect on the ode.

The unpaired epode (140–59), which is Calchas' interpretation of the portent, is in dactyls that initially alternates with iambic-choriambic rhythms, a feature found nowhere else in Aeschylus' *Oresteia*. Lines 148–59 are purely dactylic metres. Servius (Stes. Tb11 Ercoles) described the catalectic dactylic heptameter as a Stesichorean metre, which is found in the *Eriphyle* (fr. 93.3–4 Finglass = S148.3–4 PMGF) and the epode of the lyric triad (*Ag.* 148–51). The dactylic rhythm has an oracular feel, which adds weight to Calchas' prophecy.[66] The epode can be compared with the monostrophic stanzas of Alcman (fr. 1 PMGF = fr. 3 Calame), where there are strongly marked off *kola* of alternating trochaic (*lek.*) and aeolic (*hag.*) periods, followed by dactylic periods. This is also found in Stesichorus' *Iliou Persis* (ep. 6–8) and *Nostoi* (stro. 1) and the epode has aeolic elements (*Ag.* 141, 143, 146).[67] Haslam also notes that in the *Oresteia* there is 'ap-

---

[64] There are two fragments attributed to Terpander (frr. 2–3 Gostoli = frr. 697–8 PMG), which have a spondaic pentameter. Gentili and Giannini 1977, 36 and Gostoli 1990, 135 point out that line 106/7 corresponds precisely with these Terpandrian and Stesichorean pentameters: I add 124/5. See Beecroft 2008; Power 2010, 243–9, 321–3 on Terpander as a metonym of the citharodic tradition.

[65] D'Alessio 2009, 142. See Bowra 1963 = 1970, 46–58 and D'Alessio 2009, 137–9 on Eumelus. Pausanias presents a seemingly factual biographical account about Eumelus, however his historicity and the works attributed to him should remain in question, cf. West 2002 = 2011–2013, I 353–91. Bowra 1963, 145–6 also cited strophe/antistrophe 2–5 of the *Geryoneis* (e.g. F8.1–3 Finglass = S17.1–3 PMGF), though these are dactylo-anapaestic (7 *an.* and 5 *an*), not the dactylic hexameter and pentameter of Eumelus and Aeschylus. Stro./Ant. 2–5 of *Geryoneis*:

$$\underline{\smile\smile} - \smile\smile - \underline{\smile\smile} - \smile\smile -$$
$$\smile\smile - \underline{\smile\smile} - \smile\smile - - |$$
$$\underline{\smile\smile} - \smile\smile - \underline{\smile\smile} - \smile\smile -$$
$$\smile\smile - - \|$$

[66] Independently noted in Scott 1984, 35 n.26 and in Raeburn and Thomas 2011, 78.

[67] *Iliou Persis* epode

(6)– $\smile\smile - \smile\smile - \times - \smile - \times$ (D x e x)

parently a (closing?) period – – ⏑ ⏑ – ⏑ – –', which is found at verse-end in the epode (*Ag.* 141, 143, 147).[68]

The rest of the *parodos* (160–257) are acatalectic trochaic dimeters (– ⏑ – ⏑ – ⏑ – or *E*) and trimeters, the lekythion and the ithyphallic, plus a medially syncopated iambic dimeter (⏑ – ⏑ – – – ⏑ –).[69] The *vetera scholia* to Pindar (Σ Pind. *Ol.* 12 metro., *Isth.* 1 metro. Drachmann) say that the trochaic dimeter (– ⏑ – × – ⏑ – × or *e* × *e* ×) and trimeter (– ⏑ – × – ⏑ – × – ⏑ – × or *e* × *e* × *e* ×) were called 'Stesichorean.'[70] These are also found in Stesichorus' *Nostoi* (stro. 2). The *parodos* concludes with six stanzas in a predominantly iambic metre (192–257), often an iambic *metron* with an ithyphallic (⏑ – ⏑ – – ⏑ – ⏑ – –), which importantly will often appear in *Agamemnon* in connexion with or parallel to the events at Aulis. In sum, the opening metres of the *parodos* echo metres found in citharodic epic and Stesichorus. The *parodos* opens with these metres and modulates to metres that will come to be motets in the *Agamemnon* and the trilogy as a whole. The metre also correlates with the music of citharodic and Stesichorean music. Aeschylus' narrative technique and the mythical content of the *parodos* also show this orientation and departure.

4 Narrative Technique

The *parodos* is a richly ambiguous narrative that implicitly associates past, present and future events both causally and morally. In temporal terms, events are narrated in a linear sequence as in Stesichorus or in some of the compositions

---

(7) – ⏑ ⏑ – ⏑ ⏑ – (*D*)
(8) × – ⏑ – × – ⏑ – × – ⏑ – × (× *e* × *e* × *e* ×)
Barrett, according to Davies/Finglass 2014, 411, proposed (–) – ⏑ ⏑ – ⏑ ⏑ – × – ⏑ – × for ep. 8.
Metrical schemes are from Haslam 1974, 24, 48 and Schade 2003, 136.

Nostoi: strophe/antistrophe
(1) – ⏑ – × – ⏑ – – ⏑ – ⏑ – – || (*e* × *E* ×)
See Führer 1970, 14 for the reconstruction of this line of the *Nostoi*. Stes. frr. 172 ~ 173, 180, 183, 85, 93 = 210 ~ 212, 219, 222, 223, S148 *PMGF* offer a similar picture.

68 Haslam 1974, 41. Cf. also Stes. fr. 301 Finglass = fr. 244 *PMGF* for this period.
69 The lekythion or catalectic trochaic dimeter (– ⏑ – ⏑ – ⏑ – or *E*) is the most common trochaic line in Aeschylus' *Oresteia*. It is first introduced at the 'Hymn to Zeus' (160–91), and is used in passages when the chorus attempts to comprehend and interpret the events that have happened and are happening (e.g. Aesch. *Eum.* 490–565, 916–1020). These, except the trimeter, are often preceded by a full or syncopated *metron*, most commonly in the form of ⏑ – ⏑ – or ⏑ – –, occasionally – ⏑ – or – –. Aeschylus sometimes doubles or trebles it (e.g. *Ag.* 176–83).
70 Cf. *Iliou Persis* Stro. 8 (× – ⏑ – – |||) and *Nostoi* Stro. 9 ((×) – ⏑ –] × – ⏑ – – |||) for correspondences between these descriptions and the poems.

of Bacchylides and Pindar, who are indebted, but not subservient, to epic hexameter poetry.[71] The *Agamemnon* starts at the conclusion of the Trojan War, but the *parodos* (40–257) jumps back to the beginning of the expedition and starts from that point. It can be divided into five parts:

40–82: Chorus of twelve Argive elders enters. In anapaests, they tell of the expedition of the Greeks to Troy, which was justly backed by Zeus, despite the great loss of life.

83–103: Chorus, in anapaests, address Clytemnestra, who is not present, and explain that they have entered in order to see what the commotion is and if their optimism is justified.[72]

104–59: Chorus begins a dactylic lyric song and narrative.[73] It recounts the omen of the two eagles and the pregnant hare (probably at Aulis or Argos) before the expedition to Troy departed. Calchas interprets the omen to indicate that Troy will fall. The seer however also states that Artemis may be angry at the death of the young animals, prevent the departure of the expedition, and demand a compensatory sacrifice.

160–83: Chorus carries on singing in iambo-trochaics and iambo-choriambs whereby they seek to make sense of its narrative by invoking Zeus in a hymn. The 'Hymn to Zeus' is not a self-contained unit metrically, the corresponding antistrophe (184–91), which is the beginning of the Aulis narrative, metrically ties in events there with the 'Hymn'.[74]

185–257: They then narrate the sacrifice of Iphigeneia along with a monologue by Agamemnon. The chorus ends by hoping for a more positive future.

In the anapaests (40–103) the Chorus acts like citizens of a *polis* who presents past events from their own experience. Their perspective changes after the anapaests as they self-consciously take on the communal authority of a singing and dancing chorus to narrate events that they were not present at.[75] κύριός εἰμι θροεῖν...μολπᾶν ἀλκάν is a statement of authority and of beginning a new section of a song. The phrasing has no parallel in Greek poetry, but it recalls authoritative

---

71 E.g. Pind. *Ol.* 8, 9, 13; *Pyth.* 5; *Nem.* 1, 3, 4, 6; *Isth.* 8. See Slater 1983 on Pindar, and Hadjimichael 2012 on Bacchylides.
72 The sequence of marching anapaests followed by dactylo-iambic based metres is also found in Aeschylus' *Myrmidons* (frr. 131–2 *TrGF*³) and *Psychagogoi* (fr. 273 *TrGF*³). See Hermann 1834, 137; Fraenkel 1917–1918, 187; Dale 1968, 43; West 1982, 128; Cingano 1986, 141; Martinelli 1995, 176–7.
73 See Dale 1968, 25–68 for runs of anapaests and dactyls following one after the other which occur together frequently.
74 Scott 1984, 29 also notes that 'the inclusion of a long dactylic line links the hymn to the preceding dactylic section describing the prophecy of Calchas; in the second section the presence of a line of cretics foreshadows the predominant meter in which the chorus next sings of Iphigenia's murder.'
75 Aesch. *Ag.* 104–6. Schein 2009, 398.

statements found in poetry for beginning a mythical narrative.[76] The phrase acts as a transitional statement between the marching anapaests and the lyric song of the chorus. Another term for beginning a performance of song is ἐξάρχειν/ἐξάρχεσθαι, which refers usually to the instrumental solo, played by a lyre-singer[77] accompanying himself or a chorus, or to a lead singer's solo in a mixed or antiphonal type of song.[78] Aristides (Or. 33.2) says that he 'will move to another proem in the manner of Stesichorus' μέτειμι δὲ ἐπὶ ἕτερον προοίμιον (Stes. fr. 296 Finglass = fr. 241 PMGF), which brings the Palinode(s) (90 – 91j Finglass) to mind and a poetic mannerism of transitions between songs.[79] The transition, by means of an authoritative first-person statement, is a striking way to begin a lyric section of a choral ode after the introductory anapaests.[80]

The narrative technique of Stesichorus is a 'bold experimentation' with the narratives of epic poetry.[81] Aeschylus also experimented with epic narratives, notably his *Myrmidons* trilogy was a retelling of the *Iliad* (Books 9 – 18 in particular), in a different dramatic setting and the *Oresteia* is an adaptation of *Iliou Persis*/*Nostoi* epic poems and Stesichorus' *Oresteia*. His poems are not only epic poems in lyric metres, as ancient literary criticism would have it.[82] It seems that Stesichorus 'choralised' rhapsodic and citharodic epic, by which I mean the poems are probably predominantly choral songs with musical accompaniment of extended lyric narratives on heroic themes whose characters are presented within a complicated moral maze, and the main narratives are preceded by the poetic *persona* (e.g. the *Oresteia* (frr. 173 – 4 Finglass = frr. 212 – 211 *PMGF*) and the *Palinode(s)* (90 – 1j Finglass ~ 193 – 4 *PMGF*) and there is little reference

---

[76] Cf. Archil. fr. 120 *IEG*. ἀείδω or ἐννέπω or ὑμνέω or λέγω, which are used before a long narrative (e.g. Hes. fr. 1.1– 2 M-W; *Hymn. Hom. Diosc.* 17.1, 20.1; Pind. *Nem.* 10.1– 4; fr. 29 S-M), or καταλέγω (e.g. Hom. *Od.* 4.832, 16.235; Pind. *Pae.* 6.129 = D6.129 Rutherford; Hdt. 1.59, 4.83, 7.1, 7.6, 7.28) are the expected verbs.
[77] Cf. Pind. *Pyth.* 1.1; Athen. 5.180d-e.
[78] Σ Pind. *Ol.* 9.1 Drachmann.
[79] Bowie 2008, 11 n.8 suggests that this passage seems to be a reference to a particular poetic trope, rather than a quotation.
[80] Cf. also Hom. *Od.* 8.492, *Hymn. Hom. Ven.* 5.293, Xenoph. fr. 7 *IEG*, Choer. fr. 316 *SH*; Call. fr. 112.9 Pfeiffer for the general idea of moving from one poem to another.
[81] Carey 2015, 62, 59.
[82] Sim. F273 Poltera = fr. 564 *PMG*; Stes. Tb1, Tb3(a), Tb39, Tb42 Ercoles; Stes. fr. 98 Finglass = fr. 203 *PMGF*. See West 2015 for further discussion.

to a specific performative context (cf. Bacchylides).[83] A particularly noteworthy feature of the fragments of Stesichorus is the high density of direct speech.[84]

This *parodos*, unusual for a tragic choral ode, also contains direct speech, which shows the inner psychological states of the characters. Extended speeches in the Homeric manner also appear in the fragments of the *Geryoneis*, *Eriphyle*, *Iliou Persis*, and *Thebais* and would seem to be a particularly significant characteristic of the Stesichorean corpus. He presents characters in a manner that contrasts their status or type (e.g. Epeius, the Theban Queen, Helen), and continues the practice of the Homeric poems to show an interest in the psychology of these characters (e.g. frr. 15, 170, 97 Finglass = S11, 209, 222(b) *PMGF*), and ancient critics note that Stesichorus was concerned with 'the *debita dignitas* of his characters'.[85] Characters are presented in engaging speeches, which display their character traits and strengthen the drama of the storytelling. Examples include Callirhoe and Geryon, the Theban Queen (fr. 97 Finglass = fr. 222(b) *PMGF*), two unidentified Trojan speakers in *Iliou Persis* (fr. 103 Finglass = S88 *PMGF*) and Helen in *Nostoi* (fr. 170 Finglass = fr. 209 *PMGF*).[86] The last three involve the interpretation of a prophecy or omen (see below). The surviving Stesichorean material, with its prevalence of speeches, suggests that Aeschylus is making use of a Stesichorean narrative technique that has evolved from epic to add emotional intensity. Examples include Agamemnon's decision to sacrifice Iphigeneia or Calchas' interpretations, which can be divided up thus.

(i)   112–20: The omen.

---

[83] See Cingano 1993; D'Alfonso 1994 for persuasive arguments for choral performance, and Willi 2008, 76–82 for doxography on Stesichorean performance. See Carey 2015 and West 2015 for a basic reconstruction of the structure of a Stesichorean poem.

[84] The surviving parts of the *Geryoneis* has three character speeches (frr. 13, 15, 16–7 Finglass) and implies more; the *Eriphyle* (fr. 93 Finglass) and *Iliou Persis* (fr. 103 Finglass) have two, the latter has possibly a third speech (fr. 115 Finglass); the *Nostoi* has one (fr. 170 Finglass), and the *Thebais* (fr. 97 Finglass) has up to three surviving speeches. See Carey 2015 on direct speech in Stesichorus.

[85] Barrett 2007, 16. Cf. Stes. frr. 97, 180 Finglass = frr. 222(b), 219 *PMGF*. Later examples in Bacchylides and Pindar: Bacch. 3.36–9, 76–84; 5.93–6, 136–42; 151–4, 155–62 Maehler and Pind. *Ol.* 1.75–85, 4.24–7, 6.16–17, 62–3, 8.42–6, 13.67–9; *Pyth.* 3.40–2, 4.13–56, 4.87–92, 4.97–100, 4.102–19, 4.138–55, 4.156–67, 4.229–31, 8.44–55, 9.30–7, 9.39–65, *Nem.* 10.76–9, 10.80–8, *Isth.* 6.42–9, 6.52–4, 8.35a-45, *Pae.* 2.73–5, *Pae.* 4.40–57 = D2.73–5, D4.40–57 Rutherford, frr. 43.1–5, 168b.1–7 S-M. In Bacch. 11.104–5 there is a sudden transition from indirect to direct speech. Cf. also Alcm. 10 *PMGF* = 18 Calame; Sim. F271 Poltera = fr. 543 *PMG*; Pind. *Isth.* 8.31–45; Bacch. fr. 2 Maehler; Sapph. fr. 1.13–24 Voigt. Anacreon (fr. 374 fr. 1 *PMG*) likes speeches within stanzas.

[86] See Carey 2015 on speeches in *Thebais*.

(ii) 123–58: Calchas sees and interprets in *oratio recta*, but no mention of Artemis. ('Hymn to Zeus' interlude (159–183)).
(iii) 184–205: Agamemnon waits; the fleet is detained and the men suffer. Calchas states that Artemis is the cause, and implies that 'another remedy' (ἄλλο μῆχαρ), i.e. the sacrifice of Iphigeneia is needed.
(iv) 205–17: Agamemnon responds in *oratio recta*, and then commits to carry out the sacrifice (218–226).

Calchas delivers two prophecies that cause pain to Agamemnon, one at Argos or Aulis, the other at Troy.[87]

κεδνὸς δὲ στρατόμαντις ἰδὼν δύο λήμασι δισσοὺς
Ἀτρεΐδας μαχίμους ἐδάη λαγοδαίτας
πομπούς τ' ἀρχάς· οὕτω δ' εἶπε τεράζων· (125)
"χρόνῳ μὲν ἀγρεῖ Πριάμου πόλιν ἅδε κέλευθος,
πάντα δὲ πύργων
κτήνη πρόσθε τὰ δημιοπληθέα
Μοῖρα λαπάξει πρὸς τὸ βίαιον· (130)
οἶον μή τις ἄγα θεόθεν κνεφά-
σῃ προτυπὲν στόμιον μέγα Τροίας
στρατωθέν. οἴκτῳ γὰρ ἐπίφθονος Ἄρτεμις ἁγνὰ
πτανοῖσιν κυσὶ πατρὸς (135)
αὐτότοκον πρὸ λόχου μογερὰν πτάκα θυομένοισι·
στυγεῖ δὲ δεῖπνον αἰετῶν."
αἴλινον αἴλινον εἰπέ, τὸ δ' εὖ νικάτω.

"τόσον περ εὔφρων ἁ καλά, (140)
δρόσοις ἀέπτοις μαλερῶν λεόντων
πάντων τ' ἀγρονόμων φιλομάστοις
θηρῶν ὀβρικάλοισι τερπνά,
τούτων αἰτεῖ ξύμβολα κρᾶναι,
δεξιὰ μὲν κατάμομφα δὲ φάσματα † στρουθῶν. (145)
ἰήιον δὲ καλέω Παιᾶνα,
μή τινας ἀντιπνόους Δαναοῖς χρονίας ἐχενῇδας

---

[87] Sommerstein 2010b, 172–3 argues that the omen of the departure of sons of Atreus is at Argos on the grounds that the original Athenian audience would not have immediately known that the location was Aulis and that the only house mentioned so far in the play was the palace o the Atreidae. I find this unlikely as no mythographical and mythological parallel is provided, and such precise geographical detail is not required in the *parodos*. In the *Cypria* (Arg. §§6–8 *GEF*), the fleet gathers twice at Aulis, with an abortive attempt in between. At the first gathering, a snake ominously ate a brood of sparrow-chicks and their mother, who were in a plane-tree above an altar (Hom. *Il.* 2.299–330; Ov. *Met.* 12.8–38; Quint. Smyr. 6.61, 8.475; Triph. *Αλ. Ιλ.* 132–72): at the second, the ships were delayed by winds and Iphigeneia was sacrificed. Aeschylus merges the two and forms a causal link. See West 2013a, 104–11.

ἀπλοίας
τεύξῃ, σπευδομένα θυσίαν ἑτέραν, ἄνομόν τιν', (150)
ἄδαιτον,
νεικέων τέκτονα σύμφυτον, οὐ δει-
σήνορα. μίμνει γὰρ φοβερὰ παλίνορτος
οἰκονόμος δολία μνάμων μῆνις τεκνόποινος."
τοιάδε Κάλχας ξὺν μεγάλοις ἀγαθοῖς ἀπέκλαγξεν (155)
μόρσιμ' ἀπ' ὀρνίθων ὁδίων οἴκοις βασιλείοις·
τοῖς δ' ὁμόφωνον
αἴλινον αἴλινον εἰπέ, τὸ δ' εὖ νικάτω.

(Aesch. *Ag.* 123–59)

And the worthy prophet to the army saw it, and recognized the two warlike sons of Atreus, different in their temper, in the feasters on the hare who sped the rulers on their way; and thus he spoke interpreting the portent: "In time this expedition will capture the city of Priam, and in front of their walls Destiny will violently plunder all the mass of livestock the community possesses: only let no divine resentment overshadow the great curb of Troy, striking it before it can act, once it has been mustered. For holy Artemis, out of pity, bears a grudge against the winged hounds of her Father who slaughtered the wretched hare, litter and all, before it could give birth; she loathes the eagles' feast." Cry sorrow, sorrow, but may good prevail!

"So very kindly disposed is the Fair One to the unfledged seed of fiery lions, and so delightsome to the suckling whelps of all beasts that roam the wild: she demands to bring about a counterpart to this. <I interpret> the portent as auspicious but not unblemished. So I call on the healer Paian: let her not cause any persistent adverse winds that hold back the Danaan ships from sailing, bent on another sacrificial slaughter, one without music or feasting, a fashioner of strife, bred in the race, not fearing any man; for there awaits, a Wrath that remembers and will avenge a child." Such were the words that Calchas cried forth, together with great blessings, words fateful for the royal house, prompted by the birds seen by the way; and in unison with them cry sorrow, sorrow, but may good prevail!

The former leads to the sacrifice of Iphigeneia, and the latter the release of Briseis (Hom. *Il.* 1.69–105).[88] There are three extant prophecy scenes in Stesichorus (frr. 170, 103, 97 Finglass = frr. 209, S88 col. ii, 222(b) *PMGF*), and two of the three are based on ornithological omens.[89] It is unknown if there is a portent in the *Thebais* (fr. 97.274–80 Finglass = fr. 222(b).274–80 *PMGF*). Stesichorus in his *Nostoi* (fr. 170 Finglass = fr. 209 *PMGF*) draws upon the type scenes of a bird omen from epic poetry (Hom. *Od.* 15.260–78), but Stesichorus swaps the speak-

---

[88] Calchas scenes: Hom. *Il.* 1.69–105, *Il.* 2.299–322, *Il.* 13.45–70; *Cypria* Arg. §§6–8 *GEF*, *Nostoi* fr. 2 *GEF*; Hes. fr. 278 M-W; Aesch. *Ag.* 123–59; Soph. *Aj.* 746–83; Eur. *IT* 16, 531, 663; *Hel.* 749; *IA passim*; Quint. Smyr. 12.1–103.

[89] See Hom. *Il.* 13.821–3; *Od.* 15.165, 17.160 for examples of bird omens, and Hom. *Il.* 12.237–43 for the scepticism of bird omens.

ing roles around in the interpretation of a bird omen at the departure of Telemachus from Sparta.[90] In *Iliou Persis*, two Trojan speakers converse about the horse and there is an omen of a *kirkos* (Apollo's bird). This passage would possibly indicate a prophecy scene, whereby the proposed Stesichorean omen is pro-Trojan.[91]

```
τονδ[ ] . δα̣ ̣υν λ ̣[      ] ̣μ ̣ε ̣[
πρὸς ναὸν ἐς ἀκρ[όπο]λ[ι]ν σπεύδοντες [⏑ – ⏑ ⏑ –
Τρῶες πολέες τ' ἐπίκ[ου]ροι
ἔλθετε μη[δ]ὲ̣ λόγο[ις π]ε̣ιθώμεθ' ὅπως π[⏑ ⏑ – ×        (35)
τονδεκα ̣[ . . . . . ]ο̣νι ̣[] ̣ ̣
ἁγνὸν ἄ[γαλ]μα [⏑ –] ̣ ̣ αὐτεῖ καται-
σχ]ύ̣νωμε[ν ἀ]ε̣ικ[ελί]ως
×]νιν δὲ[– × – ⏑] ̣ ἁζώμεσθ' ἀν̣ά̣σ̣[σας
×]η̣σον[⏑ – ⏑ ⏑ – ⏝ –]ρ                                  (40)
 ̣] ̣[ ̣] ̣ ̣[              ] ̣α̣[ ] ̣

ὣ]ς φά[τ]ο· τοὶ [δ(ὲ) ⏑ – ⏑ ⏑ – ⏑ ⏑ – ] ̣[
φ[ρ]ά̣ζοντο ̣[⏑ – ⏑ ⏑ –
ἵπ[π]ον με ̣ ̣[⏑ – ⏑ ⏑ – × – ⏑ – ×] ̣[
ω ̣[ ̣] ̣ ̣ φυλλοφ[ορ – × – ⏑ ⏑ – ⏑ ⏑ –                   (45)
πυκινα[ῖ]ς πτερ[ύγεσσι ⏑ –
κίρκον τανυσίπ[τερον – × – ⏑ –
] ̣ες ἀνέκραγο̣ν [– × – ⏑ ⏑ – ⏑ ⏑ –
] ̣τε ̣[
```

(Stes. fr. 103.30–49 Finglass
= S88 col. ii.3–22 *PMGF*)

'... go in haste to the temple on the acropolis, you Trojans and your many allies, and let us not be persuaded by arguments so that we shamefully dishonour here this ( ) horse, the holy offering to the goddess, but let us respect with awe the anger of our lady ...' so he spoke, and they considered (how to bring) the great horse ....; and as from a leafy (bush) ... close-feathered wings ... a long-winged hawk shriek ...

In this part of the *Iliou Persis*, there are two speakers. One of them, who has a reputation for wisdom (103.24,]πρεπε καὶ πιν[υ]τᾶι), rejects a previously stated proposal to destroy the horse (35–8) and instead proposes that the horse be taken inside to Athena's temple on the acropolis (33). It is possible that Zeus in-

---

90 See Kelly 2015, 39–41 on this passage, who notes that Stesichorus is explicitly reworking this Odyssean passage in terms of vocabulary and theme. See Collins 2002 on bird prophecy in Homer and Hesiod, and Flower 2008, 134–5 on references to seers in Homer.
91 *Contra* Quint. Smyr. West 1969, inspired by Quint. Smyr. 12.11–20. Cf. also Triph. Ἁλ. Ἰλ. 247–9.

tervenes to confuse the Trojans or the second speaker (16–24).⁹² There would seem to be a portent involving two birds when the horse enters the city (45–8), where a hawk darts out of a bush and possibly attacks another bird.⁹³ This shows Stesichorean irony as it acts as a last-minute warning of the impending ruin, only to be ignored. All these examples are a type-scene and motif of an omen where a bird devours or pursues the young. Stesichorus was reputed to be as good as Simonides and Pindar but was superior to them in regard to the grandeur of the action of his theme, the care and attention to characters, and the dignity he applies to these characters through their words and actions.⁹⁴

Calchas correctly interprets that Artemis is angry with Zeus for the omen and will take her anger out on the Atreidae, who are not responsible for it. Aeschylus has tweaked things so that Agamemnon is not at fault for angering Artemis, at least. In Stesichorus, prophecy scenes have a touch of pathetic irony such as the Apolline *kirkos* in *Iliou Persis* (fr. 103 Finglass = S88 col. ii. *PMGF*). Compare the eagle of Zeus in the *parodos* of *Agamemnon*, where Zeus is all-powerful, the sole source of relief from pain, established πάθει μάθος, and causes the sacrifice of Iphigeneia.⁹⁵

Calchas is characterized in Homer (*Il.* 1.69) as οἰωνοπόλων ὄχ' ἄριστος, though remains in general a *mantis* and priest of Apollo.⁹⁶ Aeschylus (*Ag.* 122) uniquely introduces Calchas as a κεδνός...στρατόμαντις, before he is named.⁹⁷ Pindar (*Ol.* 6.33–6) and Bacchylides (5.70–7) introduce their prophets with a patronymic, and then later give a proper name. In the *Thebais*, Teiresias is Τειρ[ε]σίας τ[ερασπό]λος (fr. 97.234 Finglass = fr. 222(b).234 *PMGF*), which is an amalgamation of ὀνειροπόλος and τερασκόπος.⁹⁸ Aeschylus introduces Calchas'

---

92 Davies/Finglass 2014, 421–2.
93 West 1969, 139.
94 See Stes. Tb42 and Tb47 Ercoles.
95 Sommerstein 2010b, 148.
96 There is also a Megarian Calchas (Theogn. 11–14). Pausanias (1.43.1) says that Agamemnon set up a temple to Artemis in Megara when he went there to persuade Calchas to go to Troy. Cf. also Halitherses (Hom. *Od.* 2.158–9).
97 Aeschylus was known for his compounds, neologisms, word play, and three-word trimeters (Ar. *Ran.* 814–1434; Dion. Hal. *Imit.* 2.10, *Comp.* 20), and the *Agamemnon* and its *parodos* are particularly distinguished in this e.g. ἁγνᾷ δ' ἀταύρωτος αὐδᾷ πατρὸς φίλου τριτόσπονδον εὔποτμον παιῶνα φίλως ἐτίμα (Aesch. *Ag.* 245–7). See Marcovich 1984, 17–44 on the trimeters, Seewald 1936; Stanford 1942; Citti 1994 on the *Eigenwörter* in this *parodos*, and Rosenmeyer 1982, 92–108 on further examples of compounds, word order and neologisms.
98 Parsons 1977, 25. The supplement was the suggestion of Barrett. ὀνειροπόλος: Hom. *Il.* 1.63, 5.149; Hdt. 1.128, 5.56. τερασκόπος: Pind. *Pyth.* 4.201; Aesch. *Ag.* 977 (adj.), *Choe.* 551, *Eum.* 62; Soph. *OT* 605; Eur. *Bacch.* 248.

speech with οὕτω δ' εἶπε τεράζων, 'in this way he spoke interpreting the portent'.[99] τεράζων is a hapax, but it may hint towards the *Thebais* of Stesichorus that lies behind this Aeschylean neologism, as both Aeschylus and Stesichorus introduce their prophetic figures with neologisms to describe their mantic qualities.

Aeschylus presents Agamemnon with a choice: kill his daughter or abort the expedition.[100] Both Aeschylus and Euripides exploit the potentialities of Agamemnon's choice.[101] In contrast, Sophocles (*El.* 566–76) reduces the decision to awful necessity and Artemis wills the sacrifice (*El.* 571–2). Agamemnon is truly guilty of his daughter's murder as Aeschylus emphasizes Agamemnon's participation in the sacrifice, and the Chorus' description highlights its irreligious perversity.[102]

> ἐπεὶ δ' ἀνάγκας ἔδυ λέπαδνον,
> φρενὸς πνέων δυσσεβῆ τροπαίαν
> ἄναγνον, ἀνίερον, τόθεν
> τὸ παντότολμον φρονεῖν μέτεγνω·
> βροτοὺς θρασύνει γὰρ αἰσχρόμητις
> τάλαινα παρακοπὰ πρωτοπήμων.
>
> (Aesch. *Ag.* 218–23)

And when he put on the yoke strap of necessity, his mental wind veering in a direction that was impious, impure, unholy, from that point he turned to a mindset that would stop at nothing; for men are emboldened by miserable Infatuation, whose shameful schemes are the beginning of their sufferings.

Agamemnon's thoughts are in agony, before his mind is swept along by madness. Agamemnon speaks in a manner that is both agonized and calm. There is the θέμις of Agamemnon to desire the blood of his daughter and the ἀνάγκας ἔδυ λέπαδνον, a strong force of his madness based on the situation.[103] This speech

---

99 Aesch. *Ag.* 125. The prophecy of Medea also begins εἶπε δ' οὕτως (Pind. *Pyth.* 4.11).
100 Aesch. *Ag.* 206–26. The chorus of Argive elders are loyal to Agamemnon (*Ag.* 99–104, 165–6, 270, 1489–96); however, they acknowledge his faults (212f., 799–806, 1560–1).
101 Agamemnon's speech contrasts Eurystheus in declining to challenge Hyllus (Eur. *Heracl.* 813–6), Eteocles resolution to fight Polyneices (Aesch. *Sept.* 653–719), and Hector on his determination to fight on account of *aidōs* (Hom. *Il.* 6.441–3).
102 Lloyd-Jones 1962, 191 = 1990a, 289; Moreau 1990, 41; Sommerstein 2010a, 137–8. Cf. Aesch. *Ag.* 102–47, 1372–1555; fr. 154a.15–16 *TrGF*³.
103 'Yoke of necessity': *Hymn. Hom. Cer.* 2.216–17; [Aesch.] *PV* 108; Soph. *Phil.* 1025, fr. 591.5–6 *TrGF*⁴; Eur. *Or.* 1330, *IA* 443, 511 (quotation of Aeschylus), fr. 475 *TrGF*⁵·¹; Hdt. 8.22.2; Pl. *Phdr.* 240c; Mosch. fr. 2; Luc. *Erotes* 38; Orph. *Hymn.* 61.5.

shows resonances with the hell-for-leather resolution of Geryon (frr. 10, 12–9 Finglass = S7–15 *PMGF*) and the straight-jacketed despair of the Theban Queen (fr. 97 Finglass = fr. 222(b) *PMGF*), whereby characters in certain roles, a three-headed monster and the Queen here, speak in unconventional ways as befitting their station. Geryon speaks like a Homeric hero (fr. 15 Finglass = S11 *PMGF*),[104] and the Theban Queen is a 'menschliche Königin' (fr. 97.205–10 Finglass = fr. 222 (b).205–10 *PMGF*).[105] Before heroes depart for battle, relatives may exhort them not to fight. Geryon replies to Menoites, who had implored him not to fight Heracles, arguing it is better to die young than suffer disgrace and live long.

The seemingly composed Theban Queen is the opposite of the Homeric Agamemnon (*Il.* 1.106), who angrily rebukes Calchas, whereas she is like Aeschylean Agamemnon who is polite and respectful to Calchas (Aesch. *Ag.* 186). She tries to calmly separate the prophetic authority of Apollo from mantic powers of Teiresias. The rhythm of the passage and her words indicate that she is trying to tightly rein in her horror at Teiresias' words. The speech is one of polite exasperation, and like Agamemnon's speech, it is an attempt to rationalize the unreasonable. The heroic honour of the doomed Geryon and the desperate logic of the Theban Queen contrast and enhance the portrayal of Agamemnon in Aeschylus, who also has to calmly carry out the horrific.

As the *parodos* progresses, Aeschylus begins to distance the chorus's account of events from the mythological tradition. He also does this with the metre as noted above. The sacrifice of Iphigeneia in Aeschylus is described in an intense and pathetic manner, but also with lyric expediency and the syntax is straightforward.[106] Iphigeneia struggles against her destiny and there is no hint of Artemis rescuing her. A striking fact about the pre- and post-Aeschylean accounts of the sacrifice is that it follows a story-pattern where a mortal, often unwittingly offends a deity who then demands as punishment the sacrifice of the ruler's daughter, who in most cases is rescued at the last minute.[107] Both in Pindar and Aeschylus, Ar-

---

[104] Stesichorus modifies Sarpedon's speech at Hom. *Il.* 12.322–8. Cf. Hom. *Il.* 20.308; Tyrt. frr. 10.12, 12.30 *IEG*, contra Sol. fr. 13.32 *IEG*. I follow the text of Barrett 2007, 28–9.
[105] Willi 2008, 99.
[106] Aesch. *Ag.* 224–47. See also Pindar's account of the sacrifice in *Pythian* Eleven.
[107] Davies 2010, 334–6, cf. also Lloyd-Jones 1983, 95. In Proclus' summary of the *Cypria* (*Argumen.* §8 *GEF*), her sacrifice is ordered by Calchas, but Artemis rescues her by substituting her for a deer (Cf. *LIMC* Iphigeneia 1 (Attic, 425 BC). See Finglass 2007b, 95–6 and Davies/Finglass 2014, 484, 502–3 on the consistent or differing sequence of events in the sacrifice of Iphigeneia in different authors; and Loraux 1985 on the various ways of killing women in tragedy. Aeschylus uses the cultic totems (the saffron dress) of the cult of Artemis at Brauron, however there is no rescue of Iphigeneia, cf. Peradotto 1969 = Lloyd 2007, 211–44; Stinton 1976a = 1990, 186–9.

temis does not rescue Iphigeneia.[108] A literary parallel is completely avoided with the versions found in Stesichorus, the Epic Cycle and the Hesiodic *Catalogue of Women*, however this suits Aeschylus' purposes to display paralleled acts of vengeance and retribution. Aeschylus changes the content in his Stesichorean influenced narrative. He has, in mythological terms, distanced himself from the epic/lyric versions of the sacrifice of Iphigeneia. Iphigeneia is sacrificed in all of them: there is a gritty and pathetic realism in Aeschylus.

5 Conclusions

Aeschylus in this *parodos* was emulating the narrative, poetic and musical techniques of Stesichorean and citharodic-epic poetry. Aeschylus would seem to pay homage to them in the music and rhythm of the *parodos*. The solemn, magnificent, and high-pitched sound of the *orthios nomos* would suit the narrative and content of the *parodos* with the omen of the eagle and the hare and the sacrifice of Iphigeneia. The prevalence of speeches suggests that Aeschylus is making use of a Stesichorean narrative technique that has evolved from epic poetry. On the one hand a tragic choral ode is a type of religious song as it is performed at a competitive religious festival; on the other, the narrative content of this particular *parodos* contains ill-omened portents and human sacrifice coupled with characters that give maddeningly logical speeches and cry out forlorn apotropaic refrains. This would make his audience recall the sounds of Stesichorus, and to advertise his own version of the *Oresteia* story by the narrative content, which stays true to the *fabula*, but has undergone some changes.

Aeschylus' language is maniloquent, suffused by epic echoes, ornamented with exotic vocabulary, crammed with long, compound neologisms, and often experimental. Both Aeschylus and Stesichorus remodel passages from early Greek epic, and Aeschylus appropriates musical and mythological materials from Greek epic and lyric. The *parodos* of the *Agamemnon* is the overture to the *Oresteia* trilogy: it describes family scenes, murder, sacrifice, and retribution, and makes use of omens, prophecy and Apollo. It is an opportunity for Aeschy-

---

108 Pindar (*Pyth.* 11.22–3) associates the sacrifice with the murder of Agamemnon. It can be inferred, but it is not explicit, that Stesichorus also did this, see Davies/Finglass 2014, 489. Agamemnon did not sacrifice her in person, in Pindar and in the *Catalogue*, it was by the Achaeans in the Hesiodic version at least: Ἰφιμέδην μὲν σφάξαν ἐυκνή[μ]ιδες Ἀχαιοὶ (Hes. fr. 23a.17 M–W). The sacrifice is not mentioned in Homer. In another contrast, a *lekythos* (*c.* 470 BC) by Douris depicts Iphigeneia as a resolute figure at her sacrifice (*LIMC* Iphigeneia 3 as in Eur. *IA*), unlike in Aeschylus.

lus to imprint the key themes of the trilogy to an audience and to implant thematic, musical and rhythmical motets in their ears. By starting from a familiar point of mythical content and utilising the musico-poetic tradition of choral-lyric narratives, Aeschylus familiarises his audiences with the topic of his play and introduces complex dissonances and subversions that will enrich a trilogy what would become one of the most influential plays of Attic tragedy. According to an *apothothegm*, Aeschylus claimed that his plays were 'slices from the banquet of Homer' (Athen. 8.347e). Homer means, not just the *Iliad* and *Odyssey*, but the cycles, which applies well to this *parodos*.[109] It would seem that Aeschylus also took slices from the banquets of citharodic epic and Stesichorus.

---

109 Aeschylus' *Myrmidons* was an adaptation of *Iliad* 9–18, see Sommerstein 2010a, 241–53.

Appendix: Metrical Outline of the Lyric Triad (*Ag.* 104–59)[110]

104–21 ~ 122–39

– ⏖ – ⏑ ⏑ – ⏑ ⏑ – ⏑ ⏑ | – ⏑ ⏑ – – |	(6 *da*)
– ⏑ ⏑ – | ⏑ ⏑ – | ⏑ ⏑ – | ⏑ ⏑ – – |	(5 *da*)
– – | – – | – – | – ⏑ ⏑ – – ‖	(5 *da*)
⏑ – ⏑͡– – | ⏑ ⏑ – ⏑ ⏑ | – ⏑ ⏑ – – |	(*ia* ∫ 4 *da*)
– ⏑ ⏑ – – |	(2 *da*)
– – | – ⏑ ⏑ – ⏑ ⏑ – ⏑ ⏑ | – ⏑ ⏑ – – |	(6 *da*)
– ⏑ ⏑ – – |	(2 *da*)
– – – ⏑ ⏑ – | ⏑ ⏑ – ⏑ ⏑ – ⏑ ⏑ – ⏑ ⏑	(8 *da*)
– ⏑ ⏑ – – ‖	
⏑ – ⏑͡– – ⏑ ⏑ – ⏑ ⏑ | – ⏑ ⏑ – – |	(*ia* ∫ 4 *da*)
– – – | ⏑ ⏑ – – ‖	(3 *da*)
– ⏑ ⏑ – | ⏑ ⏑ – | ⏑ ⏑ – ⏑ ⏑ | – ⏑ ⏑ – – ‖	(6 *da*)
⏑ – ⏑ – ⏑ – ⏑ – :‖	(2 *ia*)
– ⏑ ⏑ – ⏑ ⏑ – ⏑ | ⏑ – – – – ‖‖	(5 *da*)

140–59

⏑ – ⏑ – – | ⟨⏑⟩ ⏑ – |	(*ia* ∫ *ch*)
⏑ – ⏑ – – | ⏑ ⏑ – | ⏑ ⏑ – |	(*ia* ∫ *ch* | *ia*)
– – | – ⏑ ⏑ – | ⏑ ⏑ – – |	(4 *da*)
– – | – ⏑ ⏑ – ⏑ – – :|	(*D ia*)
– – | – – | – ⏑ ⏑ – – :‖	(4 *da*)
– ⏑ ⏑ – ⏑ ⏑ – ⏑ ⏑ – ⏑ ⏑ [– –?] ‖	(5 *da*)
⏑ – ⏑ – – | ⏑ ⏑ – | ⏑ – ⏒ ‖	(*ia* ∫ *ch* | *ia*)
– ⏑ ⏑ – ⏑ ⏑ – | ⏑ ⏑ – | ⏑ ⏑ – | ⏑ ⏑	(7 *da*)
– ⏑ | ⏑ – – |	
– – | – ⏑ ⏑ – | ⏑ ⏑ – | ⏑ ⏑ – | ⏑ ⏑ – ⏑ |	(7 *da*)
⏑ – – |	
– – | – ⏑ ⏑ – ⏑ ⏑ – – – ⏑ ⏑ – – – ⏑ ⏑	(9 *da*)
– ⏑ ⏑ – – ‖	

---

110 Based on West 1998. See also Scott 1984, 30–2 and Fleming 2007, 99–101.

– ⏑ ⏑ – | ⏑ ⏑ – | – – | – – | ⏑ ⏑ – – | (6 *da*)
– ⏑ ⏑ – – | (2 *da*)
– ⏑ ⏑ – ⏑ ⏑ – | ⏑ ⏑ – – | (4 *da*)
– ⏑ ⏑ – – – | ⏑ ⏑ – | – – | ⏑ ⏑ – – | (6 *da*)
– ⏑ ⏑ – – ‖ (2 *da*)
– ⏑ ⏑ – ⏑ ⏑ – ⏑ | ⏑ – – – – – ‖‖ (5 *da*)

Pavlos Sfyroeras
Pindar at Colonus: A Sophoclean Response to *Olympians* 2 and 3

The first and third *stasima* in *Oedipus at Colonus* could not appear more antithetical in tone and theme: the celebratory praise for Colonus (668–719) gives way to a threnodic meditation on the human condition (1211–48). As is typical in tragedy, varied dramatic circumstances can certainly account for the shift of mood from one choral ode to the other. Theseus' promise to protect and defend the old suppliant elicits the laudatory mode of the first *stasimon*, as confirmed both in the chorus' own description of their song (αἶνον 707) and in the immediate impression it makes on its internal audience, the wanderer's hopeful daughter (ἐπαίνοις εὐλογούμενον...τὰ λαμπρὰ...ἔπη 720–1). By contrast, the reflection on human suffering in the third *stasimon* anticipates the wrenchingly acrimonious encounter between father and son.[1] Apart from the exigencies of the dramatic action, however, I wish to suggest that the different strands of these songs are woven onto a single canvas; and that the material for that canvas is provided, at least in part, by the two odes that Pindar composed for the Olympic chariot victory won in 476 BC by Theron of Acragas, primarily *Olympian* 3 and, to a lesser extent, *Olympian* 2.[2] As the two sets of songs, epinician and tragic, are separated by seven decades, my argument for the Sophoclean evocation of the perhaps faint Pindaric echo from a bygone era calls for a preliminary explanation.

The more general aspects of this question – the currency and visibility of *epinikia* in late fifth century Athens and its dramatic poetry – have recently attracted significant attention.[3] Even, or perhaps especially, after epinician poetry de-

---

I wish to thank the editors of this volume, as well as several participants at the conference, in particular Ewen Bowie, Michael Carroll, Douglas Cairns, Andrew Ford, Gregory Hutchinson, Nick Lowe, and Ruth Scodel. All offered invaluable suggestions that greatly improved this paper.

[1] On the Sophoclean chorus' engagement with dramatic action see Burton 1980; Gardiner 1987; Esposito 1996; Murnaghan 2012; also, with special emphasis on *OC*, Dhuga 2005. For the epinician dimensions of αἶνος and its cognates see, e.g., *Ol.* 2.95; 4.14; 6.12; 7.16; 9.14; 11.7; *Nem.* 1.6; 7.63, etc.; cf. Nagy 1990, 146–50.
[2] For some additional connections (metrical and thematic, i.e. in terms of position in plot structure) between the two odes see Carey 2009b, 120–1.
[3] See, for instance, Swift 2010, 104–72; Steiner 2010a; Carey 2012; Rodighiero 2012; also Nagy 1990, 382–413.

https://doi.org/10.1515/9783110575910-005

clined as a productive genre halfway through the 5th century, it found in Athens a hospitable environment for dissemination. Along with the practice of re-performance, which has been amply elucidated, this type of transmission demonstrates how the victory ode can transcend the strict occasionality of its first performance.[4] Athens is a special case, to be sure, given the apparent disjunction between the aristocratic values of the epinician genre and the democratic ethos of Athens in the second half of the 5th century. Yet this seemingly solid dichotomy crumbles when we consider the various contexts and modes of dissemination of choral lyric: monodic performance at *symposia*, choral practice as part of musical education, and written texts used in schools.[5] In light of such opportunities for diffusion of the lyric repertoire, primarily among the elite but also more widely, it is not surprising to find that the generic conventions of epinician are translated into the choral idiom of tragedy or to detect epinician passages and tropes in Aristophanic songs.[6] As is the case with dramatic allusiveness more broadly, the different segments of the theatrical audience, which is far from monolithic, may recognize Pindaric echoes and perceive their import in a variety of ways, but even graded familiarity creates a sufficient, indeed significant framework for my argument.

Against this general backdrop of Pindar's reception in Athens, I shall focus on the particular: why would a dramatist in the last decade of the 5th century expect his Athenian spectators, in the throes of their struggle for survival, to recognize or even appreciate the sounds of a distant time and place? I shall first examine some aspects of *Olympian* 3 that tacitly engage with Athenian ideology and may thus continue to resonate in Athens decades later. Then, in the central section of my paper, I shall offer a reading of the two Sophoclean odes that will show how, in some important ways, they constitute a diptych. This reading, while not aspiring to be exhaustive, will make the case for the need to take into account the Pindaric subtext. Finally, by exploring a set of historical circumstances not yet considered in conjunction with *Oedipus at Colonus*, I hope to demonstrate that the 'horizon of expectations' of the Athenian audience that Sophocles could count on was broader than has been assumed and to outline a frame in which this return to Pindar can be meaningfully inscribed;[7] I shall propose that the in-

---

[4] Various aspects of the reperformance of Pindar's odes have been discussed by, among others, Morrison 2007 and 2012; Carey 2007, 209–10; Currie 2004; Hubbard 2004. For some broader theoretical implications see Maslov 2015.
[5] On the extent to which written texts were involved, see Hubbard 2004, Ford 2003, and Herington 1985.
[6] See, for instance, Swift 2010; Carey 2007; 2012; Garner 1988.
[7] For the term 'horizon of expectations' see Jauss 1994.

tertextual dialogue with the celebration of a Sicilian tyrant's Olympic victory enables Sophocles and his audience to reflect on recent developments in Sicily that may affect Athens' fortunes, perhaps even on the poetics of tragedy as a receptacle for lyric genres. As important as it is, the question of how the epinician conventions are reshaped into tragic choral odes will not be addressed, except indirectly. But at the very least, I hope that this discussion may contribute to a fuller understanding of Pindar's particular place in the dramatic and political culture of late 5th century Athens.

1 *Olympian* 3, Olive Trees, and Athenian Ideology

Let us first consider the epinician background. *Olympian* 3 tells of the founding of the Olympic shrine by Heracles, dwelling in particular on the origin of the olive trees around the stadium and of the olive wreath for the victor. In this myth of apparently Pindaric invention, Heracles' pursuit of the golden-horned hind takes him to the Hyperboreans, where he is amazed at the sight of the olive trees; later, after he establishes the contests in a site still bare of vegetation, 'sweet longing' (γλυκὺς ἵμερος, *Ol.* 3.33) drives him back to the Hyperboreans, from whom he receives the olives so as to transplant them to Olympia. Pindar's non-linear narrative contains several puzzles, including the poet's reasons for connecting the Olympian olive trees with the Hyperboreans.[8] As I have argued elsewhere, the origin of the olives in the Hyperborean land, that is, in a land '*beyond* the north wind' (πνοιᾶς ὄπιθεν Βορέα ψυχροῦ, *Ol.* 3.31–2) hence blessed with perennial temperate climate, is symbolically very charged; it makes the trees, like the Hyperboreans themselves (as described both in *Olympian* 3 and in the earlier *Pythian* 10), impervious to Boreas' wintry blasts and, at the same time, immune to the symbolic effects of the North wind that we can sum up as the human condition: old age, suffering, the ravages of mortality.[9] The Hyper-

---

[8] Puzzles that have drawn the attention of critics, ancient or modern, include: the number of Heracles' trips, the role of Helen and the Tyndarids, the extent of Pindar's mythical inventiveness, the occasion of the performance and the nature of 'this festival' (*Ol.* 3.34), the classification of the composition (epinician ode or theoxenian hymn?), its novelty and relationship to *Olympians* 1 and 2; on some of these issues see Köhnken 1983; Shelmerdine 1987; Verdenius 1987; Segal 1964; Krummen 1990; Clay 2011; Morrison 2007.
[9] This summarizes part of the argument made fully in Sfyroeras 2003. In addition to Pind. *Pyth.* 10.29–46, the Hyperboreans' youthful longevity is attested in Simon. 288 Poltera = *PMG* 570; Call. *Hymn* 4.282; Strabo 15.1.57 Radt; Megasthenes *FGrHist* 715 F 27b; Plin. *HN* 4.89. Their

borean provenance of the Olympian trees endows them with a share of immortality that is in turn bestowed, through the olive wreath, on the Olympic victor and his community. This reinforces what is already implicit in the ritual treatment of the olive branch at the Olympic games. According to the ancient scholia (Σ Pind. *Ol.* 3.60 Drachmann), it must be culled by a boy with both parents living (ἀμφιθαλὴς παῖς), that is, a boy as yet untouched by death. As far as this is possible, in other words, the olive garland is not to be contaminated by the corruption of the human condition. In the logic of the Pindaric ode, athletic victory and immortality are masterfully interwoven through the olive-tree and its Hyperborean origin.

I shall pay closer attention to a couple of details that, however overshadowed by more striking puzzles in *Olympian* 3, have wider ramifications for the way Pindar intends his mythical innovation to be perceived by its various audiences and, ultimately, for the way Sophocles responds to it. The question I wish to ask concerns the exact cause of Heracles' marvel (θάμβαινε, *Ol.* 3.32), which is strong enough to motivate a second trip in the far North. Does it mean that the Hyperborean olives were perceptibly superior to the olives Heracles already knew? Or that he had not seen olive trees before his trip? By stressing Heracles' stunned wonder, Pindar raises the intriguing possibility that olives were unknown to Greece before Heracles' visit to the Hyperborean land, which therefore became the source of *all* Greek olive trees, not only of the special ones at Olympia. Heracles, in other words, would marvel not at the fairest olive trees he ever laid eyes on, but at the first specimens of olive trees altogether. The poet gives a slight nod to this rather unexpected alternative by applying to the victor's olive wreath the generic term ἐλαία instead of the specific κότινος ('wild olive'), which normally designates the Olympic olive branch. Pindar's reluctance to observe botanical distinctions – unlike Pausanias' statement that Heracles brought back the κότινος (5.7.7) – is evident in the even more generic δένδρεα, used both when Heracles notices the lack of 'fair trees' at Olympia (ἀλλ' οὐ καλὰ δένδρε' ἔθαλλεν χῶρος, *Ol.* 3.23) and when he first beholds the Hyperborean olives (*Ol.* 3.32): how can Heracles name them if he does not know what they are? Although one could assume (throughout Pindar's account) that olive trees already grew in Greece and that Heracles only brought the supreme specimens

---

land resembles Elysium (Bacchyl. 3.59; cf. Hom. *Od.* 4.561–9), the Isles of the Blessed (Hes. *Op.* 167–73; Pind. *Ol.* 2.78), or even Olympus (Hom. *Od.* 6.42–6), yet without the immortality.

to Olympia, Pindar (as we saw) scatters enough hints to tip the scales in favor of the notion that Heracles introduced olive trees to Greece as a whole.[10]

What is the purpose of this botanical vagueness? I would propose that, by fusing the Olympian olive trees with olives in general, Pindar's ode tacitly challenges several Athenian claims, namely that Athens was the birthplace of olive trees, thought of as Athena's gift (Hdt. 5.82; 8.55; Paus. 1.27.2; Apollod. *Bibl.* 3.14.1), and that the Athenian specimens surpassed all others. Our available evidence for these Athenian views postdates *Olympian* 3, to be sure, but we should not suppose them to be later inventions; quite the contrary, by all indications they may be safely assumed to be well known to Pindar and his audience.

Consider, for instance, Herodotus' account (5.82) of how the Epidaurians, advised by Delphi during a crop failure to dedicate statues made of olive wood, entreated the Athenians to let them fell Attic olive trees because they were the most sacred, or perhaps – 'it is said' – because olives could at that time be found nowhere else but Attica! While the verb λέγεται (5.82.3) describes Herodotus' own present, this episode clearly predates the Aeginetan theft of the statues, the 'old feud' between Aegina and Athens, and the brief Aeginetan independence from Epidaurus (late 7th – early 6th century).[11] To Herodotus' audience, it would certainly evoke a distant, even semi-legendary albeit post-heroic past. The presumably Athenian claim to exclusive possession of olive trees is in turn a clear corollary of the legend that the first olive was Athena's gift, the ἀστὴ ἐλαία, which Herodotus' Athenian contemporaries could point out in the shrine of 'Erechtheus the so-called Earthborn' (8.55) and assert that it was burned by the Persians and

---

10 Pindar's failure to distinguish the ἐλαία from the κότινος, already noted by Gildersleeve on *Ol.* 3.13, appears to be 'corrected' by Pausanias, yet this hardly settles the question of the olives' pre-existence; while Paus. 5.7.7 specifies the κότινος, he refers to Heracles' introduction of the tree from the Hyperboreans to Greece as a whole (ἐς Ἕλληνας), thus implying that no other olives grew there yet, since he also states (5.15.3) that the κότινος was called ἐλαία καλλιστέφανος; cf. Verdenius 1987, 18. To complicate matters further, Paus. 5.5.7 presumably means Heracles the eldest of the Dactyls/Curetes; on this version and its implications see Hubbard 2007, 36–7. On all aspects of olives see Pease 1937.

A separate issue that, while not affecting this argument, adds to Pindar's intentional vagueness, is the precise location of the Olympian olives, concerning which Paus. 5.15.3 is at odds with Pindar's notion that Heracles wished to plant olives around the race course (*Ol.* 3.33–4 with schol.); cf. Verdenius 1987, 31–2.
11 See Figueira 1993, 9–60; Buck 1981; Haubold 2007, 231–3. On various aspects of Herodotus' passage see Hornblower 2013, 233–7 [*ad loc.*]. Significantly, the Epidaurians vow to bring annual offerings to Athena Polias and Erechtheus – a clear indication of the link between olives and Athenian identity.

miraculously sprouted a fresh shoot in one day (cf. Paus. 1.27.2).¹² Such Athenian ideas must thus be traced at least as far back as the Persian wars, even earlier, if the Panathenaic amphoras containing olive oil from Athena's sacred olives and awarded as prizes are any indication (Σ Ar. *Nub.* 1005 Holwerda; Arist. *Ath. Pol.* 60). In short, there can be no doubt as to the significance of the olive tree for Athenian identity and for the patron goddess Athena; after all, the *xoanon* of Athena Polias, said to have fallen from the sky in Erechtheus' time, was of olive wood (Paus. 1.26.6; Σ Dem. 22.45 Dilts; Athenagoras, *Leg.* 17).

Given this background of mythical antagonism, Pindar's gesture in the 470s becomes more poignant if we keep Athenian olive trees in our view. While Olympia can enjoy and bestow a kind of winterless bliss, Athens by contrast has strong connections with the North wind, and this applies to its olives as well. Not too long before the first performance of *Olympian* 3, on the eve of the naval battle at Artemisium, as we learn from Herodotus (7.189), the Athenians, urged by an oracle to seek the assistance of their son-in-law, appealed to Boreas on the grounds that he had an Attic wife, Oreithyia, the daughter of Erechtheus, and thanked him afterwards by founding a shrine on the banks of Ilissus, the very site of Boreas' abduction of Oreithyia (Paus. 1.19.6).¹³ Even more à propos for the present argument, through Erechtheus Boreas receives not only marriage kinship (κῆδος) with Athens, but also a link to olive trees, for Athena's sacred olive grew in Erechtheus' shrine on the Acropolis (Hdt. 8.55).¹⁴ In fact, Boreas' connection with olive trees in Athens is also attested visually. Some representations of Oreithyia's abduction on Attic vases from the second quarter of the 5th century include an olive tree and/or depict Boreas with an olive crown.¹⁵

---

12 Strictly speaking, Athena's olive was in the Pandroseion, west of the Erechtheum (Apollod. 3.14.1–2; Philoch. *FGrHist* 328 F 67), but could still be said to be *in* the shrine of Erechtheus; cf. Bowie 2007, 143–4 [*ad loc.*]. For the ἀστὴ ἐλαία see Poll. *On.* 9.17; Hesych. α 7851 Latte; cf. Eur. *Ion* 1434. For a discussion of the passages and the ideological implications see Detienne 1973; for a more symbolic approach see Dietz 1971.
13 Ilissus is *only* the location of the cult in Herodotus and *only* the scene of the abduction in Pausanias (cf. also Ap. Rhod. 1.211–5; Apollod. 3.15.2); their combination can explain the choice of location for the cult. Abduction and cult on the banks of Ilissus are joined in Pl. *Phdr.* 229b-e, which also reports the vicinity of the Areopagus as an alternative. The cult at Ilissus may have been older (as the myth was), but acquired a new and enlarged significance after Artemisium cf. Macan on Hdt. 7.189.
14 This link is reinforced in the variant (Acusilaus *FGrHist* 2 F30) in which the occasion of Oreithyia's abduction was a sacrifice for Athena Polias on the Acropolis. For the various locations see Simon 1967, 119–20.
15 Examples: *LIMC* III.2.108–22, nos. 31, 32, 33, 53, 55, 56; cf. Kaempf-Dimitriadou 1986, 136–7, 140–1, whose interpretation of the olive crowns and branch(es) as symbols of festive celebration in an Athenian context is not incompatible with my argument.

These have been rightly interpreted as allusions to the occasion of the abduction, in some versions Athena's festival, which then shifts to the wedding celebration that makes Boreas the Athenians' son-in-law; yet I want to stress the outcome of this collocation for olive trees: in this tale, so important for Athenians in the post-war years, hence at the same time as the composition of *Olympian 3*, the emblem of Athenian pride becomes steeped in Boreatic associations.[16]

If, then, *Olympian 3* is partly intended as a challenge to Athenian ideology, it may provide a motivation for the presumably Athenian story, attested in the pseudo-Aristotelian treatise *On Marvellous Things Heard* ([*Mir. ausc.*] 51.834a), that Heracles (or the Eleans) transplanted the olives to Olympia from the *banks of Ilissus at Athens* – the very site of Boreas' abduction of Erechtheus' daughter and of his cult! It would not be surprising, in fact, if this admittedly garbled passage reflected an Athenian reaction to Pindar's subtle argument, by stressing that the olive trees at Olympia, far from coming from the Hyperboreans, actually originate in the most Boreatic of all Athenian locations.[17] This would openly contradict the logic of Pindar's myth, whereby a link with Boreas (hence with mortality) would make the Athenian olives inferior to the Olympian descendants of the Hyperborean trees. At the very least, the evidence from pseudo-Aristotle suggests that the introduction of olive trees to Olympia was far from a settled issue; on the contrary, it could be contested in ways that were possibly politically or ideologically charged.[18]

---

[16] Besides the proportionately high number of depictions on Athenian vases in this period, attributed by Agard 1966 to increased Athenian interest in Thrace, Oreithyia was mentioned in Simonides' elegy about the naval battle at Artemisium (*PMG* 534, not in Poltera, but cf. Sim. 3 *IEG*) and became the subject of tragedies (of uncertain dates) by Aeschylus (frr. 280–1 *TrGF³*) and perhaps Sophocles (frr. 768, 805, 956 *TrGF⁴*). Simonides' elegy constitutes evidence that, far from being a later invention, the story in Hdt. 7.189 arose in the 470s. As implied by Herodotus' narrative, in fact, the tale of Oreithyia and Boreas must precede Artemisium and the foundation of the altar on Ilissus, with which Simonides' elegy and perhaps Aeschylus' drama may be connected (cf. Kaempf-Dimitriadou 1986, 134; Simon 1967, 117–21). But some (admittedly uncertain) evidence, both visual (Kaempf-Dimitriadou 1986, 139; Simon 1967, 111) and literary (Pherecydes *FGrHist* 3 F 145), may push the story of Boreas and Oreithyia even earlier.

[17] The problems of this passage, quoted also in Σ Ar. *Plut.* 586 and *Suda s.v.* κοτίνου στεφάνῳ, are far too complex to treat here. They concern, briefly, (a) the distance of the olive from Ilissus, (b) the agent(s) of the transplanting(s) to Olympia, and (c) the location of the Pantheion (Athens or Olympia? cf. Σ Pind. *Ol.* 3.33); cf. Pease 1937, 2001. Even if Ilissus is to be emended and the Elean Pantheion is meant (cf. Hubbard 2007, 44 n. 55), the 'Athenianizing' mistake is telling, as it would betray an Athenian 'backlash'.

[18] See Hubbard 2007, 37–8, who discusses yet more versions placing the original olive in Olympia (Phlegon [*FGrHist* 257 F 1.10–11]; Paus. 5.14.3) or implicitly in Crete or Arcadia, and the ramifications for Elean, and more broadly Peloponnesian politics.

If, as I have argued, such nuances of Pindar's narrative are shaped partly in competition with Athens and can fruitfully be viewed as subtle statements against Athenian ideology, what is the political context for the emergence of these competing mythical accounts?[19] However difficult it may be to correlate Pindar's implicit polemic with concrete political conflicts in the wake of the Persian Wars and Athens' rise to prominence that crystallized in the new League, let me offer some necessarily speculative and by no means exhaustive suggestions, focusing almost exclusively on Athens. While Sicilian politics may be just as – if not more – crucial for the primary and secondary audiences of *Olympian 3*, the present attention to Athens is I hope justified in light of what I see as Pindar's dialogue with Athenian claims.[20]

By zooming in on the act of laying the olive wreath on the victor's head, Pindar transfers the symbolic precedence (both temporal and qualitative) of Olympian over Athenian trees to the *laudandus* Theron and his *polis* Acragas. Quite simply, this scores points for Theron in the Panhellenic competition centered on the relative contribution of Sicilian and Greek cities in the wake of their battles against Carthaginians and Persians respectively. While arguments perhaps started as early as the bitter dispute between Gelon and the Athenians (to which I shall return), the tension and resentment must have outlasted the war, morphing into claims and counterclaims as to the reasons for the Sicilian Greeks' refusal to help. I shall not rehash well-known facts, such as the tradition that the battle of Himera took place on the same day as Salamis (Hdt. 7.166) or Thermopylae (Diod. Sic. 11.24), which reflects the Sicilian desire to praise, in the words of Herodotus (7.166), 'the victory of Gelon and Theron over Hamilcar of Carthage'.[21] I simply wish to point out that the war's aftermath (the early 470s) must have been rife with debates of all sorts. We may adduce, for instance, the story about Themistocles' challenge to Hieron's participation in the Olympic games of 476 (Plut. *Them.* 25.1 drawing on Theophr. fr. 126 Wimmer) – a challenge justified, according to Ael. *VH* 9.5, on the basis of Gelon's refusal to

---

19 *Ol.* 7 provides another instance of a local version implicitly competing against an Athenian myth; see Sfyroeras 1993. *Ol.* 3 and *Ol.* 7 have more in common, including 'a close connection between the cities of the victors'; cf. Robbins 1982, 303–5.
20 On the Sicilian politics of Pindar's Sicilian odes as envisioned in performance and reperformance see, e.g., Morrison 2007; Hubbard 2001; Clay 2011.
21 Pindar will do just that in *Pyth.* 1.71–80 a few years later, under different circumstances and with none of the subtlety we find in *Ol.* 3. The suggestion of Luraghi 1994, 321, 365–8 that the parallelism between Himera and the Persian victories began with Hieron sometime later could help explain the difference between *Ol.* 3 and *Pyth.* 1.

share in the common danger earlier.[22] Whatever the historicity of this anecdote, it certainly reveals a climate conducive to such debates as could certainly extend into the area of mythical antagonism, which we should not be surprised to find reflected in Pindar's first extant odes after 480.

But in addition to the general antagonistic environment, we may correlate further some of the issues raised in Pindar's ode with the specific rhetoric in Herodotus' account (7.161–2) of the acrimonious exchange between Gelon – Theron's ally and father-in-law – and the Athenians, regarding command of the joint forces. Consider first how the Athenians justify their claim to the naval command: 'Are we not Athenians – the most ancient of all Greek peoples, the only nation never to have migrated?' (ἀρχαιότατον μὲν ἔθνος παρεχόμενοι, μοῦνοι δὲ ἐόντες οὐ μετανάσται Ἑλλήνων 7.161). As autochthony lies just under the surface here, this line of argument may easily lead to praise of the land, including olive trees and their harvest, a source of wealth and pride for both Athens and Acragas (Diod. Sic. 13.81).[23] However annoyed Theron or other Acragantines may have been at hearing repeatedly that Athenian olive trees were the first or the best, they could not claim with credibility that Acragas had priority on this score, so the next best option would be that Acragas, through Theron, had won a share of the olive trees introduced to Olympia, and to Greece at large, by Heracles, whose presence in Acragas (let it be added) was strongly felt in the temple dedicated to him.[24]

Be that as it may, I wish to turn to Gelon's riddling remark that concludes the debate, as he bids the Athenian envoys convey the message that 'the spring of the year is lost to Greece' (ἀγγέλλοντες τῇ Ἑλλάδι ὅτι ἐκ τοῦ ἐνιαυτοῦ τὸ ἔαρ αὐτῇ ἐξαραίρηται 7.162). This is so cryptic, in fact, that our manuscripts include an explanation, probably a late marginal gloss that is athetized in most editions. Some commentators, pointing out that Aristotle attributes twice the analogy to Pericles (*Rh.* 1365a31–3; 1411a2–4), argue that Herodotus, presumably unable to resist such a forceful metaphor, transferred it (rather awkwardly) to Gelon's mouth, where it is clearly less apposite.[25] But whether Gelon used the analogy or Herodotus wants us to think that he did, it is precisely *Olympian* 3 that can elucidate it. Gelon's analogy holds that Greece without Sicily is like a year with-

---

[22] Hubbard 2001, 394–5 with n. 27.
[23] See Diod. Sic. 13.81, a passage which, strictly speaking, refers to the late 5th c., and to which I shall return; cf. *CAH* iv² 777.
[24] The identification of the temple is uncertain; see Krummen 1990, 223 n. 4.
[25] Macan on 7.162; How and Wells on 7.162 leave open the possibility that Gelon may have compared 'the youthful vigour of the colony, Sicily, to the spring'. On the whole, it seems more likely that, as Grethlein 2006 re-asserted, Herodotus gave Pericles' words to Gelon.

out spring. Now, a year deprived of its spring is a year of continuous winter, that is, in Greek terms, of North wind (cf. Hes. *Op.* 503–4). As Greece without Sicily is all winter, the Sicilian cities stand for and embody winterlessness – precisely the message of *Olympian* 3: by winning the Olympic olive wreath, Theron wins 'eternal spring' for himself, his clan, his *polis* Acragas, and the larger political alliance in Sicily. Thus, if Gelon uttered the remark, Pindar shrewdly modulates his mythmaking to cater to his patron's tastes. Alternatively, if Gelon did not, Herodotus incorporates Pindar's subtle hints, which he is astute enough to perceive. In either case, Pindar's myth can resonate with an audience attuned to the dispute between Athenians and Sicilians.

But more narrowly than the Panhellenic context, the narrative of *Olympian* 3 may serve a more diplomatic purpose *within* Sicilian politics. In the 480s Theron and Gelon had cemented their alliance through intermarriage between the Emmenids and the Deinomenids, who had also brought Syracuse under their control, but after Gelon's death one year before *Olympian* 3 (478/7), latent rivalries within the Acragantine-Syracusan bloc threatened to erupt.[26] In this climate, Theron's propaganda faced a delicate task: to underline his own contribution to the effort culminating in Himera yet without ruffling too many feathers. But in his attempt to claim that *he*, an Emmenid, and not Gelon's Deinomenid successors, was the true heir of Gelon's legacy, he could suggest that *his* Olympic victory validated Gelon's statement to the Athenians, that it was only *his* olive wreath, won for Acragas, that could bring winterlessness, indeed immortality, to Sicily.

If this interpetation is correct, why does Pindar refrain from making this mythical antagonism more explicit? It is precisely this reticence that allows for multiple 'readings' by various audiences, both Sicilian and Panhellenic. Whether *Olympian* 3 was first performed at the Theoxenia in Acragas, a city (in Pindar's own declaration) hospitable to strangers, or at Olympia, to which ἐς ταύταν ἑορτάν (*Ol.* 3.34) may refer,[27] we can certainly envision performances in other cities, especially within the Acragantine epicracy, not least Himera, which Theron resettled in 476 by introducing Dorians into the local Chalcidian population. An Acragantine would of course relish the anti-Athenian devaluation of Athens' sacred emblem. An Athenian sympathizer, not only one of the Himeraean Ionians whom Theron would like to win over but also anyone at a Panhellenic venue

---

[26] *CAH* v² 149; Clay 2011 offers a different reading of *Ol.* 1–3 that considers the same political tensions.
[27] Acragas, in particular the Theoxenia, is favored by the majority of scholars (cf. Morrison 2007), although there is still dissent (e.g. Shelmerdine 1987). For a full treatment see Krummen 1990, 223–36.

such as Olympia, would be content to see only a neutral account of the Olympian olive trees, with no particular reference to Athens. Finally, in the quicksand of Sicilian dynastic politics in the 470s, other Sicilian Greeks could choose any interpretation that might suit their shifting sympathies, whether these lay with Theron or not. Anticipating such a wide range of readings is part of what makes this a tour de force of Pindaric mythmaking; its vagueness, calculated to give his ode a plasticity that can withstand the test of successive performances, helps turn an epichoric manifesto into a Panhellenic monument.[28]

Yet regardless of the specific positioning of Pindar's gesture within its historical landscape, we cannot doubt the realities of mythical antagonism in general, within which Pindar's Hyperborean version is inscribed. Without ever stating it explicitly, Pindar intimates that olives may not have been indigenous to Greece until Heracles' northern adventure. Olympia's specimens, craftily blended with ordinary olives, owe their aura of bliss not to their origin as Athena's gift but to their Hyperborean pedigree, which renders them immune to the North wind and its symbolic connection with the human condition. The quasi-divine felicity that characterizes the Hyperboreans and their trees is also the property of such mythical places as Elysium or the Isles of the Blessed, described by Pindar elsewhere, in fr. 129 and notably in *Olympian* 2. Besides *laudandus* and victory, *Olympians* 2 and 3 share also the contemplation of a utopian place – Elysium or the Hyperborean land (and by extension Olympia) – that enables the select few to transcend the limitations of mortality, whether through mystical knowledge of the afterlife or through the olive garland of the victorious athlete.[29]

2 Sophocles' Response to Pindar

Turning now to *Oedipus at Colonus*, I wish to offer a partial reading of the two Sophoclean odes as a unified response to Pindar's implicit polemic and to inscribe that response within both the broader context of the tragedy and the historical circumstances of the last decade of the 5th century, presumably the time of its composition. As noted above, recent scholarship has established that, in gen-

---

[28] For another reading of the Hyperborean version as a Panhellenic gesture meant to transcend local claims see Hubbard 2007. It must be said, however, that by implicitly rejecting both Athenian and other local claims concerning the origin of olives, Pindar tacitly furthers the interests of a new, non-traditional locality, namely Acragas.
[29] Robbins 1984, 226–7 comments on the 'realized eschatology' of *Ol.* 3, while Krummen 1990, 237–63 stresses the ode's initiatory and eschatological aspects. Pavlou 2010 starts from *Ol.* 3.42–4 to formulate a reading that complements mine.

eral, Pindar's choral lyric was still familiar, not only to members of the Athenian elite but also, less intimately, to wider segments of the public, either through the tradition of choral or sympotic re-performance or through the new institutions of education; these would certainly constitute part of Sophocles' intended audience, perhaps even the part that mattered most to the playwright.[30] But for the elite youths of Athens that, as has been proposed, performed the tragic chorus, the 'horizon of expectations' was broad enough to include Pindaric poetics. With that in mind, let us follow the threads that connect Sophocles' last play to the victory ode for Theron.

First, an essential feature of Colonus' landscape in Sophocles' praise (cf. ἄλλον δ' αἶνον 707) is the unique olive trees, noticed by Antigone already at 17 but fully described in the second strophe of the first *stasimon*.

Ἔστιν δ' οἷον ἐγὼ γᾶς
   Ἀσίας οὐκ ἐπακούω, (695)
οὐδ' ἐν τᾷ μεγάλᾳ Δωρίδι νάσῳ
   Πέλοπος πώποτε βλαστὸν
φύτευμ' ἀχείρωτον αὐτοποιόν,
   ἐγχέων φόβημα δαΐων,
ὃ τᾷδε θάλλει μέγιστα χώρᾳ, (700)
γλαυκᾶς παιδοτρόφου φύλλον ἐλαίας·
τὸ μέν τις οὐ νεαρὸς οὔτε γήρᾳ
σημαίνων ἁλιώσει χερὶ πέρσας·
   ὁ γὰρ αἰὲν ὁρῶν κύκλος
λεύσσει νιν Μορίου Διὸς (705)
χἁ γλαυκῶπις Ἀθάνα.

(Soph. *OC* 694–706)

And there is something I have not heard to have grown ever in the land of Asia, or in the great Dorian island of Pelops, a tree unvanquished, self created, a terror to the spears of enemies, that flourishes most greatly in this land, the foliage of the gray nurturer of children, the olive. This shall no young man nor any that dwells with old age destroy and bring to nothing; for it is looked upon by the ever-seeing eye of of Zeus Morios and by gray-eyed Athena.
[Tr. Lloyd-Jones, modified].

As the olive, 'the pivotal point of the whole ode' in the words of one critic,[31] comes into view, several aspects make better sense if we consider them against the Pindaric background. Let us first note the zooming effect as the chorus grad-

---

30 See nn. 4–5 above. On the ephebic chorus see Winkler 1990. For the term 'horizon of expectations' see n. 8 above.
31 McDevitt 1972, 235.

ually reveals, in the manner of a riddle, the properties and identity of this plant.[32] The shift from the generic φύτευμα to the specific ἐλαία in the last colon of the long sentence (701) is not unlike Pindar's device of narrowing down from the unknown δένδρεα (*Ol.* 3.32) to the Olympian olives. Heracles' far-flung travels all the way to the Hyperboreans find their equivalent here in the chorus' expansive geography: note that γᾶς is boldly albeit momentarily universalizing until it is limited by the epithet Ἀσίας. Note also that 'the great Dorian island' (ἐν τᾷ μεγάλᾳ Δωρίδι νάσῳ, 696) might, before we hear the genitive Πέλοπος, be understood as describing also Sicily, which is predominantly though not exclusively Dorian.[33] This dual – Peloponnesian and Sicilian – application represents a subtle conflation that acknowledges the Pindaric connection, achieved through the victor's olive wreath, between Olympia and Acragas.

Until we reach the end of the strophe, indeed, we have reason to wonder whether the chorus highlights the uniqueness of Attic olives in general, as suggested by the phrase 'blooms mightily in this land' (700), or of the sacred plants protected by Zeus Morios and Athena. The ambiguity, reminiscent of the rhetorical move we observe in *Olympian* 3, is never quite resolved; as a result, all Attic olives are endowed with extraordinary qualities in a gesture meant to counteract some of Pindar's claims.

The adjective αὐτοποιόν (697), for instance, effectively a *hapax* that means 'self-created', must refer to the report, which we find in Herodotus (8.55), of the miraculous renewal of Athena's olive in Erechtheus' precinct.[34] Yet even more than regrowth, this 'autopoetic' property evokes something akin to autochthony: Athena's self-renewing gift emerges from the soil itself, as opposed to the imported Hyperborean trees of Olympia. While αὐτοποιόν recalls Athena's tree on the Acropolis, the adjective ἀχείρωτον, which I take to mean 'unvanquished, unconquerable',[35] opens up to encompass a wider circle of olives, the μορίαι in

---

[32] On the riddling aspects of the passage see Stinton 1976b.

[33] On Dorians and Doricization in Sicily see *CAH* iii² 766; iv² 779; v² 150–1, 447. It is no accident that, on the eve of the Sicilian expedition, the Egestaeans stress the risk that a Dorian alliance between Syracusans and Peloponnesians would pose for Athens (Thuc. 6.6) and that Hermocrates appeals to the Camarinaeans' Dorian sentiment (Thuc. 6.76–80). It should be added that by the late 5th century the Peloponnese is not exclusively Dorian either. For Pindar's Dorian agenda see Hubbard 2001.

[34] The word is a *hapax* until Alex. Aphr. *in Metaph.* 563.1 (2nd-3rd c. AD). The same idea of perennial self-generation may shape Eur. *Ion* 1433–6, where the στέφανος from Athena's tree is said to remain ever fresh, never to wither: Creusa is confident that the crown, if it is among the child's tokens, will still be fresh. On Hdt. 8.55 see above; cf. Burton 1980, 275–8; Markantonatos 2002, 189–93; Rodighiero 2011, 62–4.

[35] See Jebb 1900b *ad loc.*; Kamerbeek *ad loc.*

the shrine of the Academy, mentioned explicitly at the end of the strophe. Among them are the olives, twelve (according to *Suda s.v.* μορίαι) or one (as can be inferred from Paus. 1.30.2; cf. Σ Soph. *OC* 701 de Marco), thought to have descended from Athena's tree. Like their ancestor, they show striking resilience, albeit of a different sort: the ancient scholiast (Σ Soph. *OC* 698 de Marco), drawing on Philochorus (*FGrHist* 328 F 125) and Androtion (*FGrHist* 324 F 39), connects both ἀχείρωτον and the phrase 'fear of enemy swords' with the fact that the μορίαι were spared during the Lacedaemonian and Boeotian invasions led by Archidamus.[36] Perhaps more importantly for the Pindaric intertext, the μορίαι are the source of the olive oil for the athletic victors at the Panathenaia (Arist. *Ath. Pol* 60.2; Σ Soph. *OC* 701 de Marco).[37] This, along with their location at the gymnasium of the Academy, may have prompted Sophocles, as implied by the scholia (*ibid.*, adducing Ar. *Nu.* 1005), to use the epithet παιδοτρόφος which, as has been noted, 'perhaps evokes the association of olive oil with athletics and the atmosphere of the gymnasium, where young men train in the shadow of olive trees'.[38] On the strength of their athletic aura, thus, Sophocles' olive trees prove to be worthy rivals of Pindar's specimens, especially given a certain lack of topographical precision. The Academy, i.e. the place of the μορίαι implied at the end of this strophe, and Colonus, i.e the primary subject of the chorus' praise in the *stasimon*, are distinct sites, despite their proximity. Far from careless, this geographical vagueness is fully intentional; it belongs within the broader ambiguity that serves Sophocles' rhetorical move to conflate all the olives of Attica with Athena's sacred trees (even if once removed).[39]

Sophocles' creation of concentric circles is aided by the application of the epithet γλαυκᾶς to olives (γλαυκᾶς φύλλον ἐλαίας 701). This might at first appear to be a familiar trope, hence rather unremarkable, yet a diachronic look at its development allows us to appreciate its special overtones. Before its frequent use

---

[36] *Ath. Pol.* 60 focuses on the legal aspects of their oversight, resting with the Areopagus. On the theme of security and protection see McDevitt 1972. For the connection with the Decelean war, see Hanson 1998, 159, 241.

[37] We may infer from *Ath. Pol.* 60 that *moriai* does not designate trees exclusively in the Academy and that by Aristotle's time the Panathenaic oil could even come from olives in groves where *moriai* had earlier grown; cf. Rhodes *ad loc*. This vagueness strengthens the present argument.

[38] Kamerbeek 109 *ad loc.*

[39] On the site see Travlos 1971, 42–3. The geographical imprecision, a well-known feature in *OC* (see, e.g., Rodighiero 2011), starts with the mention of Prometheus (*OC* 55–6), whose altar was in the Academy (Σ *OC* 56 de Marco; Apollod. *FGrHist* 244 F 147; Paus. 1.30.2). As implied, however, in Apollod. *FGrHist* 244 F 120 (Σ *OC* 705 de Marco), Zeus Morios and the *moriai* might not be *in* Academus' sanctuary but in its vicinity, hence closer to the hill of Colonus.

in the last two decades of the fifth century (cf. Eur. *IT* 1101; *Tro.* 802; *Supp.* 258), the only attestations of the trope take us back to Olympia: two Bacchylidean references to the victor's olive wreath (γλαυκὸν...ἄνδημ' ἐλαίας 8.14; ἐλαίᾳ γλαυκᾷ στεφανωσάμενον 11.29) and, of course, Pindar's γλαυκόχροα κόσμον ἐλαίας (*Ol.* 3.13).[40] In recalling these epinician models, therefore, Sophocles' γλαυκᾶς ἐλαίας evokes specifically the Olympian flora, while at the same time meshing with γλαυκῶπις Ἀθάνα (*OC* 706).

As this epithet returns us to the hues of the Olympian olive, we may consider the symbolic associations of the olive trees and their effect on the landscape. Like Olympia after the transplanting of Hyperborean olives, the grove of Colonus is protected from both sun and wind (τὰν ἄβατον θεοῦ φυλλάδα μυριόκαρπον ἀνάλιον ἀνήνεμόν τε πάντων χειμώνων 675–8). While the chorus attribute this effect, strictly speaking, to the ivy and vines of the place, it is still fresh in our memory when we hear of the olive foliage. Its full significance can only be appreciated in light of *Olympian 3*, but the threads that lead to Pindar are not fully woven together until we hear the epode of the third *stasimon*:

Ἐν ᾧ τλάμων ὅδ', οὐκ ἐγὼ μόνος
πάντοθεν βόρειος ὥς τις ἀκτὰ (1240)
κυματοπλὴξ χειμερίᾳ κλονεῖται,
 ὣς καὶ τόνδε κατ' ἄκρας
 δειναὶ κυματοαγεῖς
ἆται κλονέουσιν ἀεὶ ξυνοῦσαι,
αἱ μὲν ἀπ' ἀελίου δυσμᾶν, (1245)
 αἱ δ' ἀνατέλλοντος,
αἱ δ' ἀνὰ μέσσαν ἀκτῖν',
αἱ δ' ἐννυχιᾶν ἀπὸ Ῥιπᾶν.

(Soph. *OC* 1239–48)

In this the unhappy man – not I alone – is battered from all sides, like a wave-lashed cape facing north, buffeted in wintertime. Even so is this man also battered over the head by grim waves of ruin breaking over him that never leave him, some from where the sun goes down, some from where it rises, some from the place of his midday beams, and others from the Rhipaean mountains of the north, shrouded in night.
[Trans. Lloyd-Jones/ Green, combined.]

This epode concludes the threnodic meditation on the futility of longevity and the reasons why not to be born is preferable; a series of gnomic statements

---

40 Otherwise, Pindar applies γλαυκ- to snakes (*Ol.* 6.45, 8.37; *Pyth.* 4.249) and of course Athena. For later uses with olives see Nic. *Ther.* 680; Limen. *Pae. Delph.* 2.6; Phlegon *FGrHist* 257 F 36.442; Nonn. *D.* 22.72.

gives way to concrete imagery that fleshes out the connection of wind with the ravages of time.⁴¹ The human condition is defined by suffering, metaphorically imagined as storms coming from all directions, but especially northerly gales. Note the buffeted 'northern headland' that emphatically opens the epode, but also the mention of the dark Rhipaean mountains (ἐννυχίων Ῥιπᾶν).⁴² These mythical mountains are already connected with darkness in Alcman, who strikingly figures them as the 'breast of black night' (νυκτὸς μελαίνας στέρνον, *PMGF* 90; *apud* Σ Soph. *OC* 1248 de Marco).⁴³ More importantly, by Sophocles' time they become a crucial part of the Hyperborean geography. While the Sophoclean epode does not locate them explicitly in the north, it outlines a compass that starts from the north and, after moving through west, east, and south, returns to the north with the reference to the Rhipaean mountains, clearly understood as the source of the north wind. As this is entirely consonant with 5ᵗʰ century thought, such as Hellanicus (*FGrHist* 4 F 187a), Damastes (*FGrHist* 5 F 1), and the Hippocratic corpus (*Aer.* 19),⁴⁴ Sophocles' audience could hardly miss the specific emphasis on the northern winds. From the opening 'north-facing shore' to the closing Rhipaean mountains, the mental wandering of the chorus comes full circle, as they consider the storms of human suffering from their present vantage point at Colonus.

In light of both choral odes taken together, then, the olive grove of Colonus is in effect transformed into a Hyperborean place, shielded from the North wind and *ipso facto* immune to the miseries of mortality – a still point where the ills of the mortal condition cease. When we see Oedipus disappear, amidst thunder, lightning, and hail (1460–1, 1463–7, 1477–8, 1502–4, 1514–5), into the depths of the grove, to be painlessly removed 'not by blazing thunderbolt nor storm rising from the sea' (1658–60), we could not imagine a more appropriate choice for his final resting place. There are, to be sure, other poetic precedents for this type of *locus amoenus*, several from the *Odyssey*, the *nostos* narrative

---

41 The move from abstract to concrete parallels also the move from general to particular (Oedipus), typical in tragedy but unusual in this play: Carey 2009b, 121, 128–9; Dhuga 2005, 354.
42 The imagery of the epode is comparable to *Ant.* 582–92 (cf. Carey 2009b, 129), but the substitution of Rhipaean for the more typical Thracian (*Ant.* 588) is telling: the allusion is not simply to a northern direction, but specifically to a Hyperborean location.
43 Alcman's trope (στέρνον) offers another subtle hint that the locales in the two odes are symbolically linked in Sophocles' mind, whose praise for Colonus refers to Attica as στερνούχου χθονός (691): note that στερνοῦχος – a *hapax!* – represents Sophocles' only metaphorical use of στέρνον. The trope may suggest something elemental: cf. Hes. *Theog.* 117.
44 See Sfyroeras 2003, 315; Robbins 1984, 224–5.

par excellence.⁴⁵ We might recall Olympus (*Od.* 6.43–4), the Elysian fields (*Od.* 4.566–8), or even – to limit the scope to protection from both the rays of the sun and wind or rain – the more mundane wood that provided refuge to Odysseus on the Phaeacian shore (*Od.* 5.475–81) and the lair of the boar that wounded him (*Od.* 439–43, cited in Σ Soph. *OC* 676 de Marco). Yet what distinguishes Colonus from those other locations, besides the relative realism of its Athenian topography, is the numinous presence of olive trees which, I have argued, serves as a specific evocation of – and challenge to – the idealized flora in the Pindaric ode.⁴⁶ If then the connective tissue for this reading that brings the two choral odes together comes from Pindar's praise for Acragas on the occasion of Theron's chariot victory, we might very briefly broaden our purview to touch upon some implications for the tragedy as a whole.

First, there is the agonistic setting, not only in the sense that Oedipus engages in a series of hard-fought debates (646), but also in connection with the offstage battle between Theseus and Creon. Space does not permit a full discussion of the second *stasimon* that envisions Theseus' victory. It is worth noting, however, that in imagining this battle as specifically a clash of chariots (ῥιμφαρμάτοις…ἀμίλλαις 1063), the chorus employs an epithet, ῥιμφάρματος ('of swift chariots'), which occurs nowhere else – except in *Ol.* 3.37–8 (ῥιμφαρμάτου διφρηλασίας).⁴⁷ The verbal coincidence would indicate that Sophocles has that ode in mind, even were it not for the shared themes and motifs, including especially the emphasis on horses. Such emphasis can hardly come as a surprise in Pindar's 'hymn, the choicest prize for horses with untiring feet' (ὕμνον…ἀκαμαντοπόδων ἵππων ἄωτον *Ol.* 3.3–4), but *prima facie* it would be less predictable in a play about the end of Oedipus. Yet Sophocles goes out of his way to turn our attention to horses and horsemen; in addition to Theseus' troops in chariots or on horseback (899, 1062), or the somewhat puzzling Aetnaean colt on which Ismene has traveled (Αἰτναίας ἐπὶ πώλου 312–3),⁴⁸ the play draws heavily on the

---

45 The notion of return or homecoming has been recognized as an important theme in epinician poetry (Crotty 1982, 104–38; Kurke 1991, 15–61) but also, more recently, as a link with tragedy (Swift 2010, 150–1; Steiner 2010a, 23–4; Carey 2012, 18–19).
46 Of the Odyssean passages, only *Od.* 5.475–81 briefly mentions olive (477); on the symbolic importance of olives in the *Odyssey* see Dietz 1971.
47 For -αρματος compounds as Pindarisms see Rodighiero 2012, 113–4. Rodighiero 2011, 60–2 links the early description of Colonus as ἔρεισμ' Ἀθηνῶν (*OC* 58) to Pindar's praise of Athens as Ἑλλάδος ἔρεισμα (fr. 76 S-M). For other echoes of Pindaric diction and imagery in *OC* see Burton 1980, 277 (*Pyth.* 4.8), 278 (*Ol.* 13.68, 85), 287 (*Nem.* 7.99). *Pyth.* 4.263–9 – Pindar's sole reference to Oedipus – may underlie Sophocles' treatment.
48 No compelling reason why Antigone would mark the colt as 'Aetnaean' is evident (cf. Jebb 1900b *ad loc.*; Kamerbeek *ad loc.*), other than to evoke Sicily early on in the play.

actual associations of Colonus with Poseidon Hippios, at whose altar Theseus performs a sacrifice (888–9), and with Athena Hippia, honored by the horsemen along with Poseidon (1070–3).[49] These associations are foregrounded early on, when Oedipus is shown – though he cannot see – 'this Knight Colonus' (τόνδ' ἱππότην Κολωνόν 59), the eponymous hero of the deme; the demonstrative pronoun (59; cf. 65) may imply a visual signal present on stage throughout. But even without it, the language itself is unmistakeable, as in the second antistrophe that concludes the first *stasimon* (707–19).[50] The political and religious symbolism of this aspect in the wake of the oligarchic coup of 411 and the restoration of democracy has attracted plenty of attention, so I shall refrain from expanding further, except to underline the additional thread connecting tragedy and victory ode.[51] In playing up the equestrian element, Sophocles seems naturally drawn to the Pindaric model.

Second, the reception and incorporation of Oedipus at Colonus, whether or not a Sophoclean invention, may invite a comparison with Pindar's *laudandus* and his clan, the Emmenids, who traced their descent all the way to Thersander, the son of Polyneices (*Ol.* 2.42–52).[52] But while Polyneices is claimed as the ancestor of Theron – possibly of Pindar too![53] – he is fiercely repudiated by Oedipus in the play, whose mysterious power is joined to that of the Eumenides. We may recall that the inimical role of the Erinys as the agent of the double fratricide in *Ol.* 2.45 happens to coincide with the perspective of Polyneices when he makes the only two mentions of her that appear in the play (1299, 1434). By contrast, these very Erinyes, under their more auspicious names, collectively become Oedipus' allies in the tragedy. This comparison with the Pindaric intertext brings to

---

[49] Not accidentally perhaps, Paus. 1.30.4 links the altar of Poseidon Hippios and Athena Hippia with Oedipus' first arrival in Attica.

[50] The epithet εὔιππος, employed twice in the *stasimon* to refer to Colonus (668, 711), is fairly rare before Sophocles, who possibly uses it once more (1133** 51.2 *TrGF*⁴). Apart from – moving back in time – Eur. (*Andr.* 1019; *Hec.* 1090; *Phoen.* 17; *IT* 132; *Bacch.* 574), Cratinus 506 *PCG*⁴, *Hom. Hymn. Apoll.* 210, and Hes. fr. 151.21 M-W (describing the Hyperboreans!), all other attestations are Pindaric: *Ol.* 3.39; 8.47; *Pyth.* 3.8; 4.2. Thus, Pindar and Sophocles use it seven times, almost as much as all the rest combined.

[51] On horses, horsemen and such in *OC* see Edmunds 1996, 91–4; Siewert 1979.

[52] On Sophocles' mythical innovation in *OC*, see e.g. Kamerbeek 1984, 2–3, who is correct to discount Eur. *Phoen.* 1703–7 (the only reference not evidently based on *OC*) as a later interpolation, but his opinion of a pre-existing Oedipus cult in Colonus is difficult to accept: the point of *OC* is that the location of the grave is *not* known. Pausanias was shown a hero-shrine (1.30.4), but his own skepticism (1.28.7) points to a retroactive invention by later Athenians.

[53] It is worth noting that the Emmenids belonged to the race of the Aegeids (Hdt. 4.147), to whom Pindar may also have traced his descent (*Pyth.* 5.75–6; cf. Gildersleeve 1899, 140; Hubbard 2001).

light a radical shift in the ability of the *polis* to integrate the radioactive energy of a transgressive hero: the grim genealogy of the Acragantine ruling family, acknowledged in Pindar's praise, is transcended in the grove of the Eumenides, not only because the blood ties between father and son are severed, but also because, more generally, the bond of kinship gives way to the bond of friendship between host and suppliant. Conversely, given that Oedipus is by far the most problematic *xenos* to receive, Colonus deserves much greater praise for *philoxenia* than conferred by Pindar on Theron, his city, and the Dioscuri.

3 Acragas at Colonus: Keeping Sicily on their Minds

I hope to have shown that Pindar's odes for Theron's Olympic victory provide a meaningful interext for the first and third *stasimon* in *Oedipus at Colonus*, enabling us to hear their seemingly discordant tones as a symphonic texture. In fact, we cannot fully experience the numinous aura with which the olive grove is endowed in the first *stasimon* without the disquisition on suffering in the third *stasimon*, and to do so requires the foundation of *Olympian 3*. The tranquility of the olive grove and the fury of raging storms, the blessing of immortality and the realities of human suffering, triumphant praise and melancholy reflection, all these strands come together as an attempt to recreate, on the Dionysiac stage, the choral space of a past epinician performance. On this reading, Sophocles discerns, in the distant celebration of a Sicilian ruler, the implicit challenge to Athenian ideology and finds it relevant enough to respond to it. He does so not by rejecting but by adapting the Pindaric poetic universe, so as to transform his idealized Colonus into Acragas, Olympia, the land of Hyperboreans, and Elysium – all four rolled into one. I wish to conclude by offering a few inevitably speculative thoughts as to what may have prompted Sophocles to engage so creatively with Pindar's poetry. Given that, as is generally accepted, *Oedipus at Colonus*, first produced posthumously in 402/1 (*Argum.* II), was composed in the last few years before Sophocles' death in 406/5, I propose we look to the events of that period for what may have reminded the playwright of Pindar's Sicilian, and especially Acragantine odes.[54]

---

[54] On the dating of the composition and the first production, see, e.g. Tanner 1966; Edmunds 1996, 87–91; Hanink 2014, 341–4. As interesting as it might be to consider the impact on the audience of the first production, this discussion is limited to the circumstances that Sophocles himself would know.

To start with, the few years following the Sicilian disaster can hardly have erased its memory: the Athenian obsession with the island had long been ingrained too deeply in the citizens' collective consciousness for its traces to vanish. The long-standing concern with Sicily, manifest in the 'First' Sicilian Expedition (427–24), is further illustrated, for instance, in the anecdote reported by Plutarch (*Nic.* 12.1; *Alc.* 17.3) that Athenians, both young and old, would sit together to draw the shape of the island, its harbors, and its position in relation to Libya and Carthage. Nor should we discount the effect, both long- and short-term, of dramatic poetry: the promulgation of such visions on the stage undoubtedly made a lasting impression on the popular imagination.[55] It can be no accident, of course, that some of those poetic evocations of Sicily were filtered through Pindaric tropes.[56] What could thus qualify as a type of mass fixation on Sicily in the years prior to the Expedition cannot have been eradicated easily on its wake, even if we allow for a possible need to repress the traumatic memory (e.g. Ar. *Lys.* 590).

What is more, in addition to the climate of recrimination after the disaster (e.g. Thuc. 8.1; Ar. *Lys.* 392–7), there were constant reminders of its after-effects: Syracusan ships under Hermocrates were sailing the Aegean on the side of Athens' enemies, until they were recalled in 409. The very reason for their disappearance, i.e. the Carthaginian invasion, must have kept Sicily in the attention of Athenians, especially as Sicilian cities started falling to the Carthaginians: Himera in 409, then Acragas in 406. At a moment when Athens was looking both east and west for alliances, the loss of Acragas, the city that alone of all Sicily had not joined, willingly or unwillingly, the Syracusan bloc in 413 (Thuc. 7.32.2), thwarted any such hopes. At the same time, a fragmentary inscription seems to offer evidence for a favorable Athenian response to a Carthaginian overture for collaboration, apparently at the time of the siege of Acragas, in the early part of 406 (*IG* i³ 123 = M-L 92 with bibliography). The details are not recoverable,

---

[55] Some dramatic evidence is either undated or early, such as Sophocles' *Triptolemus*, in which Demeter outlines Sicilian geography for the title character's circumnavigation of the western Mediterranean (frr. 598, 600–2 *TrGF*⁴). On the poetic visions and other popular conceptions of Sicily, current in Athens prior to the expedition, that provide a more nuanced account of Athenian *apeiria* (Thuc. 6.1), see Smith 2004.

[56] To take an example, the Trojan captives' anachronistic mention of Sicily in Eur. *Tro.* 220–3, on which see Smith 2004, 50–4, is significant for its relevance in 415 but also for the chorus' crediting their knowledge to epinician poetry (ἀκούω καρύσσεσθαι στεφάνοις ἀρετᾶς). In fact, while στέφανος and ἀρετή are predictably frequent in Pindar both singly and in combination (e.g. ἀρετᾶν καὶ στεφάνων *Ol.* 5.1, a Sicilian ode that also includes καρύσσω in 5.8; στεφάνων ἀρετᾶν τε *Nem.* 3.8), the use of ἀρετή in a genitive dependent on στέφανος, as in *Tro.* 223, occurs *only once* in Pindar: *Ol.* 3.18!

as only scraps of names and 'Sicily' are securely preserved; yet in such circumstances, where discussion of Sicilian affairs is to be expected, thoughts of Sicily seem appropriate both for the playwright and his Athenian audience. There is no need to assume of course that all citizens were of the same mind on this or, for that matter, on any other issue: the argument favoring alliance with Carthage was no doubt countered by the appeal to a certain affinity with Acragas and other Greek cities of Sicily. But no matter where one stood, Sicily must have remained at the forefront of civic debates.

Acragas, in particular, may hold special resonance for the Athenians. It would hardly be possible to think of that city without picturing its olive groves, as Diodorus Siculus makes clear in his description of Acragantine prosperity and its origin during this period (Diod. Sic. 13.81): most of Acragas' territory was 'fully planted in olives' (ἐλαίαις κατάφυτον), from which they gathered an 'abundant harvest' (παμπληθῆ καρπὸν) that they sold to Carthage 'in exchange for the wealth of Libya'. Diodorus places this account – followed by the evidence of the 'incredible fortunes' (οὐσίας ἀπίστους) of Acragas, i.e. the temples (13.82) – precisely in the context of the Carthaginian invasion, perhaps suggesting, if not a peak in resources, certainly a heightened awareness of what vanished shortly afterwards. Such knowledge, if available in Athens, would be extremely poignant, not least because of the Spartan fortification of Decelea. The ravaging of the Athenian countryside must have made all Athenians even more appreciative of olive trees and their value, as they needed to import olive oil from abroad, especially after the loss of Euboea (Thuc. 8.93–5). The elimination of Acragas as a potential source provides an even more concrete context for the Sophoclean praise of Attic olives, highlighting, not unlike Pindar earlier, their mystical rather than financial properties.[57]

It may be worth paying even closer attention to Acragas and the chronology of its fate. The city was besieged in the early part of 406, surrendered in the summer, then was razed in the following winter, a little before the winter solstice of 406: all this must have occurred before Sophocles' death.[58] But one event in particular seems especially relevant: in the early stages of the siege, famous

---

[57] Another occasion, closer to home, that called olive trees to mind may have been the decision, recorded in inscriptions of 409/8 and 408/7 (*IG* I³ 474–6), to resume and complete work on the Erechtheum, the site of Athena's olive.

[58] If the generally accepted explanation of his absence from the poetic contest in *Frogs* is correct; cf. Nemeth 1983. Even a more skeptical approach (e.g. Hesk 2012, 174–9) does not preclude the possibility that Sophocles was still alive through the winter of 406/5 – even working on the play (Cic. *Sen.* 7.22); cf. Edmunds 1996, 87–8; Tanner 1966.

monumental tombs were ransacked for building materials;[59] among them, the desecration of Theron's grave clearly stood out, in part because it was struck by lightning (Diod. Sic. 13.86). The plague that followed and killed many Carthaginians including Hannibal was viewed by the attacking army as punishment for the desecration of the tomb, which however failed ultimately to protect Acragas. It would not be far-fetched to see how such a report could underlie the dramatic action of *Oedipus at Colonus* – how Sophocles' tragic script might be an attempt to rewrite and flesh out some aspects of the real-life scenario. While Theron's tomb proved ineffective in guarding against the enemy, his distant ancestor bestows on Athens the gifts of his inviolable grave which, also marked by lightning (as in Theron's case), holds the promise of eternal protection.[60]

There are, to be sure, other historical circumstances closer to home that, as critics have demonstrated, can shed light on several aspects of *Oedipus at Colonus*.[61] I would not wish to dismiss, for instance, the impact of the oligarchic coup of 411 and its aftermath on the way the audience was meant to understand this tragedy; rather, by turning to events in Sicily, not heretofore considered in conjunction with the play, I hope to have sketched some dimensions of the historical background within which the Sophoclean response to Pindar's epinician odes, confirmed by diction, theme, and ideology, can be properly and fruitfully inscribed. The lyric echoes are amplified against the Sicilian context and become clear enough that the epinician praise of a Theban poet for an olive-crowned Sicilian descendant of Thebans can be treated as competing discourse. Just as a polluted scion of hostile Thebes brings benefit to Athens in mystical fashion, so Theban poetics, originally intended as subtly anti-Athenian celebration of Sicily and Olympia, can be made to serve Attic drama and its *polis*.

---

59 On monumental tombs, some for winning horses at Olympia, see *CAH* v² 169.
60 There is precedent earlier in the century: after the fall of the Deinomenids, Hieron's tomb in Aetna was desecrated too, the expelled Aetnaeans taking the bones with them (*CAH* v² 158); there is also the matter of the bones of the Syracusans, left unburied by Diocles and collected by Hermocrates as part of a political statement: Diod. Sic. 13.75. Closer to home, we may think of the casualties of Arginusae.
61 Edmunds 1996, 87–100; Markantonatos 2007; Ferrario 2012, 457–8; more skeptically, Hesk 2012, 174–9.

Lucia Athanassaki
Talking Thalassocracy in Fifth-century Athens: From Bacchylides' 'Theseus Odes' (17 & 18) and Cimonian Monuments to Euripides' *Troades*

The *Troades* has frequently been thought of as a prolonged lament on stage responding to contemporary Athenian military cruelty and dangerous initiatives, above all the violent crushing of Melos a few months before the performance of the play and the anticipated dangers of the Sicilian expedition, a hot topic at the time of its performance.[1] The Chorus' mention in the *parodos* of the possibility of their being taken to Sicily shows that the debates about Sicily were on Euripides' mind (220–9). That Euripides responds to Athenian cruelty on Melos, on the other hand, has been challenged on the grounds that the trilogy must already have been composed when the news of Melos' suppression reached Athens.[2] From the audience's point of view, however, it is natural to assume that the lament of Trojan women would evoke Athenian violence on Melos whether these deeds weighed on Euripides' mind when he composed the play or not.[3] In what follows I argue that, although contemporary associations would be inescapable, the play is not a response to any specific single event, but voices broader political concerns that transcend the events of 416.

Focusing on the Prologue of the *Troades*, and especially on the intriguing geographical distribution of the storms that Poseidon in collaboration with Athena plans to inflict on the Achaeans, I argue that Euripides enters into dialogue

---

This version has profited from discussions following the original presentation at the 'Paths of Song' conference in London and lectures at the Scuola normale superiore di Pisa, the College of William and Mary, Johns Hopkins, Stanford and UCLA. Warmest thanks to the editors of this volume and to all discussants, and in particular to L. Battezzato, D. Bosnakis, E.L. Bowie, P. Brillet-Dubois, E. Cingano, M. Hose, R.P. Martin, S. Montiglio, K. Morgan, S.P. Morris, G.W. Most, V. Panoussi, J.K. Papadopoulos, A.-E. Peponi, H. Alan Shapiro and K. Valakas.

1 See Croally 1994, 231–4; Suter 2003; Goff 2009, 27–35 with references.
2 Scodel 1980, 139; Van Erp Taalman Kip 1987; Kovacs 1997; Kovacs 1999, 3–4 who also draws attention to the Chorus' flattering references to Athens.
3 See Croally 1994, 232 n.170: 'Most important, though, is the fact that the writing of the play is not really the issue: it was a matter for the audience to decide in March whether they saw the play as a response (as *their* response) to Melos.'

https://doi.org/10.1515/9783110575910-006

with the poetry and monumental art of Cimonian Athens, i.e. with Bacchylides' 'Theseus' dithyrambs (*Odes* 17 and 18) and the visual representations of the Theseion and the Painted Stoa (*Stoa Poikile*). Through this comparative analysis I suggest that (a) Euripides conjures up Athenian thalassocracy from the early fifth-century onward, thus reminding his audience of its original purpose and challenges; and (b) through the evocation of the times when the Persians sacked Greek cities and burnt their temples he offers a fresh and sobering perspective on the violence that the Greeks inflicted on each other during the Peloponnesian war. In the concluding section I draw attention to some interersting points of contact between the *Troades* and Aristophanes' *Lysistrata*, a play that also recalls Cimonian art and takes a long view on contemporary events.

1 The Prologue of the *Troades*

i) Trouble at Sea

In the opening of the play, Poseidon's first words show a tension between his feelings about the fall of Troy and the reaction of the Nereids who are dancing in the depths of the sea as he laments the destruction of Troy onstage:

ἥκω λιπὼν Αἰγαῖον ἁλμυρὸν βάθος (1)
πόντου Ποσειδῶν, ἔνθα Νηρῄδων χοροὶ
κάλλιστον ἴχνος ἐξελίσσουσιν ποδός.
ἐξ οὗ γὰρ ἀμφὶ τήνδε Τρωϊκὴν χθόνα
Φοῖβός τε κἀγὼ λαΐνους πύργους πέριξ (5)
ὀρθοῖσιν ἔθεμεν κανόσιν, οὔποτ' ἐκ φρενῶν
εὔνοι' ἀπέστη τῶν ἐμῶν Φρυγῶν πόλει·
ἣ νῦν καπνοῦται καὶ πρὸς Ἀργείου δορὸς
ὄλωλε πορθηθεῖσ'.[4]

(Eur. *Tro.* 1–9)

I am Poseidon, and I have come here from the briny depths of the Aegean, where choruses of Nereids turn their footsteps in graceful rounds. Ever since Phoebus and I put stone fortifications about this land of Troy with straight mason's rule, good will toward the city of the Phrygians has never left my heart. Now the city smolders, sacked and destroyed by the Argive spear.

As has been observed, Euripides does not follow the story of the *Iliad*, but capitalizes on the story of Apollo's and Poseidon's servitude to Laomedon and their

---

[4] The Greek quotations are taken from Diggle 1981; the English translations are those of Kovacs 1999 with a few small changes.

collaboration in the initial fortification of Troy.⁵ In this play Poseidon presents that collaboration as the reason for his goodwill towards Troy not only now that the city has fallen, but ever since its fortification. This claim would invite those in the audience who knew their *Iliad* well to recall that there Poseidon reported the worst possible memories of Laomedon's treatment of Apollo and himself, which served to justify his lack of sympathy for Troy and the Trojans (*Il.* 21.441–60). In the *Troades*, however, his claim prepares the audience for Athena's change of heart, which is equally dangerous.

Euripides' departure from the Iliadic tradition, however, is not total. Poseidon reports that the Nereids are dancing gracefully at the depths of the sea where he has just come from. Unlike him, the Nereids probably celebrate the news of the fall of Troy. The Euripidean representation of dancing Nereids is, in emotional terms, consistent with the Iliadic tradition which features the Nereids lamenting when Thetis does, i.e. they are sympathetic to the Greeks rather than to the Trojans.⁶

The dance of the Nereids is a favourite Euripidean theme, but Euripides mentions their dance only when they celebrate Thetis and her family. In the *Andromache*, for instance, Thetis announces her appearance in a similar way to Poseidon in the *Troades*, but she is not escorted by her dancing sisters (*Andr.* 1231–2). This is not surprising, because Thetis has come to advise Peleus on the burial of Neoptolemus. In the same speech, she announces that she will make Peleus immortal and take him to her sea-palace (*Andr.* 1253–8). Significantly, when this happy time comes, she will come to pick him up with her chorus of Nereids (*Andr.* 1266–8). Euripides' representation of the Nereids' celebrations at the wedding of Peleus and Thetis in the *Iphigenia in Aulis* (ll. 1036–57) offers yet another example of the Nereids' emotional allegiance to Thetis.⁷

I shall come back to the chorus of the Nereids. For the moment I mention only that Poseidon's pity for the Trojans, Athena's change of heart toward the Achaeans and the deal the two gods strike suggest that the dance of the Nereids will once again turn into lament. Since the destruction of the Achaean fleet falls outside the plot, however, such a lament does not find its way onto the stage. But the ironic contrast between the celebration of the Nereids and Poseidon's sadness and plan is reminiscent of the irony of the Trojans' celebration of peace with dances right before they led the Wooden horse in the city –a story that the Chorus narrates in the First *Stasimon* (*Tro.* 511–67).

---

5 Lee 1976, 67 *ad* 7.
6 See e.g. Hom. *Il.* 18.50–51 and 24.83–6.
7 In addition to the Euripidean representations of the Nereids' chorus discussed here see also *Electra* 434, 442 and *IT* 274, 428.

The *Troades* is unique in that its Prologue features the collaboration of two gods. Before exploring the significance of this collaboration in wrecking the Achaean fleet, it is also worth noting that Athena considers all Achaeans responsible, because they neither censured nor punished Ajax's impiety:

> Αθ. τοὺς μὲν πρὶν ἐχθροὺς Τρῶας εὐφρᾶναι θέλω, (65)
> στρατῶι δ' Ἀχαιῶν νόστον ἐμβαλεῖν πικρόν.
> Πο. τί δ' ὧδε πηδᾶις ἄλλοτ' εἰς ἄλλους τρόπους
> μισεῖς τε λίαν καὶ φιλεῖς ὃν ἂν τύχηις;
> Αθ. οὐκ οἶσθ' ὑβρισθεῖσάν με καὶ ναοὺς ἐμούς;
> Πο. οἶδ'· ἡνίκ' Αἴας εἷλκε Κασσάνδραν βίαι. (70)
> Αθ. κοὐ δείν' Ἀχαιῶν ἔπαθεν οὐδ' ἤκουσ' ὕπο.
>
> (Eur. *Tro.* 65–71)

ATHENA
I want to bring joy to my former enemies, the Trojans, and to give the Achaean army a journey home they will not like.
POSEIDON
But why do you leap about so, now with one character, now with another? Why hate and love whomever you chance to so excessively?
ATHENA
Are you not aware that I and my temples have been treated with contempt?
POSEIDON
Yes: it was when Ajax dragged Cassandra off by force.
ATHENA
And he was in no way punished or censured by the Achaeans.

Poseidon's surprise at Athena's volatile and extreme emotions deserves attention, for as we shall see they match the extremity of her actions. Her plan is to cooperate with Zeus and Poseidon in order to inflict maximal damage on the Achaean ships:

> Αθ. ὅταν πρὸς οἴκους ναυστολῶσ' ἀπ' Ἰλίου.
> καὶ Ζεὺς μὲν ὄμβρον καὶ χάλαζαν ἄσπετον
> πέμψει δνοφώδη τ' αἰθέρος φυσήματα·
> ἐμοὶ δὲ δώσειν φησὶ πῦρ κεραύνιον, (80)
> βάλλειν Ἀχαιοὺς ναῦς τε πιμπράναι πυρί.
> σὺ δ' αὖ, τὸ σόν, παράσχες Αἰγαῖον πόρον
> τρικυμίαις βρέμοντα καὶ δίναις ἁλός,
> πλῆσον δὲ νεκρῶν κοῖλον Εὐβοίας μυχόν,
> ὡς ἂν τὸ λοιπὸν τἄμ' ἀνάκτορ' εὐσεβεῖν (85)
> εἰδῶσ' Ἀχαιοὶ θεούς τε τοὺς ἄλλους σέβειν.
>
> (Eur. *Tro.* 77–86)

ATHENA
When they are sailing home from Ilium. Zeus for his part will send plentiful rain and hail and dark storm winds. He promises to give me the lightning bolt to strike the Achaeans and set their ships on fire. As for you, make the Aegean swell with high waves and eddies and fill the deep indentation of Euboea's coast with corpses so that henceforth the Greeks may learn to reverence my temples and show honour to the other gods as well.

Athena does not mention the possibility of any exceptions. We are thus led to understand that the punishment she is ready to inflict will affect all Achaeans, including the Arcadians, the Thessalians and the Athenians, whom Poseidon had earlier singled out for mention:

καὶ τὰς μὲν Ἀρκάς, τὰς δὲ Θεσσαλὸς λεὼς (30)
εἴληχ' Ἀθηναίων τε Θησεῖδαι πρόμοι.

(Eur. *Tro.* 30–1)

Some are taken by the Arcadian army, some by the Thessalian, and some by the sons of Theseus, leaders of the Athenians.

After his initial surprise at Athena's unexpected and rapid change of heart, Poseidon agrees to join in the destruction of the Achaean fleet:

Πο. ἔσται τάδ'· ἡ χάρις γὰρ οὐ μακρῶν λόγων
δεῖται· ταράξω πέλαγος Αἰγαίας ἁλός.
ἀκταὶ δὲ Μυκόνου Δήλιοί τε χοιράδες
Σκῦρός τε Λῆμνός θ' αἱ Καφήρειοί τ' ἄκραι (90)
πολλῶν θανόντων σώμαθ' ἕξουσιν νεκρῶν.
ἀλλ' ἕρπ' Ὄλυμπον καὶ κεραυνίους βολὰς
λαβοῦσα πατρὸς ἐκ χερῶν καραδόκει,
ὅταν στράτευμ' Ἀργεῖον ἐξιῇ κάλως.
μῶρος δὲ θνητῶν ὅστις ἐκπορθεῖ πόλεις (95)
ναούς τε τύμβους θ', ἱερὰ τῶν κεκμηκότων·
ἐρημίαι δούς <σφ'> αὐτὸς ὤλεθ' ὕστερον

(Eur. *Tro.* 87–97)

POSEIDON
It shall be so: the favour you ask requires no long discussion. I shall throw the Aegean main into confusion. The beaches of Mykonos and the reefs of Delos and Scyros and Lemnos and the promontories of Caphereus shall be filled with the bodies of many dead. So go to Olympus, take the lightning bolts from your father's hand, and wait until the Argive fleet is making full sail.
Foolish is the mortal who sacks cities and yet, after giving over to desolation temples and tombs, holy places of the dead, perishes later himself.

It has been observed that Euripides' frequent geographical references are not random, but serve specific purposes.[8] We have seen that Athena asked Poseidon to fill the bay of Euboea with corpses (*Tro.* 77–86). This is a reference to the storm at Euboean Cape Caphereus, which is linked to the Achaean shipwreck by the Cycle and other ancient sources (Proclus, *Nostoi* 18–19 Davies (p.67).[9] Poseidon's plan outdoes Athena's proposition in its zeal: he will stir the Aegean so that the beaches of Mykonos, the reefs around Delos, Scyros, Lemnos and Cape Caphereus fill with corpses (*Tro.* 87–97).

The choice of these islands for special mention is remarkable.[10] As far as the storm during the Achaean *nostos* is concerned, Cape Caphereus and Mykonos are the most relevant places. Mykonos is the place where, according to Pseudo-Apollodorus, Thetis buried the lesser Ajax after his death (*Bibl.* 6.6b.12). The other three places are relevant to the Trojan expedition at large. Delos is where Anios, the son of Apollo and Rhoeo, asked the outward-bound Greeks, who had put in the island, to stay, and revealed to them that, according to divine plan, they would conquer Troy on the tenth year (*Cypria* fr. 19 Davies). Lemnos is obviously associated with Philoctetes and Scyros with Achilles and Neoptolemus.[11] The odd combination of places relevant and irrelevant to the home-voyage of the Achaeans deserves attention, especially since these places are also associated with the Persian wars and the foundation of the Delian league.

ii) Delos and Mykonos: earthquakes before the Persian and the Peloponnesian wars

There is no need to say that the mention of Delos would trigger a wealth of associations and contemporary concerns. In contrast, Mykonos, unlike its neighboring richer islands, receives very little attention in our fifth-century sources. The most famous story about Mykonos is the one that Herodotus tells us

---

[8] Westlake 1953.

[9] The reference to Cape Caphereus also evokes Nauplius' revenge for the death of Palamedes which entailed lighting false beacons in Euboea, whereby he wrecked the Achaean fleet. See Lee 1976, 78 *ad* 89–91.

[10] According to Lee 1976, 78 and 89–91, 'The islands Mykonos, Delos, Scyros and Lemnos together with the promontory Caphereus cover most of the Aegean area and so indicate the extent to which Poseidon intends to punish the Greeks.' The great number of Aegean islands, however, offered Euripides a wide range of choices. His choice of these particular islands deserves attention.

[11] Proclus reports that Neoptolemus followed Thetis' advice and chose to come back home from Troy by land (Proclus, *Nostoi* 20, Davies p. 67).

about Datis' mysterious dream on the island, on account of which he commanded a thorough search of his fleet, found a gilded image of Apollo, sailed to Delos and handed over the statue with the request that it be returned to the Theban Delium. This story concludes with the observation that the Delians failed to do so, but twenty years later the Thebans went and took it back.[12]

This was certainly not Datis' first visit to Delos. On his way to Marathon Datis attacked Naxos and other Cycladic islands, whereupon the Delians fled to Tenos. Datis assured the Delians that he would respect the island where Apollo and Artemis were born and proceeded to make lavish offerings on the altar. But when he left an earthquake shook the island, the only earthquake Delos ever experienced. It was 'an act of God to warn men of the troubles that were on the way':

Ἐν ᾧ δὲ οὗτοι ταῦτα ἐποίευν, οἱ Δήλιοι ἐκλιπόντες καὶ αὐτοὶ τὴν Δῆλον οἴχοντο φεύγοντες ἐς Τῆνον. Τῆς δὲ στρατιῆς καταπλεούσης ὁ Δᾶτις προπλώσας οὐκ ἔα τὰς νέας πρὸς τὴν Δῆλον προσορμίζεσθαι, ἀλλὰ πέρην ἐν τῇ Ῥηναίῃ· αὐτὸς δὲ πυθόμενος ἵνα ἦσαν οἱ Δήλιοι, πέμπων κήρυκα ἠγόρευέ σφι τάδε· "Ἄνδρες ἱροί, τί φεύγοντες οἴχεσθε, οὐκ ἐπιτήδεα καταγνόντες κατ' ἐμέο; Ἐγὼ γὰρ καὶ αὐτὸς ἐπὶ τοσοῦτό γε φρονέω καί μοι ἐκ βασιλέος ὧδε ἐπέσταλται, ἐν τῇ χώρῃ οἱ δύο θεοὶ ἐγένοντο, ταύτην μηδὲν σίνεσθαι, μήτε αὐτὴν τὴν χώρην μήτε τοὺς οἰκήτορας αὐτῆς. Νῦν ὦν καὶ ἄπιτε ἐπὶ τὰ ὑμέτερα αὐτῶν καὶ τὴν νῆσον νέμεσθε." Ταῦτα μὲν ἐπεκηρυκεύσατο τοῖσι Δηλίοισι· μετὰ δὲ λιβανωτοῦ τριηκόσια τάλαντα κατανήσας ἐπὶ τοῦ βωμοῦ ἐθυμίησε. Δᾶτις μὲν δὴ ταῦτα ποιήσας ἔπλεε ἅμα τῷ στρατῷ ἐπὶ τὴν Ἐρέτριαν πρῶτα, ἅμα ἀγόμενος καὶ Ἴωνας καὶ Αἰολέας· μετὰ δὲ τοῦτον ἐνθεῦτεν ἐξαναχθέντα Δῆλος ἐκινήθη, ὡς ἔλεγον οἱ Δήλιοι, καὶ πρῶτα καὶ ὕστατα μέχρι ἐμέο σεισθεῖσα. Καὶ τοῦτο μέν κου τέρας ἀνθρώποισι τῶν μελλόντων ἔσεσθαι κακῶν ἔφηνε ὁ θεός·[13]

(Hdt. 6.97–8)

While they did this, the Delians also left Delos and fled away to Tenos. As his expedition was sailing landwards, Datis went on ahead and bade his fleet anchor not off Delos, but across the water off Rhenea. Learning where the Delians were, he sent a herald to them with this proclamation: [2] "Holy men, why have you fled away, and so misjudged my intent? It is my own desire, and the king's command to me, to do no harm to the land where the two gods were born, neither to the land itself nor to its inhabitants. So return now to your homes and dwell on your island." He made this proclamation to the Delians, and then piled up three hundred talents of frankincense on the altar and burnt it. After doing this, Datis sailed with his army against Eretria first, taking with him Ionians and Aeolians; and after he had put out from there, Delos was shaken by an earthquake, the first and last, as the Delians say, before my time. This portent was sent by heaven, as I suppose, to be an omen of the ills that were coming on the world.

---

12 Hdt. 6.118.
13 The Herodotean quotations are taken from Legrand 1932–54; the translations are those of Godley 1920.

Interestingly enough Thucydides reports a unique earthquake too, which he dates, however, a little before the outbreak of the Peloponnesian war:

ἥ τε ἄλλη Ἑλλὰς ἅπασα μετέωρος ἦν ξυνιουσῶν τῶν πρώτων πόλεων. καὶ πολλὰ μὲν λόγια ἐλέγετο, πολλὰ δὲ χρησμολόγοι ᾖδον ἔν τε τοῖς μέλλουσι πολεμήσειν καὶ ἐν ταῖς ἄλλαις πόλεσιν. ἔτι δὲ Δῆλος ἐκινήθη ὀλίγον πρὸ τούτων, πρότερον οὔπω σεισθεῖσα ἀφ' οὗ Ἕλληνες μέμνηνται· ἐλέγετο δὲ καὶ ἐδόκει ἐπὶ τοῖς μέλλουσι γενήσεσθαι σημῆναι. εἴ τέ τι ἄλλο τοιουτότροπον ξυνέβη γενέσθαι, πάντα ἀνεζητεῖτο. ἡ δὲ εὔνοια παρὰ πολὺ ἐποίει τῶν ἀνθρώπων μᾶλλον ἐς τοὺς Λακεδαιμονίους, ἄλλως τε καὶ προειπόντων ὅτι τὴν Ἑλλάδα ἐλευθεροῦσιν.[14]

(Thuc. 2.8.1–4)

Meanwhile all the rest of Hellas hung poised on the event, as the two leading cities came together in conflict. There were all kinds of prophecies and all kinds of oracular utterances being made both in the cities that were about to go to war and in other places as well. Then, too, there was an earthquake in Delos just before this time – a thing that had never happened before in the memory of the Hellenes. This was said and thought to be a sign of impending events; and if anything else of the same kind happened to occur, its meaning was always carefully examined.

Like Herodotus, Thucydides reports that it was interpreted by people as a sign of what was to come. It has been a matter of debate whether Thucydides corrects Herodotus (or vice versa), who got the date of the earthquake right, or even if there ever was such an earthquake.[15] In a recent article Jeffrey Rusten adduced archaeological and palaeoseismological evidence showing that Delos never suffered a destructive earthquake.[16] On this evidence Rusten argued for an imaginary earthquake. But anybody who has experienced earthquakes in that part of the world knows that there are strongly felt earthquakes which are not destructive. It is therefore possible that the earthquake was not imaginary. Be that as it may, it is significant that both Herodotus and Thucydides state that they report stories they heard from others. Herodotus attributes the story to the Delians, whereas Thucydides does not specify his sources. The two accounts agree on the belief that the earthquake was a portent of what was to come.

Thucydides also reports a number of earthquakes that struck various places including Athens in 426, which prevented king Agis from invading Attica. According to Thucydides, Euboea, Atalanta, and the island Peparethos (modern Skopelos) were also struck by what we would call a tsunami (3.87.4 and

---

14 Greek quotations taken from Jones and Powell 1942; the translations are those of Warner 1954.
15 For these views see Hornblower 1991, 245–6.
16 Rusten 2013.

3.89.1).¹⁷ According to Manolis Korres and Charalambos Bouras the earthquake caused damage to the Parthenon which was repaired soon afterwards.¹⁸ The earthquake seems to have caused serious damage in other areas too, i.e. the Themistoclean Wall, the Ceramicus, and the Agora.¹⁹ A year later Aristophanes may echo this event in the *Acharnians:*

ἐγὼ δὲ μισῶ μὲν Λακεδαιμονίους σφόδρα,
καὐτοῖς ὁ Ποσειδῶν, οὑπὶ Ταινάρῳ θεός, (510)
σείσας ἅπασιν ἐμβάλοι τὰς οἰκίας·
κἀμοὶ γάρ ἐστι τἀμπέλια κεκομμένα.
ἀτάρ, φίλοι γὰρ οἱ παρόντες ἐν λόγῳ,
τί ταῦτα τοὺς Λάκωνας αἰτιώμεθα;²⁰

(Ar. *Ach.* 509–14)

I hate the Spartans vehemently; and may Poseidon, the god at Tainarum, send them an earthquake and shake all their houses down on them; for I too have had vines cut down. And yet I ask—for only friends are present for this speech—why do we blame the Spartans for this?

Here Aristophanes hits two birds with one stone, for he reminds his audience of an earthquake that was fresh in their minds and simultaneously recalls the earthquake of c. 465 in Sparta.²¹

As we shall see in the last section, Aristophanes capitalizes on the c. 465 earthquake fourteen years later in the *Lysistrata*. For the moment, it is worth noting that the memory of that earthquake resurfaced right before the outbreak of the Peloponnesian war. Thucydides reports that the Athenians countered the Spartans' demand to drive out of the city the 'curse of the goddess', i.e. Pericles, by the demand that the Spartans drive out the 'curse of Taenarum', presumably those who were responsible for the sacrilege of removing and killing the Helots who had taken refuge at the sanctuary of Poseidon, an act for which the earthquake of c. 465 was believed to be a punishment.²²

In 426, however, it was Athens, not Sparta, that was hit by an earthquake. Thucydides is silent about the Athenians' perception of the 426 earthquake,

---

17 For these earthquakes see Hornblower 1991, 494 and 497 *ad loc.* For the extent of the damage see Rotroff and Oakley 1992, 53–7.
18 Korres and Bouras 1983, 114–5, 135, 328–30 (with a summary in English *ibid* pp. 678 and 688).
19 See Rotroff and Oakley 1992, 55–7.
20 The Greek quotations and the English translations are taken from Henderson 1998.
21 For the earthquake see Thuc. 1.128.1 (and 101.2) and the discussion in Cartledge 1979, 214–22; for Aristophanes' allusion see Olson 2002, 204 *ad* 510–1.
22 Thuc. 1.126–8.

but some at least must have seen it as a portent, especially since it struck the Parthenon. In any event, Herodotus', Thucydides' and Aristophanes' accounts, taken together, indicate that recent earthquakes and tsunamis would trigger the memory of earlier ones and encourage their association. Interestingly, from these earthquake stories emerges the triangle 'Delos, Sparta, Athens'.

iii) Lemnos and Scyros: memories of Miltiades and Cimon

Poseidon's threat in the *Troades* to stir up the Aegean would trigger the memory of such earthquake stories. The linked mention of Mykonos and Delos, however, would probably lead one's mind to the events before and after Marathon and to Miltiades who was a key player in the Athenian victory. Miltiades also annexed Lemnos to Athens, putting thus an end to the 'Lemnian horrors' that the Pelasgians had inflicted on the Athenians, which included abductions of Athenian women from the Brauronia:

> Οἱ δὲ Πελασγοὶ οὗτοι Λῆμνον τότε νεμόμενοι, [καὶ] βουλόμενοι τοὺς Ἀθηναίους τιμωρήσασθαι εὖ τε ἐξεπιστάμενοι τὰς Ἀθηναίων ὀρτάς, πεντηκοντέρους κτησάμενοι ἐλόχησαν Ἀρτέμιδι ἐν Βραυρῶνι ἀγούσας ὀρτὴν τὰς τῶν Ἀθηναίων γυναῖκας, ἐνθεῦτεν δὲ ἁρπάσαντες τουτέων πολλὰς οἴχοντο ἀποπλέοντες καί σφεας ἐς Λῆμνον ἀγαγόντες παλλακὰς εἶχον.
>
> (Hdt. 6.138)

> Τότε μὲν τοσαῦτα. Ἔτεσι δὲ κάρτα πολλοῖσι ὕστερον τούτων, ὡς ἡ Χερσόνησος ἡ ἐπ' Ἑλλησπόντῳ ἐγένετο ὑπὸ Ἀθηναίοισι, Μιλτιάδης ὁ Κίμωνος ἐτησιέων ἀνέμων κατεστηκότων νηὶ κατανύσας ἐξ Ἐλαιοῦντος τοῦ ἐν Χερσονήσῳ ἐς Λῆμνον προηγόρευε ἐξιέναι ἐκ τῆς νήσου τοῖσι Πελασγοῖσι, ἀναμιμνήσκων σφέας τὸ χρηστήριον, τὸ οὐδαμὰ ἤλπισαν σφίσι οἱ Πελασγοὶ ἐπιτελέεσθαι. Ἡφαιστιέες μέν νυν ἐπείθοντο· Μυριναῖοι δὲ οὐ συγγινωσκόμενοι εἶναι τὴν Χερσόνησον Ἀττικὴν ἐπολιορκέοντο, ἐς ὃ καὶ οὗτοι παρέστησαν. Οὕτω δὴ τὴν Λῆμνον ἔσχον Ἀθηναῖοί τε καὶ Μιλτιάδης.
>
> (Hdt. 6.140)

(138) These Pelasgians, dwelling at that time in Lemnos and desiring vengeance on the Athenians, and well knowing the time of the Athenian festivals, got them fifty-oared ships and lay in ambush for the Athenian women when they were celebrating a festival for Artemis at Brauron; carrying off many of the women, they sailed away further with them and brought them to Lemnos to be their concubines.

(140) But a great many years afterward, when the Chersonese by the Hellespont was made subject to Athens, Miltiades son of Cimon did, by virtue of the Etesian winds then constantly blowing, accomplish the voyage from Elaeus on the Chersonese to Lemnos; which done, he issued a proclamation to the Pelasgians bidding them leave their island, reminding them of the oracular word which the Pelasgians thought they would never see fulfilled. The men of Hephaestia, then, obeyed him; but they of Myrina would not agree that the Chersonese

was Attic land, and they stood a siege; but in the end they too submitted. Thus did Miltiades and the Athenians take Lemnos in possession.

Herodotus' account of the Hecataean vs. the Athenian version indicates that the causes of the old enmity and its resolution were discussed in Athens and elsewhere.[23] Poseidon's mention of Lemnos would therefore be sufficient to evoke its annexation by Miltiades. The joint mention of Lemnos with Scyros would reinforce the association. Shortly after the formation of the Delian league, Miltiades' son Cimon captured Skyros, repatriated the bones of Theseus and erected the Theseion, thus sparing no effort to cast himself as a second Theseus.[24]

2 The Chorus' references to Salamis

Before discussing Euripides' dialogue with Cimonian art, it is worth looking briefly at the Chorus' references to Salamis, which show that the evocation of a Delian thalassocracy under the leadership of Athens is not restricted to the Prologue. In the Second *Stasimon* the Chorus invoke the king of Salamis, Telamon, as one of the protagonists of the first sack of Troy. From a fifth-century perspective the victory at Salamis would be thought of by some in the audience as an important step towards the creation of the Delian league. Here the Chorus designates Salamis as 'the island lying opposite' to Athens, thus pointing up its proximity to the city for the patronage of which Poseidon and Athena competed once upon a time:

μελισσοτρόφου Σαλαμῖνος ὦ βασιλεῦ Τελαμών,
νάσου περικύμονος οἰκήσας ἕδραν (800)
τᾶς ἐπικεκλιμένας ὄχθοις ἱεροῖς,
ἵν᾽ ἐλαίας πρῶτον ἔδειξε κλάδον γλαυκᾶς Ἀθάνα,
οὐράνιον στέφανον λιπαραῖσί ‹τε› κόσμον Ἀθάναις,

(Eur. *Tro.* 799–803)

O Telamon, king of bee-nurturing Salamis, who dwell in a wave-washed isle that lies opposite the holy hills where the shoot of the gray-green olive was first revealed by Athena, a heavenly garland and a glory for gleaming Athens.

---

23 Hdt. 6.137.
24 For the association of Cimon with Theseus see Shapiro 1989, 143–9; Francis 1990, 43–90; Castriota 1992, 33–133; Shapiro 1992.

The Chorus here allude to one of the most popular stories in Athens that was famously the central theme of the Parthenon's West Pediment.²⁵ The allusion to Athena's competition with Poseidon over Athens would remind the play's audience of the implacable goddess making a destructive pact with the god in the Prologue.

In the Third *Stasimon* the Chorus think of 'holy' Salamis and Acrocorinth as their possible, alternative, destinations, thus adding the Peloponnese to Salamis' coordinates:

Μᾶτερ, ὤμοι, μόναν δή μ' Ἀχαιοὶ κομί-
ζουσι σέθεν ἀπ' ὀμμάτων
κυανέαν ἐπὶ ναῦν,
εἴθ' ἁλίαισι πλάταις (1095)
ἢ Σαλαμῖν' ἱερὰν
ἢ δίπορον κορυφὰν
Ἴσθμιον, ἔνθα πύλας
Πέλοπος ἔχουσιν ἕδραι.

(Eur. *Tro.* 1093–9)

Mother, ah mother, the Achaeans take me by myself away from your eyes down to their dark ship and then with seagoing oar either to holy Salamis or to the peak of the Isthmus with its two sea paths, where stand the gates to Pelops' home!

The mention of 'holy' Salamis evokes the decisive sea-battle of the Greeks against the Persians. A careful look at the Chorus's depiction of Salamis, however, shows that they do not perceive the island as a locus of union. Salamis is seen here as an alternative destination to Acrocorinth, the gate of the Peloponnese. In view of the Chorus' earlier description of Salamis' position in relation to Athens, Salamis emerges as a boundary between Athens and the Peloponnese. The mention of the gates of the Peloponnese leads the Chorus to the thought of Menelaus' ship which they wish to be destroyed, thus evoking the plan that Poseidon and Athena announced to the audience of the play:²⁶

εἴθ' ἀκάτου Μενέλα (1100)
μέσον πέλαγος ἰούσας
δίπαλτον ἱερὸν ἀνὰ μέσον πλατᾶν πέσοι
†αἰγαίου† κεραυνοφαὲς πῦρ,
Ἰλιόθεν ὅτε με πολυδάκρυτον (1105)
Ἑλλάδι λάτρευμα γᾶθεν ἐξορίζει,

---

25 For the sculptural representation see Paus. 1.24.5. See also Eur. *Ion* 1434–6 and Hdt. 8.55.
26 Lee 1976, 253 *ad* 1102–4.

χρύσεα δ' ἔνοπτρα, παρθένων
χάριτας, ἔχουσα τυγχάνει Διὸς κόρα·
μηδὲ γαῖάν ποτ' ἔλθοι Λάκαιναν πατρῶι- (1110)
  όν τε θάλαμον ἑστίας,
μηδὲ πόλιν Πιτάνας
χαλκόπυλόν τε θεάν,
δύσγαμον αἶσχος ἑλών
Ἑλλάδι τᾶι μεγάλαι (1115)
καὶ Σιμοεντιάσιν
μέλεα πάθεα ῥοαῖσιν.

(Eur. *Tr.* 1100 –17)

O that when Menelaus' ship is crossing the open sea in the midst of his oars might fall the hurled lightning blaze of Zeus as he takes me in tears from the land of Ilium as a slave to Greece while Zeus's daughter holds her golden mirrors, the delight of maidens! May he never reach the land of Sparta or his ancestral hearth, or the city of Pitana, or the goddess of the brazen gate! He has her as wife who shamed mighty Greece by her evil marriage and upon the streams of Simois brought grievous woes.

Although the Chorus do not specify the addressee of their wish, the diction (1100 – 04) leaves little doubt that the audience is invited to think of the two gods' pact in the Prologue. The evocation of Athena's and Poseidon's destructive plan in connection with Salamis in the Third *Stasimon* adds one more significant island to the web of allusions to the Persian wars and their aftermath.

3 Euripides' Dialogue with the Poetry and Art of Cimonian Athens

i) Bacchylides *Odes* 17 and 18

Poseidon's and Athena's collaboration in the destruction of the Achaean fleet stands in sharp contrast to Bacchylides Ode 17, composed a few years after the formation of the Delian league, which shows the collaboration of the two gods in helping Theseus and his companions in the previous generation:

Κυανόπρωιρα μὲν ναῦς μενέκτυ[πον]
  Θησέα δὶς ἑπτ[ά] τ' ἀγλαοὺς ἄγουσα
  κούρους Ἰαόνω[ν]
Κρητικὸν τάμνε πέλαγος·
τηλαυγέϊ γὰρ [ἐν] φάρεϊ (5)
  βορήϊαι πίτνο[ν] αὖραι
  κλυτᾶς ἕκατι π[ε]λεμαίγιδος Ἀθάν[ας·

[...]

Ἵετο δ' ὠκύπομπον δόρυ· σόει (90)
νιν βορεὰς ἐξόπιν πνέουσ' ἀήτα·
τρέσσαν δ' Ἀθαναίων
ἠϊθέων <—> γένος, ἐπεὶ
ἥρως θόρεν πόντονδε, κα-
τὰ λειρίων τ' ὀμμάτων δά- (95)
κρυ χέον, βαρεῖαν ἐπιδέγμενοι ἀνάγκαν.
φέρον δὲ δελφῖνες {ἐν} ἁλι-
ναιέται μέγαν θοῶς
Θησέα πατρὸς ἱππί-
ου δόμον· ἔμολέν τε θεῶν (100)
μέγαρον. Τόθι κλυτὰς ἰδὼν
ἔδεισε<ν> Νηρῆος ὀλ-
βίου κόρας· ἀπὸ γὰρ ἀγλα-
ῶν λάμπε γυίων σέλας
ὧτε πυρός, ἀμφὶ χαίταις (105)
δὲ χρυσεόπλοκοι
δίνηντο ταινίαι· χορῷ δ' ἔτερ-
πον κέαρ ὑγροῖσιν ἐν ποσίν.
εἶδέν τε πατρὸς ἄλοχον φίλαν
σεμνὰν βοῶπιν ἐρατοῖ- (110)
σιν Ἀμφιτρίταν δόμοις·
ἅ νιν ἀμφέβαλεν ἀϊόνα πορφυρέαν,
κόμαισί τ' ἐπέθηκεν οὔλαις
ἀμεμφέα πλόκον,
τόν ποτέ οἱ ἐν γάμῳ (115)
δῶκε δόλιος Ἀφροδίτα ῥόδοις ἐρεμνόν.
ἄπιστον ὅ τι δαίμονες
θέλωσιν οὐδὲν φρενοάραις βροτοῖς·
νᾶα πάρα λεπτόπρυμνον φάνη· φεῦ,
οἵαισιν ἐν φροντίσι Κνώσιον (120)
ἔσχασεν στραταγέταν, ἐπεὶ
μόλ' ἀδίαντος ἐξ ἁλὸς
θαῦμα πάντεσσι, λάμ-
πε δ' ἀμφὶ γυίοις θεῶν δῶρ', ἀγλαό-
θρονοί τε κοῦραι σὺν εὐ- (125)
θυμίᾳ νεοκτίτῳ
ὠλόλυξαν, ἔ-
κλαγεν δὲ πόντος· ἠίθεοι δ' ἐγγύθεν
νέοι παιάνιξαν ἐρατᾷ ὀπί.
Δάλιε, χοροῖσι Κηΐων (130)

φρένα ἰανθεὶς
ὄπαζε θεόπομπον ἐσθλῶν τύχαν.²⁷

(Bacch. 17.1–7, 90 –132)

The ship with the blue-black prow, as it carried Theseus, steadfast in the battle din, and the twice seven splendid youths and maidens of the Ionians, was cleaving the Cretan sea, for northerly breezes fell on the far-shining sail thanks to glorious Athena, the aegis-shaker

[...]

But sea-dwelling dolphins were swiftly carrying great Theseus to the house of his father, god of horses, and he reached the hall of the gods. There he was awe-struck at the glorious daughters of blessed Nereus, for from their splendid limbs shone a gleam as of fire, and round their hair were twirled gold-braided ribbons; and they were delighting their hearts by dancing with liquid feet. And he saw his father's dear wife, august ox-eyed Amphitrite, in the lovely house; she put a purple cloak about him and set on his thick hair the faultless garland which once at her marriage guileful Aphrodite had given her, dark with roses. Nothing that the gods wish is beyond the belief of sane mortals: he appeared beside the slender-sterned ship. Whew, in what thoughts did he check the Cnossian commander when he came unwet from the sea, a miracle for all, and the gods' gifts shone on his limbs; and the splendid-throned maidens cried out with new-founded joy, and the sea rang out; and nearby the youths raised a paean with lovely voice. God of Delos, rejoice in your heart at the choirs of the Ceans and grant a heaven-sent fortune of blessings.

The dithyramb commemorates the joint action of Athena and Poseidon that is instrumental for Theseus' triumph over Minos.²⁸ In the opening of the song Athena is envisaged as the deity who sends favourable north winds. Poseidon soon joins forces by ensuring Theseus' plunge into a welcoming sea and his safe transport by dolphins to his sea-palace. On arrival, he encounters the Nereids dancing, a celebration that anticipates the paean of his Ionian companions once he re-emerges triumphantly. Amphitrite welcomes him and gives him a purple-cloak and a rose-wreath, which is significantly Aphrodite's gift at her wedding with the ruler of the sea. As has been observed, Amphitrite's gifts symbolize the emergence of a new thalassocracy under the leadership of Theseus and his Ionian associates.²⁹ The Bacchylidean dithyramb brings out the synergy of Athena, Poseidon, sea-deities and creatures for Theseus' triumph.

The contrast between the Bacchylidean and the Euripidean versions could not be sharper. We have seen that in an exceptional joint appearance, the two

---

27 The Bacchylidean quotations are taken from the Maehler 1970; the translations are from Campbell 1992.
28 For the political background of this song see Severyns 1933, 56 – 9; Francis 1990, 43 – 66; Käppel 1992, 178 – 89; Van Overeren 1999; Fearn 2007, 242; Calame 2009.
29 For the symbolism of Amphitrite's gifts see Calame 2009, 172 – 6.

gods announce their pact to wreck the Achaean fleet. On the Athenian stage Poseidon claims that he has been defeated by Athena and Hera, thus disclaiming responsibility for the fate of the Trojan captives. In view of his reference to the dancing Nereids the moment he announces his feelings onstage, the audience is invited to imagine either long-standing dissension in his sea-kingdom or consider the god particularly secretive or volatile, despite his claim to his steadfast feelings towards Troy. Poseidon draws attention to Athena's emotional volatility but, as we have seen, Athena is prepared to justify her change of heart. From an Athenian point of view, Athena's decision to inflict punishment on all serves as a reminder that the descendants of Theseus will receive no preferential treatment. In comparison to the Bacchylidean dithyramb, the collaboration of the two gods for the opposite aim in the generation immediately following Theseus' thalassocracy underlines the fragility of thalassocracy that was once granted to Theseus and the Ionians by the same gods.

The possibility of Euripides' dialogue with Bacchylides is strengthened if we take into account the inclusion of Delos among the islands that will be affected by Poseidon's storm. In addition to the political significance of Delos, which has already been discussed, the mention of the island may have been intended too as link between the play and Bacchylides' dithyramb which was composed for performance on Delos, as the concluding self-referential choral statement indicates.

The inclusion of Lemnos in Poseidon's plan offers a further intriguing link between the *Troades* and another Bacchylidean song, *Ode* 18, suggesting Euripides' familiarity with Bacchylides' poetry. *Ode* 18, composed, in all likelihood, for performance at an Athenian festival, relates Theseus' wondrous deeds on his way from Troezen to Athens in the form of a dialogue between Aegeus and a group of Athenian youths. At the closure of the song Aegeus describes the as yet unknown hero as follows:

Δύο οἱ φῶτε μόνους ἁμαρτεῖν
λέγει, περὶ φαιδίμοισι δ' ὤμοις
ξίφος ἔχειν <ἐλεφαντόκωπον>,
ξεστοὺς δὲ δύ' ἐν χέρεσσ' ἄκοντας
κηὔτυκτον κυνέαν Λάκαι- (50)
ναν κρατὸς πέρι πυρσοχαίτου·
χιτῶνα πορφύρεον
στέρνοις τ' ἀμφί, καὶ οὖλιον
Θεσσαλὰν χλαμύδ'· ὀμμάτων δὲ
στίλβειν ἄπο Λαμνίαν (55)
φοίνισσαν φλόγα· παῖδα δ' ἔμμεν
πρώθηβον, ἀρηΐων δ' ἀθυρμάτων
μεμνᾶσθαι πολέμου τε καὶ

χαλκεοκτύπου μάχας·
δίζησθαι δὲ φιλαγλάους Ἀθάνας. (60)

(Bacch. 18.51–60)

He says that only two men accompany him; he has a sword with ivory hilt slung from his bright shoulders, two polished spears in his hands, a well-made Laconian cap about his fire-red hair, a purple tunic over his chest and a woolly Thessalian cloak; from his eyes flashes red Lemnian flame; he is a youth in his earliest manhood, and his thoughts are of the pastimes of Ares, war and the clashing bronze of battle; and he seeks splendour-loving Athens.

John Barron drew attention to the curious details of Theseus' description and attributed Bacchylides' choice of diction to his wish to represent Cimon as a second Theseus.[30] According to Barron the phrases κυνέαν Λάκαιναν and οὔλιον Θεσσαλὰν χλαμύδ' alluded to Cimon's sons Lacedaemonius, Ulius and Thessalus, whereas the phrase Λαμνίαν/φοίνισσαν φλόγα (54–6) served as a reminder of Miltiades' annexation of Lemnos to Athens.[31] We have seen that Euripides includes Lemnos along with Scyros in the cluster of toponyms evoking the Persian wars and their aftermath. The reference to Lemnos alone in the *Troades* (90) could be, of course, coincidental. Its joint mention with Scyros as part of Poseidon's plan to wreck the fleet of the Achaeans including the sons of Theseus (*Tro.* 31), however, shows that evocation of the Philaids was intended. Moreover, the bronze statue of Athena Lemnia on the Acropolis, dedicated by the cleruchs who were sent to Lemnos in the mid-fifth century, was a constant reminder of the Athenian involvement in the island; according to Pausanias, it was the most worth-seeing of Phidias' works (καὶ τῶν ἔργων του Φειδίου θέας μάλιστα ἄξιον Ἀθηνᾶς ἄγαλμα ἀπὸ τῶν ἀναθέντων καλουμένης Λημνίας, 1.28.2).[32] It is also worth noting that the two Theseid leaders are mentioned together with the Thessalians (and the Arcadians, *Tro.* 31).[33] Is the mention of the Thessalians intended to elicit the goodwill of a useful, if occasional, ally of Athens?[34] The answer is probably yes, but contemporary political motives do not preclude additional considerations. The joint mention of the Theseid leaders and the Thessa-

---

30 Barron 1980.
31 Barron 1980.
32 For the Athenian cleruchy on Lemnos see Graham 1964, 175–85; for Phidias' statue see Hurwit 1999, 151. See also Martin 1987, 105 who draws attention to its importance in enhancing the web of associations with Lemnian rites that inform the plot of Aristophanes' *Lysistrata*.
33 For the Arcadians see Parmentier 1959, 22; Stephanopoulos 1985.
34 See also the favourable mention of Thessaly in the *parodos* (*Tro.* 214–9) and Westlake's discussion (Westlake 1953, 185–9).

lians in this context would also evoke Cimonian Athens and could be yet another link to Bacchylides *Ode* 18.

The points of contact and contrast between the Prologue of the *Troades* and Bacchylides' *Odes* 17 and 18 are remarkable and too many to be accidental. It is impossible to know whether and to what degree Euripides' audience knew Bacchylides, but there are further reasons to believe that Euripides must have been familiar with his poetry.[35] Copies of at least Bacchylides' Athenian dithyrambic compositions must have existed in Athens and would include *Ode* 17 – probably a gift of the poet himself or the Ceans to Cimon and his circle. When Bacchylides composed for Athenian festivals Euripides was old enough at least to have heard of the Cean poet. Euripides' interest in New Music would be an incentive to contemplate the old dithyramb and especially Bacchylides' compositions, whose commissions in Athens suggest that he was considered a master. Moreover, Euripides and Bacchylides offer the most enticing early descriptions of choruses of Nereids whose number, fifty, might be thought to evoke the dithyramb. The figure of Theseus is another common interest. The *Troades* feature, of course, Theseus' descendants, Acamas and Demophon, but the Chorus refers to Athens as Θησέως εὐδαίμονα χώραν (*Tro.* 208). None of Bacchylides' extant dithyrambs treat the fortunes of Theseus' descendants but, as we shall see in a moment, Cimonian art did.

ii) The Theseion and the Painted Stoa

The meaning of Athena's and Poseidon's withdrawal of support is reinforced if we assume Bacchylides *Ode* 17 as a thalassocratic 'intertext', i.e. the collaboration of Poseidon and Athena in the first instance for Theseus' sea-triumph is replicated in the following generation to the opposite effect, i.e. to cause maximal damage to the Achaean fleet carrying the Theseid leaders, Acamas and Demophon.

Euripides, however, did not need to rely on his audience's familiarity with Bacchylides' dithyrambs, for they had also access to the visual representations of the Theseion and the Painted Stoa. We know from Pausanias that the theme of one of the walls of the Theseion was the episode of Theseus' successful response to Minos' challenge:

> τοῦ δὲ τρίτου τῶν τοίχων ἡ γραφὴ μὴ πυθομένοις ἃ λέγουσιν οὐ σαφής ἐστι, τὰ μέν που διὰ τὸν χρόνον, τὰ δὲ Μίκων οὐ τὸν πάντα ἔγραψε λόγον. Μίνως ἡνίκα Θησέα καὶ τὸν ἄλλον

---

[35] For the circulation of Bacchylides' poetry in Athens see Hadjimichael 2011, 56–111.

στόλον τῶν παίδων ἦγεν ἐς Κρήτην, ἐρασθεὶς Περιβοίας, ὥς οἱ Θησεὺς μάλιστα ἠναντιοῦτο, καὶ ἄλλα ὑπὸ ὀργῆς ἀπέρριψεν ἐς αὐτὸν καὶ παῖδα οὐκ ἔφη Ποσειδῶνος εἶναι, ἐπεὶ <οὐ> δύνασθαι τὴν σφραγῖδα, ἣν αὐτὸς φέρων ἔτυχεν, ἀφέντι ἐς θάλασσαν ἀνασῶσαί οἱ. Μίνως μὲν λέγεται ταῦτα εἰπὼν ἀφεῖναι τὴν σφραγῖδα Θησέα δὲ σφραγῖδα τε ἐκείνην ἔχοντα καὶ στέφανον χρυσοῦν, Ἀμφιτρίτης δῶρον, ἀνελθεῖν λέγουσιν ἐκ τῆς θαλάσσης.[36]

(Paus. 1.17.3)

[3] The painting on the third wall is not intelligible to those unfamiliar with the traditions, partly through age and partly because Micon has not represented in the picture the whole of the legend. When Minos was taking Theseus and the rest of the company of young folk to Crete he fell in love with Periboea, and on meeting with determined opposition from Theseus, hurled insults at him and denied that he was a son of Poseidon, since he could not recover for him the signet-ring, which he happened to be wearing, if he threw it into the sea. With these words Minos is said to have thrown the ring, but they say that Theseus came up from the sea with that ring and also with a gold crown that Amphitrite gave him.

Pausanias tells us that by his time the paint had faded and the scene was hard to make out. Another difficulty, Pausanias tells us, is that Micon did not choose to paint the whole story.[37] There is no need to say that some six or five decades after the completion of the *herōon* the painting would not have suffered so much from the passage of time. The painting's subject would have therefore been discernible to Euripides and his audience.[38]

If Pausanias had access to texts and stories that illustrated the iconography six centuries later, there is no doubt that a late fifth-century audience would have access to far more extensive material such as songs, stories and household utensils –a number of cups that have survived show that variations of the topic were popular in Attic vase-painting for several decades.[39] These vases convey the thalassocratic message which the Prologue of the *Troades* challenges. If somebody had to use any of these cups at a symposium the evening after the performance of the *Troades*, he would have plenty of reason to wonder what would hap-

---

36 The Greek quotations and translations are taken from Jones' Loeb edition.
37 For Micon's painting see Castriota 1992, 58–63.
38 For Euripides' keen interest in and dialogue with the visual arts see Zeitlin 1994; Athanassaki 2010; Stieber 2011; Athanassaki 2012a.
39 *LIMC* s.v. Amphitrite: O. Amphitrite empfängt Theseus auf dem Meeresgrund; s.v. Theseus: B. Meeting with Poseidon; C. Carried by Triton. The Euphronius cup, featuring Theseus, Amphitrite and Athena, predates the creation of the Delian league and anticipates sea-dominion, thus setting the pattern for visual representations of thalassocracy. For the Euphronius cup see Neils 1987, 58–82.

pen to Theseus and his descendants if all of a sudden Athena, Poseidon and Amphitrite got offended.⁴⁰

Euripides' dialogue with the artistic and political agenda of Cimonian Athens is not restricted to Bacchylides' 'Theseus' songs and Micon's wall painting in the Theseion. In choosing to treat the capture of Troy from the point of view of the captive Trojan women, Euripides also entered into dialogue with Polygnotus' visual representation of the *Iliou persis* in the Painted Stoa, a victory monument which was built in the late 460s.⁴¹ Pausanias mentions four different paintings: (a) the battle of Athenians against Spartans at Oenoe in the Argolid, an obscure event whose choice has puzzled scholars;⁴² (b) Theseus and the Athenians defending Athens against the invading Amazons; (c) the sack of Troy featuring the assembly of the Achaean kings to confront Ajax for the rape of Cassandra, Cassandra herself, and other Trojan captive women; and (d) the battle of Marathon with Callimachus and Miltiades among gods, heroes, fighters, Phoenician ships, etc. a subject which is treated in greater detail.

Pausanias' description of Polygnotus' Athenian version of the *Iliou persis* is very brief:

> ἐπὶ δὲ ταῖς Ἀμαζόσιν Ἕλληνές εἰσιν ᾑρηκότες Ἴλιον καὶ οἱ βασιλεῖς ἠθροισμένοι διὰ τὸ Αἴαντος ἐς Κασσάνδραν τόλμημα· καὶ αὐτὸν ἡ γραφὴ τὸν Αἴαντα ἔχει καὶ γυναῖκας τῶν αἰχμαλώτων ἄλλας τε καὶ Κασσάνδραν.
>
> (Paus. 1.15.3)
>
> After the Amazons come the Greeks when they have taken Troy, and the kings assembled on account of the outrage committed by Ajax against Cassandra. The picture includes Ajax himself, Cassandra and other captive women.

Pausanias' brief description does not allow us to infer the extent of thematic convergence between the play and the painting, except for the rape of Cassandra by

---

40 In a recent study Pucci 2016 argues that Euripides constructs a number of 'literary' or metadramatic characters in his plays in order to undermine traditional myths and to challenge the existence of anthropomorphic gods. In the *Troades* Hecuba is the metadramatic character who challenges the existence of Zeus and Aphrodite (*ibid* 71–82). It goes without saying that those in Euripides' audience, who would be sympathetic to Hecuba's challenge of Zeus and Aphrodite, would also be prepared to challenge the power of Poseidon and Athena. But Euripides must have known, as we do, that his 'under cover' revolution could not convert the traditionalists in his audience.
41 For the Painted Stoa see Castriota 1992, 76–89, 96–133. The *Iliou persis* was the theme of the metope series on the north side of the Parthenon, which are badly preserved. See G. Ferrari 2000 with references to earlier scholarship.
42 See Castriota 1992, 78–89; Stansbury O'Donnell 2005 with references.

Ajax, which I shall discuss in a moment. Polygnotus painted another *Iliou persis* for the Cnidian Lesche in Delphi, which Pausanias describes in far greater detail (10.25–7). We cannot assess the thematic relation between the two paintings, but it is worth drawing attention to some remarkable links that suggest thematic similarities.[43] For the Delphic painting Polygnotus chose again the theme of captivity. In this instance, Pausanias states that the Trojan women seem to be lamenting (γυναῖκες δὲ αἱ Τρῳάδες αἰχμαλώτοις τε ἤδη καὶ ὀδυρομέναις ἐοίκασι, 10.25.3). Did Polygnotus represent the Trojan women lamenting in the Athenian painting as well? Given their circumstances, the answer must probably be yes. If so, their lament would be yet another link with the Euripidean representation. Moreover, we learn from Plutarch that Priam's daughter Laodice was depicted in the Painted Stoa and that Polygnotus had given her the features of Cimon's sister Elpinice.[44] This is an important piece of information, because it provides a precious link between the Athenian and the Delphic version. Pausanias describes Laodice's representation in the Cnidian Lesche in some detail. These two testimonies show that the two versions must have had many more characters in common.[45] Acamas and Demophon, both represented in the Cnidian Lesche, must have featured in the Athenian version too. Another important theme the two paintings share is the assembly of the Achaeans to deliberate about Ajax's rape of Cassandra. Pausanias' account of the Delphic painting suggests that the Achaeans did not punish Ajax, because he took an oath claiming his innocence.[46] We cannot know for sure if Polygnotus represented Ajax taking an oath in the Painted Stoa too, but Pausanias' brief account leaves no doubt that the Achaeans held an assembly to discuss his *hybris* against Athena. As David Castriota observes, Polygnotus treated Ajax's outrageous act with caution:

> And what they saw [i.e. the viewers] was a version of the Fall of Troy that zealously eschewed Greek impiety, excess, and brutality, a version that drew instead upon every useful element of the established myth to assert the responsibility of a foreign enemy for their own tragic fate at the hands of a noble, restrained, and just conqueror.[47]

The summoning of an assembly to address Ajax's *hybris* is what distinguishes Polygnotus' paintings from the Euripidean play. We have seen that Athena is

---

[43] For reconstructions of the paintings of the Lesche and the Painted Stoa see Castriota 1992, 96–133.
[44] Plut. *Cimon* 4.
[45] For the similarities between the Lesche and the Stoa see Castriota 1992, 127–33.
[46] Paus. 10.26.3.
[47] Castriota 1992, 118.

angry with the Achaeans not only because they did not punish Ajax, but also because they even failed to criticize his act (κοὐ δείν' Ἀχαιῶν ἔπαθεν οὐδ' ἤκουσ' ὕπο, 71). The alleged complacency of the Achaeans must have struck all those in the audience who were familiar with Polygnotus' paintings. Some of them would have seen the Delphic version. Many more would be very familiar with the Athenian version since the Painted Stoa was a much-frequented civic space that hosted political and philosophical discussions and debates.⁴⁸

The visitors to the Stoa had good reasons to associate the visual representation of Athenian battles against mythical and historical Eastern opponents with Athens' conflict with Sparta. After their victories at Sphacteria (425 BC) and Skione (421 BC), the Athenians put on display in the Stoa the shields they had taken from the defeated:

> ἐνταῦθα ἀσπίδες κεῖνται χαλκαῖ, καὶ ταῖς μέν ἐστιν ἐπίγραμμα ἀπὸ <Σ>κιωναίων καὶ τῶν ἐπικούρων εἶναι, τὰς δὲ ἐπαληλιμμένας πίσσῃ, μὴ σφᾶς ὅ τε χρόνος λυμήνηται καὶ <ὁ> ἰός, Λακεδαιμονίων εἶναι λέγεται τῶν ἁλόντων ἐν τῇ Σφακτηρίᾳ νήσῳ.
>
> (Paus. 1.15.4)
>
> Here are dedicated brazen shields, and some have an inscription that they are taken from the Scioneans and their allies, while others, smeared with pitch lest they should be worn by age and rust, are said to be those of the Lacedaemonians who were taken prisoners in the island of Sphacteria.

The display of the spoils in the Stoa would invite visitors to see Athens' ongoing conflict with Sparta in the light of the victory of Greeks over Persia under Athens' leadership. The display would have undoubtedly revived people's interest in the paintings of the Stoa and may have contributed to Euripides choice of theme and focus in the last play of his trilogy, which may have no complex plot, but is a very powerful ζωγραφία λαλοῦσα.⁴⁹

---

48 For the *Iliou persis* in Attic vase-painting see Anderson 1997, 208–65 who also discusses Polygnotus' wall painting in the Cnidian Lesche at Delphi, *ibid* pp. 246–56.

49 Parmentier 1959, 21–2 has suggested that lines 13–4 (which are, however, athetized by many scholars) refer to Stronglyion's bronze Horse which was dedicated by Chaeredemus on the Acropolis probably a little before the performance of the *Troades*; for the sculpted horse see Pausanias 1.23.8. For a defence of lines 13–4 and their reference to Stronglylion's sculpture see Stieber 2011, 185–92 and now D'Agostino 2014, who discusses the political significance of the dedication and identifies yet another reference to the sculpted horse in *Troades* 511–67. The dedication of the Trojan Horse, if roughly contemporary with Euripides' trilogy, would also offer an additional explanation for Euripides' interest in the *Iliou persis*. The Parthenon *Iliou persis*, completed in 432, was of course another important visual intertext; see also nn. 41 and 60. For the evocation of Athenian victories through art and architecture see the fascinating article by Martin-McAuliffe/Papadopoulos 2012.

Unlike the victorious message of the Stoa's paintings and the dedicated spoils from Sphacteria, the message of the *Troades* was disquieting. Comparison of the visual representation of the Trojan captives with the Euripidean version would only heighten the unease, for in lieu of the assembled Achaeans taking Ajax to task, the emphasis of the play is on an implacable Athena collaborating with Poseidon to cause maximal damage to all those who neither punished nor condemned an act of *hybris*. Like the Painted Stoa, the *Troades* also evoked places, people, and events associated with the Persian wars from the battle of Marathon onward. Both monument and play evoked the conflict between Athens and Sparta, the former explicitly through the display of the spoils, the latter implicitly. As we have seen, Sparta does not get good press in the *Troades*.[50] The Chorus abhor at the thought of being taken to Sparta and they pray for the destruction of Menelaus' ship. Helen engages in a sophistic refutation of Hecuba's accusations, which in view of the suffering and devastation of Trojan women renders her a rather unsympathetic character.[51] In comparison, Athens receives much more favourable treatment from the Chorus, but they speak, of course, in ignorance of Poseidon's distress and Athena's wrath.

The violence in which the allied Achaean forces engaged during the capture of Troy was theologically and ethically problematic. We have seen that at the early years of the Delian league Polygnotus depicted both the suffering of the defeated and the accountability of the victors in the eyes not only of the gods but also of mortals.[52] The issue of accountability lies at the heart of the *Troades* too, but unlike Polygnotus, Euripides depicts a world in which military leaders display no sense of accountability. Those in Euripides' audience familiar with Arctinus' *Iliou persis* would know that the Achaeans had decided to stone Ajax to death, but that he took refuge at Athena's altar.[53] The elision of Achaeans' confrontation with Ajax in the *Troades* is not, of course, accidental, but in keeping with an all-pervasive sense of unaccountability in a play in which acts of violence are not debated, but reported by the messenger and other characters.[54]

---

50 As many have observed, we would not expect the captive Trojans to be favourable either to Helen and Menelaus or to Sparta. Yet the favour they show for Athens argues in favour of an anachronistic reading.
51 For the *agon* between Helen and Hecuba see Lloyd 1992, 99–112.
52 A few years after the construction of the Painted Stoa, Aeschylus treated briefly the capture of Troy and the sea-storm in the *Agamemnon* (320–47, 644–80) at the *Dionysia* of 458. For the Aeschylean representation see Leahy 1974; Anderson 1997, 107–32.
53 Proclus *Iliou persis* p. 108 Allen.
54 The decision to sacrifice of Polyxena, and to kill Astyanax, for instance, are not debated, but only reported, in this play. According to Talthybius there was a debate about Astyanax' murder, but the messenger only reports Odysseus' proposal (ll.709–21).

Acamas and Demophon are presumably among the leaders who do nothing to punish or even censure violence and are, therefore, responsible in the eyes of gods, but in this play they do not play a key-role in decision-making.⁵⁵ For this reason, Athenian military ideology and practice cannot be the only target of criticism.⁵⁶ The story of the *Iliou persis* is a foundation charter of collective responsibility which different versions modify and distribute differently. Through Athena's assertion that the Achaeans did not punish or criticize Ajax's transgression, Euripides suppresses the Achaean assembly that Polygnotus had depicted, thus attributing responsibility to all Achaean leaders.

It is also worth mentioning that four years after the performance of the *Troades*, Aristophanes asked the audience of the *Lysistrata* to look carefully at the paintings of Micon in the *Stoa Poikile* and possibly in the Theseion.⁵⁷ The chorus of men compare Lysistrata's cronies with the Amazons and with Artemisia, thus evoking the Persian wars (674–9):

ἀλλὰ καὶ ναῦς τεκτανοῦνται, κἀπιχειρήσουσ' ἔτι
ναυμαχεῖν καὶ πλεῖν ἐφ' ἡμᾶς, ὥσπερ Ἀρτεμισία, (675)
ἢν δ' ἐφ' ἱππικὴν τράπωνται, διαγράφω τοὺς ἱππέας·
ἱππικώτατον γάρ ἐστι χρῆμα κἄποχον γυνή,
κοὐκ ἂν ἀπολίσθοι τρέχοντος. τὰς Ἀμαζόνας σκόπει,
ἃς Μίκων ἔγραψ' ἐφ' ἵππων μαχομένας τοῖς ἀνδράσιν.⁵⁸

(Ar. *Lys.* 674–9)

Why, they'll even be building frigates and launching naval attacks, cruising against us like Artemisia. And if they turn to horsemanship, you can scratch our cavalry: there's nothing

---

55 In the *Hecuba*, on the contrary, they take active part in the debate (ll. 122–9), each delivering his own speech (δισσῶν μύθων ῥήτορες) despite the fact that they were of the same opinion and ended up with the same proposal, i.e. Polyxena's sacrifice. There is an interesting difference between Euripidean and visual representations; in the latter Acamas and Demophon do not take part in the fighting, their only involvement is to rescue their grandmother Aethra: see G. Ferrari 2000, 138–9.
56 Brillet-Dubois 2010–2011 argues that the murder of Astyanax is an inversion of the Athenian ceremony honoring war orphans in the *Dionysia* and concludes that the aim of the inversion is to criticize Athenian war ideology. Yet, as she points out, the custom of carrying the war-dead on their shields out of the battlefield is attested only in Sparta (*ibid* 43). The fusion of customs argues, in my opinion, against the view that Athenian war ideology is Euripides' main target and in favour of the view that Euripides criticizes war violence, regardless of the identity of the perpetrator.
57 For Aristophanes' reference to the Painted Stoa see J. Henderson 1987, 160 *ad* 678–9 and Martin 1987, 84 who also suggests the possibility of the Theseion too.
58 The Greek quotations and English translations of *Lysistrata* are taken from Henderson 2000.

like a woman when it comes to mounting and riding; even riding hard she won't slip off.
Just look at the Amazons in Mikon's paintings, riding chargers in battle against men.

It is certainly not accidental that the chorus directs the audience's attention to Cimonian iconography and not to the depictions on the west metopes of the Acropolis, for, as we shall see in the next section, Lysistrata will extol the merits of Cimonian policies as well.

4 The Thalassocratic Message of the *Troades* and its Addressees

I have argued that through his dialogue with the poetry and monumental art of Cimonian Athens Euripides evokes the Persian wars, thus inviting his audience to look at current issues and events from that perspective as well. The story of Bacchylides *Ode* 17 found its way onto the Euripidean stage, but its thalassocratic message underwent a radical transformation. The dithyramb, composed a few years after the Greek victory over the Persians, offers an optimistic account of the league's sea-dominion under the leadership of Cimon. It depicts Minos as the aggressor and Theseus as the saviour of the Ionians, thus offering justification for Athena's and Poseidon's favour that leads to Theseus' triumph. The *Troades* depict a far more complex world in which mortals are responsible not only for what they do, but for what they fail to do, when it comes to violence.

Through the reference to the perilous storm that will affect Delos, Mykonos, Skyros and Lemnos Euripides reminded his audience of the challenges that the islanders and mainland Greeks faced when the Persians sailed unchecked through the Aegean. The message was multivalent and had many addressees. The Delians, for instance, would be reminded of the time they fled to Tenos. Similarly, the Eretrians would recall that the Persians plundered and burnt their temples.[59] The evocation of Salamis in the Second and the Third *Stasima* in combination with Poseidon's mention of deserted temples in the Prologue would remind the Athenians of their own deserted city and the burning of the Acropolis when they fled to Salamis.[60]

---

59 Hdt. 6.100–2.
60 Hdt. 8.41–53. G. Ferrari 2000 argues forcefully that the placement of the *Iliou persis* in the north side metopes of the Parthenon was intentional and concludes: 'it appears more than a coincidence that the images of the sack of Troy on the north metopes looked upon the ancient temple of Athena Polias, immediately to the north, which was the visible trace of the Persian impi-

The fact, however, that the Greeks are the offenders in the *Troades* would also invite Euripides' audience to contemplate their own deeds and responsibility once they had defeated the Persians and begun fighting one another. The Athenian ambassadors who come back with the King's Eye in the *Acharnians* show that diplomatic relations with Persia were a concern voiced in the Athenian theatre already in the early years of the war (Ar. *Ach.* 61–124). Those in the audience who believed that Delos was shaken for the first time after the outbreak of the Peloponnesian war, as Thucydides reports, were encouraged to attribute the gods' anger against the Greeks to the fact that they had engaged in war with one another. By 415 BC all major players had their share in acts of violence. A look at how Thucydides describes the fortunes of the Plataeans and the Melians at the hands of the Spartans and the Athenians respectively offers full justification to the outrage of Athena and Poseidon at the Achaeans' treatment of cities, shrines and tombs:

We may first turn to the Spartans' treatment of Plataea:

αὖθις τὸ αὐτὸ ἕνα ἕκαστον παραγαγόντες καὶ ἐρωτῶντες, εἴ τι Λακεδαιμονίους καὶ τοὺς ξυμμάχους ἀγαθὸν ἐν τῷ πολέμῳ δεδρακότες εἰσίν, ὁπότε μὴ φαῖεν, ἀπάγοντες ἀπέκτεινον καὶ ἐξαίρετον ἐποιήσαντο οὐδένα. διέφθειραν δὲ Πλαταιῶν μὲν αὐτῶν οὐκ ἐλάσσους διακοσίων, Ἀθηναίων δὲ πέντε καὶ εἴκοσιν, οἳ ξυνεπολιορκοῦντο· γυναῖκας δὲ ἠνδραπόδισαν. τὴν δὲ πόλιν ἐνιαυτὸν μέν τινα [Θηβαῖοι] Μεγαρέων ἀνδράσι κατὰ στάσιν ἐκπεπτωκόσι καὶ ὅσοι τὰ σφέτερα φρονοῦντες Πλαταιῶν περιῆσαν ἔδοσαν ἐνοικεῖν· ὕστερον δὲ καθελόντες αὐτὴν ἐς ἔδαφος πᾶσαν ἐκ τῶν θεμελίων ᾠκοδόμησαν πρὸς τῷ Ἡραίῳ καταγώγιον διακοσίων ποδῶν πανταχῇ, κύκλῳ οἰκήματα ἔχον κάτωθεν καὶ ἄνωθεν, καὶ ὀροφαῖς καὶ θυρώμασι τοῖς τῶν Πλαταιῶν ἐχρήσαντο, καὶ τοῖς ἄλλοις ἃ ἦν ἐν τῷ τείχει ἔπιπλα, χαλκὸς καὶ σίδηρος, κλίνας κατασκευάσαντες ἀνέθεσαν τῇ Ἥρᾳ, καὶ νεὼν ἑκατόμπεδον λίθινον ᾠκοδόμησαν αὐτῇ. τὴν δὲ γῆν δημοσιώσαντες ἀπεμίσθωσαν ἐπὶ δέκα ἔτη, καὶ ἐνέμοντο Θηβαῖοι. σχεδὸν δέ τι καὶ τὸ ξύμπαν περὶ Πλαταιῶν οἱ Λακεδαιμόνιοι οὕτως ἀποτετραμμένοι ἐγένοντο Θηβαίων ἕνεκα, νομίζοντες ἐς τὸν πόλεμον αὐτοὺς ἄρτι τότε καθιστάμενον ὠφελίμους εἶναι.

(Thuc. 3.68.1–4)

They therefore brought the Plataeans before them again one by one and asked each of them the same question. 'Have you done anything to help the Spartans and their allies in the war?' As each man replied 'No', he was taken away and put to death, no exceptions being made. Not less than 200 of the Plataeans were killed in this way, together with twenty-five Athenians who had been with them in the siege. The women were made slaves. As

---

ety. [...] By its position the Ilioupersis drew upon, and gave epic resonance to, the artful display of ruins, which were deployed throughout the citadel and which, as we slowly have come to recognize, were as much a part of its classical plan as the new Periclean buildings (*ibid* 150). G. Ferrari also demonstrates the close parallelism between the plunder of Trojan shrines by the Achaeans in the *Agamemnon* (524–8) and of Athenian shrines by Xerxes in the *Persae* (807–12): *ibid* 145–9.

for the city, they gave the use of it for one year to some political refugees from Megara and those of the pro-Spartan party among the Plataeans who still survived. Afterwards they razed it to the ground from its very foundations and built, adjoining the temple of Hera, a large hotel 200 feet in circuit with rooms upstairs and downstairs. For these building operations they used the roofs and doors of the Plataeans, and out of the other material in the wall – the brass and the iron – they made couches which they dedicated to Hera, for whom they also built a stone temple 100 feet square. The land they confiscated and let it out on ten-year lease to Theban cultivators. It was largely, or entirely, because of Thebes that the Spartans acted so mercilessly towards the Plataeans; they considered that at this stage of the war the Thebans were useful to them.

Unlike the Spartans, the Athenians did not raze Melos to the ground, but their cruelty to men, women and children was on a par with that of the Spartans:

καὶ οἱ Μήλιοι περὶ τοὺς αὐτοὺς χρόνους αὖθις καθ' ἕτερόν τι τοῦ περιτειχίσματος εἷλον τῶν Ἀθηναίων, παρόντων οὐ πολλῶν τῶν φυλάκων. καὶ ἐλθούσης στρατιᾶς ὕστερον ἐκ τῶν Ἀθηνῶν ἄλλης, ὡς ταῦτα ἐγίγνετο, ἧς ἦρχε Φιλοκράτης ὁ Δημέου, καὶ κατὰ κράτος ἤδη πολιορκούμενοι, γενομένης καὶ προδοσίας τινός, ἀφ' ἑαυτῶν ξυνεχώρησαν τοῖς Ἀθηναίοις ὥστε ἐκείνους περὶ αὐτῶν βουλεῦσαι. οἱ δὲ ἀπέκτειναν Μηλίων ὅσους ἡβῶντας ἔλαβον, παῖδας δὲ καὶ γυναῖκας ἠνδραπόδισαν· τὸ δὲ χωρίον αὐτοὶ ᾤκισαν, ἀποίκους ὕστερον πεντακοσίους πέμψαντες.

(Thuc. 5.116.2–4)

About this same time the Melians again captured another part of the Athenian lines where there were only a few of the garrison on guard. As a result of this, another force came out afterwards from Athens under the command of Philocrates, the son of Demeas. Siege operations were now carried on vigorously and, as there was also some treachery from inside, the Melians surrendered unconditionally to the Athenians, who put to death all the men of military age whom they took, and sold the women and children as slaves. Melos itself they took over for themselves, sending out later a colony of 500 men.

Thucydides also reports that right after the destruction of Plataea both the Athenians and the Spartans were planning to send embassies to the Persian king, each in the hope to obtain his support for their own side.[61] Moreover, the Spartans decided to augment their fleet:

Γεγενημένου δὲ τοῦ ἐν Πλαταιαῖς ἔργου καὶ λελυμένων λαμπρῶς τῶν σπονδῶν οἱ Ἀθηναῖοι παρεσκευάζοντο ὡς πολεμήσοντες, παρεσκευάζοντο δὲ καὶ Λακεδαιμόνιοι καὶ οἱ ξύμμαχοι, πρεσβείας τε μέλλοντες πέμπειν παρὰ βασιλέα καὶ ἄλλοσε πρὸς τοὺς βαρβάρους, εἴ ποθέν τινα ὠφελίαν ἤλπιζον ἑκάτεροι προσλήψεσθαι, πόλεις τε ξυμμαχίδας ποιούμενοι ὅσαι ἦσαν ἐκτὸς τῆς ἑαυτῶν δυνάμεως. καὶ Λακεδαιμονίοις μὲν πρὸς ταῖς αὐτοῦ ὑπαρχούσαις

---

[61] For Athenian and Spartan embassies to the king see Meiggs 1972, 129–51 and Miller 1997, 25–8.

ἐξ Ἰταλίας καὶ Σικελίας τοῖς τἀκείνων ἑλομένοις ναῦς ἐπετάχθη ποιεῖσθαι κατὰ μέγεθος τῶν πόλεων, ὡς ἐς τὸν πάντα ἀριθμὸν πεντακοσίων νεῶν ἐσομένων, καὶ ἀργύριον ῥητὸν ἑτοιμάζειν, […]

(Thuc. 2.7.1–2)

In this affair of Plataea the treaty had quite obviously been broken, and now the Athenians made ready for war, as did the Spartans and their allies. They planned to send embassies to the King of Persia and to any other foreign power from whom they hoped to obtain support, and they tried to ally themselves with other Hellenic states who were not yet committed to either side. The Spartans, in addition, to the fleet they had already, ordered more ships to be built by the states in Italy and Sicily who were on their side: the number ordered was in proportion to the size of each city, and the total was to be a fleet of 500 ships. These cities were also asked to provide a certain sum of money.

From an early fifth-century viewpoint, the reversal is total. The opponents contend for thalassocracy in a conflict in which the Persians are no longer considered the enemy, but a prospective useful ally. It is precisely this reversal that the evocation of the Persian wars in the *Troades* brings to the surface, thus offering a long-term perspective on the ongoing conflict between Athens, Sparta and their allies. We have seen that as far as Athenian politics is concerned this is not an entirely new perspective. The display of the spoils from Sphacteria and Skione in the Stoa offered a long-term perspective on these victories linking them with Marathon and Oenoe. Nevertheless, Euripides' perspective is fresh because it adds a sobering tone to the triumphal statement of the Stoa through the dramatization of divine disaffection and the fragility of thalassocracy. The reminder of the Persian threat, however, was not and could not be addressed only to the Athenians.

Through his dialogue with the poetry and monumental art of Cimonian Athens Euripides evoked the times when the Persians were the aggressors, committing the sorts of atrocities that Poseidon condemns in the Prologue, until they were defeated at sea and land. In *Ode* 17 Bacchylides couched sea-dominion in mythical terms, as Theseus' triumph at sea thanks to the favour of Poseidon and Athena. The Prologue of the *Troades* showed the other side of the coin, namely that the favour of Athena and Poseidon is not unqualified, thus sending a powerful message to the descendants of Theseus and their associates. If we view the Prologue of the *Troades* as a meditation on thalassocracy in the fifth century, which through its dialogue with earlier thalassocratic narratives serves as a warning not only to the Athenians, but to their present or former allies and ultimately to the Greeks at large, Euripides emerges as a poet who does not simply respond to individual contemporary events, but as a poet with a broad perspective on these events' implications for the course of relations between the city-states of Greece.⁶²

As I have already suggested, Euripides' broad perspective on contemporary events, as it emerges from his dialogue with Cimonian art and poetry, has a close parallel in Lysistrata's admonition to the Lacedaemonians to stop destroying the Attic land, when they can fight the barbarians, and her reminder of Cimon's benefactions and policies:

ἄνδρες Λάκωνες, στῆτε παρ' ἐμὲ πλησίον,
ἐνθένδε δ' ὑμεῖς, καὶ λόγων ἀκούσατε.
ἐγὼ γυνὴ μέν εἰμι, νοῦς δ' ἔνεστί μοι. (1125)
αὐτὴ δ' ἐμαυτῆς οὐ κακῶς γνώμης ἔχω,
τοὺς δ' ἐκ πατρός τε καὶ γεραιτέρων λόγους
πολλοὺς ἀκούσασ' οὐ μεμούσωμαι κακῶς.
λαβοῦσα δ' ὑμᾶς λοιδορῆσαι βούλομαι
κοινῇ δικαίως, οἳ μιᾶς γε χέρνιβος (1130)
βωμοὺς περιρραίνοντες ὥσπερ ξυγγενεῖς
    Ὀλυμπίασιν, ἐν Πύλαις, Πυθοῖ—πόσους
εἴποιμ' ἂν ἄλλους, εἴ με μηκύνειν δέοι;—
ἐχθρῶν παρόντων βαρβάρῳ στρατεύματι
Ἕλληνας ἄνδρας καὶ πόλεις ἀπόλλυτε.
εἷς μὲν λόγος μοι δεῦρ' ἀεὶ περαίνεται.

(Ar. *Lys.* 1122–35)

εἶτ', ὦ Λάκωνες, πρὸς γὰρ ὑμᾶς τρέψομαι,
οὐκ ἴσθ' ὅτ' ἐλθὼν δεῦρο Περικλείδας ποτὲ
ὁ Λάκων Ἀθηναίων ἱκέτης καθέζετο (1140)
ἐπὶ τοῖσι βωμοῖς ὠχρὸς ἐν φοινικίδι / στρατιὰν προσαιτῶν; ἡ δὲ Μεσσήνη τότε
ὑμῖν ἐπέκειτο χὠ θεὸς σείων ἅμα.
ἐλθὼν δὲ σὺν ὁπλίταισι τετρακισχιλίοις
Κίμων ὅλην ἔσωσε τὴν Λακεδαίμονα.
ταυτὶ παθόντες τῶν Ἀθηναίων ὕπο (1145)
δῃοῦτε χώραν, ἧς ὕπ' εὖ πεπόνθατε;

(Ar. *Lys.* 1137–46)

Spartans, stand close to me, and you Athenians stand on this side. Now listen to what I have to say. It's true I'm a woman, but still I've got a mind: I'm pretty intelligent in my own right, and because I've listened many a time to the conversations of my father and other elders, I'm pretty well educated too. Now that you're my captive audience I'm ready to give you the tongue-lashing you deserve—both of you. You two sprinkle altars from the same cup like kinsmen, at Olympia, at Thermopylae, at Pytho—how many other places could I mention if I had

---

62 The Persian intervention on the side of Sparta a few years after the performance of the *Troades* shows that Euripides' perspective and warning were on target.

> to extend the list—yet when enemies are available with their barbarian armies, it's Greek men and Greek cities you're determined to destroy. That takes me through one of my arguments.
>
> Next, Spartans, I'm going to turn to you. Don't you remember when Pericleidas the Spartan came here once and sat at the altars as a suppliant of the Athenians, pale in his scarlet uniform, begging for troops? That time when Messenia was up in arms against you and the god was shaking you with an earthquake? And Cimon went with four thousand infantrymen and rescued all Sparta? After being treated that way by the Athenians, you're now out to ravage the country that's treated you well?

It is remarkable but not surprising that Lysistrata reminds the Lacedaemonians of the earthquake which, as we have seen, was believed to be Poseidon's punishment for the sacrilege at the god's sanctuary at Taenarum. The Athenians on the other hand would be reminded in turn of the earthquake of 426 that seems to have caused damage in the Acropolis which is the setting of the play. But far more important of course is the fact that Lysistrata's plea for cease-fire addresses all Greeks, some of whom are present on the comic stage. Aristophanes would expect of course to have a narrower audience at the Lenaea of 411 than Euripides could expect at the Dionysia of 415. It is worth noting, however, that Euripides' warning to all Greeks in a mythical context has found its way onto the comic stage: there it is explicitly voiced by Lysistrata, who has listened to the stories of her father and other elders, men who had presumably taken part in the Persian wars like those of the Chorus.

II Refiguring Lyric Genres in Tragedy

Laura Swift
Competing Generic Narratives in Aeschylus' *Oresteia*

Ever since Hellenistic scholars and librarians began to sub-divide some collections by genre, it has been a convenient filter through which to view ancient literature. Yet as scholars have increasingly come to recognise, generic boundaries are porous, and Greek writers from the archaic period onwards include material that evokes different literary forms. In this context, the relationship between Greek tragedy and earlier choral poetry is particularly rich, because tragedy is itself a choral genre, and a mimetic one. When a tragic chorus evokes (say) a paeanic or hymenaeal chorus, the choreuts do not merely allude to, but actually perform the other genre. The tragic chorus in some sense really do become the ritual chorus performing the song, and the audience sees a *paian* or *hymenaios* being enacted before their eyes. Thus lyric representations in tragedy are immediate and visceral, in a way that is quite different from literary intertexts such as allusions to famous scenes from Homer. Moreover, allusions to lyric song are more than literary guessing-games for the educated elite, since these forms of poetry are associated with particular events or stages in the life of a community or an individual. In its original performance context, choral lyric can operate as a vehicle for expressing social norms, and exploring how one should react to a significant event, whether sickness, a military victory, a wedding, or the worship of a god. Hence when a piece of ritual lyric is transferred into tragedy, it brings with it a set of shared associations and values rooted in the world beyond the play, and the tragedians can use these generic triggers to explore or test these conventional beliefs, or to show how they map onto (or fail to be compatible with) the world of the play.[1]

My previous work on this topic focuses on plays which allude to a single dominant lyric genre, whose performance context relates to the preoccupations of the tragedy itself: for example, *hymenaios* in plays that focus on dysfunctional relationships between the sexes; *paian* in plays that focus on man's relationship with the divine. In these cases, the choral odes tend to show intricate, dense, and sophisticated allusion to the tropes of the chosen lyric genre. This chapter, however, will approach the topic from a different angle, by looking at how tragedy

---

[1] I explore this topic in depth in Swift 2010. For discussions of how tragedy can engage with ritual lyric, cf. e.g. Herington 1985; Nagy 1995; Rutherford 1994–1995; Calame 1994–1995; Carey 2012; Rodighiero 2012.

can incorporate multiple lyric genres simultaneously. As we shall see, generic interaction can be used to create a narrative arc, which runs subtly throughout the play rather than being concentrated in particular odes, and can guide the audience's interpretation of the broader action. Rather than detailed allusion or intertextuality, we find something more like Wagnerian leitmotifs: small-scale references which may not seem noteworthy when taken in isolation, but which over the course of a play build up a pattern of association. Since genres carry different sets of connotations, the poet can create conflicting arcs, and bring them into tension to explore different possible outcomes, or competing motivations on the part of the characters.

Aeschylus' *Oresteia* provides a rich case-study as to how this can work in practice. A number of genres are evoked during the course of the trilogy, but I shall focus on two that recur particularly frequently: *epinikion* and *paian*.[2] As we shall see, these genres are coded so as to be associated with certain ethical standpoints in the trilogy, and these perspectives form the basis of major moral tensions. Epinician and athletic imagery is repeatedly associated with statements about the morality of tit-for-tat vengeance and the perspective that 'the doer suffers'. Set against this is another strand of genre-imagery, that of the *paian*, which is used to suggest the possibility of a different approach to questions of justice and retribution. In any given instance, the imagery occurs fleetingly, but as the plays go on, the audience would be in a position to notice the repeating patterns of association. In the first two plays, as the cycle of violence within the house of Atreus continues unfettered, the paeanic imagery is invariably presented in a way which is distorted or undermined. In *Eumenides*, however, the *paian* is presented in an uncorrupted fashion, and ultimately replaces athletic imagery, just as the action of the play itself depicts a new way of dealing with the desire for vengeance.

While features such as the *paian*-cry make paeanic imagery relatively easy to identify, it is harder to make the distinction between imagery which evokes epinician poetry, and that which is simply athletic. Claiming that a piece of athletic imagery counts as 'epinician' is a matter of context and how the imagery is used across a play. It would be implausible to claim that a single comparison of a character to an athlete evokes the genre. However, once *epinikion* has been 'triggered' for the audience by a clearly-marked reference in an important place, future references to athleticism, even if made only in passing, can be connected

---

2 A similar clash between *epinikion* and *paian* is found in Eur. *Alc.*, where the genres represent different forms of healing and resolution: see Swift 2012. For song in general as a motif in the *Oresteia* see Petrounias 1976, 291–4.

back to the genre. In the *Oresteia*, *epinikion* is evoked early, when the Chorus imagine singing *epinikia* to Zeus to celebrate his victory over Cronus, conceived as a wrestling-match (*Ag.* 167–75). This clear genre-reference is used to assign moral value to athleticism in the trilogy (discussed below). Once *epinikion* has been established as important, further examples of athletic imagery gain resonance. Similarly, the audience is guided to see 'markers' such as light imagery or language of salvation as paeanic. Taken in isolation these need not indicate the musical genre, but coming after clear references to the genre such as the ritual refrain they take on new significance.[3]

Paeanic and epinician language is scattered throughout the trilogy, but the imagery clusters around three key moments, and it is here that the two strands are directly juxtaposed. It is no coincidence that these are also turning points for the trilogy's action as a whole: Agamemnon's decision at Aulis, the murder of Agamemnon, and the vengeance of Orestes. As the characters weigh up their decisions, the language they use reinforces the connection between imagery-pattern and moral stance. Yet the way in which the athletic or paeanic imagery is presented also feeds back into the world of the play, helping the audience to encode the genres as relating to a particular standpoint.

1 Setting up the pattern: the justice of Zeus and Agamemnon's choice at Aulis

The events at Aulis are presented as crucial for understanding the action of *Agamemnon*, in terms both of character motivation and of the divine framework that underpins the world in which the humans operate. In the *parodos*, the Chorus set out the metaphysical background behind Agammenon's decision to sacrifice his daughter, and it is in this context that the language of *paian* and *epinikion* is first juxtaposed.[4] We are told of Calchas' prayer as he interprets the omen of the two eagles (146–55):[5]

ἰήιον δὲ καλέω Παιᾶνα,
μή τινας ἀντιπνόους Δαναοῖς χρονί-
    ας ἐχενῇδας ἀπλοίας
τεύξηι σπευδομένα θυσίαν ἑτέραν ἄνομόν τιν' ἄδαιτον,
νεικέων τέκτονα σύμφυτον, οὐ δει-

---

[3] On 'epinician' vs 'athletic' imagery see Swift 2010, 118–9.
[4] For further discussion of the *parodos* see Coward's paper in this volume.
[5] The Greek text is that of Page's 1972 *OCT*. All translations are mine.

σήνορα· μίμνει γὰρ φοβερὰ παλίνορτος
οἰκονόμος δολία, μνάμων Μῆνις τεκνόποινος.

I call upon Paian the healer: may she (Artemis) not bring about long-lasting adverse winds that will hold back the Danaan ships and keep them in port, eager as she is for another sacrifice, one that is lawless and comes with no feasting, an inborn architect of strife that fears no man. For a terrifying guileful housekeeper lies in wait and will rise again: a Wrath that remembers and will avenge a child.

Calchas, as a priest of Apollo, turns to his patron deity, and the audience might also expect that Apollo is chosen because he is Artemis' twin and so may be able to influence her.[6] However, he prays to the god in his capacity of Apollo Paian, and the cult name is reinforced by the ritual epithet ἰήιον, which alludes to the *paian*-cry ἰὴ παιάν.[7] In his role as paeanic Apollo, the god represents healing and purity. He stands in opposition to the cycle of kin-killing and vengeance within the house, and represents a possibility of avoiding this pattern, by preventing the death of Iphigeneia that will lead to Clytemnestra's revenge.[8] As the trilogy goes on, the *paian* will continue to be associated with the prospect of an end to the horrors within the house, but in *Agamemnon* and *Choephori*, these invocations of the *paian* are invariably futile, or are presented in a distorted fashion, associated with further vengeful feelings which will perpetuate rather than end the cycle. Here, the appeal to Apollo Paian is recalled long after the event, in order to introduce the terrible events at Aulis, and show that the anger of Artemis had exactly the consequences that Calchas feared. Thus the *paian* is invoked only to reinforce the impossibility of preventing blood-letting within the family.[9]

Calchas' appeal to Apollo is followed immediately by the Chorus' own prayer to Zeus, which sets up the play's broader moral outlook, and in particular is used to establish the principle that wrongdoing will be punished. In the middle, the Chorus describe how Zeus established his power (167–75):

οὐδ' ὅστις πάροιθεν ἦν μέγας,
    παμμάχωι θράσει βρύων,
οὐδὲ λέξεται πρὶν ὤν·
ὃς δ' ἔπειτ' ἔφυ, τρια-

---

6 See Raeburn/Thomas 2011, 83.
7 On the *paian*-tag as a generic feature see Käppel 1992, 66–67; Rutherford 2001, 68–72; Ford 2006. The refrain was identified in antiquity as a distinctive feature of the genre; cf. Ath. 15.696b-e.
8 On the gap between the Chorus' and the audience's ability to make sense of Calchas' words, see Fletcher 1999.
9 See Gruber 2009, 291.

κτῆρος οἴχεται τυχών·
Ζῆνα δέ τις προφρόνως ἐπινίκια κλάζων
τεύξεται φρενῶν τὸ πᾶν.

He who was great in the past (Uranus) and swelled with conquering boldness will not be spoken of as having ever existed. He who was born afterwards (Cronus) encountered his triple-thrower and is gone. But the man who enthusiastically cries out *epinikia* to Zeus will hit the target of sense perfectly.

Calchas' prayer is therefore answered by an alternative lyric response to the divine order: rather than singing *paianes* to Apollo, the Chorus advocate singing *epinikia* to Zeus. These *epinikia* are to celebrate an athletic triumph, since Zeus' establishment of his reign is presented as a victory in a wrestling match (τριακτῆρος, 171): the third throw is the one by which one wins the match.[10] Yet Zeus' achievement is itself part of a cycle of retaliatory violence that occurs across the generations, and the performance of *epinikia* is therefore associated with individual violent responses to injustice. Zeus' vengeance on Cronus (and Cronus' on Uranus) goes further than the traditional accounts, as the earlier deities are not merely overthrown but cease to exist altogether.[11]

Retaliatory justice has already been associated with wrestling earlier in the play, since the Chorus previously described the Trojan war as a wrestling match, and connected it to the moral order overseen by Zeus (60–7):

οὕτω δ' Ἀτρέως παῖδας ὁ κρείσσων
ἐπ' Ἀλεξάνδρωι πέμπει ξένιος
Ζεὺς πολυάνορος ἀμφὶ γυναικός,
πολλὰ παλαίσματα καὶ γυιοβαρῆ,
γόνατος κονίαισιν ἐρειδομένου
διακναιομένης τ' ἐν προτελείοις
κάμακος, θήσων Δαναοῖσιν
Τρωσί θ' ὁμοίως.

So it was that Zeus god of hospitality, the mighty one, sent the sons of Atreus against Alexandros. For the sake of a woman with many men he would impose on Danaans and Trojans alike many limb-wearing wrestling matches, the knee pressing down into the dust, the spear-shaft shattered in the pre-nuptial ceremonies.

Presenting war as an athletic struggle is a common metaphor, and on this first encounter, the audience would be unlikely to perceive the imagery as important.

---

[10] Cf. e.g. *Il.* 23.733; *Suda* τ 944 (iv.586.26 Adler). On the significance of wrestling imagery and the triple-throw in the *Oresteia* see Poliakoff 1980.
[11] See Bowie 1993, 12–13, who also notes that this version of events is softened in the kinder world of *Eumenides*, where redemption is a possibility.

When the wrestling language recurs, however, and again describes Zeus' will, its significance becomes clearer, while the mention of *epinikia* ties it more closely to a lyric genre. The *epinikion*, and henceforth athletic language in general, symbolises the concept of justice as reciprocal violence, and the cardinal principle that wrongdoers will be punished. In the case of the Trojans, the 'wrestling' is justified vengeance for the abduction of Helen, and Zeus' intervention forms the cornerstone of the Chorus' confidence that he will maintain justice.[12] In Zeus' case, his wrestling throw is the punishment for Cronus' treatment of his children, as well as being the foundational act that establishes his new order.

This initial contrast between the *paian* and the *epinikion* sets the tone for what each strand of imagery will represent, for as the action continues we see athletic imagery repeatedly used in connection with the drive for vengeance, while the *paian* is used to suggest a way of ending the cycle, whether or not this is presented as attainable. The Chorus reinforce this distinction a little later in the *parodos*, as they describe the events at Aulis that pave the way for the action of the play. As Iphigeneia is sacrificed, the Achaean chieftains who support the killing are described as 'umpires' (βραβῆς, 230), while the gag used to silence her is called a 'bit', as though she were a racehorse (χαλινῶν, 238). Similarly, when Agamemnon decides to carry out the sacrifice, he takes on the 'yoke of necessity' (ἀνάγκας λέπαδνον, 218), which presents him too as an animal harnessed for a race. In all these cases, athletic language describes the desire for violent action which will perpetuate the cycle of vengeance.

Conversely, Iphigeneia's silent plea for mercy is described through the image of her earlier performances of the *paian* in her father's house (243–7):

> ἐπεὶ πολλάκις
> πατρὸς κατ' ἀνδρῶνας εὐτραπέζους
> ἔμελψεν, ἁγνᾶι δ' ἀταύρωτος αὐδᾶι πατρὸς
> φίλου τριτόσπονδον εὔποτμον παι-
> ῶνα φίλως ἔτιμα.

Since she had often sung in her father's richly-laden banqueting chambers, and, a virgin with pure voice, she lovingly performed her father's *paian* for good fortune at the third libation.

As with Calchas' appeal to Apollo, we find a stark juxtaposition between the ideals of the paeanic performance and the reality of what is taking place. The *paian*

---

[12] Cf. *Ag.* 362–402, an extended discussion of the role of Zeus and justice in the Trojan war.

is once again corrupted, as its audience have become the umpires who approve her death.[13]

Calchas' prayer is echoed in the Herald's speech, where he prays for Apollo to look kindly upon the returning Argives (510–3):

> τόξοις ἰάπτων μηκέτ' εἰς ἡμᾶς βέλη·
> ἅλις παρὰ Σκάμανδρον ἦσθ' ἀνάρσιος·
> νῦν δ' αὖτε σωτὴρ ἴσθι καὶ παιώνιος,
> ἄναξ Ἄπολλον·
>
> Shoot missiles from your bow at us no longer – you were hostile enough to us beside the Scamander. No, now become a saviour and paeanic again, lord Apollo.

The Herald alludes to the Homeric tradition that Apollo was a pro-Trojan god, and contrasts the hostile Apollo of epic with the kindly god of ritual practice, invoking him as Apollo παιώνιος. Like Calchas' prayer, however, this is doomed to fail, since the legacy of the Trojan war is not yet over.[14] Similarly, the Herald warns of the dangers of marring good fortune with bad news by describing it as singing a *paian* to the Erinyes (παιᾶνα τόνδ' Ἐρινύων, 645), and in so doing foreshadows the way in which the *paian* is contaminated through most of the trilogy.

2 Clytemnestra's revenge

Imagery associated with lyric genres is thus introduced early in the trilogy, and embedded in the passages that establish its moral framework. The climax of *Agamemnon* is Clytemnestra's murder of her husband, and we find a cluster of paeanic and epinician language used to anticipate the killing and explore its significance. This is first signalled by the motif of the beacon that symbolises Aga-

---

13 This passage is often discussed with reference to whether or not it is plausible that Iphigeneia would have performed the *paian* at an all-male symposium (which would certainly not have been the case in a fifth-century Athenian context): e.g. Fraenkel 1950, ii.140–1; Denniston/Page 1957, 91; Raeburn/Thomas 2011, 95. The purpose of the passage, however, seems to me more symbolic, as Iphigeneia's performance of the *paian*, as well as providing pathos, introduces the motif of the 'third libation': and the perversion of the *paian*'s powers of healing and communality (discussed further below).
14 Leahy 1974 suggests a contrast between 'epic' and 'realistic' depictions of the Trojan war, though his view of the 'realistic' focuses on the grittiness of real-life warfare. I would add to this the contrast between 'epic' and 'cultic' views of the gods' role in this war.

memnon's return, which at the start of the play is greeted by the Watchman in terms that evoke paeanic salvation (22–9):

ὦ χαῖρε λαμπτὴρ νυκτός ἡμερήσιον
φάος πιφαύσκων καὶ χορῶν κατάστασιν
πολλῶν ἐν Ἄργει τῆσδε συμφορᾶς χάριν.
ἰοὺ ἰού·
Ἀγαμέμνονος γυναικὶ σημαίνω τορῶς
εὐνῆς ἐπαντείλασαν ὡς τάχος δόμοις
ὀλολυγμὸν εὐφημοῦντα τῇδε λαμπάδι
ἐπορθιάζειν,

Hail beacon, which brings the light of day in the night and will cause many choral dances in Argos in thanks for this good fortune. Iou, iou! I announce clearly to Agamemnon's wife that she should rise from her bed as quickly as she can, and lift up her voice in the auspicious *olulugmos* for the house in response to this beacon...

Light imagery is common in *paianes*, and is connected with the songs' healing function and the association between light and safety in Greek thought.[15] Here the light really exists, in the form of the beacon whose appearance signals the fall of Troy.[16] The formal greeting ὦ χαῖρε (22), the ritual cries of ἰοὺ ἰού (25), and the expectation of choral dances (23) create the mood of a religious occasion; this is amplified by the announcement at 28–9 that Clytemnestra will perform an *olulugê:* the female equivalent of the *paian*.[17] The Watchman's opening words were a prayer for divine release from suffering (θεοὺς μὲν αἰτῶ τῶν ἀπαλλαγὴν πόνων, 'I beg the gods for release from these toils', 1), while immediately before the appearance of the beacon he connects this with the appearance of light in the darkness (εὐτυχὴς γένοιτ' ἀπαλλαγὴ πόνων, 'may there be an auspicious release from toils' 20). Thus the appearance of the beacon is already charged with religious imagery, and its association with the *paian*, a song performed to celebrate release from evil, is appropriate.

In their response to the beacon, the Chorus draw on paeanic imagery to hope for an end to their worries. Rather than the beacon itself or the gods, however, it is Clytemnestra they ask to be a *paian* to them and release them from trouble (παιών τε γενοῦ / τῆσδε μερίμνης, 98–9). As with the earlier evocations of the

---

[15] Cf. Pind. *Pa.* 12.15, 3.1, 3.5, 7c(a).2 S-M; Simon. 519 fr. 120(b) *PMG*. See Haldane 1963; Rutherford 2001, 76; Swift 2010, 68–9.
[16] For light imagery more broadly in the trilogy see Peradotto 1964, 388–93.
[17] See Pulleyn 1997, 178–83. Descriptions of paeanic singing often include a group of women performing the *olulugê/ololugmos:* e.g. Sapph. fr. 44.31–3 V; Bacch. 17.124–9. On the importance of the *ololugê* in the *Oresteia* see Moritz 1979, 195; Garvie 1986, 146.

paian, there is an ironic gap between the characters' naive and optimistic invocation of the genre, and the audience's knowledge of the true state of events, since we know that the 'healing' Clytemnestra will bring is far from what the Chorus has in mind.[18] Indeed, Clytemnestra's response to the beacon redefines the paeanic language into epinician mode, by imagining the light as an athletic torch race (312–4):

> τοιοίδε τοί μοι λαμπαδηφόρων νόμοι,
> ἄλλος παρ' ἄλλου διαδοχαῖς πληρούμενοι·
> νικᾶι δ' ὁ πρῶτος καὶ τελευταῖος δραμών.
>
> Such were my arrangements for this torch-relay, and each was fulfilled one after the other in succession; the first runner and the last are both victorious.

The first and last runner are victorious in the sense that a relay victory is shared by all the members of the team; however, I agree with Sommerstein's view that there is a sinister subtext.[19] The first runner represents Agamemnon ordering the torch to be lit, and it is his victory that is being celebrated, but his return to Argos will facilitate the ultimate victory of Clytemnestra. The imagery of the torch race picks up on the earlier description of the Trojan war as wrestling, and hints at how the cycle of violence will continue, as the paeanic beacon-light is turned into vengeful fire. The association between athletic language and vengeance is made clearer as Clytemnestra's speech continues, where she imagines the terrible fate that awaits the army if the spirits of the dead cannot be placated (341–7):

> ἔρως δὲ μή τις πρότερον ἐμπίπτηι στρατῶι
> πορθεῖν ἃ μὴ χρή, κέρδεσιν νικωμένους·
> δεῖ γὰρ πρὸς οἴκους νοστίμου σωτηρίας,
> κάμψαι διαύλου θάτερον κῶλον πάλιν.
> θεοῖς δ' ἀναμπλάκητος εἰ μόλοι στρατός,
> ἐγρηγορὸς τὸ πῆμα τῶν ὀλωλότων
> γένοιτ' ἄν, εἰ πρόσπαια μὴ τύχοι κακά.
>
> But may no lust fall upon the army to plunder what they should not, defeated by greed. They still have to make a safe homecoming, turning the bend and returning for the second leg of the double run. If the army should return without committing a crime against the gods, the pain of the dead may awaken, unless sudden disaster occurs.

---

18 Thus Haldane 1965, 38.
19 Sommerstein 2008b, 39 n.71, though for a counter-view see Raeburn/Thomas 2011, 105.

Again, the Greek army's vengeance against the Trojans is conceived as an athletic event, but this time one that is not yet complete, as the second leg of the race is still to be run. While the return leg could refer simply to the journey back to Greece, the previous association of athleticism with violence primes us to expect that the 'second leg' will involve more bloodletting. Moreover, the audience can recognise that calming the pain of the dead is a veiled reference to Iphigeneia, as well as the dead of Troy, and so to Clytemnestra's own motivation for vengeance.[20]

As the action continues, Clytemnestra continues to appropriate the paeanic mode to her own agenda. She announces that she has performed the *ololugê* as the Watchman anticipated (587, 595), but while this purports to celebrate the end of war, it anticipates her own triumph over Agamemnon. This distortion of the *paian* is reinforced in her description of Agamemnon's murder, which she presents as a form of paeanic libation (1385–7):

καὶ πεπτωκότι
τρίτην ἐπενδίδωμι, τοῦ κατὰ χθονὸς
Διὸς νεκρῶν σωτῆρος εὐκταίαν χάριν.

And when he had fallen I put in a third stroke, in thanksgiving to Zeus of the underworld, saviour of the dead.

The libation to Zeus Sôtêr was the third libation to be poured before the drinking began at a symposium, and was accompanied by a *paian*.[21] Clytemnestra's language alludes to the similar imagery used of Iphigeneia's death, where we were reminded of her performance of the *paian* at the third libation (τριτόσπονδον εὔποτμον παι-/ῶνα, 246–7). The correspondence between the two passages is clear: Clytemnestra kills to avenge Iphigeneia. Yet the way in which she applies the image demonstrates her misuse of the *paian*'s generic associations, for she describes her libation as offered to Διὸς νεκρῶν σωτῆρος. The common tragic oxymoron of a *paian* to the dead is combined with the idea that Zeus Sôtêr, whose function is usually to protect the living, is concerned for the interests of the dead.[22] This dysphemic distortion echoes Clytemnestra's corruption of

---

20 See Raeburn/Thomas 2011, 107.
21 Σ Pind. *Isthm*. 6 (iii.251.24 Dr); Aesch. F 55 *TrGF*³; Ath. 15.692f-3c; Xen. *Symp*. 2.1; Plut. *Mor*. 615b and see Rutherford 2001, 50. The first two libations were to Olympian Zeus and to heroes or chthonic deities. Aeschylus also uses this order in the prayers at *Suppl*. 21–6.
22 See Raeburn/Thomas 2011, 214. On the '*paian* of death' in tragedy, see Rutherford 2001, 118–21; Loraux 2002, 65; Swift 2010, 71–2.

symbolism of the *paian*, as she turns something normally associated with communality and salvation into a tool of vengeance.²³

3 Orestes' vengeance

Another cluster of paeanic and athletic imagery is located around the vengeance of Orestes in *Choephori*. By this stage in the trilogy, the role of the Curse has been acknowledged by the characters. As the action becomes more sinister, the imagery of the triple-throw in wrestling, originally introduced to represent the justice of Zeus, comes to represent the power of the Curse, and its ability to perpetuate violence. Conversely, the *paian* continues to be associated with the possibility of peace, but in a way which distorts its true function. Thus Electra asks in her despair 'is ruin not impossible to throw three times?' (οὐκ ἀτρίακτος ἄτα, 339), to which the Chorus respond that it is possible to have a *paian* in the house instead of her songs of lament (ἀντὶ δὲ θρήνων ἐπιτυμβιδίων / παιὼν μελάθροις ἐν βασιλείοις, 342–3). The Chorus reject Electra's suggestion that no good outcome can be achieved, and use the *paian* as a marker of hope. However, like Clytemnestra they conceptualise it as corresponding to successful vengeance. This misapplication of the *paian* is shown by its proximity to the *thrênoi* it is said to replace, which again suggests the '*paian* of death' motif.²⁴

The association between vengeance, the Curse, and athletic imagery continues throughout *Choephori*. Clytemnestra, who had hoped at the end of *Agamemnon* that her own acts of violence would not be subject to the Curse (1569–76), now laments that it is a deadly wrestling opponent (ὢ δυσπάλαιστε τῶνδε δωμάτων Ἀρά, 692), while the Chorus imagine Orestes' vengeance as an athletic *agôn* (ξιφοδηλήτοισιν ἀγῶσιν, 729) and present Orestes himself as a horse running in a chariot race (794–9). The Chorus, in their support for the vengeance, continue to depict it as an act which will inspire paeanic song. They imagine performing the *ololugmos* over the deaths of Clytemnestra and Aegisthus (386–7), and later fulfil this promise, when Orestes returns to the stage after killing his mother (942–5):

ἐπολολύξατ' ὦ δεσποσύνων δόμων
ἀναφυγᾷ κακῶν καὶ κτεάνων τριβᾶς

---

23 Cf. Haldane 1965, 37; Goldhill 1984, 89. On the problematic connotations of the *ololugê* throughout the trilogy (until the closing lines of *Eum.*), see Moritz 1979, 210–1.
24 Also suggested by Electra at 151, where she describes the lament for Agamemnon as a '*paian* for the dead man' (παιῶνα τοῦ θανόντος).

ὑπὸ δυοῖν μιαστόροιν,
δυσοίμου τύχας.

Cry out the *ololugê*, for the house of our masters has escaped evil and the wasting of its goods at the hands of this polluted pair, a wretched fate.

The language of the *paian* is corrupted once more. This underscores the Chorus' mistake in supposing that the murders will end the troubles of the house, for this is an *ololugê* expressed in dysphemic language that expresses pollution and destruction (κακῶν, μιαστόροιν, δυσοίμου τύχας). As Orestes descends into madness, seeing visions of the Furies, we are soon shown the futility of the Chorus' optimism. Moreover, we are reminded that it is athletic rather than paeanic language that is more appropriate to describe the ongoing cycle of violence, as Orestes describes himself as a charioteer who has lost control of his team and is veering off the track (ὥσπερ ξὺν ἵπποις ἡνιοστροφῶ δρόμου / ἐξωτέρω, 1022–3).[25] As the Curse claims another victim, this image of an athletic triumph aborted recalls Clytemnestra's warning in the previous play of the runner unable to complete the return leg of his race (*Ag.* 343–4).

The increasing darkness of the athletic language prepares the way for the arrival of the Erinyes, and in *Eumenides* it is associated entirely with their desire to punish Orestes. Thus the Erinyes boast of how they trip up runners in a race (372–6), referring to their ability to destroy those who have committed acts of violence, while as they assert their power in preparation for the trial, they mix a metaphor of wrestling into their description of the unjust man shipwrecked by his arrogance (δυσπαλεῖ τε δίναι, 559). Once the trial begins, the wrestling imagery comes more strongly to the fore: when he admits killing his mother, the Erinyes claim that they have thrown him for the first time (ἓν μὲν τόδ' ἤδη τῶν τριῶν παλαισμάτων, 589). However, the defeat of the Erinyes marks a shift in the nature of vengeance and justice, and this is reflected by a transformation of the wrestling imagery. As Orestes blesses Athens before leaving the stage, he imagines the Athenians' power over their enemies as a wrestling-trick that cannot be defeated (πάλαισμ' ἄφυκτον, 776), presenting wrestling as a positive and protective image. Equally, the Erinyes accuse the gods of being wrestlers hard to compete against (δυσπάλαμοι, 846), and so highlight how the Olympians have redefined the nature of justice.[26] The language of athleticism is finally removed from personalised vengeance and the Curse, and can be ap-

---

25 See Myrick 1993; Fowler 2007 on this strand of imagery.
26 As Garvie 1986, 134 notes, *Eum.* 776 is the first time in the trilogy that wrestling imagery appears in a propitious context.

plied to the future order, into which the vengeful powers of the Erinyes will be harnessed for communal good.

4 Interpreting generic narratives

Throughout the first two plays in the trilogy, then, Aeschylus not only makes rich use of language which evokes *epinikion* and *paian*, but brings the two strands into juxtaposition at key moments in the plot. Athletic language is introduced alongside the *epinikion* to Zeus, and first stands for the ethics of *talio* vengeance; as the plays go on, this strand of imagery becomes increasingly dark and is associated with individual acts of violence and with the Curse on the house of Atreus, as well as the destructive and inescapable nature of this approach. Conversely, the *paian* is originally introduced to suggest a way of ending the cycle and achieving peace, but it too is either misappropriated for vengeance or presented in a distorted way. Thus it is invoked in support of an idea that the audience knows is unattainable, or it is presented as corrupted, by being juxtaposed with anathematic elements such as death and suffering. It is only in *Eumenides* that this paeanic language is allowed to return to its unsullied and positive nature. This begins early in the play, when the Pythia introduces Apollo (60–3):

> τἀντεῦθεν ἤδη τῶνδε δεσπότηι δόμων
> αὐτῶι μελέσθω Λοξίαι μεγασθενεῖ·
> ἰατρόμαντις δ' ἐστὶ καὶ τερασκόπος
> καὶ τοῖσιν ἄλλοις δωμάτων καθάρσιος.
>
> From now on let this be the concern of powerful Loxias himself, the master of this house. He is a healing seer, a diviner, and one who purifies the houses of others.

Apollo's presence in the play and his role as protector of Orestes reinforces this new image of the relationship man can have with the divine. The language of purification and healing is dense throughout *Eumenides*,[27] but its association with ritual choral song becomes clear at the end of the play, where the Processional Escort sing paeanic and euphemic cries to celebrate the conversion of the Erinyes into beneficent spirits. At 1035 and 1038 the citizens are invited to participate in the ritual celebration (εὐφαμεῖτε δέ, χωρῖται, 1035; εὐφαμεῖτε δὲ πανδαμεί, 1038); in the second strophe and antistrophe, this becomes an explicit invitation to join in the singing of an *ololugê* (ὀλολύξατέ νυν ἐπὶ μολπαῖς, 1042, 1047). The final words of the trilogy are therefore an uncorrupted and joyful paeanic per-

---

[27] On healing as a theme in the trilogy, see Petrounias 1976, 255–8.

formance in which the wider community (perhaps including the audience) is conceptualised as participants, to celebrate the restoration of harmony within the community.²⁸ The *paian* is ultimately reinstated in its proper ritual place, and is used to symbolise the establishment of a new moral order.²⁹

The contrast between *epinikion* and *paian* that runs through the trilogy is crystallised in the corresponding images of the triple throw in the wrestling and the triple libation.³⁰ As we have already seen, the *paian* performed at the third libation is a motif that connects the killings of Iphigeneia and Agamemnon (*Ag.* 246–7, 1385–7). Electra hints at it in her recognition of Orestes, when she addresses him as a saviour (σωτηρίου, *Cho.* 236) and then prays to a triple sequence of divinities culminating in Zeus (τρίτωι πάντων μεγίστωι Ζηνί, *Cho.* 244–5). While the paeanic imagery is not made explicit, the pattern of three connected with Zeus Sôtêr connects it to the previous sequences, but shows us that Electra, like her mother, imagines this *paian* of salvation as achievable through the successful realisation of vengeance. Similarly, Orestes describes the killing of Aegisthus as the third libation (τρίτην πόσιν, *Cho.* 578), linking the murder to the killings of Agamemnon and the children of Thyestes, and presenting it as a perverted act of religious worship.³¹ The motif recurs in the final lines of *Choephori*, where it acts as a bridge between the vengeful cycle of the past and the possibility of a brighter future (1068–76):

> παιδοβόροι μὲν πρῶτον ὑπῆρξαν
> μόχθοι τάλανες,
> δεύτερον ἀνδρὸς βασίλεια πάθη,
> λουτροδάικτος δ' ὤλετ' Ἀχαιῶν
> πολέμαρχος ἀνήρ,
> νῦν δ' αὖ τρίτος ἦλθέ ποθεν σωτήρ –
> ἢ μόρον εἴπω;
> ποῖ δῆτα κρανεῖ, ποῖ καταλήξει
> μετακοιμισθὲν μένος ἄτης;

> It first began with the wretched pain of child-eating; second it was the royal sufferings of a man, and the war-leader of the Achaeans died, killed in his bath. Now there is a third come from somewhere, a saviour, or should I say doom? Where will it end? Where will the power of Ruin fall asleep and cease?

---

28 See Sommerstein 2008b, 285. On the real-life evocations of this scene cf. Scott 1984, 17.
29 As Moritz 1979, 195 notes, the ritual *ololugê* echoes the refrain αἴλινον αἴλινον εἰπέ, τὸ δ' εὖ νικάτω of the *Agamemnon parodos* (121, 139, 159), and so reinforces the movement from fear to optimism.
30 For a discussion of each of these strands of imagery, see Poliakoff 1980; Burian 1986.
31 On the corruption of religious and sacrificial imagery in the trilogy, see Zeitlin 1965.

The play ends in ambiguity as to whether Orestes' actions will lead to another perverted *paian* of destruction (μόρον), or whether there is scope for a true *paian* of salvation (σωτήρ). This question paves the way for *Eumenides*, where the imagery of healing and purification will lead to an uncorrupted *paian* and a release from evil. Thus the imagery of the triple libation moves from something dark and distorted towards an optimistic resolution.

Conversely, the imagery of the triple wrestling throw moves from the positive to the negative. Originally associated with the justice of Zeus (*Ag.* 168–75), it then moves to describing the Curse (*Cho.* 339) and the Erinyes (ἓν μὲν τόδ' ἤδη τῶν τριῶν παλαισμάτων, *Eum.* 589). Yet just as the *paian* is contaminated in the first two plays, here it is the athletic language that falls short, since the Furies' anticipated triumph is not completed, and it is only the first throw that they obtain. The final resolution of these patterns of three comes when Orestes, after being acquitted, gives a triple thanks to Athena, Apollo, and thirdly Zeus Sôtêr (τρίτου Σωτῆρος, *Eum.* 759–60). The pattern echoes the triple libation, but the other deities thanked are now those who have helped free Orestes from the Erinyes, and the praise of Zeus Sôtêr finally comes in a context of true release from evils. Thus these correspondences of 'three' follow an opposing trajectory, which reflect the broader narrative attached to their respective lyric genre. The triple-throw moves from reflecting an established moral system to exposing the horrors of that system, until it is finally stopped by the trial of Orestes, and integrated into a more positive future. The third libation begins as a horrible distortion, but is ultimately allowed to succeed, since the Chorus' hope at the end of *Choephori* for a saviour is reflected in *Eumenides*, where Apollo acts as the protector of Orestes, and ushers in a new order overseen by the other gods.

5 Wider meanings: why *paian* and *epinikion*?

We have seen, then, Aeschylus makes dense use of imagery derived from lyric poetry throughout the *Oresteia*, and that these strands of imagery represent a narrative arc in the plays. It remains, however, to consider why *epinikion* and *paian* are chosen to take on these meanings, and the broader cultural connotations of these genres in an Athenian context.

The use of epinician motifs is particularly relevant to *Agamemnon* as a *nostos* play, since one function of an *epinikion* is to facilitate the re-entry of the victor into his community after completing a deed which sets him apart from it.[32]

---
32 See Kurke 1991, 15–34.

Winning at the Games was an alienating act as well as a glorious one, and real-life *epinikia* attempt to minimise the risks by presenting the victory in communal terms, while also offering warnings to the victor not to allow his new status to corrupt him.[33] In tragedy, we often find epinician language surrounding a problematic *nostos*, where it can explore the broader tragic theme of how to balance the needs of the powerful individual with that of the community.[34] In Agamemnon's case, he has committed two problematic acts: the sack of Troy, and the killing of Iphigeneia. As we have seen, both are described using athletic language. Moreover, the Chorus adopt a tone of warning when describing both acts, and raise the possibility that they will bring about danger in the future (250–4, 472–4). When Agamemnon appears on the chariot, itself a hint that he is presented in the mould of an athletic victor, he is greeted by a choral song which makes use of many of the tropes of *epinikion*.[35] The Chorus begin by greeting the victor with mention of his father and city, a common trope in *epinikia*.[36] They then explicitly refer to the dangers of praise, and the need to moderate one's language (785–7):

> πῶς σε προσείπω; πῶς σε σεβίξω
> μήθ' ὑπεράρας μήθ' ὑποκάμψας
> καιρὸν χάριτος;
>
> How should I address you? How should I honour you without overshooting or falling short of the right point of favour?

This self-conscious concern to control and moderate the praise is reminiscent of Pindaric *epinikia*, where the poet dwells on his own role, and his ability to praise his client while avoiding *phthonos*. In response comes Clytemnestra's welcome speech, where she praises Agamemnon in excessive terms (896–903).[37] Clytem-

---

33 Strategies of communality include telling a local myth or foundation story and presenting the *polis* as sharing the praise. For warning motifs, cf. e.g. Pind. *Ol.* 1.30–4, *Pyth.* 3.80–3, 7.14–18, 10.19–29, *Isthm.* 3.1–6, 17–28, 4.33–7, 5.13–16, 8.14–6; Bacchyl. 3.74–82, 5.50–5, 9.88–92, 10.45–7, 14.1–6.
34 Epinician language is found densely in Soph. *Trach.*, Eur. *HF* and *Or.*, all of which present a hero's return. For more detailed discussion of *epinikion* and *nostos* in tragedy see Swift 2010, 150–1.
35 The Pindaric resonance in this scene was first noted by Harriott 1982, 10. For fuller discussions of the epinician resonance in this scene, see Sailor/Stroup 1999; Steiner 2010a; Carey 2012. For athletic victors entering on chariots, see Sinos 1993, 78.
36 On genealogy as a feature in *epinikion*, see Golden 1998, 108–9.
37 The exaggerated levels of praise here led Dindorf 1879, xcii to condemn the lines, though most modern scholars have rightly taken it as a rhetorical strategy of Clytemnestra's.

nestra, like an epinician poet, breaks off her praise to warn of the dangers of *phthonos* (φθόνος δ' ἀπέστω, 904), but her insistence in the lines that immediately follow that Agamemnon must walk on the purple tapestries highlights the hollowness of her warning.[38] By walking on the tapestries, Agamemnon fails to touch the soil of Argos, and so his *nostos* is never completed. Whereas a successful *epinikion* defuses the potential tension in athletic victory, the praise directed at Agamemnon is presented as troubling, and the dangers of his past actions are not averted but lead directly to his downfall.

Connected to the dangers of *nostos* is the individualistic strand that runs through *epinikion*, since this is a genre whose purpose is to celebrate personal achievement. It is therefore not surprising that *epinikion* and athletic language are connected in the trilogy with the individualistic ethical code of personalised vengeance. From a fifth-century Athenian perspective, *epinikion* is also associated with an old-fashioned and aristocratic world-view. The audience at the *Oresteia* in 458 may have been familiar with contemporary *epinikia* in a way that later tragic audiences would not have been, but the last securely datable *epinikion* for an Athenian victor was from 486, and it is often supposed that *epinikia* were no longer considered suitable after the radicalisation of the democracy.[39] We should not go too far in presuming that *epinikia* were unacceptable in democratic Athens, but there certainly seems to have been a shift in taste during the fifth century, as attested directly by Eupolis (fr. 398 *PCG*[5]), who associates *epinikia* with a former age. For Aeschylus' audience, who had recently lived through political change to a radical democracy, *epinikion*'s association with times past may have been particularly marked.[40] The trilogy's overarching movement is from individual action towards a communal way of resolving problems. While individual retaliation is set up at the start as the divinely-ordained order, the characters' actions increasingly highlight the flaws of a personally-based justice system. As part of this process, the athletic language associated with such actions becomes darker, associated more with the Curse and the Erinyes, and with images of athletes crushed or failing, until it is finally redeemed by Orestes' acquittal.

---

38 This abrupt cessation of the praise is also reminiscent of the Pindaric 'Abbruchsformel', where the poet breaks away from the topic, usually to avoid incurring divine anger or *phthonos*: see Mackie 2003, ch. 1.
39 See Golden 1998, 86, though for a more cautious view see Hornblower 2004, 252–4. For a more detailed discussion of this issue see Swift 2010, 106–15.
40 A detailed discussion of the trilogy's relationship to Ephialtes' reforms and to contemporary politics is outside the scope of this paper: see Macleod 1982; Podlecki 1999, 63–100; Pelling 2000, 167–77; Sommerstein 2008b, 25–32.

Conversely, the *paian* is associated with healing and divine beneficence, and this makes it a particularly evocative choice in a trilogy that deals first with the inability to reach harmony and then with its imposition. Paeanic imagery is often found in plays with a strong divine presence, or where the religious order is explored or questioned.[41] The *paian* is also associated with the community and with an organised response to triumph or disaster.[42] In public *paianes*, the chorus not only represent the *polis* but often symbolise a group response to an event which affects their community as a whole. Similarly, military *paianes* signify the unity of the army, and when choruses from different Greek cities each perform a *paian* at a panhellenic sanctuary, the singing of the *paian* affirms the unity of the local group. Since one of the fundamental movements of the *Oresteia* is the journey from personalised violence to a communal system of justice, validated by society as a whole, the generic narrative reflects this journey on the musico-cultural level.

This discussion has only attempted to scratch the surface of a topic. Many tragedies refer to more than one lyric genre, while even within the *Oresteia*, we can see the influence of hymenaeal, threnodic, and other types of hymnic song, as well as *paian* and *epinikion*. Nevertheless, this chapter has aimed to show how the dramatic and poetic potential associated with a lyric genre can be multiplied when genres are juxtaposed, and how a tragedian can make use of this lyric imagery, not just to intensify a particular choral ode, but as a narratological device to guide the audience's interpretation. These generic narratives operate in a similar manner to the much-discussed chains of imagery in Aeschylean drama, yet they have the advantage, from the poet's perspective, that generic narratives already have their own encoded set of cultural expectations, on which a skilled poet can build. For the audience, lyric genres are not merely decorative imagery but represent a vivid part of their society's way of understanding and responding to the world, and thus these generic narratives offer them a uniquely rich and emotive experience.

---

41 Eg. Soph. *OT*; Eur. *Alc. Ion:* see Swift 2010, ch. 3.
42 See Rutherford 2001, 9, 61–3.

Andrea Rodighiero
How Sophocles Begins: Reshaping Lyric Genres in Tragic Choruses

1 Tragedy as a 'hybrid flower'

It has recently been written that 'the tragic chorus is often seen as *the* problem of Greek tragedy by modern directors and audiences.'[1] Conversely, even if the chorus is the most distinctive feature of Greek tragedy (and also 'the most vexing for any modern company'),[2] scholars dealing with choruses are fully aware that in antiquity songs and dances performed in the orchestra were not perceived as a problem or as a 'foreign body' within the drama's structure. At the very beginning of the tragic genre, the real innovation was the appearance of actors and dialogues, whereas the choral sections had been able to adapt and transform long-established performance practices into new configurations. As we all know, Aristotle in the *Poetics* (1449a 10 – 15) states that tragedy 'originated in improvisation' and from the 'leaders of the dithyramb'. With a major teleological emphasis, Aristotle portrays tragedy as progressing from a simple to a more complex form, until it reaches its maturity, that is, its 'natural form' (φύσις); at this point – we can only guess how far we are from the first stage[3] – there seems to have been a halt in the development of the new genre. In the rest of the *Poetics*, Aristotle does not examine lyric genres in any great depth, and ends up neglecting the choruses, the cultic (and danced) songs, as well as the religious festivals: in short, the ritual foundation of Attic tragedy.[4] Yet in spite of this obvious indifference, for the philosopher

---

I would like to thank Alexandre Johnston for his help with improving the English version of this paper, as well as Gary Vos, the anonymous referees, and the editors of this volume for their valuable comments.

1 Rutherford 2012, 217; on the chorus as 'the thorniest problem' in staging contemporary productions of Greek drama see Meineck 2013 (and concisely Bierl 2009, 3 – 4, with further bibliography); see also, in general, Billings/Budelmann/Macintosh 2013.
2 Goldhill 2007, 45.
3 For a recent *mise au point* see Battezzato 2013 ('if positive evidence about tragedy's origin in dithyrambic poetry is lacking, tragedy itself does not seem to show a strict affiliation with dithyramb either': 94).
4 The limits of the Aristotelian perspective on the original emergence of tragedy as an independent genre are well known: see Halliwell 1987, 78 – 84. For the ancient sources linking the tragic *stasima* to non-dramatic choral performances see Calame 1997a, 182 (with further bibliography).

https://doi.org/10.1515/9783110575910-008

the original spark of tragic drama was indisputably kindled through the medium of a lyric genre:[5] tragedy did not originate in parthenogenesis. Attic drama, therefore, remains resolutely inclusive of non-dramatic poetry.[6] As a final, hybrid flower, it stands out for its uniqueness.[7]

Modern literary theory has shown that some sections of a text are more liable to be memorized and imitated or to display standard patterns. This is especially the case for beginnings.[8] In the following pages, I shall not be looking at the motifs relating to the genesis or inspiration of specific works (such as, for instance, different treatments of myths and themes refunctionalized in a theatrical context). Rather, I shall emphasize the aforementioned 'tragic uniqueness'. By following a consistent approach, I shall demonstrate some Sophoclean stylistic features operating in three different beginnings of well-known choral songs. First I will look to *Antigone* (and to some hymnodic clues), then to *Women of Trachis*, and finally to a passage from *Ajax*.

My aim is to shed more light – where possible – on the uninterrupted attention shown by Sophocles throughout his career to forms of beginnings and openings canonized in lyric and even hexametric poetry (that is, in both cases, poetry

---

For performative occasions in Athenian culture see Goldhill/Osborne 1999; sources on Athenian choral activity in Swift 2010, 35–60.

5 Aristotle also admits that an earlier kind of tragedy originally performed in tetrameters was associated with dancing, tracing a direct, but frustratingly irrecoverable line from dithyrambic and satyr-like choruses to drama (Arist. *Po.* 1449a 22–3): διὰ τὸ σατυρικὴν καὶ ὀρχηστικωτέραν εἶναι τὴν ποίησιν, either satiric and 'suggestive of the dance' (Lucas 1968, 85), or 'mainly danced' (Janko 1987, 6), or 'more associated with dancing' (as S. Halliwell translates in the Loeb edition); see also Depew 2007, 129.

6 'Literary genres are best seen not as fixed categories but as tendencies': Carey 2009a, 22 (with Ford 2011, 71: 'it is important to think of genres not as recipes that had to be followed to the letter but as sets of expectations that might be adapted and re-negotiated for particular occasions'; see also 87–90). On the debate about style linked to the (widely general) concept of genre, see also Rutherford 2012, 1–28.

7 'Tragedy was that tradition's final, hybrid flower': Herington 1985, 96.

8 A classification has been attempted for Greek and Latin by Dunn/Cole 1992 (especially W. H. Race's pages in the same volume: 13–38); on Sophocles see Davidson 1991. Two more books on the subject must be considered – in different ways – seminal: Said 1975 and 1985 (with a new preface) and Nuttall 1992. On beginnings and endings see also Roberts/Dunn/Fowler 1997, Gemelli Marciano 2007 on the Presocratics, Roberts 2005 on tragedy, Cuny 2008 on Sophocles. Very useful – but not specifically for the aims of this chapter – is the investigation on 'how to begin a poem' in the archaic Near Eastern and Occidental tradition in West 1997, 170–3; on hymnic openings in early Greek and Mesopotamian poetry see now Metcalf 2015, 130–53 (partly in disagreement with West).

in non-dramatic contexts).⁹ We shall see that the use of poetic memory is closely related to our topic.¹⁰

It is assumed that the audience of Attic drama could clearly perceive the transition from iambic trimeters to lyric verses with the help of certain unmistakable clues: the music, the change of rhythm and metre, the accompaniment of the *aulos*. But how far can we push our investigation? How far and to what extent do Sophoclean choral odes diverge from the extant, common, and 'exemplary' forms of lyric poetry, and more specifically of lyric (or epic) beginnings?¹¹ For lack of any kind of 'original' or 'Ur-text' that functioned as a template, the only method the modern scholar can adopt is a comparative one, working on the assumption that frequently attested forms and repetitive and predominating patterns can help us to reconstruct a lost, speculative, and ultimately artificial model.¹² We will see that some of the openings of Sophocles' choruses reveal the poet's adherence to a precise and shared lexicon, especially that of traditional cultic hymns.¹³ At the same time, I should stress Sophocles' particular independence as an author capable of reshaping and transforming previous lyric imagery and language into innovative and distinctive forms, as he starts from a common creative ground and remodels it into a variety of configurations, from direct quotation to marked alteration of common patterns.¹⁴

---

9 His interest seems deeper in tragedies ascribable to his earlier career: but this impression could easily be skewed by the scantiness of the available data.
10 Cf. Richardson 2008, 1, and on classical literature Conte 1986, 70 and 82. It is well known that even for the modern critics certain lyric incipits metonymically represent the entire following song: it is the case, for instance, of the πολλὰ τὰ δεινά... (*Ant.* 332).
11 On the Sophoclean choruses in general see recently Kitzinger 2012 and Murnaghan 2012; earlier bibliography in Rodighiero 2012, 7, n. 1.
12 On the methodological problems posed by 'the extreme scarcity of authentic transmitted texts before the fourth century' see Furley/Bremer 2001, I, 14.
13 I am aware of the fact that the term ὕμνος originally designated a simple 'song', but I will use the term in a stricter sense as a song/prayer/celebration of a god: see especially Ford 2002, 12 and n. 27; the gist of the debate is summarized in Furley/Bremer 2001, I, 1–64.
14 The phenomenon is more noticeable in the extant Sophoclean plays and fragments than elsewhere: as far as I know, no systematic classification is available for the lyric opening lines of Aeschylus and Euripides (the most evident Euripidean example of reuse of a traditional pattern, though not unique – cf. e.g. Aesch. *Ag.* 160 ff. – is discussed below). On Aeschylus see also Rodighiero forthcoming-a.

2 Paeanic and hymnodic flavours in the *parodos* of *Antigone*

It is well known that the *parodos* of *Antigone* (vv. 100–61) provides a remarkable example of allusive reworking.[15] Yet in this section, I argue that behind the evidence of intertextual play in the opening verses, Sophocles resorts to a more artful and less obvious use of elements which infuse the entire choral ode with a paeanic and hymnodic flavour. A *paian* was originally a sacred hymn addressing a god called *Paian/Paieōn* – later corresponding to Apollo – which was sung and danced, usually to the accompaniment of musical instruments. However, it is notoriously difficult to isolate a satisfactory and unanimous definition of the genre.[16] Nonetheless, in the *parodos* the circumstances are indisputable: the opening invocation of Apollo – the light of day – comes after a mortal danger has been averted, and is combined with both a prayer uttered in precise hymnic style and the celebration of a military victory. If we consider the context as a whole, the *paian*-cry is implicitly expected and suggested by the situation depicted on stage, even if it is not actually pronounced by the chorus of Theban elders.[17]

Formally, the long narration includes two couples of responsive lyrics and four anapaestic systems mostly animated by a jubilant tone, as the celebratory content of the procession alternates between the description of the sinister Argive siege and the current joy displayed in the brightness of a new and hopeful day.[18] The first strophe, in aeolics, shows us the chorus exulting in the victory

---

[15] See e.g. Griffith 1999, 143, Rutherford 2001, 110 and 199–200, Furley/Bremer 2001, II, 153, Bagordo 2003, 201–2, Kitzinger 2008, 14–15.

[16] In spite of the fact that several categorizations have been put forward in recent years: on the problem of labelling the genre in formal terms see Rutherford 2001, 21–23. For a broader and practical definition see Ford 2006: the *paian*-atmosphere is suggested by the concrete situation, regardless of the presence of the refrain as ritual cry; the inconsistency of any definition is constitutive of the genre ('the *paian*'s attachability to new occasions made it easy for other genres to adopt paeanic coloring': 292; more bibliographical references in Rodighiero 2012, 124 and *passim*).

[17] 'In point of literary historical fact, not all paeans had a refrain': Ford 2011, 57.

[18] It seems impossible to establish who delivered these anapaests (probably in recitative and not *in lyricis*), whether it was the chorus-leader or the whole chorus; Griffith 1999, 139 is probably right in assigning them to the *koryphaios*, but it sounds unlikely that they were recited 'in the pauses of the choral dance,' as Jebb 1900a, 27 supposes. The *parodos* is a processional performance to be compared to the Euripidean *parodos* of the *Bacchae*, where 'a group of religious worshippers led by the god himself enter the city in order to introduce the rites of the god,' accord-

and invoking Apollo, the Sun. One can detect at the beginning a nod to a Pindaric paean:[19]

ἀκτὶς ἀελίου, τὸ κάλ- (100)
λιστον ἑπταπύλῳ φανὲν
Θήβᾳ τῶν πρότερον φάος,
ἐφάνθης ποτ', ὦ χρυσέας
ἁμέρας βλέφαρον, Διρκαί-
ων ὑπὲρ ῥεέθρων μολοῦσα (105)

(Soph. *Ant.* 100–5)[20]

Beam of the sun, the fairest light that ever shone on seven-gated Thebes, you have shone forth at last, eye of golden day, coming over Dirce's streams...

ἀκτὶς ἀελίου, τί πολύσκοπ' ἐμήσαο,
ὦ μᾶτερ ὀμμάτων, ἄστρον ὑπέρτατον
ἐν ἀμέρᾳ κλεπτόμενον; <τί δ'> ἔθηκας ἀμάχανον ἰσχύν <τ'> ἀνδράσι
καὶ σοφίας ὁδόν,
ἐπίσκοτον ἀτραπὸν ἐσσυμένα; (5)
ἐλαύνεις τι νεώτερον ἢ πάρος;
ἀλλά σε πρὸς Διός, ἱπποσόα θοάς

(Pind. *Pae.* 9.1–7 [fr. 52k.1–7 S.-M. = A1.1–7 Rutherford])

Beam of the sun! What have you contrived, observant one, mother of eyes, highest star, in concealing yourself in broad daylight? Why have you made helpless men's strength and the path of wisdom, by rushing down a dark highway? Do you drive a stranger course than before? In the name of Zeus, swift driver of horses... (trans. Rutherford).

In both texts the solemnity of the initial hymnic structure in *Du-Stil* is emphasized by means of three short sentences: in *Antigone*, they are (1) 'beam of the sun', (2) 'the fairest light that ever shone', and (3) 'eye of golden day.' This majestic incipit, an impressively elaborate invocation of the sunlight after the

---

ing to Kavoulaki 1999, 309. Religious processional events are not rare in Athens: they are listed by Parker 2005, 456–87.
19 In general, in Sophoclean and Euripidean drama 'the use of invocation to begin an ode is greatly extended and applied to odes of every type', whereas 'Aeschylus only begins an ode with an invocation where the ode is in the form of a genuine prayer': Davidson 1991, 32. For precise references to the *parodos* of Aeschylus' *Seven against Thebes* see Davidson 1983 (cf. especially *Ant.* 106–107~*Sept.* 90–91), with Johnston 2016, 27: 'la présence d'Eschyle dans la *parodos* d'*Antigone* évoque [...] une atmosphère de peur et d'angoisse qui pervertit la célébration victorieuse du Chœur.' For a full analysis of the *parodos* of *Antigone* see Rodighiero 2012, 103–37.
20 The Sophoclean text reproduced here and elsewhere is that of Lloyd-Jones and Wilson's OCT edition; the Pindaric text and its translation are from Rutherford 2001.

gloomy night, should be considered the natural consequence of the previous *epiklesis*, where the god – Apollo the deliverer – was requested for help. And now, after the (imagined) prayer, the chorus are willing to offer thanks: the phrase ἐφάνθης ποτ' (v. 103: 'you have shone forth at last'), as a confident response echoes an earlier plea expressed in the usual cletic address to the deity,[21] which is here omitted.[22]

Sophocles' engagement with Pindar is not generic and operates at a deep level, as it does not restrict itself to a simple allusion. The Sophoclean verses aim to celebrate the Theban poet whilst also challenging the content of the earlier poem. The geographical context of the two events (in both cases the city of Thebes), the celestial body which is concealing itself (v. 3: κλεπτόμενον), and the use of horse-riding imagery remind us that the Pindaric invocation of the Sun is prompted by fear: Pindar is depicting an eclipse which obscured the Greek sky (probably in 463 BC). Sophocles openly alludes to the Pindaric passage, but he adapts the lyric reference to its new dramatic circumstances, whereby the allusion is recontextualized and applied to an opposite situation. In both songs the darkness is over. In the Sophoclean passage the ominous eclipse and the apotropaic fear have been replaced by rejoicing for the coming day. The metaphorical darkness itself (terror of further violence) and the night have at long last vanished.[23] In this first strophe, the hymnodic *eulogia* is granted by the topographical references defining the area where the god exerts his influence

---

[21] As for instance ἔλθε μοι καὶ νῦν ('come again': Sapph. fr. 1.25 V.), ἔλθ' ἡμίν ('come to us', Anacr. fr. 14.7 Gentili = fr. 357.7 *PMG*); cf. also Soph. *Ant.* 1149: προφάνηθ' and *OT* 163: προφάνητε. More examples, mostly tragic, in Rodighiero 2012, 28 and n. 33 (with further bibliography); on the ἐφάνθης-motif see 111 and n. 20; on the request in prayers see Pulleyn 1997, 136–144; on the 'come...' (and 'come with...') motif in the Indo-European tradition cf. West 2007, 318–21.

[22] φάος and related terms are commonly used metaphorically as synonyms for safety: see Csapo 2008, 278. We may compare an analogous reaction in a Euripidean passage (*El.* 585–6), again with an exclamation in the second person; here the chorus greet a new day at the precise moment in which Orestes is identified: ἔμολες ἔμολες, ὤ, χρόνιος ἀμέρα, / κατέλαμψας ('you have arrived, yes, you have arrived, o long-awaited day: you have dawned').

[23] Sourvinou-Inwood 1989, 141 argues that the allusion to Pindar 'introduce[s] into the celebratory ode an intimation of threat and disorder.' See also Johnston 2016, 27–32: the allusion causes an 'échec de la célébration religieuse du Chœur d'*Antigone*' (p. 31). On the Pindaric fragment see Rutherford 2001, 189–200, who also envisages the 'remoter possibility' of a common source for both our texts and Eur. *Phoen.* 3–5; see also Furley/Bremer 2001, II, 150–60.

(vv. 104–5: '… coming over Dirce's streams'),[24] as well as by the substantial use of the so-called *Partizipialstil*.[25]

Following this prominently marked stanza, the rhetoric of prayer seems to continue in the rest of the *parodos*. A long narrative section is cut off at the opening line of the second antistrophe (v. 148) when the chorus, announcing the arrival of Victory in a joyful epiphany, return to a more celebratory tone (vv. 148–9):

> ἀλλὰ γὰρ ἁ μεγαλώνυμος ἦλθε Νίκα
> τᾷ πολυαρμάτῳ ἀντιχαρεῖσα Θήβᾳ
>
> But since Victory of glorious name has come, responding with her favourable joy to the joy of Thebes with many chariots…

In two instances Sophocles' peculiar lexical choices correspond to precise semantic fields utilized in hymns. First, the adjective μεγαλώνυμος is an epithet typically employed to designate gods 'with a great name',[26] celebrated in prayers and hymns. Secondly, it is well-known that words such as χάρις, χαίρω, χαρίζομαι are part and parcel of the hymnodist's basic vocabulary and are used to convey a mood of reciprocal pleasure, goodwill, divine favour in a synergistic endeavour, and human gratitude. No other word epitomizes so well the relationship that the worshipper tries to establish with the god.[27] In addition, we can recognize the reappearance, after the allusive incipit, of a Pindaric element in the *hapax* πολυάρματος: the adjective describing Thebes as a city 'with many chariots' contributes to the ode's epinician flavour.[28]

---

[24] The expression is comparable to Pind. *Isthm.* 1.29: ῥεέθροισί τε Δίρκας ἔφανεν, 'they appeared beside the streams of Dirce', in a hymnic celebration of Castor and Iolaus, and cf. also – again in a heavily hymnic context – Soph. *Aj.* 702–3, on which see *infra*.

[25] Soph. *Ant.* 101: φανέν, v. 105: μολοῦσα, v. 109: κινήσασα, 'you who have driven him…'. See Norden 1913, 166–76.

[26] First occurrence in Sapph. fr. 44 A.3 V. = Alc. fr. 304.3 L.-P., and cf. Ar. *Thesm.* 315 (a cletic hymn) and *Nub.* 569. Other examples in Keyßner 1932, 47, and see Furley/Bremer 2001, II, 348: 'μεγαλώνυμε, πολυώνυμε: the epithets highlight the importance of "naming" in hymns'.

[27] See Furley/Bremer 2001, I, 61–3; Race 1982, 8–10; Bremer 1998; for the reciprocal χαίρειν cf. e.g. the so-called Erythraean paean to Asclepius, fr. 934.19–23 *PMG* = *Pai.* 37.19–23 Käppel: 'I beseech you: look kindly on our city with its choral worship, hear us, Paian! grant that we enjoy the sun's abundant light…' (transl. Furley/Bremer).

[28] According to Griffith 1999, 140, 'images of athletic competition add an "epinikian" flavour' to the *parodos*. For the term πολυάρματος as a *pindarisme* see Bergson 1956, 77; examples in Rodighiero 2012, 116 and n. 35.

Ian Rutherford has rightly stated that the *parodos* in the *Antigone* is a paean to Victory, although 'no formal features corroborate this.'[29] Indeed, despite the absence of the traditional cry *iē paian* and of explicit formal features, the lyric atmosphere and the ritual setting remain fully 'paeanic.' The clear initial allusion contributes to this. We are faced with a 'false', failed and distorted paean, in which the chorus ironically express their joy before the disaster. In other words, we are dealing with what Rutherford has aptly called 'paeanic ambiguity.'[30] A first clue is offered by the nocturnal presence of Dionysus. At vv. 153–4 the god clearly adds a touch of disorder to the celebration, and his name contributes to blurring the general tone of the ode, which began, in marked contrast, under the gaze of Apollo.[31] Yet with the invocation of the Bacchic god after the narrative song, the elders, in the grip of a dithyrambic frenzy, invite him to join the dance during the forthcoming nocturnal festivals as their ἔξαρχος, their 'leader' (cf. v. 152: χοροῖς παννύχοις, and v. 154: ἄρχοι). Rather oddly, however, the evocation of a less gloomy night occurs precisely at the very moment in which the chorus are forced to stop their spinning at Creon's arrival (v. 155).[32] The paean is usually sung by young people, and the elders in the *Antigone* did not attend the battle because of their age: they are in an incongruous position, as they should represent the *entire* community of Thebes celebrating the end of the war. We know that the *paian*-cry could be shouted by warriors before and after battle,[33] but in the context of the Sophoclean tragedy – i.e. after the battle – the singers are old men clearly unable to defend their city.

Two more hints in favour of my analysis are offered by references to different and, as it were, external contexts, where the paean (the refrain, but also a more

---

[29] Rutherford 2001, 110. See also Swift 2010, 29: 'while the ode has few of the formal features of the *paian*, it could be seen to play the role of a *paian*.'
[30] Rutherford 1993; see also, for the deceptive nature of paeans in Attic drama, Rutherford 1994–1995, 118 – 'paeans in tragedy rarely have their proper force, and they are almost never what they seem' – and Swift 2010, 70–90 and 372: allusions to other choral genres in tragedy are very often ironic.
[31] ὁ Θήβας δ' ἐλελί- / χθων Βάκχιος ἄρχοι, 'and may the Bacchic god who shakes the land of Thebes be ruler'. We may quote as examples of similar Sophoclean blended songs *Trach.* 205–24 – a 'dithyrambic *paian*', cf. *Trach.* 221: ἰὼ ἰὼ Παιάν and vv. 210–1 – and the closing verses of the *OT*'s paeanic *parodos* (cf. *OT* 154: ἰήιε Δάλιε Παιάν), where Dionysus pursuing Ares is allied with a healing Apollo (*OT* 203–15). For the disquieting presence of Dionysiac elements in the *parodos* of *Antigone* see Sourvinou-Inwood 1989, 141 and Rodighiero 2012, 118–21, 162–4. A negative *nuance* is expressed at *Ant.* 136, where βακχεύων refers to Capaneus attacking the walls.
[32] 'At this point their song might have passed into a regular hymn addressed to a series of gods but their religious impulse is cut short by Kreon's entrance': Furley/Bremer 2001, I, 298.
[33] Sources in Pritchett 1971, 105–8.

elaborate song) was usually performed. The first one is found in the description of Capaneus' death. The most brutal of the seven heroes has reached the ramparts of Thebes, and before Zeus strikes him down, he raises a cry for the forthcoming triumph (vv. 132–3: ἤδη / νίκην ὁρμῶντ' ἀλαλάξαι). There is no doubt that Capaneus, an instant before being struck down by the god, 'was already hastening to shout his *nikē*, that is, he was chanting his ἐπινίκιος παιάν, the same paean to Victory that is now the burden of the victorious elders. Nike has come, but in favour of Thebes.[34] The second hidden generic element refers to an actual military practice. Many sources inform us that as the paean was performed, a trophy made of weapons was set up where the enemy's line was routed as a memorial for victory in the battlefield.[35] And precisely this action is described in a metaphorical and distorted way in the third anapaestic system of our *parodos* (vv. 141–7):

ἑπτὰ λοχαγοὶ γὰρ ἐφ' ἑπτὰ πύλαις
ταχθέντες ἴσοι πρὸς ἴσους ἔλιπον
Ζηνὶ Τροπαίῳ πάγχαλκα τέλη,
πλὴν τοῖν στυγεροῖν, ὣ πατρὸς ἑνὸς
μητρός τε μιᾶς φύντε καθ' αὑτοῖν (145)
δικρατεῖς λόγχας στήσαντ' ἔχετον
κοινοῦ θανάτου μέρος ἄμφω.

Seven captains at seven gates, man against man, for Zeus of the trophies left the tribute of their all-brazen weapons, except the two wretched, who, born of one father and one mother, set against each other their spears equally strong, sharing a common death.

In *Antigone* tragic irony prevails, and the two brothers are described as setting their spears not in the soil – as required by the ritual – but against each other: 'a mordant play on the "erecting" of a trophy.'[36]

---

34 The scholiast considers ἀλαλάξαι as a synonym of παιωνίσαι (Σ Soph. *Ant.* 133, p. 224.8–9 Papageorgiou).
35 See Pritchett 1974, 246–75; Hordern 2002, 226. Sophocles himself had been associated with both the παιάν and the most famous trophy in Athenian history: in the *Life of Sophocles* we are told that the young poet danced and raised the *paian* around the τρόπαιον erected after the battle of Salamis (*Vita Sophoclis* 3 = T 1.17–19 *TrGF*⁴, with T 28.3–4 *TrGF*⁴= Ath. 1.20e; see also – without reference to the presence of Sophocles, however – Timoth. *Pers.* fr. 791.196–201 *PMG*). On this episode see now Power 2012, 290–1 (with Rodighiero 2012, 127). The familiarity of the poet with the paean is, however, supported by the ancient sources: the fragmentary paean fr. 737(b) *PMG* = *Pai.* 32 Käppel, T 73a *TrGF*⁴= Philostr. *VA* 3.17.13–15, T 73b *TrGF*⁴ = Ps.-Luc. *Dem.Enc.* 27.8–11, T 174.12–14 *TrGF*⁴= Philostr. Jun. *Im.* 13 (p. 34.19 – p. 35.1–2 Schenkl – Reisch) = Soph. fr. 737(a) *PMG*, T 2.6–7 *TrGF*⁴= *Suda* σ 815 Adler.
36 Griffith 1999, 152. For the ritual practice see Pritchett 1974, 251, n. 19.

Thus the reference to Victory can be better understood if we remember that the παιάν (the shouting and the song), the τροπαῖον (the trophy) and the celebration of Νίκη (Victory) were strictly interrelated.[37] I do not claim that the *parodos* should be considered a 'traditional' παιάν (if such a thing exists). Rather, the Sophoclean song seems to contain some hymnic and paeanic features in disguise, suggested initially by the first verses, which are geared towards their particular dramatic context and partly faithful to non-dramatic lyric 'librettos.' The paeanic hints are very suggestive and undeniably operate as the constituents of a precise ritual action.[38] Finally, if we assume a possible connection between the choreographical movement and the vocabulary employed by the chorus, we should not overlook the fact that many terms in the *parodos* refer to a specific semantic field related to the idea of beating.[39] 'A stamping motion of the feet'[40] is indeed one of the few aspects of paeanic performance of which we know.

3 Hymnodic clues

Leaving aside a close reading of the two famous hymns of *Antigone* (to Eros and Dionysus),[41] I shall confine myself to some general reflections on certain formal devices used in shaping them. In the hymn to Dionysus (*Ant.* 1115–14), the poet seems deliberately to adhere to the expected pattern, namely an opening invocation, a narrative development, and a final request. The result, as one might have expected, is a cultic hymn combining all the elements of the genre: invocation, genealogy, epithets, *Du-Stil* and *Relativ-Stil*, praise, cultic sites and areas of influence, request for epiphany (προφάνηθι, 'appear': v. 1149), and a petition at the end of the song.

---

[37] For *Nike* and trophies in celebratory iconography see *LIMC* VI.1.891–2 with Thöne 1999, 69–70, 154.
[38] On the members of the chorus (mostly of comedy and satyr play) as 'ritual actors' see Bierl 2009, 1–82.
[39] Cf. Soph. *Ant.* 131: ῥιπτεῖ, v. 134: ἀντιτύπᾳ, v. 139: στυφελίζων, vv. 153–4: ἐλελίχθων. We can also add the words denoting noise, clash, and clangour: Soph. *Ant.* 112: ὀξέα κλάζων, v. 125: πάταγος, v. 130: καναχῆς.
[40] Rutherford 2001, 63–8, 65–6: as for the paean, 'of the types of dance involved, and their movements, we know almost nothing (alas), except that one characteristic was a stamping motion of the feet.' On this specific aspect see also Rodighiero 2012, 134–7.
[41] For a close reading see Rodighiero 2012, 139–56, with Cerbo 1993; Furley/Bremer 2001, II, 269–72 (Eros); Adami 1900, 237–44; Dorsch 1983, 66–78; Furley/Bremer 2001, II, 272–9 (Dionysus).

Let us consider now the two hymns together with a fragment from the lost *Laocoon*. The formal architecture exploited by Sophocles is repeated almost identically, as we may easily conclude from the following passages:

Ἔρως ἀνίκατε μάχαν,
Ἔρως, ὃς ἐν κτήμασι πίπτεις,
ὃς ἐν μαλακαῖς παρειαῖς
νεάνιδος ἐννυχεύεις,
φοιτᾷς δ' ὑπερπόντιος ἔν τ' (785)
ἀγρονόμοις αὐλαῖς·

(Soph. *Ant.* 781–6 – hymn to Eros)

<u>Love</u> invincible in fight, Love <u>who fall upon</u> wealth, <u>you who</u> during the night <u>keep watch over</u> the soft cheeks of a maiden, <u>and roam over</u> the sea and among the huts in the wild.

πολυώνυμε, Καδμείας (1115)
νύμφας ἄγαλμα
καὶ Διὸς βαρυβρεμέτα
γένος, κλυτὰν ὃς ἀμφέπεις
Ἰταλίαν, μέδεις δὲ
παγκοίνοις Ἐλευσινίας (1120)
Δηοῦς ἐν κόλποις, ὦ Βακχεῦ,
Βακχᾶν ματρόπολιν Θήβαν
ναιετῶν

(Soph. *Ant.* 1115–23 – hymn to Dionysus)

<u>O you of many names</u>, pride of the Cadmean bride, the son of loud-thundering Zeus: <u>you who watch over</u> glorious Italy <u>and reign over</u> the hollows of Eleusinian Demeter, common to all, Bacchic god <u>who lives</u> in Thebes, the mother-city of the Bacchants...

Πόσειδον, ὃς Αἰγαίου νέμεις
πρῶνας ἢ γλαυκᾶς μέδεις εὐανέμου
λίμνας ἐφ' ὑψηλαῖς σπιλάδεσσι † στομάτων †.

(Soph. *Laocoon* F 371 *TrGF*⁴)

<u>Poseidon, you who range over</u> the capes of the Aegean, <u>or</u> in the depths of the grey sea <u>rule over</u> the windswept waters above the lofty cliffs...

We can now better visualize the three beginnings in synoptic fashion, as follows:

Ant. 781–5:   Ἔρως... ὅς... πίπτεις, ὅς... ἐννυχεύεις, φοιτᾷς δ' ὑπερπόντιος
Ant. 1115–23: Πολυώνυμε... ὃς ἀμφέπεις... μέδεις δὲ... ναιετῶν
F 371 *TrGF* IV: Πόσειδον, ὅς... νέμεις... ἢ... μέδεις

These explicitly cultic songs are also comparable with similar compositions in which there is, by contrast, no religious atmosphere. This is the case for the celebratory 'hymn' to Salamis in the first *stasimon* of *Ajax*, which is abruptly interrupted (v. 600: ἐγὼ δ'...) by a reference to the painful situation of the sailors:

ὦ κλεινὰ Σαλαμίς, σὺ μέν που
ναίεις ἁλίπλακτος εὐδαίμων,
πᾶσιν περίφαντος αἰεί·

(Soph. *Aj.* 596–9)

O glorious Salamis, you lie beaten by the sea,
fortunate, ever famous in the sight of all.

Here the usual structure is still easily recognizable: the name is placed first in the song, and praise is achieved by the adjectives denoting fame, while the *Du-Stil* and the presence of a verb of staying (ναίεις) bring the incipit even nearer to the hymnic beginnings considered above. We know that in cultic songs, following a long-established convention, the god's name is typically in first position; further, his area of influence is specified by verbs such as 'stay', 'rule', 'live', 'control' and by means of relative clauses[42] and participial forms. We also know that it is widespread lyric practice to borrow the modes and style of hymns of praise and to incorporate them into other kinds of song.[43]

4 The *Parodos* of the *Women of Trachis*

While in the odes of *Antigone* and the *Laocoon* fragment (and even in the celebration of the island in the *stasimon* of *Ajax*) the pattern is familiar and clearly

---

42 As is noticeable already in Hes. *Theog.* 1–2: Μουσάων Ἑλικωνιάδων ἀρχώμεθ' ἀείδειν, / αἵ θ' Ἑλικῶνος ἔχουσιν ὄρος μέγα τε ζάθεόν τε, 'Let us begin to sing first the Heliconian Muses, who hold the great and sacred mount of Helicon': see Pucci 2007, 36; West 1966, 152, *ad Theog.* 2: 'the expansion by means of a relative clause of the subject of song initially named is a regular feature of epic proems (*Op.* 2–3, *Catal.* fr. 1, Hom. *Il.* 1.1–2, Hom. *Od.* 1.1, *Il. parv.* fr. 1, *Thebais* fr. 1, nearly all the hymns).'
43 As for instance Pindar often does when he places 'a hymnic "façade" [...] in front of his epinician odes': Ford 2011, 97; cf. especially Pind. *Ol.* 14.1–5 (with Lomiento 2012, 294–301, Race 1990, 97–102 and more generally 85–117): Καφισίων ὑδάτων / λαχοῖσαι αἵτε ναίετε καλλίπωλον ἕδραν, / ὦ λιπαρᾶς ἀοίδιμοι βασίλειαι / Χάριτες Ἐρχομενοῦ, παλαιγόνων Μινυᾶν ἐπίσκοποι, / κλῦτ', ἐπεὶ εὔχομαι, 'You who have inherited the waters of Kephisos, / and who reside in a land of beautiful horses, / o Graces, celebrated by songs, o queens / of bright Orchomenos, / guardians of the ancient clan of Minyans, / hear me as I pray'.

discernible, in the opening lines of the *parodos* of the *Women of Trachis* the rhetoric and form of Greek hymns seem to be used in a different way.⁴⁴

<u>ὃν αἰόλα νὺξ</u> ἐναριζομένα
<u>τίκτει</u> κατευνάζει τε φλογιζόμενον, (95)
Ἅλιον Ἅλιον αἰτῶ
τοῦτο, καρῦξαι τὸν Ἀλκμή-
νας· πόθι μοι πόθι μοι
<u>ναίει</u> ποτ', ὦ λαμπρᾷ στεροπᾷ φλεγέθων;
ἢ Ποντίας αὐλῶνας, ἢ (100)
δισσαῖσιν ἀπείροις κλιθείς;
εἴπ', ὦ κρατιστεύων κατ' ὄμμα.

(Soph. *Trach.* 94–102)

You whom glittering night brings forth when she dies and whom she lulls to sleep when you are blazing in fire: Sun, Sun, I pray you! Tell me: where, where does the son of Alcmene abide, you who shine with bright gleam? Either in the marine channels of the Black Sea or leaning between two lands? Speak, you who are the mightiest in the power of sight!

The invocation to the Sun is achieved by a sentence starting with a relative pronoun as a direct object: ὃν αἰόλα νὺξ... / τίκτει (*Trach.* 94–5). Although there is no comparable passage either in tragedy or in extant Greek lyric, the model is clear: the direct object as opening element signals the rhapsodic style and the so-called *Er-Stil*. As we have seen, the god is often addressed in the vocative form, but his name or title can also be given in the third person. Sophocles seems to combine the two forms: something is told *about* the god, his origin, and his strength, as regularly happens in rhapsodic hymns. At the same time, the typical request of cultic hymns (the so-called εὐχή, the prayer itself) is fully expressed, as Helios is urged to reply to the question about Heracles' personal condition and location. Yet the reference to the person or divinity to be invoked and praised is *not* usually announced by an opening relative pronoun, but by the full name or a connotative epithet. Sophocles hints at an established epic and hymnic *iunctura*, but makes use of it only partially, without revealing in advance the key information (that is: who is engendered?), since in the ode the name is provided *only after* the relative pronoun. A few examples of canonical

---

44 As to the reasons for such wider freedom, it is worth quoting Segal's view (slightly diverging from a strict ritualist reading): 'although the odes of tragedy are modelled upon traditional choral songs like paeans, epinicians, dithyrambs, and so on, they are not independent ritual acts. They are fictitious rituals for mythical characters': Segal 1996, 20.

patterns (most of them displaying an accusative beginning)⁴⁵ may shed light on
the relationship with the tragic passage:

Hes. fr. 357.3 M.-W.: <u>Φοῖβον Ἀπόλλωνα</u> χρυσάορον, <u>ὃν τέκε Λητώ</u>
Phoebus Apollo of the golden sword, to whom Leto gave birth

Hymn. Hom. Merc. 4.1–3 ~ *Hymn. Hom. Merc.* 18.1–3: <u>Ἑρμῆν</u> ὕμνει Μοῦσα... <u>ὃν τέκε Μαῖα</u>
Muse, sing a hymn about Hermes... to whom Maia gave birth

Hymn. Hom. Jun. 12.1: <u>Ἥρην</u> ἀείδω χρυσόθρονον <u>ἣν τέκε Ῥείη</u>
Hera with throne of gold I sing, to whom Rhea gave birth

Hymn. Hom. Herc. 15.1–3: <u>Ἡρακλέα</u> Διὸς υἱὸν ἀείσομαι, <u>ὃν</u> μέγ' ἄριστον / <u>γείνατ</u>' ἐπιχθονίων
Θήβης ἔνι καλλιχόροισιν / <u>Ἀλκμήνη</u>
Heracles the son of Zeus shall I sing, to whom – the best man upon earth – Alcmene gave
birth in Thebes with fair dancing-grounds

Eur. *Ba.* 2–3: ... <u>Διόνυσος</u>, <u>ὃν τίκτει</u> ποθ' ἡ Κάδμου κόρη / <u>Σεμέλη</u>,
... I, Dionysus: Cadmus' daughter Semele once gave birth to me

Eur. *Ba.* 87–92: <u>τὸν Βρόμιον</u>· // <u>ὅν</u>... <u>μάτηρ ἔτεκεν</u>
Bromius, to whom his mother gave birth

Philod. Scarph. *Pai.* 39.5–7 Käppel (340–339 BC): εὐοῖ ὦ Ἰό[βακχ]' ὦ ἰὲ Παιά]ν· / [ὅ]ν
Θήβαις... <u>γείνατο</u>... Θυώνα
euhoi, o io Bacchus, o iè Paean, to whom in Thebes Thyona gave birth

Limen. *Pai.* 46.5 Käppel (around 128 BC): <u>Φοῖβον</u>, <u>ὃν ἔτικτε Λατὼ μάκαιρα</u>
Phoebus, to whom the blessed Leto gave birth.

This is a particular type of opening which extends its influence throughout Greek
poetry, but if we take all the above examples as referring to the same, recurrent
model,⁴⁶ we see that the rearrangement of the typical hymnic relative clause
(necessarily) entails the postponement of the god's name only in our tragic pas-

---

45 'In conjunction with the "Let me sing"-phrase, Greek shows a marked tendency to place the name of the deity at the very beginning of the hymn': Metcalf 2015, 137. On accusative beginnings as a symptom of rhapsodic (rather than cultic) style see Lidov 1996, 134–7.
46 *Variatio* is attested e.g. in *Hymn. Hom. Aesc.* 16.1–2: Ἰητῆρα νόσων Ἀσκληπιόν... / ... τὸν ἐγείνατο δῖα Κορωνίς, 'Asclepius healer of sickness... whom the noble Coronis bore' (cf. also *Hymn. Hom. Hel.* 31.1–3, and Eur. *IA* 207–8: Ἀχιλλέα, / τὸν ἁ Θέτις τέκε, 'Achilles, to whom Thetis gave birth'). On the enunciative aspects involved in epic poetry and in the Homeric hymns see Calame 1995, 35–48: 'the relative clause thus introduced corresponds to an enunciative shift; it marks the start of the recitation, in the third person, of the qualities and exploits of the god sung by the I. The function of the initial enunciative shifting-in is therefore only to engage the description and/or the story itself' (p. 36). The same sequence (name + ὅν... τέκον/τέκε/ἔτικτε) operates even elsewhere – that is, not in opening lines – in hexametric poetry: cf. e.g. Hom. *Il.* 22.87, *Hymn. Hom. Ap.* 3.177–8, 306–7, and 317. See also Vergados 2013, 223 (on *Hymn. Hom. Merc.* 4.3).

sage. Such conventional beginnings, which Sophocles utterly disregards,[47] provide evidence that the dramatic poet allows himself much greater freedom in his re-handling of opening formulae *in lyricis*. But does this flexibility make him completely and deliberately ignore the traditional rules informing the oral composition of hexametric hymns?[48] As a matter of fact, the god's name in the accusative is neither the first element in the line, nor even in the first line, and the invocatory verb is not in a prominent position (Ἅλιον… αἰτῶ, 'Sun, I pray you'). Yet this diverging configuration preserves *all* the elements of the pattern; taken together, they give the impression of an elaborate and sophisticated style. The two opening verses effectively delay – but obviously do not remove – the information which the audience will receive only a few moments later, that is, the god's name. The formal aspects, documented in particular by the oral hexametric tradition, and the ritual character of the song are strictly related. The efficacy and effectiveness of the prayer, although it is modified, relies on the preservation of all the formulaic constituents. In order to reach their aim, the worshippers know that (all) the necessary words must be uttered. If we look at it in more detail, in the *Women of Trachis* the accusative relative pronoun is hanging, as it were, in an atypical position, whereas in the *Homeric Hymns* and elsewhere it usually follows the proper name.[49] In Sophocles we are dealing with an internal relative clause in which the so-called 'head noun' (the name of the divinity) is nevertheless only partially incorporated into the relative sentence. The syntactical configuration aligns in a sequence the relative pronoun (ὅν), the relative clause (νὺξ… τίκτει) and then the head (Ἅλιον). Albeit not unusual,[50] the

---

47 On the various forms of unpredictability in the Sophoclean sentence-structure see Budelmann 2000, 19–60, 'unpredictability is not something that makes a sentence obscure or difficult to follow, but something that spectators can make sense of' (p. 58), with further considerations in Silk 2009. The hymnodic and celebratory incipit of the first *stasimon* of the *Women of Trachis* (v. 497) offers a similar diversion from an expected form: see Rodighiero 2012, 66–9.
48 See Létoublon 2012, 22: 'les aèdes depuis l'*Iliade* posent déjà cette question : "Par quoi commencer?".' On the hymnic ἀρχή see also Race 1982, 5–8.
49 See Davies 1991, 78.
50 The same order is found in *OT* 68–9 (in trimeters): ἦν δ' εὖ σκοπῶν ηὕρισκον ἴασιν μόνην, / ταύτην ἔπραξα, 'and the only remedy – by examining every way – I could find, this one I have carried out'. In the *OT* passage the relative pronoun (ἥν) is followed by the verb of the relative clause (ηὕρισκον: the subject is Oedipus), and then by the head noun (ἴασιν). The demonstrative pronoun ταύτην ἔπραξα, which is absent in the *Women of Trachis*, comes after. On internally headed relative clauses, see bibliographical references in Bakker 2009, 81, n. 59, and for Sophoclean examples Moorhouse 1982, 270. A less forceful form of incipit can be detected in tragic lyric prayers, with the accusative personal pronoun σέ as a peculiar use of the *Du-Stil*: Eur. *Ion* 452–8 (first words of the first *stasimon*): σὲ… Ἀθάναν, ἱκετεύω… μόλε, 'I entreat you, Athena…

so-called internally headed relative clause in the *Women of Trachis* sounds extraordinarily peculiar: interpretation of the passage prompts us to understand it as a twisted pattern consciously echoing the beginning of a Homeric hymn, with the precise intention of preserving the religious and ritual functions of the echo.[51] And into this pattern Sophocles inserts the conventional motif of the god's genealogy, marked in his lyric text by the presence of the verb τίκτω, 'to bring forth', 'to give birth to.'

The previous hymnic occurences are not isolated. After this elaborate opening, the *evocatio* of the divinity and the following *preces* are fused together; the request is immediately clarified by the question, and the direct prayer to the Sun is emphasized by the repetition Ἅλιον Ἅλιον αἰτῶ / τοῦτο, καρῦξαι (*Trach.* 96–7: 'Sun, Sun, I pray you! tell me...'),[52] while an additional hymnic expansion is provided by the participial style of the *epiklesis:* the pericope ὦ λαμπρᾷ στεροπᾷ φλεγέθων (*Trach.* 99: 'you who shine with bright gleam') is 'eine Prädikation im Partizipialstil und Aretalogie in nuce'[53] (cf. v. 95: φλογιζόμενον). In a quasi-circular motion, the god's glorious deeds and virtues reappear a third time with the same participial form at the end of the first strophe: ὦ κρατιστεύων κατ' ὄμμα (*Trach.* 102: 'you who are the mightiest in the power of sight!').

By positioning the relative pronoun ὅν in an unexpected place, in the complex procedure of reshaping the beginning, Sophocles completely redirects the chorus' song while simultaneously preserving some features of traditional invocations (the god's name, his genealogy, his praise, the relative sentence and the participial style). But once again the tragic poet diverts from the expected path.

---

come...', and *Hel.* 1107–11 (first words of the first *stasimon*): σὲ... ἀναβοάσω,... ἔλθ᾽, 'I call on you... come...' (of the nightingale).

51 Cf. Létoublon 2012, 34: 'pour les formules d'ouverture et de clôture des hymnes, il s'agirait d'une parole *performative* dans le sens précis où Benveniste parle d'un performatif pour des exemples tels que "Je déclare la séance ouverte" ou "La séance est ouverte", "La séance est close".' For the significance of the genealogical motif in the Homeric hymns see Furley 2011, 229: using the model of human genealogy, Greek hexameter hymns to the gods usually took as their basic material the god's genealogy in order to establish their existence and their relations to the other generations of divinities.

52 We observe a similar structure in the paeanic *parodos* of the *Oedipus Tyrannus* (vv. 159–63): πρῶτα σὲ κεκλόμενος... Ἀθάνα,... Ἄρτεμιν,... καὶ Φοῖβον... αἰτῶ [~*Trach.* 96: Ἅλιον Ἅλιον αἰτῶ],... προφάνητέ μοι, 'first I call on you,... Athena,... and Artemis,... and Phoebus,... appear!'; This song is given some of the most common components of a hymnodic prayer, as for instance the paeanic refrain (v. 154), the request for the god to appear, and the *hypomnesis* (vv. 164–7; see Ax 1932, Swift 2010, 77–81, and Rodighiero 2012, 144–5 on some diversions from the usual formal hymnic practice).

53 See Korzeniewski 1968, 167. Since the beginning the sound 'ον' has been flowing into the musical theme of the strophe: ὅν... φλογιζόμενον... Ἅλιον Ἅλιον... τὸν Ἀλκμήνας.

We have already seen the role which verbs such as 'to stay', 'to attend', 'to live' normally feature in hymnic contexts. Yet in our choral ode the verb ναίω, 'to live', does not outline the god's cultic geography, thereby emphasizing his power; rather, it indicates some of the uncertain places visited by the missing (and mortal) Heracles: 'where, where does the son of Alcmene abide…? Is he in the marine channels of the Black Sea or leaning between two lands?' (*Trach.* 101 ἢ Ποντίας αὐλῶνας, ἢ / δισσαῖσιν ἀπείροις κλιθείς;). This is neither a rhetorical or aporetic question, nor a selective priamel.⁵⁴ The anxious chorus ask for a precise answer which cannot be given, for the time being. Therefore, the serious parody of the hymnic style is still operative, for the paradigm of multiple choices and places⁵⁵ frequently recurs elsewhere in prayers and hymns with the aim of intensifying the prestige of the divine.⁵⁶ In the *Women of Trachis*, though, it is Heracles and not the summoned god Helios who is considered ubiquitous, as if the *aretalogia* were concerned with celebrating the feats of the mortal hero: the prayer is intended to bring about the appearance not of a god, but of a missing person.⁵⁷ Yet the aporetic question to the Sun does not offer any solution. The chorus trav-

---

54 Aporetic questions (which god to invoke, which exploit to treat, where to begin the narrative) are common in rhapsodic hymns: see Bundy 1972, 57–66, Race 1990, 106, n. 58.
55 'You, god, who live either here or there, you who are coming from here or there, you who control this place or that other place…': the corresponding Greek particles are: ἢ… ἢ, εἴτε… εἴτε, καί… καί and so forth; confining ourselves to the theatre, we can quote as examples Soph. *Ant.* 1144–5 (hymn to Dionysus): μολεῖν καθαρσίῳ ποδὶ Παρνασίαν / ὑπὲρ κλειτὸν ἢ στονόεντα πορθμόν, 'come with a purifying pace over the Parnassian slope or the moaning strait!'; Ar. *Nub.* 269–73 (Socrates summons the Clouds): ἔλθετε δῆτ', ὦ πολυτίμητοι Νεφέλαι, τῷδ' εἰς ἐπίδειξιν· / εἴτ' ἐπ' Ὀλύμπου κορυφαῖς ἱεραῖς χιονοβλήτοισι κάθησθε, / εἴτ' Ὠκεανοῦ πατρὸς ἐν κήποις ἱερὸν χορὸν ἵστατε Νύμφαις, / εἴτ' ἄρα Νείλου προχοαῖς ὑδάτων χρυσέαις ἀρύτεσθε πρόχοισιν, / ἢ Μαιῶτιν λίμνην ἔχετ' ἢ σκόπελον νιφόεντα Μίμαντος, 'come then, illustrious Clouds, in an exhibition for this man, whether you now sit on Olympus' holy snow-struck peaks, or start up a holy dance for the Nymphs in father Ocean's gardens, or whether again at the Nile's mouths you scoop its waters in golden pitchers, or inhabit Lake Maeotis or the snowy steeps of Mimas' (transl. Henderson); see also Aesch. *Eum.* 292–7 (Orestes' prayer to Athena, *in trimetris*: εἴτε… ἢ… εἴτε…). More examples in Adami 1900, 227–31.
56 Differently, in *Hymn. Hom. Bacch.* 1.1–6 the priamel functions as an introduction which aims to select the real birthplace of Dionysus (οἱ μέν… οἱ δ'… οἱ δ'… οἱ δ'… ἄλλοι δ' …: 'some say… others affirm…'), identifying *via* the common formula not the name of the mother but that of the father (v. 6: σὲ δ' ἔτικτε πατὴρ ἀνδρῶν τε θεῶν τε, 'but it was the father of the mortals and the immortals who gave birth to you'; for the formal structure of the Homeric hymns in general see Janko 1981).
57 A further distortion could be recognized in Ἅλιον αἰτῶ… καρῦξαι, in the departure from the common pattern formed by vocative+imperative (ὕμνει, ἔννεπε, ἀείσεο, ἀείδεο, ὑμνεῖν ἄρχεο: on which see Létoublon 2012, 26–7).

els mentally to the ends of the earth, but the only eye which can see the location and the conditions of the hero is that of a god. The liturgical effect which seems guaranteed by this solemn beginning collapses in the antistrophe, where – with a return to the choral 'I': *Trach.* 103 – Deianeira's tragic plight becomes the main topic of the song. All in all, in the first strophe the earlier model is partially reproduced but also partially reshaped into new and unique configurations; Sophocles deconstructs several well-known generic features and readapts them to the hero's dramatic situation. From the very beginning, typical components of hymns and prayers are transformed into apparently more elusive and ambiguous, but still obvious elements, echoing traditional and widespread forms of religious and (not only) lyric poetry.

Comparing and contrasting Sophoclean and Euripidean drama yields a decisive argument that demonstrates the distinctive way in which Sophocles has handled these components, thereby proving Sophocles' aptitude for experimentation with new forms. The younger poet closely adheres to the archaic hymnic pattern in the narrative hymn praising Apollo in *IT* 1234–83 (the third *stasimon*). The text does not distance itself so far as to make the model unrecognisable: in the two opening verses (*IT* 1234–6), the god's name is followed by the accusative relative pronoun and (very likely) by the verb τίκτω: εὔπαις ὁ Λατοῦς γόνος, / ὅν ποτε... / <ἔτικτε> ('how good-looking a child is Leto's son, whom once... <she bore>').[58] A further example – although with different components – of Euripides' use of a traditional genre may be found in the initial words of the first *stasimon* in *Tro.* 511–4: ἀμφί μοι Ἴλιον, ὦ / Μοῦσα, καινῶν ὕμνων / ᾆσον σὺν δακρύοις ᾠδὰν ἐπικήδειον ('sing for me concerning Ilium, O Muse, a mourning ode of sad new songs, in tears'). This lyric incipit not only echoes the grandeur of the epic *exordia*, as for instance that of the *Little Iliad*,[59] but the appeal to the Muse also reminds the audience of the characteristic kitharodic beginnings of the *Homeric Hymns*. The formulaic ἀμφί is the first word of the performance, as in *Hymn. Hom.* 7, 22, and 33, and especially 19 (the hymn to Pan: ἀμφί μοι Ἑρμείαο φίλον γόνον ἔννεπε Μοῦσα, 'Muse, tell me about Pan, the favourite son of Hermes').[60] In the passage from the *Trojan Women* the conventional

---

58 On this narrative hymn see Furley/Bremer 2001, I, 329–36, and II, 322–9 (they read the passage as most closely resembling a kitharodic nome: *contra*, see Parker 2016, 306). At v. 1236 the almost certain ἔτικτε (Paley) is widely accepted: see Platnauer 1938, 162, Parker 2016, 309.
59 Fr. 1.1 West = fr. 28.1 Bernabé: Ἴλιον ἀείδω 'of Ilium I sing'. On the passage see West 2013a, 173.
60 For a lyric use of the same formula cf. Terp. fr. 697.1–2 *PMG* = fr. 2.1–2 Gostoli: ἀμφί μοι... ἀειδέτω with Battezzato 2005b, 85, n. 54. See also Cerbo 2016, 34–6.

models receive further confirmation by the content of the chorus' song (the fall of Troy, an epic theme *par excellence*), as well as by the dactylic 'aura' inspired by the initial *hemiepes* at *Tro.* 511 (ἀμφί μοι Ἴλιον, ὦ: –⏑⏑–⏑⏑–). Although it is transposed into lyrics, the epic syntax is fully preserved and remains easily discernible, whereas in the *Women of Trachis* the Sophoclean deconstruction provides the modern reader only with obscure hints.

5 How to begin a beginning: the second *stasimon* of *Ajax*

The last example I shall discuss is the second *stasimon* of *Ajax*. This short investigation should be preceded by a preliminary question – although many others will follow – which I borrow from Deborah Roberts: 'how does a beginning deal with what (inevitably) came before, so that it feels like an acceptable beginning? How does it prepare us for what follows?'[61]

At this point in the drama, the personal involvement of the Salaminian sailors (the chorus) is unavoidable, because – unlike the young girls of Trachis – their future depends largely on the destiny and on the mental state of their leader. The deception arising from the hero's words, and the false impression that Ajax has quickly recovered from madness makes them cheerful, and leads them to dance. From this there arises a festive choral song, which does not appear to echo any specific, known passage, but is able simultaneously to evoke the atmosphere and even the ethos of different lyric genres. As in the *parodos* of *Antigone*, the theatrical space is occupied by the chorus alone; after v. 692 Ajax leaves the stage, and the space in front of his tent remains completely empty;[62] therefore, in the absence of the actors, the audience could perceive the song as a purely lyrical performance. The sailors sing as follows (vv. 693 – 708):

ἔφριξ' ἔρωτι, περιχαρὴς δ' ἀνεπτάμαν.   στρ.
ἰὼ ἰὼ Πὰν Πάν,
ὦ Πὰν Πὰν ἁλίπλαγκτε, Κυλ-   (695)
λανίας χιονοκτύπου
πετραίας ἀπὸ δειράδος φάνηθ', ὦ
θεῶν χοροποί' ἄναξ, ὅπως μοι

---

61 Roberts 2005, 137.
62 As frequently happens before a song: about 60% of all tragic choral odes were sung to an empty stage, on which Aichele 1971, 55; see also Taplin 1977, 54 – 5, 110 – 13.

Μύσια Κνώσι' ὀρ-
χήματ' αὐτοδαῆ ξυνὼν ἰάψῃς. (700)
νῦν γὰρ ἐμοὶ μέλει χορεῦσαι.
Ἰκαρίων δ' ὑπὲρ † πελαγέων †
μολὼν ἄναξ Ἀπόλλων
ὁ Δάλιος εὔγνωστος
ἐμοὶ ξυνείη διὰ παντὸς εὔφρων. (705)

ἔλυσεν αἰνὸν ἄχος ἀπ' ὀμμάτων Ἄρης. ἀντ.
ἰὼ ἰώ, νῦν αὖ,
νῦν, ὦ Ζεῦ

I shudder with rapture, and soar up full of sudden joy. O Pan, O Pan! Ah Pan, Pan who wanders over the sea, appear from the Cyllenian rocky ridge beaten by the snow, o lord who leads the choruses of the gods, so that you can start the self-taught Mysian and Cnosian dances, joining me. Now it is my wish to dance! And coming over the Icarian sea may Apollo the lord – the Delian god, easily recognised – stay with me forever kindly!

Ares has removed dreadful distress from his eyes! O, O, now again: once more, now, Ah Zeus...

The beginning of the choral ode has been considered by John Davidson 'a classic example of the final, personal comment category [...], as the chorus, using the "instantaneous" aorist as their springboard, give utterance to the joy they feel at Ajax's apparent change of mind. This is an immediate response by the chorus, as Ajax's sailors vitally affected by their leader's situation, to the preceding dramatic development.'[63] This is not the only Sophoclean example of a chorus saying 'I' at the beginning of their song, but this moment of ecstatic joy remains unparalleled in Greek tragedy.[64] I shall consider neither the well-known hyporchematic nature of the *stasimon*, imbued with tragic irony, nor the presence of corybantic allusions.[65] Nevertheless, we should at least bear

---

63 Davidson 1991, 38–9.
64 See Stanford 1963, 43. For Sophoclean choruses saying ἐγώ in the first lines of a lyric section cf. *El.* 472, *OT* 1086; see also Kaimio 1970, 82–91.
65 'A joyous dance-song, ὑπόρχημα, which holds the place of the second stasimon' and would 'prepare for the catastrophe by a contrast' (Jebb 1896, 109). For another view of the hyporchematic nature of the ode, see Andújar in this volume. For full discussion of the hyporchematic overtones and the corybantic allusions in this *stasimon* see Rodighiero 2012, 19–60. Further evidence of exotic cult music as a possible source of inspiration is offered by the chorus of the *Tympanistae*, probably a group 'of Thracian Dionysus or Cybele devotees' ecstatically playing the *tympana* (F 636–645 *TrGF*⁴): see Power 2012, 304, after Sutton 1984, 150, and Pearson 1917, II, 263. The Phrygian mode was introduced in Athens by Sophocles according to Aristox. fr. 79 Wehrli = *Vita Sophoclis* 23 (T 1.95–7 *TrGF*⁴; on the *harmoniai* favoured by the poet see Comotti 1989b, 45–7).

in mind that ἔφριξα and ἀνεπτάμαν (which both express a violent emotion), do not necessarily represent an exclusively positive reaction. Elsewhere the two terms denote a state of disarray and fear, while in our *stasimon* the optimistic attitude of the heady Salaminian sailors appears to be made clear by the presence of περιχαρής, 'full of joy.' φρίκη is the physical symptom of a psychological (but at times even non-emotional) state as it becomes visible to others.[66] Here the verb ἔφριξα conveys the subjective choral experience in its external aspect; the symptom, an instinctive and automatic reaction, is generated by a sudden emotion.[67] This emotion is expressed both by the noun and by the adjective (ἔρως and περιχαρής), and for the shivering Salaminian sailors it turns into an involuntary physical movement which probably finds expression in the choreography.

Verse 693 constitutes an adequate prelude to the song, and provides the threshold and natural transition from the last words of Ajax, recited in iambic trimeters, to the *real* ode.[68] In dramatic poetry the exclamatory particles ἰὼ ἰὼ are commonly the symptom of a state of moral or physical suffering,[69] and their presence in our ode seems to maintain the ambiguity between joy and anxiety displayed in the first line. Nevertheless, here as in the *Women of Trachis* (v. 221: ἰὼ ἰὼ Παιάν) the ritual cry (ἰὼ ἰὼ) undoubtedly denotes a confident and hopeful reaction. The shift from the recited section is not abrupt, and after this unusual beginning the ode tries to emulate a traditional hymnic structure. As usual in prayers and requests, the repeated name of the god and the epithet

---

[66] See Cairns 2013, 85–6, 88: 'in emotional contexts, the primary reference of φρίκη and its cognates is to a certain perceptible physical movement, felt by the subject but also perceived by others.' In tragedy the verb is connected with fear in Aesch. *Ag.* 1242–4; Eur. *Hec.* 85–6; Soph. *El.* 1407, *Trach.* 1044, *OT* 1306, *Ant.* 997. Cf. also Aesch. F 387 *TrGF*³, a fragment which probably links φρίκη with the mysteries (see Cairns 2013, 100). Seaford 1994b, 284–5 even recognizes in the *Ajax* passage the 'contradictory emotions of mystic initiation.' For ἀνεπτάμαν see Soph. *Ant.* 1307: ἀνέπταν φόβῳ, 'I thrill with dread' (more examples in Finglass 2011, 343).
[67] ἔφριξ' ἔρωτι echoes v. 686: τοὐμὸν ὧν ἐρᾷ κέαρ, '... the things my heart longs for...'. In Pl. *Phdr.* 251a 'φρίκη appears as at once a symptom of ἔρως (as at Sophocles, *Ajax* 693), as a response to divine epiphany, as an experience of the mystic initiate, and as an emotion akin to both fear and σέβας': Cairns 2013, 101.
[68] I say *real* ode because the first line of the *stasimon* ('I shudder with rapture, and soar up full of sudden joy') is nothing but a final trimeter before the lyrics.
[69] Cf. Biraud 2010, 133–7; Nordgren 2015, 136–42, and 227–9: the core semantics of ἰὼ 'are emotive and denote a sensation of *grief*, perhaps also including *fear* or *anxiety*. Secondarily, ἰὼ often seems to be used as a call for attention or aid, regularly in association with divine cult, alongside vocatives and imperatives' (p. 142).

are positioned in the opening lines[70]: in 'Pan, Pan who wanders over the sea', the rare ἁλίπλαγκτε defines and describes – not only as an ornamental epithet – the god's ability to travel and intervene everywhere.[71]

Pan is 'a domestic deity to Salaminians', and the invocation sounds natural in the mouth of this specific chorus.[72] Moreover, the god enjoys dancing,[73] so the sailors ask him to come and attend their ὀρχήματα. Extraordinarily, his name appears four times; it highlights a state of excitement in which the deictic element νῦν plays a critical role as it fully expresses the mimetic self-referentiality after the description of the initial leaps ('*now* it is my wish to dance!': v. 701).[74] At this point Sophocles endows the *stasimon* with a clear generic pattern, employing 'the most intense form of a cletic hymn': the request for epiphany expressed by the conventional verb φάνηθι, 'appear.'[75]

If we look at the text more closely, we can notice the presence of an internal layout, a kind of double frame within which the name of Pan anticipates the name of Apollo. The chorus' cry should indeed be associated to quasi-παιάν refrains, as it is formed from the more common ἰὴ Παιάν that is frequently used as

---

[70] We observe the same sequence in the short Sophoclean hymn to Hypnos (*Phil.* 827–32), where the *clausula*, in addition, is a quasi-ritual refrain: ἴθι ἴθι μοι, Παιών ('come, come, Healer!'). See also e. g. Hom. *Il.* 5.31 (Ares); Alcm. 14 *PMGF* (Muse); Archil. fr. 177 *IEG* (Zeus); Aesch. *Ag.* 973 (Zeus), *Cho.* 246 (Zeus); Soph. *Ant.* 781–2 (Eros), *OC* 1559 (Aidoneus); Eur. *Tro.* 840 (Eros), *Bacch.* 370–1 (Hosia), 584 (Bromius); Theocr. *Id.* 18.50–3 (Leto, Cypris, Zeus). Cf. also Eur. *Ion* 125–7 (and 141–3): ὦ Παιάν ὦ Παιάν, / εὐαίων εὐαίων / εἴης, ὦ Λατοῦς παῖ, 'O Paean, O Paean, may you be fortunate, son of Leto' (Ion sings alone: 'he is devoted to Apollo. His ears are full of the paians which pilgrims to Delphi sang in chorus': Furley 1999–2000, 189; the Euripidean hymns are listed in Furley 2000, 197 and Furley/Bremer 2001, II, 295–329). The name of Pan is repeated in fr. 887 *PMG*; Theocr. *Id.* 1.123–4; Glauc. *AP* IX.341.5; *IG* IV² I 130 = fr. 936.19 *PMG*; on Pind. fr. 95.1 S.-M. (ὦ Πάν versus ὦ Πᾶν Πάν) see Rodighiero 2012, 23.

[71] *Pace* Jebb 1896, 109 (Lobeck 1866, 258 correctly translates 'tu, qui maria pervagari soles'). The Nymphs are ὀρίπλαγκτοι, 'mountain-wandering', in Ar. *Thesm.* 326 (a cletic hymn to Zeus already quoted above: see Austin and Olson 2004, 159–60). Eros roams ὑπερπόντιος, 'over the sea', in Soph. *Ant.* 785.

[72] Jebb 1896, 109. This familiarity has become usual since the Persian wars: there was a cult of Pan in the island of Psyttaleia, near Salamis (cf. Hdt. 8.76 and 95, with especially Aesch. *Pers.* 447–64, where the god is described as dancing on the shore).

[73] The relationship between Pan and dance is well attested: cf. *Hymn. Hom. Pan.* 19.22; Pind. fr. 99 S.-M.; Aesch. *Pers.* 448; fr. 887.2 *PMG*; *IG* IV² I 130 = fr. 936.3 and 10 *PMG* (with Lehnus 1979, 94–5 and 191–2).

[74] On choral self-referentiality in this passage see Henrichs 1994–1995, 73–5 (but I would mitigate the presence of Dionysiac hints: see Rodighiero 2012, 31–2). Other examples in the extant Sophoclean tragedies are *OT* 896, *Ant.* 152–4, *Trach.* 216–20. On self-referentiality in performative contexts see Bierl 2009, 24–47, and 275–6.

[75] Furley/Bremer 2001, II, 336 (and see n. 24 above).

a closing formula or inserted between two separate stanzas. The presence of Apollo, therefore, can be better justified and understood – with the dancing god *par excellence* apparently reduced to a secondary role –[76] if we imagine the two invocations beginning from the 'false' paean cry as the endings of a kind of dismembered refrain. Imitating common *formulae* such as the Pindaric ἰήϊε Δάλι' Ἄπολλον or Sophocles' own ἰὼ ἰὼ Παιάν (*Women of Trachis*, v. 221), ἰήϊε Δάλιε Παιάν (in the *OT*'s paeanic *parodos*), and the less characterized ἰήϊε Φοῖβε,[77] the poet capitalizes on the patent assonance between *Pan* and *Paian*. In so doing, he obtains within the same strophe two separate but related prayers: to Pan and to Apollo. The result is given by the combination of ἰὼ ἰὼ Πὰν Πάν and Ἀπόλλων ὁ Δάλιος, whereas v. 701 marks the passage from the hymnic *Du-* ('appear!': v. 697) to the *Er-Stil* ('may [Apollo] stay...': v. 705). The poetic material comes directly from a well-attested lyric tradition, and is elaborately reworked in a song (in aeolo-choriambics) which sounds primitive and spontaneous only on the surface. As the following table attempts to show, the first sequence dedicated to Pan has been duplicated and repeated for Apollo in the same words and with identical images: both named gods – praised with the same epithet, 'lord' – are asked to come from their stated birthplace (Cyllene, Delos), cross a specific stretch of sea, and appear; finally, they are invited to remain well-disposed towards the chorus and to dance:[78]

Pan	Apollo
Πάν (x4)... φάνηθ'	~ μολών... Ἀπόλλων
Pan... appear	~ coming... Apollo
ἀλίπλαγκτε, Κυλλανίας... ἀπὸ δειράδος	~ Ἰκαρίων δ' ὑπὲρ πελαγέων... ὁ Δάλιος
who wanders over the sea... from the Cyllenian ridge	~ over the Icarian sea... the Delian god
ἄναξ... μοι... ξυνῶν	~ ἄναξ... ἐμοὶ ξυνείη
the lord... joining with me	~ the lord... may stay with me.

---

[76] Sources in Calame 2001, 49–53.

[77] 'The "false" paean cry 'Io, Io, Pan, Pan' (rather than 'Ie Paean') at the start cannot fail to evoke that association (693)' (Kowalzig 2007b, 232); for the two quoted examples cf. Pind. *Pae.* 5.1 (fr. 52e S-M = D5 Rutherford), *OT* 154 and 1096. The paeanic ritual cry is widely attested: cf. e.g. fr. 867.3 *PMG* = *Pai.* 35.3 Käppel, fr. 933.1 *PMG* = *Pai.* 36a.37–9 Käppel, *P.Berol.* 6870 = *Pai.* 48.1 Käppel: Παιάν, ὦ Παιάν (with Rutherford 2001, 69–72; see also Aesch. *Ag.* 146). Cf. also the final cry in the epigraphic hymn to Pan already quoted above (*IG* IV² I 130 = fr. 936.19 *PMG*): ὦ ἰὴ Πὰν Πάν, where the poet probably plays 'deliberatamente sulla quasi-omofonia fra Πάν e Παιάν': Wagman 2000, 141.

[78] See Henrichs 1994–1995, 74–5. On the motif of the god's permanent and benevolent presence see also *OT* 275 (the verb is ξυνεῖεν) and Ariphron's hymn to *Hygieia*, fr. 813.2 *PMG*: σὺ δέ μοι πρόφρων ξυνείης, 'may you stay kindly with me', to be compared with *Aj.* 705 (with Keyßner 1932, 88–9). On the 'come, god!'-type in prayers see also Metcalf 2015, 150–2.

Returning to the opening lines, let us now consider them not only as the literary expression of a formal and metrical pattern, but also as a set of words pronounced/chanted/sung during a theatrical performance and capable of offering an emotional shift, as well as a physical transition.[79]

Certain questions inevitably arise as a result: is this choral ode entirely danced? The answer, at least in this case and as far as we can tell, must be yes; but what kind of performance can we imagine for this hyporchematic *stasimon*? Surely a very excited, fast-moving, enthusiastic, one, perhaps including some spinning. Furthermore, how should we understand the single preludeverse? In other words, how did the chorus dance this isolated iambic trimeter, and what can we say about the corresponding that opens the antistrophe?[80] Is it fanciful to assume that the plain song originally started only with the hymnic form (i.e. with the name of the god Pan), and then – in the antistrophe – with a series of repeated and 'empty' words (ἰὼ ἰώ, νῦν αὖ, / νῦν: vv. 707–8) along with the name of Zeus?[81] Was the trimeter simply chanted by the coryphaeus as a connective element which introduced the ode and, so to speak, ended the trimeters recited by Ajax? This verse is the chorus' first reaction after Ajax's *Trugrede*, and offers a display – in the same formal (i.e. metrical) terms as the hero's speech – of full approval of his beguiling words. The line also communicates a sense of relief after a long anxiety: it marks the abrupt passage between two different states of mind,[82] and constitutes for the chorus a renewed opportunity for dialogue with their leader.

Should we, therefore, define this pattern as a kind of 'double beginning' with the preliminary trimeter detached from the rest of the *stasimon*? Alternative-

---

[79] See Gagné/Hopman 2013b, 29.

[80] It is precisely in the antistrophe that the language becomes less generic and that the hymnodic tone begins to dissipate: now the chorus refer to the hero's mental state in epic terms, making use in the iambic trimeter of the Homeric *formula* αἰνὸν ἄχος ('dreadful distress': v. 706). Cf. e.g. Hom. *Il.* 4.169, 8.124, 17.83, *Od.* 18.274 ('Sophocles leaves it undetermined whether the distress is that of Ajax alone or of all his φίλοι, or of both (which is likeliest)': Stanford 1963, 153. Another hint of epic language is offered at v. 710, where θοᾶν ὠκυάλων νεῶν, 'swift ships, gliding over the sea', combines and varies Hom. *Od.* 7.34: νηυσὶ θοῇσιν τοί γε πεποιθότες ὠκείῃσι, 'trusting in the swift, fast riding ships'. More on Homeric elements in Rodighiero 2012, 54 and n. 108, with further bibliography.

[81] The insistence on the temporal aspect, with the repetition of νῦν (three times), also refers to the *hic et nunc* of choral performance. Cf. similarly Aesch. *Cho.* 719–29 and Eur. *Tro.* 515: νῦν γὰρ μέλος ἐς Τροίαν ἰαχήσω: 'now I shall sing a song of Troy'.

[82] As we can infer from the last words pronounced by the sailors at the end of the previous *stasimon* (*Aj.* 641–5), where they still consider Ajax as ill-fated and in a state of unease (cf. v. 642: δύσφορον ἄταν, 'a ruin hard to bear').

ly, are we to imagine (perhaps somewhat fancifully) something like a 'double gap' marked by Ajax's last word at v. 692, and then by the isolated opening trimeter, then again by a shorter gap before the name of Pan was shouted out? No conclusive answer is at hand. We do not know how these 'blank spaces' fitted in between the episodes and the choral songs – once formal and performative divisions, now laden with silence in front of us – were filled in ancient theatrical practice, how long they were, and at what precise point the music of the *aulos* began.

However, the well-known structural design of Greek hymns does indicate that we are dealing with a lyric shape that would have been easily recognizable to the audience. The hymnic model which underlies this very unusual and unique stylisation of a familiar pattern is set just after the first verse (not very far from the supposed beginning of the *stasimon*). As this isolated trimeter remains the sole example of its kind, not only in Sophocles,[83] we should suppose that the poet is experimenting with new forms of poetry and touching upon the (external) borders of a traditional framework rather than referring to a previous, specific 'prototype' forged by other lyric genres. The hymn and the prayer are still there, but the legacy of an age-old tradition has once more been remodelled and refurbished by a personal and distinctive creativity. This is additional proof, as Simon Goldhill tellingly puts it, of 'the extraordinary experimentation in *form* that we can see in Sophoclean handling of the chorus.'[84]

---

[83] Verse 693 (~706) is animated by the *crescendo* of four short syllables and shows a penthemimeral caesura followed by the tetrasyllable περιχαρής (⏑ – ⏑ – ⏑ | ⏑ ⏑ ⏑ – ⏑ – ⏑ –); it finds parallels in other non-lyric (i.e. recited) iambic trimeters of the drama, cf. vv. 81 (penthemimeral caesura+tetrasyllable), 332, 575, 730, 828, 896, 1033 (penthemimeral caesura+tetrasyllable), 1292; what follows in the *stasimon* at v. 694~707 is ia+sp: ⏑ – ⏑ – – –. The first verse of the *parodos* of *Philoctetes* merges perfectly with the following strophe through the presence of enjambment: yet, even this opening iambic trimeter (v. 135) 'modulates from the spoken verse of dialogue to sung verse; the corresponding verse in antistrophe α. (150) is perhaps more fully lyric, because it lacks the normal caesura of spoken trimeters at position 5 or 7': Schein 2013, 148; cf. also *Philoctetes* 676~691; the lyric nature of the opening, isolated iambic trimeter in Eur. *Heracl.* 892 is imparted by the *synapheia*. On lyric iambics in general see Denniston 1936; on *Ajax* cf. Stanford 1963, 249–50; on the undetermined execution of isolated iambic trimeters in lyric contexts cf. Gentili/Lomiento 2003, 137.

[84] Goldhill 2013a, 102. Goldhill's analysis of the interplay between lyric and iambic voices in the Sophoclean chorus focuses on sections where despite the certain shift in metre, the intonation of the voice performing the shift between speech and song nonetheless remains uncertain, as for instance in *Aj.* 364–72 (if the change of metre is abrupt, 'how abrupt is the change of [Ajax's] voice' at vv. 367~382?: p. 113). On our *stasimon* see p. 115 (= Goldhill 2012, 96).

6 Conclusions

To summarize briefly, we have attempted to examine three significant case studies, which we should note are all part of Sophocles' early production.[85] The first, the *Antigone* passage, shows how Sophocles inserts generic flavours in his lyrics and forces the spectators to follow them through obscure paths after a clearer and allusive starting point. The other examples, from *Women of Trachis* and *Ajax*, invite us to observe a complex and detailed recasting of conventional components as they are transformed into new, specific literary shapes. In each of the three cases, the process we have observed is not unconscious or naïve.

The formal *schemata* operating under the cover of the theatrical adaptation are ritually characterized, and refer to specific ritual practices via conventional language: Sophocles effectively confronts a tradition, partially respecting and partially challenging the expectations it creates. His entirely new and non-traditional *lexis* challenges a widespread poetic as well as religious and cultic repertoire consisting of a shareable and particular *langue* and specific stylistic trademarks.[86] In these beginnings, Sophocles transforms an already familiar idiom into an original and utterly brilliant creation: the difference between the starting point and his final result is one of the finest signs of his greatness as a poet.[87]

---

[85] On the formal features of Sophocles' later lyric style (which implies preference for monodies and/or lyric dialogues, and less frequent choral songs), see Esposito 1996 with Csapo 1999–2000, 407–14, Cerri 2007, Mastronarde 2010, 148–9, Rutherford 2012, 277–82, 43; on the less 'amplified' language, the less formal lyrics, and a greater simplicity in his later production, see Earp 1944, 102–19, 156–8. In his latest dramas, Sophocles is not completely aloof from other genres' traditional forms: cf. the paeanic parodos of the *OT* 151–215, with Swift 2010, 77–81, the short hymns to the Earth and to Hypnos – a lullaby – in the *Philoctetes* (vv. 391–5 and 827–32) with Rodighiero 2012, 154–5 and 148–9, and the prayer to Hades in the *OC* 1556–78.

[86] Useful considerations on tragedy's challenging a certain idea of (the epic) tradition in Cantilena 2012, 160 and *passim*. On the tradition as a 'poetic langue' and a system of literary conventions, motifs, and expressions, see also Conte 1986, 37.

[87] See Said 1975, xxiii: 'in short, beginning is *making* or *producing difference*; but – and here is the great fascination in the subject – difference which is the result of combining the already-familiar with the fertile novelty of human work in language.'

Anastasia Lazani
Constructing Chorality in *Prometheus Bound*: The Poetic Background of Divine Choruses in Tragedy

The chorus of *Prometheus Bound* consists of the Oceanides, the daughters of Oceanus and Tethys. A female chorus is a very common choice for a fifth-century tragedy. This is, however, not an ordinary female chorus. The divine nature of the chorus of *Prometheus Bound* makes it, along with Aeschylus' *Eumenides*, the only tragic divine chorus to have survived. In addition, it is the only chorus of young, peaceful divinities that has come down to us (in contrast to the horrific, threatening and disruptive Aeschylean Furies), which gives it a unique place among extant tragedies.

While divine choruses have a long tradition of choral performance in pre-dramatic poetry,[1] they seem to have been significantly less popular in Attic tragedy.[2] This makes the chorus of *Prometheus Bound* an invaluable example, and the ideal ground for exploring the use and presentation of divine choruses in drama: both their function within the tragedy and the rich poetic tradition that informs their background. The fact that the attention of modern scholarship has for long focused on the authorship of the play has often led to an oversight of other issues, and the construction of its chorality in relation to other lyric forms is one of them.[3]

I would like to thank my thesis supervisor Chris Carey for his invaluable help at various stages of writing of this chapter. My special thanks also to the participants of the *Paths of Song* conference (UCL 2013) and the editors of the volume for their most helpful feedback and remarks.

1 E.g., Hom. *Od.* 24.60; *Hymn. Hom. Ap.* 194–6; Hes. *Theog.* 24–8; Pind. *Ol.* 4.9; Sapph. fr. 103.7–9 Voigt.
2 Although, as always, accidents of survival may be generating a biased outlook, a survey of the titles and surviving fragments of the three tragedians yield little evidence in favour of an extensive presence of divinities in the choruses of fifth-century Attic drama. Sophoclean and Euripidean titles defy any reasonable attempt to detect a divine chorus, but for Aeschylus the figures may have been relatively higher: apart from *Eumenides* and the fragmentary *Nereides*, *Heliades* too may have featured a divine chorus, and so do *Lemniai* (unless the correct title is *Lemnioi*), or even *Toxotides*. *Prometheus Lyomenos* could conceivably have featured a chorus of Titans.
3 The Aeschylean authorship of the play, although never doubted in antiquity, was first questioned by Westphal in 1856, but his thesis found little support (it was scornfully rejected by Schmid in 1929) until 1977, when Griffith argued in detail on a range of grounds for a non-Aeschylean authorship. Among the more recent scholars who reject the play's authenticity are West

In this chapter, I will focus on the choral parts of the tragedy, especially the *parodos*, and I will argue that the rich poetic background, and in particular the recurring resonances of *partheneia* inform the presentation of the chorus and the audience's understanding of it. This analysis will, therefore, shed further light on our understanding of tragedy's relation with non-dramatic genre and will tentatively offer an early *testimonium* for Alcman's presence in fifth-century Attic drama and, beyond that, in Athenian culture as a whole.

In the following pages, I will first look at the emphasis on the supernatural nature of the chorus that the *parodos* creates, which emerges as a common feature of divine choruses in Attic tragedy. I will then analyze how the divine nature of the chorus is intertwined with features that they share with maidens of *partheneia* and other choral poetry. Finally, I will argue that the chorality of the chorus is based on the chorus' dual identity as divine creatures and as maidens, which is largely achieved by the rich associations both groups have in non-dramatic poetry.

1 Supernatural Entrances

Owing to the setup of the opening scene of *Prometheus*, the *parodos* of the chorus takes place under rather unusual dramatic circumstances: at the start of the play Hephaestus enters, accompanied by Kratos and Bia (as a *kophon prosopon*), and fastens Prometheus onto the rock, carrying out Zeus' orders. By the end of the scene, the main character of the play is fastened onto the rock with unbreakable bonds, unable not only to escape, but also to move (54–80, notice the 'adamantine wedge' that Hephaestus drives through Prometheus' chest after 65/6). This position of Prometheus is exploited by Aeschylus to introduce two important characteristics of the chorus, before the audience even sees the dancers: their flying and their ethereal scent. As will be shown, both elements are crucial

---

1979, who puts forward the very attractive, if unprovable, hypothesis that the play and its respective trilogy was the work of Aeschylus' son Euphorion, Bees 1993, Lefèvre 2003. So inclined is also Taplin 1977, 240–75 and appendix. Scholars who argue that our present evidence does not constitute sufficient evidence for the Aeschylean authorship of the play include, more persuasively than others, Herington 1970, and, more recently, Pattoni 1987, mainly on metrical grounds, and Podlecki 2005, 192–200. Lloyd-Jones 2002, 19 and 2003, 70 too expresses tentatively his inclination to accept the Aeschylean authorship. I am inclined to think that the play has been persuasively shown to be of non-Aeschylean authorship. As Winnington-Ingram 1983, 175–6 puts it: 'For un-Aeschylean features it is often possible to think up explanations: as they multiply, the question arises in the mind how many special hypotheses one should allow oneself!'.

for the construction of the choral persona. They highlight the supernatural nature of the maidens, introduce emphasis on their physicality, direct attention to their dance, while they also trigger Prometheus' worry and thus initiate comments on the relationship between the chorus and the protagonist.

When the chorus first approaches, Prometheus, now alone on the stage, notices them by their scent and the noise of their wings and comments:

ἆ ἆ ἔα ἔα.
τίς ἀχώ, τίς ὀδμὰ προσέπτα μ' ἀφεγγής,
θεόσυτος, ἢ βρότειος, ἢ κεκραμένη;
ἵκετο τερμόνιόν <τις> ἐπὶ πάγον
πόνων ἐμῶν θεωρός, ἢ τί δὴ θέλων;
...
φεῦ φεῦ, τί ποτ' αὖ κινάθισμα κλύω
πέλας οἰωνῶν; αἰθὴρ δ' ἐλαφραῖς
πτερύγων ῥιπαῖς ὑποσυρίζει.
πᾶν μοι φοβερὸν τὸ προσέρπον.[4]

(*PV* 114–27)

Hey, what is that?
What sound, what scent flew upon me, unseen,
sent from the gods, from mortals, or from both together?
Has someone come to this rock at the end of the world
to watch my sufferings–or what do they want?
...
Ah, ah, what is this rustling sound of birds
that I now hear close by? The air is whistling
with the light beating of wings.
Whatever approaches makes me fearful!

It is not uncommon in Greek tragedy for a character to catch sight of the approaching chorus before the dancers enter the acting area and become visible to the audience. In these instances, the character who has spotted the chorus from afar singles out the feature that caught his or her attention and comments on it, thus announcing at the same time the choral entrance. The feature that foretells the entrance of the chorus is always one that will emerge as thematically prominent in the course of the play. Since the speaking character mentions this feature before the audience have a chance to perceive it themselves, the audience is implicitly directed to notice the feature, interpret it accordingly, or even be surprised if things take an unexpected turn. For instance, the black clothes of

---

4 In this passage I follow the text as printed by Sommerstein 2008a, vol.I. All other tragic texts are from OCT. All translations are adapted from the latest Loeb editions, unless otherwise stated.

the chorus in Aeschylus' *Choephori*, which Orestes spots from afar, serve to thematize the state of the *oikos* of the Atreidai, which is trapped in grief and unable to move forward.[5] They also play with ideas of light and darkness, which are prominent throughout the *Oresteia*, and prepare us for the central *kommos*-scene around the grave of Agamemnon.

In *Prometheus*, the technique is particularly apt, since Prometheus is, as mentioned, tied and therefore unable to move. As a result, he perceives the approaching chorus through senses other than sight.[6] Now the audience, before they even see the chorus, knows it is an unusual one: it has a pleasant smell and is approaching by flying. Both are characteristics not associated with a chorus elsewhere in tragedy. Pleasant scent is never a mark of an approaching chorus in surviving Greek tragedy, or, for that matter, something that features prominently in Greek tragedy in general.[7] A pleasant aroma is, however, associated with the divine both in tragedy and elsewhere: Hera in the *Iliad*, for example, anoints herself with sweet-smelling ambrosial oil to seduce Zeus (here the smell points both to divinity and to erotic intentions).[8] More similarly to the chorus of *Prometheus*, an aromatic smell is also what reveals Artemis' divine epiphany to Hippolytus in Euripides' eponymous play.[9]

Already before the entrance of the chorus, therefore, the text is inviting us to see the imminent *parodos* as an impressive, multisensory spectacle. The exact manner of the entrance is disputed, but an entry on foot, imitating a flying movement, is compatible with the text and the physical resources of the Theatre of Dionysus[10] and would provide the impressive opening we are lead to expect. Irrespective of how one decides on this, however, repeated references to wings and

---

5 <ἔα>
τί χρῆμα λεύσσω; τίς ποθ' ἥδ' ὁμήγυρις
στείχει γυναικῶν φάρεσιν μελαγχίμοις
πρέπουσα; ποίᾳ ξυμφορᾷ προσεικάσω; (Aesch. *Cho*. 10–13, text as printed by Sommerstein 2008b, vol. II).
6 For the possibility that the chorus enters on the roof of the stage building, see n.10.
7 Unpleasant smell is perhaps slightly more common, cf. Soph. *Ant*. 412 (the decaying body of Polyneices); Soph. *Phil*. 876 and 890–1 (of Philoctetes' infected wound).
8 See, e.g. Hom. *Il*. 14.170–4.
9 ἔα
ὦ θεῖον ὀσμῆς πνεῦμα· καὶ γὰρ ἐν κακοῖς
ὢν ᾐσθόμην σου κἀνεκουφίσθην δέμας·
ἔστ' ἐν τόποισι τοισίδ' Ἄρτεμις θεά (Eur. *Hipp*. 1391–3).
10 A whole chorus would be too big a group to fit onto the *ekkyklēma*, and the business of pushing them onto the stage would mar the spectacle. Likewise, the rooftop of the stage building is better kept for Oceanus, rather than for a large crowd of twelve to fifteen dancers. See Griffith 1983, 109 for a neat survey of the different possibilities of staging.

flying suggest that the chorus were at least supposed to have flown into the acting area. A flying chorus is not found elsewhere in surviving tragedy,[11] and it is used here, in combination with the exquisite aroma to create a composite expression of the superhuman.[12] It also, as will be shown below, draws attention to the movement of the chorus, and therefore to their dancing.[13]

A *parodos* highlighting the supernatural nature of the chorus seems to have been a common technique when a divine chorus was used in tragedy, as a brief examination of *Eumenides* (our only other extant divine chorus) and the fragmentary *Nereides* will show. The Erinyes of Aeschylus' *Eumenides* differ in almost all respects from the Oceanides in *Prometheus*. Their appearance, however, is also other-worldly; so much so that it causes horror to the Pythia (and, if one were to believe the *Life of Aeschylus*, had a similar effect on members of the theatre audience):[14]

ἦ δεινὰ λέξαι, δεινὰ δ' ὀφθαλμοῖς δρακεῖν,
...
ὁρῶ δ' ἐπ' ὀμφαλῷ μὲν ἄνδρα θεομυσῆ
ἕδραν ἔχοντα προστρόπαιον, αἵματι
στάζοντα χεῖρας καὶ νεοσπαδὲς ξίφος
ἔχοντ' ἐλαίας θ' ὑψιγέννητον κλάδον,
λήνει μεγίστῳ σωφρόνως ἐστεμμένον,
ἀργῆτι μαλλῷ· τῇδε γὰρ τρανῶς ἐρῶ.
πρόσθεν δὲ τἀνδρὸς τοῦδε θαυμαστὸς λόχος
εὕδει γυναικῶν ἐν θρόνοισιν ἥμενος.
οὔτοι γυναῖκας, ἀλλὰ Γοργόνας λέγω,
οὐδ' αὖτε Γοργείοισιν εἰκάσω τύποις.
εἶδόν ποτ' ἤδη Φινέως γεγραμμένας
δεῖπνον φερούσας· ἄπτεροί γε μὴν ἰδεῖν
αὗται, μέλαιναι δ', ἐς τὸ πᾶν βδελύκτροποι·
ῥέγκουσι δ' οὐ πλατοῖσι φυσιάμασιν·
ἐκ δ' ὀμμάτων λείβουσι δυσφιλῆ λίβα·
...
τὸ φῦλον οὐκ ὄπωπα τῆσδ' ὁμιλίας

---

11 In Aristophanes' *Clouds* flying is of course also part of the chorus' supernatural persona (see *Nub.* 266, 277–81, 289–90; 323; they are described as σμῆνος by Socrates (*Nub.* 297); cf. Strepsiades' joke that his soul πεπότηται (*Nub.* 319 'has taken flight') because of their approach.
12 For the effect of foreboding that the rustling of wings could create at this stage, see p. 168.
13 See p. 174.
14 τινὲς δέ φασιν ἐν τῇ ἐπιδείξει τῶν Εὐμενίδων σποράδην εἰσαγαγόντα τὸν χορὸν τοσοῦτον ἐκπλῆξαι τὸν δῆμον ὥστε τὰ μὲν νήπια ἐκψῦξαι, τὰ δὲ ἔμβρυα ἐξαμβλωθῆναι (A1.30–2 *TrGF*[3]). Despite the apocryphal nature of the story, the comment does reflect the striking dramaturgy of *Eumenides*.

> οὐδ' ἥτις αἶα τοῦτ' ἐπεύχεται γένος
> τρέφουσ' ἀνατεὶ μὴ μεταστένειν πόνον.
>
> (Aesch. *Eum.* 34–59)
>
> Things truly fearful to speak of, fearful to behold with the eyes,
> ...
> In front of this man an extraordinary band
> of women is sleeping sitting on chairs
> – no, I shouldn't call them women, but Gorgons;
> but then I can't liken their form to that of Gorgons either.
> I did once see before now, in a painting, female creatures
> robbing Phineus of his dinner; these ones, though, clearly have no wings,
> and they're black and utterly nauseating.
> They're pumping out snores that one doesn't dare come near,
> and dripping a loathsome drip from their eyes.
> ...
> And I have never seen the tribe to which this company belongs,
> nor do I know what country boasts that it has reared this race
> without harm to itself and does not regret the labour of doing so.

The intra-dramatic focalization (through different senses) in the description of the chorus in both plays, *Eumenides* and *Prometheus*, generates a sense of foreboding. In the former the impression is created by the sheer horror entailed in the description of the Pythia; in the latter more obliquely by Prometheus' helplessness and the audience's knowledge that Zeus will send an eagle to eat out Prometheus' liver.[15] When the spectators hear of an approaching flying creature, they are bound to think of the vulture. This will heighten the effect of relief when they will instead be presented with a friendly female chorus, which will function throughout as the foil to the troubled and violent community of Olympian gods, who have recently established themselves after a fierce struggle against the older generation of gods. While the two choral entrances, in *Prometheus* and in *Eumenides*, are in the end almost antithetical in effect, they share a concern, though in different ways, to stress the outlandish or exotic and supernatural.[16] Though we are necessarily drawing conclusions based on a small surviving fraction of the

---

[15] The eagle is not mentioned until late in the play (1022), but the myth is already treated by Hesiod (Hes. *Theog.* 521–4), and Prometheus, as the patron god of potters, was more prominent a divine figure in Athens than in the rest of Greece.

[16] The scholiast's remark on the Pythia's speech may also be picking up on this emphasis: πάντα μηνύει τοῖς θεαταῖς, οὐχ ὡς διηγουμένη τὰ ὑπὸ τὴν σκηνήν – τοῦτο γὰρ νεωτερικὸν <καὶ> Εὐριπίδειον – ὑπὸ δὲ τῆς ἐκπλήξεως τὰ θορυβήσαντα αὐτὴν καταμηνύουσα φιλοτέχνως. (Σ Aesch. *Eum.*1a Smith).

original dramatic output, an entrance that stressed their non-human nature must have been common for divine choruses.

The parallel of the fragmentary Aeschylean *Nereides* corroborates this:

δελφινηρὸν πεδίον πόντου
διαμειψάμεναι

(Aesch. fr. 150 *TrGF*³)

Having crossed the expanse
of the dolphin-bearing sea

The anapaestic lines may have plausibly been delivered by the chorus in the *parodos*.

Despite vase representations of the Nereides riding on dolphins (or other sea creatures, such as sea-horses),[17] in the play the dolphins were probably no more than a reference to the Nereides' usual abode in line with the usual dramatic practice of choruses who have just arrived to mention their origin or journey. However, the association of the members of the entering chorus with the sea, a natural environment that is wild and inhospitable to humans, ties in with the emphasis on the superhuman that we saw in the case of both the Oceanides and the Erinyes. Placing verbal emphasis on the exotic nature of divinity is dramaturgically useful, since it is difficult to represent divine status visually beyond the use of physical markers. All these otherworldly features emphasize the exotic aspects of a divine chorus and their removal from normal experience.

2 The Maidens of the Dramatic Chorus

There is, however, something of a paradox in this chorus. The emphasis which Prometheus' words placed on the divine attributes of the Oceanides is downplayed by the chorus themselves when they speak their first, introductory, lines in response to Prometheus' anxious enquiries as to their identity. What they now emphasize is a different set of aspects of their existence, which brings them closer to the maidens we know from non-dramatic choral lyric:

---

[17] The majority of pictorial evidence of the Nereides listed in *LIMC* present them as riding on some sea-creature or animal, though it is possible that other figures meant to represent the Nereides cannot be recognised as such precisely because they are not equipped with such a creature.

> μηδὲν φοβηθῇς· φιλία γὰρ ἅδε τάξις
> πτερύγων θοαῖς ἁμίλλαις
> προσέβα τόνδε πάγον, πατρῴας
> μόγις παρειποῦσα φρένας·
> κραιπνοφόροι δέ μ' ἔπεμψαν αὖραι.
> κτύπου γὰρ ἀχὼ χάλυβος διῆξεν ἄντρων
> μυχόν, ἐκ δ' ἔπληξέ μου τὰν θεμερῶπιν αἰδῶ·
> σύθην δ' ἀπέδιλος ὄχῳ πτερωτῷ.

(*PV* 128–35)

> Don't be afraid: our friendly band
> has come to this rock
> on swift, striving wings,
> having with difficulty
> persuaded our father to consent.
> The swift breezes have borne and sped me here;
> for the sound of stroke on steel penetrated to the depths
> of my cave, and shocked my grave-faced modesty out of me;
> and I hurried here, unshod, on a winged cart.

Next to the supernatural elements of flying, wings and winged chariots (πτερύγων θοαῖς ἁμίλλαις and ὄχῳ πτερωτῷ), the chorus accentuate their maidenly nature: they use the word μυχός (134) for their dwellings. This is a word with different nuances which reflects the ambiguity of their nature. It is highly suited to their abode deep in the sea. But it is also a word used of the recesses of a building and so, within a world which conceives gender in spatial terms, may also suggest the 'women's part of the house'.[18] The chorus stress that they need their father's permission (πατρῴας μόγις παρειποῦσα φρένας) in order to 'leave the house', and they only shed their maidenly *aidōs* because they were struck by the intensity of the noise of the hammer (133–4). Tragic choruses do not always justify their entrance. Female choruses, however, as well as female characters, display frequently a tendency to explain their presence as the result of an emotion, as is the case here.[19] Rather than being goddesses aware of the conflict between old and new gods, and despite the emphasis on their exotic nature, the chorus seem to be timid maidens, blissfully confined within their paternal *oikos*, and in need of the parental permission in order to frequent a public

---

[18] Griffith 1983, *ad loc.*
[19] Cf., e.g. Soph. *El.* 312–3, 388; Eur. *Med.* 131ff.; Eur. *Tro.* 153ff.

place. This plays on both the realities of female life, and the literary conventions which partly reflect these.[20]

This assimilation of the chorus of female deities to the status of human *parthenoi* lays emphasis on their position as virgins. Although this is at one level a natural consequence of their dramatic identity (they are, after all, maidens), one should bear in mind that emphasis both on gender and on their status as maidens is one of the distinguishing features of *partheneia* in contrast with other lyric forms. This is particularly significant in the context of a tragedy: Attic theatre constantly engages in a creative dialogue with non-dramatic lyric forms and the constant presence of choral song in civic performances sensitises the audience to the markers of genre.[21] This applies not only to forms that were well represented in the Athenian ritual calendar, but also to forms that were remote from contemporary Athenian experience and encountered directly only by theoric groups from Athens at major panhellenic sanctuaries or by Athenian visitors to other Greek states. Here one has to bear in mind that, though the modern audience meets the lyric poets as texts, there was a widespread use of lyric poetry both in entertainment and in education long after the first performance and much lyric poetry seems to have travelled orally, irrespective of whether it was composed with the aid of writing and irrespective of whether there were texts in existence. This interest in lyric song seems to have been shared by all sectors of society even in democratic Athens, to judge by the widespread references to lyric song in comedy, which is frequently a reliable indicator of Athenian cultural awareness. All this means that points of intersection with the *partheneion* would be appreciated by at least some, and perhaps by many, in the original audience.[22]

In the following pages I will argue that parthenaic songs are thematically pertinent to *Prometheus Bound*, and that an examination of the recurrent parthenaic allusions can highlight how dramatists employed the audience's familiarity

---

20 Cf. another group of maidens, the Danaides in the *parodos* of Aeschylus' *Suppliants* (11–18), where the maiden chorus also name their father as the one who conceived of their flight and planned it. The relationship of the Danaides with their father has been extensively treated as one that is similar in many respects to that of a chorus and its *chorēgos*, see recently, Kavoulaki 2011 and Rawles in this volume.
21 The definition of lyric genres is a notoriously intricate task. See also below p. 172 specifically for the distinctive features of *partheneia*.
22 This is of course not to say that meaning would be constructed solely through the intergeneric allusiveness, here or in other uses of lyric song in tragedy, but rather that meaning is enriched by such allusion.

with non-dramatic lyric to construct or enrich the meaning of their own work.[23] In the case of maiden songs, the task of recognising allusions is further complicated by the fact that only a tiny amount of poetry has come down to us. Ancient sources seem to oscillate between understanding *partheneion* broadly as a song which was sung by *parthenoi* and had permeable generic boundaries, or treating it explicitly as a separate genre. Despite the limited evidence, however, and the indeterminacy of the ancient sources, as Swift has shown, an examination of surviving parthenaic poetry does yield a number of features that seem to be distinctive in parthenaic songs:[24] the *partheneion* placed particular emphasis on the gender and status of its maiden performers, and went so far as to mention by name a number of them. In the context of a disciplined and ordered performance under the guidance of a *chorēgos*, the maiden song highlighted through conventional imagery the female sexuality of the maidens and the sexual desirability of the dancers. At the same time it explored the anxieties of the transition from maidenhood to married life and managed the sexuality of the maidens with caveats and advice about proper behaviour and appropriate unions. Some of these features the *partheneion* shared with wedding songs. There are, however, significant differences between *partheneia* and wedding songs, the most important being that they deal with two neighbouring yet distinct phases in a woman's life: the *partheneion* focuses on the liminal state in preparation for a transition, while a wedding song celebrates the transition itself.[25]

The emphasis that maiden songs lay on the transitional state of the *parthenoi* and the sexual desirability of the maidens, which hints to their future marriage, is thematically particularly relevant to the play. Marriage, and more importantly tensions surrounding, and leading up to, marriage lie at the heart of *Prometheus Bound:* Prometheus holds a secret about Zeus's marriage that may destroy Zeus; marriage is what connects the chorus with Prometheus, since the Oceanides are sisters of Hesione, Prometheus' wife; they themselves bring up their role in the wedding ceremony (555–60, see below p. 179); finally, the

---

[23] The relation of tragedy with other lyric genres has been extensively studied in recent years (for a recent systematic treatment, focusing, however, more on Sophocles and Euripides than Aeschylus see Swift 2010).
[24] For a careful survey of the evidence and a working definition of the *partheneia* and their distinctive features, see Swift 2010, 173–89.
[25] The two genres would differ, among other things, in the occasion of their performance, as well as their emphasis on a group vs. an individual (the bride). Battezzato 2011 in reviewing Swift 2010 questions the ability of scholarship to draw a clear line between *partheneia* and wedding songs, given the affinities of the genres and the scanty evidence we possess, but as analyzed above, despite potential similarities, we have good reasons to think that the differences in scope, emphasis and performative occasion would be substantial.

story of Io, one of the central figures in the play, is the story of an attempted marriage (with Zeus), a long and painful maidenhood and is predicted to be eventually the story of a painless and successful union (848–52).

The text increases our receptivity of this reading by highlighting the chorality of the Oceanides. Already in their first words the chorus describe themselves, strikingly, as a τάξις. *Taxis* is used to denote an orderly arrangement, often of a military nature. For all Greek choral lyric, including maiden choruses, order is a central preoccupation (as it is a defining feature of chorality for the Greeks).[26] It is, therefore, no accident that the very first self-reference of our chorus is φιλία […] τάξις (128–9), 'a friendly formation'.[27] Amidst the noise and commotion caused by their entrance, the chorus carefully highlight their discipline and bond as a formal group, based on their *aidōs* (134) and their habitual obedience to their father's word (130–1). Their bond is of course initially due to the fact that they are sisters.[28] The members of divine choruses in myth invariably display an emphatically collective and homogeneous character,[29] which is often evident in their name.[30] This trait is used in this play, among other things, to create a sense of community and provide Prometheus with a disciplined sympathetic audience.[31] In selecting a group of divine sisters as the chorus of the play, and in associating their singing with the public community event that is a performance of a maiden song, the poet presents the chorus as a healthy micro-community within the violent and disrupted divine universe of the play.

This accumulated emphasis on chorality is by no means inevitable, since not all tragic choruses draw attention to their choral activity, even if often the plot has them perform choral activities in the course of the play.[32] Our chorus of Oce-

---

26 See, e.g. Pl. *Leg.* 665a. Cf. also Power 2011, 87–8.
27 The 'swift eagerness' or 'competition' of their wings (129, text cited on p. 170) could either denote an attempt of the maidens to outstrip each other, or simply their haste. If pointing to an element of friendly strife, this too could be reminiscent of Alcman's images of competition (cf. fr. 1.50 ff. *PMGF*, though the meaning of the passage is disputed).
28 Cf. Alcman's τᾶς ἐμᾶς ἀνεψιᾶς (fr. 1.52 *PMGF*).
29 Which may be a bond of origin, a geographical or family association. In the case of real-life maiden choruses the bond is often one of common age and social status, see Calame 1997b, 31.
30 Calame 1997b, 31 stresses the suffixes -ιδ- and -αδ-, used to denote subordination or geographical association. In our case, the Oceanides derive their name directly from their father Oceanus.
31 In a society where family is the central social unit and marriage seen as an institution that strengthens an *oikos* by creating connections with another family, a woman's marriage necessarily affected the members of her paternal family as well. In *Prometheus* this results in a chorus that views the hero sympathetically. For an exploration of sisterhood in tragedy, and an antithetical case of sisterhood and marriage ending badly, see Coo 2013 on Sophocles' *Tereus*.
32 Cf. Henrichs' influential article on choral self-referentiality (Henrichs 1994–1995).

anides will not use the term χορός of themselves; they will, however, employ in the *parodos* terms used elsewhere in Greek literature with reference to choral activity, and will, later in the play, refer explicitly to choral activities they themselves performed in the past at Prometheus' wedding.[33] The lightness of a dancer's step is a particularly desirable feature. In *Prometheus* the idea of lightness is taken to the extreme as the dancers actually fly.[34] This is almost a visualization of the common *topos* of the ideal, light choral step, in that here it is – supposedly – literally flying, that is, as light as it can get.[35]

Feet are further dwelled upon. The chorus say that they came without wearing their sandals, ἀπέδιλος (135), expressing together with σύθην (135, 'I/we rushed') their hurry to find out what was going on. For the idea of not having time to pause in order to get dressed we find parallels both in earlier and in later texts.[36] Sandals and words with -*pedilon* as the second compound are used elsewhere in lyric and tragedy,[37] and Pindar draws attention to Andaisistrota's sandals in his parthenaic fragment.[38] The word ἀπέδιλος however, is only found elsewhere in Alcman's first *partheneion*[39] (there qualifying ἀλκά, perhaps meant to denote hurry in that case too).[40] In this context of emphatic parthenaic chorality, and given the rarity of the word, the echo may be suggestive of a deliberate gesture specifically towards the parthenaic poetry of Alcman.[41]

---

33 See below, p. 179.
34 ... καὶ νῦν ἐλαφρῷ
ποδὶ κραιπνόσυτον θᾶκον προλιποῦσ'
αἰθέρα θ' ἁγνὸν πόρον οἰωνῶν,
ὀκριοέσσῃ χθονὶ τῇδε πελῶ (*PV* 278–81).
35 Cf., e.g. Ar. *Lys.* 1304. A delicate gait seems to have been associated particularly with women (and barbarians) in contrast to males in Ancient Greece, see Bremmer 1991, 20–1.
36 Cf., e.g. Hes. *Op.* 345: γείτονες ἄζωστοι ἔκιον; Pind. *Nem.* 1.20: καὶ γὰρ αὐτὰ ποσσὶν ἀπέπλος ὀρού/σαισ' ἀπὸ στρωμνᾶς ὅμως ἄμυνεν ὕβριν κνωδάλων; Theoc. *Id.* 24.36: ἄνστα, μηδὲ πόδεσσι τεοῖς ὑπὸ σάνδαλα θείῃς; Ap. Rhod. *Argon.* 4.43; Bion 1.21; Non. *Dion.* 5.407.
37 Though most frequently the compounds reproduce or variate the Homeric χρυσοπέδιλος. E.g. *Od.* 11.604; Hes. *Theog.* 454; Pind. fr. 94b.70, fr. 88, 6 S-M; *Hymn. Hom. Herm.* 57; Sapph. fr. 103.13 Voigt; Eur. *IA* 1042.
38 βαίνοισα πεδίλοις (Pind. fr. 94b.70 S-M).
39 Unless Lobel's reading απέ]δ{ε}ιλ[ος of the Pindaric fr. 169a.36 is correct.
40 Tsantsanoglou 2012, 18–19 has recently challenged the supplement. If our understanding of the passage as one resonating with parthenaic echoes is correct, however, it could perhaps weigh in favour of the 'traditional' reading ἀπέδιλος.
41 A similar cognate is used by Callimachus in his *Hymn to Demeter*: ὡς δ' ἀπεδίλωτοι καὶ ἀνάμπυκες ἄστυ πατεῦμες (Callim. *Hymn* 6.124). Given Callimachus' tendency to allude to archaic lyric models in constructing his own public poetry, it is not impossible that he is drawing from Alcman, or using a common archaic image. The same applies to the Theocritean passage of

In contrast to ethereal wings, reference to sandals focuses attention on a more pragmatic and physical detail, and to a body part, feet, that constitutes a traditional *topos* of female beauty. The word ἀπέδιλος may be drawn from non-dramatic poetry, and even allude specifically to Alcman's *partheneion*. Significantly what it does is draw attention to the physicality of the chorus. Emphasis on the physicality of the chorus members is another stable feature of maiden choruses, and the poet of *Prometheus* is drawing on the parthenaic understanding of the chorus to construct his own: a combination of timid maidens of real-life, ethereal nymphs of the myth, and performers invested with the authority of the community.

Mention of feet specifically, which seem to have a powerful status as sensual stimuli, does indeed recur in Alcman/maiden songs, as in the following fragment (see also further below fr. 3.10 'delicate feet', fr. 3.70 'with long feet'):

οὐ γὰρ ἀ κ[α]λλίσφυρος
Ἀγησιχ[ό]ρ[α] πάρ'αὐτεῖ

(Alcm. fr. 1.78–9 *PMGF*)

For is not fair-ankled Hagesichora present here?

Hair is also repeatedly the focal point of the poet's attention to physical detail, especially blonde hair as in the following fragments (1.70 'Nanno's hair', 3.64 'hair of the virgins' in the fragments cited further below):

... ἀ δὲ χαίτα
τᾶς ἐμᾶς ἀνεψιᾶς
Ἀγησιχόρας ἐπανθεῖ
χρυσὸς [ὡ]ς ἀκήρατος·
τό τ' ἀργύριον πρόσωπον,
διαφάδαν τί τοι λέγω;
Ἀγησιχόρα μὲν αὕτα·

(Alcm. fr. 1.51–7 *PMGF*)

... but the hair of my cousin Hagesichora blooms like pure gold,
and her silvery face– why do I tell you openly?
This is Agesichora.

... ἀ δ' ἐπιμέρωι ξανθᾶι κομίσκαι

(Alcm. fr. 1.101 *PMGF*)

---

n.36 above. The ritual associations of going unshod or letting one's hair down are often noted, and the fictional plot of tragedy makes it possible to combine them with the 'realities' of the dramatic situation.

... and she with her delightful blonde hair

ἆχι μά]λιστα κόμ[αν ξ]ανθὰν τινάξω·
 ]. σχ[ἀπ]αλοὶ πόδες

(Alcm. fr. 3.9–10 PMGF)

where I will toss forcefully my blonde hair;
...soft feet

Reference to trappings of the performance and the maidens' outfit (such as girdles and jewellery), and other details of their physical appearance, such as the face, and in particular the eyes, are also employed in constructing an image of harmonious and delicate aesthetic beauty, as well as erotic desirability:[42]

οὔτε γάρ τι πορφύρας
τόσσος κόρος ὥστ' ἀμύναι,
οὔτε ποικίλος δράκων
παγχρύσιος, οὐδὲ μίτρα
Λυδία, νεανίδων
ἰανογ[λ]εφάρων ἄγαλμα,
οὐδὲ ταὶ Ναννῶς κόμαι

(Alcm. fr. 1.64–70 PMGF)

For the abundance of purple is not sufficient for protection,
nor the intricate, all golden snake-bracelet,
no, nor the Lydian headband, ornament of the dark-eyed girls,
nor the hair of Nanno

Ἀ[σ]τυμέλοισα δέ μ' οὐδὲν ἀμείβεται,
ἀλλὰ τὸ]ν πυλεῶν' ἔχοισα
[ὥ] τις αἰγλά[ε]ντος ἀστήρ
ὠρανῶ διαιπετής
ἢ χρύσιον ἔρνος ἢ ἁπαλὸ[ν ψίλ]ον
 .˙.]ν
   ]. διέβα ταναοῖς πο[σί·]

(Alcm. fr. 3.64–70 PMGF)

But Astymeloisa is not answering me;
no, holding the garland, like a shiny star in the bright sky
or a golden branch or soft down,
she passed through with her long feet;...

---

42 For the emphasis on the female gender of the performers see Clark 1996. For the sensuality of Alcman's fragments see Swift 2010, 176. Lardinois 2011, 169–70 comments on the surprisingly sexual language used by the maidens and for the maidens, in the framework of the *parrhēsia* granted to female choruses in certain ritual contexts.

While the tone of Pindar's surviving parthenaic poetry is overall less sensual than Alcman's, the attention to physical detail relating to the virginal nature of the performers is clear here too. There is reference to the physical appearance of the performers as well as to the paraphernalia of the performance ('tender hands', 'maidenly head', 'sandals', 'robe', 'branch of laurel', 'garlands).

ἀλλὰ ζωσαμένα τε πέπλον ὠκέως
  χερσίν τ' ἐν μαλακαῖσιν ὄρπακ' ἀγλαόν
δάφνας ὀχέοισα πάν-
  δοξον Αἰολάδα σταθμόν
υἱοῦ τε Παγώνδα
ὑμνήσω στεφάνοισι θάλ-
  λοισα παρθένιον κάρα

(Pind. fr. 94b.6–12 S-M)

But tying up my robe quickly,
and carrying in my soft hands a bright branch of laurel,
I will sing of the all-glorious house of Aioladas
and his son Pagondas,
my maidenly head flourishing with garlands.

It has been shown above how the *parodos* subtly employs parthenaic echoes as part of its scene-setting. These features are not, however, confined to the *parodos*. The youthful beauty of the girls in *Prometheus Bound* is stressed elsewhere in the play as well:

δακρυσίστακτον [δ'] ἀπ' ὄσσων
ῥαδινῶν λειβομένα ῥέος παρειὰν
νοτίοις ἔτεγξα παγαῖς·

(*PV* 399–401)

I shed a flow of tears
from my tender eyes, and moistened my cheek
with their watery stream.

Cheeks come up often in tragedies in the context of grief and mourning: women – and men – wet their cheeks with tears, or scratch them with their nails in mourning (e.g. Soph. *Ant.* 530, Aesch. *Cho.* 24–5, Eur. *Tro.* 280). So do eyes that often shed tears of suffering (e.g. Aesch. *Pers.* 1056, Soph. *OC* 1709–10, Eur. *Hipp.* 245), However, both 'cheeks' and 'eyes' are at the same time traditional *topoi* of female beauty, both in drama and in non-dramatic poetry.[43] The use of the adjective ῥαδινός, and indeed for the eyes, supports this reading.[44] Even in this context of mourning, emphasis is placed on the beauty of the eyes, a major erotic *locus* in archaic and classical Greek poetry. The poet combines here the two, and makes an easy transition from the divine maidens of the *parodos* to the chorus of young females that mourn for Prometheus' fate and console him, a function frequently carried out by females in tragedy.

The physical attributes of the chorus come forward in another instance too, that is, in the scent that foretells their *parodos*. This has already been discussed above as an attribute of their divine nature.[45] However, aromatic perfumes on the hair is a feature that Alcman may have also used to emphasize the beauty (and desirability) of Astymeloisa in fr. 3:

[-κ]ομος νοτία Κινύρα χ[άρ]ις
[ἐπὶ π]αρσενικᾶν χαίταισιν ἴσδει·

(Alcm. fr. 3.71–2 *PMGF*)

giving beauty to her tresses, the moist charm of Cinyras
sits on the maiden's hair.

Thus far I have examined the *partheneion* as a model of female chorality employed in the play. This, however, is not the play's only intergeneric gesture: the female voice is also particularly associated in the Greek song tradition with wedding songs, which have come down to us in the works of Sappho.[46] As discussed earlier, though wedding songs and maiden songs are distinct, they do belong naturally together and share many motifs and concerns for a very important transition in a woman's life. As well as gesturing toward their own chorality in the present play the chorus also refer unambiguously to their own previous choral activity, significantly their performance of the bridal song at the wedding of Hesione, their own sister and wife of Prometheus:

---

[43] See, for example, the reference to the dancers' eyes in Alcm. fr. 1 *PMGF* (p. 176) or 'the soft cheeks' of a maiden in Aesch. *Supp.* 70 and Soph. *Ant.* 783–4.
[44] For the reading ῥαδινῶν and therefore its correct attribution to ὄσσων rather than to ῥέος (ῥαδινόν) or παρειὰν (ῥαδινάν), see Griffith 1983, *ad loc*. Neither of the other readings, however, significantly changes the tone of the passage, and therefore the choice does not affect our argument.
[45] See p. 166.
[46] See frr. 103; 107–17 Voigt. Less certainly also frr. 104ab and 105ac Voigt. For wedding songs in antiquity see also Contiades-Tsitsoni 1990, and for a survey of available evidence on the genre and its definition, see Swift 2010, 241–50.

τὸ διαμφίδιον δέ μοι μέλος προσέπτα
τόδ' ἐκεῖνό θ' ὅ τ' ἀμφὶ λουτρὰ
καὶ λέχος σὸν ὑμεναίουν
ἰότατι γάμων, ὅτε τὰν ὁμοπάτριον ἕδνοις
ἄγαγες Ἡσιόναν πιθὼν δάμαρτα κοινόλεκτρον.

(*PV* 555–60)

And this song that has flown to my lips is very different
from the wedding-song I sang
around your bridal bath and bed
on the occasion of your wedding, when you wooed and won
my sister Hesione to be your wife and bedfellow.

The chorus draw on their past chorality to contrast their current song, which has elements of a lament, to that *hymenaios* sung at the wedding of Prometheus. *Hymenaioi* in tragedy are elsewhere evoked to contrast the current bleak situation on stage.[47] In the context of a *hymenaios* this time, we are reminded of the common *topos* of both *partheneia*, and wedding songs, whereby one (or even two, cf. Alcm. fr. 1 *PMGF*) girl is singled out and praised separately, for example Agido, Hagesichora or Astymeloisa in Alcman, or Andaisistrota and Damaina in Pindar.[48]

The chorus of *Prometheus Bound* seem to also echo Alcman's maidens in a more specific thought about marriage:

μήποτε μήποτέ μ', ὦ
Μοῖραι <μακραίωνες>, λεχέων Διὸς εὐνά-
τειραν ἴδοισθε πέλουσαν·
μηδὲ πλαθείην γαμέτᾳ τινὶ τῶν ἐξ οὐρανοῦ.
ταρβῶ γὰρ ἀστεργάνορα παρθενίαν
εἰσορῶσ' Ἰοῦς ἀμαλαπτομέναν.

(*PV* 894–9)

Never, never,
O < long-lived > Fates, may you see me
become the sharer of Zeus's bed,
nor may I be united with any partner from among the heavenly ones:
for I am afraid when I see
Io, the man-shunning virgin, devastated.

---

47 For other tragic instances, see Swift 2010, 251.
48 See the text cited on p. 175.

The common lyric gnome that men should respect the limitations of their human condition[49] is adjusted here to the context of marriage: Io's 'marriage' to Zeus has suggested a course of thought to the maiden chorus that one needs to marry within one's rank, and they wish never to share in Zeus's bed (895–6), nor to 'be united with any partner from among the heavenly ones' (897–8). Again, the similarity, even at a linguistic level, with Alcman's fr. 1 *PMGF* is striking:

μή τις ἀνθ]ρώπων ἐς ὡρανὸν ποτήσθω
[μηδὲ πη]ρήτω γαμῆν τὰν Ἀφροδίταν.

(Alcm. fr. 1.16–7 *PMGF*)

Let no man fly to heaven
nor attempt to wed Aphrodite.

The passage comments on the suitability of marriage, a theme already mentioned as a traditional feature of weddings songs. Marriage is thematically prominent in the play, as was seen above. The chorus' ripeness for marriage and their past role in the *epithalamion* makes them an ideal voice in a play where marriage is presented as threatening, both to Io, who is visibly victimized, and ultimately to Zeus, who is threatened with destruction by his desire to marry. The appeal to non-dramatic female choruses, however, also plays to another aspect of marriage in this trilogy: the maiden in a *partheneion* moves ultimately into the state of the married woman; and the sensual emphasis on her beauty points forward to this eventual sexual ripening. The wedding song, in presenting this transition as a threat, change, or even a kind of death, highlights the anxieties which surround marriage, but also acknowledges both the need for, and the possibility of, a successful transition. This is important in a play in which marriage, though threatening, is – in the end – not necessarily painful or destructive, as developments later in the trilogy will show,[50] and as indeed is hinted by Prometheus when he predicts Io's fate (848–52). This double nature of our chorus as displaced transitional maidens and participants in the normative activity of an *epithalamion* makes them the ideal audience for the distraught Io and qualifies them to express authoritative thoughts about the ambiguities of a wedding: both the potential disaster in a marriage (as in Prometheus' case), and its socially condoned aspect.

Another feature that unites this chorus with the singers of the *partheneia* is the striking juxtaposition of profound and authoritative gnomic utterances about

---

[49] See, e.g. Pind. *Ol.* 3.59–62; *Ol.* 10.27–30.
[50] For the trilogy and a survey of possible reconstructions, see Griffith 1983, appendix.

the human condition and morality with equally emphatic expressions of maidenly modesty. This is especially important in the *partheneia* when maidens are appearing in civic space and subject themselves to the male gaze. Alcman's maidens, for instance, persistently express oblique self-praise, which they accompany with a comment on its insufficient nature:

Ϝείποιμί κ', [ἐ]γὼν μὲν αὐτὰ
παρσένος μάταν ἀπὸ θράνω λέλακα
γλαύξ·

(Alcm. fr. 1.85–7 *PMGF*)[51]

–if I may speak– I myself only a maiden
screech pointlessly, an owl from a rafter.

Pindar's maidens in his *daphnephorikon* also express more explicitly the need to match their words with proper maidenly thoughts:[52]

ἐμὲ δὲ πρέπει
παρθενήϊα μὲν φρονεῖν
γλώσσᾳ τε λέγεσθαι·

(Pind. fr. 94b.33–5 S-M)

but it is proper for me
to think maidenly thoughts
and say them with my tongue.

The chorus of *Prometheus* seems to be displaying the same self-awareness upon their entrance, when they claim that their presence in the public space contrasts their usual *aidōs*, which they call θεμερῶπις (134). This word is explained as 'grave and sedate of look' (*LSJ⁹*) and is found elsewhere only in Empedocles, where it is used in a list of nymphs as an epithet of Harmonia.[53]

ἔνθ' ἦσαν Χθονίη τε καὶ Ἡλιόπη ταναῶπις,
Δῆρίς θ' αἱματόεσσα καὶ Ἁρμονίη θεμερῶπις

(Emped. fr. 122 DK)

---

[51] Cf. Alcm. fr. 1.64–70 *PMGF* on which see p. 176.
[52] See D'Alessio 1994, 118–20 for a very useful, succinct list of 'what a maiden-chorus can do'- awareness of the conventions of their song and explicit reference to them, as here, is one of them.
[53] Also an abstract noun, as Griffith 1983, 133–4n. notes.

> There were Chthonia and the far-sighted Heliope,
> And bloody Strife and the grave-faced Harmonia

An allusion to this Empedoclean passage would be appropriate for a number of reasons: first, the passage is a catalogue of nymphs (as are our chorus), and indeed, as has been remarked, modelled on the Iliadic catalogue of another famous group of water-nymphs, the Nereides.[54] Second, because of the cosmic content of the text. Finally, the echo may function at another level given Empedocles' association with the emergence of Greek rationalism, and – at least in the tradition – his association with democracy.[55] If the word is indeed drawn from Empedocles, this would enhance the possibility that *Prometheus Bound* is a play with intertextual concerns. The word θεμερῶπις in particular would signal from the start the chorus' awareness of the proprieties of their status as *parthenoi* and at the same time it would flag the dramatic turn of events that made them shed their *aidōs*. Thus the chorus is both aligned with the sedate-looking girls of cult, and integrated in the world of the play and its events.[56]

My comparison of the chorus of *Prometheus* primarily with maiden songs (and secondarily with the tradition of wedding songs) has stressed the parthenaic features in *Prometheus*, in an attempt to analyze how this intergeneric relationship creates an additional layer of meaning for the chorus within the plot. As such, this chorus falls within a long tradition of tragedy integrating non-dramatic choral lyric into constructing its own understanding of a chorus in a fictional dramatic situation.

3 Intergeneric vs. Intertextual: Alcman in Athens?

The preceding analysis of the chorus of the play has shown how the poet of *Prometheus* employs traditional *topoi* of non-dramatic lyric poetry to construct his chorus. Alcmanic echoes suggest that the dramatist may be drawing on specific maiden songs of Alcman. While this potential poetic dialogue is revealing for the relationship of tragedy to other lyric genres, it may also be telling us something specifically about the survival and reception of Alcman in Athens.

---

54 Burnet 1945, 223n.2. Cf. Hom. *Il.* 18.39–49.
55 Another resonance of Empedoclean thought is found in this play at 191 (cf. fr. 40 DK).
56 Hesychius, however, explains the word as ἐρασμία (*s.v.*), which, if correct, may be instead yet another remark on the physicality of the chorus.

Alcman, who was active in Sparta in the seventh century BC, is sporadically mentioned by name, or alluded to, in fifth-century Athenian literature.[57] Our earliest securely dated references occur in Aristophanes' *Birds* (*Av.* 250 ff.) and in the Alcmanising song that Aristophanes presents at the end of his *Lysistrata* (*Lys.* 1296-end).[58] Alcman is also mentioned in an Aristophanic fragment (fr. 590 *PCG*$^{3.2}$), and Eupolis mentions him alongside Stesichorus and Simonides as 'classics', implying a moral evaluation as the three are contrasted to Gnesippus (fr. 148 *PCG*^{5}).[59] *Birds* and *Lysistrata* were produced in 414 and 411 BC respectively, and Eupolis was active between 429 BC and some date after 415 BC.[60] So far secure references to Alcman in fifth-century drama could not, therefore, be dated earlier than 429 BC.

Based on the most probable dating of *Prometheus Bound*, an intertextual relationship between Alcman and the poet of *Prometheus* could, as I show below, improve our understanding of Alcman's reception in Athens, and add an invaluable piece of evidence of his reception for a date earlier than it has been possible until today.

This issue is of course intertwined with the date of *Prometheus Bound*, which is in turn bound up with the issue of authenticity.[61] The extensive analysis of the technical characteristics of the play give an idea about possible production dates, but more reliable evidence must be sought in allusions to *Prometheus* in other, securely dated literary works, as well as to historical incidents that have found their way into the text. With this in mind, the play must have been produced after the eruption of Aetna in 479BC (mentioned in 351ff.), possibly after 463BC, if one accepts the case for echoes of the Aeschylean *Suppliants* in the play.[62] As to its *terminus ante quem*, a reference to *Prometheus Unbound* (of the same trilogy) in Cratinus' *Ploutoi* pushes the date to 430/29 BC.[63] West

---

[57] For the survival and dissemination of the text of Alcman see Carey 2011 with a useful appendix on the main references and allusions of lyric texts in comedy.
[58] For an analysis of the relationship between Alcman and Aristophanes in this play, and how this functions at the level of the chorus, see Bierl 2011a. Revermann 2006b, 254–9 following a suggestion in Taplin 1993, 58n.7 argues that the ending of *Lysistrata* was not originally composed for an Athenian audience but was a later addition for a Spartan or Spartan-derived audience at a re-performance.
[59] Storey 2003, 332.
[60] See Storey 2003, 52–60 for the dates of Eupolis' career and death.
[61] See n.3 in this chapter.
[62] See Ruffell 2012, 18 for an overview of the evidence for dating the play, with further references to previous scholarship on the subject.
[63] For echoes of the Prometheus trilogy in the play and its dating see Bakola 2010, 122.

suggests a date between 440 and 429 BC.[64] But on any reckoning this predates our earliest explicit references to Alcman.

If we accept this plausible dating of *Prometheus Bound*, we should then view the Alcmanic echoes found in the play as an invaluable *testimonium* for the reception of Alcman, situated at the earliest limit of, or possibly earlier than, our securely dates sources so far have allowed.

4 Conclusion

In conclusion, this analysis has highlighted striking similarities in language and sentiment between the chorus of *Prometheus Bound* and non-dramatic poetry, in particular maiden songs. The use of what appears to be Alcmanic echoes firms up the intergeneric allusion and underscores the presence of parthenaic themes. It also possibly offers an early *testimonium* for the circulation of Alcman in Athens, and corroborates the idea that Alcman seems by that point to have been acknowledged as the composer of maiden songs *par excellence*[65] and his poetry to have been fairly well known in Classical Athens.

Even if the intertextual relationship between Alcman and the poet of *Prometheus Bound* can only be argued with a degree of cautiousness, the comparison points to similarities between dramatic choral odes and non-dramatic lyric poetry, and emphasizes the prominence of the maiden identity of this chorus. This is of particular importance for the tragic chorus as a whole, since it opens up a way of thinking about divine choruses, of which so few survive. The fact that the chorus are divine creatures gives them a natural place in this context, while their maidenly nature gives them access to a wide range of feelings and song modes. Certain restrictions still apply to them (it has already been shown that they share many features and concerns with human maiden choruses), but their maiden qualities in combination with their divine nature gives the dramatist greater freedom to move them in and out of both roles for the needs of the plot and the preoccupations of the play.

The plot of *Prometheus Bound* in particular makes this chorus thematically very suitable. The Oceanides are divinities and bound to nature, the only workable chorus for a tragedy played out wholly on the divine level and in remote wilderness. They are females that have previously acted within the norms of the divine society, singing, as expected from them, in their sister's wedding.

---

[64] Griffith 1977, 9–13 and 252–4; West 1979, 146–8; Bees 1993.
[65] Cf. Alcm. fr. 13a5–7 *PMGF*.

Now they are helplessly empathizing with Prometheus, in a play where marriage is potentially threatening (Zeus and Io), but in the end not necessarily painful or destructive. Io, after her long sufferings, is impregnated by a simple-painless-touch; and in the course of the trilogy Zeus must make the right marital decision after all.[66]

Choral song, and its attributes (order, harmony, grace, beauty), are already viewed as an activity characteristic of goddesses (e.g., Muses, Charites, Sirens) in pre-dramatic poetry. Tragedy, however, is the first genre to enact the choral activity of goddesses before an audience, rather than simply describe it in word. Drawing on the long literary tradition of young female divinities singing at various occasions, and merging this with the Athenian reality of wedding songs, and the knowledge of *partheneia*, Greek tragedy attempts to catch a glimpse of the *kosmos* inherently associated with choral song and puts this in the service of its own thematic concerns.

---

[66] Zeus will eventually avoid marrying a woman who would bear 'a son mightier than his father' (*PV* 768).

Alexandros Kampakoglou
Epinician Discourse in Euripides' Tragedies: The Case of *Alexandros*

1 Introduction

Recent discussions of Attic drama have focused on the interaction of tragedy with lyric genres. Epinician poetry, the genre of lyric celebrating athletic victories, has claimed a prominent position in such analyses on account of its better textual preservation.[1] This comparative approach has proved fruitful especially in the case of characters such as Heracles who have good representation in both genres. Nonetheless, little attention has been paid to the manner in which epinician imagery is incorporated in tragic plays and its role in structuring their plot. In this chapter, I argue that Euripides employs epinician themes and motifs in specific sequences and combinations, suggesting parallels between the tragic hero and real-life victors. As I show, the appreciation of these structures is significant because it allows us to get a better understanding of the playwright's ongoing engagement with epinician poetry and its development through his career. Furthermore, determining the exact role and function that epinician discourse has in Euripides' plays is crucial for the reconstruction and discussion of fragmentary plays such as *Alexandros*.[2] As I argue in the second part of this chapter, in composing *Alexandros* Euripides not only elaborated upon epinician devices he used in other plays but also diversified their role in order to comment on the political and social circumstances prevailing in Athens in 415 BC. Specifically, several elements of the play's plot (e.g. the association of Paris' victories with the political stability of Troy; the speculations of other characters about Paris' true character and aims; the theme of envy) could reflect Athenian responses to Alcibiades' recent Olympic victories for which Euripides had composed an ode the previous year (frr. 755–756 *PMG*).[3] Furthermore, the examination of *Alexandros* in comparison to other 'epinician plays' indicates that the epinician structure in this play concerns all three plays of the so-called Trojan

---

All translations are mine unless otherwise indicated.

[1] Aeschylus: Steiner 2010a; Sophocles: Hubbard 2000; Cairns 2006; Swift 2011; Rodighiero 2012, 73–9; Kratzer 2013; Euripides: Swift 2010, 104–72; Carey 2012; Kratzer 2015.
[2] Cf. Carey 2012, 32–3.
[3] Cf. Scodel 1980, 140 with n.4; Romero Mariscal 2005, 17–18.

trilogy (i.e. *Alexandros, Palamedes, Troades*) offering us a glimpse into Euripides' experimentation with epinician discourse and trilogy structures.

2 Epinician Discourse and Euripidean Drama

Euripides' *Alexandros* is not the only Euripidean tragedy to incorporate elements of epinician discourse. The consideration of the way in which epinician language is used in other plays, especially *Heracles, Alcestis, Electra, Medea, Bacchae,* and *Andromache* can help us appreciate the reasons behind the selection of epinician discourse for the myth of Paris in *Alexandros* and better understand its significance for the plot of the lost tragedy. My aim in the first part of this chapter is to determine the means whereby epinician discourse is evoked by Euripides and the purposes to which this discourse is put. As I argue, Euripides repeatedly perverts the rituals associated with epinician praise; in his tragedies, epinician associations go hand in hand with problems in the *oikos* and signal, as a rule, negative prospects for the tragic victor. Although the tragic victor is viewed as a savior,[4] his interference leads unwittingly and inevitably to the destruction of himself and his family.[5] Tragic victors are usually beaten down by difficulties and are obliged to leave their hometowns, something that creates irony, the more so as Euripides employs the return of heroes to recall the return of the victorious athlete.[6] Building on the uniqueness of the victor as a man of excellence who approaches the heroic condition and so is set apart from his contemporaries, Euripides employs epinician imagery to throw into relief the alienation of the tragic hero from his community and accentuate the violent reversal of his fate, from glorious success to misery and dejection. This interpretation holds especially true for Euripides' *Heracles*, the emblematic epinician hero, who through his personal story sets the standard against which Euripides' tragic victors can be judged.

The incorporation of epinician discourse in *Heracles*, and in most other plays under examination, is signposted by the use of the adjective καλλίνικος 'gloriously triumphant'.[7] To a fifth-century Athenian audience, the adjective

---

[4] As in many other regards, *Medea* does not conform to this generic framework. Medea previously saved the life of Jason and the Argonauts (*Med.* 475–87). Nonetheless, Jason now treats her benefactions to him with contempt and ingratitude.
[5] The divergence of *Alcestis* from this description is predicated on the play's happy ending and its unique genre affiliation: cf. *hypothesis* b.6–7; see Parker 2007, xix-xxiv.
[6] Cf. Alexopoulou 2009, 41 and 64–5.
[7] *HF* 49, 180, 570, 582, 681, 789, 961, 1046. Cf. Swift 2010, 132–3, 145–7.

had clear epinician associations, supported first by Archilochus' use of it in a hymn, possibly an archaic specimen of epinician poetry, and second by the repeated use Pindar makes of it to refer to his poems and victors.[8] Archilochus addresses his poem to Heracles, and this choice of addressee implies that the juxtaposition of the victor with Heracles, so prominent in Pindar and Bacchylides, was part of Archilochus' epinician agenda in the seventh century. The strong epinician associations of Heracles enable Euripides to claim this genre discourse for his tragedy primarily to stress Heracles' uniqueness and heighten the violence of his destruction.[9]

When the play opens, Heracles is considered to be in an uncertain, liminal position, somewhere between life and death. He is reputed to have descended to Hades to fetch Cerberus, and both his family and the old men of the chorus believe him to be dead (116–7, 145–6). The return of Heracles, like that of other tragic victors, reflects the ritualized aspect of ancient athletics. Euripides' plays fall easily within the tripartite scheme of 'separation, transition, and incorporation' that anthropologist Arnold van Gennep developed and Kevin Crotty has employed in his discussion of epinician poetry.[10] The athlete leaves his home and family to participate in the games; he puts his life at risk by competing in the games and is so assumed to be in a state between life and death until he returns to the safety of his home. This consideration accounts for the emphasis placed in epinician celebrations on the return of the athlete and his reintegration in the community.[11] The discourse that epinician poets developed to describe the symbolic moment of the return of the victorious athlete becomes in Attic tragedy the conduit for the inclusion of epinician language in the reception of the tragic victor.[12] Agamemnon in Aeschylus' play of the same name, Orestes in Euripides' *Electra*, and Agaue in *Bacchae* are all hailed in terms strongly reminiscent of re-

---

8 For Archilochus' hymn, see fr. 324 *IEG* and Pind. *Ol.* 9.1–4. In subsequent epinician poetry, *kallinikos* is used twice for the *laudandus* and his victorious relatives (*Pyth.* 1.32; 11.46) but more commonly to describe the epinician poem: *Pyth.* 5.106, 11.46; *Nem.* 3.19, 4.15; *Isthm.* 1.12, 5.54. Cf. *HF* 180 with Bond's 1981 note *ad loc.*; *El.* 865 with Denniston 1939 on lines 862–3 and Cropp 2013 on 864–5.
9 For a discussion of the epinician discourse in this play, see Foley 1985, 147–204; Garner 1990, 110–16.
10 Cf. van Gennep 2010, 20; Turner 1995, 94–5; Crotty 1982, 108–38. See also Kurke 1991, 15–61 and 1993.
11 Cf. Kurke 1993, 139.
12 Pindar uses νόστος or the cognate verb for the return of the victor from the games: *Pyth.* 8.83; *Nem.* 2.24; 11.26.

turning athletes.¹³ The engagement with the epinician genre in these plays is marked either by the use of key-words such as καλλίνικος or by the delivery of a moralizing discourse referring to the dangers of φθόνος ('envy') for the victor or the proper use of πλοῦτος ('wealth'), both themes central to the plot of *Alexandros*. The appropriation of epinician discourse combines with an emphasis on the feeling of safety that the returning hero inspires to those present. Characters in both *Heracles* and *Electra* anticipate or welcome Heracles or Orestes, respectively, as a savior that arrived at the eleventh hour to bring salvation to his loved ones.¹⁴ This aspect of the returning tragic hero is occasioned by the crisis that besets the *oikos*. In this sense, and unlike real-life victors, returning heroes in tragedy do not return to the comfort of their homes; no banquet is prepared for them as recompense for their exertions.¹⁵ Instead, a difficult task awaits them. This involves almost always the confrontation with a formidable opponent, which is often termed by Euripides an ἀγών.¹⁶ In classical Greek, ἀγών refers very often, but not exclusively, to athletic competitions (cf. LSJ⁹ s.v. II; DGE s.v. III.1–2).¹⁷ This usage should be differentiated from the use modern scholars make of *agōn* to refer to formally circumscribed sets of verbal contests between tragic characters.¹⁸ The former is a case of athletic or epinician imagery being applied to part of the plot; the latter lacks any such implications unless these are supported by the discourse dominant in the respective play. To be more specific: it is not the case that the verbal contests (i.e. the *agōn*) between Medea and Jason, Peleus and Menelaus, or Paris and Deiphobus are described in the original text in athletic terms. Any athletic implications detected with regard to them are the result of the epinician discourse of *Medea*, *Andromache*, and *Alexandros* as plays or of specific episodes therein. To avoid confusion, I use ἀγών to refer to any physical or verbal confrontation, when Euripides does so, and *agōn* to refer to verbal contests as a formal device of Euripidean tragedy.

In all these cases, the ἀγών does not precede the athlete's νόστος, as was the case with real athletics, but follows it. It takes place out of sight, in the interior of

---

13 For tragic νόστοι, see Hall 1999, 107; Alexopoulou 2009, 37–80. For the combination of νόστος with death plot, see Alexopoulou 2009, 22; Mastronarde 2010, 67. For the unsuccessful νόστος of Agamemnon and its epinician associations, see Steiner 2010a; Carey 2012, 18–22. For Heracles' νόστος in *Trachiniae*, see Kratzer 2013.
14 Cf. *HF* 494–5; *El.* 130–6, 585–95.
15 For banquets in epinician poetry, see e.g. *Ol.* 1.15–17, *Isthm.* 6.1–3; cf. Kurke 1991, 137–40; Strauss Clay 1999; Athanassaki 2016.
16 Cf. *HF* 789; *El.* 695, 751, also 884 [ἀγώνισμα]; *Tro.* 363; *Bacch.* 964, 975, 1163; *Alc.* 1103, 1141; *Med.* 235, 366, 403.
17 Cf. *Hipp.* 1016; *Alex.* fr. 62d.12 $TrGF^{5.1}$; *Hyps.* fr. 757.102 $TrGF^{5.2}$.
18 Cf. Duchemin 1968; Lloyd 1992, 4–11. For verbal contests in other genres, see Barker 2009.

the *skēnē* (*Heracles, Electra*) or in a location outside the city (*Bacchae, Alexandros*). By staging such confrontations as competitions, Euripides relies on the epinician representation of victory as proof of lineage and character[19] and depicts the victory of the tragic victor over his adversaries as evidence of his heroic credentials.[20] Having completed the twelve labors, Heracles has proven his descent from Zeus and so is deemed worthy of a paean by the chorus prior to the killing of Lycus (*HF* 687–700).[21] Admetus hails the victorious Heracles as son of Zeus, suggesting that Heracles has exhibited his divine ancestry by defeating Death and restoring Alcestis to life. The chorus of *Andromache* sees in Peleus' success over Menelaus a reminder of his old prowess demonstrated in his participation in the Centauromachy, the Argonautic expedition, and the first sack of Troy (*Andr.* 789–801).[22] However, celebrations in tragedy are subverted by the disaster that always ensues from the success of the victor. Heracles is visited with the madness sent by Hera and kills his wife and children; Orestes is hunted down by the Furies of his mother and is exiled; Agaue realizes the painful truth of her filicide and leaves Thebes; Peleus' house is ruined: Hermione elopes with Orestes, Neoptolemus is reported to be dead, and Andromache leaves Phthia with her son for Epirus. Death, albeit an illustrious one, awaits Peleus. If lines 1076–80 indeed belong in *Medea*, Medea realizes the sad truth about her victory over Jason just before she kills her sons.[23] Medea's angry passion (*thumos*) defeats her deliberation with regard to her sons' fate and possible escape with her from Corinth (*bouleumata*).[24] Albeit victorious, Medea is in fact defeated by misfortunes (1077). Medea's admission of defeat becomes the more poignant as, up to this point in the play, Medea has feigned defeat twice, first to Creon and

---

19 E. g. Pind. *Ol.* 4.18; 8.1–2. Cf. Komornicka 1972, 238; Lehnus 1981, 138 on lines 1–2; Lomiento 2013, 437 on lines 17–18; Park 2013, 18–20.
20 Cf. *HF* 673–700; *El.* 866–89; *Alc.* 1136–9; *Bacch.* 1145–7, 1153–64; *Andr.* 766–801; *Med.* 44–5, 765–6.
21 Cf. Bond 1981, 246–7 note on line 696. The issue of nobility of birth (εὐγένεια, *HF* 696) also appears in the debate scene of *Alexandros* fr. 61b *TrGF*[5.1].
22 Cf. Stevens 1971, 190 note on line 790; Allan 2000, 220–1. Kyriakou 2016 argues that there is no clear winner in the debate and points towards the ambiguities in the praise of Peleus by the chorus. The chorus celebrate Peleus' nobility and moral probity, instead of his supposed rhetorical victory.
23 The lines are bracketed in Diggle's OCT edition, but not in van Looy's Teubner one. For a discussion of these lines with further references, see Mastronarde 2002 note on line 1079, and Appendixes A-B on pages 388–97; Mossman 2011, 317–8, 331–2.
24 I follow Kozak's (cited by Mastronarde 2002, 395n12) interpretation of *bouleumata* as 'deliberation' with reference to the 'process of internal debate carried on in the monologue' (Mastronarde 2002, 395).

then to Jason, in order to succeed in her evil plan (314–5; 912–3). Epinician language in all these plays highlights not only the illusion of grandeur that athletic victory creates but also the precariousness of the tragic heroes' status as victors.

In *Heracles*, particularly, epinician imagery underlines the isolation of Heracles as the paragon of mortal excellence:[25] Heracles enjoys a unique position between the mortal and divine conditions; this realization makes his abandonment by both gods and friends the more painful. The praise the chorus offers Heracles is presented in installments leading up to the praise offered in the second *stasimon* before catastrophe happens.[26] Combining the generic discourses of lament and hymn,[27] the first *stasimon* catalogues Heracles' twelve labors. The second choral ode is formally a paean but includes elements of epinician discourse signposted in particular by καλλίνικον at line 681.[28] The chorus rejoices, voicing the hopes of restoration of order that Heracles' return has inspired in them. This feeling of security is later undermined by Hera's unexpected interference. The old men of the chorus linger on the similarities between Apollo and Heracles to account for their decision to offer a paean to the latter (687–700). The comparison of Heracles to Apollo is intriguing from the point of view of victory songs. As a rule, epinician praise includes the comparison of the victor to a mythological hero, never a god. In most cases, this hero, the 'foil' in Bundy's terms, is Heracles, who thus offers the limit of praise of mortal athletes.[29] But the chorus of *Heracles* is faced with the impossible task of finding a proper foil for epinician poets' favorite foil. Inasmuch as Heracles like Apollo is a son of Zeus, the comparison does not look unwarranted. Additionally, as Wilamowitz (1895 *ad* 687) notes, the two brothers share another trait: they are both celebrated as averters of evil. The praise discourse renders Heracles' position ambiguous, by combining elements of both epinician odes and hymns.[30] At the pinnacle of his fame, Hera strikes Heracles down. The testimony of Lyssa indicates that there is no justification for what Heracles is about to suffer (846–55). The reason Heracles falls is Hera's envy. Iris refers to Hera's χόλος ('anger'), without indicating the reason for it. However, lines 825–42 imply that Hera is jealous first because of Zeus' infidelity (826; cf. 1308–10) and second because of the fact that Zeus protected

---

25 Cf. Swift 2010, 121–56.
26 Cf. Parry 1965, 374; Foley 1985, 177–88; Swift 2010, 124–33.
27 Cf. Bond 1981, 146–53.
28 For paeans before battles, see Rutherford 2001, 42–5. On the other hand, the emphasis on Heracles' ancestry as proved by his tasks and benefactions to humanity are epinician *topoi* that blur the genre categorization of the chorus' song; cf. Barlow 1996, 152.
29 Bundy 1962, *passim*.
30 Cf. Parry 1965, 364, 371.

Heracles for years until he completed his tasks, aggravating Hera's anger (827–8).[31] Thanks to Zeus' support Heracles attained a status, described by καλλίνικος, that approximates the divine condition of permanent happiness or success.[32] Heracles' killing of Lycus, his latest victory, is not the cause, but the event that triggers the release of Hera's pent-up anger. Specifically, at line 839, Iris refers to Heracles' children as καλλίπαις στέφανος ('crown of fair children'). Iris reverses the epinician discourse the chorus has applied to Heracles: καλλίπαις replaces καλλίνικος used throughout the play for Heracles. The wreath of victories is contrasted with the wreath of Heracles' murdered children, a juxtaposition reflected also in Heracles' discourse at 1271–80.[33] Hera's reaction is by all accounts extraordinary especially in view of Heracles' role as benefactor of Greece and mankind. Formally, however, it corresponds to the role of envy and the dangers to which it exposes the victor both in epinician poetry and Euripides' other plays.[34]

Victory is the time when the heroic, divine even, potential in mortal nature manifests itself, so much so that Pindar can claim at the opening of *Nemean* 6 that gods and men are children of the same mother (1–7).[35] Realizing this truth, the victor should neither disregard his place in the community and cosmos nor seek to go farther than what is permitted to him.[36] Any such attempt would expose the victor to the anger of gods or the other members of his community, a danger not to be taken lightly.[37] Envy has an important role in most of the other plays under consideration. In *Alexandros*, the envy of Deiphobus and Hecuba threatens Paris' life. Dionysus in *Bacchae* is enraged by members of his mother's family because they slander Semele and question his godhood.[38] During her supplication of Creon, Medea claims that people's envy of her magical skills and

---

31 Cf. Bond 1981, xxiv-xxvi; Michelini 1987, 235 n. 13, 269 n. 167; Barlow 1996, 8–9, 160.
32 Cf. Burnett 1971, 177–80; Swift 2010, 147–50.
33 Cf. Foley 1985, 154.
34 For envy in epinician poetry, see Kurke 1991, 195–224; Willcock 1995, 16–17; Athanassaki 2012b, 191–202.
35 Cf. Gerber 1999, 42–7. The final scene of *Medea* offers an interesting variation of this motif: Medea appears *ex machina* in the place of a god; cf. Rutherford 2014. The defeat of Jason is a confirmation of her innate excellence – her *phua* – reminding one that she is the daughter of a noble father and a descendant of Helios (*Med.* 406).
36 Cf. *Pyth.* 10.21–30; *Ol.* 13.91–2; *Isthm.* 7.44–7.
37 The danger that is envy is commonly exemplified by Ajax: *Nem.* 8.22–34. The wrong that Ajax' comrades committed against him (*Nem.* 7.25–30) has been put right by Homer, who has praised him among men (*Isthm.* 4.55) and preserved knowledge of his deeds for future generations (*Isthm.* 4.56–60). Cf. Hubbard 2000.
38 *Bacch.* 26–33; cf. Dodds 1960, 67 notes on lines 30, 31.

wisdom – her *sophia* – has caused her great evils (292–302). Along similar lines, Jason points out to Medea that by aiding the Argonautic cause Medea won a reputation of being *sophē* ('wise') among the Greeks (539–41). Nonetheless, envy is a necessary evil for the charismatic individual. Ironically enough, it is Medea's reputation as *sophē* that attracts Aegeus' attention.[39] As Aegeus explains, Apollo's oracle 'calls for a wise mind' (677, μάλιστ', ἐπεί τοι καὶ σοφῆς δεῖται φρενός) – *sophēs* in this line reverberates with the implications of its previous uses in the play. Pindar reminds Hieron that 'it is better to be envied than pitied' (*Pyth.* 1.85 κρέσσον γὰρ οἰκτιρμοῦ φθόνος). However, in Euripides' plays, envy is destructive to such a degree that ultimately the tragic victor moves those around him to pity and compassion (Heracles, Orestes, Agaue), or, in the case of Medea and Dionysus, to awe and fear.

Most of Euripides' victors have impeccable epinician credentials, and the audience is usually reminded of them before the ἀγών. These credentials motivate, if not account for, the tragic hero's success therein. Moreover, such credentials can help modern readers understand the reasons why Euripides selected epinician imagery in these specific plays. In *Heracles* and *Andromache*, the success praised by the chorus is situated against the background of previous victories. The enumeration of these victories by the respective choruses offers the functional equivalent of the list of the victor's previous victories in epinician poetry.[40] Heracles is καλλίνικος already before he actually appears on stage. His reputation precedes him and is based on the successful completion of the twelve tasks.[41] Heracles himself at lines 575–82 connects his reputation as heroic victor with the successful completion of the ἀγών at hand. Killing Lycus proves Heracles' prowess and sets his reputation on a more secure basis.[42] *Andromache* offers a debate involving the old and frail Peleus and Menelaus instead of a physical confrontation. Peleus interferes to save the life of Andromache and her son. He shames Menelaus into returning to Sparta, abandoning his daughter Hermione; Peleus' discourse calls into question Menelaus' supposed heroic status. The women of the chorus laud Peleus on his wealth and lineage (*Andr.* 766–

---

[39] Cf. Mastronarde 2002 on line 677.
[40] See e.g. *Pyth.* 9.79–103, *Nem.* 10.23–9. Cf. Gerber 2002, 71–8; Carne-Ross 1985, 15–17 and 97–101.
[41] Cf. Barlow 1996, 6 and 13. For Heracles' tasks as ἀγών, see *Alc.* 489, 504. See also Golden 1998, 146–57.
[42] Cf. *Alc.* 837–42.

801).⁴³ Both elements frame his present conduct, which is seen as a reminder of earlier youthful achievements.

Medea offers one *agōn* between Medea and Jason,⁴⁴ but her interaction with Creon, a supplication scene,⁴⁵ is also relevant for the discussion of epinician discourse in this play. In both debates, Medea's opponents acknowledge the credentials that render her a formidable (*deinē*) opponent, as the Nurse admits at the opening of the play (44–5).⁴⁶ Creon alludes to Medea's reputation as a powerful witch, expressing fear for the safety of his daughter (282–6). The audience does not get precise information about Medea's skills until Medea's *agōn* with Jason. Medea lists the services she offered to Jason and his comrades first in Colchis and later on in Iolcus (475–87). The epinician coloring of Medea's Colchian feats has been established by Pindar's *Pythian* 4 (220–7; 232–46): Jason's tasks serve in that ode as the mythological equivalent of sporting events. Jason calls into question the importance of Medea's contribution. Instead he attributes the success of the Argonautic expedition to Aphrodite (526–8). Jason's arrogance blinds him to Medea's powers and the ambiguity of her discourse. At line 946, Medea declares to Jason that she will take part in Jason's effort, convincing his betrothed to grant Medea's children stay in Corinth (συλλήψομαι δὲ τοῦδέ σοι κἀγὼ πόνου). The collaboration of Medea and Jason and the use of *ponos* in this line mirror events in Colchis. Jason himself has already categorized the Colchian tasks as *ponoi* at 545–6. Jason's limited view does not allow him to consider the role that Aphrodite has in the proceedings in both Colchis and Corinth. However, an important development has taken place in the meantime. In Colchis, Medea and Jason were members of the same team; in Corinth, the competition (ἅμιλλαν) is between the two of them (545–6). To the extent that events in Corinth mirror or re-enact those in Colchis, Medea's catalogue of *ponoi* prefigures her final victory over Jason.⁴⁷ Jason enlists Aphrodite's help to gain Medea's compliance. In Corinth, Jason convinces his fiancée by means of Medea's magical gifts.

---

43 For the epinician elements in this ode, see Stevens 1971, 187; Allan 2000, 217–20; Lloyd 2005, 150–3. For the ambiguities in the epinician discourse used, see Kyriakou 2016.
44 For the 'near-*agōn*' at *Med*. 1317–1414, see Lloyd 1992, 6–7.
45 For the term, see Lloyd 1992, 8–11.
46 Cf. Dionysus' ironic remark to Pentheus: 'Formidable! You are formidable! And you will suffer horribly!' (*Bacch*. 971, δεινὸς σὺ δεινὸς κἀπὶ δείν᾽ ἔρχηι πάθη).
47 In addition to the use of *kallinikos* for Medea at 45 and 765, Medea pledges to cause Jason and his new family ἀγῶνες at 366–7. At 403, Medea views her plan as a contest by means of which she will prove her courage (403). It is in the same context that Medea also references her divine pedigree. Finally, the use of *balbis* at 1245 represents Medea's revenge as a race: for the imagery, see Mastronarde 2002 and Mossman 2011 *ad loc*.

On the other hand, Orestes has no such victories to exhibit, and so the emphasis falls on those of his father.[48] At *Pyth.* 11.10–6, Orestes is used as a positive example for the victory of Trasydaeus: both of them, each in his own specific way, cause their ancestral hearth to be renowned. The epinician use of Orestes' νόστος in this ode could have provided the inspiration for the epinician imagery used by both Sophocles and Euripides in their respective versions of *Electra*. Orestes is the son of the sacker of Troy, the great Agamemnon.[49] In taking revenge on the killers of his father, Orestes proves himself to be the true son of Agamemnon. Accordingly Euripides' Electra wreathes and lauds Orestes after the killing of Aegisthus as if he were an Olympic victor and associates the discharge of Orestes' duty towards his father with his lineage (880–2). Electra hails the killing of Aegisthus as an athletic victory exactly because, to her mind, it validates Orestes' true lineage as athletic victories do in epinician poetry.[50] Epinician discourse, further, implies that, as the true son of Agamemnon, Orestes had but one path ahead of him, and this leads inexorably to the killing of Aegisthus and Clytaemestra (883–5).

Along similar lines, Sophocles, in his *Electra*, tries to compensate for Orestes' lack of previous victories by making one up. In his effort to mislead Clytaemestra, Orestes' tutor delivers a false account of a chariot race in which Orestes is supposed to have lost his life (680–763). Despite the fictional character of this, the narrative establishes Orestes' epinician credentials prior to the matricide. Orestes' victory is associated, according to epinician tradition, with his descent from Agamemnon and the Trojan expedition (693–5). The tutor's emphasis on the Argive provenance of the victor during the proclamation intimates a connection between Orestes' victory and the threat he would have posed to the usurpers of his father's throne had he survived. This epinician background shows Orestes to be an aristocratic youth bent on the pursuit of *kleos* via athletic competitions, a profile of the tragic hero quite similar to that of Paris in *Alexandros*.[51] Orestes drives his chariot himself, ignoring the risks involved in such a decision. Pindar finds such daring behavior commendable and accordingly praises the Theban Herodotus for his decision to drive his chariot himself, comparing him to both Castor and Iolaus (*Isthm.* 1.14–17).[52] Orestes' conduct exhibits

---

48 For epinician elements in this play, see Swift 2010, 156–70. For a discussion of Orestes' role in epinician tradition, see Golden 1998, 95–103.
49 Cf. Finglass 2007b, 44–5.
50 Cf. Zeitlin 1970, 655–7; Cropp 2013, 203–4.
51 Cf. Pritchard 2013, 122–3.
52 Cf. Instone 1996: 178 note on line 15. Nonetheless, driving one's chariot was expected in the heroic world; cf. the chariot-race in *Iliad* 23.

his spurning of danger in the pursuit of *kleos* and, as an effective means of characterization, prepares for the dangerous mission of avenging his father's murder. At any rate, his behavior is the natural concomitant of his lineage and predicates the revenge exacted upon the killers of his father.

In contrast to the previous cases, Dionysus and Agaue in *Bacchae* prove that epinician imagery can be applied to tragic characters with no epinician credentials. Like Heracles and Orestes, Dionysus returns home. His identity is disguised and is only revealed after the killing of Pentheus. The epinician theme is combined in this play with Dionysus' desire to solidify his divine status, enviously brought into question by Pentheus and his kinswomen.[53] *Bacchae*, like *Alcestis*, combines epinician discourse with theoxeny.[54] The self-sacrificing hospitality offered by Admetus to Heracles leads to the restoration of Alcestis to her husband. *Bacchae* offers a negative version thereof. The divine stranger is ill-received and reveals his true identity by means of an ἀγών, a choice that looks back to the role of contests in epinician discourse as proof of status. Dionysus avoids direct confrontation. He leads Pentheus to the ἀγών, and, although he does not physically participate therein, he proves victorious (964, 974–5, 1163). Dionysus exacts his revenge through Agaue, who, like Pentheus, is punished for her impiety towards the god and his mother Semele. In as much as Agaue actually defeats Pentheus in the ἀγών, *Bacchae* offers not one, but two victors.[55] Although Dionysus' status as victor is never compromised, epinician discourse underlines Agaue's tragic downfall. Like Heracles,[56] Agaue mistakes the killing of her own son for a glorious act that will bring honor to her house.[57] Agaue believes she has hunted down and killed a lion, an act imbued with heroic connotations, possibly even imitating Heracles' killing of the Nemean lion (*HF* 153–4); similar to Heracles Agaue kills the putative lion with her bare hands, an achievement she takes pride in. It is very tempting to see in their behavior a perversion of the self-esteem each victor must feel. In his illusion Heracles thinks himself to be the best competitor in the Isthmian Games (*HF* 958–62). His excellence, however, is undermined by

---

53 *Bacch.* 23–54, 219–20, 466–508, 857–61, 1340–8, 1377–8.
54 Cf. Burnett 1970, 24–29. For Heracles and Dionysus as divine guests, see Flückiger-Guggenheim 1984, 70–8, 101–19.
55 One notes here the parallel with *Medea:* Medea does not kill Creon's daughter directly; she does so through the agency of her estranged husband Jason. In this regard, both Jason and Agaue fall victim to beings of an ambiguous ontological status. Medea's divine origin, like that of Dionysus, surfaces in the last scene of the play.
56 *HF* 967–71, 981–2. For the similarities between Heracles and Agaue, see Barlow 1996, 12–13.
57 *Bacch.* 1169–71, 1173–5, 1179–84, 1195–6, 1234–43. Along similar lines, Medea resolves to proceed with her plan, which includes the slaughter of her sons, to avoid the ridicule of her enemies (*Med.* 404–6).

his attack on his own wife and offspring. On the other hand, Agaue believes that she is participating in an epinician celebration (*Bacch.* 1139–47). She returns to the city with her prize, the head of Pentheus, to share her renown with her family and community (1233–43). Agaue's return coincides with the celebration of a κῶμος in which she will participate with the members of the chorus (1172). Both Heracles and Agaue act under the baneful influence of a divine power (Hera and Dionysus respectively), and their conduct problematizes the epinician motif of the divine support that is necessary for the securing of an athletic victory.[58] Agaue evokes Dionysus as καλλίνικος; she views him as her companion in the hunt, a claim answered by the chorus, greeting Agaue as the leader of the bull (i.e. Bacchus) who brought to completion the fair contest (1153–64). Although the praise concerns both victors, it is truly praise only of the god. Agaue's hallucinations undermine the praise she receives, giving it tragic poignancy.

Unlike the tragic heroes under examination, Agaue is a woman and so an incongruous victor.[59] The clash between Agaue's sex and her status throws into relief the reversal of gender roles that Dionysus has brought to Thebes and develops the perversion of epinician rituals in Attic tragedy. The destruction of the house of Cadmus is anticipated by the confusion into which Dionysus has thrown the whole town. The conduct of the Maenads undermines gender stereotypes as these are described by Pentheus, who accuses Dionysus' followers of licentious and shameful behavior (*Bacch.* 221–5, 487).[60] Dionysus consistently does away with gender codes. Pentheus construes the feminine elements in the deportment of his opponent as unsettling and threatening to societal conventions (*Bacch.* 233–8, 352–4, 453–9).[61] Even Teiresias and Cadmus are accused by Pentheus of behaving in a manner unbecoming their age (248–54). One may compare in this regard Agaue with Medea: after all, both of them are involved in filicides and are expelled from their communities, although strictly speaking Medea is never integrated in Corinthian society, remaining instead a stranger among strangers. Both women also share a link with Heracles. If the murder of Pentheus recalls Heracles' first task, Medea shares Heracles' fate: like Heracles she kills her sons, but is welcomed in Athens – ironically, Medea is received by Aegeus, the father of the man who receives Heracles (Theseus). Nonetheless, these similarities between Agaue and Medea should not blind one to important differences. The epinician language in *Medea* lacks the Dionys-

---

58 Cf. Willcock 1995, 16.
59 I extend Prichard's (2012) concept of the 'incongruous athlete' to describe tragic victors in addition to satyrs.
60 Cf. Dodds 1960, 97 note on *Bacch.* 222–3, and 138 note on *Bacch.* 487–9.
61 Cf. Dodds 1906, 133–4 note on *Bacch.* 453–9.

iac background of gender reversal so prominent in *Bacchae*. Medea's role as a victor is predicated on her divine lineage as descendant of Helios (406), and one may suspect on her status as a foreigner: Medea's conduct confirms the status of Colchian culture as a reversal of Hellenic values. In this regard, Medea can lay claim to roles that in the Greek world were open only to men.

As I show in the second half of the chapter, the incongruity of the tragic victor is a motif central to the interpretation of Paris in *Alexandros*. But Paris' incongruity is structurally closer to that of Peleus in *Andromache* than to that of Agaue or Medea. A certain degree of incongruity appears in *Andromache* in that Peleus, despite his old age, is treated to epinician praise by the chorus. This incongruity is accentuated by the absence of both Achilles and Neoptolemus, who would be more fitting subjects for such praise. Nonetheless, Peleus' epinician credentials are impeccable and well-represented especially in the odes Pindar composed for Aeginetan victors. Pindar singles out Peleus, alongside Cadmus, as an example of human bliss in that he was deemed worthy of enjoying the company of the gods and of a divine consort, Thetis.[62] At *Nem.* 4.54–70, the most substantial treatment of Peleus in epinician poetry, he is praised for his noble bearing, his abstinence in the face of temptation, and his wedding to the daughter of Nereus in the midst of gods. At *Nem.* 4.69 the association of Peleus' career with the Pillars of Heracles sets the limits for the purest human bliss possible. Like Heracles at *Nem.* 4.21–3,[63] Peleus is the inimitable foil that sets the background for the praise of the mortal victor.[64] *Ol.* 2.78–80 represents the pinnacle of Peleus' epinician career: Peleus is mentioned, along Cadmus, as an inhabitant of the Isles of the Blessed.[65] Peleus is deemed worthy of a condition approaching the divine, symbolizing the poetic immortality that epinician poetry confers upon the victor praised. In this light, it is all the more remarkable that the women of the chorus in *Andromache* gloss over this mythological material in their praise of Peleus. Contrary to epinician practice the women of the chorus do not comment on the role of gods in Peleus' achievements, are silent on Peleus' marriage to Thetis, and miss the opportunity to celebrate the innate excellence inherent in the Aeacid line. The chorus could, for instance, comment on the fact that father (Peleus), son (Achilles), and grandson (Neoptolemus) participate in analogous endeavors (i.e. the sack of Troy).[66] This link would offer a ren-

---

[62] Peleus: *Pyth.* 3.92–5; *Nem.* 4.65–8; *Isthm.* 6.25. Cadmus: *Isthm.* 4.73–8.
[63] Cf. Pfeijffer 1999, 224–8, Burnett 2005, 142–3.
[64] Cf. *Isthm.* 6.22–5
[65] Cf. Nisetich 1989, 59–61 and 64–5 with n. 20.
[66] Our sources usually associate Peleus' brother, Telamon, with the siege of Troy by Heracles, not Peleus. See, however, *Isthm.* 5.35–8 and fr. 172 S-M. Cf. Stevens 1971, 191 note on line 796.

dition of the epinician stemma of Aeacids in Aeginetan odes.[67] Discussing these peculiarities, Poulheria Kyriakou (2016, 139–43) argues that the ambiguities of the choral ode are part of the chorus' discourse: the women are reticent on these points because of their dark or ambivalent background. Still, in the end Thetis promises to bring her husband to her aquatic abode (*Andr.* 1231–73).[68] This translates into literal terms the poetic immortality that Peleus has already achieved. In spite of his good fortune Peleus, like Euripides' other tragic victors, feels the isolation his epinician credentials bring upon him. The only consolation lies in the reunion with his son hinted by Thetis at 1259–62. Euripides agrees with epinician poets in maintaining Peleus' uniqueness: Peleus avoids the sinister future that ensues from the incorporation of epinician elements in Euripides' play, by abandoning the mortal condition altogether. Be that as it may, the application of epinician poetry to the frail Peleus underlines primarily the problems that weigh down upon Peleus' house. Like Heracles, the other paragon of epinician prowess, Peleus is left defenseless and defeated by the unpredictability of the human condition. What remains steadfast in the passage of time is the fame Peleus has achieved through his early exploits.

My discussion up to this point has detected the operation of a specific narrative sequence in Euripides' treatment of epinician discourse that slightly rearranges and reflects the stages through which an athlete would go in real life. The tragic hero comes home like an athlete returning from the games; he is then faced with problematic circumstances that threaten his family, or in *Alcestis* that of his host. He is thus expected to act by participating in a confrontation that bears athletic connotations – termed as an ἀγών. The successful outcome of the ἀγών leads to pollution, usually the shedding of kindred blood, that makes exile the inevitable expedient for the saving of the community.[69] It is at this point that one can appreciate the differences between the use of epinician discourse by Aeschylus and Sophocles, on the one hand, and Euripides, on the other. Epinician language is applied to the representation of Ajax and the *nostos* of Agamemnon and Heracles.[70] In all three cases, the tragic hero dies. To be sure, death in their case is not the result of the epinician discourse used. Nonetheless, the language of victory song highlights the failure of integration that is usually effected by means of epinician praise. In addition to this difference, in contrast to Euripides, Aeschylus and Sophocles focus on the after-

---

67 Cf. *Nem.* 3.33–63 with Pfeijffer 1999, 207–10; Bacchyl. 13.94–167.
68 One may compare this promise with the honors and hero cult awaiting Heracles in Athens (Eur. *HF* 1324–35).
69 *HF* 1417–21; *Bacch.* 1350, 1363; *El.* 1334–41.
70 Agamemnon: Steiner 2010a; Heracles: Kratzer 2013; Ajax: Hubbard 2000; Cairns 2006.

math of the hero's success and his *nostos:* thus, Agamemnon returns to Argos after he has captured Troy. Similarly Heracles in *Trachiniae* returns home after capturing Oechalia. Seen in this light, Euripides' 'failed or perverted epinicians'[71] interact creatively with a tradition that goes back to Aeschylus. Euripides, however, innovates in two points: first, he focuses on the contest that follows the *nostos* of the tragic hero rather than on the *nostos* itself; second, Euripides' tragic victors never die. Instead, they succeed by bringing death to others, in particular members of their own family. In so doing, they unsettle the community in which they fail to be re-integrated. This tendency of Euripides might be seen as a reflection of the hostility towards professional athletes expressed by several authors and particularly by Euripides in his satyric drama *Autolycus* (fr. 282 *TGrF*[5.1]).[72] However, such criticism concerns athletes' professionalism and specialization as well as the excessive material prizes meted out to the victors by their cities.[73] None of the plays discussed so far, and certainly not *Alexandros*, subscribe to this outlook.[74] One might detect a similarity between such criticism and tragic epinician discourse in that they both call into question the usefulness of the victor's athletic merits for the protection and survival of the community. Tyrtaeus, Xenophanes, and Euripides point out that athletic victories do not render athletes helpful for the protection of the *polis* against attacks. Euripides' tragic victors compromise the stability of their community in spite of their epinician credentials. Still, the focus in most cases is on the tragic story of the victor rather than his role as athlete *per se*. On the contrary, it seems more likely that Euripides' epinician imagery not only acknowledges the appeal athletics had for the public but also offers a convenient, and popular, discourse through which to sensationalize salient topics of tragic repertoire such as reversal of fortune, family conflicts, and ethical problems.[75]

---

71 Cf. Hubbard 2000, 324.
72 Cf. Kyle 1987, 124–54. Particularly for *Autolycus*, see Mangidis 1998, 19–60; Pechstein 1998, 70–85.
73 Cf. Harris 2009, 158–66.
74 Euripides' *Electra* has often been thought to offer a partial exception to this interpretation; cf. Denniston 1939 on *El.* 388–90, 388–9; and Pechstein 1998, 79–82, adding *El.* 883. Despite the similarities in language to Autolycus (fr. 282 *TGrF*[5.1]), Orestes' critique focuses on aristocratic pedigree and fortune rather than on athletics (*El.* 367–90). If lines 386–90 are meant as an attack on athletes, they hardly amount to a considerable one. Rather, they should be seen in the context of Orestes' surprise and appraisal of the Peasant's character: cf. Cropp 2013, 161–2. Along similar lines ἀχρεῖον ('ineffective') at *El.* 883 does not convey criticism of victors: cf. Denniston 1939 and Cropp 2013 *ad loc.*
75 Cf. Pritchard 2013, 121–4.

Coming back to the basic structure of Euripides' epinician plays, one also notices that this is roughly the structure of Odysseus' return, which, in turn, is based, as Emily Kearns (1982) has shown, on theoxeny myths.[76] Odysseus' true identity is revealed in *Odyssey* 21 via a contest that has Penelope as its prize. But already before this contest, Odysseus had defeated Irus, giving a sign of his true nature (*Od.* 18.66–109).[77] *Alcestis* (438 BC) represents a first stage in Euripides' experimentation with epinician discourse in his dramas: Euripides invests the contest for the woman-prize with epinician connections (*Alc.* 1025–35).[78] From here, it is a small step to *Electra*, *Heracles*, and *Bacchae*: the success of the victor in these plays reveals or solidifies his true identity, causing, at the same time, utter destruction to himself and his family. On the whole, *Alexandros*, the focus of the second part of my discussion, follows this established pattern. However, one observes significant divergences. These differences should be attributed first to the interaction of this play with its contemporaneous social and political ambience and second to the fact that *Alexandros* is not an autonomous, self-contained play but operates within the framework of the Trojan Trilogy. Although Euripides connects his trilogy loosely, it is necessary to discuss *Alexandros* in connection with the other two plays, the more so as several aspects of the structural pattern established become obvious only in the context of both *Palamedes* and *Troades*.

3 *Alexandros* and Epinician Discourse

That Euripides engages with the epinician genre in *Alexandros* is proven beyond any reasonable doubt by two facts: first, the prominent position that the funerary games organized by Priam hold in the development of the plot of the play; and second, by the messenger's detailed description of the proclamation of the victor and the celebrations that follow Paris' victories (frr. 61d.6–7, 62d.27 *TrGF*[5.1]).[79] In addition to this evidence, *Alexandros* operates on the same basic plot lines as Euripides' other 'epinician plays.' A male character is considered to be dead; a female character bewails his absence; the male hero returns under the cover

---

[76] Cf. Murnaghan 1987.
[77] Cf. Steiner 2010b, 153 and 165–7 notes *ad loc*. For Penelope as the prize of the contest, see *Od.* 21.72–3, 106–7; cf. Fernandez-Galiano 1992, 155 note on line *Od.* 21.73; Scodel 2001, 320–3. For the so-called 'Brautagonen,' see Scanlon 2002, 225–6
[78] Cf. Burnett 1971, 29–33; Garner 1990, 64–78; Swift 2011; Kratzer 2015.
[79] Cf. Huys 1986, 12. For the proclamation of the victor by the herald, see Pind. *Ol.* 13.100; *Pyth.* 1.32–3 with Cingano 1995, 339–40 *ad loc*.

of a false identity; he participates in an ἀγών that reveals his true identity.[80] The only significant difference between *Alexandros* and the plays already examined is that Paris is not cognizant of his true identity. His participation in the games inevitably stresses the innate desire for excellence and acquisition of fame.

In contrast to the plays already examined, *Alexandros* ends on a positive albeit ill-foreboding tone with the revelation of Paris' true identity and his acceptance by his family. In contrast to the other tragic victors discussed in this chapter, Paris remains in his community and so causes its utter destruction, evinced in *Troades* by the death of Astyanax and the enslavement and exile of the women of his family.[81] Destruction and exile, the final two stages in Euripides' epinician plots, are thus represented only thanks to the third part of the trilogy. Nonetheless, *Alexandros* contains explicit allusions to the events that are going to follow. This discourse culminates with Cassandra's prophecy at the last part of *Alexandros* (fr. **62 g *TrGF*$^{5.1}$), but even before that, Euripides intimates the destructive effect Paris' victories have. With regard to his family, Paris' victories fuel the anger and envy of Deiphobus and Hecuba. Fearing him to be an illegitimate son of Priam by a concubine, both of these characters view Paris as a threat to their rights in the *oikos*.[82] They come very close to shedding kindred blood but are prevented by the revelation of his true identity. Moreover, although Paris does not kill a member of his family, he competes against them, sowing the seeds of animosity between them.

The fragments of *Alexandros* suggest that Paris proves himself first in a debate (*agōn*), probably against his brother Deiphobus, and then in an athletic competition against both Hector and Deiphobus (ἀγών).[83] This reduplication of the agonistic context is a salient feature of Euripides' treatment of epinician discourse in his tragedies. The killing of Lycus by Heracles is mirrored in the slaughter of Heracles' family.[84] In *Electra* the murder of Clytaemestra is juxtaposed with that of Aegisthus and follows upon the epinician celebration of lines 859–85. The ἀγών of *Bacchae* has two layers, contrasting the victories of Agaue and Dionysus. Finally, although Medea is successful in her revenge, the death of Creon and his daughter is counterbalanced by the murder of her

---

80 The plot is thus very close to that of Sophocles' *Orestes*, too.
81 Cf. Goslin 2014.
82 Cf. Scodel 1980, 32–4; Huys 1986, 19–22; Jouan/van Looy 1998, 52; Cropp 2004, 40, 82–3 on fr. 62c *TrGF*$^{5.1}$; *contra* Timpanaro 1996, 46. Fr. 62c.5 *TrGF*$^{5.1}$ could reflect speculation about Paris' mother. For Priam's decision to invite Paris, see Timpanaro 1996, 33–5.
83 For double structures in Euripides, see Mastronarde 2010, 63–77.
84 Cf. Barlow 1996, 10–11.

sons.⁸⁵ In all of these cases the reduplication of the device undermines the morality of the tragic victor by formally offering a gruesome repetition of the first success.⁸⁶ This is not the case in *Alexandros*. The doubling of the epinician device in this play is motivated by the demands of the plot and specifically by Paris' status as a slave, which becomes a focal issue of the play. Paris is an incongruous athlete; according to historical and even mythological conventions his status as slave prevents him from participating in athletic games. In order to be allowed to participate in the funerary games organized by Priam, Paris first needs to convince his father, who probably gives him permission to compete in order to substantiate his claims of superiority over his fellow herdsmen.⁸⁷ In view of Paris' lack of previous exploits and dubious lineage, his success in the debate becomes the background for his subsequent athletic victories.⁸⁸ The debate, then, turns out to be a demonstration of Paris' natural excellence and thus foreshadows his athletic victories later in the play.⁸⁹

Euripides' tragic victors always have the choice either to avoid confrontation or to fulfill their duty, although such an improbable decision would compromise their heroic credentials and go against their character. None of them is compelled to do so in the face of mortal danger with the exception of Paris, whose life is at risk from the moment he enters the stage. Paris participates in both contests in order to secure his survival. The reason for the risk that Paris runs lies with his haughty disposition towards the other cowherds.⁹⁰ What they perceive as arrogance is for Paris an expression of his noble nature.⁹¹ This interpretation is supported by Hector's attitude towards Paris after his victories. In his confrontation with Deiphobus, Hector disregards Paris' low social standing and attributes his

---

85 In this set of analogies, Jason ought to hold a position analogous to that of Creon. However, Medea's revenge purposefully disturbs the parallel – that is, instead of being allowed to share in the fate of his children, like Creon, Jason is left alive to suffer. Letting him die would be a kindness that Medea is not willing to allow her perfidious consort.
86 Mossman (2011, *ad* 1245) notes that athletic imagery punctuates the misery of both Creon and his daughter (*Med.* 1181–2; 1214–7) and that of Medea (*Med.* 1245); thus, Medea is reduced to the same condition as her victims.
87 See Scodel 1980, 29–30; Jouan/van Looy 1998, 50; Cropp 2004, 36, 39.
88 Paris' bucolic exploits (fr. 42d *TrGF*$^{5.1}$), if they were included in Euripides' play, do not carry the same weight as previous athletic victories or heroic feats.
89 Cf. Scodel 1980, 55, 108; Romero Mariscal 2005, 16. For the semantics of power in verbal performances, see Scodel 1999–2000, 140–1. Cf. Synodinou 1977, 79 'the lack of παρρησία is a distinctive mark of slavery.' See also Mastronarde 1994, 259 on *Phoen.* 391–5; Gregory 2002, 157.
90 Cf. *Alexandros* hypothesis 15–17.
91 Cf. Scodel 1980, 29; Cropp 2004, 39.

victory to his superior nature (fr. 62b.33–4 *TrGF*⁵·¹).⁹² Paris' motives are noble. He does not seek to 'build up his estate' (οἶκο]ν αὔξων) or to make profit but rather follows a nobler desire, an expression of his true nature, an almost aristocratic pursuit (fr. 62b.30–1 *TrGF*⁵·¹).⁹³ Hector applies aristocratic patterns of thought to Paris, feeding Deiphobus' hatred of the victor. Hector's representation brings Paris close to the idealistic picture that epinician poets give of athletes,⁹⁴ according to which they compete under the influence of ἔρως or πόθος, which in the context of this genre signifies the desire for victory and the ensuing *kleos* of the victor.⁹⁵

Paris bears two more attributes that can shed some light on the issue of Euripides' innovations in *Alexandros* and help us understand the function of epinician discourse in this play. Paris is a βουκόλος ('cowherd') and a slave. There is no reason to dispute the antiquity of the depiction of Paris as the former. Princes herd flocks and ward off thieves and predators in a venerable tradition that goes as far back as the *Iliad*.⁹⁶ Moreover, there is unanimous agreement in our sources that the notorious judgment of Paris took place while he was tending his cattle.⁹⁷ It is unclear and highly unlikely though that this aspect of Paris' traditional profile is to be combined with his slave status in Euripides' play. Paris' status is in turn predicated on his abandonment by his parents. The question is, then, whether or not, according to epic tradition, Paris was left exposed as a baby to die; and, if he was, how his identity was eventually revealed. On the whole, it seems more likely than not that in the epic tradition Paris was never exposed; instead he continued living with his family in Troy. This version can accommodate Paris' pastoral activities, the judgment of the three goddesses, and the ensuing events. Alternatively, if Paris was exposed in some strand of the epic tradition, it is unlikely that he could have been restored to his family via athletic games. The participation of Paris in the games must be a later innovation either of Sophocles or Euripides.⁹⁸ Proclus' summary of the *Cypria* does not men-

---

92 Cf. fr. 61d.5 *TrGF*⁵·¹.
93 For Hector's praise of Paris cf. Pind. *Pyth.* 9.95–6; *Nem.* 3.29; *Nem.* 8.39.
94 Note especially fr. 62b.31 *TrGF*⁵·¹ πρόθυμ' ἔπρασσε. Hector's pronouncement is important because slaves were usually parodied for their love of material possessions (e.g. Ar. *Plut.* 189–92); cf. Synodinou 1977, 183.
95 Cf. Bowra 1964, 169–70; Crotty 1982, 29; Scanlon 2002, 203. at Pind. *Pyth.* 4.184, Hera instills 'desire' in the Argonauts; cf. Norwood 1945, 42; Crotty 1982, 119; Hubbard 1983, 16–17. At *Pyth.* 9.75, the fame of victory is the bride that the young Telesicrates brings home; cf. Carey 1981, 86 *ad loc.*
96 Cf. Griffin 1992, 192–6.
97 See Stinton 1990b.
98 Soph. fr. 93 *TrGF*⁴ implies some sort of victory of Paris in Sophocles' version too.

tion anything about the exposure of Paris or the funerary games. Nonetheless epic tradition knows of such games and represents famous heroes winning fame and material possessions by participating therein.[99] Still, the athletes are exclusively members of the highest social hierarchy.[100] It is quite unlikely, therefore, that any epic poet would have represented a slave, even if this slave were a prince of the royal blood, participating in funerary games.[101] Experimentations with social status and violent reversals of fate are more in tune with Attic tragedy rather than epic.

This revision of Paris' status, whether Sophoclean or Euripidean, allows Euripides to engage with the idea of the noble bearing of slaves and so undermine the epinician premise of innate excellence.[102] Paris does not win solely his freedom but climbs to the highest echelons of Trojan society. This abrupt reversal of his fortune makes him look more like an adventurer posing a threat to the stability of Troy. The first sign comes after the debate when the distinction between freemen and slaves is questioned (fr. 61b.9–10 $TrGF^{5.1}$):

μία δὲ γονὰ τό τ' εὐγενὲς καὶ {τὸ} δυσγενές,
νόμωι δὲ γαῦρον αὐτὸ κραίνει χρόνος.
τὸ φρόνιμον εὐγένεια καὶ τὸ συνετόν, ὁ <δὲ>
    θεὸς δίδωσιν, οὐχ ὁ πλοῦτος

Well-born and low-born are children of the same parent,
but time, through custom, makes the well-born arrogant.
Prudence and sound mind render one noble;
it is god who bestows this, not wealth...

Paris confounds, but only momentarily, the hierarchy described but does not lend strength to the speculations of the chorus.[103] He challenges the dichotomy between slave and free man, exactly because he is a free man reduced to the status of a slave. This interpretation is further supported by the way in which Paris'

---

[99] Cf. Davies/Finglass 2014, 212–3; Willis 1941, 392–7.
[100] Cf. Dickie 1984, 246–52; Pritchard 2013, 121–2. Epeius, the builder of the Trojan Horse, hardly represents an exception to this rule; cf. Kyle 1987, 136n64. Despite his mediocre, if not ludicrous, performance in the games of *Iliad* 23 and his absence from the catalogue of book 2 and the main fighting, Epeius is graced with a heroic pedigree at *Il.* 23.665. On Epeius, see Howland 1954–1955; Dickie 1984, 241–2; Richardson 1993, 241 note on *Il.* 23.653–99.
[101] One may perhaps consider the reaction of the suitors at *Od.* 21.320–9. It takes some special pleading by Penelope and Telemachus (*Od.* 21.330–49) to allow the disguised Odysseus to compete against them.
[102] For tragic 'polyphony', see Hall 1999, 118. For noble slaves in Euripides, see Gregory 2002: 151–62. Fr. 61b $TrGF^{5.1}$ is a case in point; cf. Di Giuseppe 2012, 101–14.
[103] Compare also Gribble's (1999, 9–10) discussion of the 'great individual.'

body is described by other characters.[104] The athletic body was part of a social structure, which underpinned the distinction between freemen and slaves.[105] The members of the chorus try to understand Paris on the basis of such preconceptions, which he obviously defies.[106] The report of Paris' victories encourages the admiration of the chorus members, who comment on his physique,[107] a point reflecting traditional epinician praise (fr. 61d.8 *TrGF*[5.1]):[108] 'his beauty is so outstanding' (ὃ δ' ὧδε μορφῆι διαφερ[]). Wonder generally combines with the attraction that especially young victors inspire in members of the audience during their proclamation by the herald or their reentry into their town.[109] Pindar correlates the victor's beauty with his athletic prowess.[110] This association alludes to the divine provenance of beauty in the Homeric epics and its connection with heroic status.[111] The comments on Paris' beauty point to his connection with the royal family but also indicate his prowess, giving the members of the chorus and the spectators a glimpse of his true identity.[112] The reversal of Paris' status becomes a central theme in the first play of the trilogy. In this respect, *Alexandros* foreshadows the violent reversal of status in *Troades*. *Troades* consistently reverses the imagery of *Alexandros*, conveying the ominous significance inherent in the epinician discourse of the latter play. The irony is heightened by the fact

---

104 If fr. 286 *TrGF*[2] (ὡς Πριαμίδηισιν ἐμφερὴς ὁ βουκόλος) belongs to this play, as has been assumed by Jouan and van Looy – fr. 7 in their edition – Paris' physique is also a sign of his descent from Priam. The assignation is, however, contested; cf. Cropp 2004, 42.
105 For the athletic body, see Brulé 2006.
106 Cf. fr. 61b-c *TrGF*[5.1]. For the physical differences between slaves and free men, see Aristotle (*Pol.* 1254b16–1255a2) and Xenophon (*Oec.* 4.2–4, 6.4–10). Cf. Synodinou 1977, 80–3; Pomeroy 1994, 236; Robertson 2000, 167–9; Wrenhaven 2012, 56–7.
107 Paris' beauty might recall that of Alcibiades; cf. Romero Mariscal 2005, 19–20. For the significance of Alcibiades' beauty in ancient sources, see Gribble 1999, 13–14, 39, 71 with n. 171.
108 Cf. Athanassaki 2012, 180–91.
109 Cf. Instone 1990; Scanlon 2002, 219–26; Fisher 2006; Papakonstantinou 2012, 1658–9.
110 Cf. Pind. *Ol.* 8.19; 9.93–4; *Ol.* 10.100–5; *Pyth.* 10.55–60; *Nem.* 3.19.
111 Cf. Hom. *Il.* 6.156. The heroes of the epic world are like the immortal gods in their good looks: *Od.* 6.18, 8.457; *Hymn. Hom. Ven.* 77. For the analogies between the representation of athletes and that of warriors, see Dickie 1984, 237–40; Perysinakis 1990.
112 A similar connection is made in the fictional narrative of the tutor in Sophocles' *Electra*, in which Orestes' beauty foreshadows his victory (*El.* 685–7). In *Trachiniae* 309, her appearance makes Iole stand out from the other slaves, suggesting to Deianeira that she is a woman of high birth; cf. Hall 1999, 111.

that Cassandra, like her brother, is represented as a victor. Cassandra, in her prophetic frenzy, invites her grief-stricken mother to crown her (*Tro.* 353–4):[113]

μῆτερ, πύκαζε κρᾶτ' ἐμὸν νικηφόρον
καὶ χαῖρε τοῖς ἐμοῖσι βασιλικοῖς γάμοις·
Mother, deck my victorious head with wreaths
and rejoice in my royal marriage.

Cassandra suffers from a perverted sense of grandeur believing that her fatal concubinage to Agamemnon signifies Trojan victory over the Greeks. Seeking the wreath of victory through her revenge, Cassandra parallels a similar statement made by Orestes in Euripides' *Electra* (614). However, Cassandra's frantic behavior brings her closer to other tragic victors such as Heracles and Agaue. The reception of Cassandra by Hecuba mirrors the reception of the victorious Paris; in both cases, the epinician discourse is undercut first by Hecuba's plot to kill Paris and second by Cassandra's delirium. The failure of Hecuba's scheme to kill the former leads to the utter destruction staged in *Troades*.[114]

In addition to the scene with Cassandra, the death of Astyanax offers further confirmation of the reversal of the epinician discourse used in *Alexandros* in the last play of the Trojan Trilogy. As Owen Goslin (2014) notes, the death of Hector's son is represented in athletic terms: the casting of Astyanax from the walls of Troy resembles the throwing of a discus (*Tro.* 1121). Furthermore, in her mourning for the boy, Hecuba defines the roles her grandson was never allowed to perform: in addition to marriage and offering funeral honors to Hecuba, these include participation in athletic competitions and the possibility of victory (*Tro.* 1209–13).[115] Goslin thus argues that Astyanax dies before he is granted the opportunity to prove his noble descent by participating in athletic contests in the manner of Paris in *Alexandros*. I would also add that Astyanax's death mirrors the infancy of Paris, when he too was cast out of the city. This symmetry tightens the structure of the whole trilogy in a ring form. This extreme measure of ejecting the infant Paris was supposed to save Troy. The failure of Priam and Hecuba's plan leads eventually to the demise of Paris' nephew. Astyanax's death, thus, offers a poignant variation of what ought to have been Paris' fate all along. Paris becomes a victor and thus thwarts the epinician prospects of

---

113 The image is ambiguous. Wreaths are used also in weddings; cf. Blech 1982, 75–81 and 109–77. But in connection with νικηφόρον it refers to an athletic victory: cf. Eur. *El.* 854, 862, 872.
114 Cf. Scodel 1980, 118–20.
115 Cf. Biehl 1989, 425 *ad loc.*

his brother's son. The irony becomes greater if one considers Hector's conciliatory tone towards Paris in the first play of the trilogy. With the death of Astyanax, the line of Priam is wiped out and with it any hope for its fame to survive the passage of time.

Heracles, *Electra*, *Bacchae*, and *Medea* undermine epinician discourse by representing the shedding of kindred blood as part of the victory of the tragic hero. In contrast to these plays, *Alexandros* focuses on the problems caused by the victor, not his victory. To a certain degree the questions that surround Paris are the result of his status as a slave, but this answer is only partially satisfactory. Cassandra reveals the victor's identity and so restores Paris to his true position. Fr. **62 g *TrGF*[5.1] implies that Cassandra, like Deiphobus, commends caution towards the tragic victor but for different reasons. Euripides emphasizes Paris' condition as a slave and the role that the funerary games have as the means whereby he is restored to his princely status. In this manner, Euripides focuses on the sinister overtones of Paris' victories and problematizes athletic performance in a manner inherently different from other plays. The reasons for doing so lie, I suggest, in the socio-political ambience in which he composed his play and specifically in the athletic victories of Alcibiades and their reception in the collective Athenian consciousness. The myth of Paris becomes in the hands of Euripides the vehicle to convey to the audience the problematic relationship of athletic victories, politics, and social stability in the times prior to the Sicilian expedition.[116] This interpretation gains strength by the fact that, unlike Heracles or Orestes, Paris has no clear athletic or epinician connotations in surviving literature. The epinician discourse used to convey this role could have been motivated by two considerations: first, Alcibiades' recent Olympic victories in the previous year; and second, the comparison of Alcibiades to an athlete often found in fourth-century sources.[117] Alcibiades' character, his commitment to Athens, and political aims were an issue of speculation already during his lifetime. Plutarch compares Alcibiades to a chameleon, thus reflecting his unique ability to adapt, excel, and survive under diverse political circumstances.[118] This ability won him admiration but also raised questions about his democratic ethos and credentials. I would suggest that the speculation touching upon Paris' identity, obvious in the discussions of Deiphobus with both Hector and Hecuba, recreates the same feeling or uncertainty that characterizes Athenian attitudes

---

[116] Eur. *Tro.* 220–3 are usually taken to imply Athenian fascination with Sicily; cf. Lee 1976, 106–7. For the possibility that *Troades* refers to the Sicilian expedition, see Delebecque 1951, 245–62; Scodel 1980, 139; Croally 1994, 231–4.
[117] E.g. Xen. *Mem.* 1.2.24; Pl. *Alc. I* 119b5–10.
[118] Plut. *Alc.* 23.3–9.

towards Alcibiades.[119] But tragedy is not history and before examining further possible connections between the two personages we need to examine the importance of mythological discourse in contemporaneous literary depictions of Alcibiades.

The association of Alcibiades with tragedy in fourth-century BC sources can help us reconstruct the cultural and political ambience in which Euripides wrote his play despite the interval of half a century. For instance, Andocides 4, a speech falsely attributed to Andocides but probably of later date (*ca.* 350 BC),[120] compares Alcibiades' behavior during the capture of Melos with that of Thyestes, who sired a son by his own daughter (Andoc. 4.22).[121] Explaining the analogy, the speaker constructs a wider one between tragic myth and contemporary politics that is of interest to our discussion (Andoc. 4.23):

> Ἀλλ' ὑμεῖς ἐν μὲν ταῖς τραγῳδίαις τοιαῦτα θεωροῦντες δεινὰ νομίζετε, γιγνόμενα δ' ἐν τῇ πόλει ὁρῶντες οὐδὲν φροντίζετε.
>
> When you watch things of this kind in tragedies, you regard them with horror; but when you see them taking place in our city, you remain unmoved.

This passage gives us a glimpse of what must have been a wider tendency in contemporaneous political discourse: to sensationalize the events in the life of prominent political figures by representing them in terms of well-known tragic myths.

The *agōn* between Aeschylus and Euripides in Aristophanes' *Frogs* brings further evidence in support of this thesis. Dionysus asks both contestants to express their opinion regarding Alcibiades. Dionysus nicely summarizes the schizophrenic infatuation of the Athenian populace with Alcibiades (*Ran.* 1425): 'they long for him, they hate him, they want him back' (ποθεῖ μέν, ἐχθαίρει δέ, βούλεται δ' ἔχειν). Nonetheless, both Aeschylus and Euripides condemn Alcibiades as dangerous for the city. Dionysus' address to Euripides as Palamedes at line 1451 could suggest that Aristophanes refers in these lines to Euripides' Trojan Trilogy

---

119 Both Paris (fr. 62d.22 *TrGF*[5.1]) and Alcibiades (Plut. *Alc.* 23.3) are said to inspire admiration in the citizens. Admiration is also found in Euripides' ode for Alcibiades (fr. 755.1 *PMG*). On Alcibiades' seeking admiration through his chariot victories, see Nicias' accusations at Thuc. 6.12.2; cf. Hornblower 2008: 333–4. Nonetheless, Alcibiades answers plausibly and wins the debate; cf. Kyriakou 2007, 149–50 and 155.
120 See Gribble 1997, 154–8.
121 Cf. Cobetto Ghiggia 1995, 227–8; Gribble 1999: 133. For a similar comparison regarding Callias' son by his mother-in-law, see Andoc. 1.129.

of 415 BC. But the strongest evidence in support of the proposed interpretation derives from the fact that Euripides composed an epinician for Alcibiades (frr. 755–756 *PMG*) the year before the Trojan Trilogy. Although the inclusion of epinician elements in Euripides' dramas antedates the commission of the ode by Alcibiades by at least one decade, if not longer than that, the production of *Alexandros* in such close proximity to the ode for Alcibiades lends strength to the proposed connection.[122] The celebration of Alcibiades' Olympic victories by Euripides in 416 BC ought not to devalue the apprehensive attitude that Euripides adopts towards Alcibiades a year later, by comparing him to Paris. On the contrary, it gives this connection further edge since Euripides has an insider's knowledge regarding Alcibiades' construal of his athletic victory and the political significance thereof.[123]

Both surviving fragments of Euripides' ode focus on two elements that resonate throughout the Trojan Trilogy: the number of chariots entered by Alcibiades in the race (i.e. his use of wealth) and his relationship to Athens.[124] Further elements of Euripides' praise discourse may be tentatively, but persuasively, restored thanks to Isoc. 16.25–8, a defense of Alcibiades by his son. Alcibiades' son tries to substantiate his father's democratic credentials by providing a catalogue of his ancestors' benefactions to Athens.[125] This catalogue focuses on Alcmaeon's Olympic victory in the chariot race. Alcmaeon demonstrated his commitment to democracy by fleeing the regime of Peisistratus. Furthermore, Alcibiades' grandfathers on both sides led the army of exiles back to Athens and restored democracy. Innate excellence combined with commitment to the *dēmos* are central to the construction of Alcibiades' public image but of an ambiguous nature, as can be deduced by the attack that Lysias (14.36–40) launches against Alcibiades and his ancestors. Alcibiades' son also mentions his father's military successes as well as his generous spending for public services (Isoc. 16.29–30). At Thuc. 6.16.2, Alcibiades himself associates his athletic victory with the prospects of Athens in the forthcoming expedition. Alcibiades construes his exorbitant spending in Olympia as a tactical maneuver meant to impress the foes of Athens and emphasize the city's resources and military supremacy.[126] However, the degree to which Alcibiades' victory benefited Athens is debated

---

[122] For the date of the epinician for Alcibiades, see Bowra 1960, 69–71.
[123] Cf. Bowra 1960, 69. Delebecque (1951, 260–1) attributes Euripides' change of heart towards Alcibiades to the latter's role in the events on Melos that intervened between the Olympic games of 416 BC and the performance of the Trojan Trilogy.
[124] Cf. fr. 755 *PMG* and fr. 756 *PMG* respectively.
[125] The same point is made by Alcibiades himself at Thuc. 6.16.1.
[126] Cf. Hornblower 2008, 342. See also Andoc. 4.29–32; Isoc. 16.32–5.

in ancient sources. Nicias and even Thucydides, himself, imply that Alcibiades sought to impress the populace in order to get elected to high offices and thus sustain his living beyond his means.[127] Despite Alcibiades' claims to the contrary, it is only natural that the average Athenian would look apprehensively on Alcibiades' excessive and illogical spending, fearing about his true aims.

Wealth and its proper use is a staple theme of epinician discourse, especially in the odes celebrating chariot victories.[128] Wealth is seen as the means of benefiting people and attracting good fame.[129] At Isoc. 16.28, Alcmaeon's Olympic victory is the 'fairest memorial of wealth' (πλούτου μέγιστον μνημεῖον) bringing fame to Athens and its citizens. It is interesting that wealth plays an important role in the first two plays of the trilogy. Paris nonchalantly disregards the use of wealth as a means of social stratification. However, and this ought to be stressed, Paris' declarations do not equal a clear-cut rejection of wealth. Wealth is the means to achieve fame, but not the goal. In this sense, it is very common for epinician poets to juxtapose *kerdos* with *kleos*. Seeking solely *kerdos* is not conducive to achieving immortal fame.[130] The two concepts are contrasted in the debate of Hector and Deiphobus in *Alexandros* (fr. 62b *TrGF*[5.1]). Paris, the messenger, and the members of the first chorus juxtapose two lifestyles (fr. 55 *TrGF*[5.1]):[131] that of the royal princes, characterized by luxury and idleness, and that of Paris, full of activity and toil (frr. 54, 61b–c *TrGF*[5.1]). Instead of employing wealth to improve his chances of *kleos*, Deiphobus egotistically guards the social prerogatives that ensue from its possession. *Palamedes*, the second play in the trilogy, must have included a discussion of the disastrous effects wealth has on men, the more so as Palamedes was put to death after being accused of bribery by the Trojans.[132] *Alexandros* discusses wealth in connection with noble birth and prowess, while *Palamedes* focuses on wealth and its meaning for the truly wise man. Like Paris, Palamedes exemplifies the case of the charismatic individual, who, on account of his wisdom, causes the envy of his community, specifically Odysseus, because of his excellence.[133]

---

[127] Thuc. 6.12.2; 6.15.2.
[128] Cf. Pind. *Ol.* 5.15; *Isthm.* 1.42; 4.47; 6.10. On δαπάνα in Pindar, see Hubbard 1985, 14–15 with n. 12, 108; Campagner 1988, 82–4; Kurke 1991, 98–9. For Alcibiades' athletic spending, see Hornblower 2004, 250–61.
[129] E.g. Pind. *Ol.* 2.53–6; *Pyth.* 1.90; 3.110–1; *Nem.* 1.31–2; Bacchyl. 3.13–14, 64–6.
[130] Pind. *Pyth.* 1.92–4; *Nem.* 7.17–18; see also *Isthm* 1.67–8; cf. Pavese 1966, 108–10; Campagner 1988, 89–91; Hubbard 1985, 93; Kurke 1991, *passim*. The idea derives ultimately from epic: cf. Hom. *Od.* 8.159–64 with Dickie's (1984, 247–51) discussion.
[131] For the attribution of this fragment to Paris, see Cropp 2004, 74–5 and 76 *ad loc*.
[132] Cf. Scodel 1980, 56–7, 90–3; Collard 2004, 94–5.
[133] Cf. Scodel 1980, 54–5.

The analogy between Alcibiades and Paris could thus account for the ominous dimensions that epinician celebrations acquire in the surviving fragments of *Alexandros*. In fr. 62d Hecuba asks Deiphobus about the whereabouts of the victor. Deiphobus responds by describing the celebrations (fr. 62d.27–8 *TrGF*[5.1]):

—ποῦ νῦ[ν ἄ]ν εἴη καλλίνικ' ἔχων στέφη;
—πᾶν ἄστυ πληροῖ Τρωικὸν γαυρούμενος.

Where could he now be, bearing the wreaths of victory?
He is filling the whole town of Troy with his exultation.

The participle γαυρούμενος ('exulting') is ambiguous. It gives an impression of arrogance and could recall the accusations made by the other herdsmen against Paris in the first part of the play. The implication is that the wreathed victor heads a festive procession through the city,[134] an event often represented as an appropriate performance scenario in epinician poetry.[135] This historical background sheds additional light on the mistrust with which Deiphobus views Paris' epinician procession. There is no information concerning Alcibiades' –return from his scandalous performance at Olympia in 416 BC. Still, as David Gribble (1999, 67–8) has suggested, one may consider Alcibiades' triumphal reception by the Athenians in 407 BC, eight years after Euripides' play, as representative of what probably transpired in 416 BC. In the descriptions of Alcibiades' return from the Hellespont given respectively by Xenophon, Plutarch, and Cornelius Nepos, the return of Alcibiades resembles that of a victorious athlete very closely. Cornelius Nepos (*Alc.* 6.3) draws an explicit analogy between the reception of Alcibiades and that of an Olympic victor. Alcibiades is surrounded by an admiring crowd; he is crowned with wreaths, golden if we believe Nepos, and paraded in the streets of Athens.[136] The reaction of the Athenians to Alcibiades' return can be easily paralleled to that of the Trojans.

Another point of comparison for Paris' κῶμος could lie with the activities of Alcibiades' group of friends, his ἑταιρεία ('political club or union').[137] Κῶμος describes any sort of merriment and is very common in the textual representation of epinician celebrations. However, κῶμοι, especially in Athens, acquired a rep-

---

[134] Cf. Plato *Resp.* 621d. Fr. 62d.50 *TrGF*[5.1] could refer to leaves left on the victor from the *phullobolia*; cf. Cropp 2004, 85. For the victor as participant or leader of the celebrations, see Agócs 2012, 198 with n. 51.
[135] Compare the procession led by Agaue in *Bacchae*; Pind. *Ol.* 9.1–4; *Nem.* 9; *Isthm.* 8.1–4. Cf. Privitera 1982, 226; Heath 1988, 183; Braswell 1998, 42, 45–6; Agócs 2012, 206.
[136] Xen. *Hell.* 1.4.13; Plut. *Alc.* 32.3–4; Corn. Nep. *Alc.* 6.
[137] Cf. Aurenche 1974, 25.

utation for disorderly and riotous behavior.[138] A fine example of this is provided by Alcibiades' arrival in Agathon's banquet in the Platonic *Symposium* (212c3–213b2). Alcibiades leads a group of drunken revelers, which upsets the order of the banquet. Alcibiades' depiction in this scene is indicative of the anxiety his behavior causes, strengthening suspicions of anti-democratic or even tyrannical behavior: Alcibiades' unexpected and violent arrival disrupts the orderliness of Agathon's banquet.[139] On the eve of the Sicilian expedition, some months after the performance of Euripides' play, a similar group of aristocratic youths headed by Alcibiades was associated with the parody of the Eleusinian mysteries and the beheading of the Hermes columns. Both incidents scandalized the Athenian population to such a degree that Alcibiades resorted to self exile in order to avoid punishment.[140] Behavior such as this exposes Alcibiades to the collective consciousness of the Athenian society as a reckless individual without any concern about or respect for the sensitivities of the people, intimating tyrannical ambitions.[141]

The political ambivalence that surrounds Paris' victories can be best illustrated by a comparison to other Euripidean tragedies staging the return of a tragic victor. In other plays of Euripides, the opponent of the tragic victor is represented as a tyrant (Lycus; Aegisthus). By killing him, the tragic victor restores political order; this is not the case in *Alexandros*, in which Paris becomes the locus of anxiety and is believed to threaten the political establishment.[142] The ominous role that Paris plays is successfully conveyed through the discord that he brings into Priam's house. Specifically, the arrival of Hector and Deiphobus betokens the rift that Paris' victories can bring into the royal family (fr. 62a.2–4 *TrGF*[5.1]):[143]

---

138 Heath 1988, 180; Agócs 2012, 198–201. For the connection between drunken κῶμοι and epinician celebrations, see Athanassaki 2012, 203–4. For the polyvalence of the term κῶμος, see Eckerman 2010; Agócs 2012, 198.
139 Cf. Gribble 1999, 251.
140 See Andoc. 1.11–18, 1.34–45; Isoc. 16.6–7; Lys. 14.42; Thuc. 6.28.1; Plut. *Alc.* 22; cf. Aurenche 1974, 160–8; Andrewes 1992, 446–53.
141 Cf. Aurenche 1974, 171–5; Gribble 1999, 81. For the fear of tyranny that Alcibiades inspired in Athenians, see Thuc. 6.15.3–4; Andoc. 4.24. Isoc. 16.5, 25, 28, 38 dispels this accusation as unfounded.
142 In both Iolcus and Corinth, Medea unsettles the political community by causing the death of the respective kings.
143 The triumphant, albeit ambiguous, return of the victor to his family's house is preceded by, and juxtaposed with that of the two defeated athletes, Hector and Deiphobus, see Huys 1986. For such juxtapositions of arrivals in tragedy, see Mastronarde 2010, 66. The juxtaposition of the νόσ-

> καὶ μὴν ὁρῶ τόνδ]' Ἕκτορ' ἐξ ἀγωνίω[ν
> περῶντα μό]χθων σύγγονόν τε παῖδε σώ [,
> ....] εἰς δ' ἅμιλλαν ἥκουσιν λόγων.
>
> "<And I see now> Hector here returning from the toils of
> the games and his brother, your two children
> ... they have entered a contest in words."

The competition now takes place in the *oikos* and is transformed into a 'conflict in words' (fr. 62a.4 *TrGF*[5.1]), ἅμιλλα also describing athletic competition. These competitions normally lay outside the household, because it was the minimal unit of integrity. The use of ἅμιλλα twice in Jason's discourse to Medea confirms the sinister implication of the word in this fragment as well. Jason engages, against his wishes, in a contest of speeches that Medea has organized (*Med.* 546, ἅμιλλαν γάρ σὺ προύθηκας λόγων). Later in the same scene he rejects the accusation that he competes in a contest against other men about the number of his sons (*Med.* 557, οὐδ' εἰς ἅμιλλαν πολύτεκνον σπουδὴν ἔχων).[144] Both instances conceptualize the breakdown of the *oikos* making use of athletic discourse. The disastrous results that such interfamilial strife could have in *Alexandros* are shown by the potential filicide that Hecuba comes close to perpetrating. Ironically, had Hecuba succeeded in her plot to kill Paris, Troy might have survived destruction.

In his speech to the Athenian assembly, before the Sicilian expedition, Alcibiades associates the charges brought against him with the φθόνος ('envy') that citizens feel at his spending; this spending concerns not only his participation in costly chariot races but also his providing choruses or discharging other public duties (Thuc. 6.16.2). Alcibiades lays the emphasis on δαπάνη ('spending') and not on the victory *per se*, following a point that Euripides must have made in his ode as well; but it cannot be denied that Alcibiades' victory and his ambition to situate himself above his co-citizens finds an attractive parallel in Paris' ambition to distinguish himself. Alcibiades employs his spending and the ensuing distinction as the evidence of his superiority over other citizens (Thuc. 6.16.4): 'nor is it wrong for a man who takes pride in himself to refuse to stand on an equal footing with others' (οὐδέ γε ἄδικον ἐφ' ἑαυτῷ μέγα φρονοῦντα μὴ ἴσον εἶναι). What Alcibiades means by μέγα φρονεῖν is indicated by his desire to excel both in athletics and politics. In his cursory description of Alcibiades' contradictory personality, Plutarch (*Alc.* 2.1) mentions Alcibiades' 'love of victory'

τος of the victor with that of the defeated athletes could be a Pindaric reminiscence: cf. Pind. *Pyth.* 8.83–7 and *Ol.* 8.69.
144 Cf. Mastronarde 2002 on line 557.

(τὸ φιλόνικον) and the 'desire to be first' (τὸ φιλόπρωτον) as his defining attributes. It is this 'aggressive competitiveness' or 'superb individualism,' as David Gribble (1999, 12–13) calls it, that brings Alcibiades closer to Euripides' Paris. In a manner similar to Euripides in *Alexandros*, Isocrates (16.29–30) associates Alcibiades' zeal to excel and claim *kleos* with his descent from noble ancestors. This family background also motivates Alcibiades' loyalty to the civic body at Isoc. 16.5 in spite of the lies Alcibiades' opponents fabricated. It is to such lies and jealousies that Isocrates (16.38) attributes the fears of Alcibiades' tyrannical ambitions.[145] Envy, a pivotal theme of *Alexandros* as it constantly surrounds and threatens Paris, figures prominently in Alcibiades' life, offering a further point of contact between the two men. After Paris' victory, the threat comes from his family. However, before his success in the games, it is the envy of his fellow herdsmen that poses the greatest threat. Paris sees them as his inferiors, and his behavior motivates them to deprive him of his freedom and potentially of his life. Paris construes the accusations leveled against him as διαβολαί ('slander'), the expression of the envy his fellow herdsmen feel about his feats of prowess (fr. 56.1 *TrGF*[5.1]). In fr. 56 *TrGF*[5.1], which is believed to derive from the debate scene, Paris adroitly describes the situation at hand in terms of the contrasting rhetorical skill and rhetorical inexperience of the participants:

ἄναξ, διαβολαὶ δεινὸν ἀνθρώποις κακόν·
ἀγλωσσίαι δὲ πολλάκις ληφθεὶς ἀνήρ,
δίκαια λέξας, ἧσσον εὐγλώσσου φέρει.

My lord, slander is a horrible evil for men;
very often a man, lacking in eloquence,
loses to an eloquent man even though he spoke justly.

The term ἀγλωσσία ('want of eloquence') that Paris chooses to describe his situation has been seen to allude to the cognate adjective ἄγλωσσος ('lacking in eloquence') that Pindar uses for Ajax at *Nem.* 8.24:[146] 'a man lacking eloquence but of brave heart.' (ἤ τιν' ἄγλωσσον μέν, ἦτορ δ' ἄλκιμον).[147] Ajax's ἀγλωσσία prevents him from successfully protecting his reputation from the 'shifty lie' of Odysseus (*Nem.* 8.25 αἰόλῳ ψεύδει). In Nemean 8, Ajax's excellence is not acknowledged by his envious comrades although it is evident by way of the courageous acts he has performed during the war. The failure of his fellow Greeks to

---

145 See, for instance, Andoc. 4.16, 4.24 with Cobetto Ghiggia's 1995 notes *ad loc.*
146 The possibility of such a connection is perhaps strengthened in light of the epinician echoes that also permeate Sophocles' *Ajax:* cf. Hubbard 2000.
147 Cf. Cropp 2004, 76 on fr. 56 *TrGF*[5.1]; Di Giuseppe 2012, 93.

appreciate his prowess leads Ajax to take his own life. Similarly, Paris' comrades and family fail to appreciate his excellence, which has been expressed through his bucolic exploits and athletic successes. The herdsmen and Deiphobus do not praise Paris; their discourse is consumed with ψόγος ('blame').[148] Despite Paris' claims to lack the rhetorical dexterity necessary to defend himself against his accusers, he demonstrates persuasive rhetorical ability in convincing Priam to allow him to participate in the games. This capability follows, not unexpectedly, from Euripides' 'universalization of rhetorical skill.'[149] Euripides could imply similarities in the situations of both Ajax and Paris, but the context also emphasizes the distance between the two characters: Paris proves himself successful where Ajax fails. In addition to this parallel, Paris exhibits something of Alcibiades' notorious rhetorical prowess, which, according to Andocides, enabled him to misrepresent himself to the Athenian population and slander his political opponents.[150]

4 Conclusions

The above discussion has shown that the incorporation of epinician imagery in Euripidean tragedy follows a specific structure that perverts the νόστος of the victorious athlete. In this manner, Euripides emphasizes the alienation of the tragic hero, the frailty of the praise he receives from other characters, and the violent reversal of his fate. The devices and motifs operating in this pattern (e.g. ἀγών; innate excellence) can be found also in *Alexandros*. However, the plot of this tragedy, as far as can be reconstructed on the basis of the available fragments, suggests that *Alexandros* diverged in significant details from the pattern detected in other Euripidean plays. These divergences arise for two reasons. First from the fact that *Alexandros* is not an autonomous play but operates within the framework of a trilogy. This consideration explains why the last two stages of Euripides' epinician pattern (i.e., destruction and exile) are not included in *Alexandros* but become clear only in the third play of the trilogy, *Troades*, which reverses the plot of *Alexandros*. Troy is destroyed and the Trojan women are led away in captivity. The second significant difference between *Alexandros* and

---

[148] Cf. Pind. *Pyth.* 2.53–6. See also Miller 1981, 139–41; Nagy 1979, 224–6, 250–2; Kurke 1991, 100–1.
[149] I borrow the term from Mastronarde 2010, 209–13. The mention of one's rhetorical inadequacy is conventional in forensic and tragic rhetoric; cf. Scodel 1999–2000, 138–9; Di Giuseppe 2012, 92–3.
[150] For Alcibiades' rhetorical skills, see Andoc. 4.16, 4.22.

other plays concerns the status of Paris as victor. The problem in *Alexandros* is not the victory, which in other plays concerns the shedding of kindred blood, but rather the victor himself. By focusing on Paris' obscure origins and on the function of games as a test of inherent excellence, Euripides succeeds in endowing Paris' victory with a political quality missing from other plays. Paris proves his innate excellence like Heracles, but his unknown identity gives rise to speculations regarding his aims with respect to the political establishment. The inspiration for these elements of the plot lies, in all probability, in Alcibiades' Olympic victories of 416 BC for which Euripides composed an epinician ode. Several of the aspects that make up Paris' persona can be paralleled with elements we know about from Alcibiades' representation in contemporaneous sources, including Euripides' ode. Both figures are overambitious individuals, and their careers threaten the survival of their community as is proved by *Troades*. However, the negativity of Euripides' conception of Paris is seriously compromised, if not relativized, by the consideration of *Palamedes*. The second play of the trilogy offers a positive version of a charismatic individual, who, like Paris, is faced with lies and slander. Euripides focused on the problems that surround the interaction of Palamedes with his community, by recapturing several of the themes discussed in the first play. In both cases, Euripides seems to examine the responsibilities of communities towards a charismatic individual, suggesting that they too bear a share of the responsibility for the catastrophe that ensues. In this light, a significant divergence of the plot of *Alexandros* from other plays is that Paris never leaves Troy; he continues his existence in the vicinity of his home but under an assumed identity. His return is not a proper return, but a transition from a bucolic to civic environment. This peculiarity underlines the role that Priam and Hecuba play in bringing about their own downfall through their actions, first, by not following Apollo's warning and, second, by not heeding Cassandra's prophecies. Both plays agree in offering visions of decadent communities torn by internal strife, mistrust, and ambition. In times such as these, traditional means whereby a man's character can be appreciated, such as prowess (Paris) and wisdom (Palamedes), are shown to be inadequate and even misleading. The issue of man's true character and the problem of his relationship with the community permeate the first two parts of Euripides' Trojan Trilogy, putting into proper proportion Achaean claims of imminent glory and triumph in *Troades*.

III Performing the Chorus: Ritual, Song, and Dance

Richard Rawles
Theoric song and the Rhetoric of Ritual in Aeschylus' *Suppliant Women*

In this paper, I consider ways in which Aeschylus' *Suppliant Women* communicates in relation to audience expectations of behaviour by choruses. I am interested in examining how the Danaids present themselves as a chorus performing ritual actions, including song, as a strategy for achieving their goals: these actions include performances associated with particular ritual situations – we might speak of genre, and of situations closely connected with genre – and these attempts at efficacious speech and song consitute a form of rhetoric. I see the Danaids as trying to achieve what they want in an anomalous situation, where they are claiming the rights of suppliants but also the rights of kin, where they are foreigners, but also Hellenes who understand and belong within a world of Greek ritual and religion. They respond to this with a kind of bricolage of rhetoric and ritual. Most importantly they claim the rights of *hiketides*, suppliants; but they also appeal to kinship through the story of Io, their genealogical link to Argos; they use exemplary mythical narrative, through the way in which they tell Io's story. In what follows, without wishing to deny the central importance of *hiketeia*, I shall unravel some other elements, especially concerning forms of chorality which are not specific to drama. I finish by considering the *exodos* of the play in terms of manipulation of features of embedded choral genres.

As such, what I do here represents a continuation in various respects of work by others, on this play and on aspects of social ritual in ancient Greece. In particular, I build on the analysis of chorality in the earlier part of the play by Athena Kavoulaki, and on the treatment of the end of the play by Laura Swift, while with regard to theoric choruses I have leant heavily on the work of Ian Rutherford.[1]

I am grateful to the editors of this volume for their help and patience, and to the organisers and participants of the conference for the stimulus of discussion and suggestions.

[1] Kavoulaki 2011; Swift 2010; Rutherford 1998, 2004, 2013.

1 Danaids as Chorus

Δαναὸς δὲ πατὴρ καὶ βούλαρχος
καὶ στασίαρχος τάδε πεσσονομῶν
κύδιστ' ἀχέων ἐπέκρινεν

(A. *Supp.* 11–3)

[DANAIDS] Our father Danaos, originator of our plan and leader of our band, surveying the situation like a gameboard, ordained this as the most honourable of sufferings...[2]

In Aeschylus' *Suppliant Women*, the chorus of the daughters of Danaus repeatedly show by word and deed their dependence on their father, even though his legal rights over them as their father are for the most part not stressed: as Kavoulaki has recently put it, 'Danaus... directs the chorus at every single step and the chorus, on their part, accept and expect his direction.'[3] Kavoulaki has further shown ways in which, at the start of the play, the vocabulary used by the Danaids draws attention to their status as a chorus in connection with their entrance procession, the identity of their group, and their relationship with Danaos. She analyses their designation of Danaos as στασίαρχος 'leader of the group' (A. *Supp.* 12), and interprets this word as suggesting Danaos' role as one who governs (ἄρχω) the established and organised band (στάσις): a term suggesting the role of a χορηγός in relation to a chorus.[4] As an analogue for the combination of the roles of father and chorus-leader, she compares Danaus with the father of Damaina, invited to 'lead' a chorus of *parthenoi* in Pindar's Theban *Daphnephorikon* (fr. 94b, 66–70):[5]

Δαμαίνας πα[τέ]ρ .. [. . .]ῳ νῦν μοι ποδὶ
στείχων ἁγέο· [τ]ὶν γὰρ ε[ὔ]φρων ἕψεται
πρώτα θυγάτηρ [ὁ]δοῦ

---

2 Here and elsewhere my Greek text of Aeschylus' play is from West's Teubner edition (West 1990a), although in a few places I have preferred different readings; translations are adapted from Sommerstein's Loeb (Sommerstein 2008a).
3 Kavoulaki 2001, 354–5 (quotation from 354), citing West 1990b, 171.
4 Kavoulaki 2011, esp. 357–63 and this should be read in the context of Kavoulaki's analysis of the vocabulary of chorality elsewhere in the play; *contra*, Friis-Johansen/Whittle 1980 ad loc., who understand 'leader or originator of sedition' and reject 'leader of a troop or party': but we may imagine that the term, which occurs here for the first time in attested Greek and does not resurface until much later times, may have been capable of conveying more than one association to members of the audience; cf. Sommerstein 1977, 67, Bowen 2013 ad loc., both speaking of 'ambiguity', and Kavoulaki 2011, 373.
5 ed. Maehler, trans. after Race (Loeb). Kavoulaki 2011, 367–8, 380–2. Cf. Murnaghan 2005, 191.

δάφνας εὐπετάλου σχεδ[ό]ν
βαίνοισα πεδίλοις

66 πα[τέ]ρ suppl. Lehnus

Father of Damaina, stepping forward now with a [...] foot, lead the way for me! Your kindly daughter will be first to follow you on the way, walking on sandals close to the branch of leafy bay.

In addition to showing how the choral character of the group of young women is written into the words of the play, this approach helps us to understand a feature of the play sometimes seen as a deficiency: the silence of Danaos from the entrance of Pelasgos at 234 until Pelasgos has announced his decision to help the Danaids in the speech ending some 250 lines later, as if Aeschylus had not yet realised how to use a second actor.[6] We might see this as reflecting the role of a χορηγός who instructs the chorus, and then stands aside while they perform.

More broadly, as many choruses do, the Danaids repeatedly perform ritual forms such as prayers and present themselves as singers or mark the ritual or performative qualities of their songs by *calling* them prayers, praise, song and so on, encouraging the audience to see them as a chorus performing in ritual contexts as choruses do.[7] From the initial procession towards an altar with statues of the gods until the departure into the city in the *exodos*, the audience sees a co-ordinated group moving in relation to sacred space: this shows the Danaids as a chorus within the play as well as in the Dionysia. The Danaids' ability to perform as an organised chorus is one of the respects in which, although foreign in costume and appearance, they know the 'language' of Greek religion and custom, as Pelasgos observes (241–3):[8]

---

[6] Before the publication of *P.Oxy.* 2256 fr.3, on which see Garvie 2006, chapter 1, the play was widely regarded as Aeschylus' earliest surviving; on the handling of Danaus and the perception that this reflected primitiveness of dramatic technique with regard to the second actor, see Garvie 2006, 126–30, with references to earlier treatments. For a particularly interesting and productive return to the play seen in terms of the earlier history of tragedy, see Murnaghan 2005, whose stress on the analogy between the Danaids and extra-dramatic chorality coheres with my own approach, and who stresses the individuation of Hypermestra and her separation from the chorus during the plot of the trilogy as an analogue for the emergence of actor from chorus in Aristotle's account of the origins of tragedy.
[7] e.g. 57–65, 69–71, 115–6, 625–9, 656–8, 808–10, 1018–25.
[8] On the complex presentation of ethnicity in the play, see e.g. Mitchell 2006.

κλάδοι γε μὲν δὴ κατὰ νόμους ἀφικτόρων
κεῖνται παρ' ὑμῶν πρὸς θεοῖς ἀγωνίοις·
μόνον τόδ''Ελλὰς χθὼν συνοίσεται στόχῳ.

[PELASGOS] And yet suppliant branches are lying beside you, before the Assembled Gods, according to our customs. Only this would confirm the conjecture that you were Greek.

2 *Hiketeia* and *Theōria*

The chorus' basic action is *arrival*. This is the etymological sense of *hiketeia*, 'supplication', from the same root as ἱκνέομαι, and the etymological connection was probably audible to classical speakers.⁹ The *process* of arrival takes up the whole play: the chorus aims to achieve what happens in the *exodos*, i.e. entry within the walls of Argos. This is partly a matter of setting: the chorus does not supplicate the Argives inside the city, but at an extra-mural altar to the Twelve Gods.

I would like to explore this pattern – a chorus from outside the city arrives and demands admission into the city – in terms of its resonances with a phenomenon which has been explored above all by Ian Rutherford: choral *theōria*, ritual travel by a chorus for religious purposes.¹⁰ This might seem a rather specific interpretation of a general pattern – again, Kavoulaki has described the arrival–reception pattern here as a much broader schema, without particular reference to *theōria*.¹¹ The pattern arrival–reception cannot be *restricted* only to particular subsets of ritual behaviour, but can also (for example) map on to cases of supplication and *xenia* which are quite separate from *theōria*.

However, there are particular reasons why I think the idea of a theoric chorus is relevant. In lines 209–21, Danaos and his daughters inspect the altar of the Twelve Gods outside Argos, with statues of the gods:

Χο. ὦ Ζεῦ, κόπων οἴκτιρε μὴ ἀπολωλότας.	(209)
Δα. κείνου θέλοντος εὖ τελευτήσει τάδε.	(211)
καὶ Ζηνὸς ὄρνιν τόνδε νῦν κικλήσκετε.	
Χο. καλοῦμεν αὐγὰς ἡλίου σωτηρίους.	
Δα. ἁγνόν τ' Ἀπόλλω, φυγάδ' ἀπ' οὐρανοῦ θεόν.	
Χο. εἰδὼς ἂν αἶσαν τήνδε συγγνοίη βροτοῖς.	(215)
Δα. συγγνοῖτο δῆτα καὶ παρασταίη πρόφρων.	
Χο. τίν' οὖν κικλήσκω τῶνδε δαιμόνων ἔτι;	

---

9 e.g. Hornblower sv. 'Supplication, Greek' in *OCD⁴*; on the ritual, Gould 1973, Haiden 2006.
10 Rutherford 2004; 2013, 236–49.
11 Kavoulaki 2011, 368–74.

ΔΑ. ὁρῶ τρίαιναν τήνδε σημεῖον θεοῦ.
Χο. ἀλλ' εὖ τ' ἔπεμψεν εὖ τε δεξάσθω χθονί.
ΔΑ. κῆρυξ ὅδ' ἄλλος τοῖσιν Ἑλλήνων νόμοις. (220)
Χο. ἐλευθέροις νυν ἐσθλὰ κηρυκευέτω.

desunt paragraphi. 210 post 206 transposuit Burges. 220 κῆρυξ Kueck (nescio an recte); Ἑρμῆς M

CHORUS Zeus, take pity on our troubles before we perish!
DANAOS If he is willing, these things will end well. Now also call upon this bird of Zeus!
CHORUS We call on the rays of the Sun, which bring salvation.
DANAOS And holy Apollo, the god exiled from heaven.
CHORUS From his knowledge of such a fate, he will sympathise with us mortals.
DANAOS Indeed, may he do so, and may he willingly stand by us.
CHORUS Who else of these gods should I call upon?
DANAOS I see this trident, symbol of a god.
CHORUS He gave us a good voyage; may he give us a good reception in this land.
DANAOS This other one is the herald, according to the Greeks' usage.
CHORUS May he be the herald of good tidings to us in freedom!

The strangers recognise the statues from seeing the gods' attributes, in a passage rich in deictic words (and note ὁρῶ at 218). This scene of visiting a previously unseen shrine and identifying the subjects of works of art is unsurprising as a representation of *theōria* in drama. We see something similar with another female chorus in Euripides' *Ion* (Eur. *Ion* 184–218, a passage similarly marked by repeated deictic vocabulary and verbs of seeing), where the chorus of Creousa's maidservants inspect and point out to one another the decoration of the temple of Apollo at Delphi, identifying and pointing out to one another different gods and mythological scenes. Other theoric dramas also probably featured scenes of this kind.[12]

When the Danaids talk to Pelasgos, they present their ritual claims in a way which connects their status as suppliants with the claims of *theoroi* (A. *Supp.* 340–53):

ΠΕΛ. πῶς οὖν πρὸς ὑμᾶς εὐσεβὴς ἐγὼ πέλω; (340)
Χο. αἰτοῦσι μὴ 'κδοὺς παισὶν Αἰγύπτου πάλιν.
ΠΕΛ. βαρέα σύ γ' εἶπας, πόλεμον ἄρασθαι νέον.
Χο. ἀλλ' ἡ Δίκη γε ξυμμάχων ὑπερστατεῖ.
ΠΕΛ. εἴπερ γ' ἀπ' ἀρχῆς πραγμάτων κοινωνὸς ἦι.
Χο. αἰδοῦ σὺ πρύμναν πόλεος ὧδ' ἐστεμμένην. (345)
ΠΕΛ. πέφρικα λεύσσων τάσδ' ἕδρας κατασκίους.
βαρύς γε μέντοι Ζηνὸς ἱκεσίου κότος.

---

12 See Rutherford 1998, *passim*; on the scene in *Ion*, 139.

Χο. Παλαίχθονος τέκος, κλῦθί μου [στρ. α.
πρόφρονι καρδίᾳ, Πελασγῶν ἄναξ.
ἴδε με τὰν ἱκέτιν φυγάδα περίδρομον, (350)
λυκοδίωκτον ὡς δάμαλιν ἂμ πέτραις
ἠλιβάτοις, ἵν' ἀλ-
κᾷ πίσυνος μέμυκε φρά-
ζουσα βοτῆρι μόχθους.

PELASGOS So how can I act piously towards you?
CHORUS By not giving us back to Aegyptos' sons when they ask.
PELASGOS Your demand is a hard one: to provoke an outbreak of war.
CHORUS But Justice stands by her allies.
PELASGOS She will – *if* she is a partner in your cause since the beginning.
CHORUS Respect the stern of the ship of state, thus garlanded.
PELASGOS I shudder, looking upon this divine abode in shadow: certainly the wrath of Zeus of suppliants is heavy.
CHORUS Son of Palaechthon, hear me with a gracious heart, lord of the Pelasgians. See me, the suppliant, wandering exile, like a wolf-chased heifer on the steep rocks, where, trusting to their protection, she lows, telling the herdsman her distress.

This is a crunch point in the dialogue, and when Pelasgos questions to what extent their case was a just one from the start it looks as if he is sceptical. So the Danaids (who give no direct answer to his question) up the pressure by appealing to their ritual status. By 'Respect the stern of the *polis*, garlanded thus!' they must mean, as commentators say, a comparison between the importance of the stern to the ship and the importance of the altar to the city.[13] They are using the familiar ship-of-state motif (and, by drawing attention to the place of the steersman, showing their assumption that Danaos is an absolute monarch; cf. 369–75). But the idea of a garlanded ship also alludes to a ship carrying a theoric delegation: in Plato's *Phaedo* (58a-b) we are told that the ship on which the Athenians sent an annual *theōria* to Delos was garlanded at the stern.[14] The garlanded ship represents the sacred status of persons involved in *theōria*, and the Danaids want this to increase the ritual pressure on Pelasgos.[15]

---

[13] See Friis Johansen/Whittle 1980 ad 345, speaking of the 'identification of the altar and the state'.
[14] Cf. Bowen 2013 ad loc., Friis Johansen/Whittle 1980 ad loc.; on the *Phaedo* passage, Rutherford 2013, 178, 299, 304.
[15] The ship sent by the Athenians to Delos was said to be the same one in which Theseus went to Crete, and the custom was said to go back to Theseus' time (Plato *Phaedo* 58a-b). The Danaids, on the other hand, despite their ancestral ties with Argos, stressed in their repeated appeals to their descent from Io, are not carrying out an anciently established custom of *theōria*: they are improvising sources of ritual pressure as they go along.

Pelasgos' response conflates *theōria* and *hikesia:* he does indeed feel αἰδώς for the sanctuary, and fears the wrath of Zeus Hikesios. Then the Danaids move into song, and appeal once more to the idea of Io by figuring themselves as a heifer pursued by a wolf.

Here the allusion to Io is indirect; elsewhere the Danaids sing and speak of Io overtly and persistently, especially before they discover that the Argive assembly has decided to admit them to the city. They sing of Io at the beginning and end of the *parodos* (16–18, 41–55, 141, 168–74); the scenes just discussed come from the following episode, in which they go through the story of Io with Pelasgos (291–315); after Pelasgos has gone to the assembly, they sing another *stasimon* in which Io features even more extensively (531–89); the final mention is in the *exodos* (1064–7). This is important in many ways; from the perspective I am adopting here it is a natural thing for them to do. The Danaids, upon arrival, immediately start performing their own identity and mythical history; specifically, performing their myth-historical relationship with Argos. This seems like a natural behaviour for a theoric chorus, using myth to articulate their relationship with their destination.[16] Similarly, *mutatis mutandis*, we can see traces of a complex and various choral discourse by which Athens and island communities play out different ways of conceiving their relationship with Delos under Athenian domination in songs which surely include songs for theoric performance on the island itself.[17]

In what seems to be a paean for performance on Delos by an Athenian chorus, for instance, a chorus describes Athenian colonisation in the Aegean, with Delos itself as the climax (Pindar *Paean* 5, D5 Rutherford, 36–42):[18]

  Εὔ-]
  βοιαν ἕλον καὶ ἔνασσαν·
  ἰήϊε Δάλι' Ἄπολλον·
  καὶ σποράδας φερεμήλους
  ἔκτισαν νάσους ἐρικυδέα τ' ἔσχον

---

16 For *theōria* and theoric song and collective identities, see Rutherford 2004, 67–9, 83–5, 89–90, Rutherford 2013, 241–2, 244–5; on *theōria* and the discourse of kinship-diplomacy (*sungeneia*), Rutherford 2013, 255, 265, 271.
17 Possible songs for theoric choruses on Delos: Bacch. 17, Pindar *Paean* 4 (D4 Rutherford), Pindar *Paean* 5 (D5 Rutherford). Cf. Fearn 2011, Kowalzig 2007a, ch. 2 (esp. 81–102), Rutherford 2000, Rutherford 2013, 240–1.
18 ed. Rutherford; trans. after Race (Loeb). For the argument that this is a song for an Athenian chorus, and discussion of its relationship to Athenian *theōria* to Delos, see Rutherford 2001, 295–8.

Δᾶλον, ἐπεί σφιν Ἀπόλλων (40)
δῶκεν ὁ χρυσοκόμας
Ἀστερίας δέμας οἰκεῖν·

They took Euboea and settled there – *Iēie*, Delian Apollo! – and founded settlements on the scattered, sheep-bearing islands, and they took famous Delos, when golden-haired Apollo gave to them Asteria's body to dwell upon.

The chorus sings the myth-historical story which explains their present relationship to the sanctuary and thus their presence as a theoric group: in this case, the story explains the Athenian control of the festival and justifies it as a gift of Apollo himself.

A story which Rutherford has related to possible theoric travel to Athens itself is even closer (868 *PMG* = Plutarch *Theseus* 16.2–3 [cf. *Quaest. Graecae* 35], citing Aristotle fr. 485 Rose):[19]

Ἀριστοτέλης δὲ καὶ αὐτὸς ἐν τῇ Βοττιαίων πολιτείᾳ δῆλός ἐστιν οὐ νομίζων ἀναιρεῖσθαι τοὺς παῖδας ὑπὸ τοῦ Μίνω, ἀλλὰ θητεύοντας ἐν τῇ Κρήτῃ καταγηράσκειν· καί ποτε Κρῆτας εὐχὴν παλαιὰν ἀποδιδόντας ἀνθρώπων ἀπαρχὴν εἰς Δελφοὺς ἀποστέλλειν, τοῖς δὲ πεμπομένοις ἀναμειχθέντας ἐκγόνους ἐκείνων συνεξελθεῖν· ὡς δ' οὐκ ἦσαν ἱκανοὶ τρέφειν ἑαυτοὺς αὐτόθι, πρῶτον μὲν εἰς Ἰταλίαν διαπερᾶσαι κἀκεῖ κατοικεῖν περὶ τὴν Ἰαπυγίαν, ἐκεῖθεν δ' αὖθις εἰς Θρᾴκην κομισθῆναι καὶ κληθῆναι Βοττιαίους· διὸ τὰς κόρας τῶν Βοττιαίων θυσίαν τινὰ τελούσας ἐπᾴδειν·
ἴωμεν εἰς Ἀθήνας.

Aristotle himself in his *Constitution of the Bottiaeans* clearly does not believe that the children were put to death by Minos, but rather that they served as labourers and grew old on Crete; and on one occasion, he says, the Cretans in fulfilment of an ancient vow sent a human sacrificial offering to Delphi, and descendants of the Athenians left Crete with the group; and when they were unable to support themselves there, they first of all crossed to Italy and settled in the region of Iapygia, and then moved again to Thrace and got the name of 'Bottiaeans'; and that is why the daughters of the Bottiaeans sing in the performance of a certain sacrifice:
'Let us go to Athens!'

Whether or not this reflects actual choral theōria from Bottiaea to Athens, it is a good example of the kind of theoric argument employed by the Danaids in our play, where they repeat the story which constitutes their claim to kinship with the Argives. It is easy to suppose that this might be regular theoric behaviour, perhaps especially at the point of arrival (rather than in the Bottiaean case, which looks like the point of departure), where the chorus makes a claim to be admitted to the sanctuary or city which is their destination.

---

[19] The translation is adapted from Campbell's Loeb edition.

3 From *prosodion* to *hymenaios:* the exodos

At the end of the play, the Danaids' programme is completed, and they process into the city: the entrance is the *exodos*. I begin with Danaos' speech immediately before (996–1009), in which he tells his daughters to be careful of their chastity, and says that they must not now suffer what they have travelled far to avoid (996–1009).

> ὑμᾶς δ' ἐπαινῶ μὴ καταισχύνειν ἐμέ,
> ὥραν ἐχούσας τήνδ' ἐπίστρεπτον βροτοῖς.
> τέρειν' ὀπώρα δ' εὐφύλακτος οὐδαμῶς·
> θῆρες δὲ κηραίνουσι καὶ βροτοί, τί μήν.
> καὶ κνώδαλα πτεροῦντα καὶ πεδοστιβῆ, (1000)
> καρπώματα στάζοντα κηρύσσει Κύπρις,
> κἄωρα μωλύουσ' ἄμ', ὡς μαίνειν ἔρῳ,
> καὶ παρθένων χλιδαῖσιν εὐμόρφοις ἔπι
> πᾶς τις παρελθὼν ὄμματος θελκτήριον
> τόξευμ' ἔπεμψεν, ἱμέρου νικώμενος. (1005)
> πρὸς ταῦτα μὴ πάθωμεν ὧν πολὺς πόνος,
> πολὺς δὲ πόντος οὕνεκ' ἠρόθη δορί,
> μηδ' αἶσχος ἡμῖν, ἡδονὴν δ' ἐχθροῖς ἐμοῖς
> πράξωμεν.

1002 incertissimum. κάλωρα κωλύουσαν θωσμένην ἐρῶ Μ; corr. Portus, West, Voss; alii alia.

[Danaos] I urge you not to bring shame upon me, since you have the youthful beauty which makes men turn their heads. Tender fruit is not at all easy to guard: beasts devour it – and men too, indeed! In the case of animals, both winged and walking, Cypris announces juicy fruits, while softening the unripe, so as to madden them with desire; and likewise with the beautiful charms of a beautiful maiden, everybody who passes by, vanquished by desire, shoots a glance of the eye at her that can melt her heart. Given these things, let us not suffer what we endured long toil and ploughed a long sea-furrow with our keel to avoid, and let us not cause disgrace to ourselves and pleasure to my enemies.

This lines may seem surprising: the Danaids have not previously seemed to need lessons in chaste behaviour, even if Friis-Johansen and Whittle are right to comment that 'the Danaids are not deficient in sexuality'.[20] Sommerstein comments that 'no other father, in a surviving text, makes such a song and dance about the matter [sc. the need for his unmarried daughters to preserve their virginity], and

---

[20] Friis Johansen/Whittle 1980 ad 996–1009; but at least sometimes it appears that the Danaids are hostile to marriage more broadly, and not only to marriage with their cousins: cf. works cited below, n.28. Arguing for hymenaeal associations of the traditional language of sexuality in this speech, see Swift 2010, 282–4.

Danaus' tirade is all the more remarkable because his daughters have not given the slightest indication of any tendency to go astray'.[21] Reasonably, many have connected this speech with the reconstruction of the trilogy, and it may well be that the passage would take on extra meaning if we knew what happened elsewhere.[22] However, this may distract from features of this speech which do not need to be connected to the reconstruction of the trilogy. It is usual for a father to be concerned with family honour and his daughters' chastity, and here this is on Danaos' mind because they are about to participate in a choral procession into a city. The same anxiety about female chastity threatened in public ritual contexts can be found elsewhere. In this passage from Aristophanes' *Acharnians*, the context for Dicaeopolis' anxiety is that he and his family are about to stage their private version of the procession of the rural Dionysia (Ar. *Ach*. 253–6):[23]

> ἄγ', ὦ θύγατερ, ὅπως τὸ κανοῦν καλὴ καλῶς
> οἴσεις βλέπουσα θυμβροφάγον. ὡς μακάριος
> ὅστις σ' ὀπύσει κἀκποιήσεται γαλᾶς
> σοῦ μηδὲν ἥττους βδεῖν, ἐπειδὰν ὄρθρος ᾖ.

> Come on, my pretty daughter, be sure you bear the basket prettily, and keep a lemon-sucking look on your face. Ah, lucky the man who'll marry you, and get a litter of kittens as good as you are at farting when the dawn is nigh!

Here Dicaeopolis clearly expects his daughter to marry – but participation in public ritual brings with it the danger of seduction, and so his daughter should look unapproachable (literally, as if she had eaten a bitter herb). Danaos' speech encourages us to understand that the *exodos* is also a staging of public ritual – in this case, choral performance. Here is the text of the song (1018–73):

ΧΟΡΟΣ	
ἴτε μὰν ἀστυάνακτας	[στρ. α.
μάκαρας θεοὺς γανόωντες	
πολιούχους τε καὶ οἳ χεῦμ' Ἐρασίνου	(1020)

---

21 Sommerstein 2010a, 102.
22 Thus Friis Johansen/Whittle 1980 ad 996–1009: 'This inference [sc. that, in referring to his enemies, Danaus foreshadows events to follow] includes the question in the class of insoluble problems connected with the following play or plays of the trilogy'. Sommerstein 2010a, 102–3 argues that in this passage Danaus does not wish his daughters to be married to anybody, and relates this to the plot of *Aegyptioi*, on this theory the first play of the trilogy (with *Suppliants* second); here he follows Rösler 1993 (cf. Sommerstein 1995).
23 Here and below I quote Aristophanes from Wilson's Oxford text; the translation is adapted from Henderson's Loeb.

περιναίουσιν παλαιόν.
ὑποδέξασθε <δ'> ὀπαδοὶ
μέλος· αἶνος δὲ πόλιν τάνδε Πελασγῶν
ἐχέτω· μηδ' ἔτι Νείλου
προχοὰς σέβωμεν ὕμνοις, (1025)

ποταμοὺς δ' οἳ διὰ χώρας [ἀντ. α.
θελεμὸν πῶμα χέουσιν
πολύτεκνοι, λιπαροῖς χεύμασι γαίας
τόδε μειλίσσοντες οὖδας.
ἐπίδοι δ' Ἄρτεμις ἁγνὰ (1030)
στόλον οἰκτιζομένα, μηδ' ὑπ' ἀνάγκας
τέλος ἔλθοι Κυθερείας·
Στύγιον πέλοι τόδ' ἆθλον.

ΑΡΓΕΙΟΙ
Κύπριδος <δ'> οὐκ ἀμελεῖν, θεσμὸς ὅδ' εὔφρων. [στρ. β.
δύναται γὰρ Διὸς ἄγχιστα σὺν Ἥρᾳ, (1035)
τίεται δ' αἰολόμητις
θεὸς ἔργοις ἐπὶ σεμνοῖς·
μετάκοινοι δὲ φίλᾳ ματρὶ πάρεισιν
Πόθος <ᾇ> τ' οὐδὲν ἄπαρνον
τελέθει θέλκτορι Πειθοῖ, (1040)
ἔδοται θ' Ἁρμονίας μοῖρ' Ἀφροδίτᾳ
ψεδυραὶ τρίβοι τ' ἐρώτων.

φυγάδεσσιν δ' ἔτι ποινὰς κακά τ' ἄλγη [ἀντ. β.
πολέμους θ' αἱματόεντας προφοβοῦμαι.
τί ποτ' εὔπλοιαν ἔπραξαν (1045)
ταχυπόμποισι διωγμοῖς;
ὅτι τοι μόρσιμόν ἐστιν, τὸ γένοιτ' ἄν·
Διὸς οὐ παρβατός ἐστιν
μεγάλα φρὴν ἀπέρατος·
μετὰ πολλᾶν δὲ γάμων ἅδε τελευτὰ (1050)
προτερᾶν πέλοι γυναικῶν.

ΧΟΡΟΣ ὁ μέγας Ζεὺς ἀπαλέξαι [στρ. γ.
γάμον Αἰγυπτογενῆ μοι.
ΑΡΓΕΙΟΙ τὸ μὲν ἂν βέλτατον εἴη.
ΧΟΡΟΣ σὺ δὲ θέλγοις ἂν ἄθελκτον. (1055)
ΑΡΓΕΙΟΙ σὺ δέ γ' οὐκ οἶσθα τὸ μέλλον.

ΧΟΡΟΣ τί δὲ μέλλω φρένα Δίαν [ἀντ. γ.
καθορᾶν, ὄψιν ἄβυσσον;
ΑΡΓΕΙΟΙ μέτριον νῦν ἔπος εὔχου.
ΧΟΡΟΣ τίνα καιρόν με διδάσκεις; (1060)
ΑΡΓΕΟΙ τὰ θεῶν μηδὲν ἀγάζειν.

ΧΟΡΟΣ
Ζεὺς ἄναξ ἀποστεροί- [στρ. δ.

ἢ γάμον δυσάνορα
δάιον, ὅσπερ Ἰὼ
πημονᾶς ἐλύσατ' εὖ (1065)
χειρὶ παιωνίᾳ
κατασχεθών, εὐμενῆ βίαν κτίσας

καὶ κράτος νέμοι γυναι- [ἀντ. δ.
ξίν. τὸ βέλτερον κακοῦ
καὶ τὸ δίμοιρον αἰνῶ, (1070)
καὶ †δίκα δίκας† ἕπε-
σθαι ξὺν εὐχαῖς ἐμαῖς,
λυτηρίοις μαχαναῖς θεοῦ πάρα.

desunt paragraphi. 1018 ἄστυδ', ἄνακτας Tucker 1019 γανόωντες Pauw: γανάεντες M. 1023 μέλος Legrand: μένος M. 1032 τέλος Weil: γάμος M. 1034 ἀμελεῖν, θεσμός Nauck. αμελεῖ θεσμός M. ἐμελὴς ἐσμὸς Weil. 1041 Ἁρμονίας... Ἀφροδίτᾳ Hartung: ἁρμονίαν... ἀφροδίτας M. (ἁρμονίαι p.c.). 1043 φυγάδεσ<σιν> Burges. ἔτι ποινὰς Burges: ἐπιπνοίαι M. 1055 θέλγεις ἀνάθελκτον M: corr. Stephanus. 1067 εὐμενῆ βίαν Valckenauer: εὐμενεῖ βίᾳ M. 1071 δίκᾳ δίκαν Haupt, δίκαι δίκαις ἕπεσθω Paley, alii alia.

CHORUS Go now, glorifying the blessed city-ruling gods, those who keep the citadel and those who dwell around the ancient stream of Erasinos. Accept our song, escorts, and let praise enfold this city of the Pelasgians; let us no longer honour the mouths of the Nile with hymns, but instead the rivers that pour their tranquil waters through this land, bringing fertility, softening the soil of the land with their gleaming streams. May chaste Artemis watch over this band in pity, and may Cytherea's consummation not come to us by force: may that prize be won only in Hades!

ARGIVES But it is a wise rule not to neglect Cypris; for she holds power very close to Zeus together with Hera, and is a goddess of cunning wiles and honoured for awesome deeds. Partners with their dear mother are Desire and the charmer Persuasion, to whom nothing can be refused, and also given to Aphrodite are a share of Harmony, and the whispering paths of love-making.

For the fugitives I foresee and fear punishments still to come, dire suffering, and bloody wars. Why did they make a good passage in their swift-sped pursuit? What is fated, will happen: the great, unfathomable mind of Zeus cannot be crossed; and this outcome, marriage, would be shared with many women before you.

CHORUS May great Zeus defend me from marriage with the sons of Aegyptos!
ARGIVES That would be best —
CHORUS You would charm the un-charm-able!
ARGIVES And you do not know the future!

CHORUS How can it be my future to see into the mind of Zeus, an unfathomable sight?
ARGIVES Then make your prayer moderate.
CHORUS What are you teaching me is the right choice?
ARGIVES Not to be excessive with regard to the gods.

CHORUS May Lord Zeus deprive us of a hateful marriage to men who are our enemies – he who gave Io a good release from her sufferings, restraining her with his healing hand, making force kindly –

– and may he give power to women. I approve the better kind of evil, the two-thirds kind, and that [judgement and justice should coincide], in accordance with my prayers, through contrivances bringing salvation at the god's hand.

The form of this performance is marked by the first word of the song, ἴτε (1018): this is a *prosodion*. One might compare the refrain of an anonymous song from papyrus, ἴτω ἴτω χορός ('Go, chorus, go!') (*SLG* 460). This song, headed in the papyrus Δή]μητρος Κείοις, is surely a *prosodion*, as Rutherford argued, citing the parallel at Aristoph. *Birds* 851–8 (where the chorus identifies the songs called for as προσόδια μεγάλα σεμνά 'great, solemn processional hymns').[24] The content serves the Danaids' rhetorical objectives: they pray for continued protection from unwanted marriage, while most of the first two strophes concerns praise of Argos. The Danaids are using praise to cement their relationship with the new city, and accordingly they mark their choral activity explicitly. They are the performers of a μέλος (1023), they want αἶνος for Argos (1023), and where they formerly produced ὕμνοι (1025), 'praise songs', for the Nile, they now do so for the rivers of Argos. Again, they mark their song as participating in standard features of praise by the word λιπαρός (1028), 'shining' and thus 'splendid, glorious': effectively a generic 'marker' of praise.[25] The pattern of praise for the city as a reward for right-treatment by the city, and to cement the relationship created, fits well with the notion of the Danaids as an arriving, theoric chorus, praising the city as they enter.

However, after the first antistrophe something surprising happens. Another voice sings, and for the remainder of the song we have a debate between two voi-

---

24 Rutherford 1995a, 41–3.
25 Note in particular the use of this word in Pindar fr. 76 M and the allusion to this celebrated Athenian dithyramb at Ar. *Ach.* 639–40 (see Lavecchia 2000 ad loc. for the large number of attestations of this song). *Prima facie*, the way in which Aristophanes treats the poetic expression and language of praise in this fragment as 'foreigner speech' (ξενικοῖσι λόγοις 634) likely to have an impact on the political judgement of the *demos* is a striking parallel to my reading of Aeschylus' play, and suggests that even in the later fifth century it made sense to think of choral song as a vehicle by which outsiders could influence the *demos* of a democratic *polis*, not only at a vaguer level of public opinion, but through a rhetoric which directly influenced the *ekklēsia* and whose force came as much from its evocation of ritual, generic forms as from its idiosyncratic content. On the interaction of the heroic world of tragedy with the politics of the world of the audience, including with reference to this play, see Carey 2003; on the democracy at Argos, Robinson 2011, 6–25; on Argos and Athens in Athenian drama, Saïd 1993.

ces: one protesting hostility towards marriage, at least with the sons of Aegyptos, and another encouraging a positive attitude towards marriage and moderation in relation to the gods. The first voice is the Danaids, but the second is more problematic: interpreters have suggested the Danaids' maids, that the Danaids split into two groups, that the second voice is Danaos, or Hypermestra stepping out of the chorus as a solo actor, and that the lines are sung by the Argive soldiers escorting the Danaids into the city. Recent opinion favours this last view, and I also find it the most probable option.[26]

In outline, I agree with the approach to this song taken by Laura Swift, developing the work of Richard Seaford and others.[27] The Danaids are a socially dangerous group. In parts of the play, they are not only hostile to marriage with their cousins but to marriage in general, normatively a necessary institution and the proper *telos* of a woman's life. They exhibit a fear of marriage characteristic of *parthenoi* in myth and song, but to an extreme degree – this will result in war and murder.[28] Here, we see this attitude countered by a male voice which points out the necessary, attractive and divinely ordained aspects of marital sexuality. For Swift, I think rightly, this represents a kind of false-*hymenaios*, which will have evoked wedding-songs of a kind involving exchanges between male and female choruses where the females sing of defloration as a loss to be mourned, while the males promote a positive view of married sexuality.[29] Our best sight of this kind of song is in Catullus 62, a poem which draws heavily upon Greek models, especially Sappho, and whose form, consisting of an exchange between choruses of young men and young women, is likely also to de-

---

[26] Relevant considerations include the masculine gender of the participle in 1019, issues of staging (the maids should be beside the Danaids, but here they need to move and dance separately), the designation of the Danaids as φυγάδες in 1043 (strange if used by the maids of their mistresses, as if they too were not fugitives), the fact that ὀπαδοί in 1022, which should be an address to the persons forming the second chorus, was previously used of the Argive soldiers in 985, and that it would be odd for the Danaids to ask the maids to 'accept' their song (1022). For fuller discussion with bibliography see Friis Johansen/Whittle 1980 ad 1018–73 (iii.306–8). The second voice is identified as the Argive soldiers in the recent editions by West 1990a, Sommerstein 2008a and Bowen 2013.
[27] Swift 2010, 279–97; Seaford 1987.
[28] Seaford 2007, 110. For the question of distaster for marriage with the Aegyptiads vs. distaste for marriage *tout court*, e.g. Sommerstein 2010a, 102, Garvie 2006, 221–2; Friis Johansen/Whittle 1980, i.30–4 emphasise that the context for apparent expressions of hostility to men and to marriage often suggests that the specific circumstances are the real point – but the specific circumstance is naturally on the Danaids' mind throughout, and does not detract from the impression given that the Danaids display at least some general distaste for marriage.
[29] Swift 2010, 282, 289–90.

rive from Greek tradition.[30] In context, this echo of marriage ritual is paradoxical: it reminds us of the transgressive qualities of the Danaids' hostility to marriage. The form of a wedding song is being given to their entry into the city, by which their virginity is being preserved at the cost of war and, later, murder.[31]

I shall now try to develop this approach further. The Danaids start by marking their song as processional, and characterised by hymnic, praise material. 'Go to the city!' describes the exit procession, and the procession is to glorify the gods of Argos; the song is also, as I have described, explicitly marked out as praise.[32] How much of a surprise is it for the Danaids, or the audience, when their song to be taken over by the escorting Argives addressed as ὀπαδοί in 1022? This depends partly on the meaning of ὑποδέξασθε (1022), sometimes translated 'take up the song', as an invitation for the Argives to sing. The lexicography of the word does not support this: ὑποδέχομαι means 'receive, welcome', and where its object is speech it means 'listen to'. This is not an invitation for the Argives to sing.[33] However, the same sentence includes the corrupt participle in 1019. The corrupt last word of this line can only been corrected to a participle from the root γαν-, whose meaning is 'make bright, make shiny'; it must mean something close to 'glorifying' (perhaps combined with a sense 'delighting').[34] We should translate 'glorifying (or delighting) the blessed gods', and the masculine participle describes a group including males. Is this an invitation for the Ar-

---

[30] Difficulties arise from the lack of substantial fragments of archaic or classical wedding songs (only some small Sappho frr.: Swift 2010, 244), so that one must approach this genre in part through imitations and reflections, such as Catullus' poem. Cf. Swift 2010, 241–50, and 255–62 on mixed-sex choruses; on Catullus 62 and its relation to Greek models, see Swift 2010, 257–60.
[31] Swift 2010, 289–96.
[32] 'Go to the city' is a paraphrase rather than a translation of the text of 1018 as I have printed it – but in context it is clear that the exit is into the city. One may consider ἄστυδ', ἄνακτας in 1018 (Tucker) in place of the ms. reading given above.
[33] Cf. Friis Johansen/Whittle 1980 ad loc. Bowen 2013 translates 'make our song welcome' and this is surely part of the point: the attendants are to 'receive' both the song and the Danaids (cf. his note ad loc.). Swift 2010, 284 translates 'take up the song', and at 280 n.91 she describes the expression (i.e., as I take it, the expression ὑποδέξασθε... γανάοντες as she prints from Page's text at 1018) as 'linguistically similar' to Eur. Hipp. 58 ἕπεσθ' ᾄδοντες ἕπεσθε where Hippolytus invites his companions to join in his processional hymn to Artemis. The latter place contains an explicit verb of singing, and thus seems at least much more explicit as an invitation.
[34] It may be impossible to decide exactly what form this participle should take (West 1990a prints the ms reading γανάεντες in cruces), but this is separable from the question of sense. For fuller discussion, see Friis Johansen/Whittle 1980 ad loc., Bowen 2013 ad loc. who translates 'gladdening'. From parallels cited by Friis Johansen/Whittle, note in particular Pl. R. 411a γεγανωμένος of the delighting or gladdening effect of *song*.

gives to sing? Perhaps not strictly speaking (it is not in any case a verb of singing). The participle might describe the effect of the whole procession, including but not restricted to the element of song; but we might understand that the Argives are invited to participate in glorifying or delighting the gods through song. One might understand lines 1022–9 as a kind of expansion of the sense of 1018–21, in which case γανόωντες corresponds to the explicitly encomiastic and hymnic language in 1023–5 (discussed above). At the least, therefore, the Danaids allow the possibility that they are inviting the Argives to participate in the sung procession which comprises the *exodos*.[35]

However, even if the Danaids invite or allow the Argives to join in their performance, they also make very clear on what grounds. They have decided on the prosodic form and encomiastic-hymnic content of the song, and instruct the Argives to continue along the same lines. Instead, the Argives hijack the Danaids' prosodic praise song for Argos, and turn it into a song with the characteristics of a *hymenaios*.

This kind of song should allow the expression of parthenaic hostility or fear concerning marriage, but then counter it with persuasion which assuages those anxieties. Are the Argives successful? Up to a point, I think they are.

In earlier parts of the play, the Danaids' hostility to marriage with their cousins becomes indistinguishable from hostility to marriage in general: this is conspicuous in the *parodos*, where they pray to 'escape the beds of men... unwedded and unsubdued' (141–3=151–3). In the *exodos*, this does not happen. The Danaids pray that the τέλος of Aphrodite not come to them ὑπ' ἀνάγκας, by compulsion (1031f.), but the appeal to Artemis suggests that they are thinking of two options: virginity, or marriage to their cousins. The Argives' response suggests that they are thinking of the same alternatives, since they move between positive aspects of marriage, and the bad consequences of the Danaids' rejection of the sons of Aegyptos. The Danaids answer by picking up the word γάμων from 1050, but respond to this statement about marriage *in general* by rejecting marriage *with the sons of Aegyptos* (1052–3). The Argives' words from 1056 onwards look like arguments that marriage should not be rejected *tout court*: 'you do not know what will come in the future... you should not go too far vis-à-vis the gods'. The Danaids respond to this pressure by appealing to the precedent of Io – the

---

[35] The same sense of a smooth 'handover' is helped by the coincidence of speaker-change with the division between strophic pairs; and while the Argives enter at the start of the second strophe, the second pair continues the ionic rhythm of the first, again reducing any sense of disruption or interruption. My treatment of this question has been substantially modified by discussion at the conference, in particular with Giambattista D'Alessio and Ruth Scodel, for both of whose contributions and suggestions I am grateful.

return to the Io theme reflects, I think, that they *do* experience this as pressure. But their prayer to Zeus is specific: to avoid a marriage which is δάιος, 'wretched' or 'hostile', and δυσάνορα 'with a bad husband' (1062–4). In this light, the Io story takes on an alternative possible interpretation: the force which tames women in marriage should be εὐμενής (1067) rather than δάιος, consensual rather than forced: thus women will have κράτος (1068). They continue by attempting to cast themselves in a reasonable, compromise position (1069–70): 'I praise the better part of evil, the two-thirds part'. They mean 'We are willing to approve the lesser of evils'. It is difficult to be sure how precisely this should be understood; perhaps the most important point is that, despite their claim in 1055 – in which they recognise the Argives' song as a form of *thelxis* – the Danaids are moderating their position. With regard to the approaching war, there is no middle way: the Argives will fight the Egyptians, or they will not. More speculatively, we might think about a possible resolution of the Danaids' position: after the murder of their Egyptian husbands (apart from Lynceus), perhaps they *will* be reconciled to what they now perceive as the lesser evil of marriage with Argive husbands. In other words, perhaps they will accept marriage not as rape, but the more attractive model of marriage offered in Aphrodite's speech from the last play of the trilogy (fr. 44, from *Danaids*):[36]

> ἐρᾷ μὲν ἁγνὸς οὐρανὸς τρῶσαι χθόνα,
> ἔρως δὲ γαῖαν λαμβάνει γάμου τυχεῖν·
> ὄμβρος δ' ἀπ' εὐνάεντος οὐρανοῦ πεσὼν
> ἔκυσε γαῖαν· ἡ δὲ τίκτεται βροτοῖς
> μήλων τε βοσκὰς καὶ βίον Δημήτριον
> δένδρων τ' ὀπώραν· ἐκ νοτίζοντος γάμου
> τελεῖθ' ὅσ' ἔστι· τῶν δ' ἐγὼ παραίτιος
>
> [APHRODITE] The holy heaven desires to penetrate the earth, and desire takes hold of Earth for marriage. Rain falls from the fair-flowing Heaven and impregnates Earth, and she bears for mortals grazing for their flocks and the life-giving grain of Demeter and the harvest of trees: by the wedlock of the rain, she comes to her fulfilment. Of this, I am in part the cause.

The continuity in the use of the imagery of fresh water and sexuality from the Danaids' praise of Argos in the *exodos* of our play, where rivers are πολύτεκνοι 'bringing fertility', is perhaps suggestive: even at the start of the *exodos*, the Danaids' language anticipates their move to a more reasonable view of marriage, both within the same song and with the trilogy as a whole.[37]

---

36 Text from Sommerstein's Loeb edition, and translation adapted from the same.
37 Cf. Swift 2010, 284–5, who argues that the hymenaeal features of the song are already evident here.

One way of describing the *exodos*, then, might be to say that the tables have been turned on the Danaids. Having exploited the authority and rhetoric of choral song throughout the play, they face a similar ploy by the Argives. By hijacking and transforming the Danaids' *prosodion* and turning it into a kind of *hymenaios*, these men use the *thelxis* of choral song (cf. 1055: even in denying their susceptibility, the Danaids concede this power) to produce a softening in the Danaids' position which anticipates the transformation in the presentation of marriage which may have been the main thematic development of the trilogy as a whole.

4 Conclusion

Paying attention to the Danaids' status as a chorus within the drama can sensitise us to aspects of their presentation which evoke features of chorality experienced outside drama. I have focused on theoric chorality as one thread in the Danaids' strategy to persuade the Argives to accept them into the city, and on the evocation of choral ritual associated with marriage to which Seaford and Swift in particular have drawn attention. These add to our awareness of the persuasive strategies adopted by the Danaids, and of how the play has been constructed around a choral protagonist through manipulation of ways in which a chorus can present itself rhetorically and make ritual demands on others. However, these demands are not irresistible. The Danaids' combination of *hiketeia* with choral authority is initially *unsuccessful* in persuading Pelasgos: they have to resort to the more drastic ploy of threatening suicide on holy ground (455–67). At the end of the play, in the song by which the Danaids attempt to define and control their entry into the city, the Argives of their escort use their own tactics against them, and with some success. While the evocation of wedding ritual exposes and emphasises the socially dangerous quality of the Danaids' rejection of marriage, it also functions as a persuasive mechanism by which, according to my reading of the play's last lines, they start to show signs of how their position will eventually soften: the plot of the trilogy itself will resemble the 'plot' of aspects of wedding ritual evoked in the *exodos*, by which parthenaic fears of marriage and sexuality are made explicit in order to be contrasted with more positive views and allayed.

Giovanni Fanfani
What melos for Troy? Blending of Lyric Genres in the First *Stasimon* of Euripides' *Trojan Women*

1 Introduction

The first *stasimon* of *Trojan Women* is a narrative account of the last day of Troy, a melic *Iliou Persis* consisting of a single triadic system and depicting the Trojans' welcoming of the Wooden Horse into the city, their rejoicing in choral dancing at night, and their violent ruin at the hand of the Achaeans. Labelled by Kranz as one of Euripides' 'dithyrambic' *stasima*,[1] the song has been seen by scholars as representative of the pictorial style that characterizes late Euripidean choral odes.[2] More recently, certain recognizable patterns informing Euripides' 'dithyrambic' and pictorial lyric have been reassessed by Eric Csapo and positioned within the wider picture of the dramatist's engagement with New Musical verse.[3] By calling attention to the growing amount of musical imagery of a Dionysiac stamp in the sung sections of Euripides' plays from ca. 420 BC onwards, Csapo defines a significant trait of poetics that locates the playwright at the fore-

---

I would like to thank V. Bers, M. Ercoles, A. Ford, A. Henrichs and N. Weiss for helpful comments on an earlier version of this chapter. I am especially grateful to P. LeVen for her valuable criticism and suggestions on different drafts of this paper, and to the editors for corrections and advice. Research for this work has been generously supported by the Danish Council for Independent Research and FP7 Marie Curie Actions – COFUND (DFF – 1321–00158) through a MOBILEX grant. The text of *Trojan Women* reproduces Diggle's OCT unless otherwise stated. English translations are adapted from the most recent Loeb editions.

[1] For structural features of these choral odes, defined as 'self-contained ballad-like narratives' ('völlig absolut stehende balladeske Erzählung') see Kranz 1933, 254, and in general 228–65, see 253, 258f. in particular on Eur. *Tro.* 511–67. Panagl 1971 offers a detailed analysis of the style, *lexis* and syntax of Euripides' 'dithyrambic' *stasima* (pp. 42–78 on our ode).

[2] See Barlow 2008, 28–31, who rightly emphasizes the dramatic quality of Euripides' pictorial style in the choral songs of *Trojan Women*: '[D]escriptive imagery of place becomes dramatic imagery also in the *Troades*'. Di Benedetto 1971, 243–7 discusses at length the pictorial qualities of *stasima* and monodies in *Trojan Women*.

[3] For a recent discussion of pictorial and musical language in the first *stasimon* of Euripides' *Electra* in relation to the category of 'dithyrambic' style, see Csapo 2009, who proposes for late Euripidean lyric the definition of New Musical verse, one that 'appeals directly to the senses, the subconscious, and the emotions' (p. 108).

front of the musical innovations introduced by the New Musicians in the theatrical genres of *nomos*, dithyramb and drama.[4] In a number of late Euripidean choral songs, descriptions and dramatizations of archetypal Dionysiac *choreia* through the device of choral projection[5] serve the purpose to archaize specific features of contemporary *mousikē* by tracing them back to primal choral formations and thus providing them with an ad hoc aetiology.[6]

Trojan Women, staged in 415 BC, is indeed the earliest tragedy of Euripides to contain marked references to music and dance in the actors' monodies:[7] these in turn present remarkable choral traits, exhibit a sustained 'dithyrambic' style and diction, and develop a metamusical motif – the nostalgic evocation of past Trojan *mousikē* – that is integrated in the narrative frame of first *stasimon* of the play through the device of choral projection. An important study by Luigi Battezzato has demonstrated that musical imagery in *Trojan Women* acts as the metaphorical vehicle through which Euripides dramatizes the interruption of a Trojan/Phrygian tradition of *choreia* and its violent incor-

---

[4] Csapo 1999–2000, esp. 417–26. See Power 2013, 240 on metamusical imagery in extant dithyramb, which is 'persistent enough to be seen as a generic trait, but it is generally turned inward. Dithyramb likes to sing about itself, to determine proleptically the terms of its reception by refashioning its sociomusical origins'.

[5] On this choral convention see especially Henrichs 1996, 49 'Choral projection occurs when Sophoklean and Euripidean choruses locate their dancing in the past or the future, in contrast to the here and now of their immediate performance, or when choruses project their collective identity onto groups of dancers distant from the concrete space of the orchestra and dancing in the allusive realm of the dramatic imagination'. An earlier attempt at pointing out the mechanism of choral projection in tragedy is represented by Davidson 1986, who (p. 40) mentions Eur. *Tro.* 542–4. Csapo 1999–2000, 417 traces back choral projection (especially its Dionysiac associations) to traditional dithyramb, in particular Pindar's: 'but whether authentically traditional or not, choral projection became a hallmark of New Musical style'. In fact, however, the device is shown by Henrichs 1996 to occur in several Euripidean plays (among which the early *Heraclidae*) as a complex pattern heightening dramatic tension. On choral projection and dithyrambic poetics in Pindar fr. 70b S-M see Calame 2013b, 339. On the question of the derivation of tragic choral projection from choral lyric conventions cf. Henrichs 1996, 49 with n. 4, who points to Alcman and Pindar's *partheneia*; Hutchinson 2001, 434 with n. 12 provides further references to Bacchylides and Pindar's instances of choral projection. On choral projection in Pindar and Bacchylides' *epinikia* see Power 2000, 67–71, who aptly remarks the distinctiveness of the device in tragedy, where 'the relation between projected and projecting choruses is often fraught with tension' (p. 70).

[6] Steiner 2011 is a fine reading of a 'dithyrambic' *stasimon* (*Hel.* 1451–511) from the point of view of the imagery of archetypal and Dionysiac *choreia*.

[7] This fact depends on the relative chronology *Trojan Women – Ion*: cf. Csapo 1999–2000, 423 (figure 3b).

poration into the new *mousikē* of the Greek invaders.⁸ Battezzato recognizes in this move a pattern of cultural appropriation of foreign music on the part of the Greeks, which he locates within the cultural discourse and poetics of the New Music: in the first *stasimon* of *Trojan Women*, and in particular through the epic/citharodic opening of the song, he sees the dramatic enactment of such a musical 'colonization'.⁹

This paper chooses a different interpretative angle, and offers a reading of the first *stasimon* of *Trojan Women* from the standpoint of generic interplay. In tragedy's complex appropriation and refashioning of the tradition of non-dramatic *melos*, references to particular song-types in choral odes may function as a literary device arousing generic expectations and/or pointing to specific melic hypotexts.¹⁰ Set against this dynamics of osmotic interaction of genres, *Tro*. 511–67 can be seen as an instance of Euripides' later lyric's inclination for mixing melic sub-genres, alluding to previous poetry, and locating itself within the discourse of contemporary music; in addition to that, it will be argued, the blending of song-types which takes place in the ode is key to an appreciation of the specific poetics of *Trojan Women*. In particular, this paper focuses on three different aspects of the *stasimon:* a) the threnodic flavour of the ode, b) its 'dithyrambic' character and c) its emphasis on *choreia*. While the aspects in question may be (and have been) considered to figure among Euripides' most pronounced New Musical traits,¹¹ they have seldom been regarded as distinctive areas of generic interaction, nor have they been treated consistently within the poetics of a single play.

The first aspect regards a pervasive thematic motif in *Trojan Women*, one that surfaces in the opening of the *stasimon* and characterizes the song as a

---

8 Battezzato 2005b, a contribution we shall often refer to throughout this paper.
9 Battezzato 2005b detects a similar pattern of 'appropriation and erasure' (p. 74) of non-Greek music at work in Sophocles' *Thamyras* and in Telestes' treatment of the myth of Marsyas in *PMG* 805 (pp. 96–101). On Melanippides' *Marsyas* see Power 2013, 241 f.
10 For tragedy's evocation of the cultural and moral assumptions of several sub-types of choral lyric see Swift 2010, *passim*. With a shift of focus, Rodighiero 2012 explores the range of generic fluidity in a selection of Sophoclean choral songs. For intertextual allusions to lyric poetry in tragedy see Garner 1990 and the systematic study of Bagordo 2003. For important methodological remarks, and terminological tools, on how to deal with tragedy's reception of lyric genres, with a special focus on *paian*, see Rutherford 1994–1995, 118–21 and *id*. 2001, 108–15. For the continuities between non-dramatic and tragic lyric at the level of the chorus' ritual utterances see Calame 1994–1995 and Henrichs 1994–1995.
11 Cf. again Csapo 1999–2000, whose purpose is to show the breadth, internal consistence, and diachronic development of the phenomenon, rather than discuss the particular function of New Musical features in the (dramatic, thematic) context of individual plays.

blending of genres: the theme of ritual lament and threnodic music as the only available for both the Chorus and the characters to express the loss of their city, culture and *mousikē*. The generic mixture of citharodic *nomos* and *thrēnos* that the *incipit* of the first *stasimon* announces grounds the claim of poetic novelty on the part of the Chorus. In turn, the 'mourning ode of new songs' (καινῶν ὕμνων ... ᾠδὰν ἐπικήδειον, 513–4) which the Muse is requested to sing in the proemial lines of the ode sublimates the range of musical imagery grounded on the recurrent figure of the '*mousa*/music of the *thrēnos*/ritual lament' that punctuates the play.

The second aspect deals with the 'dithyrambic' character of the ode in terms of its structural and stylistic features. Recent scholarship on the nature and performance context of Bacchylides' dithyrambs, and on the language and poetics of the New Music, invites further scrutiny on aspects of *lexis*, imagery and structure of lyric narrative in 'dithyrambic' *stasima*.[12] The first *stasimon* of *Trojan Women* has indeed a marked narrative shape: the single triadic structure, the opening citharodic *prooimion*, the *Iliou Persis* theme are all features of traditional narrative poetry that could be traced back to as far as Stesichorus in the history of the genre.[13] When it comes to diction, syntax and style, however, the ode presents us with a series of characteristics that seem to position Euripides at the intersection between Bacchylidean narrative dithyramb and Timotheus' experimentalism in mimetic and figurative language. Late Euripidean lyric has been convincingly demonstrated to represent a favourite hypotext and source material for Timotheus' lyric:[14] in inviting comparison with the dithyrambographer's style, the use of periphrastic compound adjectives in the first *stasimon* of *Trojan*

---

[12] See Fearn 2007, 163–99; Fearn 2013 on Bacchylides 17; Fearn forthcoming on the continuities and differences between Bacchylides' dithyrambs and Timotheus' *Persae* on the ground of narrative style. Hadjimichael 2014b explores Aristophanes' peculiar reception of Bacchylides' poetics in his parody of the 'new dithyrambic' style of Kinesias in *Av.* 1373–409: it emerges the significant role of Bacchylides in effecting the transition between 'traditional' and 'new' dithyrambic poetry in regards to stylistic, structural and musical/performative features. LeVen 2014, in particular 150–88 is a thorough and refreshing study of the style and diction of the New Music; Budelmann / LeVen 2014 tackle Timotheus' figurative language through the cognitive theory of blending.

[13] On the beginning lines of Stesichorus' *Iliou Persis* see Finglass 2013a. See Ercoles 2013, 533–6 on Stesichorus as the πρῶτος εὑρετής of the triadic system (strophe, antistrophe, epode) in the ancient paremiographic tradition.

[14] See Firinu 2009 on the intertextual dialogue between the first 'dithyrambic' *stasimon* of *Iphigenia among the Taurians* and Timotheus' *Persae* (with the latter alluding to, re-working, and often complicating Euripidean phrases, compounds, and periphrases).

Women points rather to the role played by Euripides in the transition to a 'new dithyrambic' narrative.

The third aspect encompasses a trait of late Euripidean poetics that is prominent in *Trojan Women:* the sustained strategy of musical imagery and the focus on the mechanisms of *choreia*, with the implications these might have had in performance. The motif of the nostalgic evocation of the exuberant Phrygian *mousikē* of the past, contrasted with the pervasive threnodic tone of the present *molpē* is first exploited by Hecuba in her monody through choral self-referentiality; at the level of style and imagery, the song displays New Musical features typical of many Euripidean 'dithyrambic' odes. In this respect, the case of the first *stasimon* is pretty different: we have here a strongly marked narrative frame which subsumes the episode of choral projection, and the Chorus of prisoners sing of events they have been personally involved in. At the level of imagery, the emphasis on the Phrygian connotation of Trojan *mousikē* has invited thoughts on the possibility (indeed attracting, though hard to support with evidence) that Phrygian *harmonia* (suited to both dithyramb and *thrēnos*) could accompany the Chorus' re-enactment of past Trojan *choreia* in the instance of choral projection around which the *stasimon* is built (where Λίβυς λωτός and Φρύγια μέλεα are mentioned).[15]

2 'A Mourning Ode of New Songs': A Citharodic Thrēnos?

Concluding her *rhēsis* at the end of the first episode of *Trojan Women* (a scene dramatically dominated by Cassandra's arresting performance),[16] Hecuba expresses to the women of the Chorus her desire to be placed down on her pallet on the ground and to her stony mattress, 'so that I may fall upon it and die, worn down with weeping (δακρύοις καταξανθεῖσα). Consider no prosperous man

---

[15] Battezzato 2005b, 88 has proposed this hypothesis.
[16] The prophetess delivers a monodic *hymenaios* (308–40), a rhetorically sustained *rhēsis* in iambic trimeters demonstrating Troy's blessedness (353–405), and a final speech where she announces Odysseus' fate (iambic trimeters, 426–43) and, possessed by prophetic frenzy (marked by a shift to catalectic trochaic tetrameters, 444–61), she envisages her 'marriage to death' with Agamemnon and throws away her sacred emblems of Apollonian priestess. Biehl 1989, 223, 225 and Hose 1990, 307 argue that the first *stasimon* of *Trojan Women* is to be read and understood against the background of Cassandra's first *rhēsis*. Especially significant is the motif of the deported Trojan women as 'victory crown' for the Greeks in the final lines of the *stasimon* (565), which is proleptically reversed by Cassandra's ironic claims at 353–64.

blessed until he passes away' (508–10).[17] The choral song that follows the queen's gnome on the instability of human fortune picks up both this motif and the element of tears emerging from the preceding lines: the Chorus of captive Trojan women implicitly apply the apophthegm to their own experience and present the *stasimon* as a lament for Troy, 'a mourning ode of new songs accompanied with tears':[18]

Χο. ἀμφί μοι Ἴλιον, ὦ   [στρ.
Μοῦσα, καινῶν ὕμνων
ἆσον σὺν δακρύοις ᾠδὰν ἐπικήδειον·
νῦν γὰρ μέλος ἐς Τροίαν ἰαχήσω   (515)

Sing for me about Ilium,
O Muse, a mourning ode of new songs accompanied with tears.
For now I shall rise a *melos* for Troy

What marks the first *stasimon* of *Trojan Women* as especially distinctive is the Chorus' appeal to the Muse at the opening of the ode, something unique in tragedy. Furthermore, the invocation of the Muse, embedded in the structure of a recognizable citharodic prelude, is associated with novelty and with threnodic content (511–3).

According to the social and aesthetic norm of the 'appropriateness' that binds archaic poetics to the rightness of the correspondence between songtypes and their performance and ritual context,[19] the association between *thrēnos* and the Muses (or their bards, the μουσοπόλοι) is especially ἀπρεπής ('inappropriate'): Sappho is explicit on this point in fr. 150 Voigt οὐ γὰρ θέμις ἐν μοισοπόλων <δόμῳ> / θρῆνον ἔμμεν' < . . . . > οὔκ' ἄμμι πρέποι τάδε, 'For it is not right that there should be lamentation in the house of those who serve the Muses (...) that would not befit us'.[20] The archaic antithesis between

---

[17] The *gnome* τῶν δ' εὐδαιμόνων / μηδένα νομίζετ' εὐτυχεῖν, πρὶν ἂν θάνῃ is one common in tragedy: cf. e.g. Aesch. *Ag.* 928–9; Soph. *OT* 1524–30; Eur. *Andr.* 100–2.
[18] That the song is meant to be a *thrēnos* for the city is understood by the scholiast *ad l.* (Σ Eur. *Tr.* 511 Schwartz II p. 361 περὶ τῆς Ἰλίου ποίησόν με θρηνῆσαι). Cf. Suter 2003 for a comprehensive discussion of the lament features of *Trojan Women* and their significance as both a thematic motif and a structural principle in the play.
[19] Though, as Carey 2009a, 22 aptly remarks, the actual scenario of literary genres and songtypes in archaic and early classical times was rather one characterized by generic fluidity and flexibility: '[T]he boundaries are not fixed but elastic, porous, negotiable and provisional.'
[20] On the category of archaic appropriateness see Ford 2002, 13–17 who discusses as well Alcm. *PMGF* 98 and Stes. 271 Finglass = *PMGF* 232: on these two fragments see also Fantuzzi 2007, 174 f., who points out the meta-poetic dimension of such statements of poetics.

the festive *paian* and the mournful *thrēnos*, when we look for it in tragedy,[21] is projected into the rhetorical figure of 'negated song': Euripides, more than Aeschylus and Sophocles, explores the problematic and paradoxical nature of the μοῦσα θρήνων, namely, a Muse who is the source of inspiration for ritual lament.[22]

The image of the *mousa thrēnōn* is given in *Trojan Women* a prominent poetic and thematic role: of the five occurrences of the term μοῦσα in the play,[23] three are worth a quick look since they work as gnomic corollaries to the appearance of the epic Muse at the beginning of the first *stasimon*.

1) Cassandra's aposiopesis at 384–85, 'better to say nothing of disgraceful things: may my muse not be a singer who sings disaster',[24] is curiously close to the Sapphic norm (fr. 150 V. above), and stands as an ironic counterpart to the opening of the first *stasimon*, where the epic Muse is asked to sing an 'ode of mourning accompanied by tears'.

2) The gnome at 608–9 'how sweet for those in misfortune are tears, the lamentations of *thrēnoi*, and the muse (μοῦσα) that has sorrow for its theme!',[25] is pronounced by the Chorus. Besides resonating with the Homeric motif of the *terpsis* of the lament,[26] these lines have an immediate musical and ritual

---

[21] In Aeschylus, the Erinyes' song is described as a *paian* (*Ag.* 644–5) and as a *hymnos* (*Sept.* 866–70, *Eum.* 328–33); Euripides exploits this field of imagery at full scale: see e.g. the threnodic *paian* in *Alc.* 422–3.

[22] A distinctive means of tragic self-reflection on the paradoxical nature of the μοῦσα θρήνων is the kind of 'aporetic rhetoric question' of the type we find in Eur. *Phoen.* 1498–501, 1515–8, *Hyps.* fr. 752 h, 5–9 *TrGF*[5.2].: the trope is discussed in Fantuzzi 2007, 178 f. For the 'rhetorical figure of negated song ("unmusic singing", "lyreless Muse", "unchorused dance", or the like) to express these paradoxical relations between art, beauty, ritual and tragic suffering' see Segal 1993, 16; on *alyros* as 'a central term of tragedy's own internal discourse of *mousikē*' see the remarks in Wilson 1999–2000, 433. For a survey of the occurrences and functions of the Muse/muse in tragedy see Saïd 2007.

[23] *Tro.* 120–1; 384–5; 511–5; 608–9; 1242–5. On the distinctive features of Euripides' reshaping of the epic *Mousai* into his tragic *mousa* see Fantuzzi 2007, 175, who aptly observes how the dramatist confers to his *mousa* (as source of poetic inspiration) 'un ruolo indiretto, minore, quasi in incognito [...] una dimensione da iniziale minuscola'. In the three Euripidean passages quoted below in the text, the translation of μοῦσα with 'muse' encompasses different but complementary concepts such as 'poetic inspiration', 'music' and 'song', all encompassed by the semantics of the term.

[24] σιγᾶν ἄμεινον τἀσχρά, μηδὲ μοῦσά μοι / γένοιτ' ἀοιδὸς ἥτις ὑμνήσει κακά. The lines are athetized in Diggle's and Kovacs' editions, who follow Reichenberger. Biehl 1989 *ad l.* argues convincingly for the authenticity of the passage, also given the continuity with the *praeteritio* at 361.

[25] ὡς ἡδὺ δάκρυα τοῖς κακῶς πεπραγόσιν / θρήνων τ' ὀδυρμοὶ μοῦσά θ' ἣ λύπας ἔχει.

[26] Cf. Hom. *Il.* 23.10 = 98, 24.513, *Od.* 4.102, 11.212, 19.213, 251, 513, 21.57. We find a slight variation of the iunctura θρήνων τ' ὀδυρμοὶ in Timoth. *Pers.* 103 Hord. = *PMG* 791.103 θρηνώδει ... ὀδυρμῷ.

referent in the antistrophic lyric exchange between Hecuba and Andromache (577–607), which in turn is structured as a *thrēnos*.
3) The gnomic closure 'this too is muse (μοῦσα) for those in misfortune: to shout aloud their danceless troubles' (120–1),[27] frames the first section of Hecuba's monody (98–121). The adjective ἀχόρευτος stands here both for the absence of the Chorus (Hecuba is performing a monody) and for the impossibility, for the Trojan queen lying on the ground, to accompany her words with dance. It is tempting to consider the couplet as a generalizing anticipation of the opening of the first *stasimon* (511–3), where the Μοῦσα is invoked and requested to sing a ᾠδὰ ἐπικήδειος 'mourning ode' of new songs (καινῶν ὕμνων) accompanied by tears (σὺν δακρύοις): the *thrēnos* is thus presented as the genre setting the tone of the ode – and eventually determining the claim of poetic novelty (καινότης).

Turning to matters of generic interaction in the opening lines of our *stasimon*, the typical *incipit* 'ἀμφί + object of the song (in accusative)',[28] together with the metrical texture of dactylo-epitrite sequences, evokes citharodic *prooimia* on the model of Terpander fr. 2 Gostoli = *PMG* 697 Ἀμφί μοι αὖτις ἄναχθ' ἑκαταβόλον / ἀειδέτω φρήν ('Sing to me once again about the far-shooting lord, my heart'), the *prooimion* to the *nomos Orthios*.[29] In association with the Muse, the ἀμφί-prelude is productive as well in rhapsodic context in the *exordium* of several Homeric Hymns (*h.Bacch.* (7), *h.Pan.* (19), *h.Poseid.* (22), *h.Diosc.* (33)).[30]

---

27 μοῦσα δὲ χαὔτη τοῖς δυστήνοις / ἄτας κελαδεῖν ἀχορεύτους. Other markers of the threnodic tone of this part of Hecuba's monody are the refrain αἰαῖ αἰαῖ (105), the rhetorical question τί δὲ θρηνῆσαι; (111), the woman's description of her physical prostration (112–9).
28 A structural feature shared by both dithyramb and *kitharoidia* according to *Suda* (s.v. ἀμφιανακτίζειν, A 1700 I p. 152.26 Adler). See Franklin 2013, 221f.
29 Translation mine. On the semantics of *prooimion*, a term which could refer to both autonomous introductory poems and to the introductory address to a larger poem (just as the ἀρχή/*exordium*), see Gostoli 1990, xxix-xxxiv, 128–129 on Terpander *PMG* 697, which she believes is the *exordium* of the *nomos Orthios*, relying on the testimony of Hesychius (s.v. ἀμφὶ ἄνακτα· ἀρχή τίς ἐστι νόμου κιθαρῳδικοῦ, A 3944 Latte). As Gostoli notes (p. 130), the proto-citharodic performance of the bard Demodocos in *Od.* 8.266–7 is introduced by a citharodic *prooimion* (αὐτὰρ ὁ φορμίζων ἀνεβάλλετο καλὸν ἀείδειν / ἀμφ' Ἄρεος φιλότητος εὐστεφάνου τ' Ἀφροδίτης 'he struck up on the *phorminx* an *anabolē* to a beautiful song about the love of Ares and Aphrodite of the fair crown' [trad. Power 2010, 209]). On the stylistic and structural features of the opening lines of the *stasimon* see Rodighiero forthcoming: I thank Andrea Rodighiero for sending me his refreshing and thorough analysis of the song's *incipit:* I am relieved to see that he too has focused on the ode as an instance of narrative lyric.
30 See Power 2010, 194 'probably on the model of the citharodic practice'. See Gostoli 1990, XXIX on Ps. Plut. *De Mus.* 6.1133c = test. 34.7–9 Gostoli: 'it is thus evident that (*sc.* Terpander's

As for adesp. *PMG* 938e Μοῖσά μοι ἀμφὶ Σκάμανδρον ἐύρροον ἄρχομ' ἀείδειν, the famous hexametric line from the Douris cup, it has been now demonstrated that the verse is probably the juxtaposition of two different hexametric *incipitia*.³¹ Within the diverse phenomenology and performance context of archaic *prooimia*, it has been proposed that the *prooimion* was performed monodically by the lyre player to introduce a choral *melos*:³² Power has shown that this was not always the case, and that the performative sequence *prooimion*–song was realized in different ways through different genres.³³ Suffice here to mention a fragment of Alcman (14a *PMGF* = 4 Calame) in which poetic novelty, invocation of the Muse and performance of a *melos* are associated in the context of a choral *prooimion*: Μῶσ' ἄγε, Μῶσα λίγηα πολυμμελὲς / αἰὲν ἀοιδὲ μέλος / νεοχμὸν ἄρχε παρσένοις ἀείδην ('Come Muse, clear-voiced Muse of many songs, singer always, begin a new song for girls to sing'). The claim of novelty in song, καινῶν ὕμνων (512), in the opening of the first *stasimon* of *Trojan Women* can be further compared with a couple of pronouncements by Timotheus which show the citharode's self-presentations waving between 'rhetoric of innovation' and traditionalism.³⁴ An instance of the former attitude which comes quite close, at least formally, to the opening of our *stasimon* is *PMG* 796, an open claim of *kainotomia* on the part of Timotheus: οὐκ ἀείδω τὰ παλαιά, / καινὰ γὰρ ἁμὰ κρείσσω· / νέος ὁ Ζεὺς βασιλεύει, / τὸ πάλαι δ'ἦν Κρόνος ἄρχων· / ἀπίτω Μοῦσα παλαιά ('I do not sing the ancient songs, for my new ones are better. The young Zeus rules, while it was in ancient times that Cronus had the power. Let the ancient Muse depart').³⁵

If we read the καινότης advocated by the Chorus of *Trojan Women* as a metaliterary claim on the part of Euripides,³⁶ the novelty of the *stasimon* could rely

---

citharodic *prooimia*) must have been compositions entirely analogous to the *Homeric Hymns*' (my translation).
31 See Palumbo Stracca 1994, Sider 2010.
32 This is the hypothesis of Koller 1956.
33 Power 2010, 185–215 is an exhaustive account of citharodic *prooimion*, its morphology and history. See especially pp. 201–10 for the hypothesis of a choral origin of *citharōidia*, and 202 on Pindar's proemial introductions and mirror descriptions of archetypal choral performances introduced by a *prooimion*.
34 See Power 2010, 534–8 (quote from p. 534) on Timotheus' 'eunomian strategies'.
35 Inspired by a different poetic agenda are the claims of the citharode in the *sphragis* of the *Persians*, where he reverses the terms of the polemics new-old by lamenting Spartan hostility to him (*PMG* 791.211–2 ὅτι παλαιοτέραν νέοις / ὕμνοις Μοῦσαν ἀτιμῶ 'on the ground that I dishonour the older Muse with my new songs') and positioning his own musical innovation 'within the validating "paternal" Aeolic tradition of Pierian Orpheus and Lesbian Terpander': Power 2010, 535.
36 With 'metaliterary' it is meant here 'referring self-reflexively to the nature and literary dimension of the actual poem/song'.

on the juxtaposition of citharodic *nomos* – indeed a fitting genre, *qua* lyric narrative, for an account of the sack of Troy (as Stesichorus' *Iliou Persis* seems to confirm)³⁷ – and the melic genre of *thrēnos*, within the structure of a narrative dithyramb. The audacity of this generic fusion might have been in place in the context of the struggle for innovation in the genres of *nomos* and dithyramb taking place in the lively New Musical scene of late fifth century Athens.³⁸ If, on the other hand, the proemial claim of 'new songs' should be explained entirely within the logic and events of the play, we could see in the opening of the ode an archaeology of the genre of women's lament, the *thrēnos*,³⁹ to which *aulos* music and Phrygian *harmonia* were at time associated by ancient sources.⁴⁰

---

37 A reconstruction *exempli gratia* of the first triad of Stesichorus' *Iliou Persis* is attempted by Finglass 2013a, 14. See Power 2010, 267–71 on the citharodic *Little Iliad* by Lesches. Di Benedetto in Di Benedetto / Cerbo 1998, 178 f. (*ad loc.*) proposes as a possible model for the opening of the stasimon the *incipit* of the Cyclic *Little Iliad* (fr. 28 Bernabè Ἴλιον ἀείδω καὶ Δαρδανίην εὔπωλον).
38 D'Angour 2011, 184–206, has recently pointed out how the contest for poetic novelty is part of a traditional discourse among Greek poets (for pre-classical lyric he focuses on Pindar *Ol.* 3.4–6, *Nem.* 8.20–1, and Bacchylides fr. 5 M), and a reinvigoration of this aspect accompanied the raise of the New Music; in this regard, see 72–3 on the conceptual associations and semantics of καινός. In the case of Eur. *Tro.* 511–5, D'Angour observes that '[G]iven the reference to *melos*, we may speculate that melic novelty was also an issue' (p. 194). See also Power 2013 *passim* (also on the intersections *nomos*-dithyramb-drama) and 2010, 272–3.
39 In proposing the equipollence ritual lament = *thrēnos* in tragedy (while this was not the case in archaic poetry) I follow Swift 2010, 303.
40 The Phrygians are described as μάλιστα θρηνητικοί ('especially inclined to express mournful emotions through the *thrēnos*') in Σ Aesch. *Pers.* 1055 [pp. 268 f. Dähnhardt]. In an opposite direction Pindar 128c S-M, where the poet theorizes the opposition between *paian* and dithyramb on one hand (as song-types celebrating the gods), and *thrēnos* on the other. An interesting source dealing with appropriateness in the use of *harmoniai* in relation to dithyramb and *thrēnos* is P. Vindob. 19996a, fragment a I, which is now discussed in Battezzato 2013, 99–102: according to Battezzato's reconstruction, in the papyrus' theoretical discussion on what is πρέπον to dithyramb, it seems to be debated the fact that the dithyrambic genre (and thus Phrygian *harmonia*) is inappropriate to express the *pathos* of lamentation. On the Asian origin of lament in Euripides see *Hyps.* fr. 752 g.9–10 *TrGF*⁵·².; *Erecht.* fr. 369d *TrGF*⁵·¹.; *IT* 178–85; *Phoen.* 1302–3. In Pind. *Pyth.* 12 the invention of aulodic music originates from the primordial dirge of the Gorgons (θρῆνος 8, γόος 22), which Athena transforms into a πάμφωνον μέλος (19): see Steiner 2013 for a reading of the poem which accounts for Pindar's active participation in the experimentalism in aulodic music of his time.

3 Metaliterary *Kainotēs*

The nature of the καινότης claimed by the Chorus for this song has been much debated among scholars. In fact, following the citharodic *prooimion*, a first-person self-referential utterance on the part of the Chorus announces their performance as a *melos* for Troy (νῦν γὰρ μέλος ἐς Τροίαν ἰαχήσω 515), thus adding a further layer to be harmonized within this composite poetic opening. Two particular aspects of *Tro.* 511–67, related to generic expectations and gender of the singers respectively, have been seen as factors at odds with the epic/citharodic characterization of the opening lines of the *stasimon* and with the theme of the ode, and as such have been singled out as bearing the novelty of the song: a) the mournful content of this song, with its threnodic take on the *Iliou Persis* myth, and b) the fact that the events are narrated and interpreted through the eyes of the Chorus of captive Trojan women.[41] A different approach to the metaliterary stance of καινότης has been proposed (independently, and grounded on different interpretations of the ode) by Battezzato and Sansone: the Trojan Women of the Chorus assert the birth of tragedy as a new literary genre which is 'the successor to, even the supplanter of, epic poetry',[42] and which 'not only incorporates earlier genres of Greek poetry, but can also include the narrative about their origin'.[43]

A first reading of the *stasimon* opening lines as a statement of poetics on the part of Euripides was offered by Kranz in 1933 and became classic; since it associated the poetic novelty claimed by the Chorus with Euripides' embracing the 'dithyrambic' lyric style, it provides a fitting starting point to ground a discussion on the 'dithyrambic' features of *Tro.* 511–67. In Kranz's interpretation, the open-

---

41 Lee 1976, 164 proposes two layers of meaning for making sense of the καινότης of the *stasimon:* while for the Chorus the καινοὶ ὕμνοι denote the present song of woe, different from the joyous *mousikē* enjoyed by the Trojans in times of peace and depicted in the *stasimon*, the novelty embraces an extra-dramatic aspect, i.e. 'the present song is 'new' when compared to the well-known epic treatment of the subject'. Barlow 1986, 184 and Croally 1994, 245 correlate the novelty of the ode with the female perspective on the events narrated. Quijada 2006 provides a survey of the scholarly debate on the *stasimon*.
42 Sansone 2009, 194. Sansone sees in the threnodic tonality of the *stasimon* a reference to the contents of *Iliad* 24, and in a fine intertextual reading of the ode he is able to show Euripides' indebtedness to Homer at both the level of situational allusion and in the reuse of specific terms. Torrance 2013, 219–45 argues for a different Homeric hypotext for our *stasimon*, namely the *hymnos* performed by Demodocus in *Odyssey* 8.426–534, itself a narrative *Iliou Persis*.
43 Battezzato 2005b, 90.

ing of the ode⁴⁴ represented the programmatic manifesto of a new phase of Euripides' lyric, inaugurated in 415 BC and largely documented in the last decade of the dramatist's production. Within this chronological frame, Kranz argues that as many as eleven choral odes present a character of narrative self-containment – in lacking any direct reference to the events on stage – and certain structural features typical of the narrative lyric of Bacchylides' dithyrambs.⁴⁵ As for the charge of dramatic irrelevance, the first *stasimon* of *Trojan Women* has been long redeemed, and the very category of 'dithyrambic *stasima*', together with Kranz's chronology, questioned and reassessed by Eric Csapo's influential work on the New Musical traits of late Euripidean tragedy.⁴⁶ More recently, David Fearn's studies have repositioned Bacchylides' dithyrambs within a tradition of archaic narrative lyric and in the performance context of fifth century festivals, shedding new light on the nature and performance of κύκλοι χοροί.⁴⁷ This allows him to

---

44 Which he quotes in the epigraph of his chapter 'Das neue Lied' as ἀμφί μοι Ἴλιον, ὦ Μοῦσα, καινῶν ὕμνων ἄεισον, thus omitting the funereal connotation conveyed by the terms qualifying the ᾠδά, i.e. the adjective ἐπικήδειος and the instrumental σὺν δακρύοις. This is pointed out, among others, by Sansone 2009, 193f., who argues that Kranz's omission of the tears and of the sorrowful nature of the song is due to the fact that these elements 'are antithetical to the character of dithyramb'. At 513 ᾆσον σὺν δακρύοις is Burges' conjecture (printed by Diggle) on the manuscripts' (VPQ) ἄεισον ἐν δακρύοις: for a defense of the manuscripts' reading see Panagl 1971, 43 and Di Benedetto in Di Benedetto and Cerbo 1998, 178f. n. 139.
45 See *infra* n. 1. See Kranz 1933, 253–4 on the ballad-like features of Bacchylides' dithyrambs (odes 16, 17, 19 and 20): in particular, Kranz points out the similarities in structural patterns (antistrophe responding to a question/point raised at the end of strophe) between Soph. *Trach.* 504 and Bacchyl. 19.15 (where Kranz p. 155 reads the papyrus TIHN as τί ἦν 'how was it..', thus making the clause an interrogative one), and between Eur. *Hel.* 1317–9 and Bacchyl. 17.89 (and respective antistrophes).
46 Lee 1976, 168, Biehl 1989, 223–5, Di Benedetto / Cerbo 1998, 178f. and Hose 1991, 302–8 all offer convincing explanations of the ways by which the ode, through explicit references to the role of Athena in the fall of Troy – the goddess is the addressee (536) of the wooden horse, δόλιος ἄτη (530) for the Trojans – links the *stasimon* to the prologue (10 μηχαναῖσι Παλλάδος) and to the core religious issues of the play. For criticism of Kranz's argument in relation to the alleged dramatic irrelevance of this *stasimon* see already Neitzel 1967, 42–68. Csapo 1999–2000, 407–9 revises at length Kranz's categorization against the background of a systematic reconstruction of late Euripidean production in terms of musical innovations – thus offering evidence for Euripides' engagement with New Music. On the socio-politic conditions for the rise of the New Music, and on the musical and stylistic innovation of the 'New Musicians' (and Euripides among them) see Csapo 2004. A recent and highly innovative study of late classical Greek lyric is LeVen 2014: the poetics, style and language of the New Musical verse is exhaustively treated; the lyric of late classical tragedy is not dealt with, though LeVen's approach invites application to the language and style of late Euripidean tragic odes.
47 Fearn 2007, 163–99, esp. 188–92 on the relation between dithyramb and New Music.

argue against Csapo's claim of a Dionysiac revival in New Musical dithyramb (as a move toward the re-appropriation of genuine dithyrambic traits), and against his perplexity over Kranz's concept of 'dithyrambic *stasima*' as self-contained narratives, a trait, according to Fearn, which seems in fact to characterize narrative lyric in both dithrambs and late (or New Musical) Euripidean lyric."[48] The following discussion takes its start from a re-consideration of the 'dithyrambic' features that Kranz (and Panagl for matters of style) attributed to the first *stasimon* of *Trojan Women*.

4 Structural and Stylistic Features of a 'Dithyrambic' *Stasimon*

The formal structure of the *stasimon* presents a single triadic antistrophic system: as in Aesch. *Ag.* 104–59 and Soph. *Tr.* 497–530, similarly consisting of a single triad, the chorus as lyric narrator adopts here an authoritative poetic stance by means of the appeal to the Muse embedded into a citharodic *prooimion*.[49] Such a formally sustained attack of the song, which announces the theme of the piece and makes it a self-contained ballad, detaching it from the dramatic reality of the play, is what characterizes 'dithyrambic' *stasima* in Kranz's view.[50] The shift from the proemial invocation to first-person choral self-referentiality at 515 (νῦν γὰρ μέλος ἐς Τροίαν ἰαχήσω) reinforces the impression of solemnity of this opening and declares the subject of the song, Troy. The two following subordinate clauses further specify the content of the *melos* (516–21):

---

48 Cf. Fearn forthcoming.
49 Cf. Hutchinson 2001, 436 n. 16. Kranz 1933, 256 pairs the opening of our *stasimon* and Soph. *Trach.* 497–502 on the ground of their rhetorically elaborate openings. See Rodighiero forthcoming on Aesch. *Ag.* 104–7, and Coward in this volume on Aesch. *Ag.* 105–59.
50 Further structural features of these odes happen to be shared by *Tro.* 511–67. Suffice here to mention just a couple of them: i) the gnomic statement of a turn of events at the closing of a strofe, which the beginning of antistrophe will pick up and develop, as in Bacchylides 17.89 (μοῖρα δ' ἑτέραν ἐπόρσυν' ὁδόν 'but Fate was preparing another course'): see Eur. *Tro.* 529–30 κεκαρμένοι δ' ἀοιδαῖς / δόλιον ἔσχον ἄταν ('rejoicing in song they took for themselves ruin in disguise'); ii) the 'return' to the first-person singular, and thus to a more intimate and domestic dimension of the song, at the opening of the epode (and in a iambic ambience) after a tighter narrative in the strophic pair (often a mix of dactylo-epitrite and iambics): this, Kranz 1933, 258 argues, is shared by *Trojan Women* (551) and *Trachiniae* (517). See Bacchylides 19.37, matching only partially the pattern. On the pattern of the 'return to the I' in *Trachiniae* 517–530 see Rodighiero 2012, 89–95.

νῦν γὰρ μέλος ἐς Τροίαν ἰαχήσω, (515)
τετραβάμονος ὡς ὑπ' ἀπήνας
Ἀργείων ὀλόμαν τάλαινα δοριάλωτος,
ὅτ' ἔλιπον ἵππον οὐράνια
βρέμοντα χρυσεοφάλαρον ἔνο- (520)
   πλον ἐν πύλαις Ἀχαιοί·

For now I shall rise a *melos* for Troy,
how that Argive four-feet conveyance
wrougth my destruction and cause my enslavement,
when the horse, reaching high heaven
with its clatter, decked with gold cheekpieces,
full of arms within, was left at the gates by the Achaeans.

The formal structure of 516–7 is noteworthy. Firstly, we have here a *kephalaion*, a poetic device typical of ring structures and particularly dear to Pindar and Bacchylides,[51] by which in the first sentence of a ring the course of the events is anticipated by the mention of 'the extreme temporal points of the action recounted'.[52] In the case of this ode, the introduction of the Trojan Horse in the city (519–21) and the enslavement of the women (565–6) represent the first and the last event in a temporal perspective. Secondly, the word pattern within the *kephalaion* shows symmetry of design: two five-syllable words, τετραβάμονος (516) and δοριάλωτος (517), frame a structure with three trisyllabic words that in turn circumscribe the main verb (ὀλόμαν), with ἀπήνας and τάλαινα forming a further frame and Ἀργείων functioning as a ἀπὸ κοινοῦ.[53]

The following temporal clause shows a sequence of three pairs of words (ἔλιπον ἵππον – οὐράνια βρέμοντα – χρυσεοφάλαρον ἔνοπλον, 519–21) characterized by a conspicuous use of sound figures (homoteleuton and assonance), but it is the accumulation of compound epithets, *hapax legomena* and periphrases referred to the Horse that seems to point to 'new-dithyrambic' features in this colon (515–21). The periphrasis τετραβάμων ἀπήνη 'conveyance with four feet' is an apt starting point for exploring Euripides' use of riddling expressions in this *stasimon*. In a recent discussion of τετραβάμων in Eur. *El.* 476, where the adjective is referred to horses,[54] Csapo illustrates the history of the word (literally 'moving with four'), which 'is probably a Euripidean coinage' and which shares with other compound adjectives ending in –βάμων the characteristic to be am-

---

[51] Pindar: Illig 1932, 20; Bacchylides: Cairns 2010, 104 and n. 6, with further bibliography.
[52] Pelliccia 1989, 100 n. 45.
[53] I am drawing here and in the next paragraph on Panagl 1971, 44–6.
[54] Csapo 2009, 107f.

biguous 'about who is doing the walking and how'.⁵⁵ Being attached to ἀπήνη ('conveyance', 'wagon') but referring to the Wooden Horse, τετραβάμων becomes especially ambiguous: a 'wagon moving with four feet/legs'. Panagl notes that the periphrasis generates an 'alienating effect', and that the position at the opening of the *kephalaion* adds to the ambiguity of the Horse, pointing at the divergence between its outer appearance and its real nature.⁵⁶ In describing Euripidean periphrases as the accumulation of a series of adjectives which modify the 'natural' relationship with the noun they qualify by means of unexpected associations, Panagl comes closer to LeVen's innovative treatment of the effect generated by dithyrambic periphrasis and compounds in terms of 'defamiliarizing' the relationship between language and things.⁵⁷ One further interesting trait of New Musical poetics that LeVen has convincingly brought to light and systematically verified in the case of Timotheus' *Persians* regards the ways dithyrambic compounds activate a poetic memory through reworking Homeric formulae, *hapax* or compound adjectives into novel words.⁵⁸ It would be tempting to read the periphrasis τετραβάμων ἀπήνη in *Tro.* 516 as Euripides' variation on the Homeric τετράκυκλον ἀπήνην (*Il.* 24.324): the dramatist reworks a rare Homeric compound to create his ambivalent and 'defamiliarizing' image of a 'conveyance with four feet'.⁵⁹ Timotheus' intertextual use, blending, and reshaping of Euripidean periphrases into more complex (if obscure) expressions and riddling metaphors has been demonstrated by Firinu in the case of the relation be-

---

55 In the Euripidean occurrences τετραβάμων is referred to Callisto transformed into a bear (*Hel.* 376), the Sphinx (*Phoen.* 808) and to chariots drawn by winged horses (*Phoen.* 793): see Csapo 2009, 107.
56 Panagl 1971, 46.
57 LeVen 2014, 161f., 167–72. See in part. 161: '[D]ithyrambic compounds offer a way to describe the world in an unfamiliar way that gives listeners fresh access to things'. Panagl (p. 49) considers periphrastic compounds as part of Euripides' narrative technique in 'dithyrambic' *stasima*; he is skeptical though about the narrative functionality of Timotheus' periphrases.
58 LeVen 2014, 178–87. Budelmann / LeVen 2014. On the formal features and poetics of the 'new dithyramb'-New Musical style see Ford 2013 with further bibliography; for a valuable survey of generic traits of dithyramb and *nomos* and their use in Timotheus see Hordern 2002, 33–43; on the dithyrambic *lexis*, especially concerning compounds, see Napolitano 2000, 132–6.
59 The compound adjective τετράκυκλος occurs only twice in Homer (*Il.* 24.324 and *Od.* 9.242). For a discussion of ἀπήνη in *Tro.* 516 as an allusion to *Il.* 24.324 (where the word refers to the wagon bringing the ransom for Hector's body) see Sansone 2009, 198 f. On ἀπήνη as metatextual vehicle of the relation between the periphrases ναΐα ἀπήνη 'marine cart' (Eur. *Med.* 1122–3) and πλωταὶ ἀπῆναι 'sailing carts' (*PMG* 1027(*f*)), grounded on the metaphorical relation between cart and ship, see Firinu 2009, 117 f.

tween the first *stasimon* of *Iphigenia among the Taurians* and the *Persians*.⁶⁰ When we look at the first *stasimon* of *Trojan Women*, the only metatextual segment that seems to point to a direct relation with Timotheus' *Persians* is the periphrasis πεύκα οὔρειος 'mountain pinewood' (534): this is a metonym referring to the Wooden Horse and introducing the motif of the analogy between the Trojan Horse and a ship, further developed in the comparison at 537–8 κλωστοῦ δ' ἀμφιβόλοις λίνοιο, ναὸς ὡσεὶ / σκάφος κελαινόν ('with nooses of spun flax they brought it, like the dark hull of a ship').⁶¹ In the *Persians* we encounter the periphrasis πεῦκαι ὀρίγονοι 'mountain-born pines' (78–9) referred to ships (or, as commonly in Timotheus, to oars) in the context of a sustained texture of figurative images expressing the idea of the blurring of 'the boundaries between maritime and land elements':⁶² νῦν δὲ σ' ἀναταράξει / ἐμὸς ἄναξ ἐμὸς πεύ- / καισιν ὀριγόνοισιν, ἐγ- / κλήσει δὲ πεδία πλόιμα νομάσι ναύταις (75–8 'and now my lord, yes mine, will stir you up with his mountain-born pines and enclose your navigable plains with his roaming seamen').⁶³ The amount and concentration of periphrastic compounds in *Persians* is an essential trait of Timotheus' dithyrambic style: Euripides' exploitation of the potential of defamiliarizing periphrases and compound adjectives in his 'dithyrambic' odes might have contributed to the development of the device. In the first *stasimon* of *Trojan Women* it is the Wooden Horse that generates and attracts most periphrastic and metaphoric

---

60 Firinu 2009, who includes in her analysis similarities of metrical patterns. The passages discussed are: *IT* 407–12 ~ *PMG* 791.4–6, 7–13; *PMG* 1027(*f*) ~ *IT* 410, *Med*. 1122–3; *IT* 422–6 ~ *PMG* 791.79–81, 35–9; *IT* 439–46 ~ *PMG* 791.126–31.
61 A further possible instance of the association of πεύκα with the Wooden Horse in the context of a fragment of lyric narrative which shows remarkable New Musical stylistic traits and (especially in diction) seems to point to Euripides is P.Mich. inv. 3498 + 3250b verso and 3250c verso, which has recently benefited by a new edition and a rich commentary Sampson in Borges/Sampson 2012, 36–129. The text, which is likely to presuppose a Trojan setting (among other topographical references pointing to this, a specific mention of the wood of Mt. Ida is found in fr. 1, col. II.5 Ἰδαί[ων] … δενδρέων), has been convincingly located by Sampson (in terms of its mythical plot) within the context of the Achaean construction of the Wooden Horse (Borges / Sampson 2012, 62–75). It would thus be tempting to speculate on the occurrence of πεύκα (fr. 1 col. II.2) as a reference to the Wooden Horse, like in *Tro*. 534. Even more interesting is the fact that on narrative, stylistic, and linguistic ground this fragmentary piece of lyric narrative is ascribable to either Euripides' New Musical verse or (as Sampson proposes) 'to a poet of New Musical dithyramb or citharodic *nomos* from the late fifth of fourth century who is herein imitating Euripides. Timotheus is the likeliest alternative candidate' (Borges/Sampson 2012, 75). I would like to thank Thomas Coward for drawing this papyrus to my attention.
62 LeVen 2014, 181 f.
63 LeVen 2014, 182 notes that in this passage ὀριγόνοισι seems to replace πλωσίμους, which we find referred to πεῦκαι at 12.

expressions: its function of vehicle containing humans and weapons, its exterior shape of wooden offering for Athena, and its analogy with a ship all contribute to define the ambiguous nature of the structure.

Going back to the strophe and to the paratactic series of three adjectives (plus the adverb οὐράνια) at 519–21 (οὐράνια / βρέμοντα χρυσεοφάλαρον ἔνο- / πλον 'reaching high-heaven with its clatter, decked with gold cheek-pieces, having arms within'), we can see how each term evokes a sense, in coherence with a broader pattern of this ode:[64] οὐράνια βρέμοντα (lit. 'producing a sound which reached to high heaven') appeals to sound, the *hapax* χρυσεοφάλαρος evokes sight, and ἔνοπλος (normally 'armed', but here 'arms within') brings to mind the real nature and function of the Horse. The sequence of periphrases at 534–5 πεύκαν οὐρείαν, ξεστὸν λόχον Ἀργείων / καὶ Δαρδανίας ἄταν, θεᾷ δώσων ('to give this mountain-borne pinewood, Greek polished ambush, this ruin for Dardanus' land, to the goddess') features 'an example of bold hypallage'[65] in ξεστόν, which should logically go with πεύκαν (in the sense of 'polished pinewood') but is grammatically attached to the abstract λόχος: the metonymy ξεστός λόχος may in turn be a reworking of the Homeric κοῖλον λόχον (*Od.* 4.277, 8.515).[66] The most remarkable series of complex periphrases in the *stasimon* is left to the epode (562–7):

σφαγαὶ δ' ἀμφιβώμιοι
Φρυγῶν ἔν τε δεμνίοις
καράτομος ἐρημία
νεανίδων στέφανον ἔφερεν (565)
Ἑλλάδι κουροτρόφον,
Φρυγῶν δὲ πατρίδι πένθος.

The slaughtering of Phrygians about the altars
and, in our beds, beheaded desolation
brought a victory garland of young women
to Greece to bear them children,
but grief to the land of Phrygians.

The passage presents a predominance of nominal constructs, with only one verbal form (ἔφερεν, 565) in the six lines. The progress of the narrative is provided

---

64 Barlow 1986, 183 explains that the reality of past Troy in the ode 'is built up by the dramatist in a series of images suggesting sight, sound and texture'. See as well Barlow 2008, 30.
65 Lee 1976, 167.
66 See Di Benedetto and Cerbo 1998, 181. On the aetiological association of the concept of λόχος (of which the Trojan Horse offers a paradigmatic instance) with pyrrich dance see Ceccarelli 1998, 202–206.

by two condensed periphrases: σφαγαὶ δ' ἀμφιβώμιοι Φρυγῶν, which contains the *hapax* ἀμφιβώμιοι, points back to Priam's death as described by Poseidon in the prologue (16–7); καρατόμος ἐρημία νεανίδων is a further convoluted riddling phrase where a rare compound adjective is attached to a noun in an unfamiliar way.[67]

When considering Euripides' 'dithyrambic' use of defamiliarizing expressions in his *stasima* with an eye to the style and *lexis* of Timotheus – and his sustained use of periphrastic compounds to produce poetic and narrative texture – it is tempting to think of the dramatist as an innovator in the genre of dithyrambic narrative lyric, and of Timotheus and the new dithyrambographers and *kitharodes* as building on the playwright's New Musical experimentations.

After the 'poetic' opening, the narrative develops in a series of descriptive and pictorial canvases: the syntax is paratactic and plain, and the lyric burden is borne by images and words (in particular adjectives) related to visual, aural and more properly musical experience, often in association with the Wooden Horse. Intruding in the sequence of beautiful descriptions, sinister associations, ambiguous images and anticipations of future ruin punctuate the *stasimon*.[68] Besides being traits of Euripidean tragic lyric, certain stylistic features of the *stasimon* seem to come close to Bacchylides' narrative style: the predilection for descriptive epithets and compounds,[69] chosen in order to emphasize the contrast between the beauty of an image and its sinister effect;[70] the increasing tension in the narration progressing to its dramatic climax;[71] and the 'elliptical' narrative strategy where just a few trait of the story are given, leaving the audience to fill in the rest.[72] In a forthcoming contribution on the continuity of stylistic and structural features linking Bacchylides and Timotheus' dithyrambs – features that are applied to an intertextual reading of some passages of the *Persians* as alluding to Bacchylides 17 – David Fearn argues for a substantial similarity of narrative style of the two poets, grounded on the juxtaposition of plain syntax

---

[67] See Lee 1976, 173 who adds that this is 'a somewhat violent hypallage for ἐρημία καρατόμων ἀνδρῶν'.
[68] E. g. the oxymoron μέλαιναν αἴγλαν closing the antistrophe (549). See also Mastronarde 1994, 331 (*ad* Eur. *Phoen.* 638–89) on 'the paradoxical wedding of beautiful language and sensuous description to violent content' which characterizes Euripides' 'dithyrambic' style.
[69] Colour: χρυσεοφάλαρον 520; divine prerogatives: ἀμβροτοπώλου 536; aspect: τετραβάμωνος 516; status: δοριάλωτος 517; feelings: ἐπικήδειον 514.
[70] χρυσεοφάλαρον 520; κουροτρόφον 566.
[71] 551–61.
[72] 555–7. For these features of Bacchylidean poetry see Maehler 2004, 19–21; cf. now Hadjimichael 2014a on Bacch. 60 M., a discussion of the fragment's narrative style against the background of Bacchylides' dithyrambs.

and richness of visual texture (effected by the pictorial character of epithets) in large narrative sequences.⁷³ I submit that Euripides' narrative lyric, in turn, can be positioned within this same tradition of dithyrambic narrative. Differences between Euripides' narrative lyric style, and his New Musical verse can be appreciated by looking at Hecuba's monody in *Trojan Women*.

5 New Musical Features in Hecuba's Monody

The second part of Hecuba's astrophic monody (122–52), in lyric anapaests, while reinforcing the threnodic tonality of the song through features such as ritual refrains and invocations,⁷⁴ offers a remarkable instance of Euripides' New Musical style in *Trojan Women* and introduces the motif of the interruption of the normalcy of Phrygian *choreia*. The opening of this section of the monody develops the rhetorical motif of the *arkhē kakōn* ('the origin of woes') through the evocation of the arrival of the Greek fleet to Troy (122–8). The pervasive use of parataxis, with relative clauses and appositions linking together pictorial descriptions of single images, the boldness of riddling periphrases (πλεκτὰν Αἰγύπτου / παιδείαν ἐξηρτήσασθε 'you hung down the interlaced culture of Egypt' 128–9, referring to the ropes fabricated with papyrus fibres), the reference to music (with the juxtaposition of the 'hateful *paian* of the *auloi*' and 'the voice of tuneful σύριγγες' 126–7), the blending of Homeric quotations in the opening lines⁷⁵ – all produce a picture where the sensual and musical texture of the images seems to obliterate the pathos of the situation.⁷⁶ As has been recently pointed out,⁷⁷ Hecuba can be described as a 'displaced chorus leader' in her self-ref-

---

73 Cf. Fearn forthcoming.
74 Refrains: αἰαῖ 130, ὤμοι 138. Invocation: ὦ τῶν χαλκεγχέων Τρώων / ἄλοχοι μέλεαι, / καὶ κοῦραι δύσνυμφοι, / τύφεται Ἴλιον, αἰάζωμεν 'o unhappy wives of the Trojans swords of bronze, girls unblest in your husbands, Ilium is burning: let us cry aloud!' 142–5. At 144 I print Musurus' conjecture, which gives a catalectic anapaestic dimeter.
75 Battezzato 2005b, 83 points out that Hecuba's opening lines are 'a pastiche of Homeric phrases'; in particular, the expressions describing the sea and the harbours (ἅλα πορφυροειδῆ at 124, λιμένας ... εὐόρμους at 125) echo and rework Homeric verses, in a way that can at least be compared with the refined use of Homeric *formulae* and *hapax* to produce novel compounds exploited by poets like Timotheus and Telestes, and demonstrated by Le Ven 2014, 150–88.
76 On the style and features of Euripides' 'new lyric' see Di Benedetto 1971, 239–72.
77 Murnaghan 2013, 160 f.

erential address to her role of ἔξαρχος of the ritual Phrygian dance (146–52) in the past.

μάτηρ δ' ὡσεί τις πτανοῖς,
κλαγγὰν ἐξάρξω 'γὼ μολπάν,
οὐ τὰν αὐτὰν οἵαν ποτὲ δὴ
σκήπτρῳ Πριάμου διερειδομένου (150)
ποδὸς ἀρχεχόρου πλαγαῖς Φρυγίαις
εὐκόμποις ἐξῆρχον θεούς.[78]

> Like a mother bird to her winged brood,
> I shall lead off the cry of lamentation, a song,
> not at all the same song
> that I led off, as Priam leaned upon his sceptre,
> with the confident Phrygian beats
> of the foot leader of the dance
> in praise of the gods.

The double occurrence of the verb ἐξάρχω at 147 and 152 stresses the distance between the joyful Trojan *choreia* of the past (ἐξῆρχον) with its distinctive Phrygian *mousikē*,[79] and the present disruption where ritual ἐξαρχία can only allow for a song of lamentation (κλαγγὰν ἐξάρξω 'γὼ μολπάν, 147), which the 'performative' future ἐξάρξω suggests being executed by Hecuba through her monody. Hecuba's reference to the rhythmical stamping of the dancers' feet in Phrygian ritual dance (ποδὸς ἀρχεχόρου πλαγαῖς Φρυγίαις / εὐκόμποις, 151–2) represents an anticipation of, and a strong link to, the mimetic description of that same trait of Φρύγια μέλεα in the first *stasimon* (545–7): what in Hecuba's monody is the nostalgic evocation of choral (*qua* ritual) normalcy, will become in the first *stasimon* (through choral projection) the re-enactment of past Trojan *choreia*, and the dramatization of its violent end.

---

[78] I give for lines 146–148 Kovacs' text. Following Battezzato 2005b, 83f., at 151 I diverge from Kovacs (and Diggle) in conserving the codices' reading Φρυγίαις, which qualifies the rhythm of the ritual dance as 'Phrygian', coherently with a major motif of the play.

[79] The 'Phrygian beat' (πλαγαῖς Φρυγίαις, 152) recalls Φρύγια ... μέλεα in the first *stasimon* (545).

6 Choral Projection within Narration: Phrygian *Choreia*

Within the narrative frame of the first *stasimon*, the chorus of Trojan prisoners project themselves in the past, when as a choral formation of *parthenoi* they performed ritual dance for Artemis at the climax of the Trojans' euphoric celebrations taking place around the Wooden Horse.[80] This in turn activates a peculiar declension of the 'joy before disaster' pattern, subsumed into a narrative structure and realized through the abrupt shift of tone following the syntactic pause after χοροῖσι at 555.[81]

> ἐπὶ δὲ πόνῳ καί χαρᾷ
> νύχιον ἐπεὶ κνέφας παρῆν,
> Λίβυς τε λωτὸς ἐκτύπει
> Φρύγιά τε μέλεα, παρθένοι δ'   (545)
> ἀέριον ἅμα κρότον ποδῶν
> βοάν τ' ἔμελπον εὔφρον', ἐν
> δόμοις δὲ παμφαὲς σέλας
> πυρὸς μέλαιναν αἴγλαν
> †ἔδωκεν ὕπνῳ†.   (550)
> ἐγὼ δὲ τὰν ὀρεστέραν   [ἐπῳδ.
> τότ' ἀμφὶ μέλαθρα παρθένον
> Διὸς κόραν ἐμελπόμαν
> χοροῖσι· φοινία δ' ἀνὰ   (555)
> πτόλιν βοὰ κατέσχε Περ-
>   γάμον ἕδρας·

> And when their labour and joy
> the night's blackness overtook,
> the Libyan pipe sounded
> and Phrygian songs were played, and young girls
> stamping and lifting their feet in the dance

---

80 A further layer, this time of generic interaction, enriches the episode of choral projection. As pointed out by Swift 2010, 191, parthenaic imagery aptly functions here as a metaphorical foil to the violent (and perverted) transition of the Trojan women to their future condition of concubines of the Achaeans

81 For the 'joy before disaster' choral odes – a characteristic dramatic device in Sophocles (e.g. *Aj.* 693–705, *Trach.* 205–21, *Ant.* 1142–52; cf. Gardiner 1987, 66 f.) where premature choral rejoicing and Dionysiac exuberance on the part of the chorus prelude to tragic reversal – as a matrix for choral self-referentiality and choral projection see Henrichs (1994–1995, 73–85, on Sophocles; Henrichs 1996, 52 f. on Eur. *Heracl.* 892–927, 60 on *HF* 761–821). See also Andújar's discussion of such odes in connection to the *hyporchēma* in this volume.

sang a song of joy,
while within the doors the radiant blaze
of fire gave forth its sinister gleam
to banish sleep.[82]
In that hour in honour of her of the wilds,
Zeus's *parthenos* daughter,
I was performing choral dancing around the temple,
when a murderous cry throughout the city
possessed the seats of Pergamon.

Especially interesting for the purpose of this paper is the reference to circular choral dance provided by the mention of the temple (μέλαθρα 553) around which (ἀμφί) the chorus of *parthenoi* perform their dance (ἐμελπόμαν 554).[83] The identity between this projected chorus and the dramatic Chorus of captive Trojan women singing and dancing the *stasimon* strengthens the impression that a mimetic realization of the circular choral dance described in these lines could have taken place in performance – the Chorus, having abandoned their usual rectangular formation, arrange themselves in circular shape around the orchestral altar.[84] A further feature of Phrygian *choreia* that the Chorus is likely to have executed while performing the *stasimon* occurs some lines earlier, in the antistrophe (545–7): the dancing and singing of the *parthenoi* is described mimetically by the two objects of the verb ἔμελπον, κρότος ('beat, thud of dancing feet', here qualified by the adjective ἀέριος) and βοή ('song').[85] The description of the music and dance performed at Troy during the last night before the fall of the city provides the mention of the Libyan pipe (544) and the Phrygian songs (545). On the ground of the association between the Phrygian *harmonia* and

---

[82] The translation of 550 (Kovacs) presupposes accepting Tyrrell's emendation ἀντέδωκεν ὕπνου.

[83] Cf. Calame 1997b, 36; see as well 86f. on the semantics of μέλπω (as both song and choral dancing) and its use in Bacchylides and Pindar.

[84] Cf. Calame 1997b, 35f. for references to circular choral formations in Euripides and for the semantics of 'centrality' as expressed by the adjective μέσος accompanied by a preposition. An instance of a similar use (Soph. *Trach*. 514–5 οἳ τότ' ἀολλεῖς / ἴσαν ἐς μέσον) is discussed at length in Rodighiero 2012, 79–89, who surveys ancient testimonia and modern scholarship on tragic and epinician choral dance and proposes for the first *stasimon* of *Trachiniae* a movement toward the centre of the orchestra of two rows of *choreutai*.

[85] We find a similar image, again in the context of choral projection associated with parthenaic choral dancing, in the third *stasimon* of *Heraclidae*, where the Chorus mentions 'on the windswept hill loud shouts of gladness resound to the beat of maiden dance steps (ὑπὸ παρθένων ἰαχεῖ ποδῶν κρότοισιν) all night long' (782–3). On choral self-referentiality and choral projection in *Heraclidae* see Henrichs 1996, 50–4.

the dithyramb, which seems in fact to be a cultural construct of the 'archaizing' musical discourse of the New Music,[86] it has been proposed by Battezzato that the Phrygian mode may have been used at this point in the *stasimon* to accompany the Chorus' description of Phrygian songs.[87]

The motif of the refashioning of Phrygian music on the part of the Achaeans is reflected at the level of text through the ambivalent semantics of the term βοά, whose associations with the *aulos* and with joyful music acquire a sinister tone in the *stasimon*:[88] the shout of joy of the Trojans at the sight of the wooden horse (522), indeed an expression of ritual jubilation (544–7), becomes the musical medium of the Greek violent appropriation of the Phrygian *choreia* in the murderous shout of the Achaeans at the moment of their attack (555–6 φοινία δ' ἀνὰ / πτόλιν βοὰ κατέσχε Περ- / γάμον ἕδρας·). The architecture of 555 is especially noteworthy, with the rhetorically marked and emotionally arresting juxtaposition of χοροῖσι and φοινία (separated by syntactic and metrical pause) amplifying the sense of impending catastrophe.

When examined from the point of view of chorality, the first *stasimon* of *Trojan Women* is characterized by the 'poetic' posture of the Chorus in the opening invocation, followed by the self-referential 'performative' future ἰαχήσω (515) which expresses the immediacy of choral singing. The description of parthenaic dance is vivid and detailed (545–7), and the return to the first person at the beginning of the epode (ἐγὼ δὲ ... ἐμελπόμαν, 551–4, a typical feature of non-dramatic choral lyric) gives further strength to the duplicating effect of choral pro-

---

[86] See, among other passages, Arist. *Pol.* 8.1342b; of opposite advice (peaceful character of the Phrygian *harmonia*) Plato (*Resp.* 3.399a-c). Prauscello 2013, 91 observes that 'it is with the New Musical developments that dithyramb and the Phrygian mode become virtually indistinguishable'. On the motif of the opposition of musical modes in the New Music see Csapo 2004, 233 f. and the cautionary remarks by Fearn 2007, 176 f. Two attestations of Φρύγιον μέλος in archaic lyric (Alcm. 126 *PMGF* Φρύγιον αὔλησε μέλος τὸ Κερβήσιον and Stes. 173.2 Finglass = *PMGF* 212.2 ὑμνεῖν Φρύγιον μέλον †ἐξευρόντα†) are certainly not references to dithyramb.

[87] See Battezzato 2005b, 88: this is certainly an attractive hypothesis, though not easy to demonstrate on the basis of just verbal references and metre. In similarly speculative terms, a further moment in the *stasimon* for which a shift of musical modes could be proposed is the rhythmical change from dactylo-epitrite to iambic sequences at the beginning of strophe and antistrophe, with the shift occurring at 517–37 (*hemiepes* + iambic dimeter). A possible dithyrambic parallel for such a rhythmic and harmonic shift is represented by Lasos of Hermione's *Hymn to Demeter* (*PMG* 702) where a shift from a dactylo-epitrite start to a different pattern of iambic/aeolic cola is explicitly referred to in the text with the mention of the Aeolian *harmonia*, as recently pointed out by Prauscello 2013, 89–92 and 2012, 69.

[88] I draw here on Battezzato 2005b, 76 f., 88 n. 66 who offers a rich discussion of βοή in the stasimon, and of the term's association with Phrygian music and the sound of the *aulos*.

jection. Constantly taking place in a markedly ritualized ambience,[89] choral projection is here under the realm of Artemis.[90]

7 Conclusions

To conclude, the first *stasimon* of *Trojan Women* presents an interesting case of generic mixture, one in which each lyric/melic component – citharodic, threnodic, dithyrambic – is chosen to evoke different stylistic features and, thus, various expectations in the audience. The opening citharodic *prooimion*, solemn as it sounds, features a claim of poetic καινότης associated with threnodic content, and this unusual combination could have brought to the spectators' mind the experimentations and melodramatizations of coeval *nomos* and dithyramb.

Notwithstanding the fundamental fact that the first *stasimon* of *Trojan Women* is a tragic ode and, as such, deeply linked to its dramatic context, in terms of poetic form the very definition and nature of 'dithyrambic' *stasima* is capable of conveying more than just one poetic reality. The tradition of fifth century narrative lyric (in particular Bacchylides' dithyrambs) reveals itself in the structural architecture of the *stasimon*, in the disposition of the narrative sequence and in the paratactic texture of the narration. In turn, certain stylistic traits in the ode seem to reveal a predilection for periphrastic compound adjectives, a remarkable 'density' of nominal constructs and sound figures: these are some of the characteristics which Timotheus was bringing to a new level of (hyper)expressiveness in those same years, and the first *stasimon* of *Trojan Women* might attest to Euripides' role in the transition to a 'new dithyrambic' narrative. As evident in Hecuba's monody, Euripides' New Musical style was (in terms of both motifs and *lexis*) already fully developed at the time of the composition of *Trojan Women:* the dramatist's choice is rather to offer in the first *stasimon* of the play, in coherence with the mythical material, a melic *Iliou Persis* in

---

[89] See Henrichs 1996, *passim*.
[90] The association between a group of παρθένοι, Artemis and the sound of the pipe is also productive in Soph. *Tr.* 205–15, though there the ritual and religious ambience is paianic and Apollinean: see Henrichs 1994–1995, 81. Furthermore, the pattern of the abduction of a group of *parthenoi* performing circular choruses in honour of Artemis seems to be a characteristic feature in Spartan myth, thus making a case for dithyrambs performed by women in a Spartan context, a combination apparently matching Bacchylides 20, as D'Alessio 2013b, 124–5 has recently pointed out. For an exhaustive account of the cults of Artemis in a Spartan context as connected to myth of rape and abduction of *parthenoi* celebrating the goddess see Calame 1997b, 143f. (Artemis *Limnatis*); 151f. (Artemis *Karyatis*).

the footstep of traditional narrative lyric,[91] punctuating it with features of his New Musical verse and exploiting at full scale the dramatic and mimetic effects of choral projection 'within narration'.

---

[91] See Prodi in this volume on the choral odes of Euripides' *Phoenician Women* as a melic *Thebais*.

Rosa Andújar
Hyporchematic Footprints in Euripides' *Electra*

This chapter explores the tragic path of one of the most elusive and least understood choral lyric genres: the *hyporchēma*. Despite the fact that the hyporcheme is included in prominent accounts of ancient lyric music and dance as early as the fifth century,[1] testimonies regarding both the basic nature and specific characteristics of these 'dancing songs' are scarce and often contradictory. The few surviving ancient sources frequently disagree with one another regarding the basics of the *hyporchēma*, including its place of origin and distinguishing features, though they emphasise its ubiquity and importance. To add to this complication, until recently the term was liberally applied by modern scholars to certain tragic choral odes perceived as especially lively or vigorous, particularly those found in Sophocles expressing sudden joy and which stand in marked contrast to the disaster that immediately follows. Recent insights into the nature of tragic *stasima* as well as into the practice of choral self-referentiality and projection, however, have led most scholars to banish the previously ubiquitous concept from discussions of tragedy, with the result that the term is now synonymous with misconception and is subsequently rarely mentioned in the most recent commentaries of plays featuring passages previously labelled as *hyporchēmata*.[2]

Both the difficulty of the evidence of the genre and the many uncertainties surrounding choral dancing in tragedy might suggest that any attempt wishing to account for hyporcheme as a lyric genre, and particularly for the manner in which tragedians might have evoked it in their plays, is futile. However, this chapter suggests that the term may still have some use in discussions of the tragic chorus' dancing, and in particular might help us better understand a brief

---

I am grateful to Lyndsay Coo, Lucy Jackson, and my co-editors Thomas Coward and Theodora Hadjimichael for reading and commenting on an earlier version of this chapter.

1 Pl. *Ion* 534c includes the hyporcheme in a list of different types of established lyric compositions. See my discussion of the surviving evidence on the genre below.
2 E.g. Finglass' recent commentary on Sophocles' *Ajax* (2011), though admirably comprehensive in its learnedness, breadth and range, does not mention the word anywhere, not even in his discussion (p. 341) of the second *stasimon* (693–718), which in earlier scholarship tended to be cited as a prime example of a tragic hyporcheme. It is worth noting that in scholarship outside the Anglophone world, the term is still employed, e.g. Rodighiero 2012, esp. pp. 19–60, in which he analyzes precisely the second *stasimon* of the *Ajax*.

strophic song by the chorus of women in Euripides' *Electra* (860–79) containing a unique performative dynamic between heroine and chorus. This ode, in which the women celebrate Orestes' murder of Aegisthus, has been previously examined in relation to non-dramatic choral lyric: recent work has analysed its many epinician evocations,[3] and, until the mid-twentieth century, scholars formerly listed it among examples of tragic *hyporchēmata* simply because of its overt references to dancing.[4] Still left unremarked is the fact that this ode is not only quite emphatic in its repeated indications of the physical movement of the tragic chorus, but it is also exceptional in its invitation to – *and* response by – Electra to sing a song that will accompany the chorus' celebratory dance.

In this chapter, I suggest that Euripides potentially flirts with one conception of the hyporcheme involving a separation between singers and dancers as he introduces the notion of two distinct movements performed by the chorus and Electra which occur at the same time. This brief choral ode remarkably documents a unique process of separation in which both parties refuse to join the other in their activity. My reading depends on a critical review of the surviving evidence of the *hyporchēma* and its more recent (mis)applications to tragedy; the first section of this chapter therefore re-evaluates the ancient testimonies which discuss the term to salvage a plausible sketch of the *hyporchēma*, whereas the second re-examines the genre's obscure footprints in tragedy. These two sections touch on important points regarding the study of choral lyric genres and their perceived presence in tragedy, such as the vague and inconsistent manner in which the Alexandrians and their followers classified terms like *hyporchēma*,[5] and the pitfalls caused by the uncritical application of such terms by modern scholars. Nevertheless my main aim in resuscitating this poorly understood concept is to discuss the performance and representation of the chorus' dance in tragedy, a subject which is frequently neglected in accounts of *mousikē*, even though dance was one of its key components along with song and poetry. Though the nature of ancient Greek dance is incredibly difficult to capture based on the lack of surviving evidence, I argue that understanding the dynamics of this brief ode from Euripides' *Electra* in light of a potential hyporchematic imprint allows us to reconsider the various performative and orchestic modes that were possible on the tragic stage. While it may be impossible to reconstruct the details of any particular ancient choral movement or bodily gesture, an analysis of the ode's unique presentation of a strategic disjunction between singing

---

[3] Swift 2010, 156–70; Carey 2012: 22–5.
[4] Denniston 1939, 154.
[5] Cf. Carey 2009a.

and dancing may allow a glimpse into the self-reflexive way in which tragedians may have alluded to the *hyporchēma* and to the performance of tragic dance more generally.

1 Evidence of an Elusive Genre

The *hyporchēma* may be the most baffling ancient lyric genre for us moderns to understand: though it is discussed by the foremost sources on ancient musical culture such as Athenaeus and Plutarch (and Pindar was said to have written two books of hyporchemes, and Bacchylides another), a persuasive account of its nature has been nearly impossible to produce. The extant fragments of Pindar's *hyporchēmata* have mostly survived as quotations from later sources, and taken together barely add up to fifty verses covering a range of unremarkable topics, from praise of Hieron (fr. 105ab) to stories of Hercules (fr. 111).[6] The diachronic nature of the testimonies is especially problematic, since they were all separated by at least one or many removes from the classical period, rendering it impossible to reconstruct the assumptions and misconceptions regarding Athenian song-culture and choral lyric genres under which each source operated. If all sources are to be believed equally, conflicting conceptions of the genre emerge: either the hyporcheme is a song sung to, or by, a group dancing uniformly in simultaneous dance and song, or the *hyporchēma* was a choral dance whose performance separated singers from a chorus of dancers; either the dance itself was mimetic, or an entirely frivolous affair. Essentially we have a genre which to some extent involved song and dance, much like *any other* choral lyric from antiquity. Accounts regarding its origin, place and mode of practice do not shed any further light and in fact frequently disagree with one another: some report that the hyporcheme may have originated in Crete like the *nomos* or the paean potentially in connection with the weapon dances of the Curetes, some claim that it had special prominence in Sparta, while others note that the *hyporchēma* was associated in particular with ceremonies for Apollo.[7] Given that performance function is of central importance for un-

---

6 Cf. Suda s.v. Πίνδαρος, Stob. 3.11.19, Athen. 14.631c. There are even fewer for Bacchylides, the longest comprising five verses (fr. 14). Only one of the Pindaric fragments (fr. 107ab) contains a reference to rapid dancing; see Carey 2009a, 25 n.20.
7 According to the scholiast to Pindar, *Pyth.* 2.127 and Ps.-Plu. *Mus.* 1134b, Thaletas of Gortyn (7th century BC) was the inventor of the form. The scholiast to Pindar furthermore connects it to the Curetes and to Pyrrhichus the Cretan; cf. Ath. 5.10.19, which states: Κρητικὰ καλοῦσι τὰ ὑπορχή-

derstanding Greek genres, these contradictions coupled with the lack of any surviving ancient musical or orchestic schemes translate into modern uncertainty.

It is nevertheless possible to differentiate among the sources in order to produce a coherent conception of the genre. In one of the last comprehensive reviews of this elusive form, Massimo Di Marco highlights three sources in particular which contain the key to understanding *hyporchēmata* as well as the reasons why the original characteristics of the genre might have become distorted with time: Plutarch, Athenaeus, and Lucian.[8] These three offer much fuller accounts of the genre than other sources, such as Photius' *Bibliotheca* (essentially a summary of Proclus' *Chrestomathia*), which merely include the hyporcheme in a list of important lyric genres. Quoting Proclus, Photius divides melic poetry according to religious, secular and mixed categories (that is, types assigned to the gods, others to men, and others to gods and men), and assigns the *hyporchēma* to the type allotted to the gods along with hymns, paeans, and the dithyramb.[9] Plato's *Ion* 534c is a similar source: the hyporcheme is included in a list of other established genres such as dithyramb and iambos as examples of types of song specialties that each poet can compose through divine dispensation.[10] What these sources make clear is that in antiquity the *hyporchēma* already existed as a technical term that designated a particular species of melic song.[11]

In contrast, the accounts in Plutarch, Athenaeus and Lucian give some indication as to the nature of the *hyporchēma*: essentially, the hyporcheme is a choral melos that combines dancing and poetry into a unique song that is characterized by mimetic action. In Book IX of the *Quaestiones convivales* Plutarch

---

ματα. However, the survey of music in Ps.-Plu. *Mus.* 1134c-d also connects it to Sparta, whereas Luc. *Salt.* 16 associates it with performances for Apollo. See also Robbins 1998, 815.

8 Di Marco 1973–1974.

9 Photius, *Bibl.* 319b-320a: Περὶ δὲ μελικῆς ποιήσεώς φησιν ὡς πολυμερεστάτη τε καὶ διαφόρους ἔχει τομάς. Ἃ μὲν γὰρ αὐτῆς μεμέρισται θεοῖς, ἃ δὲ <ἀνθρώποις, ἃ δὲ θεοῖς καὶ> ἀνθρώποις, ἃ δὲ εἰς τὰς προσπιπτούσας περιστάσεις. Καὶ εἰς θεοὺς μὲν ἀναφέρεσθαι ὕμνον, προσόδιον, παιᾶνα, διθύραμβον, νόμον, ἀδωνίδια, ἰόβακχον, ὑπορχήματα ('Regarding melic poetry, he [Proclus] says that it has a great many parts and different divisions. Some types are assigned to the gods, others to men, others to gods and men, and still another group to various circumstances. The ones that refer to the gods are the hymn, the *prosodion*, the paean, the dithyramb, the *nomos*, *adonidia*, the *iobakchon*, and *hyporchēmata*.')

10 Pl. *Ion* 534c: ἀλλὰ θείᾳ μοίρᾳ, τοῦτο μόνον οἷός τε ἕκαστος ποιεῖν καλῶς ἐφ' ὃ ἡ Μοῦσα αὐτὸν ὥρμησεν, ὁ μὲν διθυράμβους, ὁ δὲ ἐγκώμια, ὁ δὲ ὑπορχήματα, ὁ δ' ἔπη, ὁ δ' ἰάμβους· ('But it is by a divine dispensation that each one is able to compose successfully that to which the Muse has stirred him: this man dithyrambs, another *encomia*, another *hyporchēmata*, another epic, and another iambic verse.')

11 Other sources of this type include Ps.-Plu. *Mus.* 1134c-d, and Tz. *Trag. Poes.* 97.

tells of how the *hyporchēma* unites both dancing and poetry in order to create a single work that consists of an imitation through forms and words:

> ὀρχηστικῇ δὲ καὶ ποιητικῇ κοινωνία πᾶσα καὶ μέθεξις ἀλλήλων ἐστί, καὶ μάλιστα [μιμούμεναι] περὶ <τὸ> τῶν ὑπορχημάτων γένος ἓν ἔργον ἀμφότεραι τὴν διὰ τῶν σχημάτων καὶ τῶν ὀνομάτων μίμησιν ἀποτελοῦσι.
>
> (Plutarch, *Quaest. conv.* IX.748a-b)
>
> Dancing and poetry share much in common and are in partnership with one another, especially when they are mixed together in the type of composition known as *hyporchēmata*, in which they both produce a single work, an imitation through poses and words.[12]

According to Plutarch, the genre contains a crucial defining mimetic component, and it is precisely this lively mimetic and scenic representation of the words that links poetry and dancing, the latter bringing the poetry to life. Further in the same passage, he highlights one of the most successful composers of *hyporchēmata*, a poet believed to be Pindar (fr. 107ab),[13] as the one who most persuasively shows that poetry and art need each other (πιθανώτατος ἑαυτοῦ τὸ δεῖσθαι τὴν ἑτέραν τῆς ἑτέρας, 748b):

> Πελασγὸν ἵππον ἢ κύνα (6)
> Ἀμυκλαίαν ἀγωνίῳ
> ἑλελιζόμενος ποδὶ μίμεο καμπύλον μέλος διώκων.
>
> Imitate the Pelasgian horse or dog
> from Amyclaea in the contest
> while you whirl with your foot following the curved song.

Here, a specific instruction to dance not only opens the song but more importantly drives it forward.[14] In particular, the chorus is instructed to imitate (μίμεο) as they 'whirl' their foot (ἑλελιζόμενος). Ἑλελίζω, 'to whirl', is an epic reduplication of ἑλίσσω, a word which Euripides employs frequently in his later plays to indicate a choral circular dance, one tied to Dionysiac cultic practice.[15] Strikingly,

---

12 Cf. Poll. *Onomasticon* 4.103–5.
13 Authorship is contested, since Plutarch only quotes the text and does not name the author. Schneider (1776, Hyporchem. 6 = 122 Turyn = 96 Bowra = 107ab S-M) proposed Pindar, whereas Reinach 1898 suggested Bacchylides. Most recently, Poltera 2008, 428–35 believes the author to be Simonides.
14 On διώκω, see Lefkowitz 1991, 12: 'to "pursue" a song probably means to "follow the music in dance".'.
15 Csapo 1999–2000, 422. On images of whirling, see Weiss' discussion in this volume.

these two verbal forms suggest a simultaneous choreography blending the chorus' mimicry with their circular movement.

Similarly, Athenaeus makes clear that *hyporchēmata* are representational or mimetic dances in which the dance imitates what is expressed in the lyrics of the song which accompanies it:

οἶδε δὲ ὁ ποιητὴς καὶ τὴν πρὸς ᾠδὴν ὄρχησιν· Δημοδόκου γοῦν ᾄδοντος (θ 262) κοῦροι πρωθῆβαι ὠρχοῦντο· καὶ ἐν τῇ Ὁπλοποιίᾳ δὲ παιδὸς κιθαρίζοντος ἄλλοι ἐναντίοι μολπῇ τε ὀρχηθμῷ τε ἔσκαιρον (Σ 572). ὑποσημαίνεται δὲ ἐν τούτοις ὁ ὑπορχηματικὸς τρόπος, ὃς ἤνθησεν ἐπὶ Ξενοδήμου καὶ Πινδάρου. καί ἐστιν ἡ τοιαύτη ὄρχησις μίμησις τῶν ὑπὸ τῆς λέξεως ἑρμηνευομένων πραγμάτων·

(Athenaeus 1.15d)

The poet also knows of the practice of dancing with song accompaniment. For Demodocus (*Od.* 8.262–4) sang while young boys danced, and in the *Forging of the Arms* a boy played the lyre while others opposite him frisked about to the song and the dance (*Il.* 18.569–72). Here there is an allusion to the style of the hyporcheme, which became popular in the time of Xenodemus and Pindar. This variety of dance is an imitation of acts which can be interpreted by words.

The passage illustrates that the hyporcheme is both a song and a dance in the sense that the dance itself also carries meaning. More importantly, Athenaeus provides two examples from Homer which accentuate the crucial role of the dance in the genre, since these are passages in which the epic poet explicitly differentiates between dancers and singers. In the *Odyssey*, Demodocus is in the centre singing of Ares and Aphrodite while adolescent boys, who are described as 'experienced in dancing' (δαήμονες ὀρχηθμοῖο, 8.263), perform a dance around him.[16] The poet gives no indication that the boys also sang, but instead draws attention to their bodies, both at rest and in motion: first the youths stood around the bard (ἀμφὶ δὲ κοῦροι / πρωθῆβαι ἵσταντο, 262–3), and then they beat the divine dance-floor with their feet (πέπληγον δὲ χορὸν θεῖον ποσίν, 264). As they dance, Odysseus marvels at the 'twinkling of their feet' (μαρμαρυγὰς...ποδῶν, 265). It is clear that in this passage, which subsequently focuses on Demodocus' singing, dancers and singers are kept entirely separate. The Linos-song represented on the shield of Achilles in *Iliad* 18 similarly involves a strategic separation of dancers and singers: the maidens and youths there dance and beat the earth around the boy who sings the song as an accompaniment to his music (567–72). A few verses later we find another description of

---

[16] Mullen 1982, 13: 'The seated blind bard in this seems to be a leader with voice and lyre presiding over some kind of elaborate mime.'

maidens and youths dancing, who are differentiated from the three performers who lead the song and also the dance: one singer (θεῖος ἀοιδός, 604), and two lead dancers (κυβιστητῆρε, 605, who are described as ἐξάρχοντες, 606). It is significant that the word used to identify the two performers as dancers (κυβιστητῆρε) is elsewhere in the *Iliad* used of fish who *leap* above the surface (as in 21.354),[17] an action which will recur in other descriptions of choral dance. In contrast to the two examples of *hyporchēmata* provided by Athenaeus, in which a dancing chorus of youths surrounds a lone singer, the last example from *Iliad* 18 further differentiates among the dancers by introducing two further 'leaping' dancers who lead the chorus. This might be perhaps explained in terms of skill: in the *Odyssey*, the entire group of dancers was singled out by virtue of their experience, whereas presumably these two leaping dancers stood out from the rest on account of their 'leaps'.

Lucian's description of choirs of boys at Delos likewise describes *hyporchēmata* as choral performances in which dancers and singers are separated, in particular stating that a select few dancers were differentiated from the horde:[18]

> Ἐν Δήλῳ δέ γε οὐδὲ αἱ θυσίαι ἄνευ ὀρχήσεως ἀλλὰ σὺν ταύτῃ καὶ μετὰ μουσικῆς ἐγίγνοντο. παίδων χοροὶ συνελθόντες ὑπ' αὐλῷ καὶ κιθάρᾳ οἱ μὲν ἐχόρευον, ὑπωρχοῦντο δὲ οἱ ἄριστοι προκριθέντες ἐξ αὐτῶν. τὰ γοῦν τοῖς χοροῖς γραφόμενα τούτοις ᾄσματα ὑπορχήματα ἐκαλεῖτο καὶ ἐμπέπληστο τῶν τοιούτων ἡ λύρα.
>
> (Lucian *Salt.* 16)

> At Delos, even the sacrifices were not without dancing, but were performed with dancing and the aid of music. Choruses of boys came together, and as they sang to the accompaniment of the *aulos* and *kithara*, those who had been selected from among them as the best danced. Indeed, the songs that were written for these choruses were called hyporchemes, and lyric poetry is full of them.

Though we have now lost the lone bard figure that was prominent in the Homeric examples, and around which the chorus danced, this description unmistakably separates two groups from within the chorus itself: the general chorus of boys who ἐχόρευον to the *aulos* and *kithara*, and a select few among them, highlighted as the best, who ὑπωρχοῦντο. Though both χορεύω and ὀρχέομαι can gener-

---

17 Edwards 1991, 231.
18 Mullen 1982, 232, n.11 points out that Callimachus' *Hymn to Delos* 304–306 similarly implies that 'the singers and dancers are different people at the Delian performances.' In that passage, as he describes, 'the women in chorus strike the ground with their feet while the men "sing in accompaniment" (*hupaeidousi*) the ancient nome of Olen.' It is worth noting, however, that Mullen also point out that Callimachus may not be describing the same dance at Delos as Lucian.

ally mean 'to dance', their opposition here strongly indicates that the latter designates 'to dance' (as evident by the strong etymological connection in *orcheisthai* emphasising the role of the dance) as opposed to the former's 'taking part in a chorus'.[19] It is clear that Lucian is describing a stratified chorus, in which the best dancers were separated from the singers, as opposed to the more normal practice in which the chorus performs both activities of singing and dancing.[20] Thus far, these sources present the hyporcheme as a type of mimetic dancing that somehow imitates what is expressed in the lyrics, an action which seemed to have required skilled dancers, leading to a general separation between singers and dancers. The dancing group may have been furthermore led by particularly skilled dancers, as in the second example from the *Iliad* and in Lucian's description. Nevertheless it appears that the both song and dance work actively together to create meaning; there is no explicit suggestion of the subordination of one to the other.

However, Athenaeus' further references to the *hyporchēma* in the 14th book of his *Deipnosophistae* muddle our understanding of the nature of the genre. These three references not only provide contradictory information, but they also deviate from the earlier discussion found in book 1 in which the dance was singled out as the essential characteristic. In particular, these examples undermine the general sense of the *hyporchēma* involving mimetic dancing that is separate from singing, and instead describe a genre which emphasises the dance's dependence on the lyrics. This major deviation from the earlier formulation in book 1 is unfortunate, particularly given the importance of book 14 to the study of *mousikē*, which is one of the book's two main topics, and the fact that the book contains one of the most extensive surviving discussions of ancient dance.[21] The first of the three references to the *hyporchēma* in Book 14 seems to place, for the first time in the *Deipnosophistae*, special emphasis on the etymology of the word, suggesting that the dance in the *hyporchēma* is *subordinate* to the words accompanying it:

> καὶ γὰρ ἐν ὀρχήσει καὶ πορείᾳ καλὸν μὲν εὐσχημοσύνη καὶ κόσμος, αἰσχρὸν δὲ ἀταξία καὶ τὸ φορτικόν. διὰ τοῦτο γὰρ καὶ ἐξ ἀρχῆς συνέταττον οἱ ποιηταὶ τοῖς ἐλευθέροις τὰς ὀρχήσεις καὶ ἐχρῶντο τοῖς σχήμασι σημείοις μόνον τῶν ἀδομένων, τηροῦντες αἰεὶ τὸ εὐγενὲς καὶ ἀνδρῶδες ἐπ' αὐτῶν, ὅθεν καὶ ὑπορχήματα τὰ τοιαῦτα προσηγόρευον. εἰ δέ τις ἀμέτρως

---

19 Cf. Bosher 2008–2009, 15–8 who points out a distinction between the two verbs in tragedy.
20 Nagy 1990, 351 cites a similar testimony regarding the Spartan Feast of the Hyacinthia, in which dancers were separated from singing choruses of youths. Cf. Pickard-Cambridge 1988, 255 n. 2.
21 E.g. Ath. 14.615a-e, 616e-623d, 623e-632e.

διαθείη τὴν σχηματοποιίαν καὶ ταῖς ᾠδαῖς ἐπιτυγχάνων μηδὲν λέγοι κατὰ τὴν ὄρχησιν, οὗτος δ' ἦν ἀδόκιμος.

(Athenaeus 14.628d)

For in both dancing and walking, elegance and orderliness are noble, while disorder and vulgarity are shameful. This is why composers from the beginning composed dances for free men, and used the movements as expressions only of that which was sung, consistently maintaining their nobility and manliness: and that explains why such compositions were called *hyporchēmata*. But if someone did choreography unrestrainedly or said something with the songs that did not coordinate with the dances, he was discredited.

In other words he suggests that dances were secondary to – and exclusively in support of – the themes and the words of the poetry. This is one of the earliest indications of dance possessing the specific and subordinate function of illustrating language, rather than expressing that the two work in conjunction with one another. A few passages later he continues to limit the notion of *hyporchēma*, this time linking the hyporchematic to a particular type of dramatic poetry:

τρεῖς δ' εἰσὶ τῆς σκηνικῆς ποιήσεως ὀρχήσεις, τραγική, κωμική, σατυρική. ὁμοίως δὲ καὶ τῆς λυρικῆς ποιήσεως τρεῖς, πυρρίχη, γυμνοπαιδική, ὑπορχηματική... ἡ δὲ γυμνοπαιδικὴ παρεμφερής ἐστι τῇ τραγικῇ ὀρχήσει, ἥτις ἐμμέλεια καλεῖται· ἐν ἑκατέρᾳ δὲ ὁρᾶται τὸ βαρὺ καὶ σεμνόν. ἡ δ' ὑπορχηματικὴ τῇ κωμικῇ οἰκειοῦται, ἥτις καλεῖται κόρδαξ· παιγνιώδεις δ' εἰσὶν ἀμφότεραι.

(Athenaeus 14.630c-e)

There are three kinds of dancing associated with dramatic poetry, tragic, comic and satyric; and similarly there are three associated with lyric poetry, the *pyrrhichē*, the *gymnopaidikē* and the *hyporchēmatikē*...The *gymnopaidikē* is similar to the tragic dance known as the *emmeleia*; for seriousness and gravity are apparent in both. The *hyporchēmatikē* is related to the comic dance called the *kordax:* both are frivolous.

Finally, Athenaeus supplies a final definition of the hyporchematic, in what may be the most vague formulation of the genre to be found in all the extant ancient testimonies:

ἡ δ' ὑπορχηματική ἐστιν ἐν ᾗ ᾄδων ὁ χορὸς ὀρχεῖται.

(Athenaeus 14.631c)

The *hyporchēmatikē* is that in which the chorus dances while singing.

These last two passages in particular raise more questions than they provide answers. The fact that the hyporcheme is uniquely associated with the comic dance *kordax* potentially suggests that in the postclassical era the hyporcheme may have been confused and assimilated with pantomime.²² The last example directly contradicts the picture of a separation of dancers and singers provided by Athenaeus in 1.15d. If anything, these three examples reveal that Athenaeus has not used the term consistently throughout his work.

How are we to explain this wide range of discrepancy in this important source? Recent work on Athenaeus has pointed out the challenges of relying on him as a source on musical matters, given his lack of interest in chronology or even in the evolution of music.²³ Other scholars have pointed out the distinct influence of particular philosophical views and concepts, especially those stemming from Plato on the 'proper' form of music and its crucial role in the education of citizen men.²⁴ In a recent analysis of the structure and contents of book 14 of the *Deipnosophistae*, Paola Ceccarelli points out that the book contains some of the most general philosophical reflections on the effects of *mousikē* on the mind and soul found in the entire work, with the result that citations from ancient sources now appear as blurred, and it is unclear who is being cited as an authority, whether it is an ancient source or a figure from Athenaeus' time.²⁵ This analysis of the wider functioning of authority in Athenaeus's work allows us, I would argue, to reassess his description of the hyporcheme, and explain its apparent contradictions, such as the alignment of a lively and mimetic dance with the *kordax*, which ultimately reflects a moralising statement on the place of non-solemn dances that is more in keeping with Plato, who banishes ecstatic dancing from the educational repertoire of citizen men.²⁶ It is also in the fourteenth book that we find one of the most prominent, and contested, examples of the genre, the so-called *hyporchēma* by Pratinas (14.617b-f, *PMG* fr. 708). Scholarship on this seventeen verse lyric piece has tended predominantly to discuss its performance context as well as the many textual difficulties that it presents.²⁷ The general sense of the complaint in the fragment is that the dance

---

22 Theophrastus' *Characters* 6 mentions the *kordax* as a 'lewd, grotesque, and shameless dance' in direct connection to the comic chorus. See also Ath. 14.630c-d and Luc. *Salt.* 26.
23 Barker 2000, 433, Naerebout 1997, 191–2. On Athenaeus' citation as 'performance', see Jacob 2004, and also Leven 2010, who discusses the problems with using Athenaeus as a source for the New Music revolution.
24 Cf. Ley 2007, 204. Mirhady 2012, 395: 'The definition of hyporchēma that Athenaeus suggests seems suspiciously like one that a philosopher might device on the basis of etymology…The word is normally used much more widely, even in Athenaeus, to refer to lively and/or mimetic dances both within and outside dramatic productions. So it seems that in Athenaeus we have a sort of philosophical definition doing battle with practical usages of the term.'
25 All this blurring of sources prompts Cecarelli 2000, 81 to ask: 'whose times are these?'
26 Pl. *Lg.* vii. 815c, cf. Pickard-Cambridge 1988, 246–8, Griffith 2013a, 46–7.
27 Seaford 1977–1978, Napolitano 2000, D'Alessio 2007, D'Angour 2013, 202.

has now become subordinate to the *aulos*, in that the aulete no longer accompanied the chorus but vice versa. The fragment is presented in a rather incoherent discussion of the *aulos*, which flits from accounts that belittle the music produced by the pipes (e.g. Melanippides on Athena in 14.616e) to those that offer a description of their usefulness (e.g. Telestes' description in 14.617b). As Pauline LeVen has recently argued, this particular section of Athenaeus' text seems more concerned with illustrating the validity of Aristotle's beliefs regarding the *aulos* through a variety of poetic examples,[28] and we may extend this to the entire fourteenth book, which, by presenting such a collection of conflicting testimonies, appears to be a discussion of music ultimately in the service of philosophical debate. These examples do not provide empirical descriptions, and they should not be mistaken as such.

Even if we restrict the evidence, ignoring Athenaeus' 14th book, thus making the *hyporchēma* mean two types of orchestic movements involving song and dance, we must admit the evidence is still fairly unspecific: any choral dance with song might be so designated. How can it be that the hyporcheme's only distinctive characteristic is dance when dance already accompanied most choral songs? In *Poetics* 1447a27 Aristotle points out the mimetic capacity of *all* dancers, who through physically translating rhythms can 'create mimesis of character, sufferings, and actions' (διὰ τῶν σχηματιζομένων ῥυθμῶν μιμοῦνται καὶ ἤθη καὶ πάθη καὶ πράξεις). It comes as no surprise that scholars in the modern period have denounced the term as an unhelpful one, especially when trying to trace its elusive footprints in surviving literature. In a discussion of the character and form of the dithyramb, Wilamowitz declared that the grammarians are to blame for assigning the name *hyporchēmata* and arranging them in special books: it is a bad name because they are all dance songs (*Tanzlieder*).[29] However, as we have seen the term existed in Plato's time to designate a particular type of choral *melos*. Furthermore, Wilamowitz's complaint regarding 'bad names' can easily be extended to other lyric genres.[30] As other scholars have pointed out, ancient categories were not ex-

---

28 Leven 2010.
29 Wilamowitz-Moellendorf 1907, 76: 'Und nicht einmal das ist dem Dithyrambos ausschliesslich eigen, sondern fand sich auch in anderen Liedern als denen, welche für den Dionysosdienst verfasst waren; die Grammatiker haben sie, weil sie keinen bezeichnenden Namen hatten, als Tanzlieder (ὑπορχήματα) bezeichnet und in besonderen Bücher geordnet. Es ist ein schlechter Name; denn Tanzlieder sind sie ja alle.' ('And not even that is unique to the dithyramb, but was also found in other songs than those dwhich were composed for Dionysos' cult; the grammarians have classed them as dance songs (ὑπορχήματα) because they had no better name to classify them with, and arranged them into special books. It is a bad name; for they are all dance songs.')
30 Cf. Swift 2010, 22.

clusive, and vague and inconsistent use of terms for lyric compositions is the norm, making the reconstruction of ancient conceptions of genre a challenging and frustrating endeavour. It is useful here to note Chris Carey's recent comments on the especially fluid nature of the categories and boundaries relating to lyric genres, in which he reminds us that these labels are worth retaining so long as we do not either apply or reject them too simplistically.[31] Nevertheless, this careful review of the available evidence on the *hyporchēma* allows us tentatively to define it as a choral genre that separated the chorus into two visible groups of dancers and singers, as opposed to the normal practice of having the chorus perform both singing and dancing, in order to accommodate a more mimetic dance.[32] In the hyporcheme, singing and dancing are not entirely disconnected forms, but rather might be better thought of as one end of a spectrum, in which the dynamic between the activities that is typically present in all ancient Greek choral forms is pushed to the point of separation.

2 The *Hyporchēma* and Dancing in Tragedy

The previous section analysed the most important ancient testimonia regarding the hyporcheme. As we saw, one of the examples of the genre that Athenaeus provides was the song by Demodocus in *Od.* 8.264. In his famous commentary on the epic poem, the Byzantine scholar Eustathius echoes Athenaeus' judgement that this dance belongs to the hyporchematic genre (τὸ ὑπορχηματικὸν εἶδος), providing a definition that closely quotes Athenaeus 1.15 on the mimetic aspect of the dance (ἔστι δέ φασιν ἡ τοιαύτη ὄρχησις μίμησις τῶν ὑπὸ τῆς λέξεως ἑρμηνευομένων πραγμάτων.)[33] However, he lists a further example of this kind of dance: a certain Telestes, an Aeschylean actor who, when he performed in the *Seven Against Thebes*, made the action clear through dancing (ὥστε ἐν τῷ ὀρχεῖσθαι τοὺς ἑπτὰ ἐπὶ Θήβας φανερὰ ποιῆσαι τὰ πράγματα δι'

---

[31] Carey 2009a, 22: 'the boundaries are not fixed but elastic, porous, negotiable and provisional. Literary genres are best seen not as fixed categories but as tendencies, firm enough to allow affinities and influences to be discernible and to generate a set of audience expectations, but sufficiently flexible to allow and even tacitly invite frustration and redefinition of those expectations.'

[32] Lada-Richards 2007, 26 posits a similar definition of the *hyporchēma* that is likewise centred on the separation of singer and dancers, additionally commenting that this is 'at the very threshold of the pantomime genre'.

[33] Eust. *ad Od.* I.296.30.

ὀρχήσεως).³⁴ Though Eustathius seems to be quoting another section of the *Deipnosophistae* that does not otherwise mention the *hyporchēma* (1.22a, when Athenaeus quotes Aristocles), the link which he makes between the choral genre and tragedy is nevertheless suggestive, given that tragedy is not only a choral genre but also a deeply mimetic one.

Despite its presence in Plato's list of lyric compositions, there is no single ancient surviving testimony that discusses the *hyporchēma* in direct connection to tragedy. The term is absent in Aristotle's *Poetics*, but this is unsurprising given the inadequate attention that the philosopher gives to choral matters (χορικόν),³⁵ as well as the fact that Aristotle makes no reference to other genre types such as epinician or the paean, both of which are invoked throughout tragedy.³⁶ Nevertheless, postclassical scholars have claimed to find evidence of the *hyporchēma* in tragedy, as a result of various modern misconceptions regarding the general nature of the tragic choral dance, much of which stems from poor coverage of the tragic chorus by ancient sources like Aristotle. Most prominent among these misunderstandings is the erroneous idea that choral movement was limited to the processions of the entering and departing chorus in the *parodos* and *exodos* of any given play. As a result, scholars, whenever confronted with what appeared to be particularly 'lively' odes throughout the tragic corpus, tended to associate them with the hyporcheme, as evident in the following passage by A. E. Haigh:

> Sometimes, however, on the arrival of joyful tidings, even the tragic chorus relaxed its usual gravity, and gave vent to its delight in an ode accompanied by lively and ecstatic movements. Such odes were called 'hyporchēmata' or 'dance-songs,' and were written in rapid and vigorous measures. They are often inserted with striking effect just before the catastrophe of the play, when the chorus, misled by false news, abandon themselves to a feeling of exultation which is speedily to be dashed to the ground.³⁷

---

34 Eust. *ad Od.* I.296.32. On this Telestes (or Telesis), cf. Pickard Cambridge 1988, 248 n. 6.
35 According to *Poetics* 1452b17–8, the choral part of tragedy consists of only three main choral contributions: *parodoi*, *stasima*, and *kommoi*. See Halliwell 1986, 250 for a discussion of the *Poetics* and its negative impact on modern views of the tragic chorus, and the introduction to this volume.
36 Rutherford 1994–1995, Swift 2010. As Pickard-Cambridge 1988, 256 n. 4 explains, 'the absence of all mention of hyporchēmata by Aristotle in the *Poetics* (especially ch. xii) probably means that he regarded ὑπόρχημα in the strict sense as a species of poetry no less distinct from drama than (for example) the paean or the hymn.
37 Haigh 1896, 357. Haigh (*ibid.*) furthermore outlines that the *hyporchēma* was a particular 'lively kind of *stasimon*, in which the dancing was the prominent feature, instead of being subordinate to poetry.'

Haigh's comment rests on two important (but incorrect) assumptions about tragic *stasima:* that they were motionless and solemn.[38] These assumptions were so widespread that any deviation that scholars detected in the surviving tragic plays tended to be easily explained in direct connection to *hyporchēmata*, the 'dancing songs' mentioned by Plato and elaborated upon by Athenaeus. The first notion has mostly been debunked by A. M. Dale's influential article 'Stasimon and Hyporcheme', at least in the Anglophone world.[39] Dale revealed that scholiasts and postclassical grammarians tended to operate under the false notion that all *stasima* were 'stationary songs',[40] and as a result they began to invent other categories for songs containing dance and movement, in particular the ὑπορχηματικόν that was developed by Eucleides and quoted by the Byzantine Tzetzes.[41]

Whereas Dale's piece has debunked the strange tendency expressed here of imagining tragic choral odes to be songs without dance, the general idea of the solemnity that was believed to be inherent to tragic odes still persists, and has been a major deterrent in finding true traces of the *hyporchēma* in tragedy. This notion stems from Athenaeus' association of tragic dancing with the *emmeleia*,[42] which is frequently contrasted with the comic *kordax* (1.20e, 14.630e): at 14.631d, for example, he summarises that the *kordax* is 'low-class' (φορτικός), whereas the *emmeleia* is 'serious' (σπουδαία).[43] These moralising statements on dance can themselves be traced to Plato's ideas of dancing as an educative art for citizen men in his discussions of the role of music in moral education (e.g. Pl. *Lg.* 814e-816d). As my discussion above illustrated, it is important to recognise that some of these sources in certain instances may be more concerned with finding examples to support particular philosophical ideologies instead of providing evidence for the historical context of musical genres in antiquity. Modern scholars must be wary when relying on these more philosophical discussions for evidence of actual practice in the ancient world.

A quick survey of extant tragic choral odes confirms that these songs were not always 'serious', as this connection with the *emmeleia* might suggest. Even

---

38 Cf. Smyth 1900, lxxiii who believes that the hyporcheme 'was impressed into the service of tragedy as a dramatic device for relieving the monotony resulting from the regular recurrence of the *stasima*, which were necessarily of a certain amplitude and accompanied by the solemn ἐμμέλεια dance.' Kranz 1933, 114 also describes it as a restrained song.
39 Dale 1950. The term *hyporchēma* continues to be applied in Italian scholarship, see Rodighiero 2012, esp. 19–60.
40 E.g. schol. E. *Phoe.* 202 and Suidas *s.v. stasimon*. On the term *stasimon* and its varying interpretations, *cf.* West 1990, 21.
41 Dale 1968, 210, Tz. *de Trag.* 114–6 (which links ἐμμέλεια with ὑπόρχησις).
42 Cf. Luc. *Salt.* 26, Schol. Ar. *Nu.* 540, Suidas and Hesychius s.v. *emmeleia*, Pollux 4. 99.
43 Cf. Ath. epit. vol. 2,2 page 133 line 29.

if we exclude the ecstatic and extraordinary odes of the Maenads found in Euripides' *Bacchae*, many tragic choral songs are full of references to dancing, much of which is celebratory and in no way solemn:[44] for example, in *Ant.* 148–54 the chorus call for 'all-night dances' (χοροῖς παννυχίοις, 152–3) to celebrate the victory of Thebes, and in *HF* 763–97 the chorus turn to joyous dancing after the death of Lycus, inviting the streams and streets of Thebes to join them (ἀναχορεύσατ' ἀγυιαί, 783). In fact, choruses throughout extant tragedy frequently express their joy in terms of dancing, either making a reference to their own movement or calling for other choruses to perform the dance, with a majority occurring in Sophocles' earlier plays (*Aj.* 693–718, *Ant.* 1115–54, *OT* 1086–109, *Trachiniae* 633–62).[45] In these cases the choruses either assume an extra-dramatic identity as performers of a ritual dance or project their identity onto other groups of dancers located outside the dramatic space, in phenomena famously described by Albert Henrichs as choral 'self-referentiality' and 'projection', respectively.[46] It was precisely this self-conscious mentioning and awareness of dance that encouraged earlier scholars to label such moments as hyporchematic.[47] Two such cases of odes previously assumed to be clear examples of *hyporchēmata* are worth discussing briefly, since they were widely assumed to be as such due to the fact that they contain elaborate and even deictic references to their own performance, suggesting that such a dance may be taking place in the 'here and now' of the choral ode. The first example is the astrophic song sung by the chorus in *Trachiniae* 205–25, in which the chorus respond to Deianira's command to raise the ὀλολυγή at 202–3. Upon closer reading, the song appears to be more of an evocation of a paean given the usage of the genre-term (e.g. ὢ ἰὼ Παιάν at 221) as well as the appeal to the relevant deities Apollo and Artemis in 209 and 214.[48] However, the song appears additionally to invoke a particular type of Bacchic dancing in 216–20:

αἴρομαι οὐδ' ἀπώσομαι
τὸν αὐλόν, ὦ τύραννε τᾶς ἐμᾶς φρενός.
ἰδού μ' ἀναταράσσει,
εὐοῖ,
ὁ κισσὸς ἄρτι Βακχίαν
ὑποστρέφων ἅμιλλαν.

---

44 e.g. A. *Eum.* 307, S. *OT* 896, E. *HF* 761–4.
45 See Kranz 1933, 213, De Falco 1958, 56–88, Rode 1971: 107, and Burton 1980, 30–1.
46 Cf. Henrichs 1994–1995 and Henrichs 1996.
47 Henrichs 1994–1995, 59–60, esp. notes 20–4. Other moments include E. *Ba.* 1153–64.
48 Swift 2010, 381. De Falco 1958, 79 counts this along with S. *OT* 1086, and *Aj.* 693 as παιᾶνες ὑπορχηματικοί.

> I leap up and I will not I reject
> the *aulos*, you who rule my mind.
> See, it excites me
> Euoi
> the ivy
> whirling me around in the bacchic rush.

Apart from the important references to Dionysus (e.g the ivy and the use of the adjective 'Bacchic'), the general picture is of dancers in frenzied, and specifically circular, motion. Here, the chorus leaps (αἴρομαι) and whirls (ὑποστρέφων), because they are excited (ἀναταράσσει) by the music of the *aulos*. The deictic ἰδού suggests that they are performing such a dance as they are singing it.[49] It was precisely this excited Dionysian movement, presumably thought to be incompatible with the Apolline paean,[50] which prompted an ancient scholiast to comment on the apparent singularity of this song:

> τὸ γὰρ μελιδάριον οὐκ ἔστι στάσιμον, ἀλλ' ὑπὸ τῆς ἡδονῆς ὀρχοῦνται.
>
> (Schol. to S. *Tr.* 216)
>
> This little song is not a *stasimon*, but they [the chorus] dance for joy.[51]

As we established above, the scholiast is operating under the misunderstanding that the tragic chorus did not dance during *stasima*, and so such a 'lively' description would strike him as exceptional. However, we find an analogous scene of excited circular dancing in connection with the paean in Euripides' *Iphigenia at Aulis* 1466–1531, precisely at the moment when Iphigenia bids the chorus to sing a celebratory paean (1468) for her death. Specifically, she instructs the chorus to 'whirl around' the altar of Artemis (ἑλίσσετ' ἀμφὶ ναόν / ἀμφὶ βωμὸν Ἄρτεμιν, 1480–84).[52] The heroine employs the verb 'to whirl' (ἑλίσσω), which is frequently tied to Dionysian cultic practice, as I discussed above. Though here it is not the chorus themselves who utter such a statement, but rather Iphigenia who bids them to do so, nevertheless the scene presents a compelling similarity to the brief song in *Trachiniae*, that is, a paean containing elements of Dionysiac dancing.

---

49 D'Alessio 2007, 109–10 notes the deitic connection with Pratinas.
50 Cf. Rutherford 1994–1995, 120.
51 Xenis 2010, 99 notes that this scholia is found in Laurentian, Triclinian and Roman manuscripts. Burton 1980, 50: 'the note in the scholia was prompted by the explicit reference in 216 and 218 ff. to the physical movements of a dance (ἀείρομαι and ἀναταράσσει...ἅμιλλαν).
52 Cf. Rutherford 2001, 65.

Similarly, the second *stasimon* in *Ajax* (693–719), likewise labelled hyporchematic, demonstrates a unique concern with dancing. Here, the chorus, who are wrongly convinced by Ajax's speech, sing a hymn to the god Pan as the χοροποίος of the gods invoking his help with their own dance.[53] In particular the first strophe indicates that a lively dance is presently being performed:

ἔφριξ᾽ ἔρωτι, περιχαρὴς δ᾽ ἀνεπτάμαν.
ἰὼ ἰὼ Πὰν Πάν,
ὦ Πὰν Πὰν ἁλίπλαγκτε, Κυλ- (695)
λανίας χιονοκτύπου
πετραίας ἀπὸ δειράδος φάνηθ᾽, ὦ
θεῶν χοροποί᾽ ἄναξ, ὅπως μοι
Μύσια Κνώσι᾽ ὀρ-
χήματ᾽ αὐτοδαῆ ξυνὼν ἰάψῃς. (700)
νῦν γὰρ ἐμοὶ μέλει χορεῦσαι.

I thrill with longing, and leap up in my delight!
iō, iō, Pan, Pan!
Pan, Pan, he who wanders over the sea,
appear from the snow-beaten rocky ridge of Cyllene,
lord who creates the dances among the gods,
so that you can be with me and tread the
Mysian and Cnosian measures that you have taught yourself!
Now I intend to dance.

The emphasis on the dance here is obvious: besides invoking Pan as a 'creator of dances' the chorus specifically request that he teach them particular types of dances, Mysian and Cnosian, as they declare their intention to dance (701). In addition, the insistent repetition of Pan's name, coupled with the 'snow-beaten' epithet (χιονοκτύπου) produce a beating sound that must have echoed the actual dance.[54] The energy and vigour found in this choral ode, as evidenced with specific references to dancing and echoes of dancing rhythms, made it an attractive candidate to many scholars seeking examples of this new category of lively song. However, despite this self-conscious interest in dancing, we must assume that all *stasima* in tragedy were accompanied by rhythmic movements of some kind, so a direct reference to or even emphasis on dancing, no matter how energetic, is not necessarily a sign of the hypocheme.

---

53 For Pan as the god of dancing, see *Hom. Hym* 19.20–1, Pindar. fr. 99, A. *Pers.* 448–9. Ar. *Thesm.* 978). See also Finglass 2011, 344 on Pan's iconography.
54 Stanford 1963, 151: 'one can almost hear the thud of the dancers' feet beating out the resonant word.'

Where in tragedy are we then to find the hyporcheme, which according to Lucian, filled (ἐμπέπληστο) lyric poetry (*Salt.* 16)? And how, if a persistent or singular reference to dancing is not enough? As we saw in the previous section, the surviving ancient references to the hyporcheme stress that it was a very common dance song used for a large range of themes and occasions. It therefore makes sense that some of these *hyporchēmata* would wind their way into the great voracious tragic monster which liked to gobble up all sorts of lyric genres, especially one that had mimetic action at its core. Though there is not a single ancient testimony referring directly to a hyporcheme in tragic drama, we do have only one possible mention of the *hyporchēma* in the entire surviving tragic corpus; a curious instance of the verb ὑπορχεῖσθαι, which is found in Aeschylus' *Choephori*:

ἀλλ' ὡς ἂν εἰδῆτ', οὐ γὰρ οἶδ' ὅπῃ τελεῖ,
ὥσπερ ξὺν ἵπποις ἡνιοστροφῶ δρόμου
ἐξωτέρω· φέρουσι γὰρ νικώμενον
φρένες δύσαρκτοι, πρὸς δὲ καρδίᾳ φόβος
ᾄδειν ἑτοῖμος ἠδ' ὑπορχεῖσθαι κότῳ. (1025)

But so that you may know – for I do not know how it will end,
Just as a charioteer, I am driving rather off the track.
For my mind is out of control and carries me, who am conquered,
and fear is near my heart,
ready to sing and to dance to the tune of anger.

In this crucial passage, which occurs immediately before the appearance of the Furies, Orestes discusses his madness for the first time through an extended metaphor. Specifically, he describes his *phrenes* as the uncontrollable chariot horses, and narrates that his personified fear is both ready to sing (ᾄδειν) and dance (ὑπορχεῖσθαι). Orestes not only uses loaded choral terms (describing their main activity, song and dance) in order to express conflicted emotions, but he also echoes the chorus' sentiments earlier in the play: at the precise point when Electra finds the lock that was left behind by Orestes on Agamemnon's tomb, the chorus of slave women beg her to reveal her new discovery by also relating that their 'heart dances with fear' (ὀρχεῖται δὲ καρδία φόβωι, 167). Through this formulation, the chorus transforms a common trope found elsewhere in Greek literature in which the heart (ἦτορ, θυμός, καρδία) is described as leaping in fear (with the verb πάλλω) into a more specific choral formulation, centred on the verb ὀρχέομαι, of the heart dancing or beating with fear.[55] Orestes, however,

---

[55] Cf. Hom. *Il.* 22. 452, A. *Choe.* 410–1, A. *Supp.* 567 and 785, and S. *OT* 153 (though used of φρήν).

takes the usage even further as his personified fear is itself carrying out both the singing and dancing, in what is the very first mention of his madness in the play. Here we find a stronger formulation of the separation that Lucian describes at Delos, of the chorus of boys who ἐχόρευον to the *aulos* and *kithara*, and a subset comprised of the best of them who ὑπωρχοῦντο. Crucially Orestes here employs the verb 'to sing' (ᾄδειν) rather than two forms of verbs connected to dance, as in Lucian. This lone tragic reference to the *hyporchēma* therefore suggests that singing and dancing are actions that are separated, which would be in accord with some of the ancient testimonies explored in my first section. Though the evidence is scant, it is significant that this lone tragic moment likewise suggests that the *hyporchēma* might involve a strategic disjunction between song and dance rather than their seamless conjunction.

3 Euripides' *Electra* 860–79

As we have seen, there is not much evidence of the *hyporchēma* in tragedy beyond the incorrect assumption that any self-referential language employed by the tragic chorus automatically indicates vigorous dancing. Dramatic choruses frequently draw attention to their own or another chorus' song, music or dance, as Henrichs established in his studies of choral self-referentiality and projection, and such a practice does not indicate that any special type of dancing is actually taking place on stage. Only Orestes' singular use of ὑπορχεῖσθαι in the very first mention of his madness in Aeschylus' *Choephori* intimates that the *hyporchēma* might have involved a separation between song and dance, just as my earlier reading of selected passages from the scant surviving sources on the genre. This possibility, according to which the *hyporchēma* might represent a strategic disjunction between song and dance rather than their seamless conjunction, helps illuminate a brief ode from Euripides' *Electra* (860–79), which as I argue, might offer an even more secure base for the *hyporchēma* in tragedy. The ode occurs at a crucial juncture in the play, at the point immediately following the anticipated death of Aegisthus. This is a song of joy and celebration, like the supposed Sophoclean hyporchemes: as soon as the chorus hear that Aegisthus is dead, they immediately express their happiness through singing and dancing. Uniquely, they invite Electra to accompany their dancing with song (ὑπάειδε), but she immediately refuses, proposing instead to fetch adornments inside with which to crown Orestes. Her refusal not only interrupts and alters the course of the choral song, but also draws attention to the performance of an alternative activity beyond the dancing space. I would like to suggest that this short and lively strophic song, which is strongly imbued with epinician language, imagery, and rhythm, additionally evokes the *hyporchēma* not only in its persistent references to dancing but also in its specific introduction of two distinct types of performances by the chorus and Electra. However, the playwright may be taking to an extreme a separation that is already incipient in this Aeschylean moment: Euripides depicts what might have been a joint performance between Electra and the chorus as a decisive process of separation.

Before analysing the potential hyporchematic connections, we must note that this ode strongly evokes the epinician, a link which has been much remarked in the scholarship.[56] The chorus not only call this a καλλίνικον ᾠδὰν (865), but they also explicitly compare the murder of Aegisthus to an athletic contest (in 863 'the banks of Alpheaus' is a clear reference to the Olympic games). The ode's metre is dactylo-epitrite with the alternating dactylic and iambo-trochaic sequences, rhythms that are familiar from Pindar's and Bacchylides' victory songs. The ode furthermore opens with the use of a simile at 860, which is a common epinician trope also found in epinicia such as Pind. *Ol.* 6 and *Nem.* 5.[57] Scholars have also noted that the specific image of a fawn leaping is also found in Bacchylides 13.84–90.[58] Finally, the chorus employ one of Pindar's favourite words, *aglaia*, at 861.[59] Given the rich nexus of athletic imagery woven into the *Oresteia* and into the *Electra* plays,[60] this clear and obvious evocation of the epinician is not surprising. This device of setting up Orestes as hero-athlete is ironically intended to diminish the horror of the matricide precisely by comparing it to an athletic event.

However, to identify the ode as merely epinician in flavour would be incorrect. The ode opens with an explicit indication of vigorous dancing, and a direct invitation to Electra to join their performance:

θὲς ἐς χορόν, ὦ φίλα, ἴχνος, ὡς νεβρὸς οὐράνιον (860)
πήδημα κουφίζουσα σὺν ἀγλαΐᾳ.
νικᾷ στεφαναφόρα κρείσσω τῶν παρ' Ἀλφειοῦ

---

[56] Swift 2010, 156–70, Carey 2012, 22–5; Cerbo 2012. Roisman/Luschnig 2011, 197 call it an 'epinician in reverse', since 'usually athletes are compared to mythological characters.'
[57] Swift 2010, 160.
[58] Cropp 2013, 203. Henrichs 1994–1995, 88 connects it to Dionysus: 'the metaphor of the leaping fawn recurs in one of the choral odes of the *Bakkhai* as an image of maenadic freedom and escape from oppression.'
[59] On *aglaia*, cf. Carey 2012, 23: 'a term much loved by Pindar, who uses the noun and its cognates over fifty times in the extant corpus.'
[60] Swift 2010, 165–9.

ῥεέθροις τελέσας
κασίγνητος σέθεν· ἀλλ' ὑπάειδε
καλλίνικον ᾠδὰν ἐμῷ χορῷ. (865)

Set your feet to the dance, dear friend, as a fawn
nimbly leaps to the sky with joy.
Your brother has won, has completed a crown-
   contest surpassing those
by Alphaeus' streams. Come, sing
a song of glorious victory to accompany my dance.

These direct references to a lively dance performance crucially differs from the epinicia of Pindar and Bacchylides, which as Carey points out, are 'notoriously unforthcoming about the nature of their performance.'[61] In particular the image of a fawn leaping to the sky, though used in Bacchylides 13, activates other cultural expectations and ideas of dancers leaping. The chorus furthermore lays emphasis on their role as dancers by inviting Electra to sing a song (ὑπάειδε... ᾠδὰν)[62] – though a particular kind, the *kallinikos* – which would accompany their dance (ἐμῷ χορῷ). This invitation creates the unusual possibility that an accompanied performance between Electra and the chorus might take place.

This possibility briefly becomes a reality: in a situation unparalleled in extant drama, the song's addressee interrupts and replies to the chorus' song in 866–72. Instead of the choral antistrophe, Euripides inserts a rather lengthy response by Electra, who, in addressing chorus' invitation to join them in dance, echoes the same epinician flavouring introduced by the women in their strophe; specifically, she will crown the head of her victorious brother (στέψω τ' ἀδελφοῦ κρᾶτα τοῦ νικηφόρου, 872).[63] However, though she continues the imagery and language of victory of the chorus, she replies in *iambics*, which effectively put a stop to the chorus' song. The effect of this jarring response is multiplied by Electra's suggestion that they all instead go inside the house in order to fetch hair-adornments for Orestes (φέρ', οἷα δὴ 'χω καὶ δόμοι κεύθουσί μου / κόμης ἀγάλματ' ἐξενέγκωμεν, φίλαι, 870–1). In including Electra's response, Euripides has not only interrupted choral song, but he has also uniquely created two distinct performances on stage. That he makes Electra, a character whom Edith Hall calls 'almost pre-programmed to sing in tragedy',[64] *speak* to the chorus and in particular invite them to an activity that does not involve singing and dancing

---

[61] Carey 2012, 24.
[62] On ὑπάειδε, see Diggle 1980, 39–40.
[63] Immediately after this brief ode, Electra continues to address Orestes in epinician terms (ὦ καλλίνικε, 880).
[64] Hall 2010, 319.

is remarkable: when called to accompany the chorus with her famous singing, the Athenian viewing audience may have expected that such a possibility might actually happen, given her lengthy and at times unusual singing role in all plays which involve her.⁶⁵ Instead of a joint performance depicted between Electra and the chorus, Euripides sketches out two simultaneous but competing activities that are to be carried out by the chorus and Electra, thus staging a certain and irreparable process of separation.

Her reply in iambics fundamentally changes the choral song. Though the women acknowledge her reply and interruption, they ultimately decide to continue dancing without her, while adopting even more self-referential language:

> σὺ μέν νυν ἀγάλματ' ἄειρε κρατί· τὸ δ' ἀμέτερον
> χωρήσεται Μούσαισι χόρευμα φίλον. (875)
> νῦν οἱ πάρος ἀμετέρας γαίας τυραννεύσουσι φίλοι βασιλῆς
> δικαίως, τοὺς ἀδίκους καθελόντες.
> ἀλλ' ἴτω ξύναυλος βοὰ χαρᾷ.

> You bring adornments, then, for his head; but we
> shall dance our dance which is dear to the Muses.
> Now shall the former dear rulers of our land be masters in it,
> with justice, now they have cast down the unjust.
> Come, let us shout with the aulos, joyfully.

The contrast is clear: in 874 their response is formulated in terms of a strong opposition between Electra and themselves (σὺ μέν νυν...τὸ δ' ἀμέτερον), which not only continues to emphasise the disjunction between the two parties, but also further accentuates the role of the chorus as dancers (χωρήσεται Μούσαισι χόρευμα φίλον, 875). The dance is again stressed as the chorus' business, one that is furthermore held in high regard by the Muses, whereas Electra is instructed to go inside and fetch the adornments of victory. This contrast here forces us to think about the staging of this strange moment, and specifically whether Electra at this precise moment enters her hut to look for the crown which she is to place on Orestes' head as the chorus sing their antistrophe. If Electra were to move inside the *skēnē*, would her movements distract from the chorus' song

---

65 The dating of Euripides' and Sophocles' *Electra*, and specifically which version came first, continue to plague scholars. Denniston 1939 dated Euripides' version to 413 because of the concern of the Dioscuri about sailing to Sicily in lines 1347–8 (read as an allusion to the Athenian expedition to Sicily; cf. Thuc. 7.20.2, 7.42.1) as well as their references to Helen's eidolon in Troy while she physically was in Egypt in 1280–3 (Euripides' *Helen* was performed in 412). *Communis opinio* dictates that Sophocles' version is also a late play, based on perceived formal similarities with the *Philoctetes* and *Oedipus at Colonus*.

and dance? Equally important, what is the chorus doing while Electra is speaking and interrupting her song? Might it be possible that while Electra utters her addresses to the sun, the women of the chorus go through the movements of the dance to the tune of the lyre or flute while they themselves keep silent? The specifics of the tragic chorus' dance are impossible to reconstruct and understand, given the paucity of surviving evidence on the topic.[66] The little that there is suggests that during an ode, the chorus moved around the altar during the strophe, promptly changed direction during the antistrophe (literally 'turning the other way'), and stood still for the epode, perhaps in an imitation of cultic worshippers.[67] Electra's alternative suggestion of moving inside at the precise moment of a possible joint performance between protagonist and chorus illuminates the many orchestic possibilities on the fifth century stage. It is remarkable that in this particular case Euripides has effectively separated the chorus and Electra at the precise moment when the prospect of an accompaniment and a collaborative performance between the two is promised. Instead of a joint performance, both parties refuse to join the other and end up performing two separate activities.

The emphasis on such a glaring disjunction between the chorus and Electra, initially highlighted as possible joint performers, might be best explained in terms of a hyporchematic echo. As we saw in the previous sections, it is possible to construct a particular conception of the *hyporchēma* based on the strategic separation of singers and dancers, a notion which is furthermore supported by the only use of *hyporcheisthai* in the *Choephoroi* used in direct contrast to *aidein*. The invitation extended by the chorus for Electra to join their performance is framed in terms of *hypaeide* (864), which in turn is differentiated from their dance (ἐμῷ χορῷ, 865). This suggests that in this epinician-filled ode, Euripides introduces, or rather blends, the prospect of a hyporchematic performance between the two parties, in which the chorus would dance while Electra sings. The possibility of such a hyporchematic operation becomes more striking when we consider the various references to choral dancing throughout the play,[68] and, in particular, to Electra's possible participation in them. In the play's *parodos* (167–212), the chorus ask Electra to join them in a festival to

---

66 The lack of evidence has led to multiple debates by modern scholars regarding the dance that was performed in the ancient Greek theatre, including the prominent disagreement on whether the chorus danced in a circular or rectangular space. See, for example, Wiles 1997, 87–97; Foley 2003, 9–11; Csapo 2008, 280–2; Bosher 2008–2009; and Lech 2009.
67 Ar. *Th.* 953–1000; Schol. E. *Hec* 647; Färber 1936, 14–8; D'Alfonso 1994; Csapo 2008, 280–1.
68 The play's second *stasimon* (432–86), for example, prominently showcases several famous mythic choruses: the Nereids, the Pleiades and Hyades.

Hera, a request which Electra famously refuses. Though much of the criticism in this *parodos* has been focused on Electra's 'self-centred' character,[69] critics typically fail to see that the chorus' invitation – and Electra's subsequent rejection – to the festival of Hera is formulated in ritual terms: the crucially chorus employ στείχειν at 174, which suggests a processional form,[70] whereas Electra's response at 178 further suggests that she has been invited by the chorus precisely to take up the role of choral leader (οὐδ' ἱστᾶσα χοροὺς).[71] Towards the end of the play when Euripides stages Orestes and Electra's sudden revulsion at the matricide that they have recently committed, Electra's first worry is also expressed in terms of her future role in the choral dance; specifically she wonders which chorus will take her at 1198–9 (ἰὼ ἰώ μοι. ποῖ δ' ἐγώ, τίν' ἐς χορόν, / τίνα γάμον εἶμι;).[72] The *Electra*, for all its accusations of realism, thus contains several important references to ritual performances and especially to Electra's role in them. Her refusal to attend Hera's festival is significant, given the goddess' role as protector of marriage and the transition from virgin to wife.[73] Electra's status as a virgin who is now married is clearly problematic in the framework of these rituals, as is the fact that she is wed to someone who is her social inferior. By birth, she should lead the Argive dances but her ambiguous status means that she has no role in festival, and therefore no way to perform. Euripides' echo of the *hyporchēma*, if taken to mean a strategic disjunction between dancers and singers, would be an important way to illustrate and further emphasise Electra's unique but separate situation in his play.

This chapter began by showing how difficult it is to make an argument on the nature of *hyporchēmata* based on fragmentary and biased evidence. Even when certain testimonies do elaborate on the nature of this elusive genre, we may often find contradictory definitions, particularly if the quote is found in an ideologically or theoretically charged context. Furthermore, what these few sources do stress is the role of dance in *hyporchēma*, leaving us at a grave disadvantage when attempting to understand its nature and characteristics, since dancing is assumed to be an essential part of all other choral lyric genres. With any other lyric genre it is possible to assemble a case for its presence in tragedy based on imagery, diction, and context, but not so with the *hyporchēma*. Nonetheless this chapter has aimed to show that there are sufficient hints to be

---

[69] Cf. Cropp 2013, 9–11, Michelini 1987, 187–8.
[70] Cf. Calame 1997b, 39–40.
[71] Cf. Calame 1997b, 45–6.
[72] Euripides' *Electra* 1198–9: ἰὼ ἰώ μοι. ποῖ δ' ἐγώ, τίν' ἐς χορόν, / τίνα γάμον εἶμι; On the play's end, see Andújar 2016.
[73] Zeitlin 1970.

found regarding its nature that enable us to reconstruct a meaning of the choral genre involving a separation of singers and dancers. Furthermore, such a definition allows us to look afresh at the practice and representation of dance on the tragic stage. Recent studies on the self-conscious language employed by the chorus has alerted us to the myriad ways in which the chorus foregrounds dance in their odes. Many of these moments had been previously assumed by scholars as direct evidence for the *hyporchēma*, by the simple fact that they mention dance. Though some choruses draw unusual attention to their own dancing in the 'here and now' of the tragic performance, they nevertheless contain references to other types of choral lyric, such as paeans and hymns, which crucially also contained dancing. Nevertheless, I believe that a more secure example of the elusive 'dancing song' can be found in a brief and unique ode in Euripides' *Electra*, a song which is interrupted by its own addressee. Electra's singular *iambic* response in the ode, especially after the chorus had specifically extended her a special invitation to join the performance, creates an irreparable separation between her and the chorus at a moment when a joint performance is expected. As I argue, understanding this moment in light of a hyporchematic echo allows us to reflect on the many times the chorus and Electra are suggested as ritual performers throughout the play, only to have their separation stressed at the end. My discussion of this brief ode furthermore attempts to show that though mired in doubt, a particular reading of the *hyporchēma* involving a separation between singers and dancers may shed light on the orchestic dynamics of the tragic stage, and specifically the varying types of physical movements that are possible between chorus and actors. Scholars of the ancient Greek world frequently discuss the song-culture context in which lyric poetry was performed. The *hyporchēma* reminds us that choral lyric crucially involved dance, and therefore that in discussions of choral lyric the term 'song-and-dance' culture should be adopted.

Enrico Emanuele Prodi
Dancing in Delphi, Dancing in Thebes: The Lyric Chorus in Euripides' *Phoenician Women*

Despite the great popularity of Euripides' *Phoenician Women* throughout antiquity, its chorus had a bad press already at that time.[1] When Aristophanes' Dicaeopolis jibes that, as he puts on Telephus' garb for his peroration to the old men of Acharnae, 'the audience [must] know me, who I really am, but the members of the chorus [must] stand there like idiots' (*Acharnians* 442–3), an unnamed critic remarks:

> τοὺς δ' αὖ χορευτάς : καὶ διὰ τούτων τὸν Εὐριπίδην διασύρει. οὗτος γὰρ εἰσάγει τοὺς χοροὺς οὔτε τὰ ἀκόλουθα φθεγγομένους τῆι ὑποθέσει, ἀλλ' ἱστορίας τινὰς ἀπαγγέλλοντας, ὡς ἐν ταῖς Φοινίσσαις, οὔτε ἐμπαθῶς ἀντιλαμβανομένους τῶν ἀδικηθέντων, ἀλλὰ μεταξὺ πίπτοντας.[2]

> (Schol. ΕΓLh Ar. *Ach.* 443 Wilson)

'But the members of the chorus' : With these words too he is ridiculing Euripides, for the choruses that the latter brings on the stage do not say something relevant to the plot, but tell some stories, as in the *Phoenician Women*, nor do they emotionally side with those suffering injustice, but are simply interposed.

I am deeply indebted to audiences in Oxford, Seattle, Liverpool, and Venice, which heard versions of this paper and helped it develop into its present shape; to the editors of this volume, for their feedback as well as for kindly requesting it *in lieu* of the one originally delivered at the *Paths of Song* conference; and to Vanessa Cazzato, who much improved it. Quotations from the *Phoenician Women* are taken from Mastronarde's Teubner text (Leipzig 1988). All translations are my own. This paper was first delivered at the memorial colloquium for James Worthen in 2010, and the written version, though much changed, remains dedicated to his memory.

1 On the popularity of the *Phoenician Women* see for instance Bremer 1983, 294; 1984; Cribiore 2001.
2 πίπτοντας is found in place of the transmitted ἀντιπίπτοντας only on the TLG-E (the newer online version has again ἀντι-). Filippomaria Pontani, who alerted me to this fact, must be right that the reading – be it due to a rogue scribe or a mere mistake – is the correct one. The sense of the text as transmitted is unclear, as is shown by the paraphrases given by Riemschneider 1940, 55 ('sondern gegen den Zusammenhang dazwischenfallen') and Nikolaidou-Arabatzi 2015, 26 n. 2 ('but their narration lies somewhere in between the plot of the myth', significantly ignoring ἀντι-); conversely, μεταξὺ πίπτειν is amply attested and unproblematic in context.

https://doi.org/10.1515/9783110575910-014

He was not alone. A commentator on the *Phoenician Women* itself curtly notes the ostensible irrelevance of the third *stasimon* to the present events – specifically, to Menoeceus' heroic self-sacrifice – to which it ought to have reacted:

ἔβας ἔβας ὦ πτεροῦσσα : πρὸς οὐδὲν ταῦτα· ἔδει γὰρ τὸν χορὸν οἰκτίσασθαι διὰ τὸν θάνατον Μενοικέως ἢ ἀποδέχεσθαι τὴν εὐψυχίαν τοῦ νεανίσκου, ἀλλὰ τὰ περὶ Οἰδίπουν καὶ τὴν Σφίγγα διηγεῖται τὰ πολλάκις εἰρημένα.

'You came, you came, O winged one' : This is pointless. The chorus should have expressed pity for Menoeceus' death or approval for the young man's courage; instead it narrates the story of Oedipus and the Sphinx, stuff told over and over.

ἀραῖσι τέκεα μέλεος : ἀπὸ τούτων ἐχρῆν εὐθέως ἄρξασθαι τὸν χορόν. ἐκεῖνα γὰρ περιττά ἐστιν.

'With curses his children, wretched one' : The chorus should have begun from this straightaway. What comes before is superfluous.

(Schol. MTAB E. *Ph.* 1019, 1053 Schwartz)

Contemporary scholarship has put much effort into investigating the role of the chorus and qualifying these rather ungracious statements.[3] On this occasion we shall focus on a particular and hitherto undervalued aspect of the Phoenician women's relevance to the play named after them: namely, the intimated characterisation of the chorus as a (cultic) chorus within the dramatic fiction, a characterisation which is parallel to, but independent of, their being a chorus in the theatrical reality.[4] Helene Foley put her finger on this characterisation over three decades ago: 'This chorus, unlike Aeschylus' chorus of native-born women [sc. in *Seven against Thebes*], is almost a chorus by profession ... The Phoenician maidens dedicate themselves to Apollo and to a life of celebrating myth in a foreign land through dance, song, and prayer in honor of the gods'.[5] However, she did not pursue this valuable insight further or investigate

---

[3] Beside the relevant parts of the commentaries by Balmori 1945, Craik 1988, Mastronarde 1994, and Amiech 2004, see Riemschneider 1940; Arthur 1977; Parry 1978, 166–73; Cerbo 1984–1985; Foley 1985, 118–19, 136–9; Mueller-Goldingen 1985 *passim*; Nancy 1986; Calame 1994–1995; Gould 1996, 224–5; Medda 2005 (condensed into 2006, 18–27); Papadopoulou 2008, 78–87; Lamari 2010 *passim*; Hilton 2011, 41–6.

[4] By arguing for a further, exceptional layer of chorality in the *Phoenician Women*, this approach complements and enriches the argument made by Calame 1994–1995 on the enduring cultic function of the tragic chorus with reference to the same play. Compare also Zimmermann 2002 on the 'duplice carattere del coro, contemporaneamente *dramatis persona* e coro cultuale' (p. 122) in Aeschylus' *Seven against Thebes*.

[5] Foley 1985, 119, 144; see also Hilton 2011, 42. A similar argument is compellingly made by Murnaghan 2006, 99–100 with reference to Euripides' more obviously metatheatrical *Bacchae*,

its significance for the chorus and for the play more broadly. Doing so shall therefore be our purpose on this occasion. The first part of this paper investigates the elements of choral characterisation that are subtly but persistently woven into the chorus' self-presentation in the early phases of the play, with parallels from cultic (and para-cultic) lyric and dedicatory epigrams; the second and final part explores the Phoenician women's status as a theoric chorus sent from Tyre to Thebes and Delphi and how such status is integral to the narratives they sing and to the role that they perform in the rest of the play.

The Phoenician women introduce themselves twice: first to the audience in the first strophic pair of the *parodos* (202–25), then to Polynices in the first episode (280–5). The latter passage almost sounds like a more prosaic résumé of the bare facts of the first,[6] and we shall return to it shortly. But let us first examine the opening of the *parodos*:

Τύριον οἶδμα λιποῦσ' ἔβαν
    ἀκροθίνια Λοξίαι
    Φοινίσσας ἀπὸ νάσου,
Φοίβωι δούλα μελάθρων   (205)
    ἵν' ὑπὸ δειράσι νιφοβόλοις
    Παρνασσοῦ κατενάσθη,
    Ἰόνιον κατὰ πόντον ἐλά-
    ται πλεύσασα, περιρρύτων
    ὑπὲρ ἀκαρπίστων πεδίων   (210)
    Σικελίας Ζεφύρου πνοαῖς
    ἱππεύσαντος ἐν οὐρανῶι
    κάλλιστον κελάδημα.

πόλεος ἐκπροκριθεῖσ' ἐμᾶς
    καλλιστεύματα Λοξίαι   (215)
    Καδμείων ἔμολον γᾶν,
κλεινῶν Ἀγηνοριδᾶν
    ὁμογενεῖς ἐπὶ Λαΐου
    πεμφθεῖσ' ἐνθάδε πύργους.
ἴσα δ' ἀγάλμασι χρυσοτεύ-   (220)
    κτοις Φοίβωι λάτρις ἐγενόμαν·
    ἔτι δὲ Κασταλίας ὕδωρ
    περιμένει με κόμας ἐμᾶς
    δεῦσαι παρθένιον χλιδὰν
    Φοιβείαισι λατρείαις.   (225)

---

where '[t]he chorus of Asian bacchantes is playing a role, but it is the role, effectively, of a chorus' (p. 100).
6 On the relation between the two passages see Lamari 2010, 51.

> Leaving the Tyrian swell I have come as a choice offering for Loxias from the Phoenician island, a slave of the halls for Phoebus where he dwells below the ridge of snow-strewn Parnassus; I sailed through the Ionian sea by ship as Zephyr with his blasts galloped in the sky over the barren plains that wash around Sicily, a most beautiful sound.
>
> Chosen out of my city as the fairest gift for Loxias, I have come to the land of the Cadmeans, sent here to the towers of Laius, kin to the glorious Agenorids. Equal to the gold-wrought statues I became a servant of Phoebus; but the water of Castalia is still waiting for me to steep the maidenly finery of my hair in Phoebus' service.

What invites attention is the interlacing of the language of servitude, offering, and desirability across strophe and antistrophe. Servitude to Apollo is first mentioned at line 205 (δούλα), when the song icastically moves, like the Phoenician women themselves, from Tyre to Delphi, from origin to destination.[7] The chorus returns to it in the second half of the antistrophe, with the repetition in close proximity of the co-radicals λάτρις (221) and λατρείαις (225): the former looking back to their dedication to Phoebus at the point of origin, the latter looking forward to their eventual entering his service at Delphi (though pointedly avoiding all mention of their journey there). Consistently with their projected status as sacred slaves gifted to the divinity, at the very beginning of their song they describe themselves as ἀκροθίνια 'choicest offerings' (or, in a military context, 'spoils') (203). As though prompted by the West Wind's κάλλιστον κελάδημα, in the antistrophe they dwell on their beauty. They are καλλιστεύματα 'most beautiful things' for Loxias (215), chosen as such out of their entire city (214). In their service to Phoebus they are like golden ἀγάλματα, statues or pleasing gift-offerings (220–1). The reference to the 'maidenly finery of [their] hair' (223–4) completes and specifies the picture as one of almost eroticised female attractiveness. The focal point of this complex description is the chorus' self-definition as ἀκροθίνια, which connects the Phoenician women's sacred role with their physical attributes. This connection is highlighted by the very structure of the antistrophe: καλλιστεύματα Λοξίαι (215) resumes the tautometric ἀκροθίνια Λοξίαι of the strophe (203), while the two further references to their desirability accompany the two references to their subordination (221 λάτρις, 225 λατρείαις).

An emphasis on the beauty or worth of the offering is integral to ancient Greek discourse on dedication; so is self-reference as a dedication. A handful of examples from Maria Letizia Lazzarini's collection of archaic dedicatory in-

---

[7] On the language of servitude, labour, and submission in Greek religion (which becomes prevalent in Hellenistic and Roman times, but with a few fifth- and fourth-century antecedents) see Pleket 1981, 159–71 (164 on the *Phoenician Women*).

scriptions will suffice to illustrate this point.⁸ An ἀκροθίνιον can openly refer to itself as such: Lazzarini 704 ἀqροθίνια τõ Διὸς τõ Ὀλυμπίο, 'choicest offerings for Olympian Zeus'; 705 τõ Διὸς τõ Ὀλυμπίο *h*ακροθίνιον τõ πεδι[, 'choicest offering of ... for Olympian Zeus'; 981 Ἀθεναῖοι τ[õι] Ἀπόλλον[ι ἀπὸ Μέδ]ον ἀκ[ροθ]ίνια τẽς Μαραθ[õ]νι μ[άχες, 'the Athenians (dedicate) to Apollo the spoils of the battle of Marathon'.⁹ Ἄγαλμα is another frequently employed term, either on its own or coupled with words or expressions highlighting the beauty of the object offered:¹⁰ Lazzarini 720 = CEG 363 Χαλϙοδάμανς με ἀνέθεκε θιιοῖν περικαλλὲς ἄγαλμα, 'Chalcodamas dedicated me, a most beautiful offering for the gods'; 728b = CEG 422 Χηραμύης μ' ἀνέθηκε θ⟨ε⟩ῆι περικαλλὲς ἄγαλμα, 'Cheramyes dedicated me, a most beautiful offering for the goddess'; 856.1 = CEG 302.1 [Φοί]βο μέν εἰμ' ἄγαλ[μα Λ]ατ[οί]δα καλ[ό]ν, 'I am a beautiful offering for Phoebus son of Leto'. The whole a part of which is selected as an offering can also be mentioned, providing a parallel for the reference to the choice of the Phoenician women at line 214: Lazzarini 636 = CEG 193 Νέαρχος ἀνέθεκε[ν *h*ο κεραμε]ὺς ἔργον ἀπαρχὲν τἀθ[εναίαι, 'Nearchus the potter dedicated a tithe from his work to Athena'; 638.1–2 = CEG 205.1–2 Παλάδι Ἀθαναίαι Λύσον ἀνέθεκεν ἀπαρχέν / *h*õν αὐτõ κτ[εά]νον, 'Lyson dedicated to Pallas Athena a tithe from his own possessions'; 803.1–2 = CEG 414.1–2 Δημοκύδης τόδ' ἄγαλμα Τελεστοδίκη τ' ἀπὸ κοινῶν / εὐχσάμενοι στῆσαν παρθένωι Ἀρτέμιδι, 'Democydes and Telestodice set up this offering from their common possessions to the virgin Artemis in fulfilment of a vow'.

Several of the examples just cited refer to two further elements in the dedication process: the name of the dedicator(s) and the act of dedication itself. Reference to these is absent from the *parodos* (though note the hint at 219, πεμφθεῖσ' ἐνθάδε) but appears explicity in the chorus' subsequent self-presentation to Polynices (280–5):

Φοίνισσα μὲν γῆ πατρὶς ἡ θρέψασά με, (280)
Ἀγήνορος δὲ παῖδες ἐκ παίδων δορὸς
Φοίβωι μ' ἔπεμψαν ἐνθάδ' ἀκροθίνιον·
μέλλων δὲ πέμπειν μ' Οἰδίπου κλεινὸς γόνος
μαντεῖα σεμνὰ Λοξίου τ' ἐπ' ἐσχάρας,
ἐν τῶιδ' ἐπεστράτευσαν Ἀργεῖοι πόλιν. (285)

The soil of Phoenicia is the fatherland that nurtured me. The sons of Agenor's sons sent me here, spoils of the spear for Phoebus; but when Oedipus' glorious son was about to send me to the revered oracle and altars of Loxias, just then the Argives marched upon the city.

---

8 Lazzarini 1976.
9 On the dedication of spoils see Jim 2014, 176–202.
10 On ἄγαλμα as a key word and concept in dedicatory inscriptions see Day 2010, 85–129.

The similarity between the first three lines of this extract and dedicatory epigrams such as Lazzarini 856 = *CEG* 302 (cited above) is remarkable. It strengthens the impression that the first strophic pair of the *parodos* persistently and deliberately echoes the language of dedication as familiar from dedicatory epigrams, thereby underscoring the Phoenician women's envisaged role as human offerings to Apollo.

The dedication of human beings in sanctuaries abroad is not unique in Greek mythology, or indeed history.[11] In literature it is attested as early as the cyclic *Epigoni*, where Tiresias' daughter Manto was said to have been dedicated as an offering in Delphi (fr. 3 Bernabé = 4 West *ap.* schol. A.R. 1.308b Wendel). Upon hearing Ion call himself a 'slave of the god', Euripides' Creusa politely inquires whether he is the dedication of a city (ἀνάθημα πόλεως) or was sold by somebody (*Ion* 310), showing no sign of finding either option strange. Several foundation myths employ a story pattern according to which a group of people, or sometimes an entire population, is dedicated or tithed to a temple (using explicit terms such as ἀνάθημα 'dedication', ἀπαρχή 'tithe', δεκατεύω 'to tithe', ἀκροθίνιον) and then goes on to found a city.[12] The Mycenaean record also offers examples of what appears to be construed as a gift of men or women to divinities, although it is unclear how it worked in practice.[13]

But are we to think that the service the Phoenician women see themselves performing in the 'kultisches Idyll'[14] of Delphi is limited to being there quite beautifully and belonging to Apollo, like the golden statues and the other offerings in his temple? The mesode (226–38) points us towards a more complex and far-reaching solution:

---

[11] A well-known historical case is that of the so-called Locrian Maidens, on which see Graf 1978. On human dedications in the Hellenistic and Roman East see now Caneva/Delli Pizzi 2015, emphasising that this cluster of phenomena 'cannot be framed within a single interpretative paradigm, beyond the mere fact that they all shared in a special relationship with a sanctuary' (190).

[12] See the evidence collected by Ducat 1974, 100–6 and Jim 2014, 281–8; one instance is also recalled at p. 307 below.

[13] The example that first comes to mind is a tablet from Pylos, PY Tn 316 (*DMG* 172) where a series of divinities are allocated gold bowls, gold cups, women, and/or men. The human offerings have been variously interpreted, from cup-bearers (Ventris/Chadwick in *DMG* p. 284) to victims for human sacrifice (Chadwick in *DMG*² p. 460) to temple-servants (Hughes 1991, 199–202), the latter seemingly the likelier. Human beings also exchange hands, with a deity as the recipient in at least two cases, in PY An 1281 (*DMG*² 312). Several other Pylian tablets (and possibly one from Cnossus, KN X 966) refer to named individuals as *te-o-jo do-e-ro* or *do-e-ra* 'slave of the god', see Gérard-Rousseau 1968, 76–8.

[14] Mueller-Goldingen 1985, 66.

ὦ λάμπουσα πέτρα πυρὸς
δικόρυφον σέλας ὑπὲρ ἄκρων
βακχείων Διονύσου,
οἴνα θ' ἃ καθαμέριον
στάζεις, τὸν πολύκαρπον οἰ- (230)
νάνθας ἱεῖσα βότρυν,
ζάθεά τ' ἄντρα δράκοντος οὔ-
ρειαί τε σκοπιαὶ θεῶν
νιφόβολόν τ' ὄρος ἱερόν, εἱ-
λίσσων ἀθανάτας θεοῦ (235)
χορὸς γενοίμαν ἄφοβος,
παρὰ μεσόμφαλα γύαλα Φοί-
βου Δίρκαν προλιποῦσα.

O rock that flashes the twin-peaked light of fire over Dionysus' rapturous heights; vine that drips every day as it sends forth the grape of the vine which bears much fruit; divine cave of the serpent; mountain lookouts of the gods; holy snow-strewn mountain; – may I become a fearless chorus of the immortal goddess, whirling round by the hollow of Phoebus, the navel of the earth, once I have left Dirce.

After remarking their absence from Delphi at the end of the preceding antistrophe, the women elaborate in almost fantasising terms on the singing and dancing that awaits them there. This is easily related to the phenomenon that Albert Henrichs – in a paper whose title the present one consciously echoes – terms choral projection: 'when Sophoklean and Euripidean choruses locate their own dancing in the past or in the future, in contrast to the here and now of their immediate performance, or when choruses project their collective identity onto groups of dancers distant from the concrete space of the orchestra and dancing in the allusive realm of the dramatic imagination'.[15] Choral projection, yes, but with a twist. Firstly, in its context within the play it is not an escapist fantasy like many other occurrences of this topos, but rooted in the reality of a determined, explicit, and indeed divinely sanctioned destination (however hindered and rendered uncertain by the present war, as will be explained in the second strophic pair). Moreover, and more importantly, the choral singing and danc-

---

15 Henrichs 1996, 49. In that publication he lists the *Phoenician Women* among plays which feature 'a complex pattern of choral projection and choral self-reference that extends over three or more choral odes' (51) but does not elaborate further beyond noting καλλίχορος at line 786 and chastising Mastronarde 1994, 378 n. 1 for excluding a metatheatrical interpretation of that adjective. My argument proceeds in a somewhat different direction, although the two are not mutually exclusive. For recent treatments of choral projection that include its ritual dimension (which is crucial for the *Phoenician Women*, as the rest of our discussion will show) see Kowalzig 2007b, esp. 232–42, Nikolaidou-Arabatzi 2015.

ing that they envision themselves doing upon their arrival in Delphi is not only the actual occupation of the Athenian choreutes in the reality of the tragic performance, but also consistent with the characterisation of the Phoenician women throughout the action of the play, as we shall see. This is a consequence of the way in which the cluster of dedicatory self-references in the first strophic pair of the *parodos* and the choral tension of the mesode resonate with an established network of associations between song – especially, but not exclusively,[16] choral songs for public worship, or 'hymns' – and dedication.

In Simon Pulleyn's words, '[t]he hymn is clearly seen as a gift or offering, an ἄγαλμα for the god'.[17] Two ancient anecdotes, or perhaps two variants of one, have Pindar state that he composed a dithyramb or a paean for the purpose of a sacrifice, θύσων.[18] As Mary Depew has convincingly shown, 'hymns' partake of a discourse of self-referential deixis that is shared with material dedications.[19] 'Dedicatory statues, votive reliefs, inscriptions, and hymns have one thing in common: they typically present, in deictic terms fitting to their medium, the act of dedication itself'.[20] So, as we have seen, does our chorus, both in the first strophic pair of the *parodos* and (in more concise and explicit terms) upon their meeting Polynices in the first episode. Greek cult songs from the archaic to the Hellenistic age offer parallels for several of the dedicatory self-references whereby we have linked the *parodos* to dedicatory inscriptions. Firstly, prayers for reception imply to an extent one's self-representation as an offering. In the final stanza of Pindar's *Paean 5* (D5 Rutherford, quoted in full at pp. 309–10 below) the speaker entreats Apollo and Artemis to receive (δέξασθε) him, their servant, kindly, together with the sweet-sounding paean he brings.[21] A similar prayer, addressed to Apollo as Παιάν, concludes what is commonly known as the third triad of *Paean 6* (D6 Rutherford). The opening of the same poem – if it is indeed the same poem – is an elaborate prayer to Delphi that she might receive (δέξαι) the speaker, the 'songful mouthpiece of the Pierian

---

[16] See for instance Steiner 1993 on Pindar's association of song and material artefacts such as statues and stelae (with their respective inscriptions) in the victory odes.
[17] Pulleyn 1997, 49.
[18] Dithyramb: Phld. *Mus.* 4.135 p. II 261 Delattre (fr. *86a Sn.-M.). Paean: Pi. *apophth.* p. I 3 Drachmann, Eust. *prooem. in Pi.* 31.1 Kambylis = p. III 302 Drachmann. See Svenbro 1984, 926 (suggesting that the anecdote on the paean may refer to *Pae.* 6.127–8), 929; Pulleyn 1997, 49–50, who notes that the *topos* of the 'smokeless' sacrifice of poetry persists in post-Classical poetry (Call. fr. 494 Pf., Leon. Alex. 1.3 Page = *FGE* 1866); compare Kowalzig 2004: 49–50.
[19] Depew 2000. Parts of her arguments had been anticipated by Svenbro 1984; Day 1994, 55–6; Pulleyn 1997, 49–51.
[20] Depew 2000, 64.
[21] Day 1994, 55–6.

Ones', together with the Graces and Aphrodite.[22] The latter is a thinly veiled reference to the charm and attractiveness of the performance (and of the performers);[23] a similar allusion can be found in '*Paean*' 12.5–8 (G1 Rutherford, actually a *Prosodion*),[24] where the sacrifices sent from Naxos to Delos are said to come Χαρίτεσσι μίγδαν 'together with the Graces'. Furthermore, the notion of the pleasantness of the offering stands behind the emphasis on χαίρειν that pervades both dedicatory inscriptions and hymnic poetry.[25] Beside the obvious example of the *Homeric Hymns*, where χαῖρε normally introduces the conclusion of the poem, similar expressions are used in explicit connection with the song itself in the refrain of the Dictaean hymn to the Kouros (*IC* III/2 2 = *CA* pp. 160–1),[26] Aristonous' hymn to Apollo (*FD* III/2 192.45 = *CA* p. 164),[27] and the so-called Erythraean paean to Asclepius in the version found at Ptolemais (*IGR* I/5 1154.30–1 = *CA* p. 138).[28] Isyllus' paean (*IG* IV²/1 128 = *CA* p. 135) and the history of its composition are explicitly equated with a dedication by the inscription that preserves it: ταῦτα τοί, ὦ μέγ' ἄριστε θεῶν, ἀνέθηκεν Ἴσυλλος (83), 'to you, O far the best of the gods, Isyllus dedicated these'[29] – an equation emphasised by the fact that, like the other hymnic compositions just cited, its text was really set up as a dedication in a sacred space.

One can thus argue that the Phoenician women's self-presentation in the *parodos* and the associations that it evokes bestow on them a clear overtone of chorality that is internal to the dramatic fiction and consequential with it, overlapping with and emphasised by (but not exclusively relying on) the obvious fact that they actually are a chorus in the reality of the stage. It is important to note, with Leslie Kurke, that the analogy with sacrifice and dedication concerns 'not the poem per se … but the poem in full choral performance, sung and danced in unison and in perfect synchronization by a well-trained, beautifully outfitted chorus'.[30] In Pindar's fifth and sixth *Paeans*, as we have just seen, what Leto's

---

22 Day 1994, 61; Depew 2000, 64, 75–6.
23 See Rutherford 2001, 307 with Day 2010, 252–3.
24 On *P.Oxy.* 1792 (whose fr. 1 preserves '*Pae.*' 12) as a manuscript of Pindar's *Prosodia* not *Paeans* see D'Alessio 1997, 25–7.
25 See Day 2000, 46–57; Depew 2000, 62–4; Day 2010, 234–8, 248–54, 262–3. On the functioning of χάρις between the divine and the human sphere see also Jim 2014: 22–3, 60–84.
26 Depew 2000, 63.
27 On Aristonous' hymn see Furley / Bremer 2001, II 45–52; LeVen 2014, 299–304, esp. 304.
28 Day 2010, 249–51. On the Erythraean paean see Furley / Bremer 2001, II 161–7; LeVen 2014, 286–94, esp. 292–3.
29 Depew 2000, 64. On Isyllus' paean and the inscription in which it is embedded see Furley / Bremer 2001, II 180–92; Kolde 2003, esp. 47–8, 220; LeVen 2014, 317–28, esp. 318, 328.
30 Kurke 2012, 221.

children and Delphi are asked to receive is the speaking first person with his accoutrement of gracefuless and song, not merely the song as such. Just as a dedication in a temple inseparably joins the original act of dedication with the permanence of the dedicated artefact (with the inscription on the latter testifying to and memorialising the former),[31] so an offering of song involves both the text in its envisioned permanence through time and the original performance in its embodied totality. This is the key to solving one potential oddity that may otherwise affect our interpretation as outlined above, namely the Phoenician women's equation of themselves – not specifically of their song and dance – to dedicated objects. This is obviously mandated by the back-story that Euripides assigns to them, but does not conflict with their characterization as a chorus. For the time of the performance, the singer and dancer is herself a part of the offering she brings into visible and audible existence, at once dedicator and dedication. The allusions to the Phoenician women's attractiveness (215, 220–1, 223–4) are part and parcel of this conceptualisation of choral performance, as is more obviously the case in Alcman's maiden songs (*PMGF* 1 and 3 *passim*)[32] but also, for instance, in the opening of Pindar's sixth *Paean*, with its emphatic reference to Aphrodite as an attendant to the (male) speaker.

The portrayal of a group of women as a dedication, arguably in connection with a musical performance, finds two hitherto unremarked parallels from the early decades of the fifth century. Neither of them is an exact equivalent of the situation we have unpicked in the *parodos* of the *Phoenician Women* – far from it – but they allow us better to contextualise Euripides' representation of his chorus and its implications. The first of these texts is a notorious poem of Pindar, four fragments of which – covering just over fifteen verses, perhaps a substantial proportion of the original poem[33] – are transmitted by Athenaeus, who quotes them from Chamaeleon's monograph *On Pindar* (fr. 31 Wehrli = 35 Martano *ap*. Ath. 13.573c–574b). As Chamaeleon's notoriously imaginative storytelling would have it, the Corinthian athlete Xenophon vowed that he would

---

31 Day 1994, 43–6, 54 (see also 1989, 22–5 on funerary epigrams).

32 On visual self-referentiality in maiden song (both *partheneia* proper and references to choruses of young women in other literature) see now Swift 2016. The often neglected but crucial point that such emphasis on the performers' attractiveness has a divine as well as a human audience in mind is at p. 282.

33 The minimum possible total is twenty lines (four stanzas). It is endorsed as the true figure by Snell and Maehler as well as Burnett 2011, 50–1 and Liberman 2016, 55 n. 65; this is not without problems, as it necessarily implies that a single verse is missing between 16 and 18. A slightly higher figure, such as twenty-five lines, may be closer to the truth: see van Groningen 1960, 49–50 (at least twenty-five); Currie 2011, 289 and n. 80 ('We do not know how much of the original poem is missing').

bring (ἀπάξειν) courtesans to Aphrodite, according to a supposed local custom, if he won at the Olympic games; his wish was granted, whereupon this *skolion* – the only surviving poem of Pindar that was certainly called so by its author[34] – was performed during the sacrifice in which said courtesans took part. If Chamaeleon is right at least in connecting the poem to Xenophon's double Olympic victory, which Pindar commemorated more directly in *Olympian* 13, then its composition and performance are to be dated to 464 BC; given the explicit reference to Xenophon, we cannot be very far off that date in any case. The first passage that Chamaeleon quotes (fr. *122.18–20 Sn.-M.) probably constituted the end of the poem:

ὦ Κύπρου δέσποινα, τεὸν δεῦτ' ἐς ἄλσος
φορβάδων κορᾶν ἀγέλαν ἑκατόγγυιον Ξενοφῶν τελέαις
ἐπάγαγ' εὐχωλαῖς ἰανθείς. (20)

O mistress of Cyprus, here to your sanctuary Xenophon brought a hundred-limbed herd of grazing girls, rejoicing in the accomplishment of his prayers.

Following Heinz Alexander Schmidt, Leslie Kurke has rightly remarked the sacrificial undertones of φορβάδων, ἀγέλαν, and ἑκατόγγυιον (the latter recalling a hecatomb).[35] However, the picture should be broadened slightly. The entirety of these three remarkably self-contained verses is essentially a dedicatory inscription in lyric formulation.[36] As Schmitz pointed out, it contains all the elements that we would expect from one:[37] references to dedicator, dedicatee, dedicated

---

[34] Hubbard's 2011, 353–5 contention that ἀρχὰν σκολίου at line 14 does not designate the poem itself as a *skolion*, but as 'a subtext of witty σκόλια at future symposia' is not justified by the text, see Currie 2011, 289 n. 82. On the generic label and its implications see Liberman 2016, esp. 54–7; see also Carey 2009a, 31–2, suggesting that the label *skolion* here is less than serious. As Thomas Coward points out to me, Pindar may have used the word *skolion* also in another poem (presumably the one which included frr. *124–*126 Sn.-M.) if [Plut.] *Mus.* 28 = *Mor.* 1140f is correct to claim that he credited Terpander with the invention of *skolia*.
[35] Schmitz 1970, 73 n. 70; Kurke 1996, 58; see also Budin 2008b, 122–5, but note Pirenne-Delforge 2009 and Burnett 2011, 58–9 on some over-interpretations in her analysis of the poem.
[36] The initial asyndeton is noteworthy; so is the aorist ἐπάγαγ(ε), which is more at home in a dedicatory epigram – memorialising an event that took place in the past, from the reader's perspective at any rate – than in a song purportedly referring to a contemporaneous event. A possible explanation is that lines 18–20 were presented as reported speech, as though they were read out or proclaimed by a third party: maybe the same Ἰσθμοῦ δεσπόται whose speech is referenced at 13–14, or the usual τις of projected reception (*Il.* 6.459, 462; 7.87, 91; etc.)?
[37] Schmitz 1970, 71 n. 50; see also Hubbard 2011, 354.

'object', act of dedicating, and occasion of the dedication (the fulfilment of a prayer, itself a common trope in dedicatory epigrams).[38]

Stephanie Budin may very well be right to suggest that an ἄλσος of Aphrodite, coupled with the deictic δεῦτ(ε) in a poem that calls itself a σκόλιον, should be taken less than literally, as gesturing to the sympotic *andron* rather than to an actual temple.[39] She is certainly correct on two further points: that, contrary to some earlier interpretations, no permanent dedication in a temple for the purpose of 'sacred prostitution' is suggested by what survives of Pindar's text (or of Chamaeleon's for that matter); and that Chamaeleon's account of the occasion of the *skolion* is likely to be his own reconstruction based on no other evidence than the poem itself.[40] Nevertheless, the 'bringing' of the women is implicitly but clearly *presented* as a dedication in a space that is, at least imaginatively, portrayed as sacred. Any contrast with the reality of the occasion would only highlight the significance of Pindar's description as well as the tongue-in-cheek interplay between the sacred intimations of his language and its rather more earthly referent. And, much like true dedicatory epigrams do the objects they accompany, it is the quasi-epigram embedded in the song that memorialises and reperforms (and, if Budin is right, altogether creates) Xenophon's 'dedication' of the courtesans to whatever service of Aphrodite the occasion entailed. If the courtesans themselves played a role in the performance of the *skolion*, as Bruno Currie has recently suggested (the masculine *persona loquens* in line 14 need not be an obstacle),[41] the parallel with the Phoenician women becomes even more striking; but the relevance of this poem to the broader theme of dedication in song does not require this to have been the case.

The second example is an epigram attributed to Simonides (14 Page = *FGE* 732–5). It is quoted in slightly diffent wording by three ancient authorities: Cha-

---

38 On ἐπάγω (and its variant ἀπάγω, perhaps supported by Chamaeleon's use of the same verb in his narrative) see van Groningen 1960, 44–6; Budin 2008b, 138–9; Currie 2011, 289 n. 81. For references to an earlier prayer or vow in connection with the act of dedication in inscriptional texts see Lazzarini 1976, 280–2; Pulleyn 1997, 41. Here εὐχωλαῖς probably means prayers rather than vows, given the reference to joy at their fulfilment; nevertheless, considering the racy occasion of the performance, a *double entendre* may well have been intended, with Xenophon quite as glad of his own fulfilment of his vow as of the goddess' fulfilment of his prayer.
39 Budin 2006, 85–6 and 2008b, 115–9, 140; see also Burnett 2011, 58–60. Differently, Cingano 2003, 42–4 and Currie 2011, 289–92 argue for a public, choral performance in a temple, but largely on the precarious authority of Chamaeleon.
40 Budin 2008b, 140, 150–2, with references.
41 Currie 2011, 290 n. 83. Whatever the case, the poem would certainly have been a good candidate for sympotic reperformances involving *hetairai*, see Hubbard 2011, 354–5 (though with the *caveat* recalled above).

maeleon immediately before his discussion of Pindar's *skolion*, Theopompus as reported in a scholion to Pindar's thirteenth *Olympian* (*BNJ* 115 F 285b *ap.* schol. 32b p. I 365 Drachmann), and Plutarch in his essay *On the Malice of Herodotus* (39 = *Mor.* 871b).[42] All three sources agree that the epigram accompanied an object representing the Corinthian women who prayed to Aphrodite for the salvation of Greece at the time of the Persian invasion. This is the text printed by Sir Denys Page, a slightly amended version of that given by the Pindaric scholion:

> αἵδ' ὑπὲρ Ἑλλάνων τε καὶ ἀγχεμάχων πολιητᾶν
> ἔστασαν εὐχόμεναι Κύπριδι δαιμόνια·
> οὐ γὰρ τοξοφόροισιν ἐβούλετο δῖ' Ἀφροδίτα
> Μήδοις Ἑλλάνων ἀκρόπολιν δόμεναι.

> These stood in wondrous prayer to Cypris on behalf of the Greeks and their close-fighting fellow-citizens, for divine Aphrodite did not wish to give the citadel of Greece to the bow-carrying Medes.

In their commentary to the epigram, the three sources disagree as to the identity of the unnamed αἵδ(ε) of the opening verse – Corinthian women generally according to the Pindaric scholion and Plutarch, Corinthian courtesans according to Chamaeleon – as well as to the object(s) to which the epigram referred, a set of bronze εἰκόνες (Plutarch) or a πίναξ (Chamaeleon); in turn, the latter can be understood as either a painting of the *hetairai* or a catalogue of their names.[43] Another important variant concerns the main verb at line 2, which both in Plutarch and in Athenaus' quotation of Chamaeleon is given as ἔσταθεν – a passive form (perhaps with intransitive meaning) which has a considerable likelihood of being the true reading.[44]

The first couplet effectively conflates the image (if this is what it was) with the women it represents. Both the women and their likeness stood in prayer for Greece and Corinth; both this prayer and the artefact that memorialises it are, each in its own way, dedicated to Aphrodite. As Bruna M. Palumbo Stracca suggests, the γάρ that introduces the second couplet is more easily accounted for if the main verb refers to the dedication of the image as well as (or instead of) to

---

[42] On this epigram and its different transmitted versions see Boas 1905, 47–71; Page in *FGE* pp. 207–11; Palumbo Stracca 1985, 58–65; Budin 2008a and 2008b, 140–9.
[43] See Palumbo Stracca 1985, 61–2.
[44] See Palumbo Stracca 1985, 61–3 (passive); Sider 2008 (intransitive).

the original prayer.⁴⁵ The aorist of ἵστημι can be used to denote the act of 'setting up' an object as a dedication to a divinity:⁴⁶ see for instance Lazzarini 688.1–2 = CEG 429.1–2 αὐδὴ τεχνήεσσα λίθο, λέγε τίς τόδ' ἄ[γαλμα] / στῆσεν Ἀπόλλωνος βωμὸν ἐπαγλαΐ[σας 'skilful voice of the stone, tell who set up this offering gracing the altar of Apollo', 679 = CEG 194 Παλ]άδι μ' ἐγρεμάχαι Διονύσιο[ς ἐνθά]δ' ἄγαλμα / στέσε Κολοίο παῖς 'Dionysius, the son of Coloius, set me up here as a gift-offering for battle-rousing Pallas', and 803.1–2 = CEG 414.1–2 quoted above. This – especially, but not exclusively, if ἔσταθεν is the true reading – supports the interpretation of the epigram as portraying not only the actual dedication of the image, but also the notional dedication of the women it depicts. But there may be more to it than this. The verb ἵστημι, in both the active and the middle, is also a favourite designator for the act of setting up a χορός or participating in one.⁴⁷ In Pindar's second *Paean* (D2 Rutherford), the bright-headbanded maidens of Delphi sing ἱστάμεναι χορὸν / [ταχύ]ποδα 'setting up a swift-footed chorus' (99–100). The title character of Euripides' *Iphigenia in Aulis* asks στήσομεν ἄρ' ἀμφὶ βωμόν, ὦ πάτερ, χορούς; 'shall we set up chorus around the altar, father?' (676). In the same poet's *Electra*, the heroine laments that she will not be able to dance ἱστᾶσα χορούς / Ἀργείαις ἅμα νύμφαις 'setting up choruses with the brides of Argos' (178–9).⁴⁸ The twelve Spartan maidens of Theocritus' *Epithalamian of Helen* πρόσθε νεογράπτω θαλάμω χορὸν ἐστάσαντο 'set up a chorus in front of the newly painted bedchamber' (18.3). So one could easily suggest, with David Sider, that the Corinthian women 'stood as a chorus ... that is, that their prayer took the form of a choral ode'.⁴⁹

Once we discount the intriguing but untrustworthy stories spun by Chamaeleon, the details of the background and performance of these two short poems elude us. In neither case can choral performance by the women in question

---

45 Palumbo Stracca 1985, 63. However, if Bernardakis' conjecture δαιμόνια is accepted (as it is by Page), γάρ can also be taken as referring to the adjective specifically: the women's prayer was a thing of wonder and miracle, *as is shown by the fact that* Aphrodite did not allow the Persians to conquer Corinth.
46 Palumbo Stracca 1985, 60, 64.
47 See Alonge 2012.
48 I reproduce the text printed by James Diggle in his OCT (Oxford 1991). Alonge 2012 advocates rejecting Reiske's ἱστᾶσα in order to retain the manuscripts' στᾶσα and instead emend the transmitted χορούς into Seidler's χοροῖς, on the strength of *IT* 1143 χοροῖς δὲ σταίην and fr. 122 Kannicht (*Andromeda*) οὐ χοροῖσιν . . . ἔστηκ'. Seidler's emendation is plausible, but no less so is Reiske's: as the Pindaric and Theocritean parallels suggest, ἵστημι (or ἵσταμαι) χορόν (or χορούς) can refer to simply taking part in a chorus – which, as Alonge remarks, is the sense the context demands – with no necessary implication of being the chorus leader.
49 Sider 2008.

be proved. However, in both cases we are presented with a performance – of whatever kind – by women who are conceived of as an offering. In one case they are explicitly presented as such; in the other, the dedication is only intimated by the text, but made evident by the actual setup of the artefact in the temple of Aphrodite. So, the intimated chorality of the dedicated Phoenician women is not as unique as it might seem. What remains to be done is to tease out the significance of this choral characterisation of the chorus. On the external, contextual level, as Smaro Nikolaidou-Arabatzi has recently put it, 'Whenever a Euripidean chorus introduces its own dancing into ritual choral events from the past or future, it broadens its choreia with fictional mirrors of its own performance, thus validating its initial role of offering praise to the honoured god Dionysus'[50] – an effect that is all the more powerful if what is introduced is not only a momentary imagination of chorality but a consistent characterisation. But the details, implications, and significance of this characterisation within the tragedy itself also invite exploration, and it is to such exploration that the second part of this paper is dedicated.

Already Claire Nancy, in one of the most perceptive analyses of the choral odes of the *Phoenician Women* published to date, recognised a broadly 'lyric' quality to their discourse on the level of themes and imagery: 'Lyrique en ce sens d'abord qu'il procède par une disposition de motifs, par un jeu de contrepoint: image contre image, scène contre scène. Qu'il réagence librement les données légendaires pour faire émerger un sens enfoui jusqu'ici dans la trame de l'histoire'.[51] But the choral odes are 'lyric' – beside the concrete sense of being sung and danced on the stage – under another aspect too. As we know from Pindar and the other late archaic lyricists, the normal disposition of large-scale choral cult song is to begin by introducing the speaker and the song itself before launching into an extended mythical narrative, typically related to the cult in which they are taking part or the locality in which it takes place, only to return to the present of the performance at the very end. The countless variations and the different combinations of specific topics in the poems that survive only emphasises the persistence of this basic structure. And the Phoenician women's singing throughout the play can be seen, on a deep level, to partake of a similar fundamental disposition.[52]

---

50 Nikolaidou-Arabatzi 2015, 28.
51 Nancy 1986, 474; see also Cerbo 1984–1985, 190, who finds structural echoes of the 'forme specifiche della lirica arcaica – ditirambo, inno, *threnos*'.
52 The connection between the Phoenician women's myth-telling and their dramatic persona is observed by Foley 1985, 144 (quoted above, p. 292).

After introducing themselves, their provenance, their purpose, and their present situation in the *parodos*, during the greatest part of the *stasima* (most of the first, the antistrophe and epode of the second, and the whole of the third) they engage in a series of interwoven mythical narratives about Thebes and its royal house. That the *stasima* can be taken together to constitute one such song cycle was noticed already by Wilhelm Riemschneider almost eight decades ago.[53] As Marilyn Arthur notes, 'The choral odes of the *Phoenissae* explain this connection between the city's present ills and the conditions of its foundation. They are organized in the form of a survey of the history of Thebes which leaves off only as the last chapter is about to be added in the form of an assault on the city and the duel between the brothers'.[54] (It is often remarked that Euripides' *Phoenician Women* and the eponymous chorus stand in marked and self-conscious contrast with Aeschylus' *Seven against Thebes*.[55] One wonders if there is a touch of competition also in Euripides' telescoping of the entire Theban tetralogy of 467 BC into the choral parts of a single play.[56]) So, not a series of independent songs interlaced one by one with the dramatic action, as the ancient critics quoted at the beginning of this paper would have wanted, nor the occasional pointless rambling that they saw in them, but rather steps in one long path of song that winds its way alongside the action and becomes conspicuous when the action recedes into the background only to bow out for a time when the action comes to the fore again. If the argument presented in the first half of this paper is correct and the Phoenician women present themselves in the *parodos* with a clear suggestion of choral characterisation, then this fact becomes easier to account for. The template of choral lyric is (granted) blown out of proportion and to some extent distorted, but its imprint is recognisable nonetheless.

But we should not stop here, as there is another level on which the model of choral lyric in action, as it were, is relevant to our understanding of what the Phoenician women do and why. If the argument made so far in this paper is ac-

---

[53] Riemschneider 1940, 16, 25. In his view, this 'Liederzyklus' includes the *parodos* and excludes the fourth *stasimon*. However, the latter is a natural end-point for the song cycle, whose retracing of Thebes' history since its foundation culminates in the present situation and its immediate future (the duel of Eteocles and Polynices and their mutual fratricide), in which the fourth *stasimon* is absorbed. This return to the present, however, provides far from a sense of closure: see below, pp. 313.
[54] Arthur 1977, 163–4; similarly Parry 1978, 167. On time, myth, and narrative in the choral sections of the *Phoenician Women* see Lamari 2010, chapters 2, 3, and 5 *passim*.
[55] See e.g. Rawson 1970, 112; Aélion 1983, I 197–227; Cerbo 1984–1985, 186; Foley 1985, 113–39; Hilton 2011, 28–46; Torrance 2013, 94–133.
[56] On the *Phoenician Women* as 'a Theban mythical 'megatext'' see Lamari 2010, 17, 135–7.

cepted, upon their arrival on the stage they characterise themselves as a choral offering sent by their Tyrian sovereigns to the sanctuary of Apollo in Delphi via Thebes. Two aspects of this endeavour need highlighting in this connection. Firstly, that the women's journey from Phoenicia to Greece is a mythically significant one; secondly, that the path of their song partly retraces this journey and plays out the complex relation between that myth (and others) and the present.[57] '[L]e voyage des Phéniciennes – writes Nancy – est une réédition: elles ont mis leurs pas, si l'on peut dire, dans ceux de leur ancêtre Cadmos, qui n'est autre que le fondateur de Thèbes'.[58] The opening of the first *stasimon* makes it clear (638–42):

> Κάδμος ἔμολε τάνδε γᾶν
> Τύριος, ὧι τετρασκελὴς
> μόσχος ἀδάματον πέσημα
> δίκε τελεσφόρον διδοῦσα
> χρησμόν ...

> Cadmus came to this land, the Tyrian man, for whom the four-legged calf fell to the ground without compulsion and gave fulfilment to the oracle ...

The deictic τάνδε brings Cadmus' journey into the chorus' present space, and the very location of this reference at the beginning of their extended myth-making casts him as the foundational figure to look to – for them no less than for Thebes. This passage stands in a triangular relationship with two other significant nodes of the play.[59] One is the opening of the *parodos*, which we examined above: both describe in similar language a journey from Tyre to a mythically charged present space (note 216 Καδμείων ἔμολον γᾶν),[60] thus establishing an implicit but clear link between Cadmus and the Phoenician chorus that retraces his steps in song no less than in deed. The other is the very beginning of the tragedy, where Jocasta describes Cadmus' journey from Phoenicia into the present space in terms which the opening of the first *stasimon* replicates almost verbatim (3–6):[61]

---

57 Arthur 1977, 166; Nancy 1986, 463.
58 Nancy 1986, 463.
59 See Riemschneider 1940, 25.
60 Mastronarde 1994, 334 (see also 8 and n. 2 on the 'arrival motif' more generally in the play).
61 There is a continuing controversy over whether the play opened with what is now line 1 or rather, as several ancient sources appear to suggest, with line 3 itself. See most recently Meccariello 2014 with references to earlier bibliography.

Ἥλιε, θοαῖς ἵπποισιν εἰλίσσων φλόγα,
ὡς δυστυχῆ Θήβαισι τῆι τόθ' ἡμέραι
ἀκτῖν' ἐφῆκας, Κάδμος ἡνίκ' ἦλθε γῆν (5)
τήνδ', ἐκλιπὼν Φοίνισσαν ἐναλίαν χθόνα.

Sun, who on swift mares drive your blaze around, how wretched was the beam you shed on Thebes that day when Cadmos came to this land, leaving the coastal soil of Phoenicia.

The parallel between Cadmus' arrival as described in the prologue and that of the chorus as described in the *parodos* validates and authorises the chorus' beginning of their narrative in Cadmus' name at the opening of the first *stasimon*. In turn, this nexus authorises the chorus' narrative in the *stasima* as a lens through which to reflect on the present situation of Thebes, echoing Jocasta's lengthy exposition in the prologue (though as an individual character she has, understandably, a more pressing concern for her immediate family) but enriching it with different and broader perspectives.[62] The Phoenician women's kinship with Thebes and its ruling house, which they emphasize repeatedly, especially during the early stages of the play (216–9, 243–9, 291–2, cf. 819), has a similarly authorising function for their utterances.[63]

But where does their chorality come in? Part of the answer, I suggest, lies in the well-established Greek practice of *theōria:* in Ian Rutherford's terse definition, 'extraterritorial religious activity in which a city-state or other political entity sends sacred delegates to act on its behalf '.[64] Such sacred delegations often included a chorus, whose task it was to perform upon reaching their destination (and, in some cases, at chosen points along the way too):[65] a choral offering consistent with the conceptualisation we examined earlier in this paper. Although not strictly identical to this practice, the sending of a group of women to a pan-Hellenic sanctuary as sacred dedications with an offering of song and dance distinctly resonates with it.[66]

Theōriai too are often represented as retracing (in either direction) a mythical journey, from which the delegation's own journey draws its *raison d'être*. A few examples variously related to Athens will suffice. The yearly Athenian mission to Delos was thought to retrace the steps of Theseus and the 'twice seven' at least as

---

[62] See Lamari 2010, 23–4, 41.
[63] Cerbo 1984–1985, 186; Nancy 1986, 464. See also Hilton 2011, 250–1 for the 'moral and intellectual authority' (251) displayed by the chorus at various stages in the play.
[64] Rutherford 2013, 4.
[65] On the choral component of *theōria* see Rutherford 2004; Kowalzig 2005 and 2007a *passim*; Rutherford 2013, 41–2, 237–49.
[66] On *theōria* as 'a kind of cultural metaphor through which to express inter-state relations' in Attic drama, especially comedy, see Kowalzig 2005, 60–1 (quotation from 61).

early as Plato, who claims that, 'as the Athenians say', the ship used by the *theōria* was the very one on which the hero and his companions had sailed (*Phaedo* 58a–b).[67] It can be argued that Bacchylides 17, though not an Athenian poem, suggests that this idea goes back at least to the first half of the fifth century.[68] An intriguing intersection of (envisaged) *theōria*, human dedication, mythical travelling, and song is testified by a fragment of Aristotle's *Constitution of the Bottiaeans* paraphrased twice by Plutarch (fr. 485 Rose *ap. Thes.* 16.2–3, *QG* 35 = *Mor.* 298f–299a). The treatise traces back the inhabitants of the northern Greek city of Bottiaea to the Athenian human tribute sent to Minos before Theseus' time. According to this myth, their descendants were later sent by the Cretans to Delphi as an ἀνδρῶν ἀπαρχή and subsequently migrated to Iapygia in present-day Italy before coming back to the Greek peninsula and settling in Bottiaea; and for this reason, Aristotle concludes, at one of their festivals the young women of Bottiaea sing ἴωμεν εἰς Ἀθήνας 'Let us go to Athens!'.[69] If Pindar's fifth *Paean* (D5 Rutherford) is an Athenian commission, as has been commonly maintained since its first publication,[70] its final part displays a similar preoccupation with mapping the chorus' theoric voyage to Delos onto the quasi-mythical Athenian colonisation of the Aegean isles that justifies it:[71]

>   Εὖ-]   (35)
>   βοιαν ἕλον καὶ ἔνασσαν·
>
> ἰήϊε Δάλι' Ἄπολλον·
> καὶ σποράδας φερεμήλους
> ἔκτισαν νάσους ἐρικυδέα τ' ἔσχον
> Δᾶλον, ἐπεί σφιν Ἀπόλλων   (40)
> δῶκεν ὁ χρυσοκόμας
>   Ἀστερίας δέμας οἰκεῖν·
>
> ἰήϊε Δάλι' Ἄπολλον·
> Λατόος ἔνθα με παῖδες
> εὐμενεῖ δέξασθε νόωι θεράποντα   (45)
> ὑμέτερον κελαδεννᾶι
> σὺν μελιγάρυϊ παι-
>   ᾶνος ἀγακλέος ὀμφᾶι.

---

67 On this and other Athenian *theōriai* to Delos see Rutherford 2004, 82–9; see also Kowalzig 2007a, 56–128.
68 See Kowalzig 2007a, 88–94, esp. 92.
69 See Rutherford 2004, 71–2.
70 Grenfell / Hunt 1908, 20; see also Rutherford 2001, 296–8; Kowalzig 2007a, 84. In Wilamowitz's opinion (1922, 327–8) it was a Euboean commission.
71 Rutherford 2001, 297; 2004, 83–5; 2013, 240–1; Kowalzig 2007a, 83–6.

... they took Euboea and settled it. *Ieie*, Delian Apollo! And they peopled the scatterd isles that bear flocks, and held famous Delos, since Apollo the gold-haired gave them the body of Asteria to inhabit. *Ieie*, Delian Apollo! There, children of Leto, welcome me, your servant, with kindly disposition, to the resounding, honey-voiced strain of a glorious paean.

In this last case, the parallel with the Phoenician women is particularly close, not least because the latter's journey too retraces and recalls a mythical path of colonisation. Another example worth citing is the Pythaïs, a state-sanctioned *theōria* sent by Athens to Delphi at irregular intervals since relatively early times.[72] The earliest explicit evidence for it is the so-called Nicomachus Calendar, compiled probably in the last decade of the fifth century on the basis of earlier religious legislation,[73] but an allusion to the Pythaïs can be detected already in the opening of Aeschylus' *Eumenides* (9–14 with schol. E 12, M 13 Smith), produced in 458 BC,[74] and it has been plausibly argued that a paean by Simonides – so no later than the first half of the century – is also connected with this rite (*PMG* 519 fr. 35(b).1–10 = fr. 100 Poltera).[75] While in Aeschylus' tragedy there is only a hint that the mythical episode in question – Apollo's landing in Attica and his march to Delphi escorted by an Athenian contingent – finds an echo in contemporary cult practice, Apollo's journey and that of the Pythaïs are explicitly identified by Ephorus in a passage quoted by Strabo (*BNJ* 70 F 31 *ap.* 9.3.12): ἐξ Ἀθηνῶν δ' ὁρμηθέντα ἐπὶ Δελφοὺς ταύτην ἰέναι τὴν ὁδόν, ᾗ νῦν Ἀθηναῖοι τὴν Πυθαΐδα πέμπουσι 'and when from Athens he set out to Delphi he journeyed on the very road on which the Athenians now send the Pythaïs'.[76] The 'paean and prosodion' composed by Limenius for choral performance by the Athenian 'Craftsmen of Dionysus' at a much later Pythaïs, probably in 128/7 or 106/5 BC (*CID* III 2 = *CA* pp. 149–59),[77] leaves implicit the connection between the mythical journey and the procession, but explicitly connects the former with the song

---

[72] On the Pythaïs see Boëthius 1918; Rutherford 2004, 76–81; Rutherford 2013, 222–30, 312–3, and *passim*.
[73] On the Nicomachus Calendar see most recently Parker 1996, 43–8; Lambert 2002. The data relevant to the Pythaïs are brought together by Rutherford 2013, 312–3, 376–7.
[74] Boëthius 1918, 31–7.
[75] Rutherford 1990, 173–6. Poltera 2008, 370 disagrees, on the argument that fr. 100 and fr. 102 (*PMG* 519 fr. 32) – probably a Delian poem, or at least one concerned with the Delian myth – 'were probably not far apart in the roll': Lobel 1959, 54.
[76] Πυθαΐδα is Radt's palmary emendation of the transmitted Πυθιάδα (2002–11: III 92); that the passage refers to the Pythaïs was already assumed by Boëthius 1918, 31, 35–6.
[77] On the poem see Bélis in *CID* III pp. 84–129; Vamvouri 1998; Furley / Bremer 2001, II 92–100. Bowie 2015b, 110–7 and Thomas 2015, 33–7 focus particularly on its spatial aspect. On the date see Bélis in *CID* III pp. 133–42 (assuming 128/7); Schroeder 1999, 71–4 (arguing for 106/5).

itself, for which it serves as an aetiology and which, accordingly, it validates (13–21):[78]

> τότε λιπὼγ Κυυνθίαν νᾶασον ἐπ[έβα θεό]ς πρῳ[τό-
> κα⟨α⟩ρπὸγ κλυτὰν Ἀτθίδ' ἐπὶ γαα[λόφωι   ] Τριτωωνίδος·
> μελίπνοον δὲ Λίβυς αὐδὰγ χέω[ν λωτὸς ἀνέμελ]πεν [ἀ-
> δεῖειαν ὄπα μειγνύμενος αἰειόλ[οις κιθάρι]ο̣[ς μέλεσιν,
> ἅ]μα δ' ἴαχεμ πετροκατοίκητος ἀχ[ὼ παιὰν ἰὲ παιάν.] Ὁ δὲ̣ γέγα-
> θ' ὅτι νόωι δεξάμενος ἀαμβρόταν δω̣[   ]γ, ἀνθ' ὥων
> ἐκείνας ἀπ' ἀρχᾶς Παιήονα κικλῄισκ[ομεν   ] λᾳὸς αὐτ̣[ο-
> χθόνων ἠδὲ Βάκχου μέγας θυρσοπλὴ[ξ ἑσμὸς ἱ]ερὸς τεχνι-
> τῶων ἔνοικοος πόλει Κεκροπίαι.

Then, leaving the Cynthian island, the god reached the glorious land of the first crop, Attica, on the hilly ... of Tritonis. The Libyan reed poured its honey-breathing voice and sang a sweet strain, mingling with the varied tunes of the *kithara*, and at the same time the echo that dwelt in the rock rang out, 'Paean ie Paean!' And he rejoiced because he understood the immortal ... Therefore since that primeval time we call on Paean, we the ... indigenous people and the great thyrsos-stricken holy swarm of the Craftsmen which lives in Cecrops' city.

As we have seen, the journey of the Phoenician women, like the Pythaïs, is a mythically significant one. If anything, on the play's own terms their mid-way stop in Thebes seems to be *more* significant, from this point of view, than their envisaged end-point in Delphi. It is incorrect to imply, as sometimes is done, that their true destination was Delphi and they merely got stranded in Thebes more or less by chance on their way there. Firstly, the chorus leader's statement at lines 282–3 explicitly contradict this view: 'the sons of Agenor's sons sent me *here*, spoils of the spear for Phoebus'. Secondly, attention should be paid to the first strophe of the *parodos*, lines 208–11, where the chorus describe their voyage through the 'Ionian Sea' with the West Wind blowing over Sicily. This ostensibly counter-intuitive itinerary has led to (in Donald Mastronarde's words) 'a great deal of nonsense',[79] which there is no point in rehearsing here; as he has shown, a route clockwise around the Peloponnese is a perfectly reasonable solution for anyone wanting to sail to Delphi coming from the east, even more so in the light of the precedent offered by the *Homeric Hymn to Apollo* (404–43).[80] But this itinerary also creates a further effect. If one is sailing to Delphi across the Ionian Sea, Thebes is not on one's way; one can simply dis-

---

78 See Vamvouri 1998, 56–7; Rutherford 2004, 81; Bowie 2015b, 116.
79 Mastronarde 1994, 210.
80 Mastronarde 1994, 209–10.

embark at Cirrha and walk the few miles up to Delphi from there. So if the Phoenician women have sailed that way and now find themselves in Thebes, it means they were positively going to Thebes as much as to Delphi.[81] Despite the obvious divarication of their spatial (and temporal) perspective, which conspicuously encompasses their Delphic destination and their Phoenician origin as well as their present location,[82] the centrality of Thebes in their journey – not only in the play as such – ought not to be allowed to slip out of sight.

As John Gould recognised, collective memory is key to the chorus' engagement with Thebes, even more than kinship per se: 'From the first *stasimon* to the last, the memory of the chorus plays over, and their songs rehearse, the long history of Thebes'.[83] This provides a stark contrast with the individual characters (with the partial exception of Jocasta and Tiresias); the Phoenician women are 'far more firmly conscious of the rootedness of the play's events than are the heroic protagonists'.[84] This contrast in attitude is mirrored by the drastically limited amount of actual interaction between the chorus and the characters during most of the play, noted by Enrico Medda and especially glaring in the finale, where an elaborate lamentation such as the one sung by Antigone and Oedipus could have been expected to include a more substantial choral element than the handful of anapaests at 1480 – 4.[85] For all its knowledge of Theban myth, Medda argues, this 'estranged' chorus behaves like an external observer who has no business intervening in the action.[86] For the most part, the Phoenician women speak to the audience, not to the characters in the play; indeed they come close to being an internal spectator of the dramatic action, suspended between detachment and involvement and possessed of a broader viewpoint than any of the characters have.[87] Still, their detachment should not be overplayed: their rel-

---

[81] Compare the reconstruction proposed by Mastronarde 1994, 209 – 10 (the chorus made their way to Thebes in order for their Theban kin to escort them to Delphi from there).
[82] See Arthur 1977, 169; Calame 1994 – 1995, 144; Lamari 2010, 43 – 8, 167 – 9.
[83] Gould 1996, 225.
[84] Gould 1996, 225. See also Foley 2003, 21 – 2; Medda 2005, 128 – 9.
[85] Medda 2005, 126 – 8. See also Arthur 1977, 165; Cerbo 1984 – 1985, 189; Foley 1985, 139 – 40. Medda notes the expectations raised by the futures ἰαχήσω and θρηνήσω in the fourth *stasimon* (1295, 1303) and subsequently frustrated.
[86] Medda 2005, 129. See also the slightly different argument put forward by Hilton 2011, 252, who highlights rather the chorus' powerlessness – 'their role as victims in a war over which they have no control'.
[87] Medda 2005, 129 – 30. Compare Murnaghan's argument on the metatheatrical function performed by the chorus of the *Bacchae* and the 'shadow chorus' of Theban women that joins them: 'Euripides gives us two models of choral experience, and so presents within tragedy the terms of a debate about the role of the chorus and the closeness of its relationship to the

ative lack of personal involvement with the individual characters does not belie their deep, ancestral involvement with Thebes, her mythical history, and her destiny – with Thebes as cultural patrimony, one might say, or cultural inheritance, more than as a physical place or civic community.[88]

The Phoenician women's intimated characterisation as a theoric chorus is instrumental to their 'combination of foreignness and remote kinship' (Foley)[89] and to the complex and peculiar role that they take up in the play. As we have seen, a theoric chorus is naturally invested with the task of performing links between time and time, place and place. And what the Phoenician women perform, with their songs and their long journey, is the thread that links Thebes and Phoenicia, their present and their past.[90] After the almost idyllic association of dancing with Dionysiac worship at the close of the strophe of the first *stasimon* (655–7), song and dance are repeatedly evoked as a foil for the horrors of Thebes' history, which are explicitly characterised by a lack of music or by its perversion. Ares is Βρομίου παράμουσος ἑορταῖς 'out of tune with the festivals of Bromius' (785) and does not partake in (fulsomely described) choral songs, leading instead a κῶμον ἀναυλότατον 'utterly pipe-less revel' (790); the Sphinx came ἀμουσοτάταισι σὺν ὠιδαῖς 'with most unmusical songs' (807) and ἄλυρον ἀμφὶ μοῦσαν 'on a lyre-less tune' (1028), giving rise to songs of mourning throughout the city (1033–8). As Nancy notes, the chorus implicitly counters this unmusicality with its own song and dance as well as by the alternative histories that it narrates.[91] But musical resistance can only go so far. Once they have finally rejoined the present and faced its sheer horror in the fourth *stasimon*, the Phoenician women and their song all but fade from sight.[92] In this light, their iridescent song-cycle and its strange relation to the events in the play can also serve as a *mise en abyme* of mythical narrative and its relation to the present, of the poetic act and its relation to the world. By reference to the all-pervasive medium of choral song in one of its most solemn, liturgical manifestations, Euripides is able to enrich his play with further perspectives and meanings – and perhaps to reflect, and invite reflection, on the possibilities and limits of tragedy itself.

---

main actors that we still struggle with' (2006, 100). Arguably, also the chorus of the *Phoenician Women* can be viewed from a similar metatheatrical angle.
88 Cf. Gould 1996, 225.
89 Foley 1985, 119 n. 25.
90 Cf. Aélion 1983, I 210, who notes 'cette façon d'utiliser le chœur pour voyager à travers le temps'. On time and space in the *Phoenician Women* see Lamari 2010, chapter 5.
91 Nancy 1986, 471–4, see also Di Benedetto 1971, 261.
92 Cf. Arthur 1977, 165.

Naomi A. Weiss
Performing the Wedding Song in Euripides' *Iphigenia in Aulis*

Greek tragedy was, to a large extent, musical theater. The spoken dialogue in each play was punctuated by big song-and-dance numbers performed by the chorus (occasionally by an actor), and these must have been some of the most memorable parts of the show, just as they are for modern audiences of Broadway, Bollywood, opera, and musical television dramas. Unfortunately, however, tragedy's *mousikē*—a word that conveys the totality of song, music, and dance—is almost entirely lost to us, its modern readers. We have two surviving scraps of papyri that show musically notated lyrics from *Orestes* and *Iphigenia in Aulis*, yet these cover only a few lines of choral song and tell us little about the musical design of a whole tragedy.[1] Through the comments on and parodies of Aeschylean and Euripidean lyric in Aristophanes' comedies we have a glimpse of the impact of these tragedians' different styles (at least on a late fifth-century Athenian audience), but we still have only very limited access to the *mousikē* itself.[2] And while we might be able to grasp something of the effect of *mousikē* in the performance of tragedy by likening it to our own experience of musical theater, we do not really have a contemporary dramatic tradition similar to the mix of actors' dialogue and choral performance that characterizes Athenian theater.

A similar version of this essay appears in chapter 5, section 3 of my book, *The Music of Tragedy: Performance and Imagination in Euripidean Theater* (University of California Press, 2018).

1 For a transcription and description of these two papyri, see West 1992, 284–87, Pöhlmann/West 2001, 12–21. They both demonstrate Euripides' use of *melisma* (the practice of extending a syllable over more than one note), which is also highlighted in the parody of his choral lyric in Aristophanes' *Frogs* (1314). In addition, the *Orestes* papyrus demonstrates that melody could be divorced from the words' pitch accent in Euripidean strophic lyric. D'Angour 2006, 276–83 hypothesizes that this practice was the result of New Musical experimentation in the late fifth century BC, culminating in Euripides 'breaking free of the traditional principles of matching word pitch with musical pitch in the responsional choruses of tragic drama' (p.282).
2 See esp. Ar. *Ran.* 1298–363. Other evidence for tragic *mousikē* includes Plato's complaints about New Musical styles (e.g. *Leg.* 669cd, 700d; cf. *Rep.* 397a); Aristotle's brief mention of *melopoiia* in *Poetics* (which I discuss below), as well as his much lengthier discussion of the types of *harmoniai*, melodies, rhythms, and instruments to be used in 'theatrical *mousikē*' in *Politics* (1339b-42b); and a few possible images of tragic choruses on Attic vases (numerous representations of scenes from tragedies survive on South Italian vases from the fourth century, but these do not include musical performances).

We also lack (at least in contemporary Western European and Northern American society) a song culture comparable to that of fifth-century Athens, where *choreia* (choral song and dance) frequently occurred both within and outside of the theater, and most citizens within the audience had previously themselves been choral performers.[3] We are therefore left with just the text of the plays themselves.

The surviving tragedies are not, however, entirely silent. Many of them, particularly a cluster of tragedies from the last two decades of Euripides' career, contain an extraordinary amount of metamusical language—that is, the chorus and actors describe scenes of music-making while they themselves are singing and dancing. While we should not assume a one-to-one relationship between such performances described in song and the live ones in the theater, the simultaneity of the two must have been designed to encourage the audience to link them together in certain ways. The aim of this chapter is to show the dramatic effects of this sort of interplay between imagined and performed *mousikē* in the third *stasimon* of *Iphigenia in Aulis*, one of the Euripides' very latest plays.[4] This song not only abounds in musical images but is also framed as a particular type of musical performance itself—that of a *hymenaios* (wedding song). Yet despite the ways in which it evokes this genre, both in performance and through drawing on the traditional imaginary of hymeneal *choreia*, the ode ultimately is not—*cannot*—be a *hymenaios* itself, and it is this disturbing disconnect that I wish to draw out here.

I begin with a broader discussion of how we can approach the *mousikē* of tragedy, and situate my analysis of this ode from *Iphigenia in Aulis* within broader scholarship on musical trends in the late fifth century BC. The main part of this essay is a close reading of the song itself, alongside various comparanda from nondramatic lyric that help to shed light on Euripides' deployment of hymeneal motifs and styles of performance. I then compare the ode to other songs from the tragedian's later work: first the 'Achilles Ode' from *Electra*, which follows a similar pattern of 'narrative followed by application'; then Cassandra's frenzied monody from *Troades*, which, like the third *stasimon* of *Iphigenia in Aulis*, is a distorted *hymenaios* that underscores the absence of a 'real' one.

---

[3] On ancient Greek song-culture and its connection with the Athenian audience's experience of tragedy, see Herington 1985, 3–5; Bacon 1994; Revermann 2006a. On the likelihood that many of the citizens in the audience would themselves have performed in a Dionysiac chorus (dithyrambic or dramatic), see Gagné/Hopman 2013b, 26.

[4] The play was posthumously produced, probably in 405 BC: according to schol. on Ar. *Ran.* 66–7 (= *TrGF*[1] DID C 22), it appeared in a tetralogy that included *Bacchae* and *Alcmeon in Corinth*.

1 Approaching tragic *mousikē*

Until recently, the musical element of tragedy was largely ignored in Classical scholarship. This neglect of such an important component of the genre is partly a result of how little evidence we have for it, but it also stems from Aristotle, who says very little about the role of *mousikē* in his *Poetics* and famously claims that, as in the case of epic, one can appreciate a tragedy's effects simply through reading it.⁵ He also calls tragedy's lyric element (*melopoiia*) one of its 'seasonings' (*hēdusmata*), secondary in importance to plot (*mythos*), character, thought, and diction; spectacle (*opsis*) comes last of all (1450a8-b20).⁶ 'Seasonings' could actually be more important than we might at first assume: for a Middle Eastern meal in particular, the seasonings are absolutely crucial for giving meat taste;⁷ in the context of tragedy, Aristotle's culinary metaphor of *hēdusmata* applies to the elements of tragedy that produce pleasure (*hēdonē*), which would be vital for a drama's success in the theater.⁸ In general, however, Aristotle is much more interested in the more cerebral aspects of tragedy, at least in this surviving book of the *Poetics*.⁹

A particularly influential passage of the *Poetics* in terms of scholarly views on choral song in tragedy is Aristotle's brief and rather confusing criticism of a recent trend of including odes that he calls *embolima*—songs that are 'thrown in' without any relevance to their dramatic context (Arist. Poet. 1456a25–31). Although he states that the chorus should be 'part of the whole' and integrated within the action of the play (μόριον εἶναι τοῦ ὅλου καὶ συναγωνίζεσθαι), he

---

5 Arist. Poet. 1462a10–11, 17. See also the introduction to this volume.
6 This ranking does not, however, mean that Aristotle disregards the impact of *mousikē* and *opsis* altogether: indeed, in the final chapter of *Poetics* he explicitly states that they play 'no small part' in a tragedy (οὐ μικρὸν μέρος, 1462a15).
7 Cf. Sifakis 2001, who argues that Aristotle uses the metaphor of ἡδύσματα to refer to essential ingredients of tragedy, since music is a form of ethical characterization (56–70).
8 At 1462a15–6 Aristotle explicitly states that *mousikē* and *opsis* produce the most vivid pleasures (...τὴν μουσικὴν καὶ τὰς ὄψεις, δι' ἃς αἱ ἡδοναὶ συνίστανται ἐναργέστατα), though he goes on to claim that tragedy has such vividness in reading as well as performance.
9 It is possible that Aristotle expanded on the subject of tragedy's musical component elsewhere, since in the *Politics* he refers to '[the work] on the art of poetry' (τὰ περὶ ποιητικῆς) for a discussion of *catharsis* as one of the functions of *mousikē* (1341b40). This may have been part of the second book of the *Poetics* or a lost portion of the *Politics*: see Halliwell 1986, 190–1; Kraut 1997, 209; Sifakis 2001, 54, 166 n. 1. Given his examination in the last book of the *Politics* of the potent, soul-changing effects of *mousikē* within education and leisure in general (1339a11–1342b35, esp. 1339e43–1340b19), it seems rather unlikely that he would not have appreciated its role within tragedy.

does not elaborate on why he deems Sophocles to be particularly successful in this respect, nor does he clarify whether or not Euripides is guilty of composing such *embolima*. Following this passage of the *Poetics*, however, it was often argued in nineteenth and twentieth century scholarship on tragedy that the chorus becomes increasingly irrelevant in Euripides' plays, and that several of the choral odes in his later work are representative of the *embolima* criticized by Aristotle.[10] The idea of these as self-contained musical performances that are disconnected from a play's *mythos* also contributed to the standard view that the tragic chorus' role and significance steadily declined towards the end of the fifth century BC and into the fourth, especially as more and more lyric was assigned to actors.[11]

Though the idea that particular choral odes are irrelevant to the surrounding drama is now generally out of fashion, the last two decades have seen a related surge of interest in the so-called New Music, the umbrella term referring to changes in musical style, performance, instruments, and language through the fifth century. Eric Csapo in particular has pointed us towards Euripides' New Musical experimentation, and this seems to be especially clear in those same choral odes of his later plays (including the third *stasimon* of *Iphigenia in Aulis*), which often contain strikingly metamusical language.[12] Several of such odes are often called 'dithyrambic' in modern scholarship, in large part because they seem to be free-standing narratives like dithyrambs were. 'Dithyrambic' therefore tends (somewhat misleadingly) to be used as virtually a synonym for Aristotle's *embolima*, the songs that are just 'thrown in', and the labels 'dithyrambic' and New Musical become almost interchangeable, since the dithyrambic genre was one of the sites of particularly great musical experimentation and novelty, and such songs often include vivid descriptions of musical performance.[13] As Csapo has shown, 'dithyrambic' or New Musical songs often include highly self-referential descriptions of *mousikē*, and in particular highlight both the *aulos*—the double pipe that accompanied dithyrambic and dramatic choruses

---

10 On increasing choral irrelevance in Euripides and his 'self-contained' choral odes, see e.g. Schlegel 1846, 299; Kranz 1933, 228–62, esp. 251–4; Helg 1950, 53–7; Pohlenz 1954, 440; Lesky 1971, 454; Panagl 1971; Rode 1971, 111–3. For a discussion of this tradition of scholarship, see Neitzel 1967, 5–7; Csapo 1999–2000, Battezzato 2008, 161, 164.
11 On the rise of the actor's song in tragedy during this period, see esp. Csapo 1999–2000, 409–12; Hall 1999, 2002.
12 On Euripides and the New Music, see esp. Kranz 1933; Panagl 1971; Csapo 1999–2000; 2003, 71–4; 2008; 2009; Wilson 1999–2000; Steiner 2011.
13 The dithyramb was by no means the only genre to exhibit such a self-conscious display of musicality. Satyr play and *kitharoidia* in particular can be highly metamusical: see esp. Power 2010: 500–49, 2013, and in this volume; Griffith 2013b; LeVen 2014.

—and circular choreography with verbs like ἑλίσσω ('whirl'). They also tend to refer to archetypal dancing figures and choral groups such as dolphins and Nereids; the latter are usually fifty in number, just like a dithyrambic chorus was.

Scholarship on the New Musical character of Euripides' work has been extremely valuable in turning our attention to tragedy's *mousikē* by linking it to extradramatic trends within Athens' broader sociocultural landscape. As a result, however, Euripides' musical innovation tends to be viewed independently from the more traditional aspects of his *mousikē*, notably the employment of established lyric genres like *partheneion* (maiden's song), *hymenaios* (wedding song), and *epinikia* (victory song), elements of which, as Laura Swift has shown, frequently appear in his tragedies, as well as those of Aeschylus and Sophocles.[14] The focus on New Music in late fifth-century tragedy can also perpetuate a sense of the increasing disengagement of tragic *mousikē* from its dramatic context, so that we are left with the question: what did the music and dance *do* within a tragedy? Given that Aristotle ranks *melopoiia* among the tragedy's constitutive parts, we must assume that it was an integral and powerful element of any performance. What effect, then, might it have had on the audience? And was the *mousikē* of Euripides' late tragedies really as removed from the *mythos* as is so commonly assumed?

To answer these questions, we must consider the dramatic role of the plays' richly metamusical language and its relationship with the live musical performance in the theater. This combination of music and the musical imaginary could produce a doubling effect, whereby the audience would simultaneously experience two registers of *mousikē*, which can be either in harmony or in dissonance with each other.[15] When the chorus sing about the *aulos* (double pipe), for example, their description must have been intensified by the sound of this instrument, the chorus' accompaniment, in the theater. Images of other instruments may either be complemented by the auletic accompaniment or create a deliberately uncomfortable auditory disconnect between the musical description and actual performance. This sort of merging of different registers of *mousikē* can be called

---

14 Swift 2010. Of course the dithyramb (which Swift does not discuss) was also a traditional choral genre, but the extensive employment of dithyrambic imagery and even styles of performance in tragedy seems primarily to have been a late fifth-century phenomenon. See Battezzato 2013 for a recent analysis of dithyramb and tragedy. On the incorporation of traditional styles and motifs within a display of musical innovation, see LeVen 2014: she demonstrates how the New Musical poets combine old and new in constructing their position within a lyric tradition.
15 This phenomenon has been examined by several scholars in the field of Sound Studies, in terms of the mix of imagined and perceived sound: see e.g. Handel 1989, 181–2; Smith 1999: 242–5; Ihde 2003.

choral projection, the term originally coined by Albert Henrichs to describe moments when choruses refer to other singing and dancing choral groups beyond the world of the play itself.[16] We can also see it as part of a broader process of imaginative suggestion through *choreia*, whereby the audience are encouraged to see and hear the *mousikē* in the theater as (or in contrast to) the *mousikē* described in song.

2 Imagined and performed *mousikē* in *Iphigenia in Aulis*

Iphigenia in Aulis, like *Bacchae*, contains a striking accumulation of allusions to and descriptions of *mousikē* that play into its actual performance, from the chorus' description of Paris playing his *syrinx* (panpipes) in the first *stasimon* to Iphigenia's musical exchange with the chorus in what was probably meant to be the closing scene of the tragedy.[17] The climax of such (meta)musicality is the third *stasimon*, in which the chorus vividly describe the wedding celebrations of Achilles' parents, Peleus and Thetis. This ode has in the past been seen as a typical example of one of Euripides' 'dithyrambic' songs and of the new types of tragic odes that Aristotle labeled *embolima*.[18] But a close analysis of the use of hymeneal *mousikē* (wedding song and dance) in this ode, both in its actual performance and in its musical imaginary, can demonstrate the ways in which the song might be embedded within the dramatic fabric of the tragedy through its very musicality. As I hope the following close reading of the ode also makes clear, even in his latest tragedies Euripides combines both new and traditional *mousikē:* such moments of intensely self-conscious musicality draw on traditional images of music-making and *choreia* just as much as they showcase the tragedian's innovative skill, suggesting that we should view his innovation in terms of a nuanced mix of generic motifs and new styles of language and performance.[19]

The chorus perform this intensely metamusical ode at a point of uncertain hope in the play: Iphigenia and her mother, Clytemnestra, have arrived at Aulis in the expectation of a marriage ceremony for Iphigenia and Achilles,

---

16 Henrichs 1994–1995, 1996.
17 On this passage of the first *stasimon*, see Weiss forthcoming. On the antiphonal performance at the end of the play, see Weiss 2014.
18 See esp. Kranz 1933, 254–9; Panagl 1971, 208–22. Csapo 1999–2000, 421 notes its dithyrambic and New Musical language.
19 Cf. LeVen 2011, 2014 on New Musical poets' 'rhetoric of tradition'.

but have discovered that Agamemnon has summoned them there in order to sacrifice the girl so that the Greek army can depart for Troy. In the scene immediately preceding the chorus' ode, however, Achilles has confidently claimed that he will be able to persuade Agamemnon not to sacrifice Iphigenia, even if Clytemnestra's attempts to do so fail. The chorus then sing of the wedding of Peleus and Thetis, thus inviting us to suspend disbelief and to imagine the happy marriage of Achilles and Iphigenia. By transporting us to a scene that is so at odds with the dramatic reality, however, their song also works to undermine Achilles' hollow promises and to intensify our expectation of Iphigenia's imminent death, since we all know that she is indeed going to be sacrificed.

This song is full of language about *mousikē*—instrumental, vocal, and choreographic. The opening strophe in particular abounds in self-reflexive descriptions of movement and sound, which would at the same time be partly or allusively performed by the chorus as they themselves sing and dance in the theater:

τίν' ἄρ' Ὑμέναιος διὰ λωτοῦ Λίβυος
μετά τε φιλοχόρου κιθάρας
συρίγγων θ' ὑπὸ καλαμοεσ-
　σᾶν ἔστασεν ἰαχάν,
ὅτ' ἀνὰ Πήλιον αἱ καλλιπλόκαμοι　　　　　　　　　　　　　　　　(1040)
Πιερίδες †ἐν δαιτὶ θεῶν†
χρυσεοσάνδαλον ἴχνος
ἐν γᾶι κρούουσαι
Πηλέως ἐς γάμον ἦλθον,
μελωιδοῖς Θέτιν ἀχήμασι τόν τ' Αἰακίδαν　　　　　　　　　　　　(1045)
Κενταύρων ἐν ὄρεσι κλέουσαι
Πηλιάδα καθ' ὕλαν;
ὁ δὲ Δαρδανίδας, Διὸς
λέκτρων τρύφημα φίλον,　　　　　　　　　　　　　　　　　　　　(1050)
χρυσέοισιν ἄφυσσε λοι-
　βὰν ἐκ κρατήρων γυάλοις
ὁ Φρύγιος Γανυμήδης.
παρὰ δὲ λευκοφαῆ ψάμαθον
εἱλισσόμεναι κύκλια　　　　　　　　　　　　　　　　　　　　　　(1055)
πεντήκοντα κόραι Νηρέως
γάμους ἐχόρευσαν.[20]

What wedding hymn was it that raised its cry amid the Libyan pipe and along with the chorus-loving *kithara* [lyre] and to the accompaniment of the reedy *syrinxes* [panpipes], when, along the ridge of Mount Pelion, at the feast of the gods, the beautiful-haired Pierians, beating their golden-sandaled foot on the earth, came to the marriage of Peleus, celebrating with melodious strains Thetis and the son of Aeacus, in the mountains of the Centaurs,

---

[20] All quotations from Euripides' *Iphigenia in Aulis* are taken from Diggle (OCT 1994).

down through the woods of Pelion? And the Dardanian boy, the dear darling of Zeus' bed, drew off the libation wine amid the golden hollows from the mixing bowls, the Phrygian Ganymede. And along the gleaming white sand, whirling in circles, the fifty daughters of Nereus celebrated the marriage in dance. (1036–57)

This initial image of the sounds of multiple instruments accompanying the cry of the wedding song immediately establishes a correspondence between the chorus' own performance and the one they describe, since they too are raising their voices in song to instrumental accompaniment, the music of the *aulos*. As in other choral odes in Euripides' later plays, the 'Libyan *lōtos*' in the first line of this song denotes the *aulos* itself.[21] The 'chorus-loving' (φιλόχορος) *kithara* and 'reedy' (καλαμόεις) *syrinx* would probably not have been on stage— they belong to the imagined *mousikē* of the song—but for the audience they could also merge with and be encompassed by the sound of the *aulos* that they actually hear. The *aulos* would be well suited to such acoustic representation, since it was long associated with mimetic flexibility: Pindar, for example, describes its tune as 'every-sound' (πάμφωνος), while in Plato's *Republic* it is this trait that causes Socrates to exclude makers and players of the *aulos* from the city; Plato's condemnation of it as 'the most many-stringed' instrument (πολυχορδότατος), in addition to referring to its capacity for modulation, may also suggest its (perceived) ability even to imitate an instrument like the *kithara*.[22] The chorus of *Iphigenia in Aulis* draw on the conceptualization of the *aulos* as an especially mimetic instrument earlier in the tragedy too, when in the first *stasimon* they suggest an imitative overlap of the *aulos* and *syrinx* with the image of Paris playing on his pipes on Mount Ida:

†ἔμολες, ὦ Πάρις, ᾗτε σύ γε†
βουκόλος ἀργενναῖς ἐτράφης
Ἰδαίαις παρὰ μόσχοις, (575)
βάρβαρα συρίζων, Φρυγίων
αὐλῶν Ὀλύμπου καλάμοις
μιμήματα †πνέων†.

---

21 On the 'Libyan *lōtos*' see Barker 1984, 67 n.34; 268 n.38; Biehl 1989, 234–5; West 1994, 113 n.145. Cf. Eur. *Hel.* 170–71, *IA* 1036. For just *lōtos* as a designation for the *aulos*, cf. Eur. *Heracl.* 892, *El.* 716, *Phoen.* 787, *Bacc.* 160, *IA* 438, *Erechtheus* fr. 370 *TrGF⁵*, line 8; also Pind. fr. 94b SM, line 14. See also Theoph. *Hist. Plant* 4.3.3–4 on the Libyan *lōtos* as an apt material for *auloi*; also Ath. 14. 618b-c on why the *aulos* is called Libyan.
22 Pind. *Pyth.* 12.19, *Ol.* 7.12, *Isth.* 5.27; Pl. *Rep.* 399d; cf. *Leg.* 669c-e. On the conceptualization of the *aulos* as the most mimetic instrument, see esp. Wilson 1999, 87–93; Weiss forthcoming.

You came, Paris, to the place where you were reared as a herdsman among the shining white heifers of Mount Ida, piping foreign tunes on the *syrinx*, breathing on the reeds imitations of the Phrygian *auloi* of Olympus.[23]

As in this previous song, the merging of imagined and performed *mousikē* at the very start of the third *stasimon* has the effect of transporting the audience immediately into this vivid scene of the past, making them not only hear about such *mousikē* but experience it too.

Following this intensely acoustic beginning, perfectly coordinated and highly attractive choral dance takes over from the instrumental accompaniment as the song's focus: the Muses with their beautiful hair (καλλιπλόκαμοι, 1040) beat their golden-sandaled feet on the ground in unison, while they sing in praise of Peleus and Thetis.[24] The attraction of the Muses' *choreia* then becomes erotically charged as the focus soon shifts from them to Ganymede, Zeus' beautiful plaything, whose golden mixing bowl corresponds with the gold of their feet (1049–53).[25]

The chorus of Muses seems to have been traditionally included in representations of the marriage of Peleus and Thetis, often with an emphasis on their beauty and attractiveness: in Pindar *Nemean* 5, for example, the κάλλιστος χορός of Muses sing to the accompaniment of Apollo's lyre (18–43); in *Pythian* 3 both Peleus and Cadmus are said to have enjoyed at their weddings the 'golden-crowned Muses singing in the mountains' (χρυσαμπύκων / μελπομενᾶν ἐν ὄρει Μοισᾶν, 89–90).[26] As in those songs, the chorus in Euripides' ode present an image of pro-

---

[23] In my translation of lines 576–8 I follow that of Kovacs 2002, 223, but the alternative given by Barker 1984, 92 ('breathing imitations of Olympus on the reeds of Phrygian auloi') is also possible. The broadly suggestive ambiguity of the grammar here is surely deliberate so as to effect a crossover of the two instruments. On the perceived intimacy of the *aulos* and *syrinx*, see Weiss forthcoming.
[24] Cf. the description of the Muses as καλλίκομοι in Sappho fr. 128 Voigt and of Dawn as χρυσοπέδιλλος in frr. 103 and 123. On the attractiveness of the Muses here, see Panagl 1971, 211.
[25] Cf. Barlow 1971, 112 on the correspondence of different 'dazzling impressions' in this scene. See also Michelini 2000, 53: '[t]hese moments of glowing, ideal beauty belong to the legendary and lyrical view of the erotic.' The erotic focus of Ganymede with his golden bowl may recall that of Aphrodite in Sappho fr. 2 Voigt, whom the singer bids to pour nectar χρυσίαισιν ἐν κυλίκεσσιν (14). On the erotic potential of *choreia*, see Kurke 2012, 2013.
[26] Note too the presence of the Muses in the scene of the wedding of Peleus and Thetis on the François Vase and the Sophilos Dinos (both Attic black figure from the late sixth century BC): see Stewart 1983, 62 for a list of the figures shown on each vase. See also Theogn. 15–7 (the Graces and Muses at Cadmus' wedding). Both Graces and Muses also appear, apparently in connection with wedding song, in Sappho fr. 103 Voigt, a highly fragmentary wedding song; Contiades-Tsitsoni 1990, 71–91, suggests that the mythical marriage is that of Hebe and Heracles (*ibid* 82).

totypical *choreia*, through which the audience can momentarily see and hear the choral dancing in the theater as divine, merging with that of the Muses. The chorus also focus on the Muses' song, their *hymenaios* for Peleus and Thetis, emphasizing its 'melodious strains' (μελωιδοῖς...ἀχήμασι, 1045) as well as its content. The Muses' *choreia* thus fuses with that of the dramatic chorus, not only in dance but also in song, as both choruses, imagined and performing, sing a song in celebration of Peleus and Thetis. Through the process of imaginative suggestion all three registers of *mousikē*—instrumental accompaniment, song, and dance—seem to correspond with the chorus' own performance in the theater.[27]

At the end of the strophe the spotlight shifts to dancing once again, but now a new choral group takes over from the Muses: the fifty Nereids, Thetis' sisters, are described as 'whirling in circles' in their dance (εἱλισσόμεναι κύκλια...ἐχόρευσαν, 1055–57). This is one of the most explicitly choreographic descriptions in all of Euripides, and the clearest textual stage direction for the dramatic chorus to dance with similarly circular movement, whether twirling on the spot or joining hands in concentric circles (or a mixture of both).[28] It is also an example of Euripides' New Musical or 'dithyrambic' style, which, as I mentioned at the start of my discussion, often includes both dancing Nereids and vocabulary denoting circular dancing (especially the verb ἑλίσσειν, which is used here).[29] At this moment, then, the dramatic chorus, presumably also dancing in circles, would be fusing themselves through their performance with the Nereids, just as they had previously done with the Muses. Through dance the performance space is transformed too: the 'gleaming sand' (λευκοφαῆ ψάμαθον, 1054) beside which the Nereids dance becomes the floor of the *orchēstra*. The inclusion of the fifty dancing Nereids here may be a marker of Euripides' innovative *mousikē* at the end of his career; it is also a very apt addition to the narrative of the wedding of Peleus and Thetis, since the bride herself is one of Nereus' daughters.

As we have already seen, the chorus' reenactment of the celebrations for Peleus and Thetis through their own musical performance, which merges with the

---

[27] Cf. Panagl 1971, 210, who thinks the Muses are the musicians as well as the dancers: '[a]uf der Schilderung der Klänge folgt also der Auftritt der göttlichen Musikantinnen, die wie der Dramenchor in seinen Liedern – als Göttinnen natürlich in gleicher Person – zu den instrumentalen Tönen den von Inhalt erfüllten, konkreten Gesang treten lassen'. See also *ibid.* 213 on the combination of dancing and instrumental and vocal sound.

[28] The combination of ἑλίσσω and κύκλος only occurs in the surviving plays of Euripides: *Hel.* 1362–3, *IT* 1103–4. It also occurs twice in actors' spoken lines, but with a less obviously choreographic reference: *Pho.* 1185–6 (the messenger describing Capaneus' death) and *Or.* 444 (Orestes telling Menelaus that he is surrounded by hostile Argives).

[29] On this verb see also the discussion by Andújar in this volume.

described *mousikē* in their song, is similar to other lyric descriptions of this prototypical marriage ceremony. The account of the chorus of Muses in Pindar's *Nemean* 5 offers a particularly noteworthy parallel, with multiple interactions between the mythic narrative and the present choral performance: not only does the κάλλιστος χορός correspond with the choral performance of the epinician, but the figure of Apollo playing on his phorminx in the middle (ἐν δὲ μέσαις, 24) is like the *chorēgos* in the center of the circular chorus.[30] The Muses' performance and that of the epinician even merge into one as the ode continues, since Pindar does not indicate an end to the prototypical song.[31] We also have several similar visual representations of this famous marriage. The best preserved of these is Kleitias' François Vase (ca. 570 BC), which shows on its shoulder the procession of gods and chariots to the wedding of Peleus and Thetis (fig. 1). This in-

Fig. 1: Detail from the François Vase, Attic black-figure volute krater, ca. 570 BC, Museo Archeologico di Firenze. Photo courtesy of Alinari / Art Resource, NY.

cludes the Muses, with Kalliope, standing apart from her sisters, facing out toward the viewer and playing the *syrinx*; the Horai making coordinated gestures with their hands, which could represent dancing; and, next to them, Dionysus dancing with bent legs and arms as he carries an amphora. A similar

---

30 See Mullen 1982, 149, 158–60; Power 2000, 68. On the position of the *chorēgos* in the center of a choral circle, see Calame 1997b, 36; on Apollo and the Muses in *Nemean* 5, see *ibid:* 50.
31 On the crossover between the idealized performance of the Muses and the actual performance of the epinician here, see Power 2010, 202.

scene is also shown on two roughly contemporary vases by Sophilos: a very fragmentary *dinos* from the Acropolis (Akr. 587), and the huge Erskine *dinos* in the British Museum, on which one of the Muses is also playing a *syrinx* (fig. 2). If

Fig. 2: Detail from the Sophilos *Dinos*, Attic black-figure *dinos*, ca. 580 BC, The British Museum. ©The Trustees of the British Museum. All rights reserved.

vases like these were originally intended as wedding gifts, then the images of music and dance shown on them could have visually corresponded to the hymeneal music actually performed during the celebrations—a type of interaction comparable to that between the mythical narrative and choral performance in *Iphigenia in Aulis*.[32]

The depiction of the musical celebrations at the wedding of Peleus and Thetis in *Iphigenia in Aulis* is similar to representations of other mythical marriages

---

[32] On the function of the François Vase, see Stewart 1983, 69–70; Iozzo 2013, 54–61; Neils 2013, 120–3.

too, some of which may form parts of actual *hymenaioi*.³³ In Sappho fr. 44 the marriage of Hector and Andromache is described with a striking emphasis on music, both instrumental and vocal, building up a multilayered soundscape rather like that in the *Iphigenia in Aulis* ode:

αὖλος δ' ἀδυ[μ]έλης [κίθαρίς] τ' ὀνεμίγνυ[το
καὶ ψ[ό]φο[ς κ]ροτάλ[ων, λιγέ]ως δ' ἄρα πάρ[θενοι
ἄειδον μέλος ἄγγ[ον, ἴκα]νε δ' ἐς αἴθ[ερα
ἄχω θεσπεσία....³⁴

And the sweet-sounding *aulos* and [*kithara*] were combined, and the noise of *krotala* [clappers], and maidens sang [shrilly] a holy song, and the wondrous echo reached the sky.... (fr. 44 Voigt, lines 24–7)

Whether or not this description of the mythical wedding is a fragment of an actual *hymenaios*,³⁵ it would most probably have been performed as a monody to the accompaniment of the *kithara*,³⁶ which would then sonically represent all three instruments (the *aulos*, *kithara*, and *krotala*) just as the *aulos* would in the performance of Euripides' ode. Greek hymeneal songs seem to have traditionally contained mythic narrative sections describing prototypical marriages, including that of Peleus and Thetis, implicitly comparing the bride and bridegroom with these divinities and heroes.³⁷ The description of their wedding in this choral ode therefore appears to resemble the content of an actual *hymenaios*. Likewise the self-reflexive language, along with the chorus' own dancing, would give the audience the impression that they are witnessing the performance of a wedding

---

33 In what follows I use the term *hymenaios* to refer to the wedding song rather than *epithalamion*, since the latter word is not used in extant pre-Hellenistic literature: see Contiades-Tsitsoni 1990, 31; Swift 2010, 242–3. *Hymenaioi* referred particularly to the songs sung at the wedding procession, like those the Muses are said to sing for Peleus and Thetis.
34 Text is taken from Voigt 1971.
35 On fr. 44 as a hymeneal fragment, see Rösler 1975; Hague 1983: 134; Lasserre 1989: 81–106; Contiades-Tsitsoni 1990, 102–9. The choice of the wedding of Hector and Andromache, however, seems a rather ominous theme for such a celebration, particularly if, as Nagy 1974, 138 has suggested, the epithets used of Paean Apollo ironically allude to the Homeric Apollo, who deserts Hector just before he dies, and if the epithet θεοείκελος used of Hector in line 34 refers to Achilles, his killer (cf. *Il.* 1. 131, 19. 155). See also Kakridis 1966 and Schrenk 1994.
36 On the poem as monodic, see Lasserre 1989, 81–106; Contiades-Tsitsoni 1990, 102–8; Lardinois 1996, 159.
37 Cf. Sappho frr. 103 and 144 Voigt, both of which seem to refer to a divine wedding. See Hague 1983, 133–4; Swift 2010, 247. In Aristophanes' *Birds* the chorus perform a *hymenaios* in which they describe the wedding of Zeus and Hera (1731–43). See too Sappho fr. 141 Voigt, a fragment describing a divine marriage which may also be from a wedding song.

song, not just the description of one, even though the ode as a whole is not a formal *hymenaios*.³⁸

The chorus in *Iphigenia in Aulis* thus do not just 'perform' the celebratory *mousikē* of the wedding of Peleus and Thetis by complementing their account of that event with their own song and dance: they also seem to enact the *hymenaios* of Iphigenia and Achilles themselves.³⁹ Indeed the content of this song, particularly its musical focus, corresponds with the rites that the messenger in ignorance bids Agamemnon to set up upon Iphigenia's arrival:

> ἀλλ' εἶα τἀπὶ τοισίδ' ἐξάρχου κανᾶ, (435)
> στεφανοῦσθε κρᾶτα, καὶ σύ, Μενέλεως ἄναξ,
> ὑμέναιον εὐτρέπιζε, καὶ κατὰ στέγας
> λωτὸς βοάσθω καὶ ποδῶν ἔστω κτύπος·
> φῶς γὰρ τόδ' ἥκει μακάριον τῆι παρθένωι.

> But come now, given these events, set up the basket, wreathe your head, and you, lord Menelaus, make ready the *hymenaios* song, and let the *lōtos* pipe shout out through the tents and let there be the beat of feet! For this day has come, a blessing for the maiden. (435–39)

The hymeneal song that the audience hears in the third *stasimon* contains both in language and in performance the cry of the *lōtos* pipe—the *aulos*—and the beat of the dancing chorus' feet.⁴⁰ The messenger's description of the day as 'blessed' (μακάριον, 439) for Iphigenia may also refer to the *makarismos* within a *hymenaios*—just such a blessing occurs in the antistrophe of the third *stasimon*, when the gods establish the divine marriage as μακάριος (μακάριον τότε δαίμονες...γάμον...ἔθεσαν, 1076–9). As we shall see, the wreathing of heads is also taken up as a motif in the third *stasimon*, though of course it refers to neither Menelaus nor Agamemnon: the centaurs are garlanded in Dionysiac celebration (1058); Iphigenia for sacrifice (1080). There is thus a complete merging of identity between the chorus and the Muses on the one hand, and the chorus and the Nereids on the other: just as the chorus of Chalcidean women are (momentarily) celebrating the union of Iphigenia and Achilles by performing a *hymenaios*, so the Muses and Nereids sing and dance in honor of that of Achilles' parents. Unlike the performance context of a *hymenaios*, however, the marriage of Iphigenia and Achilles is impossible, so the enactment of their hymeneal song

---

38 See Rösler 1975, 277–8; Hague 1983, 132–8, Contiades-Tsitsoni 1990; Swift 2010, 242–9 on elements of the *hymenaios*. It seems very likely that the *melody* too could have imitated that of wedding songs, but it is impossible for us to know to what extent this might have been the case.
39 Cf. Wilson 2005, 189 on the 'restaging' of different kinds of musical performances in tragedy.
40 Cf. Walsh 1974, 243.

paradoxically also underscores the lack of any such celebratory *mousikē* for Iphigenia.⁴¹

We become increasingly aware of this lack through the rest of the ode. The Dionysian imagery established by the whirling Nereids continues into the antistrophe with the entrance of the *thiasos* of centaurs,⁴² but this is an image of chaotic revelry rather than the sort of coordinated *choreia* that is described and enacted in the previous strophe:

ἅμα δ' ἐλάταισι στεφανώδει τε χλόαι
θίασος ἔμολεν ἱπποβάτας
Κενταύρων ἐπὶ δαῖτα τὰν (1060)
  θεῶν κρατῆρά τε Βάκχου.
μέγα δ' ἀνέκλαγον....

And with fir trees and wreathed greenery, the horse-mounted revel-rout of Centaurs came to the feast of the gods and the mixing-bowl of Bacchus. And they shouted out loudly.... (1058–62)

Given the centaurs' attempted rape at the wedding of Perithoos and Hippodameia, their takeover from the Muses and Nereids as a performing group introduces a particularly unsettling tone within this hymeneal context.⁴³ Now, instead of melodious singing, there is loud shouting (ἀνέκλαγον, 1068) as they address Thetis and recount Chiron's prophecy regarding her son.⁴⁴ This prophecy draws the audience away from the immersive celebrations of the past toward the dramatic present and future, to Achilles as sacker of Troy:⁴⁵

ὃς ἥξει χθόνα λογχήρεσι σὺν Μυρμιδόνων
ἀσπισταῖς Πριάμοιο κλεινὰν
γαῖαν ἐκπυρώσων, (1070)
περὶ σώματι χρυσέων
ὅπλων Ἡφαιστοπόνων
κεκορυθμένος ἐνδύτ', ἐκ
  θεᾶς ματρὸς δωρήματ' ἔχων
Θέτιδος, ἅ νιν ἔτικτεν. (1075)

---

41 Cf. Foley 1982: 163–4, 168 on the multiple ironies of this ode's epithalamic themes.
42 See Panagl 1971, 214; Stockert 1992, 505.
43 Cf. Walsh 1974, 244–5. For the wedding of Perithoos and Hippodameia, see *Od.* 21. 295–304; Pind. fr. 166 SM.
44 Kovacs 2003, 283 rightly corrects previous translations of these lines that make Chiron the subject governing ἀνέκλαγον: Chiron himself is not present, and his prophecy is embedded within the centaurs' cry.
45 The prophecy also emphasizes Achilles' ancestry, which has already been recounted by Agamemnon to a quizzical Clytemnestra at 695–713; cf. 208–9, 926–7.

[A son] who will come to the land with the spear-wielding shieldbearers of the Myrmidons, to burn the famous country of Priam to ashes, clad about his body in the clothing of golden armor made by Hephaistos, holding the gifts from his divine mother, Thetis, who bore him. (1068–75)

Although the song is still framed within a hymeneal context, its mood continues to become more ominous with this shift forwards, particularly as Achilles' presence at Troy precludes Iphigenia's survival.[46] In these lines the visual focus of desire is also transformed, shifting from the golden-sandaled Muses and Ganymede with his golden mixing-bowl to Achilles with his golden armor (χρυσέων / ὅπλων, 1071–2) in the antistrophe. The previously carefree eroticism of *choreia* is here directed at a much more destructive subject.

The theme of Achilles' future (his death as well as his warring) seems to have been common in representations of the marriage of Peleus and Thetis. The bottom section of the François Vase shows Achilles' pursuit of Troilus; on the neck are the funeral games of Patroklos; on the handles is Achilles' lifeless corpse, being carried by Ajax away from the battle. It has also been argued that the amphora that Dionysus carries in the procession shown on the central frieze is meant to represent the urn that will hold the ashes of Achilles and Patroklos.[47] Likewise in Pindar *Isthmian* 8 the story of Thetis' marriage to Peleus is followed by the later bloody exploits of Achilles:

ὃ καὶ Μύσιον ἀμπελόεν
αἵμαξε Τηλέφου μέλα-
   νι ῥαίνων φόνωι πεδίον

γεφύρωσέ τ' Ἀτρεΐδαι-
σι νόστον, Ἑλέναν τ' ἐλύσατο, Τροΐας
ἶνας ἐκταμὼν δορί....[48]

He even bloodied the vine-clad plain of Mysia, sprinkling it with Telephos' dark gore, and he bridged a return home for the sons of Atreus, and released Helen, having cut out Troy's sinews with his spear.... (Pind. *Isth*. 8. 49–52).

A similar transition from the joy of the wedding to the destruction of the Trojan War is evident in Alcaeus fr.42: after the birth of Achilles is mentioned, we are given the chilling reminder that 'they perished, however, for Helen's sake, both the Phrygians and their city' (οἱ δ' ἀπώλοντ' ἀμφ' Ἑ[λέναι Φρύγες τε /

---

[46] See Walsh 1974, 244–7; Foley 1982, 168; 1985, 83; Sorum 1992, 535–6; Stockert 1992, 496, 506–7.
[47] For this interpretation see Stewart 1983.
[48] All quotations from Pindar's *epinicia* are taken from Snell and Maehler (Teubner 1987).

καὶ πόλις αὐτῶν, 15–6).⁴⁹ In the context of *Iphigenia in Aulis*, however, the prediction of Achilles' destruction at Troy is particularly charged as a result of the assurances he has just made to Clytemnestra that Iphigenia will be spared (in which case there would be no Trojan War).⁵⁰ The striking absence of vivid musical imagery in the antistrophe reflects this return to the more unsettling present and immediate future of the *mythos*, away from the previous celebratory scenes of *mousikē*.

It is possible, however, that even in the strophe there was some hint of this more ominous turn through the focus on the two complementary choral groups of Muses and Nereids, since one of the most memorable occasions when they appear together is at the funeral of Achilles, as described by the ghost of Agamemnon in Book 24 of the *Odyssey*:

ἀμφὶ δέ σ' ἔστησαν κοῦραι ἁλίοιο γέροντος
οἴκτρ' ὀλοφυρόμεναι, περὶ δ' ἄμβροτα εἵματα ἕσσαν.
Μοῦσαι δ' ἐννέα πᾶσαι ἀμειβόμεναι ὀπὶ καλῆι
θρήνεον· ἔνθα κεν οὔ τιν' ἀδάκρυτόν γ' ἐνόησας
Ἀργείων· τοῖον γὰρ ὑπώρορε Μοῦσα λίγεια.

And about you stood the daughters of the old man of the sea, mourning pitifully, and clothed you in immortal garments. And all nine Muses, answering one another with their beautiful voice, were singing a dirge. There you would have seen not one of the Argives tearless, for such was the shrill Muse's power to move. (*Od.* 24.58–62)

The combination of the two choruses may herald the disturbing shift toward the present and future through the rest of the ode, which further stresses the impossibility of a *hymenaios* for Iphigenia and Achilles, and at the same time undermines its enactment. The wedding song can be present in performance, but it is poignantly absent in the reality of the play.

Despite this shift away from the joyful *mousikē* with which the ode begins, there may still be some correspondence between the language of the antistrophe and the musicality of the strophe. David Wiles has argued for the 'choreographic identity' of strophe and antistrophe, with the result that the same visual image

---

49 Text taken from Voigt 1971. The song of the Parcae in Catullus 64 also concentrates on both the destructive exploits of Achilles and his death (338–70).

50 It also suggests a disconnect between the traditional, heroic image of powerful Achilles (as he is presented in the third *stasimon*, and also in the *parodos*) and Achilles as a character in this play, who will be unable to resist the sway of the army (even his own men): see Walsh 1974, 245–7.

can receive two meanings.[51] There is something of this sort of association between the strophe and antistrophe in the third *stasimon*, although the choreography may not be exactly identical: it might be surprising, for example, to imagine the same dancing accompanying the start of Chiron's reported prophecy in lines 1062–5 as that performed in imitation of the Muses in lines 1040–3. But the simultaneous merging and transformation of images between the two stanzas, partly realized by the chorus' *mousikē* (both singing and dancing), adds to the increasingly unsettling effect of the antistrophe. Not only do the chorus shift from the Muses and Nereids to the centaurs, a much more problematic performing group, but the Muses' song becomes the prophecy of Chiron, 'who knows the music of Phoebus' (ὁ φοιβάδα μοῦσαν / εἰδώς, 1064–5).[52] Instead of the 'quoted' *hymnos* of the Muses that we hear in Pindar, *Nemean* 5, it is Chiron's prophecy that is enframed, though without any indication of beautiful, orderly *mousikē*.[53] At the end of the antistrophe the previous image of the Nereids' joyful dancing turns into that of the gods blessing the marriage (1076–9). If, as Wiles contends, the chorus' choreography here would recall their earlier circular movements, such correspondence would underscore the ironic disconnect between past and present, divine and human: the marriage of Peleus and Thetis might be blessed, but that of Achilles and Iphigenia is impossible.

3 Narrative followed by application: returning to the present

With the epode, the chorus fully shift away from the hymeneal scene of the past and return to the horror of the immediate dramatic present. Now the second person address changes from that of the centaurs to Thetis, the bride of Peleus, to that of the chorus in their own person to Iphigenia, the sacrificial bride of Achilles:[54]

---

51 Wiles 1997, 87–113. I am more inclined to agree with Dale 1968, 212–4 that the choreographic mirroring of strophe and antistrophe need not have been an absolute rule, and instead could have allowed for some variation of gesture and movement between them, according to the requirements of the dramatic action.
52 Although μοῦσαν can metaphorically mean 'prophecy' (see Stockert 1992, 506), its literal meanings of both 'music' and 'Muse' are extremely apposite here.
53 See Power 2000, 75 on the Muses' song in Pind. *Nem.* 5.
54 On the unaccompanied σὲ referring to Iphigenia, see Mastronarde 1979, 99–100.

σὲ δ' ἐπὶ κάραι στέψουσι καλλικόμαν (1080)
πλόκαμον Ἀργεῖοι, βαλιὰν
ὥστε πετραίων
ἀπ' ἄντρων ἐλθοῦσαν ὀρέων
μόσχον ἀκήρατον, βρότειον
αἱμάσσοντες λαιμόν·
οὐ σύριγγι τραφεῖσαν οὐδ' (1085)
ἐν ῥοιβδήσεσι βουκόλων,
παρὰ δὲ ματέρι νυμφοκόμον
Ἰναχίδαις γάμον.

But you, upon your head the Argives will crown your beautiful hair, your locks, like a dappled, untouched calf that's come from rocky caves of mountains, they bloodying your mortal neck: not raised with the *syrinx* nor among the whistlings of herdsmen, but dressed as a bride at the side of your mother, a wedding for the sons of Inachus. (1080–88)

The ode as a whole is thus an example of a particularly Euripidean pattern of what Donald Mastronarde calls 'narrative followed by application', whereby a choral song opens with a mythic narrative and eventually turns to the immediate situation in the *mythos*.[55] The use of this pattern here, with the shift from a seemingly carefree scene of the past to a more ominous present, is especially similar that of the first *stasimon* of *Electra*, which is the earliest extant play of Euripides containing multiple, extended descriptions of *mousikē* (it is now usually dated to around 420 BC on metrical grounds).[56] This song (the 'Achilles Ode') is another so-called 'dithyrambic' song, and begins with seemingly carefree musical imagery describing the Greeks' sea journey to Troy:

κλειναὶ νᾶες, αἵ ποτ' ἔβατε Τροίαν
τοῖς ἀμετρήτοις ἐρετμοῖς
πέμπουσαι χορεύματα Νηρῄδων,
ἵν' ὁ φίλαυλος ἔπαλλε δελ- (435)
φὶς πρώιραις κυανεμβόλοι-
σιν εἱλισσόμενος,
πορεύων τὸν τᾶς Θέτιδος
κοῦφον ἅλμα ποδῶν Ἀχιλῆ
σὺν Ἀγαμέμνονι Τρωίας (440)
ἐπὶ Σιμουντίδας ἀκτάς.[57]

---

55 Mastronarde 2010, 141. Other examples include *Andr.* 274–308, *El.* 699–746, *Phoen.* 638–89, 1019–66, and most likely *Hel.* 1301–68 (but the corrupt lines at the end of this ode make the pattern harder to recognize); also Aesch. *Cho.* 585–662; Soph. *Ant.* 332–75, *OT* 863–910: see Mastronarde 2010, 140–3, 148–49.
56 On the dating of *Electra*, see Cropp/Fick 1985, 23, 60–1; Cropp 2013, 31–3.
57 Text taken from Diggle (OCT 1981).

> Glorious ships, which once went to Troy with countless oars, escorting the choral dances of the Nereids, where the *aulos*-loving dolphin would leap, whirling by the dark-blue prows, carrying Thetis' son, Achilles, swift in the leap of his feet, with Agamemnon to the banks of the Simois, Troy's river. (432–41)

As in the *Iphigenia in Aulis* ode, here the chorus refer to the dancing of Nereids; they continue to draw on the dithyrambic musical imaginary by picturing the '*aulos*-loving dolphin' (ὁ φίλαυλος…δελφίς, 435–6) who whirls (εἰλισσόμενος, 437) by the prows. As it continues into the second strophic pair, however, the song becomes much more unsettling, since these typically celebratory figures of chorality are transformed into more ominous images of *mousikē* as the chorus describe the emblems that are 'terrors' (the metrically problematic δείματα in line 456) on Achilles' armor:[58]

στρ. β Ἰλιόθεν δ' ἔκλυόν τινος ἐν λιμέσιν
  Ναυπλίοις βεβῶτος
  τᾶς σᾶς, ὦ Θέτιδος παῖ,
  κλεινᾶς ἀσπίδος ἐν κύκλωι   (455)
  τοιάδε σήματα †δείματα
  Φρύγια† τετύχθαι·
  περιδρόμωι μὲν ἴτυος ἕδραι
  Περσέα λαιμοτόμαν ὑπὲρ ἁλὸς
  ποτανοῖσι πεδίλοις κορυφὰν Γοργόνος ἴσχειν,   (460)
    Διὸς ἀγγέλωι σὺν Ἑρμᾶι,
    τῶι Μαίας ἀγροτῆρι κούρωι.

ἀντ. β ἐν δὲ μέσωι κατέλαμπε σάκει φαέθων
  κύκλος ἀλίοιο   (465)
  ἵπποις ἄμ πτεροέσσαις
  ἄστρων τ' αἰθέριοι χοροί,
  Πλειάδες Ὑάδες, †Ἕκτορος
  ὄμμασι† τροπαῖοι·
  ἐπὶ δὲ χρυσοτύπωι κράνει   (470)
  Σφίγγες ὄνυξιν ἀοίδιμον ἄγραν
  φέρουσαι· περιπλεύρωι δὲ κύτει πύρπνοος ἔσπευ-
    δε δρόμωι λέαινα χαλαῖς
  Πειρηναῖον ὁρῶσα πῶλον.   (475)

ἐπωιδ. ἄορι δ' ἐν φονίωι τετραβάμονες ἵπποι ἔπαλλον,
  κελαινὰ δ' ἀμφὶ νῶθ' ἵετο κόνις.
  τοιῶνδ' ἄνακτα δοριπόνων
  ἔκανεν ἀνδρῶν, Τυνδαρί,   (480)
  σὰ λέχεα, κακόφρον κόρα.

---

58 On the shift in the ode's mood, see esp. Csapo 2008.

τοιγάρ σοί ποτ' οὐρανίδαι
πέμψουσιν θανάτου δίκαν.
ἔτ' ἔτι φόνιον ὑπὸ δέραν (485)
ὄψομαι αἷμα χυθὲν σιδάρωι.

I used to hear, from someone who came from Ilium to the harbor of Nauplia, that on the circle of your famous shield, O son of Thetis, were wrought these emblems, terrors for the Phrygians: on the surrounding base of the shield's rim, Perseus the throat-cutter, over the sea with winged sandals, was holding the Gorgon's head, with Hermes, Zeus' messenger, the rustic son of Maia.

In the center of the shield the gleaming circle of the sun was shining on winged horses, and the heavenly choruses of stars, Pleiades, Hyades, turning back the eyes of Hector; and upon his gold-beaten helmet were sphinxes, carrying in their talons song-caught prey. On the rib-encircling hollow a fire-breathing lioness sped at a run with her claws, seeing Peirene's colt.

On the bloody sword four-footed horses were leaping, and about their backs black dust was thrown up. The lord of such spear-toiling men, your [adulterous] bed killed, evil-minded daughter of Tyndareus! For this the heavenly gods will one day [soon] send to you the punishment of death. Still, still beneath your bloody throat I shall see blood pouring forth at the sword. (452–86)

Like the opening strophe, this ecphrasis contains allusions to choreography, especially circular movement, as when the chorus picture the 'heavenly choruses of stars' (ἄστρων τ' αἰθέριοι χοροί, 467) around the gleaming 'circle of the sun' (κύκλος ἁλίοιο, 465) in the second antistrophe, yet these stars are ominously described as τροπαῖοι, causing the rout of Hector. At the start of the epode, the leaping of the four-footed horses depicted on Achilles' sword in line 476 replaces the image of the leaping, dancing, *aulos*-loving dolphin with which the song began. The chorus of Argive women then address Clytemnestra directly, turning from the bloodiness of Achilles' weapons to her murder of Agamemnon, and finally imagining her own bloody death (479–86). Through this movement back towards the present, the chorus not only 'apply' the narrative of the ode to the immediate dramatic situation, but also anticipate a pivotal point in the plot—Clytemnestra's murder at the hands of Orestes and Electra.[59]

In the epode of the *Iphigenia in Aulis* third *stasimon* the imagery of *mousikē* is similarly used for a deeply unsettling effect, as the chorus allude to details of music and dance from the previous verses, but transfer them from the context of

---

[59] There is a similar movement towards the present dramatic situation in the second *stasimon*: see Gagné/Hopman 2013b, 11–7 on Eur. *El.* 699–746.

marriage to that of sacrifice.⁶⁰ In doing so, the chorus here, as in *Electra*, anticipate the inevitable turning point in the plot of the play, as Iphigenia submits to her sacrifice. The garlanding of her head (στέψουσι, 1080) recalls the shouting, reveling *thiasos* of centaurs with their 'wreathed foliage' (στεφανώδει χλόαι, 1058), while the focus on her beautiful hair (καλλικόμαν / πλόκαμον, 1080–1) reminds us of the καλλιπλόκαμοι Muses dancing and singing.⁶¹ Through the course of the ode, then, the focus of erotic attraction has shifted from the Muses' *choreia* and Ganymede in the strophe, to Achilles in the antistrophe, and finally—and most disturbingly—to Iphigenia, the sacrificial bride, in the epode.

The chorus also once again refer to the *syrinx* (1085), which takes on a twofold meaning as a result of the instrumental sound with which the ode began.⁶² On the one hand, the fact that Iphigenia was not raised to the sound of the *syrinx* and the whistling of herdsmen emphasizes the difference between her and the mountain calf, a more usual sacrificial animal, to which the preceding simile compares her. In this respect the mention of the *syrinx* reminds us of the image of Paris as a βουκόλος piping on his *syrinx* at the end of the first *stasimon* (574): it is another image of pastoral innocence that is used to contrast with the surrounding dramatic context, while the similar language here points to the causal connection between the moment of the judgment scene and Iphigenia's sacrifice.⁶³ On the other hand, the absence of a *syrinx* for Iphigenia here contrasts with the inclusion of the 'reedy *syrinxes*', along with the *aulos* and *kithara*, in the opening of the ode (1038). The *syrinx* therefore also functions as a representative of wedding music, just as it does in the hands of Calliope on the François Vase and the Sophilos *Dinos*, and so the mention of it here highlights the absence of any such celebratory *mousikē* for Iphigenia. This absence would have been further stressed through the performance of the third *stasimon* as a whole, if, given the lack of references to choreography here, we can assume that the chorus would dance less in the epode, or even that they might be stationary (as William

---

60 On the combining of marriage and sacrificial imagery in *Iphigenia in Aulis*, see Foley 1982; 1985, 82–3; Seaford 1987, 108–10; Michelakis 2006, 70–1. Cf. Rehm 1994 and Swift 2010, 250–5 on the conflation of marriage and funerary rituals in Greek tragedy.
61 Lines 1080–1 also foreshadow Iphigenia's words at 1477–9 as she goes to be sacrificed: στέφεα περίβολα δίδοτε, φέρετε / –πλόκαμος ὅδε καταστέφειν– / χερνίβων τε παγάς.
62 ῥοιβδήσεσι, translated here as 'whistlings', may also refer to both the sound and the way of playing the *syrinx*: Stockert 1992, 509 understands lines 1085–86 to mean essentially 'nicht beim schrillen Klang der ländlichen Syringen'.
63 This image also recurs with Paris as a βουκόλος in Iphigenia's lament, lines 1291–9.

Mullen has suggested might happen in the performance of epodes in Pindaric *choreia*).[64]

4 The absent *hymenaios*

This paradoxical effect of an absent *hymenaios* can be compared to Cassandra's solitary performance of hymeneal *mousikē* in Euripides' *Troades*, which similarly creates a poignant contrast to the surrounding drama. In this earlier tragedy, Cassandra interrupts the lament that so dominates the music of the play by rushing on stage and singing her own *hymenaios*, a much more energetic and lyrical song, even though a marriage celebration is of course far from the reality of her fate:

ἄνεχε, πάρεχε, φῶς φέρε· σέβω φλέγω—
ἰδοὺ ἰδού—
λαμπάσι τόδ' ἱερόν. ὦ 'Υμέναι' ἄναξ· (310)
μακάριος ὁ γαμέτας,
μακαρία δ' ἐγὼ βασιλικοῖς λέκτροις
κατ' Ἄργος ἁ γαμουμένα.
Ὑμὴν ὦ 'Υμέναι' ἄναξ.
ἐπεὶ σύ, μᾶτερ, †ἐπὶ δάκρυσι καὶ† (315)
γόοισι τὸν θανόντα πατέρα πατρίδα τε
φίλαν καταστένουσ' ἔχεις,
ἐγὼ δ' ἐπὶ γάμοις ἐμοῖς
ἀναφλέγω πυρὸς φῶς (320)
ἐς αὐγάν, ἐς αἴγλαν,
διδοῦσ', ὦ Ὑμέναιε, σοί,
διδοῦσ', ὦ Ἑκάτα, φάος
παρθένων ἐπὶ λέκτροις
ἇι νόμος ἔχει.

πάλλε πόδ' αἰθέριον, <ἄναγ'> ἄναγε χορόν— (325)
εὐὰν εὐοῖ—
ὡς ἐπὶ πατρὸς ἐμοῦ μακαριωτάταις
τύχαις. ὁ χορὸς ὅσιος.
ἄγε σὺ Φοῖβέ νιν· κατὰ σὸν ἐν δάφναις
ἀνάκτορον θυηπολῶ. (330)
Ὑμὴν ὦ 'Υμέναι' Ὑμήν.
χόρευε, μᾶτερ, χόρευμ' ἄναγε, πόδα σὸν
ἕλισσε τᾷδ' ἐκεῖσε μετ' ἐμέθεν ποδῶν
φέρουσα φιλτάταν βάσιν.

---

[64] Mullen 1982, 90–142.

βόασον ὑμέναιον ὦ (335)
μακαρίαις ἀοιδαῖς
ἰαχαῖς τε νύμφαν.
ἴτ', ὦ καλλίπεπλοι Φρυγῶν
κόραι, μέλπετ' ἐμῶν γάμων
τὸν πεπρωμένον εὐνᾶι (340)
πόσιν ἐμέθεν.⁶⁵

Lift up, bring, carry the light: I worship, I make gleam [for you]. See, see—with torch fire this holy place, O lord Hymenaios! Blessed is the bridegroom, blessed too am I, to a king's bed in Argos wedded. Hymen, O lord Hymenaios! For you, mother, in tears and groans my dead father and dear fatherland keep lamenting, but I at my marriage kindle the light of fire to a beam, to a gleam, giving it, O Hymenaios, to you, giving, O Hekate, a light for a maidens' marriage bed as custom ordains.

Shake your foot in the air, <raise up,> raise up the choral dance—*Euan euoi!* Just as if for my father's most blessed fortunes. The choral dance is holy. You, Phoebus, lead it! [Crowned] in laurels I perform sacrifices at your temple. Hymen, O Hymenaios, Hymen! Dance, mother, start up the choral dancing, whirl your foot this way and that, following my feet, moving your most dear step. Shout out *hymenaios*, O, with blessed songs and cries for the bride. Come, O beautiful-robed daughters of the Phrygians, sing for me of the one ordained for my marriage bed, my husband. (308–41)

As in the case of the *Iphigenia in Aulis* ode, it is the performance of this song that underscores the absence of an actual *hymenaios*, since it should be sung and danced by a chorus, not Cassandra herself as the supposed bride. Her monodic distortion is made explicit through the typically choral refrain of ὦ Ὑμέναιε (ἄναξ), which is similar to the repeated cry of ὑμήναον that we find in Sappho fr. 111 Voigt. The characterization of the maiden immediately before and after her song as a raving maenad, in addition to her own Dionysiac cultic cry of εὐάν εὐοῖ in line 326, further undermines her self-presentation as a bride, since, as Richard Seaford has shown, in tragedy the subversion of wedding ritual and corresponding destruction of the household is often expressed in terms of maenadism.⁶⁶

---

65 Text taken from Diggle (OCT 1981).
66 Seaford 1994a, 330–62, esp. 356. Cf. Papadopoulou 2000: 515–21, who points out that the hymeneal nature of the song is also undermined by Cassandra's addresses to Hecate (323) and Apollo (329). When Andromache is described as a maenad in the *Iliad*, it is at the moment when, upon seeing her husband's dead body, she flings from her head the *krēdemnon* that Aphrodite gave to her on her wedding day (22.468–72). In doing so, she not only symbolically reverses that marriage ritual but also represents her own rape in the future, since the loss of this veil often acts as an analogy for the loss of chastity: see Nagler 1974, 44–58; Seaford 1994a, 333–4.

But both the third *stasimon* of *Iphigenia in Aulis* and Cassandra's song in *Troades* are more connected to the dramatic fabric of their respective plays than through simply providing a contrast with the reality of the immediate dramatic situation. The emphasis on the lack of a chorus in Cassandra's performance plays into the motif of absent *choreia* that runs throughout the tragedy, emphasizing the complete breakdown of communal worship and civic structure in the wake of Troy's destruction. At the same time, the lack of *hymenaioi* sung by a chorus of *parthenoi* (rather than by the bride herself) points forward beyond the span of the play itself to Cassandra's doom, rather as the ironic emphasis on the lack of any such celebratory *choreia* for Iphigenia anticipates her sacrifice rather than her marriage.

The idea that the distortion or absence of a proper hymenaios signals both the hopelessness of the union and the bride's own destruction may have been a common one in archaic and classical Greek thought. We see it also in Pindar's *Pythian* 3, in which the account of Coronis' adultery against Apollo and consequent death begins with the observation that she waited for neither the marriage feast nor the *hymenaioi*:

> οὐκ ἔμειν' ἐλθεῖν τράπεζαν νυμφίαν,
> οὐδὲ παμφώνων ἰαχὰν ὑμεναίων, ἅλικες
> οἷα παρθένοι φιλέοισιν ἑταῖραι
> ἑσπερίαις ὑποκουρίζεσθ' ἀοιδαῖς.

(Pind. *Pyth.* 3.16–19)

> She waited neither for the marriage feast to come, nor for the cry of full-voiced *hymenaioi*, the sorts of things with which maiden companions of the same age love to murmur in evening songs.

As David Young has pointed out, Pindar places a particular emphasis here on the importance of *hymenaioi* in this marriage, and so 'establishes the absence of song as the primary motif in the disastrous nature of Coronis' new union'.[67] Likewise in *Iphigenia in Aulis*, as in *Troades*, the absence of a *hymenaios*, ironically made clear as the chorus appear to perform one, spells doom for the female protagonist.

---

[67] Young 1968, 35.

5 Conclusion: *mousikē* in Euripidean tragedy

This close analysis of the third *stasimon* of *Iphigenia in Aulis* demonstrates that we can use the surviving text of Euripides' corpus to think about how the *mousikē* of a play might have worked within its *mythos*, and thus move beyond viewing the metamusicality of such odes as merely a self-conscious display of his experimentation with new styles of musical performance and language. Though the ode does transport us to a time and place beyond the play, it is by no means just an *embolimon*, since the language and performance of *mousikē* simultaneously create a close link with the surrounding drama. The inclusion of such imagery as the fifty Nereids dancing in circles seems to be typical of the dithyramb and New Music, but it is also part of a broader pattern of performed and imagined *mousikē* that suggests that, in this and other plays from the last fifteen years or so of his career, Euripides was experimenting with the ways in which choral performance could relate to the *mythos*. We can also see that the vivid focus on *mousikē* in this ode is not all new. Its highly metamusical language and the way in which it draws on the musical imaginary within and through its performance derive from traditional hymeneal choral lyric, and it is through the audience's acquaintance with this long-established genre that the song achieves its devastatingly ironic impact, directing us forward not towards Iphigenia's marriage, but towards her death.

The ode also fits within a larger pattern of *mousikē* that runs through the whole play. The first two thirds of the tragedy are rich with choral song: over a quarter of the lines are sung by the chorus in the *parodos* and three *stasima*. But this third *stasimon* is the last intensely lyrical outburst of choral song. The shift of focus onto Iphigenia herself in the epode heralds not only a turning point in the play as her death becomes more certain (as we know it must), but also a change in terms of the dominant voice of the tragedy, since about half of all the lines in the last third are hers. It also heralds a different type of *mousikē*, since she, not the chorus, performs the next two songs.[68]

This example of *mousikē* in the *Iphigenia in Aulis* therefore suggests that Euripides could give a far more central role to the lyric element than the one Aristotle seems to suggest in *Poetics*. Even in this late play, *choreia* ties in closely with the play's dramatic structure, indicating that the chorus could still play a significant, relevant part in Euripides' tragedies towards the end of the fifth century. Indeed *Iphigenia in Aulis*, like *Bacchae*, has overall a higher proportion of choral song than many of Euripides' earlier plays, a fact which also contradicts

---

[68] On this musical shift through *Iphigenia in Aulis*, see Weiss 2014.

the standard narrative of choral song steadily giving way to that of the actors towards the end of the fifth century. The sharp increase in the amount of *choreia* in these two plays from the very end of Euripides' life cannot be explained away simply as part of his archaizing in Macedonia: the innovative combination of new and traditional choral motifs in the third *stasimon* of the *Iphigenia in Aulis* suggests a continuance of his more experimental tendencies rather than a return to traditionalism. It is also unlikely that Euripides was forced to rely less on highly skilled actors in Macedon and therefore focus more on the chorus: though professional choruses were probably available, Archelaus must have drawn to his city the great actors of the day too as he transformed it into a cultural center. [69] Finally, it is worth remembering the fact that, when Plato in the fourth century writes about tragedy in his *Laws*, he still sees it in terms of *choreia*. So however much limelight actors gained during this period, tragedy could still be viewed as an essentially choral genre, while its *mousikē* could still play a closely integrated role within a drama as a whole. [70] The singing and dancing of the chorus—tragedy's 'seasonings'—must have been vital to a play's performance and impact.

---

69 Cf. Csapo 1999–2000, 414–5. On tragic performances in Macedon, see Revermann 1999–2000, esp. 254–6; Duncan 2011.
70 On tragedy as a largely choral event, see esp. Bacon 1994–1995; Gagné/Hopman 2013b, 19–22.

Timothy Power
New Music in Sophocles' *Ichneutae*

1 Music in the (Funhouse) Mirror

Among the welcome outcomes of the 'musical turn' taken in Classical Studies over the past few decades has been a fuller appreciation of the crucial role played by music in Attic drama. This has meant not only a renewed understanding of the ways in which drama was musical in its structure and performance, but also a more profound recognition of the ways in which verbal references to and narrative discourse about musical matters imported real sociocultural meaning into a play's fictive economy, even as they reflected back onto contemporary Athens, offering up commentary on the city's rapidly evolving musical culture, of which drama itself was a major component. Comedy's engagement with the real-world musical scene around it is of course the most explicit and sustained of the dramatic genres, and it has accordingly stimulated the greatest scholarly response.[1] But we are becoming more attuned to critical reflections of contemporary musical experience embedded in the mythically removed plots and texts of tragedy as well.[2]

Satyr drama has attracted relatively less socio-musicological scrutiny. Yet, as Mark Griffith reminds us in an important recent article, the fragmentary remains of classical satyr plays exhibit a marked interest in *mousikē* (musical instruments, sounds, song and dance performances) and contain an abundance of self-referential musical and performative language.[3] It is unlikely that this pervasive attention to music in the plays was devoid of deliberate relevance to the musical world outside them. For inasmuch as Athenian citizens were invited to see in satyrs a cartoonish alter-image of their own appetites and endeavors, surely theatrical satyrs' engagement with music must have echoed, in ways both ridiculous and critically insightful, the experiences and inclinations of their audience: as in other things, when it came to music, satyrs could be as good to think with as to laugh at.[4] Such echoes, as we will see, are muted, often expressed in double entendres—satyr drama is, like tragedy, situated in the distant

---

[1] See e.g. Zimmermann 1993; Dobrov/Urios-Aparisi 1995; Barker 2004.
[2] Cf. Wilson 1999–2000, 2009; Steiner 2011; Power 2012. See also Coward and Weiss in this volume.
[3] Griffith 2013b.
[4] Lissarrague 1990 (the oft-cited 'funhouse mirror' metaphor appears on p. 235); Griffith 2002, 211.

world of myth, and generally guards the integrity of its dramatic fiction—but they are not inaudible, not for us, and certainly not for the original audience. The playful commentary on musical culture in satyr plays would seem to lie somewhere between comedy's frank, boisterous, and often parodic music criticism and tragedy's cautious obliquity.

Griffith detects a number of probable allusions to contemporary developments in music and dance in the satyric fragments of Aeschylus and Sophocles. He argues too that the song said by Athenaeus to be a hyporcheme of Pratinas (*TrGF¹*, 4 F 3) in which someone, probably a satyric chorus, berates an aulete for overstepping his role as accompanist with too-showy playing, quite likely derives from a satyr play by Pratinas of Phlius (ca. 500 BC), and not from a later-fifth-century dithyramb by another Pratinas, as others hold. The metamusically saturated language of this text, which points toward a critique of broader trends in Athenian musical life—Athenaeus states that recent virtuosic innovations in *aulos* playing, which put Dionysian choruses in the shade of their accompanists, inspired Pratinas' invective (14.617b)—was, in Griffith's view, as much a generic feature of satyr drama as of the dithyramb.[5]

There are other indications that satyr plays could flirt quite openly with real-world music from the remove of their fantastic settings. Polion's painting of three silens playing 'Thracian' *kitharai* before a dramatic aulete on a bell krater of the 420s very probably depicts a scene from a satyr play (New York, Metropolitan Museum of Art 25.78.66; *ARV²* 1172, 8). A label above the silens' heads identifies them as ΟΙΔΟΙ ΠΑΝΑΘΕΝΑΙΑ, 'Singers at the Panathenaia'. It is reasonable to suppose that the artist was inspired by a satyr play featuring a parody of the celebrated musicians who competed at the Panathenaic citharodic *agōn*.[6] The popular culture of *mousikoi agōnes* might also have been the target of a satyr play by Sophocles' son Iophon entitled *Aulōidoi* (*Aulos-Singers*). Clement of Alexandria (*Strom.* 1.3.24.3 = *TrGF¹*, 22 F 1) preserves the only fragment, two lines describing the appearance of a 'well-rehearsed crowd of many *sophistai*' (πολλῶν σοφιστῶν ὄχλος ἐξηρτυμένος). Since Clement says that Iophon here refers to

---

[5] Griffith 2013b, 266–74. See too D'Alessio 2007 for the older dating. Zimmermann 1986 remains the strongest argument for Pratinas' hyporcheme as a later-fifth-century dithyramb. (Cf. Andujar's discussion in this volume.) Prauscello 2012, 73 observes that the metamusical content of two other fragments (712a–b PMG) attributed to Pratinas (of Phlius) would not be inconsistent with satyr play.

[6] Kárpáti 2012 argues that the scene comes from a comedy with a satyric chorus; cf. Roos 1951, 227–8. The argument is entirely reasonable, but I would disagree with the notion that the 'cultural politics' (Kárpáti 2012, 235) implied by Polion's image disqualifies satyr drama as the source.

'rhapsodes and others', these *sophistai* must be expert performers in *mousikē*, presumably readied and assembled *en masse* for a festival contest, the usual context for performance by rhapsodes as well as skilled *aulos*-singers.[7] The title suggests that the members of the satyr chorus played the role of *aulōidoi*, perhaps to similarly parodic effect as the satyric 'Singers at the Panathenaia'.[8]

In the present chapter, the spotlight falls on our second-best-preserved satyr play, the *Ichneutae* of Sophocles, which happens to be largely concerned with *mousikē*. First, however, a few general remarks about Sophocles' handling of music are in order. The texts of the preserved tragedies of Sophocles show comparatively few of the musical references that mark Aeschylean and especially Euripidean tragedy. Yet the fragments, of the tragedies and the satyr plays, tell a different tale, that Sophocles was in fact quite intent on treating all sorts of musical matters in his plays, and may even have scored them to quite adventurous music.[9]

Besides *Ichneutae*, the most outstanding example is the tragedy *Thamyras* (*TrGF*[4], F 236–45), in whose production Sophocles himself apparently impersonated the titular citharode.[10] Peter Wilson has explored what must have been the metamusical complexity of this work: plot and fragments suggest that an exploration of generic and musical contrasts between *aulos*-based tragedy and *kitharōidia* formed the subtext to the mythical plot. Wilson goes further, however. Arguing that the tragedy was staged in the 440s, later than has usually been thought, he suggests that Sophocles depicted the hubristic Thamyras as a proto-exponent of the New Music, which in Athens of the 440s was already beginning to coalesce into a recognizable 'movement'. Indeed, it was probably during this decade that a newer style of *kitharōidia* in particular came to greater public awareness in Athens. The citharode Phrynis of Mytilene, known for his

---

[7] Cf. Kaimio *et alii* 2001, 48. See Almazova 2008 on *aulōidoi* and festival contests in *aulōidia*. Athletic *agōnes* were apparently the setting of Aeschylus' satyr play *Isthmiastai*; cf. Kárpáti 2012, 234. For *sophistēs* as 'expert musician', Sophocles *TrGF*[4], Adesp. F 906; *Rhesus* 924. As Wilson 2009, 60 n.56 observes, the word so used of musicians (and those skilled in other arts, too) implies not only extraordinary expertise but a slant toward cultural innovation. Iophon's satyrs may then be mocking those aulodes specifically associated with the innovations of the New Music. Wilson 2004, 287 n.45 raises this possibility for Polion's citharodic satyrs, though these may as well, he notes, parody the 'old guard' of citharodes.
[8] Cf. KPS, 549–50.
[9] For detailed discussion, see Power 2012.
[10] This is strongly suggested, though not explicitly stated, by Athen. 1.20e and *Life of Sophocles* 5.

novel techniques, won his first Panathenaic victory in 446 BC.[11] It is Euripides and Agathon whom we associate with the New Music of the second half of the fifth century, but there is little reason to believe that Sophocles did not confront it as well, as a poet, interrogating the social and cultural implications of contemporary musical innovation through mythical drama, and perhaps even as a composer, integrating new stylistic developments into his own musical idiom.[12]

Ichneutae, like *Thamyras*, was once considered by a majority of scholars to be a very early work of Sophocles, for no very compelling reason. Its fragmentary preservation, combined with the lack of testimony about its production, renders even approximate dating a guessing game based on uncertain criteria (metrical, dramaturgical, intertextual, biographical). Nowadays, a somewhat lower date for the play, in the 440s, has won broader acceptance, though the possibility of its influence on Euripides' *Antiope* (produced around 408) may support an even later date.[13]

Particularities of the representation of music in *Ichneutae* could also support dating its production to the second half of the fifth century. I refer to what seems a canny conflation of different notions of 'new music' in the play. The plot, staging, and text involve new music in a basic, literal sense: the satyr chorus reacts to the music of Hermes' freshly invented lyre, which is entirely new to them. At this level, Sophocles follows, and plays variations upon, the *Homeric Hymn to Hermes*, which provides material, rich in social-burlesque and metatheatrical potential, for conventional *topoi* in satyr drama, including the satyrs' comical reaction to a novel invention and their learning new tricks.[14] In the following section, I consider the new music of *Ichneutae* in this sense, exploring the theatrical and metatheatrical, thematic, generic, and intertextual aspects of its prominent role in the drama. But, as I argue further in the third section, the never-before-heard

---

[11] Σ Ar. *Clouds* 971a actually says Phrynis was victorious in the archon year of Kallias, 456 BC, but this was not a Panathenaic year. Most emend to Kallimachos, archon in 446. See discussion in Miller 1997, 222.

[12] Aristoxenus apparently viewed Sophocles as a musical innovator, claiming he was the 'first poet among the Athenians to adopt the Phrygian manner of melody for his own songs and to mix in the dithyrambic style' (fr. 79 Wehrli = *Life of Sophocles* 23).

[13] Sutton 1980, 47–8 argues for a date in the 440s based on perceived thematic continuities between *Ichneutae* and *Ajax*; the two plays, he thinks, belonged to the same tetralogy. Bethe 1919, 27 was an early proponent of a later dating (430–420 BC). For the relationship between *Ichneutae* and *Antiope*, with a survey of views on dating, see Maltese 1982, 12–17; cf. Wilamowitz 1912, 460–1.

[14] For the relation of *Ichneutae* to the *Hymn to Hermes*, see Allègre 1913, Vergados 2013, 79–86. For invention and discovery in satyr play, see now Lämmle 2013, 371–80, with further bibliography. KPS, 312 summarizes other generic *topoi* in *Ichneutae*.

music made by Hermes is also anachronistically loaded. Its textual representation (and perhaps too its actual sound in performance) cleverly assimilates it to the New Music, which was, from at least the 440s on, one of the leading stories in the cultural life of Athens, and as such would inevitably have attracted comment from the satyric stage.

2 From *Psophos* to *Tonos*: Satyric Encounters with 'New Music'

A brief review of the play, or at least the first half of it that is preserved in a papyrus fragment of around 450 lines, will bring us to (lower-case) new music.[15] *Ichneutae* begins with Apollo's proclamation of a reward of gold for the recovery of his stolen cattle. Silenus takes him up, recruiting his band of satyrs to hunt down the animals. Apollo promises him, and presumably also the other satyrs, freedom if they succeed (63). As the satyrs near the cave of Maia in their hunt, they are frightened by the first notes of Hermes' lyre, which sounds from within the cavern and is thus invisible to them. Silenus, not hearing the instrument, berates his sons for their cowardice as they move prostrate on the ground in fear (124–6); their howls greet perhaps another lyric flourish at line 131. The satyrs recover sufficiently to tell Silenus about the strange noise (*psophos*, 144). Silenus, however, continues to deride the satyrs as worthless cowards, and then rallies them to continue their chase, saying he will spur them on by whistling (*syrigma*, 173). A frenetic choral song-and-dance begins at line 176, which is interrupted by another burst of the lyre immediately before line 203, which this time Silenus hears and flees in panic.

The satyrs, now at the entrance of the cave, perform an orchestically wild *paraclausithyron*, stomping their feet and yelling to draw the attention of the noisemaker in the cave (217–9; 222). At this point Hermes' nurse Cyllene appears, annoyed and bewildered by the satyrs' aggressive dance (221–42). The satyrs demand to learn the identity of the sound. Cyllene eventually tells of Hermes' secret birth and finally reveals, after a riddling exchange with the chorus, the identity of the lyre (324–8). Probably after another lyric flourish, the satyrs, now enlightened, sing praise of the music they hear (329–31). They then turn back to 'the

---

15 *P.Oxy.* 1174 + 2081a = *TrGF*⁴, F 314. Throughout this chapter, I cite Diggle's text in *Tragicorum Graecorum Fragmenta Selecta*, with the two divergences noted here: (1) for Diggle's οἴῳ 'κπλαγέντες (142; cf. Guida 2010, 6–8), οἴῳ πλαγέντες; (2) for <ὀμ>οψάλακτος (329), <χ>οψάλακτος.

matter at hand' (τὸ πρᾶγμα, 332), the missing cattle, and we hear no more of the lyre for the remainder of the papyrus fragment.

The satyrs' encounter with the lyre obviously alludes to Apollo's first encounter with Hermes' lyre playing in the *Homeric Hymn*. There the newly invented lyre also has the potential for terror: it 'rings out σμερδαλέον' at the touch of the newborn god (420; cf. 54, 502). Adverbial σμερδαλέον elsewhere in early hexameter poetry qualifies sounds that shock and terrify, yet the lyric music of Hermes inspires joyful awe in Apollo rather than the abject terror felt by the satyr chorus (421–3).[16] We should keep in mind, however, that Sophocles dramatically dials up the 'fear factor' by making the lyre invisible: the satyrs cannot see what is making the weird noise.

This uncanny detachment of musical sound from sight is a dramaturgical device that Sophocles may have been the first to exploit in extended fashion.[17] His *Inachus*, very likely a satyr play, featured a variant of it. Hermes, made invisible by his 'cap of Hades', came on stage making music on his *syrinx* (*TrGF*[4], F 269c.7), which someone, very likely the bewildered chorus, heard as 'noises', *psophêmata* (*TrGF*[4], F 269c.22). The same word, *psophos*, is used repeatedly by the satyrs and Silenus in *Ichneutae* to describe the sound of Hermes' lyre (*Ichn.* 144, 145, 160, 204; cf. 157). The unseen *syrinx*, like the unseen lyre, instills fear in its listeners (*TrGF*[4], F 269c.27, 39). But the *syrinx* would only have been invisible in the fictional world of the play. The actor playing Hermes, along with the *syrinx*, would presumably have been visible to the audience. Further, if the dramatic aulete piped the 'part' of Hermes' *syrinx* while the actor simply mimed playing it, as seems probable, then the source of the music would have been visible to the audience members, since the aulete, who was stationed in the orchestra, was normally visible to them.[18]

---

[16] Cf. Guida 2013, 146. For σμερδαλέον, see Cantilena 1993, who discusses the satyrs' reaction to the lyre in *Ichneutae* in light of the *Hymn* at pp. 122–3.

[17] Sophocles as innovative dramaturge: *Life of Sophocles* 4. Seale 1982 examines the expression of themes of vision (and its lack) in Sophoclean stagecraft (but makes no mention of the satyr plays). On blindness and sight in Sophocles' *Thamyras*, see Coo 2016.

[18] Cf. Kaimio *et alii* 2001, 49, citing Taplin 1993, 74: '[I]t is generally assumed that when a character in comedy played the *aulos* he or she mimed, while the actual sound was supplied by the official piper'. The extensive mimetic capacity of the *aulos* (cf. Wilson 1999, 92–3) would have permitted the aulete to imitate the sound of the panpipes (at Eur. *IA* 576–8, the *syrinx* imitates the *aulos*), as it would Silenus' whistling (*syrigma*, 173) in *Ichneutae* (see below). An obvious modern parallel is presented by Mozart's opera *The Magic Flute*, in which Tamino's wooden prop flute is voiced by the professional flautist in the orchestra. Cf. Kovacs 2013, 485. Abbate 2001 offers stimulating analyses of instrumental ventriloquism in Western opera. Kane 2014 reflects more generally on the phenomenon of visually sourceless ('acousmatic') sound.

In the production of *Ichneutae*, the disjunction of sound from sight was likely more extreme, since the text would suggest that the lyre was invisible to the audience as well as the satyr chorus, played out of sight down in Maia's cave, i.e. inside the *skēnē*.[19] Other scenarios are imaginable, of course. Cyllene and the satyrs both refer to the loudness of Hermes' lyre (289, 299), and it may thus be objected that a lyre, more at home in the symposium than the theatre, would be too quiet to project at sufficient volume to the audience when played offstage. An easy solution to the problem of acoustics, however, would have been to have the louder 'concert' *kithara*, which was routinely played before large theatrical audiences, sound the offstage part of Hermes' tortoiseshell *lyra*.[20]

Conceivably, the citharist supplying music for the still-hidden lyre might have stood visibly in the orchestra along with the aulete and chorus.[21] Yet it seems improbable that the wooden *skēnē* would so severely muffle a strategically positioned and forcefully struck *kithara* as to necessitate this measure. More crucially, even if having the citharist in the orchestra might render the string music more audible, it would surely subtract from the dramatic suspense and cumulative impact of the scenes leading up to and including, as seems almost certain, Hermes' emergence from the cave with his mysterious instrument.[22]

The visible presence in the orchestra of an aulete supplying music for a prop instrument such as the *syrinx* in *Inachus* is one thing: the aulete was a fixed, familiar piece of theatrical furniture, like the orchestra in the pit of an opera hall, and he would presumably not distract too much from dramatic illusion (even if his presence, particularly in comedy, always had the potential for metatheatrical play).[23] But the lyre and *kithara* were far from being fixtures in the Theatre of Di-

---

19 Cf. Kaimio *et alii* 2001, 48–9.
20 Several people at the UCL conference suggested to me the possibility that a backstage battery of lyres (or *kitharai*) was used in the production to create a fully audible volume. This would not, I think, have been entirely necessary, but it is certainly conceivable. Multiple lyres and *kitharai* were in fact sometimes played synchronously and homophonically, particularly, it would seem, in processional contexts. Polycrates *FGrHist* 588 F 1 describes a procession of Spartan youths strumming *kitharai* in unison. Marching 'satyr choruses' in Archaic Athenian vase painting occasionally appear with stringed instruments, which they appear to play in unison. Cf. Hedreen 2007, 164–9; Kárpáti 2012, 224–6, who discusses the relation of these images to Polion's 'Singers' krater. See further Almazova 2012.
21 Thus Kovacs 2013, 495.
22 Cf. Robert 1912, 560. For the effectiveness of the lyre as the unseen 'director' of the stage action, see Maltese 1991, 65–6.
23 However, the Bari Pipers kalyx-krater (Apulian, ca. 365–50 BC; Taplin 1993, Figs. 14.11*a* and *b*) suggests that, even in some cases of auletic ventriloquism, an attempt was made to remove the aulete from the audience's direct line of sight in the orchestra in order to maintain greater verisimilitude: a piper who would appear to be the official dramatic aulete crouches down be-

onysus; when they do appear, as in *Thamyras* or *Ichneutae*, they tend to be deeply integrated into the plot and dramatic action. Whatever the acoustical or practical benefits might have been of having a string-player appear visibly before the spectators of *Ichneutae* and apart from the dramatic fiction, these, it seems to me, would have been far outweighed by the dramatic, visual, and psychological value of keeping him hidden, at least until the actor playing Hermes appeared with his lyre.[24] At that point, a *lyra*, now unobstructed by the *skēnē*, may well have been sufficiently audible to the audience, and so could have been played by the actor impersonating Hermes. Alternately, the offstage, surrogate citharist could have continued to play while the actor mimed; perhaps he could have even moved into a more visible and audible spot now that the mystery of the lyre was revealed. Again, other stagings are certainly imaginable, but the completely-invisible-lyre/*kithara* scenario is the one most obviously implied by the text, and the one that would seem best to enhance the spectators' experience of the drama.[25]

The complete invisibility of the lyre certainly would have been a powerful means of involving the audience affectively in the stage action. Film theorists once spoke often of 'suture', the process through which certain cinematic and narrative techniques imperceptibly 'stitch' viewers into the fictional world of a film, making them forget their status as spectators removed from that illusory world and its inhabitants.[26] Hermes' offstage lyre, invisible to both satyrs and

---

hind a tree onstage, while two actors with pipes of their own take center stage, presumably only pretending to play them while the 'hiding' aulete actually supplies their musical parts. Taplin thinks it likely that the aulete was screened only from the actors, not the theatrical spectators (1993, 74–5). But why bother hiding the aulete at all in that case, unless some larger metatheatrical game were being played? The image is obviously difficult to interpret, but it might offer some *a fortiori* support for a stringed instrument hidden from the audience of *Ichneutae*.

24 And comic value as well: Wilamowitz 1912, 456.

25 One other alternative is worth mentioning: Could the *aulos*, that hyper-mimetic instrument, have played the part of the lyre all along? Auletic imitation of stringed instruments was not unknown in drama; see e.g. Ar. *Wealth* 290 with scholia. This scenario appeals both for its apparent simplicity as well as its potentially complex metamusical implications (cf. Power 2013 on mimetic one-upmanship between pipes and strings). But the odds are great that strings were actually used in other plays such as the *Thamyras*, unless we assume the testimonia are wrong and there too the *aulos* voiced a silent *kithara*. It is possible that Sophocles either did not want to deal with the practical challenges of using a real lyre (or *kithara*) in the production of *Ichneutae* or that he was intent on making some conceptual point about the mimetic mastery of tragedy and the *aulos* over lyric genres, but it is far more likely that he simply incorporated real strings into the production.

26 This is a necessarily reductive definition, as suture is an enormously complex theoretical concept. For overviews, see Hayward 2000, 378–85, Žižek 2001, 31–54.

spectators alike, would function dramaturgically like a technique of suture, aligning the latter with the subject position of the former in the world of the play. Such suturing would effect a reaction more visceral than mere sympathetic identification.[27] Though the spectators were of course all familiar with the lyre, and most likely the *Homeric Hymn to Hermes* as well, the initial, unexpected eruption of the instrument would nevertheless have shocked, or at least surprised them as much as it did the satyrs. After that initial jolt passed, the suture was broken, but perhaps the audience members, despite their superior knowledge, would have more sympathetically 'played along' with the satyrs as they puzzled out the source of the frightening noise. For a moment, after all, the lyre was as 'new' to them as it was to the primitive satyrs.

The lyre's unseen sounds may have carried a metatheatrical charge as well – invisibility as a way of conceptualizing the novelty and indeed the fundamental alienness of the lyre in the Athenian theatrical context. For although it was the normative cornerstone of Hellenic *mousikē*, the instrument primarily identified with Apollo was a stranger in the Theatre of Dionysus, where the *aulos* was at home, and cameos there by its players tend to be fraught, problematic, dark.[28] There is, for instance, Sophocles' Thamyras, the overly ambitious citharode violently stripped of his art by the Muses; Orpheus in Aeschylus' *Bassarids* (*TrGF*³, pp. 138–40), torn apart by Maenads for his refusal to recognize Dionysus; Euripides' lyre-singing Amphion, whose devotion to *mousikē* alienates him from his twin brother in the *Antiope* (*TrGF*⁵·¹, F 179–227). Lyre-singers generally do not have an easy time on the comic stage, either. Their indelicate treatment is vividly emblematized by the much-discussed image of the citharode Phrynis being manhandled by an angry old man ('Pyronides') on a Paestan bell-krater by Asteas (ca. 350 BC), which very likely represents a scene from Eupolis' comedy *Demes* (produced between 417 and 410 BC).[29]

As creatures of Dionysus and the theatre, Sophocles' satyrs, like other dramatic satyrs, are happy intimates of the *aulos*; their dance-songs are accompanied by it, after all.[30] Thus, when the satyrs first relate to Silenus their reaction to the lyre, their words come with a metatheatrical doubleness:

---

27 Cf. relevant remarks on identification in Heath 1987, 15.
28 The subject is explored in Wilson 2008, 185–6 and 2009; Power 2012, 298–300 and 2013. Kovacs 2013 surveys dramas that probably featured string playing.
29 Cf. Csapo 2010, 61–3. Power 2013 examines antagonism to *kitharōidia* in comedy as well as dithyramb, another song genre practiced in the Theatre of Dionysus.
30 For the role of the aulete in satyr drama, see now the essays on the Pronomos Vase in Taplin and Wyles 2010, especially Wilson 2010 and Griffith 2010. It is worth noting here the presence of two lyres on the Pronomos Vase, one residing near the poet Demetrios, the other in the hands of

> ἄκουσον αὐτ[.] ... [πά]τερ, χρόνον τινὰ
> ο]ἵῳ πλαγέντες ἐν[θάδ'] ἐξενίσμεθα
> ψόφῳ, τὸν οὐδε[ὶ]ς π̣[ώπ]ο̣τ' ἤκουσεν βροτῶν.

(*Ich.* 142–4)

Listen [yourself], father, for a moment, to what sort of noise has left us here terror-struck and astonished; no one in the world has ever heard it!

In the papyrus text, the word at the end of line 143 is illegible. The variant recorded in the margin, ἐξενίσμεθα, has been generally accepted by editors. The passive verb would seem to mean here 'to be astonished, surprised (by a strange phenomenon)', a sense not otherwise attested until the Hellenistic period (LSJ s.v. ξενίζω II.1). In Sophocles' time, ξενίζεσθαι would normally mean 'to be entertained, offered hospitality as a guest', but that definition, at least in a literal sense, seems unsuited to the context.³¹ For this reason, some scholars have sought alternatives to ἐξενίσμεθα, but the word is attractive just because its uncustomary usage demands reflection on the part of the audience.³² It operates, I suggest, within two frames of reference at once, indicating both the strangeness of the lyre in the world of the play as well as its defamiliarization of the theatrical milieu framing that world. The deictic adverb ἐνθάδε 'here' complements this referential layering. As characters in the dramatic fiction, the satyrs are stunned by the sound of lyre, which is, being brand new, naturally a stranger (*xenos*) 'here', in the rustic setting of the drama (and indeed the larger world). Speaking as members of a dramatic chorus in an Athenian satyr play, however, the satyrs/*khoreutai* imply with ἐξενίσμεθα that they too are notionally rendered strangers (*xenoi*), alienated from 'here', their Dionysian home-turf of the theatre, by the in-

---

Kharinos, whom Wilson 2010, 206 identifies attractively as the *khorēgos*. Neither lyre is shown being played, in contrast to the *auloi* on which Pronomos actively pipes. They seem to serve entirely symbolic functions in the image, and there is little reason to assume they point to the use of a lyre in the actual dramatic production to which the image refers.

31 Griffith 2013b, 269, however, translates lines 143–4 as 'entertained and smitten by such a sound'. This translation nicely picks up on a possible erotic subtext: no doubt we are to understand the satyrs are stirred to some inchoate desire for the lyre (as is Apollo in the *Hymn to Hermes*). But abject fear determines their behavior in this scene, and it is difficult to understand their words to communicate such a differently oriented message at the primary, surface level.

32 For alternative conjectures, none of them obviously more satisfactory than ἐξενίσμεθα, see Guida 2010, 2013, 149–51. Guida himself prefers ἐξ[η]ιγίσμεθα, from the unattested verb ἐξαιγίζω, a conjecture of Walker 1919, 452–3, which Walker translates as 'we have been broken as with a tempest'.

trusion of this instrument foreign to the conventions of the theatre.³³ There is, however, a neat irony in the chorus' reaction to its 'estrangement' by the lyre: they perform a frenetic dance spectacle of a type entirely appropriate to satyr drama, which elicits the metatheatrically loaded question from Silenus, 'Why are you acting crazy/going Bacchic (βακχεύεις)?' (133).

Furthermore, it is tempting to speculate that the metatheatrical intrusiveness of the lyre was manifested in an actual sonic confrontation with the *auloi* played in the orchestra. Silenus says he will 'urge on the satyrs with a dog-spurring whistling' (κυνορτικὸν σύριγμα διακαλούμενος, 173). This announcement is very likely a cue for the pipes to accompany the wild dance-song beginning at 176, in which the chorus members imitate hounds, exhorting one another toward the hunt. But that song, which lasts for 26 lines (the papyrus is severely lacunose after 182, however), is clearly terminated by a fresh lyric outburst right before line 203. Silenus had most probably been miming at whistling on the stage while the *aulos* played and the satyrs sang and danced. The satyrs' question, 'Father, why do you fall silent?' (πάτερ, τί σιγᾷς;, 203), thus asks to be heard as a metatheatrical reference to the sudden silencing of the *aulos* by the lyre, addressed both to Silenus and the aulete.³⁴

Mock *paideia* was a recurring theme of satyr play—satyrs learning to do the things, athletic, cultural, and social, that were part of the formation of Athenian citizens.³⁵ We see it here too in *Ichneutae*. The satyrs' move from fear and loathing to rapturous acceptance of the lyre unfolds as a spoof of the education in lyre playing that was a central aspect of the *paideia* undergone by Athenian youths, or at least those of better-off families, among whom most, if not all, of the chorus members could count themselves.³⁶ The *Homeric Hymn to Hermes* already has fun with the institution of lyric *paideia* in imagining the older, aristocratic Apollo

---

33 In its metatheatrical frame of reference, ἐξενίσμεθα anticipates the later-attested meanings 'make strange' and, be a stranger, foreigner' (LSJ s.v. ξενίζω II.2, III.1).
34 The papyrus scribe indicates in the margin at line 176 that the song at 176–202 is delivered by the chorus. Antonopoulos 2014 argues, against the scribal indication and prevailing scholarly opinion (but following the lead of Robert 1912, 547–9), that it was a lyric dialogue between Silenus and the chorus, and that πάτερ, τί σιγᾷς; must mean Silenus has stopped speaking or singing, not whistling. I am, however, more inclined to read the exhortations in the song as self-exhortations (which are amply attested in choral melic), and less inclined to read σε προσβιβῶ λόγῳ in 172 literally, as an indication that Silenus intends to move the satyrs with words (*logos*); Lloyd-Jones's (1996, 157) 'I'll win you to my way of thinking' seems closer to the mark.
35 Cf. Griffith 2013b, 265; Lissarrague 1990.
36 The social status of the *khoreutai* in Athenian dramatic productions was probably not uniformly aristocratic, but it did likely tilt toward the educated and well-off. See Wilson 2000, 75, 126–9. For lyric *paideia* in fifth-century Athens, see Power 2007.

tutored in lyre playing by the young upstart Hermes. Like Sophocles' satyrs, Apollo knows only the 'blooming dance-song and the seductive roar of *auloi*' (μολπὴ τεθαλυῖα καὶ ἱμερόεις βρόμος αὐλῶν, 452) before he is exposed to the newly invented lyre and the refined pleasures it brings.

Here it is Cyllene who tutors the satyrs in the appreciation of lyric *mousikē*, leading them on a 'hunt' for the identity of the lyre that is really a process of cultural initiation. Their progress is marked by their verbal and physical responses to the lyre. At first, they react to what seems to them its inarticulate noise (*psophos*, 144) with their own inarticulate howls (ὒ [ὒ] ὒ ὒ, 131) and animalistic movements across the ground (127–8). The second wave of lyric *psophos* drives them into a rage, which they express through their wild stamping on the earth over Maia's cave (217–20). But after Cyllene emerges to issue a stern reprimand (221–42)—the satyrs are acting like θῆρες 'animals' (221), caught up in 'strange and maniacal whirlings' (στροφαὶ νέαι μανιῶν, 229–30)—it is as if a civilizing process begins to take effect. The satyrs inquire after the source and maker of the sound, with increasing verbal sophistication, first in song (lines 243–50 are in lyric meter, presumably accompanied by the *aulos*):

<XO.> ἀλλ' [εὐ]πετῶς μοι πρ[
μ' ἐν [τ]όποις τοῖσ[
στως ἐγήρυσε θέσπιν αὐδά[ν.

(*Ich*. 248–50)

But readily to me .... in this place .... uttered a divine voice.

Cyllene continues to chide the satyrs for their aggressiveness, but begins to soften, encouraging them to try again (251–7). The satyrs repeat their request, in speech this time (iambic trimeters), presumably exhibiting still more self-control:

<XO.> τόπων ἄνασσα τῶν[δ]ε, Κυλλήνης σθένος,
ὅτου μὲν οὕνεκ' ἦλθ[ο]ν, ὕστερον φράσω·
τὸ φθέγμα δ' ἡμῖν τοῦθ' ὅπερ φωνεῖ φράσον
καὶ τίς ποτ' αὐτῷ διαχαράσσεται βροτῶν.

(*Ich*. 258–61)[37]

---

[37] Lloyd-Jones 1996, 163 translates διαχαράσσεται 'exasperates', Pearson 1917, 257 'sets our teeth on edge'. Pearson is probably right to detect an allusion to the plectrum 'as it *scrapes across* the strings of the lyre'. Perhaps too διαχαράσσεται playfully and learnedly foreshadows the flaying of the satyr Marsyas by Apollo after their musical contest. The early Byzantine writer Agathias uses the verb of a historical flaying (of the satrap Nacoragan), which he contrasts with the fictional story of Marsyas' flaying (*Histories* 4.23).

Queen of this region, might of Cyllene,
why I came I will explain later.
But explain to us this voice which sounds,
and who in the world is scraping at us with it?

What was before called noise is now significantly characterized as an aesthetically articulate, even anthropomorphized sound, a 'voice' (ἐγήρυσε, αὐδᾴ[ν, 250; τὸ φθέγμα ... φωνεῖ 260; cf. φθέγμα, 284, 328; γῆρυν, 297). The satyrs' language notably takes on the heightened tone of hexameter poetry. Cyllene is addressed with the epic periphrasis Κυλλήνης σθένος 'might of Cyllene'; θέσπιν αὐδᾴ[ν in particular recalls the epicism θέσπις ἀοιδή 'divine song', used of the lyric songs sung by the bards Phemius and Demodocus, respectively, at *Od.* 1.328 and 8.498 (both times in the accusative case at verse end, as here).[38] A still more apposite echo are the words of Apollo in the *Hymn to Hermes*, soon after he has first heard Hermes' lyre song:

ἠέ τις ἀθανάτων ἠὲ θνητῶν ἀνθρώπων
δῶρον ἀγαυὸν ἔδωκε καὶ ἔφρασε θέσπιν ἀοιδήν;
θαυμασίην γὰρ τήνδε νεήφατον ὄσσαν ἀκούω.

(*Homeric Hymn to Hermes* 441–3)

Or did some immortal or mortal give you this brilliant gift and show you its wondrous song?
For amazing is this new-spoken voice I hear.

Cyllene responds to this newfound politesse of the satyrs by confiding the secret of Hermes' birth and describing his precocious creation of the 'contrivance' (μηχανῇ, 284), created from some dead creature, that produces the strange voice. The identity of that creature is presented in a riddle: what is mute while alive, yet possessed of voice in death (300)? The solution is revealed to the satyrs— the creature is the tortoise, and Hermes calls the resonant object made from it a lyre (324)—after Cyllene leads them through a stichomythic exchange that simultaneously evokes a number of discursive scenarios associated with education, enculturation, and enlightenment: a schoolroom lesson, a philosophical dialogue, a sympotic riddle contest, even mystical initiation.[39]

---

38 Hermes is not yet heard singing to the lyre, so αὐδᾴ[ν, elsewhere used of the lyre's 'voice' (*Od.* 21.411), is an appropriate substitution for ἀοιδή. Cf. Maltese 1982, 88–9. Additionally, the 'voice' of the lyre will figure prominently in the riddling exchange with Cyllene that follows. Diggle 1996, 13 has more on the lyre's 'voice'.
39 For riddling in sympotic poetry, see Martin 2001, 61–3, Collins 2005, 111–34; for riddles about musical instruments, Power 2007, 201–2. The mute tortoise/speaking lyre paradox is im-

With Cyllene as their teacher and notional hierophant, the satyrs become virtual connoisseurs of the lyre. Their transformation is indicated by the rapturous opening lines of the choral strophe beginning at line 329, which are presumably prompted by another, perhaps this time more florid burst of music from the cave:

<XO.> < x >οψάλακτός τις ὀμφὰ κατοιχνεῖ τόπου,
πρεπτὰ <δ' ἤ>δη τόνου φάσματ' ἔγ-
χωρ' ἐπανθεμίζει.

(*Ich.* 329–31)

A [?-]plucked voice spreads over the region! Conspicuous now are the apparitions of musical tone (*tonos*) it scatters like flowers all over this place![40]

Now initiated, the satyrs are able properly to comprehend, to *see*, as it were, the 'conspicuous apparitions of tone' produced by the still-invisible lyre.[41] They employ technically and poetically sophisticated language to describe what they perceive. The word *tonos*, whose basic meaning is 'tension, stretching', is first used in a musical sense in the second half of the fifth century to denote a stable pitch or tone, particularly one produced by a string (cf. *heptatonos* 'seven-pitched', used of the lyre in Eur. *Alc.* 447 and *HF* 683 and Ion of Chios fr. 32.3 *IEG*, a text heavy with music-theoretical inflection). We may suppose that here it still has a certain *au courant* technical glamour, marking its users as true *mousikoi*.[42] In the elaborate periphrasis of line 329, the compound adjective < x >οψάλακτος could imply some special knowledge of string-playing technique, while ὀμφὰ expresses a heightened appreciation of the lyre's 'voice', and recognition too of its

---

plicit already in Sappho fr. 118 Voigt (cf. Svenbro 1992, 141 n.42), and was probably long the subject of sympotic *ainigmata*. Cf. Borthwick 1970. Lämmle 2013, 433–5 notes the intimation of Dionysian mysteries in the riddling stichomythia. In view of the centrality of the lyre in Cyllene's riddling, and the paradoxical theme of 'living voice in death', however, we may want to consider Orphic mysticism to be the specific reference point. The author of the Derveni Papyrus notes how the poetry of Orpheus is 'strange and riddling', and claims that Orpheus wanted to reveal 'great things through riddles' (Col. VII.4–7). For riddles as a *topos* in satyr drama, see Seaford 1984, 41–2.

40 I follow the translation of Lloyd-Jones 1996, 169. For ἐπανθεμίζει as probably transitive, with ὀμφά as subject, see Maltese 1982, 93, Stahl 1913, 308. Or, taken another way: 'Conspicuous apparitions of tone now come to bloom in this place'. Pearson 1917, 263, Nooter 2012, 171, and Griffith 2013b, 271 offer other interpretations.

41 Lämmle 2013, 433–4 detects undertones of mystical-initiatory themes and imagery in this phrase.

42 For the later applications of *tonos* in Greek music theory, see Hagel 2010.

maker's divinity.⁴³ In Homer, ὀμφή is reserved for the voice of gods uttered to mortals in dreams, oracles, and epiphanies.⁴⁴ In the elaborate metamusical vocabulary of Pindar and Bacchylides, ὀμφά describes the beautiful voices of singers and instruments (e.g. Pind. *Nem.* 10.34, Bacch. 14.13).

While stringed instruments were relative strangers to the Theatre of Dionysus, they are commonly played with gusto and apparent expertise by the imaginary satyrs depicted in *thiasos* and *kōmos* scenes on Archaic and Classical Attic vases, not only the 'Dionysian', sympotic *barbitos*, but also the more distinctly 'Apollonian' tortoise-shell lyre and *kithara*.⁴⁵ Such depictions, which arguably carry a whiff of ludic transgression and cultural mischief—Apollonian strings in bestial hands—would seem to raise the question of backstory. When and how did satyrs gain their evident enthusiasm for strings? It is tempting to read *Ichneutae* as an attempt to answer that question. That is, Sophocles may have intended the *paideia* of his lyre-less satyrs as a sort of mock *aition* for the attachment of satyrs to stringed instruments that we see depicted in the iconography and that was surely part of their mythopoetic representation more broadly. It is conceivable that this aetiology received further elaboration in the lost second half of *Ichneutae*. In one obvious scenario, Hermes eventually appeared on stage, where he probably sang, was reconciled with Apollo, and finally handed the lyre over to his brother, as in the *Homeric Hymn to Hermes*.⁴⁶ But might Apollo in turn have promised to share its pleasures with the satyrs, as a reward for

---

43 On ὀμφά, cf. Nooter 2012, 171. Although it was more common to strike (*krouein*) lyre- and kithara-strings with the plectrum than to pluck them with fingers (*psallein*, to which *psalassein/psalaktos* is related), lyre players did employ pizzicato, cf. West 1992, 66–7. But realistic detail of lyre-playing seems less the point of this epithet than the clever way it calls back to ὀρθοψάλακτον (255), which likely describes some aspect of the satyrs' initially quarrelsome demeanor toward Cyllene (the text is too lacunose to be more specific). Most scholars have understood ὀρθοψάλακτον to mean 'loud, shrill sounding', as if it were ὀρθιοψάλακτον. But Zagagi 1999, 255 n. 84 proposes an appealing alternative, 'erect, as a result of being touched lightly': 'The reference would be to the phallic situation of the satyrs…responsible for the satyrs' aggressive attempt to gain entrance to her [Cyllene's] cave'. Whatever the full form of the epithet in 329 was – Lloyd-Jones' χεροψάλακτος 'plucked by hand' seems to me slightly better than any other proposed supplement; see discussion in Diggle 1996, 13 – the repetition of -οψάλακτος marks a significant change of tone, underlining the (momentary, at least) transformation of the satyrs from hypersexual louts into cultured *mousikoi*. Cyllene's invective epithet is neatly transmuted into the satyrs' 'learned' praise for the lyre.
44 Ford 1993, 175.
45 See Voelke 2001, 91–130 on musical satyrs. For Archaic images of 'satyr choruses' playing stringed instruments, which might represent some sort of historical pre-dramatic song-and-dance performances in Athens (dithyrambs?), see Hedreen 2007, 164–9 and Kárpáti 2012, 224–6.
46 Cf. KPS, 311.

their help? Lloyd-Jones makes the appealing argument that the freedom apparently promised by Apollo to the satyrs was freedom from servitude to Dionysus, and that Apollo ultimately reneged on the promise, leaving the satyrs still in (happy) thrall to Dionysus.[47] A share in Hermes', now Apollo's lyric *mousikē*, which the satyrs gladly carry over into their Dionysian *thiasos*, might have been their consolation prize.

All that must remain speculation. But it is suggestive that Euripides has the satyrs of his *Cyclops* make what seems a fairly clear allusion to *Ichneutae* by way of expressing their enthusiasm for string music. Odysseus tells the satyrs he has devised a punishment for the Cyclops and a plan for escaping their captivity to him (441–2). The satyrs reply, 'Speak, as we could hear no sound (*psophos*) sweeter than the Asiatic *kithara*, save word of the Cyclops' death' (λέγ', ὡς Ἀσιάδος οὐκ ἂν ἥδιον ψόφον / κιθάρας κλύοιμεν ἢ Κύκλωπ' ὀλωλότα, 443–4). *Psophos* is not a *Lieblingswort* of Euripides, and only once elsewhere does he use it of musical sound (*Ba.* 687, λωτοῦ ψόφῳ 'noise of the pipe', referring to *auloi*). Given that Sophocles' satyrs and Silenus make several emphatic references to the *psophos* of the lyre, a wink back to *Ichneutae* is a real possibility.[48]

If this is so, the allusion would imply a certain degree of maturation in satyric musical culture. The long-ago exposure of the Sophoclean satyrs to the 'new' tortoiseshell-lyre has developed into the Euripidean satyrs' appreciation for the Asiatic *kithara*, that is, the large 'concert' *kithara* played by virtuoso professional citharodes.[49] We may wonder too whether the play depicted on the

---

[47] Lloyd-Jones 1996, 143; cf. Zagagi 1999, 182 n.10. If the satyrs were enslaved to and then released by Apollo, as others hold, a similar scenario is nonetheless conceivable: the satyrs took up and continued to practice the lyric art of their former master. See relevant comments in Griffith 2013b, 269 n.44.

[48] Seaford 1982 argues compellingly for the production of *Cyclops* in 408 BC, but, if we remain open to a later dating for *Ichneutae*, we need not assume that the time between the productions of the two plays was so great.

[49] Asiatic *kithara*: Ps.-Plut. *De mus.* 6.1133c; Douris fr. 81 Jacoby. Barker 1984, 211 n. 45 thinks it likely that *Asias kithara* at *Cyclops* 443–4 (as in other fifth-century texts) refers to the *barbitos*, an instrument associated, like the *kithara*, with Lesbos and Lydia (cf. Pindar fr. 125 S-M). It is true that in *Cyclops* Silenus introduces the *parodos* by evoking a memory of the satyr chorus once upon a time 'swaggering to the songs of *barbitoi*' (ἀοιδαῖς βαρβίτων σαυλούμενοι) as they approached the house of Althaea (39–40). But we need not assume that satyrs cannot be aficionados of both *barbitos* and *kithara*; the vase paintings indicate they are. It is worth noting that Silenus' recollection of the satyrs dancing (presumably) while holding *barbitoi* may allude to a previous satyr play featuring a chorus of *barbitos*-playing satyrs, similar perhaps to the citharodic satyrs on the 'Singers' krater (and the string-playing 'satyr choruses' on Archaic vases). We hear of a comedy by Magnes entitled *Barbitistai* (Σ Ar. *Eq.* 522a).

'Singers' krater by Polion, with its citharodic satyrs, may also have engaged *Ichneutae* in some related fashion.

3 Double Vision: From 'New Music' to The New Music

The *Asias kithara* presents an opportune segue into the New Music. It is in Euripides that we first find the *kithara* called 'Asiatic'.[50] T.B.L. Webster had the appealing idea that Euripides adopted it as a coded show of support for his fellow traveller in the New Music, Timotheus of Miletus, when the latter found himself a pariah in Athens on account of his too-radical innovations in *kitharōidia*.[51] Be that as it may, the epithet *Asias* would seem to register more broadly an increasingly 'exotic' turn taken by innovative citharodes of the later fifth century, above all Timotheus and his older rival, Phrynis of Mytilene, who opened their music to novel influences from the Theatre of Dionysus, both tragedy and dithyramb.[52] Thus, it may be that Euripides' satyrs are enthusiasts not only of the *kithara*, but specifically of the novel *kitharōidia* emerging in Athens.

Citharodic New Music may, however, already be peeking through the representation of Hermes' lyric 'new music' in *Ichneutae*, as well as in the characterization of the satyrs as a listening audience. With the addition of strings beyond the traditional seven (*polychordia*) and the novel sonic effects being created on them, the *kithara* was very much in a state of accelerated evolution during the years when *Ichneutae* was probably produced, even if that was as early as the 440s. The instrument was a *mēchanē* 'contrivance', to borrow Cyllene's word, suggestive of technical cunning and wondrous artifice, for Hermes' brand-new lyre (284), that was subject to ongoing reinvention.[53] It is thus not so far-fetched to view the satyrs as stand-ins for a fascinated, yet confused and even hostile

---

50 Besides *Cyclops* 443–4, *Hypsipyle* $TrGF^{5.2}$ F 752 g.9–10 and *Erechtheus* $TrGF^{5.1}$ F 369d.
51 Webster 1967, 18.
52 Cf. Power 2013.
53 Ion fr. 32 *IEG*, which celebrates the novelty of an 'eleven-stringed *lyra*' (by which a *kithara* is probably meant) is remarkable testimony for such reinvention. Pherecrates *Chiron* fr. 155.14–25 PCG^7 details in sexually metaphorical language the organological and technical innovations of the citharodes Phrynis and Timotheus. See Power 2007 on Ion, Dobrov-Uparisi 1995 and Restani 1983 on Pherecrates.

Athenian public coming to terms with this ongoing renewal of lyric/citharodic tradition.[54]

Whether the actual music played on Hermes' lyre—which, recall, was very likely voiced by the louder *kithara*—echoed in some manner the style of 'new citharodes' such as Phrynis and Timotheus is obviously a question we cannot answer. However, we might want to leave open this intriguing possibility, which becomes still more intriguing if we follow Wilamowitz in speculating that Sophocles himself played the part of Hermes, as he (probably) did Thamyras.[55] But the language of the text does invite us to hear the mythical sounds as modern, and to imagine the mischievous and innovative god as an Athenian 'new citharode'.

Griffith similarly reads New Music discourse out from between the lines of *Ichneutae*, though his focus is more on the satyrs' dancing than Hermes' music. Arguing for satyr drama as a site of choreographical innovation, he hears in the verbal responses to the wild orchestic displays of Sophocles' satyr chorus language that is redolent of New Music criticism. Thus Silenus asks the satyrs, as they fearfully contort themselves on the ground, what new *technē* they have invented, saying that their style, *tropos*, of dance is one of which he has no previous experience (124–30; cf. 223). Later, when Cyllene describes the satyrs' 'strange and maniacal whirlings' (στροφαὶ νέαι μανιῶν, 229–30), she evokes the imagery of twists, bends, and turns that so commonly appears in both the programmatic language and criticism of the New Music.[56]

But Hermes' music too elicits such pregnant language. A hint of this comes as early as Silenus' mock-Nestorian screed, in which he reproaches his sons for their cowardly reaction to the *psophos*—an insult, he tells them, to his own virility and past acts of valor (read: sexual bravado in his relations with nymphs), acts 'whose lustre is now tarnished by you, all because of an unexpected wheedling noise from some shepherds' (ἃ] νῦν ὑφ' ὑμῶν λάμ[πρ' ἀ]πορρυπαίνεται / ψ] όφῳ νεώρει κόλακ[ι] ποιμένων π[ο]θέν, 159–60). The phrase ψόφῳ νεώρει κόλακι has frustrated all translators, no doubt because its subtext vies so strongly with the text to be heard. What is rendered here, forcedly, as 'unexpected wheedling noise'—Silenus apparently has in mind the panpipes used by shepherds to call their flocks—means far more naturally, and no doubt would have been heard

---

54 For Athenian hostility toward Timotheus' radical musical innovations (*kainotomia*), see Satyrus *Life of Euripides* (P. Oxy. 1176 fr. 39 col. xxii).
55 Wilamowitz 1912, 461. Robert 1912, 560 would have Sophocles playing Apollo's part instead, and singing to the newly acquired lyre at play's end.
56 Griffith 2013b, 269–70. On such imagery, see now Franklin 2013.

by the audience primarily to mean, 'a new noise, a fawning one'.⁵⁷ In that contextually awkward yet more natural sense, the New Music subtext unavoidably comes through, and Silenus becomes an unwitting mouthpiece of moralizing criticism against musical innovation, with the new lyre, not some pastoral *syrinx*, as the understood target. The causative role assigned to 'new noise' in this rant about generational decline, feminization, and the loss of discipline and order cannot but resonate with the critique of the New Music we find in Old Comedy and other culturally conservative texts.⁵⁸

This impression is strengthened by κόλακι 'flatterer, fawner', a word that resists easy comprehension at the surface level of Silenus' speech. It must be understood figuratively—the pipe as flatterer of flocks, telling them what they want to hear in order to move them—but the sense is badly strained, with a subtlety unsuitable to the immediate rhetorical context. One scholar has suggested emending to δόνακι, the reed of the *syrinx*.⁵⁹ It is better, I think, to keep κόλακι and recognize that its difficulty becomes more sensible when considered against the backdrop of the New Music. As such, the word takes on a proleptic force, looking ahead to the characterization of the popular New Musician as a vulgar panderer to the masses, a shameless crowd-pleaser, that appears in the conservative musical criticism.⁶⁰

Finally, it should be noted that *psophos* itself carries New Musical connotations.⁶¹ Aristotle denigrated dithyrambic songs—and these would be dithyrambs in the new style of the later-fifth and fourth century—as 'full of noise' (ψοφώδεις, *Rh.* 1406b2). Dionysius of Halicarnassus, echoing critical language of the Classical period, writes of the 'noises (*psophous*) and natterings of dithyrambs' (*Dem.* 7). What is truly incomprehensible noise to satyrs and Silenus is

---

57 'Wheedling' is how Lloyd-Jones renders κόλακι (1996, 157); cf. Pearson 1917, 247, 'soothing'. 'Unexpected' is suggested for νεώρει by Guida 2013, 152.
58 Csapo 2004 remains the best study of these and related critical themes; see too Csapo 2011. Silenus' speech especially recalls (though we should not assume any direct relationship to) that of Better Argument in Ar. *Clouds* 961–99. This aged reactionary laments the corruption of the old education that bred the victors at Marathon by, among other things, the intrusion of popular novelties into lyric *paideia*, in particular the flashy 'bends' of Phrynis the citharode.
59 Guida 2013, 152–5, who reviews other interpretations and emendations, none satisfying.
60 Thus Plato puts the 'new dithyrambographer' Cinesias and his citharode father, Meles, on a level with popular orators and politicians, whose desire to gratify the mob at any cost is a base form of *kolakeia* 'pandering, flattery' (*Gorg.* 501e-502c). Related views inform the portrait of the popular musician in Arist. *Pol.* 8.1339a–1342a. Cf. Power 2010, 83–4. These are fourth-century texts, but their critical assumptions have roots in fifth-century cultural elitism.
61 Griffith 2013b, 269, 271 n. 50 makes the same observation. Cf. Porter 2010, 379–80.

thus, from the contemporary Athenian view, innovative music that invites dismissal as 'noise' by conservative critics.

But it is in the closing words of Cyllene on the subject of the lyre, and then in the subsequent choral song, where the modern musical subtext emerges most clearly:

> <ΚΥ.> καὶ τοῦτο λύπης ἔστ' ἄκεστρον καὶ παραψυκ[τ]ήρ[ιο]ν
> κείνῳ μόνον, χαίρει δ' ἀλύων καί τι προσφων[ῶν] μέλος.
> ξύμφωνον ἐξαίρει γὰρ αὐτὸν αἰόλισμα τῆς λ[ύ]ρας.
> οὕτως ὁ παῖς θανόντι θηρὶ φθέγμ' ἐμηχανήσατο.
> <ΧΟ.> < x >οψάλακτός τις ὀμφὰ κατοιχνεῖ τόπου,
> πρεπτὰ <δ'> ἤ>δη τόνου φάσματ' ἔγ-
> χωρ' ἐπανθεμίζει.

(*Ich*. 325–31)

> Cyllene: And that [the lyre] is the only cure and comfort for unhappiness he's got. He enjoys letting go and giving voice to song; for the quick succession of varied tones played harmoniously on the lyre elates him [lit. 'lifts him up']. So that is how the child contrived a voice for the dead creature.
>
> Chorus: A [?-]plucked voice spreads over the region! Conspicuous now are the apparitions of musical tone (*tonos*) it scatters like flowers all over this place!

Throughout Cyllene's account of Hermes' music making, allusions to the *Homeric Hymn to Hermes* jockey for attention alongside sly references to contemporary trends in *kitharōidia*, creating a palimpsestic layering of new and New musics.[62] While Cyllene's anodyne description of the lyre as emotional 'cure and comfort' goes back to the *Hymn* (447), Hermes' enjoyment in 'letting himself go' (ἀλύων) through his music evokes the more controversial 'Bacchic' ethos of freedom and experimentation that infused New Music composition and performance, and perhaps too the extreme, often maddened and unhinged emotional states its composers and performers, citharodes included, gravitated toward representing (the better to display their virtuosic technique and creative experimentation).[63]

---

[62] In what follows, I return, with slightly different emphases, to some of the observations made in Power 2012, 301–3.

[63] Cf. Csapo 2004, especially pp. 229–30; Power 2013, 245–6 on the 'new citharodic' predilection for representing states of emotional, mental, and physical extremity. For musical experimentation figured as Bacchic frenzy, see Plato *Laws* 700d–e. The verb ἀλύω could indeed attribute a certain Dionysian excess to Hermes' lyric performance. Pearson 1917, 262 translates 'he is crazy with delight'. Cf. Aesch. *Sept*. 391, where ἀλύων describes Tydeus' raving. Diggle 1996, 12 finds ἀλύων, Hunt's slight correction of the papyrus' (curiously Aeolic: *Et. Mag.* 254.17) αλυιων, 'insipid' and prefers Bucherer's ἀθύρων 'playing'. While ἀθύρων would provide a neat allusion

The verb ἐξαίρει and its subject αἰόλισμα add further colour to the portrait of Hermes as avant-garde citharode. On the one hand, both echo keywords in the narrative of the lyre's invention in the *Hymn*, αἰόλισμα the 'dappled' (αἰόλον, 33) shell of the lyre, ἐξαίρει Hermes' initial 'lifting up' (ἀείρας, 39) of the tortoise from the ground. On the other hand, both words suggest the same aesthetic of expressive freedom as ἀλύων. Here, it is Hermes' lyre music that lifts *him* up (ἐξαίρει), an image that calls to mind the aerial motif not uncommon in the representation of New Musicians.[64] What specifically lifts Hermes up is called αἰόλισμα, a congener of that term so central to New Music discourse, ποικιλία, 'complexity' in musical form and performance (Plato *Crat*. 409a actually says αἰολλεῖν and ποικίλλειν are identical in meaning); αἰόλισμα suggests the flashy technique of a new citharode, in which virtuosic manual speed of play (cf. Plato *Laws* 669e) and tonal and harmonic complexity and variability come together.[65] (I thus render the word as 'the quick succession of varied tones'.)

We may compare Telestes 805c and 808 PMG, both fragments from 'new dithyrambs', which highlight manual speed in *aulos* and harp playing, respectively. Oblique echoes of ἐξαίρει γὰρ αὐτὸν αἰόλισμα in *Ichn*. 327 may perhaps be heard in the former fragment, which focuses on Athena's 'uplifted, flash-winged breath' (ἀερθὲν πνεῦμ' αἰολοπτέρυγον) and the 'swiftness of her shining hands' (σὺν ἀγλαᾶν ὠκύτατι χειρῶν) as she plays the newly invented *auloi*, whose mastery she gives over to Dionysus.[66] We may also wonder whether

---

to *Hymn to Hermes* 32, 40, 52 (where the lyre is called a 'plaything', *athurma*), the passage would, I think, be at greater risk of insipidness if we lose the more challenging ἀλύων.

64 See Wilson 1999–2000, 441 for the aerial motif; cf. Power 2012, 302–3. Notable is the appearance of *aeirein* in the context of lyric innovation in Ion fr. 32 IEG (see n. 53 above); there it is the old-time players of the seven-stringed lyre who 'raise up a paltry music' (σπανίαν μοῦσαν ἀειράμενοι, 3). The participle ἀειράμενοι may be ironically marked, since it belongs more properly to players of the novel eleven-stringed lyre or *kithara* (e.g. Timotheus), who elevate music to new heights of sonic and technical complexity.

65 Cf. Griffith 2013b, 271. For *aiol-* terms in music criticism, see Csapo 2004, 269; Hunter 1996, 101–2. New Musical *poikilia*: Franklin 2013, LeVen 2013. The adjective modifying αἰόλισμα, ξύμφωνον, recalls the συμφώνους … χορδάς 'consonant strings' of Hermes' lyre at *Homeric Hymn to Hermes* 52, which is the first attestation of σύμφωνος. As Franklin 2003, 303–4 argues, the *Hymn* likely borrowed the word directly from the professional language of practicing musicians. Sophocles would thus be retaining a word that in its original poetic context was already a technical novelty.

66 Cf. Telestes 806.3–4: the reeds of *auloi* are αἰολομόρφοις 'of swift-changing forms'. The (probably) satyric chorus of Sophocles' *Inachus*, hearing Hermes' (perhaps newly invented, see Carden 1974, 81) *syrinx* for the first time, seems to liken its sound to 'very rapid whisperings' (fr. ψιθυρᾶν μάλ' αἰολᾶ[ν). For possible New Musical colouring to this scene, see Power 2012, 297–8.

Sophocles intended αἰόλισμα as a punning allusion to one of the best-known new citharodes of his day, Phrynis, from the Aeolian island of Lesbos, which had a long history of producing famous citharodes.⁶⁷

Finally, the satyrs' sung response to Cyllene, and to the lyre that has presumably once again sounded, further gestures towards the New Music. In the previous section, we examined how the technical and elevated language in these lines might reflect the satyrs' 'education' under Cyllene's tutelage. However, there is also a synaesthetic, highly impressionistic quality to their song, which remarkably manages to be at once both airy and flowery in its imagery; particularly in combination with the musical-technical language we examined above (τόνος, < x >οψάλακτος), this abstruse, substance-less style triggers associations with the poetry of the New Music, both the dithyramb and the citharodic *nomos*.⁶⁸ The compound neologisms < x >οψάλακτος (in a characteristic periphrasis with ὀμφᾷ) and ἐπανθεμίζει, which frame the lines, are consistent with New Music poetic expression, as is the centrality of the aerial motif. Previously, the god's lyre had sounded threateningly from down in the cave; now, its 'apparitions of musical tone' float gently down from above like flowers. It is even as if the chorus members themselves, like Hermes, are uplifted by the lyre on a flight of fancy. Their *peripeteia* is complete: not only have they learned to appreciate the music of the lyre, they now show themselves to be connoisseurs of the latest trends in *kitharōidia*, initiated, as it were, into the mysteries of the New Music.

It is indeed tempting to imagine that the citharist, cued by Cyllene's description of Hermes' musical enthusiasm in 325–8, had played behind the *skēnē* an αἰόλισμα in the style of Phrynis or Timotheus to prompt the satyrs' appropriately 'elevated' response.⁶⁹ Such a virtuoso flourish would serve as a fitting instrumen-

---

67 Cf. Power 2010, 349–50 on other potential 'Aeolic' citharodic puns. Griffith 2013b, 271 sees a possible reference in αἰόλισμα to '"Aeolic" tunings and articulations appropriate to the monodic tradition'.
68 For New Musical poetry, see Ford 2013 and LeVen 2014, 150–88; cf. Csapo 2004, 216–29.
69 Diggle 1996, 13 would seem to suggest that the chorus hears Hermes already *singing* to the lyre by the time they begin their song at 329 (thus his rationale for adopting von Blumenthal's <ὀμ>οψάλακτος: 'the "voice twanged in unison" is the voice of the lyre, twanged in unison with that of Hermes'). The idea has intriguing implications: Hermes might not only have offered up a snatch of solo citharistic novelty, he might instead have delivered a full-blown parody of 'new citharodic' song. We might expect, however, that the words of such a song would be scripted into the text. I think it more likely that Hermes' lyre (or, more precisely, the *kithara* that dubbed it) alone sounded, in such a way as to give an impression of the modern style. And if we permit ourselves to imagine that the string playing bled over into the choral song, then Hermes' singing seems even less likely.

tal prelude, *anabolē*, to their song with its modern airs.[70] And if we permit ourselves yet more speculation, we might wonder whether the citharist continued to play in such a style as the satyrs began their *aulos*-accompanied choral song. The resulting *synaulia* of instruments, choral voices, and song genres—whatever it might have sounded like—would have been a *coup de théâtre* to rival anything in the very New Music it was sending up.

---

70 The *anabolē*, in both dithyramb and *kitharōidia*, was a key site of musical innovation and experimentation, independent as it was from the exigencies of a poetic text. Ar. *Av.* 1372–1409 imagines the dithyrambographer Cinesias gathering his *anabolai* from the clouds, a vivid elaboration of the aerial motif. See West 1992, 205; Comotti 1989a; Franklin 2013 (especially p. 222).

Andrew Ford
Afterword: On the Nonexistence of Tragic Odes

The essays in *Paths of Song*, in the context of a decade of work stressing the importance of Greek chorality, add impetus to an old view that is currently being revived, that tragedy was fundamentally a choral art. Such a view can find support in Aristotle's tracing of the origins of tragedy to ritual choruses, which may suggest that what the editors of *Paths of Song* call the 'choral nucleus of fifth-century tragedy' is an inheritance from the formative stage of the genre. Yet the studies assembled above show tragedy interacting with such a variety of lyric forms that it is hard to see them all as evolving out of such archaic cult songs as were performed by the 'tragic choruses' (τραγικοὶ χοροί, Hdt. 5.67) in sixth-century Sicyon.[1] A different perspective on the centrality of choral song to tragedy can be outlined by following up Aristotle's scenario for the origin of the genre. On his account, tragic drama became differentiated from ritual when one of the singers who had traditionally 'led off' (οἱ ἄρχοντες) the dithyramb stepped apart from the group and created the space that would come to be filled by 'actors' speaking trimeters (*Poet*. 1449a9–18). But that change would have entailed another of equal importance: as actors made it possible to dramatize new stories, new songs would have been needed to enhance them and so choruses would have had to expand their repertoires beyond hymns to the god or hero at hand. If we ask where tragic poets were to get the new songs demanded by the new genre, *Paths of Song* suggests that the most obvious source was what John Herington called the song-culture enveloping them. The studies above find tragic choruses singing in the accents of *partheneia* (Lazani) and of *citharodia*, both in its early heroic manner (Coward) and in its New Musical mode (Fanfani); the influence of Stesichorus is examined (Finglass, Coward), and Pindaric hymns get notice (Rodighiero), as does Bacchylidean dithyramb (Athanassaki, Fanfani). The interest in *epinikion* shown by a number of studies (Athanassaki, Sfyroeras, Kampakoglou, Swift) will raise a question about how much our picture is influenced by the fact that those are the lyric texts we happen to have in greatest abundance; but there is also attention to song forms that are barely preserved outside of drama, such as the *hymenaios* (Rawles, Weiss), the theoric hymn (Prodi), or the elusive *hyporchēma* (Andújar). A tragedian eager to exploit the power of song to guide his audience's

---

[1] A recent wide-ranging review of the evidence for tragedy's ritual origins is Csapo/Miller 2007.

expectations and sharpen the emotional impact of his play needed only to tune in to the ambient soundscape for an anthology of highly charged musical forms, both old songs fondly and more or less faithfully recalled and new ones constantly being made.

The best way to give an overview of these studies may be to think a little further about the two poles involved in this exchange, and to think of them in terms of genre. To speak glibly of tragedy as 'inheriting' the lyric tradition does not do justice to the dynamism and complexity of that exchange, and similarly to say that a particular lyric form is 'imported into' or 'evoked' or 'drawn on' by tragedy presumes two manifestly distinct genres that can prove difficult to disentangle in practice, let alone to define in clear-cut terms. The project of *Paths of Song* thus requires reflecting both on the micro-distinctions by which the innumerable kinds of Greek singing were sorted into recognisable genres and on the macro-distinction that separates dramatic from lyric choruses.

On the 'lyric' side, to detect when a specific song form is being presented on the tragic stage requires a subtle and flexible approach to genre, and the contributors to *Paths of Song* offer a variety of approaches that enable us to go beyond the limitations of prescriptive formalism in identifying lyric kinds. At the same time, this task of detection must be careful to acknowledge the limitations in our knowledge about Athenian song-culture in the classical age: How far did poets depend on a close familiarity with lyric in the audience, and how can this be gauged? What role did a cultural elite play, both as audience members and as poets? Is there a way we can control for, if we cannot cure, our blind spots that may not see important aspects of choral culture (most notably dance) that are barely recorded in the texts? The other party to the exchange is even more difficult to pin down, for we do not even have a satisfactory name that captures the peculiar status of a song in a tragedy. Here it is necessary to avoid, as Laura Swift does in her ground-breaking *The Hidden Chorus*, taking the tragic chorus for granted 'as an institution in its own right ... a convention of drama' (2010, 2). In what follows I will address these two questions chiastically, first putting pressure on the idea of a generic 'tragic ode' to argue that tragedy's commerce with the lyric tradition was intrinsic to the art and not a case of songs coming in from the 'outside' and ousting some presumed native form. This suggests in turn that the many cases of lyric-tragic interaction identified in this volume are but a sample of a far more extensive phenomenon. If we then outline, in emic terms, the system of Greek lyric genres, we can turn to the questions surrounding classical Athenian song-culture and consider how ancient audiences – and modern scholars as well – might be prompted to recognize specific kinds of lyric coming out of the mouths of tragic performers.

1 From Tragic Ode to *Stasimon*

It used to be common in tragic scholarship to speak about 'tragic odes' as if they were a distinct and definite kind of lyric, indeed as if they constituted a sort of Platonic form.² According to the template laid up in heaven, every tragedy had to have three or four strophic songs in lyric metre (especially Aeolics or dactylo-epitrites); they were to be performed by the whole chorus in the orchestra with no contribution from the actors on stage; their function was to separate 'episodes' or scenes. Current tragic criticism accords a less central role to ideal 'tragic odes' in order to attend to the wide variety of song forms that choruses may execute: there are choral songs within scenes as well as between them, and scene-dividing choral songs that are astrophic in form or in iambo-trochaic rhythms; a chorus may even split into two parts that sing to each other, or enter into a duet with an actor who may reply in either lyric or recited verse.³ In view of this variety, the expression 'tragic ode' becomes nearly empty and so is now less frequently to be found in commentaries (along with another critical fiction of the same vintage, the 'tragic hero'); commentators today are more likely to use the more neutral expression 'choral ode' or the emic term *stasimon*. 'Choral ode' is unimpeachable as a formal description but has the disadvantage of being unable to distinguish between choral songs performed in the orchestra as part of a play and those performed outside the theatre in non-dramatic contexts. *Stasimon*, as will be seen, has deficiencies of its own, but it is at least a fifth-century term and remains the most precise available word to designate a choral song as part of a tragedy. The word is introduced to us in Chapter 12 of Aristotle's *Poetics*, a problematic chapter in a work that, as is noted in the Introduction and in the essay by Naomi Weiss, has long drawn criticism for the short shrift it gives to tragic choruses and to lyric generally. It is true that Aristotle's plot-centred approach to *mimesis* sometimes leads him to describe songs disparagingly as a mere 'seasoning' added to the meat of the *muthos* (1449b28), but he never denies them a vital role in the genre: lyrics or 'songs' (μέλη) are defined as essential to tragedy (1450a9–10) and music is recognized as a powerful means of enhancing tragedy's proper pleasure (1450b15–16); the 'composition of songs', μελοποιία, was 'in no small part' what made tragedy superior to music-less epic (1462b16–7; cf. 1449b32–4). For all his limitations, Aristotle's testimony reflects a vast amount of historical research and experience of theatre and his discussion of

---

[2] E.g. Haigh 1896, 353–61; cf. Kranz 1933, 113, and Ch. 4 generally.
[3] See Battezzato 2005a for an excellent conspectus; cf. Goldhill 2013a, 109–29 on the relationship between the choral and iambic portions of tragedy.

stasima, read critically, can provide unique insights into classical conceptions and attitudes about what tragic choruses sang.[4]

In contrast to the definition of tragedy in *Poetics* Chapter 6, which specified six 'qualitative' or functional parts that any tragedy had to have to be a tragedy (plot, character, song etc.), Chapter 12 defines the parts of tragedy in 'quantitative' or formal terms. Indeed, this schematic definition of *stasima* in Chapter 12 is in large part responsible for the phantom notion of a 'tragic ode':

> κατὰ δὲ τὸ ποσὸν καὶ εἰς ἃ διαιρεῖται κεχωρισμένα τάδε ἐστίν, πρόλογος ἐπεισόδιον ἔξοδος χορικόν, καὶ τούτου τὸ μὲν πάροδος τὸ δὲ στάσιμον, κοινὰ μὲν ἁπάντων ταῦτα, ἴδια δὲ τὰ ἀπὸ τῆς σκηνῆς καὶ κομμοί.

> The parts of tragedy that can be distinguished on a quantitative basis are: the prologue, the episode, the final scene, the choral part (χορικόν); the latter consists of the *parodos* and *stasimon*. These are common to all tragedies while some plays have songs sung by actors 'from the stage' and '*kommoi*'.

(Arist. *Poet.* 1452b15–18)

Of tragedy's four quantitative parts, the first three are conducted in recited meters (usually iambic or trochaic *stichoi*) and are listed in order of occurrence; the fourth, the choral part (χορικόν), is distributed in different parts of the play (as the definition of tragedy specified: 1449b25–6) and has subdivisions. Aristotle privileges two of its forms because they are found in all tragedies: the entrance song (πάροδος) and 'standing songs' or *stasima* (στάσιμα). He is fully aware that other kinds of singing are found in the plays and mentions their main kinds briefly: some tragedies feature shared singing between an actor and the chorus, a form Aristotle terms 'dirges' (κομμοί); for the sake of completeness he also includes (even though they do not strictly speaking belong to 'the choral part') solo songs performed by actors 'from the stage' (ἀπὸ τῆς σκηνῆς) as opposed to choral song in the orchestra.

Of these four sung parts, the three that involve the chorus can be subdivided according to their location in the play, their meters and performative mode:

> χορικοῦ δὲ πάροδος μὲν ἡ πρώτη λέξις ὅλη χοροῦ, στάσιμον δὲ μέλος χοροῦ τὸ ἄνευ ἀναπαίστου καὶ τροχαίου, κομμὸς δὲ θρῆνος κοινὸς χοροῦ καὶ ἀπὸ σκηνῆς.

(Arist. *Poet.* 1452b22–5)

---

[4] For criticism of *Poetics* 12, see Taplin 1977, 470–6; Else 1957, 360–3 would excise the chapter but it is thoroughly Aristotelian in conception.

Of the choral part, a *parodos* is the whole of the first utterance of the chorus; a *stasimon* is a choral song without anapaests or trochaics; a *kommos* is a song of lament shared between the chorus and the actors on the stage.

Parodoi and *stasima* are distinguished from *kommoi* by being purely choral, and are distinguished from each other by the fact that *parodoi* came first in the play and could use runs of anapaests or trochaics in recitative, which *stasima* did not.[5] As Aristotle had defined an 'episode' as the part of a play between choral songs (1452b20 – 1: μεταξὺ ὅλων χορικῶν μελῶν), the implicit function of *stasima* is to separate scenes.

How *stasima* got the name of 'standing songs' is unclear, but the word seems to go back to the working theatre of the fifth century;[6] it is now usually understood as designating songs that were performed (by no means standing still) after the *parodos* when the chorus had come to 'stand' in its place in the orchestra.[7] Oliver Taplin has pointed out numerous ways in which this originally choreographic term is seriously inadequate to describe the ways choruses actually perform in our plays (e. g. by neglecting many instances of choral singing within scenes and downplaying *amoibaia*). An additional defect of the term relevant to this volume is that it is too generic: as *The Hidden Chorus* documented, under this colourless label may lie perfectly good *paianes, epinikia, partheneia, hymenaioi,* or *thrēnoi*.

In Chapter 12, then, the chorus' part takes two basic forms: first of all, every tragedy needs an entry song if only to get the chorus into the orchestra; secondly, there must be other songs performed by the chorus at intervals before the finale. In formal terms, it might be thought that these two types of song are an inheritance from tragedy's ritual origins, for each represents an archetypal cultic form – processional songs for *parodoi* and songs sung standing or dancing around an altar for *stasima*. But if we turn to consider the contents of *stasima*, a lineal descent from archaic cult singing seems far less relevant than a dynamic and continuously renewed engagement with a broad range of song that had been established for other contexts.

The quantitative analysis of Chapter 12 does not address the question of what the chorus is to sing, but Aristotle does give a hint in his recommendation

---

5 So Dale 1969, 35. On recitative, see Pickard-Cambridge 1968, 156 ff.
6 Cf. στάσιν μελῶν in Ar. *Av.* 1280; Taplin 1977, 474. On the etymology, cf. Dale 1969, 36 against Kranz 1933, 14, 115. Aristotle's metrical terms in Ch. 12 may have a similar provenance: 'anapaests' is attested in Aristophanes as a metonym for the comic *parabasis* (*Eq.* 504, *Pax* 735); Plato refers to an analysis of the τροχαῖος, 'trochee', by Damon: *Rep.* 400b.
7 Dale 1969, 34 – 6.

that 'the chorus should be conceived as one of the actors and participate in the action, not as in Euripides but as in Sophocles' (1456a25–7).[8] It is difficult to be sure of what he means and why he thought that Sophocles was better than Euripides in this regard. It cannot be supposed that the Lyceum was in possession of plays with more active and integrated choruses than the ones we know, for the *Problems* defines the chorus as 'an inactive attendant, offering only its good will to those on stage' (*Pr.* 19.48 922b26–7). But there is one respect in which even the most passive choruses are like protagonists: they react to the situation emerging before them and express their reaction in heightened speech. Tragedies are representations of *praxeis*, purposeful actions expressive of character, and in some situations the most appropriate thing for a group of people to do is to form a chorus and, mixing their *logos* with rhythm and *harmonia*, to make a μέλος that prays to the gods or pleads or argues with others on stage; the singers may, like any speaker, call up gnomic wisdom or pointed stories from the past, or stir up passions like pity, fear and anger (*Poet.* 1456a36–1456b1), or simply give vent to strong emotion. What Aristotle considers essential is that 'what the chorus sings' (τὰ ᾀδόμενα, 1456a28) should fit its context. The key point, as Aristotle goes on to say, is that choral performances should not be *entr'actes*, despite a tendency traced to late fifth-century tragedians like Agathon to compose songs so detached from the action that they might as well have come from another play (1456a27–32).

This actorial function of the chorus brings *stasima* once again closer to lyric traditions than to archaic cult, for the Greek system of lyric genres can be compendiously described as a set of highly charged situations calling for a collective verbal acknowledgement by the particular groups affected. Reaching maturity, marriage, war, displacement and death are among the momentous events in individual and communal lives that generated their own kinds of song, and such situations are also inherently dramatic. The tragedian whose plot turned on such issues had no shortage of models for articulating a plausible group response on the part of involved and often anxious observers.

Let us imagine a playwright, as Aristotle does in Chapter 17 of the *Poetics*, who has worked out a plot and broken it down into episodes; mindful of custom and of his audience's expectations, he will want to punctuate the plot with choral songs. Imagine further that his first scene shows a city beset by plague that has received not altogether clear instructions from Apollo for how it may be purified. A priest leading a delegation of beleaguered citizens petitions the king for

---

8 *Poet.* 1456a25–7 καὶ τὸν χορὸν δὲ ἕνα δεῖ ὑπολαμβάνειν τῶν ὑποκριτῶν, καὶ μόριον εἶναι τοῦ ὅλου καὶ συναγωνίζεσθαι μὴ ὥσπερ Εὐριπίδῃ ἀλλ' ὥσπερ Σοφοκλεῖ.

help. He replies that he has sent to the Pythia a second time, and the scene closes as the new emissary is about to return. In such circumstances what is needed is not some generic 'choral ode' but a song to Apollo, and indeed the priest ends the episode with a call for a paean in trimeters that, in a manner, 'lead off' the song: 'May Phoebus Apollo who sent this oracle prove saviour and stopper of plague': Φοῖβος δ' ὁ πέμψας τάσδε μαντείας ἅμα /σωτήρ θ' ἵκοιτο καὶ νόσου παυστήριος (*OT* 149–50). The priest's rare word 'stopper' (παυστήριος) cues a *paian*, which folk etymology connected with 'stop' (παύειν); and Teiresias' syncretizing the god of plague with the god of prophecy constitutes an argument for the appropriateness of singing a paean now.[9] Thereupon the chorus renders a song in cult metre that includes the paeanic cry (*OT* 154) and all the *topoi* of a cult hymn.[10]

All this is not to say that every ode in Greek tragedy can be identified with a particular lyric genre; there are many reasons why this will not always be so. For one, a number of *stasima* are best analysed not as a version of any single genre but as a mixture of several (Rawles, Andújar). For another, as tragedy took on a history in the course of the fifth century the vacuous category of 'tragic ode' came to be filled with exemplars, in the sense that memorable songs and musical strategies from old plays could inspire new compositions that would reflect intra-tragic poetics as much as the outer song world. An especially rich version of this kind of song is found when a poet contrives a dramatic situation that claims to be unprecedented and so lacks a traditional musical form in which to express one's reaction. The ode that follows is thus presented not as embodying any known kind of song but as the founding archetype of a new form, since grown into a familiar genre; for example, the setting of the *Trojan Women* allows its first *stasimon* to pose as the original song about Troy's fall of which epic and *citharodia* will be imitators (Rodighiero, Fanfani).[11] A third complication is the gaps in our knowledge of contemporary musical production which means we may not register the presence of minor and less well known genres, such as the (monodic) lullaby in *Hypsipyle* (fr. 752f.9–10 *TrGF*$^{5.2}$). Despite these and other complications, however, the essays in this volume must encourage readers, when they come upon a 'tragic ode', to make their first question: what kind of song it this and where does it come from? What stance authorized in the past does the chorus assume to give them the right to sing? Is the crisis they face

---

9 On *paian*'s etymologies, A. von Blumenthal, *Paian RE* 18 1949, col. 2344. On the importance of the paeanic cry, Ford 2006.
10 On the *parodos* of the *OT* as a formal cult song, Ax 1932.
11 Also Tsolakidou 2012, Ch. 1. Cf. Weiss on *epithalamia* in the *IA* and, on the richly ironic *Helen*, Ford 2011; Steiner 2011.

one that has earlier found potent forms of expression to which the chorus recurs? The songs of tragedy may mix genres, refashion them ('Praise wine that is old but songs that are new', says Pindar: *Ol.* 9.48–9), or create new ones for the stage; but no song has no genre, and to label one a 'tragic ode' or a 'choral ode' or a *stasimon* is just to begin to read it.[12] The necessary next step is to consider how distinct kinds of lyric song were identified at the time.

2 Lyric Genres

Scholars of Greek poetry have for some time now dispensed with the Romantic notion of 'lyric' as a timeless and universal category of literature and no longer think of individual lyric genres as purely literary essences.[13] Archaic and classical songs depended for much of their power on their embeddedness in social, religious and political practices that are easily missed by Alexandrian taxonomies in terms of form and content; in addition, the context of any performance (or re-performance) of a song profoundly shaped its reception in ways that cannot be captured in essentialising approaches to lyric genres such as Plato recommends (*Laws* 700). As a consequence there can be no single method for detecting a tragic allusion to a lyric form; different genres were formally marked in different ways and to different degrees, and even within the same genre the practice of composing poets could differ.

Accordingly, the contributors to *Paths of Song* take an array of approaches to identifying lyric genres. The *parodos* of the *Oedipus the King* discussed above is a case in which its paeanic character is strongly marked by converging formal, thematic and contextual cues: an appropriate metrical form, sacred diction and myths, the fictive occasion, the speaker's ethical stance and associated *topoi*. Some other genres allow for such 'clustered' marking (Rodighiero): *epinikia*, for example, are associated with a definite occasion and range of forms and also tend to feature a regular set of *topoi* (e. g. advice on the right use of wealth or how to avoid envy) and themes (*kleos*, inherited excellence) (Kampakoglou). In the case of victory songs, however, all of the 'content' can also be found in gnomic elegy such as the Theognidea, and so a tragic poet wishing to signal the epinician mode specifically may add a key-word such as καλλίνικος (Fanfa-

---

[12] Taplin 1977, 52 and 473–4 notes that the ghost of the 'Tragic Ode' can still be sensed when commentaries describe scene-dividing lyrics that do not fit the mould (for example, that are astrophic or not wholly choral or) as 'standing in place of a *stasimon*'.
[13] E. g. Calame 1998; Battezzato 2005a; Ford 2006; Bakola/Prauscello/Telò 2013; Foster/Kurke/Weiss, forthcoming.

ni). Other genres provide fewer canonical exemplars which makes their identification less easy: in such cases we may need to seek evidence from further afield, as Enrico Prodi adduces cultic and para-cultic lyric and dedicatory epigrams to delineate the characterization of the chorus in Euripides' *Phoenissae*.

Form, content and the immediate performative context are for us the most legible aspect of these song texts, but a number of studies here show that such markers are not always decisive. Andrea Rodighiero suggests that generic markers may even be present in the 'zero degree', as he argues is the case in the *parodos* in the *Antigone* which in all respects functions as a *paian* to Victory, although 'no formal features corroborate this'. Swift offers a model that sits somewhere in between relying on explicit and implicit cues: she argues that early, strongly marked allusions to lyric kinds can 'trigger' less well marked subsequent allusions and the ensemble can function like Wagnerian leitmotifs running through an entire trilogy; on this view even quite brief mentions of a topic such as athletics can put in play the *Oresteia*'s overarching contrast between paeanic and epinician values.

To these markers should be added powerful intangible effects the song would have had in performance but which are harder to extract from our texts. Because song genres were correlated with functions and situations of performance, they could be associated with specific kinds of social experience and imbued with corresponding ethics. In addition, the critic may find help in choral self-referential and meta-poetic remarks that promote certain expectations in the audience (Fanfani, Power) as well in the meta-performative and meta-musical features in our texts. Thomas Coward's analysis of the *parodos* of the *Agamemnon* seeks echoes of Stesichorus and citharodic epic not only on the lexical and mythical level but in its very rhythms and likely its music. Rosa Andújar adds that the movements of the chorus suggested in the text are clues not to be neglected.

Even after methods like these have led us to conclude that an identifiable lyric form has entered tragedy, defining its genre *in situ* remains a complicated affair. In a sense, as Swift says, a chorus performing a *paian* or *hymenaios* on stage 'really do[es] become the ritual chorus performing the song, and the audience sees a *paian* or *hymenaios* being enacted before their eyes'. In another sense, any lyric produced at Dionysus' festivals becomes *ipso facto* a ritual song to that god. Within a play at the Dionysia, then, a chorus' identity as Athenians performing for the god is always doubled by its other identity as performers in a distant time and place.[14] This doubleness of the masked singers can find expression in the figure called choral projection by Albert Henrichs, by which a chorus modulates between its Athenian present and its heroic setting. It may be, as some argue, that the lability of choral identity in tragedy is the most characteristic feature of *stasima*,[15] but I would note that this wavering status can only be appreciated if one senses the generic constituents put in play.

3 Allusions in a Song-Culture

Readers who seek to identify lyric genres in our *stasima* must also be prepared for less clear-cut forms of allusiveness: playwrights, for example, may deliberately mismatch song and context to create effects of irony or dissonance, and it was always possible for poets to bend the 'rules' and try out a traditional theme in a non-traditional style (Rodighiero). The large sample of case studies in *Paths of Song* offers ways to cope with these subtleties, but a more difficult obstacle is that our knowledge of extra-dramatic lyric in the fifth century has enormous gaps; the fact is obvious enough, but becomes worrying when we reflect that our lyric canon is not necessarily the same as the lyric canon of the second half of the tragic century when most of the plays we have were composed. Of course, there is overlap between the archaic songs Athenians loved, those canonized in Alexandria and the texts we have. But in the song world there is always jostling as new waves try to sweep old favourites out of the repertoire. In the Peloponnesian-war generation such upheavals are documented by Aristophanes who makes the young Euripidean Pheidippides declare that singing Simonides and Aeschylus at symposia is *passé* (ἀρχαῖον, *Nub.* 1357) and by Eupolis who adds Stesichorus, Alcman and Simonides to the roster of *passé* poets (148 *PCG*⁵). Eupolis also says that the works of Pindar 'are now consigned to silence because of failure of most men to appreciate beauty' (398 *PCG*⁵),[16] and this raises a question in view of the number of studies above arguing for the influence of *epinikion* (Athanassaki, Sfyroeras, Kampakoglou, Swift). This prominence seems to go against evidence suggesting that *epinikion* was a quiescent if not moribund genre in the second half of the fifth century. We have a short, dactylo-epitritic *epinikion* attributed to Euripides for Alcibiades' Olympic victory in 416 (Kampakoglou), but a genera-

---

14 Calame 2013a, 35, 40. It is worth remembering that the theatre was the setting for a number of non-musical sacred and secular rituals: Chaniotis 2007.
15 See the essays in Gagné/Hopman 2013a.
16 Eupolis 398 *PCG*⁵: ὡς τὰ Πινδάρου <ὁ> κωμῳδιοποιὸς Εὔπολίς φησιν ἤδη κατασεσιγασμένα ὑπὸ τῆς τῶν πολλῶν ἀφιλοκαλίας.

tion separates this poem from the latest known *epinikia* of Pindar and Bacchylides; and when *epinikion* was revived and remade for the Hellenistic age it had lost its contact with the song-culture and took the form of recitable elegy and epigram.[17] So how was it possible that tragic poets should have been so invested in *epinikion*? The concern is that our picture is distorted by the fact that the survival of exemplars by Pindar and Bacchylides from the first half of the century make *epinikion* the best known genre of classical lyric. One response would be that, even if the heyday of *epinikion* had passed, it remained a particularly useful form for tragic scenarios because it was associated with welcoming or 'reintegrating' an outstanding figure back into the community (Swift, Kampakoglou). Alternatively, as Pavlos Sfyroeras suggests, perhaps Eupolis exaggerates and *epinikion* was better preserved than other genres, possibly even in writing which made it better able to weather changes in fashion.[18]

A larger question, implicit in all these studies and directly addressed by some, is the nature of the song-culture in fifth-century Athens. Sfyroeras' contribution asks how well Sophocles could have expected an Athenian audience of 406 to know their Pindar. He argues for the possibility of an 'intertextual dialogue' between two *stasima* from the *Oedipus at Colonus* and two Pindaric odes to Theron some seventy years earlier by pointing out that the play was produced amidst significant political developments in Sicily that would have resonated with issues raised in the earlier works. Following some recent studies arguing that *epinikia* retained a measure of a 'visibility in late fifth-century Athens', he concludes that knowledge of this repertoire must have been diffused 'primarily among the elite but also more widely' at the end of the century. In harmony with this view Patrick Finglass concludes (again, *pace* Eupolis) that 'Stesichorus was certainly familiar to theatrical audiences in fifth-century Athens' at the time of Aristophanes' *Peace*; as mechanisms for preservation he suggests sympotic re-performance that perhaps encouraged texts to be circulated among the elite.

A different approach is adopted by Lucia Athanassaki in arguing that Euripides knew Bacchylides' 'Theseus dithyrambs' and used them some sixty years later to suffuse the prologue of his *Trojan Women* with Cimonian ideology. On Athanassaki's reading, the audience need not have had first-hand acquaintance with the songs since their thalassocratic imagery would have been inscribed into material culture on the Theseion and Painted Stoa. It is good to be reminded that

---

17 See Barbantani 2012.
18 The fact that Eupolis uses Pindar's favourite trope for obscurity when he says the poet has been 'silenced' (κατασεσιγασμένα) indicates that he exaggerates at least to some extent (cf. *Ol.* 9.103, *Pyth.* 9.92; *Nem.* 9.7; *Isthm.* 2.44; frr. 94a.10, 121.4). Hubbard 2004 argues for a written dissemination of Pindar's *epinikia*; cf. West 2011, 64–7.

song can be carried forward in memory not only through texts and performances but also through associated artefacts (cf. Weiss on the François vase and the Sophilos dinos). Athanassaki points out as well that songs may ride less tangible cultural waves, as in her argument that Poseidon's threat of an earthquake in *Trojan Women* would have resonated with a series of portentous earthquakes in Greece about a decade before the play. In a similar vein, Rodighiero argues that an eclipse of around 463 BC could have made Pindar's fearful invocation of the sun in his *Paian* for Thebes available to be exploited by the *Antigone* in 441.

Attempts to address such questions when arguing for a close relation between a lyric and tragic text, even if they will be inevitably speculative at points, are a welcome alternative to the easy model of a completely ahistorical intertextuality in which words are matched up with words without any attempt at historical framing. On the other hand, the historicist's demand for specific evidence of the currency of a given genre must be temperate, for Anastasia Lazani reminds us that a poetic text like *Prometheus Bound* may be as valid an indication of Alcman's presence in the Athenian song-culture (*pace* Eupolis again) as the explicit testimony of Aristophanes' plays from the 'teens.

Most of the authors who take into account the audience's horizon of expectation invoke, at least implicitly, a model familiar from Shakespearean criticism which separates the audience into a sophisticated elite who will appreciate the same nuances savoured by modern scholars while the 'groundlings' fill out the rest of the theatre. Such a division is Aristotle's as well (*Pol.* 1342a19–24; *Poet.* 1462a2–4) and is probably inescapable in some form (cf., e.g., Ar. *Eccl.* 1154–7). But reservations are in order: Athenian musical culture was shaped along crisscrossing economic, political, age and gender lines that a simple binary model may not capture; moreover, scholars who posit such 'elites' run the risk of projection if they assume that ancient sophisticates valued the same songs for the same reasons as we do, and they risk idealization if they think musical connoisseurs had a commanding authority in the fractious democratic culture. No doubt among the many thousands who crowded into the Theatre of Dionysus an indeterminate percentage were highly literate, devoted and even scholarly experts in lyric from the past; such a description would certainly seem to fit Euripides who, like *epinikion*, has attracted a large number of studies here (Sfyroeras, Athanassaki, Kampakoglou, Fanfani, Andújar, Prodi, Weiss). But whatever percentage one assumes, a considerable part of the rest of the crowd, as John Herington famously pointed out in 1985, had experience of lyric choirs as participants and as audience members; there were old men in 422 who still relished the sweet songs of Phrynichus (Ar. *Vesp.* 220). This makes credible the story Plutarch tells, that some Athenian sailors who lived off the country after the defeat in the battle of Syracuse were able to get food by teaching their protectors selected Euripidean songs (τῶν μέλων ᾄσαντες, *Nicias* 29.4); it can take only one lyric aficionado on board a ship (someone like Dionysus, the *Andromeda*-reading marine of *Frogs* 52–4) to spread a song to the whole crew.[19]

Finally, Swift and Weiss make an important point that must qualify the 'groundlings' model: many people were attached to songs from the past not because they relished the recherché but because such songs were associated with important points in their lives; as a consequence, tragic allusions to lyric should be seen as something more than displays of literary sophistication for the educated; they offered poets not reference for reference's sake but a way of drawing on profound associations that could be awakened by traditional forms. The embeddedness of lyric in significant occasions of life is a far more important reason than a taste for literary allusion why 'In tragedy, whoever sings locates himself or herself in a literary tradition'.[20]

In future work the readings and methods proposed in this volume might profitably be applied across the rest of the tragic corpus, and indeed extended, via the Satyr play (Power), to comedy with its mixture of close parody and wild lyric freedom.[21] It is perhaps worth stressing in conclusion that these findings can also shed light on the supposed 'donor' form, fifth-century lyric and the pre-Hellenistic song tradition generally. Most of our editions and anthologies of Greek lyric poetry have erected a wall of separation between 'proper' lyric and the ones found in tragedies, as if the latter weren't lyric poems but some sort of 'tragic ode'. Happily, there are signs of that wall being breached, or to change the metaphor, of the back cover of the anthologies being detached to make room to bring in lyrics from fifth-century drama. G. O. Hutchinson's *Greek Lyric Poetry* includes several *stasima* and the collection of *Greek Hymns* by David Furley and Jan Bremer admits examples from tragedy. This is a trend worth expanding, for tragedy has the potential to tell us things about lyric performance that cannot be gleaned from an isolated lyric text that comes, say, from a book of songs in Sapphic stanzas or even from a book labelled 'Bacchylides' dithyrambs'. Tragic poets give us not only songs but song situations; the audience is presented not with a bare epinician, say, but with a hero, an outstanding accomplishment, a city (including envious onlookers), a group of celebrants and an ethic. These song situations must of course be read as fictional and, as noted,

---

19 Cf. Ford 2003, 19–20. I have profited from discussing Plutarch's passage with Timothy Duff.
20 Battezzato 2005a, 149.
21 Suggestive essays in Bakola/Prauscello/Telò 2013.

the genres they call forth may be transmogrified by the mere fact of being framed in a play. Notwithstanding these complexities, if read with tact and a sophisticated conception of genre, the songs of Greek drama have the potential to add to our understanding of the performance, situation and context of archaic and classical lyric performance.

If this be thought a potentially fruitful line of research, one is tempted to add a final suggestion that may strike some as blasphemous: while we're about the business of mistreating books, might it not also be interesting to remove the covers from the corpus of Athenian drama and then tear the songs right out of the plays (as we know Agathon did). The result would be a windfall, a sudden accession of literarily hundreds of lyric poems, mostly from the little known second half of the fifth century. As said, these framed lyrics need careful handling, and it will always be legitimate to ask whether a given *stasimon* belongs to a song cycle or in other ways ties deeply into the imagery and themes of the play that hosts it. Doubtless it is possible to go too far along this path, but the excesses will provide some redress for the previous generation of tragic criticism in which the focus on the civic *agōn* relegated the chorus to a secondary role at best. Furthermore, not every play was a *Gesamtkunstwerk,* and nothing prevents even a *stasimon* that is well integrated in its environment from finding a resonant second home in a symposium or on board a ship. With due allowance for the complexities that dramatic framing entails, we stand to gain an immense and largely untapped resource for the study of classical Greek lyric if we open up the great Athenian song book.

Bibliography

Abbate, C. (2001), *In Search of Opera*, Princeton.
Adami, F. (1900), 'De poetis scaenicis Graecis hymnorum sacrorum imitatoribus', in: *Philologische Jahrbücher* suppl. 26, 215–62.
Aélion, R. (1983), *Euripide héritier d'Eschyle*, I-II, Paris.
Agard, W. R. (1966), 'Boreas at Athens', in: *CJ* 61, 241–6.
Agócs, P. (2012), 'Performance and Genre: Reading Pindar's κῶμοι', in: P. Agócs / C. Carey / R. Rawles (eds.) (2012a), 191–223.
Agócs, P. / Rawles, R. / Carey, C. (eds.) (2012a), *Reading the Victory Ode*, Cambridge.
Agócs, P. / Rawles, R. / Carey, C. (eds.) (2012b), *Receiving the Komos: Ancient and Modern Receptions of the Victory Ode*. BICS Suppl. 112, London.
Aichele, K. (1971), 'Das Epeisodion', in: W. Jens (ed.), *Die Bauformen der griechischen Tragödie*, Munich, 47–83.
Alexopoulou, M. (2009), *The Theme of Returning Home in Ancient Greek Literature: The Nostos of the Epic Heroes*, Lewiston NY and Lampeter.
Allan, W. (2000), *The* Andromache *and Euripidean Tragedy*, Oxford.
Allen T. W. (1912), *Homeri opera. Tomus V*, Oxford.
Almazova, N. (2008), 'On the meaning of αὐλῳδία, αὐλῳδός', in: *Hyperboreus* 14, 5–34.
Almazova, N. (2012), 'Lyre in Public Performance?', in: D. Castaldo / F. Giannachi / A. Manieri (eds.) *Poetry, Music, and Contests in Ancient Greece*, 2 vols. (Series: Rudiae. Ricerche sul mondo classico 22–23, 2010–2011), Galatina, II 457–88.
Amiech, C. (2004), *Les Phéniciennes d'Euripide*, Paris.
Anderson, M. J. (1997), *The Fall of Troy in Early Greek Poetry and Art*, Oxford.
Andrewes, A. (1992), 'The Peace of Nicias and the Sicilian Expedition', in: D. M. Lewis / J. Boardman / J. K. Davies / M. Ostwald (eds.), *The Cambridge History of Ancient History; Volume V: The Fifth Century*, 2nd edn., Cambridge, 433–63.
Andújar, R. (2016), 'Uncles *ex machina*: Familial Epiphany in Euripides' *Electra*', in: *Ramus* 45.2, 165–91.
Antonopoulos, A. P. (2014), 'Sophocles' *Ichneutai* 176–202: A lyric dialogue (?) featuring an impressive mimetic scene', in: *Hermes* 142, 246–54.
Arrighetti, G. (1994), 'Stesicoro e il suo pubblico', in: *MD* 32, 9–30.
Arthur, M. B. (1977), 'The curse of civilization: the choral odes of the *Phoenissae*', in: *HSPh* 81, 163–85.
Athanassaki, L. (2010), 'Performing Myth through Word, Deed, and Image: The Gigantomachy in Euripides' *Ion*', in: A. M. Gonzalez de Tobia (ed.), *Mito y Performance. De Grecia a la Modernidad. Quinto Coloquio Internacional. Acta* (Universidad Nacional de la Plata), La Plata, 199–242.
Athanassaki, L. (2012a), 'A Magnificent Birthday Party in an Artful Pavilion: Lifestyle and Leadership in Euripides' *Ion* (on and offstage)', in: V. Bers / D. Elmer / D. Frame / L. Muelner (eds.), *Donum natalicium digitaliter confectum Gregorio Nagy septuagenario a discipulis collegis familiaribus oblatum*, Washington DC: chs.harvard.edu/CHS/article/display/4680.

Athanassaki, L. (2012b), 'Recreating the Emotional Experience of Contest and Victory Celebrations: Spectators and Celebrants in Pindar's Epinicians', in: X. Riu / J. Pòrtulas (eds.), *Approaches to Archaic Greek Poetry*, Messina, 173–219.

Athanassaki, L. (2016), 'The Symposion as Theme and Performance Context in Pindar's Epinicians', in V. Cazzato / D. Obbink / E. E. Prodi (eds.), 85–112.

Athanassaki, L. / Bowie, E. L. (eds.) (2011), *Archaic and Classical Choral Song: Performance, Politics and Dissemination*, Berlin and Boston.

Austin, C. / Olson, S. D. (2004), *Aristophanes. Thesmophoriazusae*, Oxford.

Ax, W. (1932), 'Die Parodos des *Oidipus Tyrannos*', in: *Hermes* 67.4, 413–37.

Bacon, H. (1994–1995), 'The Chorus in Greek Life and Drama', in: *Arion* 3, 6–24.

Bagordo, A. (2003), *Reminiszenzen früher Lyrik bei den attischen Tragikern. Beiträge zur Anspielungstechnik und poetischen Tradition*, Munich.

Bakker, S. J. (2009), *The Noun Phrase in Ancient Greek: A Functional Analysis of the Order and Articulation of NP Constituents in Herodotus*, Leiden and Boston.

Bakola, E. (2010), *Cratinus and the Art of Comedy*, Oxford.

Bakola, E. / Prauscello, L. / Telò, M. (eds.) (2013), *Greek Comedy and the Discourse of Genres*, Cambridge.

Balmori, C. H. (1945), *Eurípides. Las Fenicias*, Tucuman.

Barbantani, S. (2012), 'Hellenistic Epinician', in: P. Agócs / R. Rawles / C. Carey (eds.) (2012b), 37–55.

Barker, A. (1984), *Greek Musical Writings: I The Musician and his Art*, Cambridge.

Barker, A. (2000), 'Athenaeus on Music', in: D. Braund / J. Wilkins (eds.), *Athenaeus and His World: Reading Greek Culture in the Roman Empire*, Exeter, 334–44.

Barker, A. (2001), 'La musica di Stesicoro', in: *QUCC* NS 67.1, 7–20.

Barker, A. (2004), 'Transforming the Nightingale: Aspects of Athenian Musical Discourse in the Late Fifth Century', in: P. Murray / P. Wilson (eds.), 185–204.

Barker, E. T. E. (2009), *Entering the Agon: Dissent and Authority in Homer, Historiography, and Tragedy*, Oxford.

Barlow, S. A. (1971), *The Imagery of Euripides: A Study in the Dramatic Use of Pictorial Language*, London.

Barlow, S. A. (1986), *Euripides. Trojan Women*, Warminster.

Barlow, S. A. (1996), *Euripides. Heracles*, Warminster.

Barlow, S. A. (2008), *The Imagery of Euripides*. 3rd edn., London.

Barrett, W. S. (1968), *Euripides. Hippolytos*, Oxford.

Barrett, W. S. (2007), *Greek Lyric, Tragedy, and Textual Criticism. Collected Papers*, ed. M.L. West, Oxford.

Barron, J. P. (1980), 'Bakchylides, Theseus and a Woolly Cloak', in: *BICS* 27, 1–8.

Battezzato, L. (1995), *Il monologo nel teatro di Euripide*, Pisa.

Battezzato, L. (2005a), 'Lyric', in: J. Gregory (ed.), 149–66.

Battezzato, L. (2005b), 'The New Music of the Trojan Women', in: *Lexis* 23, 73–104.

Battezzato, L. (2009), 'Metre and Music', in: F. Budelmann (ed.), *The Cambridge Companion to Greek Lyric*, Cambridge, 130–46.

Battezzato, L. (2011), Review of Swift, L. (2010) *The Hidden Chorus: Echoes of Genre in Tragic Lyric*, Oxford, in: *JHS* 131, 180–1.

Battezzato, L. (2013), 'Dithyramb and Greek Tragedy', in: B. Kowalzig / P. Wilson (eds.), 93–110.

Beecroft, A. (2008), 'Nine fragments attributed to Terpander', in: *CJ* 103.3, 225–41.
Bees, R. (1993), *Zur Datierung des* Prometheus Desmotes, Stuttgart.
Bergson, L. (1956), *L'épithète ornementale dans Eschyle, Sophocle et Euripide*, Lund.
Bethe, E. (1919), 'Die *Ichneutai* des Sophokles', in: *Ber. über d. Verhandl. d. sächs. Gesellsch. d. Wiss. zu Leipzig Phil.-hist. Klasse* 71, 1–29.
Biehl, W. (1989), *Euripides. Troades*, Heidelberg.
Bierl, A. (2009), *Ritual Performativity. The Chorus in Old Comedy*, Washington DC.
Bierl, A. (2011a), 'Alcman at the End of Aristophanes' *Lysistrata:* Ritual Interchorality', in: L. Athanassaki / E. L. Bowie (eds.), 415–36.
Bierl, A. (2011b), 'Il drama satiresco di Pratina e il *Ciclope* di Euripide', in: A. Rodighiero / P. Scattolin (eds.), *Un enorme individuo: funzioni, interpretazioni*, Verona, 67–96.
Billings, J. (2014), *Genealogy of the Tragic: Greek Tragedy and German Philosophy*, Princeton.
Billings, J. / Budelmann, F. / Macintosh, F. (eds.) (2013), *Choruses, Ancient and Modern*, Oxford.
Biraud, M. (2010), *Les interjections du théâtre grec antique. Étude sémantique et pragmatique*, Louvain.
Blech, M. (1982), *Studien zum Kranz bei den Griechen*, Berlin and Boston.
Blinkenberg, C. (1915), *Die lindische Tempelchronik*, Kleine Texte für Vorlesungen und Übungen 131, Bonn.
Boas, M. (1905), *De epigrammatis Simonideis*, I: *Commentatio critica de epigrammatum traditione*, Amsterdam.
Boëthius, A. (1918), *Die Pythaïs: Studien zur Geschichte der Verbindungen zwischen Athen und Delphi*, Uppsala.
Bond, G. W. (1981), *Euripides. Heracles*, Oxford.
Borges, C. / Sampson, C. M. (2012), *New Literary Papyri from the Michigan Collection. Mythographic Lyric and a Catalogue of Poetic First Lines*, Ann Arbor.
Borthwick, E. K. (1970), 'The Riddle of the Tortoise and the Lyre', in: *Music and Letters* 51, 373–87.
Borthwick, E. K. (1994), 'New Interpretations of Aristophanes *Frogs* 1249–1328', in: *Phoenix* 48.1, 21–41.
Bosher, K. (2008–2009), 'To Dance in the Orchestra: A Circular Argument', in: *ICS* 33–34, 1–24.
Bowen, A. J. (2013), *Aeschylus. Suppliant Women*, Oxford.
Bowie, A. M. (1993), 'Religion and Politics in Aeschylus' *Oresteia*', in: *CQ* 43.1, 10–31.
Bowie, A. M. (2007), *Herodotus Histories Book VIII*, Cambridge.
Bowie, E. L. (2008), 'Aristides and Early Greek Lyric Elegiac and Iambic Poetry', in: W. V. Harris / B. Holmes (eds.), *Aelius Aristides Between Greece, Rome, and the Gods*. Columbia Studies in the Classical Tradition 33, Leiden and Boston, 9–29.
Bowie, E. L. (2015a), 'Stesichorus at Athens', in: P. J. Finglass / A. Kelly (eds.), 111–24.
Bowie, E. L. (2015b), 'Time and Place, Narrative and Speech in Philicus, Philodamus and Limenius', in A. Faulkner / O. Hodkinson (eds.), *Hymnic Narrative and the Narratology of Greek Hymns*, Leiden and Boston, 87–118.
Bowra, M. (1960), 'Euripides' Epinician for Alcibiades', in: *Historia* 9, 68–79.
Bowra, M. (1961), *Greek Lyric Poetry*. 2nd edn., Oxford.
Bowra, M. (1963), 'Two Lines of Eumelus', in: *CQ* 13, 145–53 [= (1970), 46–58].
Bowra, M. (1964), *Pindar*, Oxford.

Bowra, M. (1970), *On Greek Margins*, Oxford.
Braswell, B. K. (1998), *A Commentary on Pindar* Nemean 9, Berlin and Boston.
Bremer, J. M. (1983), 'Papyri Containing Fragments of Eur. *Phoenissae*. Some corrections to the first editions', in: *Mnemosyne* s.4.36, 293–305.
Bremer, J. M. (1984), 'The Popularity of Euripides' *Phoenissae* in Late Antiquity', in: J. Harmatta (ed.), *Proceedings of the VIIth Congress of the International Federation of the Societies of Classical Studies*, Budapest, I 282–8.
Bremer, J. M. (1998), 'The Reciprocity of Giving and Thanksgiving in Greek Worship', in: C. Gill / N. Postlethwaite / R. Seaford (eds.), *Reciprocity in Ancient Greece*, Oxford, 127–37.
Bremmer J. (1991), 'Walking, Standing, and Sitting in Ancient Greek Culture', in: J. Bremmer / H. Roodenburg (eds.), 15–35.
Bremmer, J. / Roodenburg, H. (eds.) (1991), *A Cultural History of Gesture from Antiquity to the Present Day*, Cambridge.
Brillet-Dubois, P. (2010–2011), 'Astyanax et les orphelins de guerre Athéniens. Critique de l' idéologie de la cité dans les *Troyennes* d' Euripide', in: *REG* 123, 29–50.
Brulé, P. (2006), 'Le corps sportif', in: F. Prost / J. Wilgaux (eds.), *Penser et représenter le corps dans l'Antiquité: actes du colloque international de Rennes, 1–4 septembre 2004*, Rennes, 263–87.
Buck, R. J. (1981), 'Epidaurians, Aeginetans and Athenians', in: G. S. Shrimpton / D. J. McCargar (eds.), *Classical Contributions: Studies in Honour of M. F. McGregor*, Locust Valley NY, 5–13.
Budelmann, F. (2000), *The Language of Sophocles. Communality, Communication and Involvement*, Cambridge.
Budelmann, F. (ed.) (2009), *The Cambridge Companion to Greek Lyric*, Cambridge.
Budelmann, F. / LeVen, P. A. (2014), 'Timotheus' Poetics of Blending: A Cognitive Approach to the Language of the New Music', in: *CPh* 109, 191–210.
Budelmann, F. / Power, T. (2013), 'The Inbetweenness of Sympotic Elegy', in: *JHS* 133, 1–19.
Budin, S. L. (2006), 'Sacred prostitution in the First Person', in: C. A. Faraone / L. K. McClure (eds.), *Prostitutes and Courtesans in the Ancient World*, Madison WI, 77–92.
Budin, S. L. (2008a), 'Simonides' Corinthian epigram', in: *CPh* 103, 335–53.
Budin, S. L. (2008b), *The Myth of Sacred Prostitution in Antiquity*, Cambridge.
Bundy, E. L. (1962), *Studia Pindarica*, Berkeley.
Bundy, E. L. (1972), 'The "Quarrel between Kallimachos and Apollonios" Part I: The Epilogue of Kallimachos's "Hymn to Apollo"', in: *CSCA* 5, 39–94.
Burian, P. (1986), 'Zeus σωτήρ τρίτος and Some Triads in Aeschylus' *Oresteia*', in: *AJP* 107, 332–42.
Burnet, J. (1945), *Early Greek Philosophy*, New York.
Burnett, A. P. (1970), 'Pentheus and Dionysus. Host Guest', in: *CPh* 65: 15–29.
Burnett, A. P. (1971), *Catastrophe Survived: Euripides' Plays of Mixed Reversal*, Oxford.
Burnett, A. P. (1988), 'Jocasta in the West. The Lille Stesichorus', in: *ClAnt* 7, 107–54.
Burnett, A. P. (2005), *Pindar's Songs for Young Athletes of Aigina*, Oxford.
Burnett, A. P. (2011), 'Servants of Peitho: Pindar fr.122 S.', in: *GRBS* 51, 49–60.
Burton, R. W. B. (1980), *The Chorus in Sophocles' Tragedies*, Oxford.
Cairns, D. (2006), 'Virtue and Vicissitudes: The Paradoxes of the *Ajax*', in: D. Cairns / V. Liapis (eds.), *Dionysalexandros: Essays on Aeschylus and his Fellow Tragedians in Honour of Alexander F. Garvie*, Swansea, 99–131.

Cairns, D. (2010), *Bacchylides. Five Epinician Odes (3,5,9, 11, 13)*, Cambridge.
Cairns, D. (2013), 'A short history of shudders', in: A. Chaniotis / P. Ducrey (eds.), *Unveiling Emotions* II. *Emotions in Greece and Rome: Texts, Images, Material Culture*, Stuttgart, 85–107.
Calame, C. (1994–1995), 'From Choral Poetry to Tragic Stasimon: The Enactment of Women's Song', in: *Arion* 3.1, 136–54.
Calame, C. (1995), *The Craft of Poetic Speech in Ancient Greece*, Ithaca and London.
Calame, C. (1997a), 'De la poésie chorale au stasimon tragique. Pragmatique de voix féminines', in: *Mètis* 12, 181–203.
Calame, C. (1997b), *Choruses of Young Women in Ancient Greece: Their Morphology, Religious Role, and Social Function*, tr. D. Collins and J. Orion, Lanham Md. [rev. edn. of Calame, C. (1977) *Les choeurs de jeunes filles en Grèce archaïque*, vol. I, Morphologie, fonction religieuse et sociale, Rome].
Calame, C. (1998), 'La poésie lyrique grecque: un genre inexistant?' in: *Littérature* 111, 87–110.
Calame, C. (2001), *Choruses of Young Women in Ancient Greece: Their Morphology, Religious Role, and Social Function*, Lanham Md.
Calame, C. (2009), 'Apollo in Delphi and in Delos. Poetic Performances between Paean and Dithyramb', in: L. Athanassaki / R. P. Martin / J. F. Miller (eds.), *Apolline Politics and Poetics*, Athens, 169–97.
Calame, C. (2013a), 'Choral Polyphony and the Ritual Functions of Tragic Songs', in: R. Gagné / M. G. Hopman (eds.), 35–57.
Calame, C. (2013b) 'The Dithyramb, a Dionysiac Poetic Form. Genre Rules and Cultic Contexts', in: B. Kowalzig / P. Wilson (eds.), 332–52.
Campagner, R. (1988), 'Reciprocità economica in Pindaro', in: *QUCC* NS 29.2, 77–93.
Campbell, D. A. (1992), *Greek Lyric IV. Bacchylides, Corinna and others* (LCL 461), Cambridge MA and London.
Caneva, S. G. / Delli Pizzi, A. (2015), 'Given to a Deity? Religious and Social Reappraisal of Human Consecrations in the Hellenistic and Roman East', in: *CQ* 65, 167–91.
Cantilena, M. (1993), 'Il primo suono della lira', in: R. Pretagostini (ed.), *Tradizione e innovazione nella cultura greca da Omero all'età ellenistica. Scritti in onore di Bruno Gentili*, Rome, 115–27.
Cantilena, M. (2012), 'Intorno alla tradizione', in: *SemRom* I.2, 147–63.
Carden, R. (1974), *The Papyrus Fragments of Sophocles*, Berlin.
Carey, C. (1981), *A Commentary on Five Odes of Pindar*, Salem.
Carey, C. (2003), 'The Political World of Homer and Tragedy', in: *Aevum antiquum* NS 3, 464–84.
Carey, C. (2007), 'Pindar, Place, and Performance', in S. Hornblower / C. Morgan (eds.), *Pindar's Poetry, Patrons, and Festivals: From Archaic Greece to the Roman Empire*, Oxford, 199–210.
Carey, C. (2009a), 'Genre, Occasion and Performance', in: F. Budelmann (ed.), 21–38.
Carey, C. (2009b), 'The Third Stasimon of *Oedipus at Colonus*', in: S. Goldhill / E. Hall (eds.), 119–33.
Carey, C. (2011), 'Alcman: From Laconia to Alexandria', in: Athanassaki L. / Bowie, E. L. (eds.), 437–60.

Carey, C. (2012), 'The Victory Ode in the Theatre', in: P. Agócs / R. Rawles / C. Carey (eds.) (2012b), London, 17–36.
Carey, C. (2015), 'Stesichorus and the Epic Cycle', in: P. J. Finglass / A. Kelly (eds.), 45–62.
Carne-Ross, D. S. (1985), *Pindar*, New Haven.
Carter, D. M. (ed.) (2011), *Why Athens? A Reappraisal of Tragic Politics*, Oxford.
Cartledge, P. (1979), *Sparta and Lakonia. A Regional History 1300–362 B.C*, London.
Castriota, D. (1992), *Myth, Ethos, and Actuality. Official Art in Fifth-Century B.C. Athens*, Madison WI.
Cazzato, V. / Obbink, D. / Prodi, E. E. (eds.) (2016), *The Cup of Song. Studies on Poetry and the Symposion*, Oxford.
Ceccarelli, P. (2000), 'Dance and Desserts: An Analysis of Book Fourteen', in: D. Braund / J. Wilkins (eds.), *Athenaeus and His World: Reading Greek Culture in the Roman Empire*, Exeter, 272–91.
Cerbo, E. (1984–1985), 'Il coro nelle *Fenicie* di Euripide: una testimonianza della nuova espressività teatrale', in: *Dioniso* 55, 183–91.
Cerbo, E. (1993), 'Gli inni ad Eros in tragedia: struttura e funzione', in: R. Pretagostini (ed.), *Tradizione e innovazione nella cultura greca da Omero all'età ellenistica*, "Scritti in onore di Bruno Gentili", II, Rome, 645–56.
Cerbo, E. (2012), 'Il corale 'ibrido' della καλλίνικος ᾠδή nell'*Elettra* di Euripide (vv. 859–879)', in: *SemRom* 12, 131–52.
Cerbo, E. (2016), 'Un epicedio per Troia. Lettura metrico-ritmica di Eur. *Troad*. 511–567', in: *Rationes Rerum* 7, 33–68.
Cerri, G. (2007), 'Nuovi generi corali nell'*Edipo a Colono* di Sofocle', in: F. Perusino / M. Colantonio (eds.), 159–81.
Chaniotis, A. (2007), 'Theater Rituals', in: P. Wilson (ed.), *The Greek Theater and Festivals: Documentary studies*, Oxford, 48–66.
Chantry, M. (1999), *Scholia in Aristophanem III I*ᵃ*: Scholia Vetera in Aristophanis Ranas*, Groningen.
Cingano, E. (1986), 'Il valore dell'espressione στάσις μελῶν in Aristofane, "Rane", v. 1281', in: *QUCC* NS 24.3, 139–43.
Cingano, E. (1993), 'Indizi di esecuzione corale in Stesicoro', in: R. Pretagostini (ed.), *Tradizione e Innovatione nella Cultura Greca da Omero all'Età Ellenistica: Scritti in Onore di Bruno Gentili*, 3 vols., Rome, I 347–61.
Cingano, E. (1995), '[Introduction and Commentary on *Pythian* 1, 2]', in: B. Gentili et al. (eds.), *Pindaro: Le Pitiche*, Milan.
Cingano, E. (2003), 'Entre skolion et enkomion: réflexions sur le "genre" et la performance de la lyrique chorale grecque', in: J. Jouanna / J. Leclant (eds.), *Colloque: La poésie grecque antique. Actes*, Paris, 17–45.
Citta, V. (1994), *Eschilo e la lexis tragica*, Amsterdam.
Clark, C. A. (1996), 'The Gendering of the Body in Alcman's *Partheneion* 1: Narrative, Sex, and Social Order in Archaic Sparta', in *Helios* 23.2, 143–69.
Clay, J. S. (2011), '*Olympians* 1–3: A Song Cycle?', in: L. Athanassaki / E. L. Bowie (eds.), 337–45.
Cobetto Ghiggia, P. (1995), *[Andocide], Contro Alcibiade: introduzione, traduzione, e commento*, Pisa.

Collard C. (2004), 'Euripides. *Palamedes*' in: C. Collard / M. J. Cropp / J. Gibert (eds.), 92–103.
Collard, C. / Cropp, M. J. (2008), *Euripides. Fragments* (LCL 506), Cambridge MA and London.
Collard, C. / Cropp, M. J. / Gibert, J. (eds.) (2004), *Euripides. Selected Fragmentary Plays*, Vol. 2: Philoctetes, Alexandros (with Palamedes and Sisyphus), Oedipus, Andromeda, Hypsipyle, Antiope, Archelaus, Oxford.
Collins, D. (2002), 'Reading the Birds: *Oiônomanteia* in Early Epic', in: *Colby Quarterly* 38.1, 17–41.
Collins, D. (2005), *Master of the Game: Competition and Performance in Greek Poetry*, Washington DC.
Colonna, A. (1951), *Himerii Declamationes et orationes cum deperditarum fragmentis*, Rome.
Comotti, G. (1989a), 'L'anabole e il ditirambo', in: *QUCC* 31, 107–17.
Comotti, G. (1989b), *La musica nella tragedia greca*, in: L. de Finis (ed.), *Scena e spettacolo nell'antichità*, Atti del Convegno Internazionale di Studio, Trento, 28–30 marzo 1988, Firenze, 43–61.
Conte, G. B. (1986), *The Rhetoric of Imitation. Genre and Poetic Memory in Virgil and Other Latin Poets*, Ithaca and London.
Contiades-Tsitsoni, E. (1990), *Hymenaios und Epithalamion: Das Hochzeitslied in der frühgriechischen Lyrik*, Stuttgart.
Coo, L. (2013), 'A Tale of Two Sisters: Studies in Sophocles' Tereus', in: *TAPhA* 143.2, 349–84.
Coo, L. (2016), 'Blindness and Sight: The Mask of Thamyris', in: M. Squire (ed.), *Sight and the Ancient Senses*, London, 237–48.
Cousland, J. R. C. / Hume, J. R. (eds.) (2009), *The Play of Texts and Fragments. Essays in Honour of Martin Cropp*. Mnem. Suppl. 314, Leiden and Boston.
Craik, E. (1988), *Euripides*. Phoenician Women, Warminster.
Cribiore, R. (2001), 'The Grammarian's Choice: The popularity of Euripides' *Phoenissae* in Hellenistic and Roman education', in: Y. L. Too (ed.), *Education in Greek and Roman Antiquity*, Leiden and Boston, 242–59.
Croally, N. T. (1994), *Euripidean Polemic:* The Trojan Women *and the Function of Tragedy*, Cambridge.
Cropp M. J. (2004), 'Euripides. *Alexandros*', in: C. Collard / M. J. Cropp / J. Gibert (eds.), 35–87.
Cropp M. J. (2013), *Euripides*. Electra. 2nd edn., Oxford.
Cropp, M. J. / Fick, G. (1985), *Resolutions and Chronology in Euripides: The Fragmentary Tragedies*. BICS Suppl. 43, London.
Cropp, M. J. / K. Lee / D. Sansone (eds.), (1999–2000), *Euripides and Tragic Theatre in the Late Fifth Century, ICS* 24–5.
Crotty, K. (1982), *Song and Action. The Victory Odes of Pindar*, Baltimore and London.
Csapo, E. (1999–2000), 'Later Euripidean music', in: M. Cropp / K. Lee / D. Sansone (eds.), 399–426.
Csapo, E. (2003), 'The Dolphins of Dionysus', in: E. Csapo / M. C. Miller (eds.), *Poetry, Theory, Praxis: The Social Life of Myth, Word and Image in Ancient Greece. Essays in Honour of William J. Slater*, Oxford, 69–98.
Csapo, E. (2004) 'The Politics of the New Music', in: P. Murray / P. Wilson (eds.), 207–48.

Csapo, E. (2007) 'The Men who built the Theatres: *Theatropolai, Theatronai*, and *Arkhitektones*' with an Archaeological Appendix by Goette, H. R., in: P. Wilson (ed.) *The Greek Theatre and Festivals: Documentary Studies*, Oxford, 87–121.
Csapo, E. (2008), 'Star Choruses: Eleusis, Orphism, and New Musical Imagery and Dance', in: M. Revermann / P. Wilson (eds.), 262–90.
Csapo, E. (2009) 'New Music's Gallery of Images: The "Dithyrambic" First Stasimon of Euripides' *Electra*', in: J. R. C. Cousland / J. R. Hume (eds.), 95–109.
Csapo, E. (2010), *Actors and Icons of the Ancient Theater*, Chichester and Malden MA.
Csapo, E. (2011), 'The Economics, Poetics, Politics, Metaphysics, and Ethics of the New Music', in: D. Yatromanolakis (ed.), *Music and Cultural Politics in Greek and Chinese Societies: Volume 1: Greek Antiquity*, Cambridge MA, 65–132.
Csapo, E. / Miller, M. C. (eds.) (2007), *The Origins of Theater in Ancient Greece and Beyond*, Cambridge.
Csapo, E. / Slater, W. J. (1995), *The Context of Ancient Drama*, Ann Arbor MI.
Csapo, E. / Wilson, P. (2009), 'Timotheus the New Musician', in: F. Budelmann (ed.), 277–93.
Cuny, D. (2008), 'Les mots de la fin chez Sophocle', in: B. Bureau / C. Nicolas (eds.), *Commencer et finir. Débuts et fins dans les littératures grecque, latine et néolatine.* Actes du colloque organisé les 29 et 30 septembre 2006 par l'Université Jean Moulin – Lyon 3 et l'ENS – LSH, I-II, Paris, 573–83.
Currie, B. (2004), 'Reperformance Scenarios for Pindar's Odes', in: C. J. Mackie (ed.), 49–69.
Currie, B. (2011), 'Epinician *Choregia:* Funding a Pindaric Chorus', in: L. Athanassaki / E. L. Bowie (eds.), 269–310.
Dähnhardt, O. (1894), *Scholia in Aeschyli Persas*, Leipzig.
Dale, A. M. (1968), *The Lyric Metres of Greek Drama*. 2nd edn., Cambridge.
Dale, A. M. (1969), 'Stasimon and Hyporcheme', in: T. B. L. Webster / E. G. Turner (eds.) *Collected Papers of A. M. Dale*, Oxford, 34–40 [repr. from *Eranos* 48 (1950) 14–20].
D'Alessio, G. B. (1994), 'First-person Problems in Pindar', in: *BICS* 39, 117–39.
D'Alessio, G. B. (1997), 'Pindar's *Prosodia* and the Classification of Pindaric Papyrus Fragments', in: *ZPE* 118, 23–60.
D'Alessio, G. B. (2007), "Ἠν ἰδού: ecce satyri (Pratina, PMG 708 = TrGF 4 F 3). Alcune considerazioni sull' uso della deissi nei testi lirici e teatrali', in: F. Perusino / M. Colantonio (eds.), 95–128.
D'Alessio, G. B. (2009), 'Defining Local Identities in Greek Lyric Poetry', in: R. Hunter / R. Rutherford (eds.), 137–67.
D'Alessio, G. B. (2013a), 'The wanderings of the Thestorids (Stesichorus fr. 193.16–22 *PMGF*)', in: *ZPE* 186, 36–7.
D'Alessio, G. B. (2013b), '"The Name of the Dithyramb". Diachronic and Diatopic Variations', in: B. Kowalzig / P. Wilson (eds.), 113–32.
D'Alfonso, F. (1994), *Stesicoro e la performance: studi sulle modlità esecutive dei carmi stesicorei*, Rome.
D'Angour, A. (2006), 'The New Music—so what's new?', in: S. Goldhill / R. Osborne (eds.), Cambridge, 264–83.
D'Angour, A. (2011), *The Greeks and the New. Novelty in Ancient Greek Imagination and Experience*, Cambridge.
D'Angour, A. (2013), 'Music and Movement in the Dithyramb', in: B. Kowalzig / P. Wilson (eds.), 198–210.

Danielewicz, J. (1990), 'Il *nomos* nella parodia di Aristofane (*Ran.* 1264sgg.)', in: *Annali dell' Istituto universitario orientale di Napoli. Dipartimento di studi del mondo classico e del mediterraneo antico, sezione filologico-letteraria* 12, 131–42.
Davidson, J. F. (1983), 'The Parodos of the "Antigone": A Poetic Study', in: *BICS* 30, 41–51.
Davidson, J. F. (1986), 'The Circle and the Tragic Chorus', in: *G&R* 33.1, 38–46.
Davidson, J. F. (1991), 'Starting a Choral Ode: Some Sophoclean Techniques', in: *Prudentia* 23, 31–44.
Davies, M. (1988), *Epicorum Graecorum Fragmenta*, Göttingen.
Davies, M. (1991), *Sophocles*. Trachiniae, Oxford.
Davies, M. (2010), ' "Sins of the fathers": Omitted Sacrifices and Offended Deities in Greek Literature and the Folk-tale', in: *Eikasmos* 21, 333–55.
Davies, M. / Finglass, P. J. (2014), *Stesichorus. The Poems*, Cambridge Classical Texts and Commentaries 54, Cambridge.
Day, J. W. (1989), 'Rituals in Stone: Early Greek Grave Epigrams and Monuments', in: *JHS* 109, 16–28.
Day, J. W. (1994), 'Interactive Offerings: Early Greek Dedicatory Epigrams and Ritual', in: *HSPh* 96, 37–74.
Day, J. W. (2000), 'Epigram and Reader: Generic Rorce as (Re-)Activation of Ritual', in: M. Depew / D. Obbink (eds.), 37–57.
Day, J. W. (2010), *Archaic Greek Epigram and Dedication. Representation and Reperformance*, Cambridge.
De Falco, V. (1958), *Studi Sul Teatro Greco*, Napoli.
Delebecque, E. (1951), *Euripide et la guerre du Péloponnèse*, Paris.
Denniston, J. D. (1936), 'Lyric Iambics in Greek Drama', in: G. Murray / C. Balley (eds.) *Greek Poetry and Life. Essays Presented to Gilbert Murray on His Seventieth Birthday*, Oxford, 121–44.
Denniston, J. D. (1939), *Euripides*. Electra, Oxford.
Denniston, J. D. / Page, D. L. (eds.) (1957), *Aeschylus*. Agamemnon, Oxford.
Depew, M. (2000), 'Enacted and Represented Dedications: Genre and Greek Hymn', in: M. Depew / D. Obbink (eds.), 59–79.
Depew, D. (2007), 'From Hymn to Tragedy: Aristotle's Genealogy of Poetic Kinds', in: E. Csapo / M. C. Miller (eds.), 126–49.
Detienne, M. (1973), 'L'olivier: un mythe politico-religieux', in: M. I. Finley (ed.), *Problèmes de la terre en Grèce ancienne*, Paris, 293–306.
Dhuga, U. S. (2005), 'Choral Identity in Sophocles' *Oedipus Coloneus*', in: *AJPh* 126.3, 333–62.
Di Benedetto, V. (1971), *Euripide: Teatro e società*, Turin.
Di Benedetto, V. / Cerbo, E. (1998), *Euripide*. Troiane, Milan.
Dietz, G. (1971), 'Das Bett des Odysseus', in: *Symbolon. Jahrbuch der Symbolforschung* 7, 9–32 [repr. in: G. Dietz (2000), *Menschenwürde bei Homer*, Heidelberg, 1–25].
Dickie, M. (1984), 'Phaeacian Athletes', in: F. Cairns (ed.), *Papers of the Liverpool Latin Seminar: Fourth Volume 1983*, Liverpool, 237–76.
Diels, H. / Kranz, W. (1951–1952), *Die Fragmente der Vorsokratiker*, 3 vols., Berlin.
Diggle, J. (1980), *Studies on the Text of Euripides*. Supplices, Electra, Heracles, Troades, Iphigenia in Tauris, Ion, Oxford.

Diggle, J. (1981), *Euripidis fabulae. Tomus II.* Supplices, Electra, Hercules, Troades, Iphigeni in Tauris, Ion, Oxford.
Diggle, J. (1996), 'Sophocles, *Ichneutae* (fr. 314 Radt)', in: *ZPE* 112, 3–17.
Di Giuseppe, L. (2012), *Euripide.* Alessandro, Lecce.
Di Marco, M. (1973–1974), 'Osservazioni sull'iporchema', in: *Helikon* 13–14, 326–48.
Dindorf, W. (1879), *Aeschyli Tragoediae.* 5th edn. Leipzig.
Dobrov, G. / Urios-Aparisi, E. (1995), 'The Maculate Music: Gender, Genre, and the *Chiron* of Pherecrates', in: G. Dobrov (ed.), *Beyond Aristophanes: Transition and Diversity in Greek comedy*, Atlanta, 138–74.
Dodds, E. R. (1960), *Euripides.* Bacchae, Oxford.
Dorsch, K.-D. (1983), *Götterhymnen in den Chorliedern der griechischen Tragiker. Form, Inhalt und Funktion*, Münster.
Dougherty, C. / Kurke, L. (eds.) (1993), *Cultural Poetics in Archaic Greece: Cult, Performance, Politics*, Oxford.
Drachmann, A. B. (1903–1927), *Scholia Vetera in Pindari Carmina*, 3 vols., Leipzig.
Ducat, J. (1974), 'Les thèmes des récits de la fondation de Rhégion', in: *Mélanges helléniques offerts à Georges Daux*, Paris, 93–114.
Duchemin, J. (1968), *L'ΑΓΩΝ dans la tragédie grecque.* 2nd edn., Paris.
Duncan, A. (2011), 'Nothing to do with Athens? Tragedians at the Courts of Tyrants', in: D. M. Carter (ed.), 69–84.
Dunn, F. M. / Cole, T. (eds.) (1992), *Beginnings in Classical Literature*, Cambridge (= *YCS* 29).
Earp, F. R. (1944), *The Style of Sophocles*, Cambridge.
Easterling, P. (ed.) (1997a), *The Cambridge Companion to Greek Tragedy*, Cambridge.
Easterling, P. (1997b), 'Form and Performance', in: P. Easterling (ed.), 151–77.
Eckerman, C. (2010), 'The κῶμος of Pindar and Bacchylides and the Semantics of Celebration', in: *CQ* 60.2, 302–12.
Edmunds, L. (1996), *Theatrical Space and Historical Place in Sophocles'* Oedipus at Colonus, Lanham MD and London.
Edwards, M. (1991), *The Iliad: A Commentary vol. V, Books 17–20*, Cambridge.
Else, G. (1957), *Aristotle's* Poetics: *The Argument*, Cambridge MA.
Ercoles, M. (2013), *Stesicoro: Le Testimonianze Antiche*, Bologna.
Ercoles, M. / Fiorentini, L. (2011), 'Giocasta tra Stesicoro (*PMGF* 222(b)) ed Euripide (*Fenicie*)', in: *ZPE* 179, 21–34.
Esposito, S. (1996), 'The Changing Roles of The Sophoclean Chorus', in: *Arion* 3rd s. 4.1, 85–114.
Färber, H. (1936), *Die Lyrik in der Kunsttheorie der Antike*, Munich.
Fantuzzi, M. (2007), 'La *mousa* del lamento in Euripide, e il lamento della Musa nel *Reso* ascritto ad Euripide', in: *Eikasmos* 18, 173–99.
Fearn, D. (2007), *Bacchylides: Politics, Performance, Poetic Tradition*, Oxford.
Fearn, D, (2011), 'The Ceians and Their Choral Lyric', in: L. Athanassaki / E. L. Bowie (eds), 207–34.
Fearn, D. (2013), 'Athens and the Empire: The Contextual Flexibility of Dithyramb, and its Imperialist Ramifications', in: B. Kowalzig / P. Wilson (eds.), 133–52.
Fearn, D. (forthcoming) 'Lyric Reception and Sophistic Literarity in Timotheus' *Persae*', in: B. G. F. Currie / I. C. Rutherford (eds.), *The Reception of Greek Lyric Poetry. Transmission, Canonization, and Paratext*, Leiden and Boston.

Fernandez-Galiano, M. (1992), '[Commentary] on Book XXI', in: J. Russo / M. Fernandez-Galiano / A. Heubeck (eds.), *A Commentary on Homer's Odyssey, Volume 3: Books XVII–XXIV*, Oxford, 148–206.
Ferrari, G. (2000), 'The Ilioupersis in Athens', in: *HSPh* 100, 119–50.
Ferrari, G. (2008), *Alcman and the Chorus of Sparta*, Chicago.
Ferrari, W. (1938), 'L'*Oresteia* di Stesicoro', in: *Athenaeum* NS 16, 1–37.
Ferrario, S. (2012), 'Political Tragedy: Sophocles and Athenian History', in: A. Markantonatos (ed.), 447–70.
Figueira, T. J. (1993), *Excursions in Epichoric History: Aiginetan Essays*, Lanham MD.
Finglass, P. J. (2007a), *Sophocles. Electra*, Cambridge Classical Texts and Commentaries 44, Cambridge.
Finglass, P. J. (2007b), *Pindar. Pythian Eleven*, Cambridge Classical Texts and Commentaries 45, Cambridge.
Finglass, P. J. (2011), *Sophocles. Ajax*, Cambridge Classical Texts and Commentaries 48, Cambridge.
Finglass, P. J. (2012), 'Ethnic Identity in Stesichorus', in: *ZPE* 182, 39–44.
Finglass, P. J. (2013a), 'How Stesichorus Began His *Sack of Troy*', in: *ZPE* 183, 1–17.
Finglass, P. J. (2013b), 'Demophon in Egypt', in: *ZPE* 184, 37–50.
Finglass, P. J. (2013c), 'Stesichorus and The Leaping Lot', in: *ZPE* 184, 10.
Finglass, P. J. (2014a), 'Introduction', in: M. Davies / P. J. Finglass (eds.), 1–91.
Finglass, P. J. (2014b), 'Text and Critical Apparatus', in: M. Davies / P. J. Finglass (eds.), 93–204.
Finglass, P. J. (2014c), '*Thebais?*', in: M. Davies / P. J. Finglass, (eds.), 356–92.
Finglass, P. J. (2014d), '[Commentary on frr. 187–369]', in: M. Davies / P. J. Finglass (eds.), 531–57.
Finglass, P. J. (2014e), 'The Glorious Water-Carrier: Stesichorus' *Sack of Troy*', in: *Omnibus* 67, 1–3.
Finglass, P. J. (2015a), 'Simias and Stesichorus', in: *Eikasmos* 26, 197–202.
Finglass, P. J. (2015b), 'Stesichorus, Master of Narrative', in: P. J. Finglass / A. Kelly (eds.), 83–97.
Finglass, P. J. (2017), 'The Sack of Troy in Stesichorus and Apollodorus', in: *QUCC* NS 115, 11–20.
Finglass, P. J. (2018), *Sophocles. Oedipus the King*, Cambridge Classical Texts and Commentaries 57, Cambridge.
Finglass, P. J. (forthcoming-a), 'Μεθοδολογικά ζητήματα στην έκδοση του Στησιχόρου', in: M. Tamiolaki (ed.), *Μεθοδολογικά Ζητήματα στις Κλασικές Σπουδές. Παλαιά Προβλήματα και Νέες Προκλήσεις*, Herakleion.
Finglass, P. J. (forthcoming-b), 'Editing Stesichorus', in: M. Alexandrou / C. Carey / G. B. D'Alessio (eds.), *Song Regained. Working with Greek Poetic Fragments*, Sozomena, Berlin and Boston.
Finglass, P. J. (forthcoming-c), 'Stesichorus', in: L. Swift (ed.), *A Companion to Greek Lyric*, Chichester and Malden MA.
Finglass, P. J. (forthcoming-d), 'Labour 10: The Cattle of Geryon and The Return from Tartessus', in: D. Ogden, (ed.), *The Oxford Handbook to Heracles*, Oxford.
Finglass, P. J. / Kelly, A. (eds.) (2015a), *Stesichorus in Context*, Cambridge.

Finglass, P. J. / Kelly, A. (2015b), 'The State of Stesichorean Studies', in: P. J. Finglass / A. Kelly (eds.), 1–17
Firinu, E. (2009), 'Il primo stasimo dell'*Ifigenia Taurica* euripidea e i *Persiani* di Timoteo di Mileto: un *terminus post quem* per il *nomos?*', in: *Eikasmos* 20, 109–31.
Fisher, N. (2006), 'The Pleasures of Reciprocity: *Charis* and the Athletic Body in Pindar' in: F. Prost / J. Wilgaux (eds.), *Penser et représenter le corps dans l'Antiquité: actes du colloque international de Rennes, 1–4 septembre 2004*, Rennes, 227–45.
Fleming, T. (1973), 'The Musical *Nomos* in Aeschylus' *Oresteia*', in: *CJ* 72, 222–33.
Fleming, T. (2007), *The Colometry of Aeschylus*, Amsterdam.
Fletcher, J. (1999), 'Choral Voice and Narrative in the First Stasimon of the *Agamemnon*', in: *Phoenix* 53, 29–49.
Flower, M. (2008), *The Seer in Ancient Greece*, Berkeley and London.
Flückiger-Guggenheim, D. (1984), *Göttliche Gäste: die Einkehr von Göttern und Heroen in der griechischen Mythologie*, Bern.
Foley, H. P. (1982), 'Marriage and Sacrifice in Euripides' *Iphigenia in Aulis*', in: *Arethusa* 15.1, 159–80.
Foley, H. P. (1985), *Ritual Irony: Poetry and Sacrifice in Euripides*, Ithaca NY and London.
Foley, H. P. (2003), 'Choral Identity in Greek Tragedy', in: *CPh* 98.1, 1–30.
Ford, A. L. (1993), *Homer: The Poetry of the Past*, Ithaca NY.
Ford, A. L. (2002), *The Origins of Criticism. Literary Culture and Poetic Theory in Classical Greece*, Princeton and Oxford.
Ford, A. L. (2003), 'From Letters to Literature: Reading the 'Song Culture' of Classical Greece' in: H. Yunis (ed.), *Written Text and the Rise of Literate Culture in Ancient Greece*, Cambridge, 15–37.
Ford, A. L. (2006), 'The Genre of Genres: Paeans and *Paian* in Early Greek Poetry', in: *Poetica* 38.3–4, 277–96.
Ford, A. L. (2011), *Aristotle as Poet. The Song for Hermias and Its Contexts*, Oxford.
Ford, A. L. (2013), 'The Poetics of Dithyramb', in: B. Kowalzig / P. Wilson (eds.), 313–31.
Foster, M. / Kurke, L. / Weiss, N. (eds.) (forthcoming), *The Genres of Archaic and Classical Greek Poetry: Theories and Models*, Boston and Leiden.
Fowler, B. H. (2007), 'Aeschylus' Imagery', in: *C&M* 28, 1–74 [partially repr. In: Lloyd (2007), 302–15].
Fraenkel, E. (1917–1918), 'Lyrische Daktylen', in: *RhM* NS 72, 161–97, 321–52 [= (1964), 165–233].
Fraenkel, E. (1950), *Aeschylus. Agamemnon*, 3 vols., Oxford.
Fraenkel, E. (1964), *Kleine Beiträge zur klassischen Philologie*, 2 vols., Rome.
Francis, E. D. / Vickers, M. J. (1990), *Image and Idea in Fifth Century Greece: Art and Literature After the Persian Wars*, London.
Franco, A. (2008), *Periferia e frontiera nella Sicilia antica. Eventi, identità a confronto e dinamiche antropiche nell'area centro-settentrionale fino al IV sec. a.C.*, Kokalos 19, Pisa.
Franklin, J. C. (2003), 'The Language of Musical Technique in Greek Epic Diction', in: *Gaia* 7, 295–307.
Franklin, J. C. (2013), 'Songbenders of Circular Choruses', in: B. Kowalzig / P. Wilson (eds.) 213–36.
Friis-Johansen, H. / Whittle, E. W. (1980), *Aeschylus. The Suppliants*, 3 vols., Copenhagen.

Führer, R. (1970), 'Zum "Stesichorus redivivus"', in: *ZPE* 5, 11–16.
Furley, W. D. (1999–2000), 'Hymns in Euripidean Tragedy', in: M. Cropp / K. Lee / D. Sansone (eds.), 183–97.
Furley, W. D. (2011), 'Homeric and Un-Homeric Hexameter Hymns: A Question of Type', in: A. Faulkner (ed.), *The Homeric Hymns. Interpretative Essays*, Oxford, 206–31.
Furley, W. D. / Bremer, J. (2001), *Greek Hymns. Selected Cult Song from the Archaic to Hellenistic Period*, 2 vols., Tübingen.
Gagné, R. / Hopman, M. G. (eds.) (2013a), *Choral Mediations in Greek Tragedy*, Cambridge.
Gagné, R. / Hopman, M. G. (2013b), 'Introduction: The Chorus in the Middle', in: R. Gagné / M. G. Hopman (eds.), 1–34.
Gaisford, T. (1848), *Etymologicum magnum*, Oxford. [repr. (1967), Amsterdam]
Gantz, T. (1983), 'The Chorus in Aischylos' Agamemnon', in: *HSPh* 87, 65–86.
Gardiner, C. P. (1987), *The Sophoclean Chorus. A Study of Character and Function*, Iowa City.
Garner, R. (1988) 'Death and Victory in Euripides' *Alcestis*', in: *ClAnt* 7.1, 58-71.
Garner, R. (1990), *From Homer to Tragedy: The Art of Allusion in Greek Poetry*, London.
Garrod, H. W. (1920), 'The Hyporcheme of Pratinas', in: *CR* 34.7/8, 129–36.
Garvie, A. F. (1986), *Aeschylus.* Choephori, Oxford.
Garvie, A. F. (2006), *Aeschylus'* Supplices: *Play and Trilogy*, 2nd edn., Bristol.
Gemelli Marciano, M. L. (2007), 'Quelques observations sur les *incipit* des présocratiques', in: *PhilosAnt* 7, 7–37.
Gennep, A. van (2010), *The Rites of Passage*, Oxford. [Orig. Publ. 1960 London and Henley; tr. M.B. Vizedom / G.L. Caffee].
Gentili, B. (1952), *La metrica dei Greci*, Messina-Firenze.
Gentili, B. / Giannini, P. (1977), 'Preistoria e formazione dell'esametro', in: *QUCC* 26, 7–51.
Gentili, B. / Lomiento, L. (2003), *Metrica e ritmica. Storia delle forme poetiche nella Grecia antica*, Milan.
Gérard-Rousseau, M. (1968), *Les mentions réligieuses dans les tablettes mycéniennes*, Rome.
Gerber, D. E. (1999), 'Pindar, *Nemean Six*: A Commentary', in: *HSPh* 99, 33–91.
Gerber, D. E. (2002), *A Commentary on Pindar* Olympian 9, Stuttgart.
Gildersleeve, B. L. (1899), *Pindar: The Olympian and Pythian Odes*. Rev. edn, New York.
Godley, A. D. (1920), *Herodotus. With an English translation*, Cambridge.
Goff, B. (2009), *Euripides*. Trojan Women, London.
Golden, M. (1998), *Sport and Society in Ancient Greece*, Cambridge.
Goldhill, S. (1984), *Language, Sexuality, Narrative: The* Oresteia, Cambridge.
Goldhill, S. (1996), 'Collectivity and Otherness – The Authority of the Tragic Chorus: Response to Gould', in: M. S. Silk (ed.), 244–56.
Goldhill, S. (1999) 'Programme Notes', in: S. Goldhill / R. Osborne (eds.), 1–29
Goldhill, S. (2007), *How to Stage Greek Tragedy Today*, Chicago.
Goldhill, S. (2012), *Sophocles and the Language of Tragedy*, New York.
Goldhill, S. (2013a), 'Choreography. The Lyric Voice of Sophoclean Tragedy', in: R. Gagné / M. G. Hopman (eds.), 100–29.
Goldhill, S. (2013b), 'The Greek Chorus: Our German Eyes', in: J. Billings / F. Budelmann / F. Macintosh (eds.), Oxford, 35–52.
Goldhill, S. / Hall, E. (eds.) (2009), *Sophocles and the Greek Tragic Tradition*, Cambridge.
Goldhill, S. / Osborne, R. (eds.) (1999), *Performance Culture and Athenian Democracy*, Cambridge.

Goslin, O. (2014), 'Astyanax and the Discus: Athletic Discourse in Euripides' Troades', Abstract 145th Annual Meeting of the Society for Classical Studies, Chicago IL.
Gostoli, A. (1990), *Terpander: veterum, testimonia, collegit, fragmenta edidit*, Rome.
Gostoli, A. (1993), 'Il nomos citarodico nella cultura greca arcaica', in: R. Prestagostini (ed.), *Tradizione e Innovatione nella Cultura Greca da Omero all'Età Ellenistica: Scritti in Onore di Bruno* Gentili, 3 vols., Rome, I 167–78.
Gostoli, A. (2015), 'Glauco di Reggio musico e storico della poesia greca nel V secolo a.C.', in: *QUCC* NS 110.2, 125–42.
Gould, J. (1973) '*Hiketeia*', in: *JHS* 93, 74–103 [repr. in: Gould, J. (2001), *Myth, Ritual, Memory and Exchange. Essays in Greek Literature and Culture*, Oxford, 22–77].
Gould, J. (1996), 'Tragedy and Collective Experience', in: M. S. Silk (ed.), 217–43 [repr. in: Gould, J. (2001), *Myth, Ritual Memory, and Exchange. Essays in Greek Literature and Culture*, Oxford, 379–404].
Graf, E. (1888), 'Orthios Nomos', in: *RhM* 43, 512–23.
Graf, F. (1978), 'Die Lokrischen Mädchen', *SSR* 2/1: 61–79 [repr. in: Buxton, R. (ed.) (2000), *Oxford Readings in Greek Religion*, Oxford, 250–70].
Graham, A. J. (1964), *Colony and Mother City in Ancient Greece*, Manchester.
Grandolini, S. (2002), 'Natura e caratteristiche del ΜΕΛΟΣ ΑΡΜΑΤΕΙΟΝ', in: *GIF* 54, 3–11.
Gregory, J. (2002), 'Euripides as Social Critic', in: *G&R* 49.2, 145–62.
Gregory, J. (ed.) (2005), *A Companion to Greek Tragedy*, Chichester and Malden MA.
Grenfell, B. P. / Hunt, A. S. (1908), '841. Pindar, *Paeans*', in: *The Oxyrhynchus Papyri* V, 11–110.
Grethlein, J. (2006) 'The Manifold Uses of the Epic Past: The Embassy Scene in Herodotus 7.153–63', in: *AJPh* 127.4, 485–509.
Gribble, D. (1999), *Alcibiades and Athens: A Study in Literary Presentation*, Oxford.
Griffin, J. (1992), 'Theocritus, the *Iliad*, and the East', in: *AJPh* 113.2, 189–211.
Griffith, M. (1977), *The Authenticity of* Prometheus Bound, Cambridge.
Griffith, M. (1983), *Aeschylus*. Prometheus Bound, Cambridge.
Griffith, M. (1999), *Sophocles*. Antigone, Cambridge.
Griffith, M. (2002), 'Slaves of Dionysos: Satyrs, Audience, and The Ends of the *Oresteia*', in: *ClAnt* 21.2, 195–258.
Griffith, M. (2008), 'The Poetry of Aeschylus (in its traditional contexts)', in: J. Jouanna / F. Montanari (eds.), *Eschyle à l'aube du theater occidental*, Entretiens Hardt 55, Vandoeuvres-Genève, 1–57.
Griffith, M. (2010), 'Satyr-Play and Tragedy Face to Face, from East to West', in: O. Taplin / R. Wyles (eds.), 47–63.
Griffith, M. (2013a), 'Cretan Harmonies and Universal Morals: Early Music and Migrations of Wisdom in Plato's *Laws*', in: A.-E. Peponi (ed.), *Performance and Culture in Plato's* Laws, Cambridge, 15–66.
Griffith, M. (2013b), 'Satyr-play, Dithyramb, and the Geopolitics of Dionysian style in Fifth-century Athens', in: B. Kowalzig / P. Wilson (eds.), 257–81.
Gruber, M. A. (2009), *Der Chor in den Tragödien des Aischylos: Affekt und Reaktion*, Tübingen.
Guida, A. (2010), 'Due varianti negli Ichneutai di Sofocle (fr. 314, 143 Radt)', in: *ZPE* 175, 5–8.

Guida, A. (2013), 'Sofocle, I Segugi: alla scoperta di un 'suono adulatore di pastori', in: G. Bastianini / A. Casanova (eds.), I papiri di Eschilo e di Sofocle. Atti del Convegno Internazionale di Studi. Firenze, 14–15 giugno 2012, Florence, 143–58.
Hadjimichael, Th. A. (2011), *Bacchylides and the Emergence of the Lyric Canon* (PhD diss. University College London).
Hadjimichael, Th. A. (2012), 'Epinician Competitions: Persona and Voice in Bacchylides', in: D. Castaldo / F. Giannachi / A. Manieri (eds.) *Poetry, Music, and Contests in Ancient Greece* (Series: Rudiae. Ricerche sul mondo classico 22–23, 2010–2011), Galatina, I 333–56.
Hadjimichael, Th. A. (2014a), 'Bacchylides Fr. 60 M. and the *Kassandra*', in: *BASP* 51, 77–100.
Hadjimichael, Th. A. (2014b) 'Aristophanes' Bacchylides: Reading *Birds* 1373–1409', in: *GRMS* 2, 184–210.
Hagel, S. (2010), *Ancient Greek Music: A New Technical History*, Cambridge.
Hague, R. H. (1983), 'Ancient Greek Wedding Songs: The Tradition of Praise', in: *Journal of Folklore Research* 20, 131–43.
Haigh, A. E. (1896), *The Tragic Drama of the Greeks*, Oxford.
Haldane, J. A. (1963), 'A Paean in the *Philoctetes*', in: *CQ* NS 13.1, 53–6.
Haldane, J. A. (1965), 'Musical Themes and Imagery in Aeschylus', in: *JHS* 85, 33–41.
Hall, E. (1999), 'The Sociology of Athenian Drama', in: P. E. Easterling (ed.), 93–126.
Hall, E. (2010), *Greek Tragedy: Suffering Under the Sun*, Oxford.
Halliwell, S. (1986), *Aristotle's* Poetics, London.
Halliwell, S. (1987), *The "Poetics" of Aristotle: Translation and Commentary*, London.
Handel, S. (1989), *Listening: An Introduction to the Perception of Auditory Events*, Cambridge MA.
Hanink, J. (2014), 'The Great Dionysia and the End of the Peloponnesian War', in: *ClAnt* 33, 319–46.
Hanson, V. D. (1998) *Warfare and Agriculture in Ancient Greece*, Berkeley.
Harriott, R. M. (1982), 'The Argive Elders, the Discerning Shepherd and the Fawning Dog: Misleading Communication in the *Agamemnon*', in: *CQ* NS 32.1, 9–17.
Harris, J. P. (2009), 'Revenge of the Nerds: Xenophanes, Euripides, and Socrates vs. Olympic Victors', in: *AJPh* 130.2, 157–94.
Harrison, G. / Liapis, V. (eds.) (2013), *Performance in Greek and Roman Theatre*, Leiden and Boston.
Haslam, M. (1974), 'Stesichorean Metre', in: *QUCC* 17, 7–57.
Haslam, M. (1978), 'The Versification of the New Stesichorus (*P.Lille* 76abc)', in: *GRBS* 19.1, 29–57.
Haubold, J. (2007), 'Athens and Aegina: 5.82–9', in: E. Irwin / E. Greenwood (eds.), *Reading Herodotus: A Study of the* Logoi *in Book 5 of Herodotus' Histories*, Cambridge, 226–44.
Hayward, S. (2000), *Cinema Studies: The Key Concepts*. 2nd edn., London.
Heath, M. (1987), *The Poetics of Greek Tragedy*, Stanford.
Heath, M. (1988), 'Receiving the κῶμος. The Context and Performance of Epinician', in: *AJPh* 109.2, 180–95.
Hedreen, G. (2007), 'Myths of Ritual in Athenian Vase-Paintings of Silens', in: E. Csapo / M. Miller (eds.), 150–95.

Helg, W. (1950), *Das Chorlied der griechischen Tragödie in seinem Verhältnis zur Handlung*, Zurich.
Henderson, J. (1987), *Aristophanes. Lysistrata*, Oxford.
Henderson, J. (1998), *Aristophanes I. Acharnians, Knights* (LCL 178), Cambridge MA and London.
Henderson, J. (2000), *Aristophanes II. Acharnians, Knights* (LCL 179), Cambridge MA and London.
Henrichs, A. (1994–1995), '"Why should I Dance?": Choral Self-referentiality in Greek Tragedy', in: *Arion* 3.1, 56–111.
Henrichs, A. (1996), 'Dancing in Athens, Dancing on Delos. Some Patterns of Choral Projection in Euripides', in: *Philologus* 140, 48–62.
Herington, J. (1970), *The Author of the Prometheus Bound*, Austin.
Herington, J. (1985), *Poetry into Drama. Early Tragedy and the Greek Poetic Tradition*, Berkeley.
Hermann, G. (1834), *Opuscula*, Vol. 5, Leipzig. [Repr. (1970), New York]
Hesk, J. (2012), 'Oedipus at Colonus', in: A. Markantonatos (ed.), 167–89.
Higbie, C. (2003), *The Lindian Chronicle and the Greek Creation of their Past*, Oxford.
Hiller, E. (1886), 'Die Fragmente des Glaukos von Rhegion', in: *RhM* NS 41, 398–436.
Hilton, I. (2011), *A Literary Study of Euripides' Phoinissai* (PhD diss. University College London).
Holwerda, D. (1977), *Scholia in Aristophanem Pars I Fasc. 3.1: Scholia vetera in Nubes*, Groningen.
Holwerda, D. (1978), *Scholia in Aristophanem Pars II Fasc. 2: Scholia vetera et recentiora in Aristophanis Pacem*, Groningen.
Hopman, M. G. (2013), *Scylla: Myth, Metaphor, Paradox*, Cambridge.
Hordern, J. H. (2002), *The Fragments of Timotheus of Miletus*, Oxford.
Hornblower, S. (1991), *A Commentary on Thucydides. Volume I: Books I-III*, Oxford.
Hornblower, S. (2004), *Thucydides and Pindar: Historical Narrative and the World of Epinikian Poetry*, Oxford.
Hornblower, S. (2008), *A Commentary on Thucydides. Volume 3: Books 5.25–8.109*, Oxford.
Hornblower, S. (2013), *Herodotus Histories Book V*, Cambridge.
Hose, M. (1991), *Studien zum Chor bei Euripides*, Vol. II, Stuttgart.
How, W. W. / Wells, J. (1936), *A Commentary on Herodotus*, Oxford.
Howland, R. L. (1954–1955), 'Epeius, Carpenter and Athlete', in: *PCPS* 183, 15–16.
Hubbard, T. K. (1985), *The Pindaric Mind: A Study of Logical Structure in Early Greek Poetry*. Mnem. Suppl. 85, Leiden and Boston.
Hubbard, T. K. (2000), 'Pindar and Sophocles: Ajax as Epinician Hero', in: *Echos du Monde Classique / Classical Views* 19, 315–32.
Hubbard, T. K. (2001), 'Pindar and Athens After the Persian Wars', in: D. Papenfuss / V. M. Strocka (eds.), *Gab es das Griechische Wunder? Griechenland zwischen dem Ende des 6. und der Mitte des 5. Jahrhunderts v. Chr.*, Mainz, 387–400.
Hubbard, T. K. (2004), 'The Dissemination of Epinician Lyric: Pan-Hellenism, Reperformance, Written Texts', in: C. J. Mackie (ed.), 71–93.
Hubbard, T. K. (2007), 'Pindar, Heracles, the Idaean Dactyl, and the Foundation of the Olympic Games', in: G. P. Schaus / S. R. Wenn (eds.), *Onward to the Olympics: Historical Perspectives on the Olympic Games*, Waterloo ON, 27–45.

Hubbard, T. K. (2011), 'The Dissemination of Pindar's Non-Epinician Choral Lyric', in: L. Athanassaki / E. L. Bowie (eds.), 347–63.
Hughes, D. D. (1991), *Human Sacrifice in Ancient Greece*, London and New York.
Hummel, P. (1997), 'Les composés en λιπ(ο)- dans la poésie lyrique grecque. Étude d'un micro-système lexical', in: *Philologus* 141, 145–8.
Hunter, R. (1996), *Theocritus and the Archaeology of Greek Poetry*, Cambridge.
Hunter, R. / Rutherford, R. (eds.) (2009), *Wandering Poets: Travel and Locality in Greek Poetic Culture*, Cambridge.
Hurwit, J. M. (1999), *The Athenian Acropolis. History, Mythology, and Archaeology from the Neolithic Era to the Present*, Cambridge.
Hutchinson, G. O. (2001), *Greek Lyric Poetry: A Selected Commentary on Larger Pieces*, Oxford.
Huxley, G. (1968), 'Glaukos of Rhegion', in: *GRBS* 9.1, 47–54.
Huys, M. (1986) 'The Plotting Scene in Euripides' *Alexandros:* An Interpretation of Fr. 23, 23a, 23b, 43 Sn. (Cf. Hypothesis ll. 23–5)', in: *ZPE* 62, 9–36.
Ieranò, G. (1997), *Il ditirambo di Dioniso: Le testimonianze antiche*, Pisa and Rome.
Ihde, D. (2003), 'Auditory Imagination', in: L. Back / M. Bull (eds.), *The Auditory Culture Reader*, Oxford, 61–6.
Illig, L. (1932), *Zur Form der Pindarischen Erzählung*, Berlin.
Instone, S. (1990), 'Love and Sex in Pindar: Some Practical Thrusts', in: *BICS* 37, 30–42.
Instone, S. (1996), *Pindar. Selected Odes*, Warminster.
Iozzo, M. (2013), 'The François Vase: Notes on Technical Aspects and Function', in: H. A. Shapiro / M. Iozzo / A. Lezzi-Hafter (eds.), *The François Vase: New Perspectives*, Zurich, 53–66.
Jacob, C. (2004), 'La citation comme performance dans les *Deipnosophistes* d'Athénée', in: C. Darbo-Peschanski (ed.), *La citation dans l'Antiquité*, Grenoble, 147–74.
Janko, R. (1980), 'Aeschylus' *Oresteia* and Archilochus', in: *CQ* 30.2, 291–3.
Janko, R. (1981), 'The Structure of the Homeric Hymns: A Study in Genre', in: *Hermes* 109.1, 9–24.
Janko, R. (1987), *Aristotle, Poetics I With the Tractatus Coislinianus, Reconstruction of Poetics II, and the Fragments of the On Poets*, Indianapolis.
Janko, R. (2001), 'Aristotle on Comedy, Aristophanes and Some New Evidence From Herculaneum' in Ø. Andersen / J. Haarberg, (eds.), *Making Sense of Aristotle. Essays in Poetics*, London, 51–71.
Janko, R. (2011), *Philodemus On Poems Books 3–4, With The Fragments of Aristotle On Poets*, Oxford.
Jauss, H. R. (1994), *Toward an Aesthetic of Reception*, tr. T. Bahti, Minneapolis.
Jebb, R. C. (1896), *Sophocles. The Ajax*, Cambridge [repr. London 2004].
Jebb, R. C. (1900a), *Sophocles. The Antigone*, Cambridge [repr. London 2004].
Jebb, R. (1900b), *Sophocles: The Plays and Fragments*, vol. 2: Oedipus Coloneus, Cambridge.
Jim, T. S. F. (2014), *Sharing with the Gods. Aparchai and Dekatai in Ancient Greece*, Oxford.
Johnston, A. (2016), '"Rayon du soleil": un écho pindarique dans l'*Antigone* de Sophocle', in: *Les Cahiers d'ALLHiS* 4, 21–35.
Jones, H. S. / Powell, J. E. (1942), *Thucydidis Historiae*, 2 vols., Oxford.
Jones, H. S. (1918), *Pausanias. Description of Greece. Books I-II* (LCL 93), Cambridge MA and London.

Jouan, F. / van Looy, H. (1998), *Euripide. Tome VIII: Fragments 1re partie* Aigeus-Autolykos, Paris.
Kaempf-Dimitriadou, S. (1986), 'Boreas', in: *LIMC* III.1, 133–42.
Kaimio, M. (1970), *The Chorus of Greek Drama Within the Light of the Person and Number Used*, Helsinki.
Kakridis, J. (1966), 'Zur Sappho 44 LP', in: *WS* 79, 21–6.
Kambitsis, J. (1972), *L'Antiope d'Euripide*, Athens.
Kamerbeek, J. C. (1984), *The Plays of Sophocles: Commentaries. Part 7:* The Oedipus Coloneus, Leiden and Boston.
Kane, B. (2014), *Sound Unseen. Acousmatic Sound in Theory and Practice*, Oxford.
Käppel, L. (1992), *Paian: Studien zur Geschichte einer Gattung*, Berlin.
Kárpáti, A. (2012), 'A Satyr-Chorus with Thracian Kithara: Toward an Iconography of the Fifth-Century New Music Debate', in: *Phoenix* 66.3/4, 221–46.
Kavoulaki, A. (1999), 'Processional Performance and the Democratic Performance', in: S. Goldhill / R. Osborne (eds.), 293–320.
Kavoulaki, A. (2011), 'Choral Self-awareness: On the Introductory Anapaests of Aeschylus' *Supplices*', in: L. Athanassaki / E. L. Bowie (eds.), 365–90.
Kearns, E. (1982), 'The Return of Odysseus: A Homeric Theoxeny', in: *CQ* NS 32.1, 2–8.
Kelly, A. (2015), 'Stesichorus and Homer', in: P. J. Finglass / A. Kelly (eds.), 21–44.
Keyßner, K. (1932), *Gottesvorstellung und Lebensauffassung im griechischen Hymnus*, Stuttgart.
Kitzinger, R. (2008), *The Choruses of Sophokles'* Antigone *and* Philoktetes. *A Dance of Words*, Leiden and Boston.
Kitzinger, R. (2012), 'Sophoclean Choruses', in: A. Markantonatos (ed.), 385–407.
Köhnken, A. (1983), 'Mythical Chronology and Thematic Coherence in Pindar's Third *Olympian* Ode', in: *HSPh* 87, 48–63.
Kolde, A. (2003), *Politique et religion chez Isyllos d'Épidaure*, Basel.
Koller, H. (1956), 'Das kitharodische Prooimion: Eine formgeschichtliche Untersuchung', in: *Philologus* 100, 159–206.
Komornicka, A. A. (1972), 'Quelques remarques sur la notion d' Ἀλάθεια et de Ψεῦδος chez Pindare', in: *Eos* 60, 235–53.
Korres, M. / Bouras, Ch. [= Κορρές, Μ. και Μπούρας, Χ.] (1983), Μελέτη αποκαταστάσεως του Παρθενώνος, Athens.
Korzeniewski, D. (1968), *Griechische Metrik*, Darmstadt.
Koster, W. J. W. (1978), *Scholia in Aristophanem, Pars II. Scholia in Vespas, Pacem, Aves et Lysistratam; Fasc. I, continens Scholia vetera et recentiora in Aristophanis Vespas*, Groningen.
Kotsidu, H. (1991), *Die musischen Agone der Panathenäen in archaischer und klassischer Zeit: eine historisch-archäologische Untersuchung*, Quellen und Forschungen zur antiken Welt, Bd. 8, Munich.
Kovacs, D. (1997), 'Gods and Men in Euripides' Trojan Trilogy', in: *Colby Quarterly* 33, 162–76.
Kovacs, D. (1999), *Euripides IV.* Trojan Women, Iphigenia Among the Taurians, Ion (LCL 10), Cambridge MA and London.
Kovacs, D. (2002), *Euripides VI.* Bacchae, Iphigenia at Aulis, Rhesus (LCL 495), Cambridge MA and London.

Kovacs, D. (2003), 'Toward a Reconstruction of "Iphigenia Aulidensis"', in: *JHS* 123, 77–103.
Kovacs, G. (2013), 'Stringed Instruments in Fifth-Century Drama', in: G. Harrison / V. Liapis (eds.), Leiden and Boston, 477–99.
Kowalzig, B. (2004), 'Changing Choral Worlds: Song-dance and Society in Athens and Beyond', in: P. Murray / P. Wilson (eds.), 39–65.
Kowalzig, B. (2005), 'Mapping out *Communitas:* Performances of *Theōria* in their Sacred and Political Context', in: J. Elsner / I. Rutherford (eds.), *Pilgrimage in Graeco-Roman & Early Christian Antiquity. Seeing the Gods*, Oxford, 41–72.
Kowalzig, B. (2007a), *Singing for the Gods. Performances of Myth and Ritual in Archaic and Classical Greece*, Oxford.
Kowalzig, B. (2007b), ' "And Now All the World Shall Sance!" (Eur. *Bacch.* 114): Dionysus' *Choroi* Between Drama and Ritual', in: E. Csapo / M. C. Miller (eds.), 221–51.
Kowalzig, B. / Wilson, P. (eds.) (2013), *Dithyramb in Context*, Oxford.
Kranz, W. (1933), *Stasimon: Untersuchungen zu Form und Gehalt der griechischen Tragödie*, Berlin.
Kratzer, E. (2013), 'A Hero's Welcome: Homecoming and Transition in the *Trachiniae*', in: *TAPhA* 143.1, 23–63.
Kratzer, E. (2015), 'Mortality is Hard to Wrestle with: Cosmology and Combat Sports in the *Alcestis*,' in: T. Scanlon (ed.) *Greek Poetry and Sport*, special issue, *Classics@13:* http://chs.harvard.edu/CHS/article/display/6050.
Kraut, R. (1997), *Aristotle. Politics Books VII and VIII*, Oxford.
Krumeich, R. / Pechstein, N. / Seidensticker, B. (eds.) (1999), *Das griechische Satyrspiel*, Darmstadt (=KPS)
Krummen, E. (1990), *Pyrsos Hymnon. Festliche Gegenwart und mythisch-rituelle Tradition als Voraussetzung einer Pindarinterpretation (Isthmie 4, Pythie 5, Olympie 1 und 3)*, Berlin and Boston.
Kuch, H. (1998), 'Euripides und Melos', in: *Mnemosyne* s.4 51.2, 147–53.
Kurke, L. (1991), *The Traffic in Praise: Pindar and the Poetics of Social Economy*, Ithaca NY and London.
Kurke, L. (1993), 'The Economy of *Kudos*', in C. Dougherty / L. Kurke (eds.), 131–63.
Kurke, L. (1996), 'Pindar and the Prostitutes: or, Reading Ancient "Pornography" ', in: *Arion* s.3 4.2, 49–75.
Kurke, L. (2012), 'The Value of Chorality in Ancient Greece', in: J. K. Papadopoulos / G. Urton (eds.), *The Construction of Value in the Ancient World*, Los Angeles, 218–35.
Kurke, L. (2013a), 'Pindar's *Pythian* 11 and the *Oresteia:* Contestatory Ritual Poetics in the 5th c. BCE', in: *ClAnt* 32.1, 101–75.
Kurke, L. (2013b), 'Imagining Chorality: Wonder, Plato's Puppets, and Moving Statues', in: A.-E. Peponi (ed.), Cambridge, 123–70.
Kyle, D. G. (1987), *Athletics in Ancient Athens*, Leiden and Boston.
Kyriakou, P. (2007), '*Epidoxon Kydos:* Crown Victory and its Rewards', in: *C&M* 58, 119–58.
Kyriakou, P. (2016), 'Wisdom, Nobility, and Families in *Andromache*', in: P. Kyriakou / A. Rengakos (eds.), *Wisdom and Folly in Euripides.* Trends in Classics Suppl. Vol. 31, Berlin and Boston, 137–54.
Lämmle, R. (2013), *Poetik des Satyrspiels*, Heidelberg.

Lada-Richards, I. (2002), 'Reinscribing the Muse: Greek Drama and the Discourse of Inspired Creativity', in: E. Spentzou / D. Fowler (eds.) *Cultivating the Muse: Struggles for Power and Inspiration in Classical Literature*, Oxford, 69–91.
Lada-Richards, I. (2007), *Silent Eloquence: Lucian and Pantomime Dancing*, London.
Lamari, A. A. (2010), *Narrative, Intertext, and Space in Euripides' Phoenissae*, Berlin and Boston.
Lambert, S. (2002), 'The sacrificial calendar of Athens', in: *ABSA* 97, 353–99.
Lanata, G. (1963), *Poetica pre-Platonica: testimonianze e frammenti*, Firenze.
Lardinois, A. P. M. H. (1996), 'Who Sang Sappho's Songs?', in E. Greene (ed.), *Re-Reading Sappho: Reception and Transmission*, Berkeley, 150–62.
Lardinois, A. P. M. H. (2011), 'The Parrhesia of Young Female Choruses in Ancient Greece', in: L. Athanassaki / E. L. Bowie (eds.), 160–72.
Lasserre, F. (1989), *Sappho: Une Autre Lecture*, Padua.
Latte, K. (1953–1966), *Hesychii Alexandrini Lexicon*, 2 vols., Copenhagen.
Latte, K. / Erbse, H. (1965) (eds.), *Lexica Graeca Minora*, Hildesheim.
Lavecchia, S. (2000), *Pindari dithyramborum fragmenta*, Rome.
Lawler, L. B. (1964), *The Dance of the Ancient Greek Theatre*, Iowa.
Lazzarini, M. L. (1976), *Le formule delle dediche votive nella Grecia arcaica*, Rome.
Leahy, D. M. (1974), 'The Representation of the Trojan War in Aeschylus' *Agamemnon*' in: *AJPh* 95.1, 1–23.
Lech, M. L. (2009), 'Marching Choruses? Choral Performance in Athens', in: *GRBS* 49.3, 343–61.
Lee, K. H. (1976), *Euripides. Troades*, Basingstoke.
Lefèvre, E. (2003), *Studien zu den Quellen und zum Verständnis des Prometheus Desmotes*, Göttingen.
Lefkowitz, M. (1991), *First-person Fictions: Pindar's Poetic 'I'*, Oxford.
Legrand, Ph. E. (1932–1954), *Hérodote. Histoires*, 9 vols., Paris.
Lehnus, L. (1979), *L'inno a Pan di Pindaro*, Milan.
Lehnus, L. (1981), *Pindaro. Olimpiche*, Milan.
Lesky, A. (1971), *Geschichte der griechischen Literatur*, 3rd edn., Bern.
Létoublon, F. (2012), 'Commencer à chanter', in: R. Bouchon / P. Brillet-Dubois / N. Le Meur-Weissman (eds.), *Hymnes de la Grèce Antique. Approches littéraires et historiques*, Lyon, 21–35.
LeVen, P. A. (2011), 'Timotheos' Eleven Strings: A New Approach', in: *CPh* 106.3, 245–54.
LeVen, P. A. (2013), 'The Colors of Sound: *Poikilia* and Its Aesthetic Contexts', in: *GRMS* 1, 229–42.
LeVen, P. A. (2014), *The Many-Headed Muse. Tradition and Innovation in Late Classical Greek Lyric Poetry*, Cambridge.
Ley, G. (2007), *The Theatricality of Greek Tragedy: Playing Space and Chorus*, Chicago.
Liberman, G. (2016), 'Some Thoughts on the Symposiastic *Catena*, *Aisakos*, and *Skolia*', in: V. Cazzato / D. Obbink / E. E. Prodi (eds.), 42–62.
Lidov, J. B. (1996), 'Pindar's "Hymn to Cybele" (fr. 80 SM): Meter, Form, and Syncretism', in: *GRBS* 37.2, 129–44.
Lissarrague, F. (1990), 'Why Satyrs are Good to Represent', in: J. J. Winkler / F. Zeitlin (eds.), 228–36.
Lloyd, M. A. (1992), *The Agon in Euripides*, Oxford.

Lloyd, M. A. (2005), *Euripides. Andromache.* 2nd edn., Warminster.
Lloyd, M. A. (2007), *Oxford Readings in Aeschylus*, Oxford.
Lloyd-Jones, H. (1962), 'The Guilt of Agamemnon', in: *CQ* 12.2, 187–99. [= (1990), 283–99]
Lloyd-Jones, H. (1983), 'Artemis and Iphigeneia', in: *JHS* 103, 87–102.
Lloyd-Jones, H. (1990a), *Greek Epic, Lyric, and Tragedy: The Academic Papers of Sir Hugh Lloyd-Jones*, Oxford.
Lloyd-Jones, H. (1990b), 'Problems of Early Greek Tragedy: Pratinas and Phrynichus', in: Lloyd-Jones, H., *Greek Epic, Lyric and Tragedy: The Academic Papers of Sir Hugh Lloyd-Jones*, Oxford, 227–37.
Lloyd-Jones, H. (1996), *Sophocles. Fragments* (LCL 483), Cambridge MA and London.
Lloyd-Jones, H. (2002), 'Ancient Greek Religion and Modern Ethics', in: *SIFC* 20 (1–2), 7–23.
Lloyd-Jones, H. (2003), 'Zeus, Prometheus, and Greek Ethics', in: *HSPh* 101, 49–72.
Lobeck, C. A. (1866), *Sophoclis Aiax*, 3rd edn., Berlin.
Lobel, E. (1959), '2430. Choral Lyric in the Doric Dialect (?Simonides), in: *The Oxyrhynchus Papyri* XXV, 45–87.
Lomiento, L. (2012), 'Inno alle Cariti con epinicio in Pindaro, "Olimpica" 14', in: D. Castaldo / F. Giannachi / A. Manieri (eds.) *Poetry, Music, and Contests in Ancient Greece* (Series: Rudiae. Ricerche sul mondo classico 22–23, 2010–2011), Galatina, I 287–305.
Lomiento, L. (2013), "[Introduction and Commentary on *Olympian* 4, 5, 10, 11, 13, and 14]," in: Gentili *et al.* (eds.), *Pindaro. Le Olimpiche*, Milan.
Loraux, N. (1985), *Façons tragiques de tuer une femme*, Paris.
Loraux, N. (2002), *The Mourning Voice: An Essay on Greek Tragedy*, Ithaca.
Lucas, D. W. (1968), *Aristotle. Poetics*, Oxford.
Lucas de Dios, J. M. (2008), *Esquilo. Fragmentos y Testimonios*, Madrid.
Luraghi, N. (1994), *Tirannidi arcaiche in Sicilia e Magna Grecia*, Florence.
Maas, P. (1962), *Greek Metre*. trans. H. Lloyd-Jones, Oxford.
Macan, R. W. (1908), *Herodotus: The Seventh, Eighth, and Ninth Books*, London.
Mackie, C. J. (ed.), (2004), *Oral Performance and Its Context*. Mnem. Suppl. 248, Leiden and Boston.
Mackie, H. (2003), *Graceful Errors: Pindar and the Performance of Praise*, Ann Arbor.
Macleod, C. W. (1982), 'Politics and the *Oresteia*', in *JHS* 102, 124–44 [repr. in Macleod, C. W. (1983), 20–40, and Lloyd (2007), 265–301].
Macleod, C. W. (1983), *Collected Essays*, Oxford.
Maehler, H. (post B. Snell) (1970), *Bacchylidis carmina cum fragmentis*. 10th edn., Leipzig.
Mancuso, G. (2013), 'Nota a *P.Oxy.* 2506 (fr. 26 col. i. 21 = Stesich. *PMGF* 193)', in: *ZPE* 186, 38–9.
Mangidis, I. (1998), *Euripides' Satyrspiel* Autolykos, Frankfurt a. M.
Marcovich, M. (1984), *Three-Word Trimeter in Greek Tragedy*, Königstein.
Markantonatos, A. (2002), *Tragic Narrative. A Narratological Study of Sophocles'* Oedipus at Colonus, Berlin and Boston.
Markantonatos, A. (2007), Oedipus at Colonus: *Sophocles, Athens, and the World*, Berlin and Boston.
Markantonatos, A. (ed.) (2012), *Brill's Companion to Sophocles*, Leiden and Boston
Marshall, C. W. (2014), *The Structure and Performance of Euripides'* Helen, Cambridge.

Martano, A. / Matelli, E. / Mirhady, D. C. (eds.) (2012), *Praxiphanes of Mytilene and Chamaeleon of Heraclea: Text, Translation, and Discussion*. Rutgers University Studies in Classical Humanities (RUSCH) 18, New Brunswick and London.

Martano, A. (2012), 'Chamaeleon of Heraclea: The Sources, Texts and Translations' in: A. Martano / E. Matelli / D. C. Mirhady, (eds), 159–338.

Martin, R. P. (1987), 'Fire on the Mountain: "Lysistrata" and the Lemnian Women', in: *ClAnt* 6.1, 77–105.

Martin, R. P. (2007), 'Ancient Theatre and Performance Culture' in: M. McDonald / M. Walton (eds.), *The Cambridge Companion to Greek and Roman Theatre*, Cambridge, 36–54.

Martin-McAuliffe, S. / Papadopoulos, J. K. (2012), 'Framing Victory: Salamis, the Athenian Acropolis, and the Agora', in: *JSAH* 71, 332–361.

Martinelli, M. C. (1995), *Gli strumenti del poeta: elementi di metrica greca*, Bologna.

Maslov, B. (2015), *Pindar and the Emergence of Literature*, Cambridge.

Mastronarde, D. J. (1979), *Contact and Discontinuity: Some Conventions of Speech and Action in the Greek Tragic Stage*, Berkeley and Los Angeles.

Mastronarde, D. J. (1994), *Euripides. Phoenissae*, Cambridge.

Mastronarde, D. J. (2002), *Euripides. Medea*, Cambridge.

Mastronarde, D. J. (2010), *The Art of Euripides. Dramatic Technique and Social Context*, Cambridge.

Matijašić, I. (2014), 'Timachidas di Rodi. Introduzione, edizione dei frammenti, traduzione e commento', in: C. Ampolo / D. Erdas, / A. Magnetto (eds.), *La Gloria di Athana Lindia ASNP* Sr. 5 6.1, 113–86.

Mayer, M. (1883), *De Euripidis mythopoeia capita duo* (PhD diss. Berlin).

McDevitt, S. (1972), 'The Nightingale and the Olive: Remarks on the First Stasimon in *Oedipus Coloneus*', in: R. Hanslik / A. Lesky, / H. Schwabl (eds.), *Antidosis: Festschrift für Walther Kraus zum 70. Geburtstag*, Vienna, 227–37.

Meiggs, R. (1972), *The Athenian Empire*, Oxford.

Meillier, C. (1976), 'Callimaque (P.L. 76 d, 78 abc, 82, 84, 111 c). Stésichore (?) (P.L. 76 abc)', in: *Études sur l'Egypte et le Soudan anciens = Cahiers de recherches de l'Institut de papyrologie et d'égyptologie de Lille* 4, 255–360.

Meineck, P. (2013), '"The Thorniest Problem and the Greatest Opportunity". Directors on Directing the Greek Chorus', in: R. Gagné / M. G. Hopman (eds.), 352–83.

Metcalf, C. (2015), *The Gods Rich in Praise: Early Greek and Mesopotamian Religious Poetry*, Oxford.

Michelakis, P. (2002), *Achilles in Greek Tragedy*, Cambridge.

Michelini, A. N. (1987), *Euripides and the Tragic Tradition*, Madison WI.

Miller, A. M. (1981), 'Pindar, Archilochus and Hieron in P. 2.52-56', in: *TAPhA* 111, 135–43.

Miller, M. C. (1997), *Athens and Persia in the fifth century BC. A Study in Cultural Receptivity*, Cambridge.

Moore, T. (2008), '*Parakatalogē*: Another look', in: *Philomusica on-line* 7.2, 152–61.

Moorhouse, A. C. (1982), *The Syntax of Sophocles*. Mnem. Suppl. 75, Leiden and Boston.

Moreau, A. (1990), 'Les sources d'Eschyle dans l'*Agamemnon*: Silences, Choix, Innovations', in: *REG* 103, 30–53.

Moritz, H. E. (1979), 'Refrain in Aeschylus: Literary Adaptation of Traditional Form', in: *CPh* 74.3, 187–213.

Morrison, A. D. (2007), *Performance and Audiences in Pindar's Sicilian Victory Odes*, BICS Suppl. 95, London.
Morrison, A. D. (2012), 'Performance, Re-performance, and Pindar's Audiences', in: P. Agócs / C. Carey, / R. Rawles (eds.) (2012a), 111–33.
Mossman, J. (2011), *Euripides. Medea*, Oxford.
Mueller-Goldingen, C. (2000), 'Tradition und Innovation Zu Stesichoros' Umgang mit dem Mythos', in: *AC* 69, 1–19.
Mullen, W. (1982), *Choreia: Pindar and Dance*, Princeton.
Murnaghan, S. (1987), *Disguise and Recognition in the* Odyssey, Princeton.
Murnaghan, S. (2012), 'Sophocles' Choruses', in: K. Ormand (ed.), *A Companion to Sophocles*, Chichester and Malden MA, 220–35.
Murray, G. (1897), *A History of Ancient Greek Literature*, London.
Musso, O. (1967), 'Esiodo e Stesicoro nel fr. 109 M (= 74 N²) degli "Eraclidi" di Eschilo (un nuovo frammento della "Gerioneide")', in: *Aevum* 41, 507–8.
Myrick, L. D. (1993), 'The Way Up and Down: Tracehorse and Turning Imagery in the Orestes Plays', in: *CJ* 89.2, 131–48.
Naerebout, F. G. (1997), *Attractive Performances. Ancient Greek Dance: Three Preliminary Studies*, Amsterdam.
Nagler, M. N. (1974), *Spontaneity and Tradition: A Study in the Oral Art of Homer*, Berkeley.
Nagy, G. (1974), *Comparative Studies in Greek and Indic Meter*, Cambridge MA.
Nagy, G. (1979), *The Best of the Achaeans: Concepts of the Hero in Archaic Greek Poetry*, Baltimore and London.
Nagy, G. (1990), *Pindar's Homer: The Lyric Possession of an Epic Past*, Baltimore and London.
Nagy, G. (1995), 'Transformations of Choral Lyric Traditions in the Context of Athenian State Theatre', in: *Arion* 3.1, 41–55.
Nancy, C. (1986), 'La voix du choeur', in : *ASNP* s.3 16, 461–79.
Napolitano, M. (2000), 'Note all'iporchema di Pratina', in: A. C. Cassio / D. Musti / L. E. Rossi (eds.), *Synaulia. Cultura musicale in Grecia e contatti mediterranei*, Naples, 111–55.
Nauck, A. (1889), *Tragicorum Graecorum Fragmenta*. 2nd edn., Leipzig.
Neils, J. (1987), *The Youthful Deeds of Theseus*, Rome.
Neils, J. (2013), 'Contextualizing the François Vase', in: H. A. Shapiro / M. Iozzo / A. Lezzi-Hafter (eds.), *The François Vase: New Perspectives*, Zurich, 119–30.
Neitzel, H. (1967), *Die dramatisch Funktion der Chorlieder in den Tragödien des Euripides*, Hamburg.
Nemeth, G. (1983), 'On Dating Sophocles' Death', in: *Homonoia* 5, 115–28.
Neschke, A. (1986), 'L'*Orestie* de Stésichore et la tradition littéraire du myth des *Atrides* avant *Eschyle*', in: *AC* 55, 283–301.
Nikolaidou-Arabatzi, S. (2015), 'Choral Projections and *Embolima* in Euripides' Tragedies', in: *G&R* 62.1, 25–47.
Nisetich, F. (1989), *Pindar and Homer*, Baltimore.
Nooter, S. (2012), *When Heroes Sing: Sophocles and the Shifting Soundscape of Tragedy*, Cambridge.
Norden, E. (1913), *Agnostos Theos. Untersuchungen zur Formengeschichte religiöser Rede*, Leipzig and Berlin.

Nordgren, L. (2015), *Greek Interjections. Syntax, Semantics and Pragmatics*, Berlin and Boston.
Norwood, G. (1945), *Pindar*, Berkeley.
Nuttall, A. D. (1992), *Openings: Narrative Beginnings from the Epic to the Novel*, Oxford.
Olson, S. D. (2002), *Aristophanes. Acharnians.* Oxford.
Page, D. L. (1963), '2506. Comment on Lyric Poems', in: *The Oxyrhynchus Papyri* 29, 1–48.
Page, D. L. (1972) *Aeschyli septem quae supersunt tragoediae*, Oxford.
Palumbo Stracca, B. M. (1985), 'Lettura critica di epigrammi greci (I)', in: *BollClass* s.3 6, 58–75.
Palumbo Stracca, B. M. (1994), 'Sull'iscrizione della coppa di Duride (*PMG* adesp. 938e)', in: *SMEA* 23, 119–29.
Panagl, O. (1971), *Die "dithyrambischen Stasima" des Euripides: Untersuchungen zur Komposition und Erzähltechnik*, Vienna.
Papadopoulou, T. (2000), 'Cassandra's Radiant Vigour and the Ironic Optimism of Euripides' *Troades*', in: *Mnemosyne* s.4 53.5, 513–27.
Papadopoulou, T. (2008), *Euripides. Phoenician Women*, London.
Papakonstantinou, Z. (2012), 'The Athletic Body in Classical Athens: Literary and Historical Perspectives', in: *The International Journal of the History of Sport* 29, 1657–68.
Park, A. (2013), 'Truth and Genre in Pindar', in: *CQ* 63.1, 17–36.
Parker, L. P. E. (2007), *Euripides. Alcestis*, Oxford.
Parker, L. P. E. (2016), *Euripides. Iphigenia in Tauris*, Oxford.
Parker, R. (1996), *Athenian Religion. A History*, Oxford.
Parker, R. (2005), *Polytheism and Society at Athens*, Oxford.
Parmentier, L. (1959), *Euripide. Tome IV*, Paris.
Parry, H. (1965), 'The Second Stasimon of Euripides' *Heracles* (637–700)', in: *AJPh* 86.4, 363–74
Parry, H. (1978), *The Lyric Poems of Greek Tragedy*, Toronto and Sarasota.
Parsons, P. (1977), 'The Lille Stesichorus', in: *ZPE* 26, 7–36.
Pattoni, M. P. (1987) *L'autenticità del Prometeo incatenato di Eschilo*, Pisa.
Pavese, C. (1966) 'ΧΡΗΜΑΤΑ, ΧΡΗΜΑΤ' ΑΝΗΡ ed il motivo della liberalità nella seconda *Istmica* di Pindaro', in: *QUCC* 1, 103–12.
Pavlou, M. (2010), 'Pindar *Olympian* 3: Mapping Acragas on the Periphery of the Earth', in: *CQ* NS 60.2, 313–26.
Pearson, A. C. (1917), *The Fragments of Sophocles*, I-III, Cambridge.
Pearson, L. (1975), 'Myth and *Archaeologia* in Italy and Sicily – Timaeus and his Predecessors', in: D. Kagan (ed.) (1975), *Studies in the Greek Historians*. Yale Classical Studies 24, Cambridge, 171–95.
Pease, A. S. (1937), 'Ölbaum', in: *RE* 17.2, 1998–2022.
Pechstein, N. (1998), *Euripides Satyrographos: ein Kommentar zu den euripideischen Satyrspielfragmenten*, Stuttgart.
Peek, W. (1958), 'Die Nostoi des Stesichoros', in: *Philologus* 102, 169–77.
Pelliccia, H. (1989), 'Pindar, *Nemean* 7.31–36 and the Syntax of Aetiology', in: *HSPh* 92, 71–101.
Pelling, C. B. R. (2000), *Literary Texts and the Greek Historian*, London.
Peponi, A.-E. (ed.) (2013a), *Performance and Culture in Plato's* Laws, Cambridge.

Peponi, A.-E. (2013b), 'Theorizing the Chorus in Greece', in: J. Billings / F. Budelmann/ F. Macintosh (eds.), 15–34.
Peradotto, J. J. (1964), 'Some Patterns of Nature Imagery in the *Oresteia*', in: *AJPh* 85.4, 378–93.
Peradotto, J. (1969), 'The Omen of the Eagles and the Ethos of Agamemnon' in: *Phoenix* 23.3, 237–63. [Repr. in M. Lloyd (ed.) (2007), *Oxford Readings in Classical Studies: Aeschylus*, Oxford, 211–44]
Perusino, F. / Colantonio, M (eds.) (2007), *Dalla lirica corale alla poesia drammatica*, Rome.
Perysinakis, I. N. (1990), 'The Athlete as Warrior: Pindar's *P.* 9.97–103 and *P.* 10.55–59', in: *BICS* 37, 43–49.
Petrounias, E. (1976), *Funktion und Thematik der Bilder bei Aischylos*, Göttingen.
Pfeijffer, I. L. (1999), *Three Aeginetan Odes of Pindar: A Commentary on* Nemean V, Nemean III & Pythian VIII, Mnem. Suppl. 197, Leiden.
Phoutrides, A. E. (1916), 'The chorus of Euripides', in: *HSPh* 27, 77–170.
Pickard-Cambridge, A. W. (1968), *The Dramatic Festivals of* Athens. 2nd edn., Cambridge.
Pickard-Cambridge, A. W. (1988), *The Dramatic Festivals of Athens*. Rev. edn with a new supplement by J. Gould and D. M. Lewis, Oxford.
Pirenne-Delforge, V. (2008), Review of Budin 2008b, in: *BMCR* 2009.04.28.
Platnauer, M. (1938), *Euripides*. Iphigenia in Tauris, Oxford.
Pleket, H. W. (1981), 'Religious History as the History of Mentality: The 'Believer' as Servant of the Deity in the Greek World', in: H. S. Versnel (ed.), *Faith Hope and Worship: Aspects of Religious Mentality in the Ancient World*, Leiden and Boston, 152–92.
Podlecki, A. J. (1971), 'Stesichoreia', in: *Athenaeum* NS 49, 313–27.
Podlecki, A. J. (1999), *The Political Background of Aeschylean Tragedy*, 2nd edn., London.
Podlecki, A. J. (2005), Prometheus Bound, Oxford.
Pohlenz, M. (1954), *Die griechische Tragödie*, 2nd edn., Göttingen.
Poliakoff, M. (1980), 'The Third Fall in the *Oresteia*', in: *AJPh* 101.3, 251–9.
Poltera, O. (2008), *Simonides lyricus, Testimonia und Fragmente: Einleitung, kritische Ausgabe, Übersetzung und Kommentar*, Basel.
Pomeroy, S. B. (1994), *Xenophon*, Oeconomicus: *A Social and Historical Commentary*, Oxford.
Porter, J. (2010), *The Origins of Aesthetic Experience in Ancient Greece: Matter, Sensation, and Experience*, Cambridge.
Pöhlmann, E. / West, M. L. (2012), 'The Oldest Greek Papyrus and Writing Tablets: Fifth-Century Documents from the 'Tomb of the Musician' in Attica', in: *ZPE* 180, 1–16.
Power, T. (2000), 'The parthenoi of Bacchylides 13', in: *HSPh* 100, 67–81.
Power, T. (2007), 'Ion of Chios and the Politics of Polychordia', in: V. Jennings / A. Katsaros (eds.), *The World of Ion of Chios*, Leiden and Boston, 179–205.
Power, T. (2010) *The Culture of kitharôidia*, Hellenic Studies Series 15, Washington DC.
Power, T. (2011), 'Cyberchorus: Pindar's Κηληδόνες and the Aura of the Artificial', in: L. Athanassaki / E. L. Bowie (eds.), 104–13.
Power, T. (2012), 'Sophocles and Music', in: A. Markantonatos (ed.), 283–304.
Power, T. (2013), 'Kyklops *kitharoidos:* Dithyramb and nomos in play', in: B. Kowalzig / P. Wilson (eds.), 237–56.
Prag, A. J. N. W. (1985), *The* Oresteia. *Iconographic and Narrative Tradition*, Chicago.
Prauscello, L. (2006), *Singing Alexandria: Music Between Practice and Textual Transmission*, Mnem. Suppl. 274, Leiden and Boston.

Prauscello, L. (2012), 'Epinician sounds: Pindar and Musical Innovation', in: P. Agócs / C. Carey / R. Rawles (eds.) (2012a), 58–82.
Prauscello, L. (2013), 'Demeter and Dionysos in the sixth-century Argolid. Lasos of Hermione, the cult of Demeter Chthonia, and the origins of Dithyramb', in: B. Kowalzig / P. Wilson (eds.), 76–92.
Pritchard, D. M. (2012), 'Athletics in Satyric Dramas', in: *G&R* 59.1, 1–16
Pritchard, D. M. (2013), *Sport, Democracy, and War in Classical Athens*, Cambridge.
Pritchett, W. K. (1971), *Ancient Greek Military Practices*, Part I, Berkeley and London.
Pritchett, W. K. (1974), *The Greek State at War II*, Berkeley and London.
Privitera, G. A. (1982), *Pindaro. Le Istmiche*, Milan.
Prudhommeau, G. (1965–1966), *La danse grecque antique*, 2 vols., Paris.
Pucci, P. (2007), *Inno alle Muse (Esiodo, "Teogonia", 1–115)*, Pisa.
Pucci, P. (2016), *Euripides' Revolution Under Cover. An Essay*, Ithaca NY.
Pulleyn, S. (1997), *Prayer in Greek Religion*, Oxford.
Quijada, M. (2006), "'Por Ilión, ¡oh Musa!, cántame entre lágrimas un canto de duelo, un himno nuevo' (Eurípides, *Troyanas* 511 ss.)', in: E. Calderón / A. Morales / M. Valverde (eds.), *Koinòs Lógos. Homenaje al profesor José García López*, Murcia, 841–53.
Race, W. H. (1982), 'Aspects of Rhetoric and Form in Greek Hymns', in: *GRBS* 23.1, 5–14.
Race, W. H. (1990), *Style and Rhetoric in Pindar's Odes*, Atlanta.
Radt, S. (2002–2011), *Strabons* Geographika, *I-X*, Göttingen.
Raeburn, D. / Thomas, O. (2011), *The* Agamemnon *of Aeschylus: A Commentary for Students*, Oxford.
Rawson, E. (1970), 'Family and Fatherland in Euripides' *Phoenissae*', in: *GRBS* 11.2, 109–27.
Rehm, R. (1992), *Greek Tragic Theatre*, London and New York.
Rehm, R. (1994), *Marriage to Death: The Conflation of Wedding and Funeral Rituals in Greek Tragedy*, Princeton.
Reinach, T. (1898), *Poèmes choisis de Bacchylide*, Paris.
Renehan, R. F. (1998), 'The Euripidean Studies of James Diggle: Part II', in: *CPh* 93.2, 249–70.
Restani, D. (1983), 'Il Chirone di Ferecrate e la 'nuova' musica greca," in: *Rivista italiana di musicologia* 18, 139–92.
Revermann, M. (1999–2000), 'Euripides, Tragedy and Macedon: Some Conditions of Reception', in: M. Cropp / K. Lee / D. Sansone (eds.), 451–68.
Revermann, M. (2006a), 'The Competence of Theatre Audience in Fifth- and Fourth-Century Athens', in: *JHS* 126, 99–124.
Revermann, M. (2006b), *Comic Business: Theatricality, Dramatic Technique, and Performance Contexts of Aristophanic Comedy*, Oxford.
Revermann, M. / Wilson, P. (eds.) (2008), *Performance, Iconography, Reception: Studies in Honour of Oliver Taplin*, Oxford.
Richardson, B. (ed.) (2008), *Narrative Beginnings. Theories and Practices*, Lincoln and London.
Richardson, N. (1993), *The Iliad. A Commentary. Volume VI: Books 21–24*, Cambridge.
Riemschneider, W. (1940), *Held und Staat in Euripides' Phönissen*, Würzburg.
Robbins, E. (1982), 'Heracles, the Hyperboreans, and the Hind: Pindar, *Ol. 3*', in: *Phoenix* 36.4, 295–305.

Robbins, E. (1984) 'Intimations of Immortality: Pindar, *Ol*. 3.34–35', in: D. E. Gerber (ed.), *Greek Poetry and Philosophy: Studies in Honour of Leonard Woodbury*, Chico CA, 219–28.
Robbins, E. (1998), *'Hyporchēma'*, in: *Der Neue Pauly* 5, 815–16.
Robert, C. (1912), 'Aphoristische Bemerkungen zu Sophokles' ΙΧΝΕΥΤΑΙ', in: *Hermes* 47.4, 536–61.
Roberts, D. H. (2005), 'Beginnings and Endings', in: J. Gregory (ed.), 136–48.
Roberts, D. H. / Dunn, F. M. / Fowler, D. (eds.) (1997), *Classical Closure. Reading the End in Greek and Latin Literature*, Princeton.
Robertson, B. G. (2000), 'The Scrutiny of New Citizens at Athens', in: V. Hunter / J. Edmondson (eds.), *Law and Social Status in Classical Athens*, Oxford, 148–74.
Robinson, E. W. (2011), *Democracy Beyond Athens: Popular Government in the Greek Classical Age*, Cambridge.
Rode, J. (1971), 'Das Chorlied,' in: W. Jens (ed.), *Die Bauformen der griechischen Tragödie*, Munich, 85–116.
Rodighiero, A. (2011), 'The Sense of Place: *Oedipus at Colonus*, 'Political' Geography, and the Defence of a Way of Life', in: A. Markantonatos / B. Zimmerman (ed.), *Crisis on Stage: Tragedy and Comedy in Late Fifth-Century Athens*, Berlin and Boston, 55–80.
Rodighiero, A. (2012), *Generi lirico-corali nella produzione drammatica di Sofocle*, Drama NS 12, Göttingen.
Rodighiero, A. (forthcoming-a), 'Aeschylus, *Agamemnon* 104–105, Homer, and the Epic Tradition: A New Survey', in: *JHS* 138.
Rodighiero, A. (forthcoming-b), 'Raccontare cantando nella tragedia greca: due casi da "Agamennone" e "Troiane" ', in: G. Ieranò / P. Taravacci (eds.), *Il racconto a teatro. Dal dramma antico al Siglo de Oro alla scena contemporanea*, Trento.
Roisman, H. / Luschnig, C. A. E. (2011), *Euripides' Electra: A Commentary*. Oklahoma Series in Classical Culture 38, Norman OK.
Romero Mariscal, L. (2005), *'Alejandro* de Euripides: la configuración de un motivo folklórico', in: *Ágora. Estudios Clássicos em Debate* 7, 11–23.
Roos, E. (1951), *Die tragische Orchestik im Zerrbild der altattischen Komödie*, Lund.
Roselli, D. K. (2011), *Theater of the People: Spectators and Society in Ancient Athens*, Austin.
Rosenbloom, D. / Davidson, J. (eds.) (2011), *Greek drama IV: Texts, Contexts, Performance*, Oxford.
Rosenmeyer, T. G. (1982), *The Art of Aeschylus*, Berkeley.
Rossbach, A. / Westphal, R. (1868), *Metrik der Griechen*, Leipzig.
Rotroff, S. I. / Oakley, J. H. (1992), *Debris from a Public Dining Place in the Athenian Agora*, Hesperia Supplement 25, Princeton NJ.
Rösler, W. (1975), 'Ein Gedicht und sein Publikum: Überlegungen zu Sappho Fr. 44 Lobel-Page', in: *Hermes* 103.3, 275–85.
Rösler, W. (1993), 'Der Schluss der "Hiketiden" und die Danaiden-Trilogie des Aischylos', in: *RhM* 136.1, 1–22 [translated into English in: M. Lloyd (ed.) (2007), *Aeschylus*. Oxford Readings in Classical Studies, Oxford, 174–98].
Ruffell, I. A. (2012), *Aeschylus. Prometheus Bound*, London.
Rusten, J. S. (2013), 'ΔΗΛΟΣ ΕΚΙΝΗΘΗ: An "Imaginary Earthquake" on Delos in Herodotus and Thucydides', in: *JHS* 133, 135–45.
Rutherford, I. (1990), 'Paeans by Simonides', in: *HSPh* 93, 169–209.

Rutherford, I. (1993), 'Paeanic Ambiguity: A Study of the Representation of the παιάν in Greek Literature', in *QUCC* NS 44.2, 77–92.
Rutherford, I. (1994–1995), 'Apollo in Ivy: The Tragic Paean', in: *Arion* 3.1, 112–35.
Rutherford, I. (1995), 'The Nightingale's Refrain: *P. Oxy*. 2635 = *SLG* 460', in: *ZPE* 107, 39–43.
Rutherford, I. (1998), 'Theoria as Theatre: Pilgrimage in Greek Drama', in: F. Cairns / M. Heath (eds.), *Papers of the Leeds International Latin Seminar* 10, 131–56.
Rutherford, I. (2000), 'Keos or Delos? State Pilgrimage and the Performance of *Paean* 4', in M. Cannatà Fera / S. Grandolini (eds.), *Poesia e religione in Grecia* (Festschrift Privitera), Naples, ii. 605–12.
Rutherford, I. (2001), *Pindar's Paeans. A Reading of the Fragments with a Survey of the Genre*, Oxford.
Rutherford, I. (2004), 'χορὸς εἷς ἐκ τῆσδε τῆς πόλεως (Xen. *Mem*. 3.3.12): Song-dance and State-pilgrimage at Athens', in: P. Murray / P. Wilson (eds.), 67–90.
Rutherford, R. (2012), *Greek Tragic Style: Form, Language, and Interpretation*, Cambridge.
Rutherford, I. (2013), *State Pilgrims and Sacred Observers in Ancient Greece. A Study of Theōriā and Theōroi*, Cambridge.
Rutherford, R. (2014), 'The Final Scene', in: D. Stuttard (ed.), *Looking at* Medea: *Essays and a Translation of Euripides' Tragedy*, London, 89–97.
Said, E. (1975), *Beginnings: Intention and Method*, New York.
Saïd, S. (1993), 'Tragic Argos', in A. H. Sommerstein / Halliwell, S. / Henderson, J. / Zimmermann, B. (eds.) *Tragedy, Comedy and the Polis*, Bari, 167–89.
Saïd, S. (2007), 'Les transformations de la Muse dans la tragédie greque', in: F. Perusino / M. Colantonio (eds.), 21–47.
Sailor, D. / Stroup, S. C. (1999), 'ΦΘΟΝΟΣ Δ' ΑΠΕΣΤΩ: The Translation of Transgression in Aiskhylos' *Agamemnon*', in: *ClAnt* 18.1, 153–82.
Sansone, D. (2009), 'Euripides' New Song: the First Stasimon of *Trojan Women*', in: J. R. C. Cousland / J. R. Hume (eds.), 193–203.
Sansone, D. (2015), 'The Place of the Satyr-Play in the Tragic Tetralogy', in: *Prometheus* 41, 3–36.
Scanlon, T. F. (2002), *Eros & Greek Athletics*, Oxford.
Schade, G. (2003), *Stesichoros. Papyrus Oxyrhynchus 2359, 3876, 2619, 2803*, Mnem. Suppl. 237, Leiden and Boston.
Schein, S. (2009), 'Narrative Technique in the *Parodos* of Aeschylus' *Agamemnon*', in: J. Grethlein / A. Rengakos (eds.), *Narratology and Interpretation. The Content of Narrative Form in Ancient Literature*, Berlin and Boston, 377–98.
Schein, S. (2013), *Sophocles*. Philoctetes, Cambridge.
Schmid, W. (1929), *Untersuchungen zum Gefesselten Prometheus*, Stuttgart.
Schmitz, H. A. (1970), *Hypsos und Bios. Stilistische Untersuchungen zum Alltagsrealismus in der archaischen griechischen Chorlyrik*, Bern.
Schrenk, L. P. (1994), 'Sappho Frag. 44 and the *Iliad*', in: *Hermes* 122.2, 144–50.
Schroeder, S. (1999), 'Zwei Überlegungen zu den Liedern vom Athenerschatzhaus in Delphi', in: *ZPE* 128, 65–75.
Schütrumpf, E. (ed.) (2008), *Heraclides of Pontus: Texts and Translations*. Transl. P. Stork / J. van Ophuijsen, / S. Prince. Rutgers University Studies in Classical Humanities (RUSCH) 14, New Brunswick and London.
Schwartz, E. (1887–1991), *Scholia in Euripidem*, 2 vols., Berlin.

Scodel, R. (1980), *The Trojan Trilogy of Euripides*, Hypomnemata 60, Göttingen.
Scodel, R. (1999–2000), 'Verbal Performance and Euripidean Rhetoric', in: M. Cropp / K. Lee / D. Sansone (eds.), 129–43.
Scodel, R. (2001), 'The Suitor's Games', in: *AJPh* 122.3, 307–27.
Scott, W. C. (1984), *Musical Design in Aeschylean Theatre*, Hanover and London.
Seaford, R. (1977–1978), 'The "Hyporchema" of Pratinas', in: *Maia* 29–30, 81–99.
Seaford, R. (1982), 'The Date of Euripides' *Cyclops*', in: *JHS* 102, 161–72.
Seaford, R. (1984), *Euripides. Cyclops*, Oxford.
Seaford, R. (1987), 'The Tragic Wedding', in: *JHS* 107, 106–30.
Seaford, R. (1994a), *Reciprocity and Ritual: Homer and Tragedy in the Developing City-State*, Oxford.
Seaford, R. (1994b), 'Sophokles and the Mysteries', in: *Hermes* 122.3, 275–88.
Seale, D. (1982), *Vision and Stagecraft in Sophocles*, London.
Seewald, J. (1936), *Untersuchungen zu Stil und Komposition der Aeschyleischen Tragödien*, Greifswalder Beiträge 14, Greifswald.
Segal, C. P. (1964), 'God and Man in Pindar's First and Third *Olympian* Odes', in: *HSPh* 68, 211–67.
Segal, C. P. (1993), *Euripides and the Poetics of Sorrow: Art, Gender, and Commemoration in Alcestis, Hippolytus, and Hecuba*, Durham N.C.
Segal, C. P. (1996), 'The Chorus and the Gods in "Oedipus Tyrannus"', in: *Arion* s.3 4.1, 20–32.
Severyns, A. (1933), *Bacchylide: essai biographique*, Liége.
Sfyroeras, P. (1993), 'Fireless Sacrifices: Pindar's *Olympian* 7 and the Panathenaic Festival', in: *AJPh* 114, 1–26 [repr. in: G. Nagy (ed.) (2001), *Greek Literature*, vol. 3, New York].
Sfyroeras, P. (2003), 'Olive Trees, North Wind, and Time: A Symbol in Pindar, *Olympian* 3', in: *Mouseion* s.3, 313–24.
Shapiro, H. A. (1989), *Art and Cult Under the Tyrants in Athens*, Mainz.
Shapiro, H. A. (1992), 'Theseus in Kimonian Athens: The Iconography of Empire', in: *Mediterranean Historical Review* 7, 29–49.
Shelmerdine, S. C. (1987), 'Pindaric Praise and the Third *Olympian*', in: *HSPh* 91, 65–81.
Sider, D. (2008), Review of L. Bravi, *Gli epigrammi di Simonide e le vie della tradizione*, Rome 2006, in: *BMCR* 2008.02.47.
Sider, D. (2010), 'Greek Verse on a Vase by Douris', in: *Hesperia* 79, 541–54.
Sifakis, G. M. (2001), *Aristotle on the Function of Tragic Poetry*, Herakleion.
Silk, M. S. (ed.) (1996), *Tragedy and the Tragic: Greek Theatre and Beyond*, Oxford.
Silk, M. S. (2009), 'The Logic of the Unexpected: Semantic Diversion in Sophocles, Yeats (and Virgil)', in: S. Goldhill / E. Hall (eds.), 134–57.
Simon, E. (1967), 'Boreas und Oreithyia auf dem silbernen Rhyton in Triest', in: *A&A* 13, 101–26.
Sinos, R. H. (1993), 'Divine Selection, Epiphany and Politics in Archaic Greece', in: C. Dougherty / L. Kurke (eds.), 73–91.
Slater, W. (1983), 'Lyric Narrative: Structure and Principle', in: *ClAnt* 2.1, 117–32.
Slatkin, L. (1986) '*Oedipus at Colonus:* Exile and Integration', in: J. P. Euben (ed.), *Greek Tragedy and Political Theory*, Berkeley and Los Angeles, 210–21.
Smith, B. R. (1999), *The Acoustic World of Early Modern England: Attending to the O-Factor*, Chicago.

Smith, D. G. (2004), 'Thucydides' Ignorant Athenians and the Drama of the Sicilian Expedition' in: *SyllClas* 15, 33–70.
Smith, O. L. (1976), *Scholia Graeca in Aeschylum quae exstant omnia. Pars I: Scholia in Agamemnonem Choephoros Eumenides Supplices continens*, Leipzig [repr. with corrections 1993].
Smyth, H. W. (1900), *Greek Melic Poets*, New York.
Sommerstein, A. H. (1977), 'Notes on Aeschylus' *Suppliants*', in: *BICS* 24, 67–82.
Sommerstein, A. H. (1995), 'The Beginning and the End of Aeschylus' Danaid Trilogy', in: B. Zimmermann (ed.), *Griechische-römische Komödie und Tragödie*. Drama 3, Stuttgart, 111–34.
Sommerstein, A. H. (2008a), *Aeschylus I*. Persians, Seven against Thebes, Suppliants, Prometheus bound (LCL 145), Cambridge MA and London.
Sommerstein, A. H. (2008b), *Aeschylus II*. Oresteia, Agamemnon, Libation-bearers, Eumenides (LCL 146), Cambridge MA and London.
Sommerstein, A. H. (2010a), *Aeschylean Tragedy*. 2nd edn., London.
Sommerstein, A. H. (2010b), *The Tangled Ways of Zeus: And Other Studies in and Around Tragedy*, Oxford.
Sorum, C. E. (1992), 'Myth, Choice, and Meaning in Euripides' *Iphigenia at Aulis*', in: *AJPh* 113.4, 527–42.
Sourvinou-Inwood, C. (1989), 'Assumptions and the Creation of Meaning: Reading Sophocles' *Antigone*', in: *JHS* 109, 134–48.
Stahl, J. M. (1913), 'Zu den Ἰχνευταί des Sophokles', in: *RhM* 68, 307–9.
Stanford, W. B. (1942), *Aeschylus in his Style: A Study in Language and Personality*, Dublin.
Stanford, W. B. (1963), *Sophocles. Ajax*, London.
Stansbury-O'Donnell, M. D. (2005), 'The Painting Program in the Stoa Poikile', in: J. M. Barringer / J. M. Hurwit (eds.), *Periklean Athens and its Legacy. Problems and Perspectives*, Austin, 73–87.
Steiner, D. (1993), 'Pindar's "oggetti parlanti"', in: *HSPh* 95, 159–90.
Steiner, D. (2010a), 'The Immeasures of Praise: The Epinician Celebration of Agamemnon's Return', in: *Hermes* 130.1, 22–37.
Steiner, D. (2010b), *Homer, Odyssey: Books XVII and XVIII*, Cambridge.
Steiner, D. (2011), 'Dancing with the Stars: Choreia in the Third Stasimon of Euripides' *Helen*', in: *CPh* 106.4, 299–323.
Steiner, D. (2013), 'The Gorgon's Lament: Auletics, Poetics, and Chorality in Pindar's *Pythian* 12', in: *AJPh* 134.2, 172–208.
Stephanopoulos, T. K. (1980), *Umgestaltung des Mythos durch Euripides*, Athens.
Stephanopoulos, T. K. (1985), 'Euripides und die Arkader (*Troades* 30–31)', in: *Hermes* 113.1, 115–9.
Stevens, P. T. (1971), *Euripides. Andromache*, Oxford.
Stewart, A. (1983), 'Stesichoros and the François Vase', in: W. G. Moon (ed.), *Ancient Greek Art and Iconography*, Madison, 53–74.
Stieber, M. (2011), *Euripides and the Language of Craft*, Mnem. Suppl. 327, Leiden.
Stinton, T. C. W. (1976a), 'Iphigeneia and the Bears of Brauron', in: *CQ* 26.1, 11–13. [= (1990a), 186–9]
Stinton, T. C. W. (1976b) 'The Riddle at Colonus', in: *GRBS* 17.4, 323–8. [= (1990a), 265–70]
Stinton, T. C. W. (1990a), *Collected Papers on Greek Tragedy*, Oxford.

Stinton, T. C. W. (1990b), 'Euripides and the Judgment of Paris', in: T. C. W. Stinton (1990a) 17–75.
Stockert, W. (1992), *Euripides, Iphigenie in Aulis*, vol. II, Vienna.
Storey, I. C. (2003), *Eupolis, Poet of Old Comedy*, Oxford.
Strauss Clay, J. (1999), 'Pindar's Sympotic Epinicia', in: *QUCC* NS 62.2, 25–34.
Suter, A. (2003), 'Lament in Euripides' "Trojan Women"', in: *Mnemosyne* s.4 56.1, 1–28.
Sutton, D. F. (1980), *The Greek Satyr Play*, Meisenheim am Glan.
Sutton, D. F. (1984), *The Lost Sophocles*, Lanham MD.
Svenbro, J. (1984), 'Il taglio della poesia. Note sulle origini sacrificali della poetica greca', in: *StudStor* 25, 925–44.
Svenbro, J. (1992), '"Ton luth, à quoi bon?" La lyre et la pierre tombale dans la pensée grecque', in: *Mètis. Anthropologie des mondes grecs anciens* 7, 135–60.
Swift, L. A. (2010), *The Hidden Chorus. Echoes of Genre in Tragic Lyric*, Oxford.
Swift. L. A. (2011), 'Epinician and Tragic Worlds: The Case of Sophocles' *Trachiniae*', in: L. Athanassaki / E. L. Bowie (eds.), 391–413
Swift, L. A. (2012), 'Paeanic and Epinician Healing in Euripides' Alcestis', in: J. Davidson / D. Rosenbloom (eds.), 149–68.
Swift, L. A. (2015), 'Stesichorus on Stage', in: P. J. Finglass / A. Kelly (eds.), Cambridge, 125–44.
Swift, L. A. (2016), 'Visual Imagery in Parthenaic Song', in: V. Cazzato / A. Lardinois (eds.), *The Look of Lyric. Greek Song and the Visual*, Leiden and Boston, 255–87.
Swift, L. A. (ed.) (forthcoming), *A Companion to Greek Lyric*, Chichester and Malden MA.
Synodinou, K. (1977), *On the Concept of Slavery in Euripides*, Ioannina.
Tanner, R. G. (1966), 'The Composition of the *Oedipus Coloneus*', in: M. Kelly (ed.), *For Service to Classical Studies. Essays in Honour of Francis Letters*, Melbourne, 153–92.
Taplin, O. (1977), *The Stagecraft of Aeschylus. The Dramatic Use of Exits and Entrances in Greek Tragedy*, Oxford.
Taplin, O. (1986), 'Fifth-Century Tragedy and Comedy: A *Synkrisis*', in: *JHS* 106, 163–74.
Taplin, O. (1993), Comic *Angels: And Other Approaches to Greek Drama Through Vase-Paintings*, Oxford.
Taplin, O. (1995), 'Opening Performance: Closing Texts?" in: *Essays in Criticism* 45, 93–120.
Taplin, O. (1999), 'Spreading the Word Through Performance' in: S. Goldhill / R. Osborne (eds.), 33–57.
Taplin, O. (2012), 'How was Athenian Tragedy Played in the Greek West?' in: K. Bosher (ed.), *Theater Outside Athens. Drama in Greek Sicily and South Italy*, Cambridge, 226–50.
Taplin, O. / Wyles, R. (eds.) (2010), *The Pronomos Vase and its Context*, Oxford.
Theodoridis, C. (1982–2013), *Photii Patriarchae Lexicon*, 3 vols., Berlin and Boston.
Thöne, C. (1999), *Ikonographische Studien zu Nike im 5. Jahrhundert v. Chr. Untersuchungen zur Wirkungsweise und Wesensart*, Heidelberg.
Thomas, O. (2015), 'Greek Hymnic Spaces', in: E. Barker / S. Bouzarovski / C. Pelling / L. Isaksen (eds.), *New Worlds from Old Texts. Revisiting Ancient Space and Place*, Oxford, 33–46.
Timpanaro, S. (1996), 'Dall'*Alexandros* di Euripide all'*Alexander* di Ennio', in: *RFIC* 124, 5–70
Torrance, I. (2013), *Metapoetry in Euripides*, Oxford.
Tsantsanoglou, K. (2012), *Of Golden Manes and Silvery Faces: The Partheneion 1 of Alcman*, Trends in Classics Suppl. Vol. 16, Berlin and Boston.

Tsolakidou, K. (2012), *The Helix of Dionysus: Musical Imagery in Later Euripidean Drama* (PhD diss. Princeton University).
Turner, V. (1995), *The Ritual Process: Structure and Anti-Structure*, New York [Orig. Publ. (1969) Chicago].
Ucciardello, G. (2005), 'Sulla tradizione del testo di Ibico', in: S. Grandolini (ed.) (2005), *Lirica e teatro in Grecia. Il testo e la sua ricezione. Atti del II incontro di studi, Perugia, 23–24 gennaio 2003*, Perugia, 21–88.
Vamvouri, M. (1998), 'Fiction poétique et réalité historique à propos du *Péan* de Liménios', in: *Gaia* 3, 37–57.
van Erp Taalman Kip, A. M. (1987), 'Euripides and Melos', in: *Mnemosyne* s.4 40.3/4, 414–9.
van Groningen, B. A. (1960), *Pindare au banquet. Les fragments des scolies*, Leiden.
van Overen, C. D. P. (1999), 'Bacchylides Ode 17. Theseus and the Delian League', in: I. L. Pfeijffer / S. Slings (eds.), *One Hundred Years of Bacchylides*, Amsterdam, 31–42.
Verdenius, W. J. (1987), *Commentaries on Pindar*, vol. 1: *Olympian Odes 3, 7, 12, 14*, Mnem. Suppl. 97, Leiden and Boston.
Vergados, A. (2013), *The Homeric Hymn to Hermes: Introduction, Text, and Commentary*, Berlin and Boston.
Vernant, J.-P. / Vidal-Naquet, P. (1981), *Tragedy and Myth in Ancient Greece*, trans. J. Lloyd, New York.
von Schlegel, A. W. (1846), *Sämmtliche Werke* vol. V, ed. E. Böcking, Leipzig.
Wagman, R. (2000), *L'inno epidaurico a Pan. Il culto di Pan a Epidauro*, Pisa.
Walker, R. J. (1919), *The Ichneutae of Sophocles*, London.
Wallace, R. L. (2003), 'An Early Fifth-century Athenian Revolution in Aulos Music', in: *HSPh* 101, 73–92.
Walsh, G. B. (1974), '*Iphigenia in Aulis:* Third Stasimon', in: *CPh* 69.4, 241–8.
Warner, R. (1954) *Thucydides. The Peloponnesian War*, Suffolk.
Webster, T. B. L. (1967), *The Tragedies of Euripides*, London.
Weiss, N. (2014), 'The Antiphonal Ending of Euripides' *Iphigenia in Aulis* (1475–1532)', *CPh* 109.2, 119–29.
Weiss, N. (forthcoming), 'Hearing the Syrinx in Euripidean Tragedy', in A. D'Angour / T. Phillips (eds.), *Music, Texts, and Culture in Ancient Greece*, Oxford.
West, M. L. (1966), *Hesiod. Theogony*, Oxford.
West, M. L. (1969), 'Stesichorus Redivivius', in: *ZPE* 4, 135–49 [= (2011–2013), II 98–106].
West, M. L. (1971), 'Stesichorus', in: *CQ* NS 21, 302–14 [= (2011–2013), II 78–97].
West, M. L. (1979a), 'The Prometheus Trilogy', in: *JHS* 99, 130–48.
West, M. L. (1979b), 'Where Eagles Dare: The *Parodos* of the Agamemnon', in: *CQ* 29.2, 1–6 [= (2011–2013), II 215–22].
West, M. L. (1981), 'The Singing of Homer and the Modes of Early Greek Music', in: *JHS* 101, 113–29.
West, M. L. (1982), *Greek Metre*, Oxford.
West, M. L. (1986), 'The Singing of Hexameters: Evidence from Epidauros', in: *ZPE* 63, 39–47.
West, M. L. (1990a), *Aeschyli Tragoediae cum incerti poetae Prometheo*, Stuttgart.
West, M. L. (1990b), *Studies in Aeschylus*, Stuttgart.
West, M. L. (1992), *Ancient Greek Music*, Oxford.
West, M. L. (1997), *The East Face of Helicon. West Asiatic Elements in Greek Poetry and Myth*, Oxford.

West, M. L. (1998), *Aeschylus Tragoediae*. 2nd edn., Stuttgart.
West, M. L. (2002), 'Eumelos: A Corinthian Epic Cycle?', in: *JHS* 122, 109–33. [= (2011–2013), I 353–91]
West, M. L. (2007), *Indo-European Poetry and Myth*, Oxford.
West, M. L. (2011), 'Pindar as a Man of Letters', in: D. Obbink / R. Rutherford (eds.), *Culture In Pieces: Essays on Ancient Texts in Honour of Peter Parsons*, Oxford, 50–68.
West, M. L. (2011–2013), *Hellenica: Selected Papers on Greek Literature and Thought*, 3 vols., Oxford.
West, M. L. (2013a), *The Epic Cycle. A Commentary on the Lost Troy Epics*, Oxford.
West, M. L. (2013b), 'The Writing Tablets and Papyrus from Tomb II in Daphni', in: *GRMS* 1, 73–92.
West, M. L. (2015), 'Epic, Lyric Epic, and Lyric', in: P. J. Finglass / A. Kelly (eds.), 63–80.
Westlake, H. D. (1953), 'Euripides, *Troades* 205–29', in: *Mnemosyne* 6, 181–91.
Westphal, R. (1856), *Metrik der Griechischen Dramatiker und Lyriker, 3. Teil*, Leipzig.
Wilamowitz-Moellendorff, U. von (1895), *Euripides. Herakles*, 2 vols., Berlin.
Wilamowitz-Moellendorff, U. von (1900), *Die Textgeschichte der griechischen Lyriker*, Berlin.
Wilamowitz-Moellendorff, U. von (1907), *Einleitung in die griechische Tragödie*, Berlin.
Wilamowitz-Moellendorff, U. von (1912), 'Die Spürhunde des Sophokles', in: *Neue Jahrbücher für das klassische Altertum* 29, 449–76.
Wilamowitz-Moellendorff, U. von (1913), *Sappho und Simonides. Untersuchungen über griechische Lyriker*, Berlin.
Wilamowitz-Moellendorff, U. von (1922), *Pindaros*, Berlin.
Wiles, D. (1997), *Tragedy in Athens: Performance Space and Theatrical Meaning*, Cambridge.
Willcock, M. M. (1995), *Pindar, Victory Odes: Olympians 2, 7, and 11, Nemean 4, Isthmians 3, 4 and 7*, Cambridge.
Willink, C. W. (1986), *Euripides. Orestes*, Oxford.
Willis, W. H. (1941), 'Athletic Contests in the Epic', in: *TAPhA* 72, 392–417.
Wilson, N. (1975), *Prolegomena de Comoedia scholia in Archarnenses, Equites, Nubes: Scholia in Aristophanis Acharnenses Fasc. IB*, Groningen.
Wilson, P. (1999), 'The Aulos in Athens', in: S. Goldhill / R. Osborne (eds.), 58–95.
Wilson, P. (1999–2000), 'Euripides' Tragic Muse', in M. Cropp / K. Lee / D. Sansone (eds.), 427–49.
Wilson, P. (2000), *The Athenian Institution of the Khoregia: The Chorus, the City and the Stage*, Cambridge.
Wilson, P. (2005), 'Music', in J. Gregory (ed.), 183–93.
Wilson, P. (2009), 'Thamyris the Thracian: The Archetypal Wandering Poet?', in: R. Hunter / R. Rutherford (eds.), 46–79.
Wilson, P. (2010), 'The Man and the Music (and the Choregos?)', in: O. Taplin / R. Wyles (eds.), 181–212.
Winkler, J. J. (1990) 'The Ephebe's Song: *Tragôidia* and *Polis*', in: J. J. Winkler / F. I. Zeitlin (eds.), 20–62.
Winkler, J. J. / Zeitlin, F. (eds.) (1990), *Nothing to Do with Dionysos?: Athenian Drama in its Social Context*, Princeton NJ.
Winnington-Ingram, R. P. (1983), *Studies in Aeschylus*, Cambridge.
Wrenhaven, K. L. (2012), *Reconstructing the Slave: The Image of the Slave in Ancient Greece*, London.

Wyles, R. (2011), *Costume in Greek Tragedy*, Oxford.
Xenis, G. A. (ed.) (2010), *Scholia vetera in Sophoclis Trachinias*, Berlin.
Young, D. C. (1968), *Three Odes of Pindar: A Literary Study of* Pythian *11,* Pythian *3, and* Olympian *7*, Leiden and Boston.
Zagagi, N. (1999), 'Comic Patterns in Sophocles' Ichneutae', in: J. Griffin (ed.), *Sophocles Revisited. Essays presented to Sir Hugh Lloyd-Jones*, Oxford, 177–218.
Zardini, F. (2009), *The Myth of Herakles and Kyknos. A Study in Greek Vase-Painting and Literature*, Verona.
Zeitlin, F. I. (1965), 'The Motif of the Corrupted Sacrifice in Aeschylus' *Oresteia*', in: *TAPhA* 96, 463–508.
Zeitlin, F. I. (1970), 'The Argive Festival of Hera and Euripides' *Electra*', in: *TAPhA* 101, 645–69.
Zeitlin, F. I. (1994), 'The Artful Eye: Vision, Ekphrasis and Spectacle in Euripidean Theatre', in: S. Goldhill / R. Osborne, (eds.), 138–96.
Zeitlin, F. I. (2008), 'Intimate Relations: Children, Childbearing, and Parentage on the Euripidean Stage', in: M. Revermann / P. Wilson (eds.), 318–32.
Zimmermann, B. (1986), 'Überlegungen zum sogenannten Pratinas-Fragment', in: *MH* 43, 145–54.
Zimmermann, B. (1992), *Dithyrambos: Geschichte einer Gattung*, Göttingen.
Zimmermann, B. (1993), 'Comedy's Criticism of Music', in: N. W. Slater / B. Zimmermann (eds.), *Intertextualität in der griechisch-römischen Komödie*, Stuttgart, 39–50.
Zimmermann, B. (2002), 'Coro e azione drammatica nei *Sette contro Tebe* di Eschilo', in: A. Aloni / E. Berardi / G. Besso / S. Cecchin (eds.), *I* Sette a Tebe. *Dal mito alla letteratura*. Atti del Seminario Internazionale, Torino 21–22 Febbraio 2001, Bologna, 117–24.
Žižek, S. (2001), *The Fright of Real Tears. Krzysztof Kieslowski between Theory and Post-Theory*, London.

Notes on Contributors

Rosa Andújar is Lecturer and Deputy Director of the new Department of Liberal Arts at King's College London. She has published articles on various aspects of ancient Greek tragedy as well as its modern reception. She is currently completing a monograph which examines the various roles and capabilities of the fifth-century tragic chorus beyond the choral ode, both as a dynamic actor and a versatile physical performer.

Lucia Athanassaki is Professor of Classical Philology at the University of Crete, presently serving a four-year term as Dean of the School of Philosophy (2014–2018). Her research interests focus on melic and dramatic poetry and more recently on Plutarch's works. She is particularly interested in the dialogue with material culture of poetry and now of prose as well. Her publications include ἀείδετο πᾶν τέμενος: οι χορικές παραστάσεις και το κοινό τους στην αρχαϊκή και πρώιμη κλασική περίοδο (Heraklion 2009), *Apolline Politics and Poetics*, edited jointly with Richard P. Martin and John F. Miller (Athens 2009), *Archaic and Classical Choral Song*, edited jointly with Ewen Bowie (Berlin 2011), Ιδιωτικός βίος και δημόσιος λόγος στην ελληνική αρχαιότητα και τον διαφωτισμό, edited jointly with Tasos Nikolaidis and Dimos Spatharas. Among her current projects is *Plutarch's Cities*, which she is editing jointly with Frances B. Titchener, and a monograph on Art, Cult and Politics in Euripidean Drama.

Thomas R.P. Coward is Term Assistant Professor of Classics at George Mason University, VA. His main interests are Greek poetry and music, ancient scholarship, fragmentary literary texts, and difficult and obscure authors. He has several articles on these topics. He is currently preparing a monograph on Pindar and Greek lyric poetry for Oxford University Press. He is also co-editing with Enrico Emmanuele Prodi (Ca Foscari) a volume on Didymus and Greco-Roman learning for BICS. His next project will be on ancient knowledge economies, in particular intellectual life and learning on the island of Rhodes.

Giovanni Fanfani is postdoctoral researcher in the ERC Consolidator Project 'PENELOPE: A Study of Weaving as Technical Mode of Existence', hosted at the Research Institute for the History of Science and Technology, Deutsches Museum, Munich. His current work focuses on textile technology, especially weaving imagery, in Archaic and Classical Greek poetry, and on the contribution of ancient weaving to the development of early Greek mathematics. His research interests include intertextuality in Euripidean tragedy, in particular in *Trojan Women*. He has co-edited the volume *Spinning Fates and the Song of the Loom. The Use of Textiles, Clothing and Cloth Production as metaphor, Symbol and Narrative Device in Greek and Latin Literature* (2016, with Mary Harlow and Marie-Louise Nosch).

P. J. Finglass is Henry Overton Wills Professor of Greek and Head of the Department of Classics and Ancient History at the University of Bristol. He has published editions of Sophocles' *Oedipus the King* (2018), *Ajax* (2011), and *Electra* (2007), of Pindar's *Pythian Eleven* (2007), and of Stesichorus (2014) with Cambridge University Press.

Andrew Ford is the Ewing Professor of Greek Language and Literature and professor of Classics at Princeton University. His work has focused on the history of Greek literary criticism from Homer to Aristotle, most recently exploring the intersections between poetic and critical discourses in the classical period.

Theodora A. Hadjimichael is WIRL Marie Skłodowska-Curie COFUND fellow at the Institute of Advanced Study at the University of Warwick. She has published on the poetics of Bacchylides and on his reception in antiquity, and has forthcoming contributions on the Peripatos and on anecdotography on the lyric poets. Her monograph *The Emergence of the Lyric Canon* is forthcoming with Oxford University Press UK. She is currently working on her project on Plato and Greek Lyric Poetry.

Alexandros Kampakoglou teaches Greek Language and Literature at Trinity College, Oxford. His research concerns Hellenistic poetry; in particular, it focuses on its interaction with archaic lyric poetry and intercultural traditions. He has published papers on the poetry of Theocritus, Callimachus, and Bacchylides. He is currently preparing a monograph on the Reception of Pindar in Ptolemaic court poetry.

Anastasia Lazani is working on her PhD on the Aeschylean chorus at UCL. Her research interests include Greek tragedy and its interaction with lyric and epic poetry; performance and notions of chorality in Greek culture; and ancient perceptions of identity, especially gender and ethnicity.

Timothy Power is an Associate Professor of Classics at Rutgers University. He has published scholarship on music, poetry, and performance in ancient Greece and Rome, and is currently writing a book on sound and listening in early Greek religion.

Enrico Emanuele Prodi is Marie Skłodowska-Curie Fellow at Ca' Foscari University, Venice. His research interests encompass Greek lyric, ancient scholarship on Greek literature, papyrology, and the history of the book in antiquity. After a doctoral dissertation on Pindar's *Prosodia* he is working on ancient scholarship on archaic Greek iambic poetry.

Richard Rawles is Lecturer in Greek at the University of Edinburgh. He is the author of articles on Greek lyric and drama, on Thucydides and on Theocritus, and of the forthcoming book *Simonides the Poet: intertextuality and reception* (Cambridge University Press).

Andrea Rodighiero is Associate Professor of Greek Language and Literature at the University of Verona. He is the author of several articles relating to Greek literature, the Attic drama, and its tradition. His books include commentaries on Sophocles' *Oedipus at Colonus* (1998) and on *Women of Trachis* (2004), *Una serata a Colono: Fortuna del secondo Edipo* (2007), *Generi lirico-corali nella produzione drammatica di Sofocle* (2012), and *La tragedia greca* (2013).

Pavlos Sfyroeras is Professor of Classics at Middlebury College, Vermont. He has published a number of articles on Greek poetry, both dramatic (Aristophanes, Euripides, Sophocles) and lyric (Pindar). In addition to his forthcoming book *The Feast of Poetry: Sacrifice and Performance in Aristophanic Comedy* (Center for Hellenic Studies), he is currently working on a book-length project, tentatively entitled *Pindar and Athens: Epichoric Traditions of Mythmaking*.

Laura Swift is Senior Lecturer in Classical Studies at the Open University. She has published widely on Greek tragedy and early Greek poetry. She is the author of *Euripides: Ion* (Bloomsbury 2008), *The Hidden Chorus: Echoes of Genre in Tragic Lyric* (Oxford University Press 2010), and *Greek Tragedy: Themes and Contexts* (Bloomsbury 2016), and has a commentary on Archilochus forthcoming with Oxford University Press.

Naomi A. Weiss is Assistant Professor in the Department of the Classics at Harvard University. She has published articles on tragedy, Pindar, and ancient Greek musical culture, and is the author of *The Music of Tragedy: Performance and Imagination in Euripidean Theater* (University of California Press, 2018). She is currently co-editing a volume on the genres of archaic and classical Greek lyric poetry, and another on the relationship between music and memory in the ancient Mediterranean.

Index of Proper Names and Subjects

accompaniment, musical 41, 45f., 53, 139f., 270f., 287, 319, 321–324, 327
Achaean 61, 87, 89–92, 98f., 102–104, 106–110, 112, 124, 132, 218, 239, 252, 254, 259, 261
Acharnians 95, 112, 230, 291
Achilles 15, 92, 150, 199, 270, 316, 320f., 327–336
Acropolis 5f., 57, 70, 77, 103, 108, 111, 116, 326
actor 39, 137, 146, 155, 223, 234, 240, 276, 289, 313, 315f., 316, 318, 324, 341, 348, 350, 367, 369–372
Aegean 84, 88, 91f., 96, 111, 147, 227, 309
Aegisthus 129, 132, 196, 203, 214, 266, 283f.
Aegyptos, Aegyptus 226, 232, 234, 236
aeolics 140, 369
Aeschylus 8–9, 25–9, 32–7, 39–64, 119–36, 141, 163, 166–7, 171, 221–38, 282–3, 292, 310, 376
Agamemnon 15, 26, 28, 32f., 35f, 40, 47, 51f., 54f., 55, 58–61, 121f., 124–129, 132–135, 166, 189f., 196, 200f., 208, 243, 282, 321, 328f., 334f.
Agamemnon 9, 39–43, 46–49, 51, 52, 58–61, 109, 112, 122, 132–135, 189, 196
Agathon 214, 346, 372, 380
Agenor 295, 311
agōn, agōnes, ἀγῶνες, athletic 46, 190, 194, 195, 197, 200, 203, 210, 217
agōn, agōnes, ἀγῶνες, dramatic 46, 190, 210, 344f., 380
agora 95
aidōs, αἰδώς 59, 170, 173, 181f.
Ajax 90, 92, 106–110, 155–157, 160–162, 193, 200, 216f., 281, 330,
Ajax 11, 138, 148, 155–157, 160–162, 216f., 265, 281, 346
Alcestis 12, 27, 188, 191, 197, 200, 202
Alcmaeon 211f.
Alcman 12, 41, 48–50, 80, 164, 173–184, 240, 247, 300, 376
Alexandrians 43, 266, 374

Alexandros 12, 123, 187f., 190f., 193, 196, 199, 201–205, 207–209, 211–218
allusion 22f., 71, 80, 95, 98f., 119f., 142, 144, 156, 171f., 182–184, 203, 227, 233, 241, 249, 253, 270, 286, 299f., 310, 320, 335, 344, 354, 358, 362, 364, 374–376, 379
allusiveness 66, 171, 376
altar 55, 71, 78, 82, 93, 109, 115f., 223f., 226, 255, 260, 280, 287, 295, 304, 371
Amphion 35
anapaest(s) 46, 52f., 140, 145, 169, 257, 312, 371
Andromache 12, 89, 188, 190f., 194, 199, 246, 327, 338
animal 26, 40, 52, 124, 169, 229, 336, 347, 354
Antigone 11, 29, 76, 81, 138, 140–142, 144–146, 148, 155, 162, 312, 375, 378
Antiope 346, 351
aoidos, ἀοιδός, bard 4, 45, 148, 244f., 270f., 355,
Aphrodite 101, 106, 180, 195, 232, 236f., 246, 270, 299–305, 323
Apollo, Apolline 3, 5, 9, 33f., 47, 57f., 60f., 88f., 92f., 122–125, 131, 133, 140–142, 144, 150, 154, 156, 158f., 192, 194, 218, 225, 228, 267f., 279, 292, 294–296, 298f., 304, 307, 310f., 323, 325, 327, 338f., 347f., 351–355, 357f., 360, 372f.
appropriation, cultural 190, 241, 251, 261
arc 48, 120, 133
Argive, Argives 52, 59, 88, 91, 125, 196, 224, 227f., 232, 234–238, 252, 288, 295, 324, 331, 333, 335
Argos 14, 29, 52, 55, 126f., 135, 201, 221, 224, 226f., 233, 235–237, 304, 338
Aristonous 299
Aristophanes 9, 12, 20–23, 39, 41f., 44, 88, 95f., 103, 110, 116, 167, 183, 210, 230, 233, 242, 291, 315, 327, 371, 376–378

Index of Proper Names and Subjects

Aristotle 6f., 41, 71, 73, 78, 137f., 207, 223, 228, 275, 277, 309, 315, 317–320, 340, 361, 367, 369–372, 378
Artemis 35, 52, 55f., 58–61, 93, 96, 122, 152, 166, 232, 235f., 259, 262, 279f., 295, 298
Asclepius 143, 150, 299
Asteria 228, 310
astrophic 257, 279, 369
Atalanta 26, 94
Athena 57, 69–71, 75–79, 82, 85, 87, 89–92, 97–99, 101–107, 109–112, 114, 133, 152f., 221, 248, 250, 255, 275, 295, 363
Athenaeus 267f., 270–278, 300, 344
Athenian 1, 5–10, 13, 22, 28, 41, 55, 66f., 69–76, 81–88, 91, 95–97, 102–104, 106–108, 110–116, 125, 130, 133, 135, 138, 145, 164, 171, 183, 185, 187f., 209f., 212–215, 217, 226–228, 233, 267, 286, 295, 298, 308–310, 315f., 343f., 346, 349, 351–353, 360, 362, 368, 375–378, 380
Athens 5, 7–10, 12, 15, 19f., 22, 40, 46, 65–67, 69–77, 81, 84–88, 94–99, 102–104, 106, 108f., 111, 113f., 130, 135, 141, 156, 168, 171, 182–184, 187, 198, 200, 209, 211–213, 227f., 233, 248, 308–310, 316, 319, 343, 345, 347, 353, 357, 359, 377
athlete 75, 120, 135, 188–190, 192, 198, 200f., 204–207, 209, 213–215, 217, 284, 300
athletic 3, 68, 78, 120f., 123f., 127–131, 133–135, 143, 187, 189f., 192, 196, 198, 200f., 203–205, 207–209, 211f., 215, 217, 284, 345, 353, 375
Attic drama 86, 138f., 144, 163f., 187, 308, 343
audience 1f., 5f., 10f., 14, 20, 22–25, 28, 30, 35, 37, 39, 41, 44, 48, 55, 61f., 65–69, 72, 74, 76, 80, 83, 85–89, 95, 97–99, 102, 104–106, 108–112, 115f., 119–123, 125, 127f., 131f., 135–137, 139, 151, 154f., 161, 164–168, 171, 173, 180, 183, 185, 188, 194f., 207, 209, 221–223, 233, 235, 256, 262, 276, 286, 291, 293, 300, 312, 315f., 319f., 322–324, 327–329, 340, 343f., 348–352, 359, 361, 367f., 372, 375, 377–379
aulete, auletic 43–46, 48, 275, 319, 344, 348–351, 353
Aulōidoi 344f.
aulos 42, 45f., 139, 161, 248, 261, 271, 275, 280, 283, 286, 318f., 322f., 327f., 334–336, 344f., 348, 350f., 353f., 363, 365
authenticity 163, 183, 245
authorship 163f., 269

Bacchae 12, 140, 188f., 191, 193, 197, 199, 202f., 209, 213, 279, 292, 312, 316, 320, 340
Bacchic 144, 147, 279f., 353, 362
Bacchylides 8, 10, 49, 52, 54, 58, 87f., 99, 102–104, 106, 111, 114, 189, 240, 242, 248, 250–252, 256, 260, 262, 267, 269, 284f., 309, 357, 377, 379
Bassarids 351
beginning 30, 34, 40f., 47f., 52f., 59, 137–139, 141, 147f., 150–152, 154–157, 159–162, 226f., 242, 245, 251, 261, 273, 294, 306–308, 323, 345, 353, 356
Birds 12, 183, 233, 327
Bollywood 315
book 25, 40, 42, 53, 138, 206, 267f., 272, 274f., 315, 317, 331, 379f.
Bottiaea 228, 309
bridal song 178
bride 147, 172, 205, 304, 324, 327, 332f., 336, 338f.
Broadway 315
Bromius (see also Dionysus) 150, 158, 313

Cadmus 24, 150, 198f., 307f., 323
Calchas 29, 47, 50, 52, 54–56, 58, 60, 121–125
Carians 26
Cassandra 47f., 90, 106f., 203, 208f., 218, 243, 245, 316, 337–339
Castalia 294
cave 170, 297, 333, 347, 349, 354, 356f., 364
celebration 10, 13, 15, 67, 70f., 83, 86, 89, 101, 131, 139f., 143f., 146, 148, 189, 191,

Index of Proper Names and Subjects — **421**

198, 202f., 211, 213f., 259, 283, 320, 324, 326–329, 337
celebratory ode 142
centaur 27, 321, 328f., 332, 336
Cerberus 26, 189
characterisation 14, 34, 40f., 249, 292f., 298, 300, 305f., 313, 317, 338, 361, 375
chariot 65, 81, 129, 134, 143, 170, 196, 210–212, 215, 253, 282, 325
chastity 229f., 338
Chiron 329, 332
Choephori 122, 129, 132f., 166, 282f.
choral 1, 6–9, 11–15, 39–41, 45, 48f., 53, 62, 66, 76, 83, 102, 119, 126, 131, 134, 137f., 140, 143f., 149, 154f., 157f., 161f., 164f., 168, 171, 173f., 178, 185, 221, 223f., 227f., 230, 233, 238–241, 243f., 247, 251, 258–263, 265–269, 271, 275–277, 279, 282f., 285–289, 293, 297f., 305–308, 312f., 315–320, 323–325, 331, 333f., 338, 340f., 347, 353, 356, 362, 364f., 367–372, 374–376
choral lyric 6, 8f., 12, 39, 41f., 48, 66, 76, 119, 169, 173, 182, 240f., 261, 265–267, 288f., 306, 315, 340
choral ode 1, 3, 9, 14, 39, 41f., 48, 53f., 61, 65, 67, 80f., 119, 136, 139f., 153, 155f., 160, 184, 192, 200, 239, 250, 259, 263, 265f., 278f., 281, 284, 297, 304–306, 318, 322, 327, 369, 373f.
choral performance 1, 46, 54, 137, 160, 163, 230, 247, 271, 299f., 302, 304, 310, 315, 325f., 340, 372
choral projection 5, 14, 240, 243, 258, 259f., 263, 297, 320, 376
choral self-referentiality 23, 173, 251, 259f., 265, 283
chorality 12–14, 163f., 173f., 178f., 221–223, 238, 261, 292, 299, 305, 308, 334, 367
chorēgos, χορηγός 171, 172, 325
choreia 15, 240f., 243, 258, 305, 316, 320, 323f., 329f., 336f., 339–341
choreia, Phrygian 257, 259–261
choreographical movement 146
choreography 41, 157, 270, 273, 319, 332, 335f.

choreutai 119, 260, 298
chorus 1–6, 9, 12–15, 20, 22, 32, 39, 42, 47, 51–53, 59f., 65, 76–81, 84, 87–89, 97–99, 104, 109–111, 116, 119, 121–124, 126f., 129f., 133f., 136–140, 142–144, 146, 152–156, 158–161, 163–176, 178–184, 189, 191–194, 198–200, 206f., 212, 215, 221–228, 232–235, 238, 240–247, 249, 251, 257, 259–262, 265–267, 269–277, 279–289, 291–295, 297–300, 304–309, 311–313, 315–325, 327f., 331f., 334–336, 338–341, 344–349, 352f., 357f., 360, 362–364, 367–376, 380
Cimon 10, 96f., 103f., 107, 111, 115f.
circular 152, 260, 262, 269f., 280, 287, 318, 324f., 332, 335
circumstances 10, 30, 65f., 72, 75, 83, 85f., 107, 140, 142, 164, 187, 200, 209, 234, 268, 373
citharode 43, 45f., 247, 345, 351, 358–364
citharodic, citharody (see also *kitharōidia*) 9, 14, 40–48, 50f., 53, 61f., 241–244, 246–249, 251, 254, 262, 344f., 358–360, 362, 364, 375
civic 85, 108, 171, 181, 216, 218, 313, 339, 380
Clement of Alexandria 344
cletic 142f., 158
Clouds 153, 167, 346, 361
Clytemnestra 9, 15, 28, 32–35, 37, 47, 52, 122, 125–130, 134f., 320f., 329, 331, 335
Cnosian 156, 281
collective 84, 110, 173, 209, 214, 227, 240, 297, 312, 372
Colonus 65, 76, 78–83
comedy 22, 27, 146, 171, 183, 308, 343f., 348f., 351, 358, 361, 379
communality 125, 129, 134
community 56, 68, 119, 132–134, 136, 144, 168, 173, 175, 188f., 193, 198, 200f., 203, 212, 214, 218, 313, 377
competition 1, 5, 7, 72, 98, 143, 173, 190f., 195f., 203, 208, 215, 306

composition 31, 36, 39, 51, 67, 71, 75, 83, 104, 147, 151, 247, 262, 265, 269, 273, 276 f., 299, 301, 362, 369, 373
connotation 42 f., 120, 129, 133, 197, 200, 209, 243, 250, 361
Constitution of the Bottiaeans 228, 309
contest 5, 46, 67, 85, 190, 195, 197 f., 201 f., 204, 208, 215, 248, 269, 284 f., 345, 354 f.
context 2, 7 – 10, 12 – 14, 32, 40 f., 43, 47, 54, 66, 70, 72, 74 f., 85 f., 104, 116, 119 – 121, 125, 130, 133, 138 – 140, 142 – 144, 146, 153, 157 f., 161, 171 f., 174, 176 – 180, 184, 195, 201 – 203, 205, 217, 222 f., 230, 234 f., 241 f., 244, 246 – 248, 250, 254, 260, 262, 274, 278, 288 f., 291, 294, 297, 304, 317, 319, 328 – 331, 335 f., 345, 349, 351 f., 361, 363, 367, 369, 371 f., 374 – 376, 380
Corinth 191, 195, 214, 303 f., 316
Coronis 150, 339
Corybantic 156
Craftsmen of Dionysus 310
creatures 101, 164, 168 f., 184, 351
Crete, Cretan 71, 226, 228, 267
cult 1, 60, 70 f., 82, 122, 156 – 158, 182, 200, 262, 275, 298, 305, 310, 367, 371 – 373
cultic 12, 14, 60, 125, 137, 139, 146 – 150, 153, 162, 280, 287, 292 f., 338, 371, 375
Cyclops 358 f.
Cyllene 159, 281, 347, 349, 354 – 357, 359 f., 362, 364
Cypris (see also Aphrodite) 158, 229, 232, 303

dactylo-epitrites 44 – 46, 49, 246, 251, 261, 284, 369
Danaids 13, 221 – 223, 225 – 229, 233 – 238
Danaos, Danaus 222 – 226, 229 f., 234
dance, dancer (s), dancing 4, 7, 13 – 15, 20, 41, 45, 52, 88 f., 101 f., 126, 137 f., 140, 144, 146, 150, 153, 155 f., 158 – 160, 165, 167, 229, 234, 239 f., 245 f., 255, 258 – 261, 265 – 267, 269 – 283, 285 – 289, 291 f., 300, 304 f., 308, 313, 315 f., 319 – 324, 326 – 328, 332, 334 – 336, 338, 340 f., 343 f., 347, 351, 353 f., 357 f., 360, 368, 371
daphnephorikon 181, 222
darkness 80, 126, 130, 142, 166
Daughters of Pelias 27
dedicatory epigram 14, 293, 296, 301 f., 375
Deipnosophistae 272, 274, 277
deixis 298
Delos 4, 91 – 94, 96, 101 f., 111 f., 159, 226 – 228, 271, 283, 299, 308 – 310
Delphi 69, 107 f., 158, 225, 228, 291, 293 f., 296 – 298, 300, 304, 307, 309 – 312
Demes 351
democracy 82, 135, 182, 211, 233
democratic culture 378
Demodocus 249, 270, 276, 355
dialogue (see also exchange) 8, 10, 47, 67, 72, 87, 97, 99, 102, 105 f., 111, 114 f., 127, 161 f., 171, 182, 226, 242, 315, 353, 355,
Dicaeopolis 230, 291
diction 11, 81, 86, 99, 103, 240, 242, 254, 288, 317, 374
Dionysia 5, 109 f., 116, 223, 230, 280, 329, 344, 352, 356 – 358, 362, 375
Dionysiac cultic practice 269
Dionysus 144, 146 f., 150, 153, 156, 193 – 195, 197 f., 203, 210, 280, 284, 297, 305, 325, 330, 351, 358, 363, 375, 379
diplomacy 227
dirge (see also *thrēnos*) 3, 248, 331, 370
dissemination 12, 66, 183, 377
dithyramb, dithyrambic 5 f., 8, 10, 13 f., 88, 101 f., 104, 111, 137, 149, 233, 240, 242 f., 246, 248, 250 f., 253 f., 256, 261 f., 268, 275, 298, 318 f., 340, 344, 351, 357, 359, 361, 363 – 365, 367, 377, 379
dithyrambic 1, 5, 13 – 15, 41, 104, 137 f., 144, 239 – 243, 248 – 254, 256 f., 261 f., 316, 318 – 320, 324, 333 f., 346, 361
dithyrambographers 256
divine 3, 10 – 12, 24, 56, 75, 92, 114, 119, 121, 123, 126, 131, 135 f., 143, 153, 157, 163 f., 166 – 169, 173, 178, 184, 191 – 193, 195, 197 – 199, 207, 226, 256, 268, 270, 297, 299 f., 303, 324, 327 f., 330, 332, 354 f.

divinity 149, 151f., 166, 169, 294, 304, 357
dolphin 101, 169, 319, 334f.
drama 7f., 12f., 15, 27, 41, 43, 54, 71, 136–138, 141, 154f., 161–163, 178, 183, 188, 201f., 211, 221, 225, 233, 238, 240, 248, 277, 282, 285, 315, 317f., 337, 340f., 343, 346, 350–352, 367f., 379f.
dramatic 1, 5–7, 9, 11–13, 15, 26, 34, 39, 41, 43, 53, 65–67, 84, 86, 136, 142, 146, 151, 154, 156f., 164, 168f., 171, 175, 182, 184, 223, 239–241, 249–251, 256, 259f., 262f., 273f., 278f., 283, 292, 297, 299, 305f., 312, 315–321, 324, 329, 332, 335f., 339f., 343f., 348–353, 357, 368, 372f., 376, 380
dramaturgy 167

earthquake 92–96, 116, 378
education 46, 66, 76, 171, 274, 278, 317, 353, 355, 361, 364
Egypt 28, 257, 286
Egyptian 237
ekkyklēma 166
Electra 9, 12, 14, 28, 36, 89, 129, 132, 188–191, 196, 201–203, 207–209, 239, 265f., 282–289, 304, 316, 333, 335f.
elegy 41, 71, 374, 377
ἑλίσσω 269, 280, 319, 324
elite 22, 66, 76, 119, 368, 377f.
emmeleia 273, 278
emotion 31, 90, 156f., 170, 239, 248, 282, 372
emotional impact 368
encomium, *enkōmion*, encomiastic (see also praise) 4, 6, 25, 236, 268
entrance 144, 164–166, 168–170, 173, 181, 222f., 229, 329, 347, 357, 370
envy 187, 190, 192–194, 203, 212, 215f., 374
epic 9, 23, 26, 31, 39f., 42, 46, 48–54, 56, 61f., 112, 125, 139, 148–150, 154f., 160, 162, 205–207, 212, 241, 245, 249, 268–270, 276, 317, 355, 369, 373, 375
epigram 300, 302–304, 377
epiklesis 142, 152
epinician (see also victory ode), *epinikia/on* 3, 11–14, 65–67, 79, 81, 83f., 86, 120f., 125, 127, 133–135, 143, 148f., 187–209, 211–214, 216–218, 260, 266, 277, 283–285, 287, 325, 374f., 379
epiphany 143, 146, 157f., 166
episode 26f., 30f., 45, 69, 104, 145, 161, 190, 227, 243, 259, 293, 298, 310, 369–373
epithalamia/on 180, 304, 327, 329
Erinyes 34, 36, 82, 125, 130f., 133, 135, 167, 169, 245
Eriphyle 9, 26, 49, 50, 54
Erskine *dinos* 326
ethics 131, 375
ethos 41, 66, 94, 155, 209, 362
eulogia 3, 142
Eumenides 34, 49, 82f., 120, 123, 130f., 133, 163, 167f., 310
Euphronius, vase of 105
Eupolis 22, 135, 183, 351, 376–378
Euripidean poetics, late 243
Euripides 1f., 8–10, 12, 14f., 23f., 26–34, 37, 41f., 49, 59, 87–89, 92, 97, 99, 102–106, 108–112, 114–116, 139, 154, 166, 172, 187–191, 193f., 196, 200–206, 208–211, 213–218, 225, 239–243, 245, 247–250, 252–254, 256f., 260, 262f., 265f., 269, 279f., 283–289, 291f., 296, 300, 304, 306, 312f., 315f., 318–324, 327, 333, 337, 340f., 346, 351, 358–360, 372, 375–378
Europa 26
Eustathius 276f.
exchange (see also dialogue) 12, 73, 85, 234, 246, 296, 320, 347, 355, 368
exodos 221, 223f., 227, 229f., 236–238, 277
exordium, exordia 154, 246

fame 148, 192, 200, 203, 205f., 209, 212
family 2f., 24f., 29, 33, 36, 39, 61, 83, 89, 122, 173, 188f., 193, 195, 198, 200–203, 205, 207, 214, 216f., 230, 308
female 12, 126, 163, 168, 170–172, 175f., 178, 180, 184f., 202, 225, 230, 234, 249, 294, 339
festival 1, 5, 7, 61, 67, 71, 96, 102, 104, 137, 144, 228, 250, 287f., 309, 313, 345, 375

focalization 168
Frogs 9, 41–43, 85, 210, 315, 379
funerary games 202, 204, 206, 209

games 27, 44, 49, 68, 72, 119, 134, 189, 200, 203–206, 211, 215–218, 284, 301, 330
Ganymede 322f., 330, 336
gender 170–172, 176, 198f., 234, 249, 378
genealogy 28, 83, 134, 146, 152
generic 2, 7, 10–12, 14, 47, 66, 68, 77, 119f., 122, 128, 131, 136, 142, 145, 154, 158, 160, 162, 172, 188, 192, 233, 240–242, 244, 246, 248f., 253, 259, 262, 301, 320, 344–346, 368, 371, 373, 375f.
genre 1–3, 5–8, 10f., 13–15, 19, 35, 39, 42f., 66f., 119–122, 124f., 127, 133, 135–138, 140, 144, 146, 154f., 161f., 164, 171f., 178, 182, 185, 187–190, 192, 202, 205, 221, 235, 239–242, 244, 246–249, 256, 265–270, 272–279, 282f., 288f., 316–319, 340f., 343, 350f., 365, 367–369, 372–378, 380
genre-imagery 120
Geryoneis 9, 27, 44, 49f., 54
gnome 180, 244f.
gnomic 79, 180, 245f., 251, 372, 374
god 20f., 34, 89–91, 93, 95, 98f., 101f., 106, 109f., 112, 116, 119, 122f., 125–127, 130, 133, 139f., 142–145, 147–154, 156–160, 165, 168, 170, 192f., 197–199, 206f., 223–225, 232–236, 248, 258, 268, 281, 292, 295–299, 305, 311, 321, 325, 328f., 332, 335, 348, 357, 360, 364, 367, 372f., 375
Greece 25, 68f., 73–75, 99, 115, 128, 168, 174, 193, 221, 255, 303, 307, 378
gymnopaidikē 273

hapax legomena 252
harmonia 181f., 243, 248, 260f., 372
healing 120, 122, 125–127, 131, 133, 136, 144, 233
hecatomb 301
Hector 59, 203–205, 208f., 212, 214f., 253, 327, 335

Hecuba 26, 106, 109f., 193, 203, 208f., 213, 215, 218, 243, 246, 257f., 262
Helen 9, 23, 27–29, 37, 49, 54, 67, 109, 124, 286, 292, 304, 330, 373
Hera 33, 102, 113, 150, 166, 191–193, 198, 205, 232, 288, 327
Heracles, Hercules 2–4, 12, 25, 27, 60, 67–69, 71, 73, 75, 77, 149f., 153, 187–194, 197–203, 208f., 218, 323
Heraclidae 240, 260
Hercules Furens 2
herdsmen 204, 213, 216f., 333, 336
Hermes 154, 214, 335, 346–355, 357–360, 362–364
hero 60, 82f., 102, 106, 128, 134, 145, 153–155, 160, 173, 187f., 190, 192, 194, 196, 198, 200–202, 206f., 209, 217, 284, 309, 327, 367, 369, 379
Herodotus 10, 69–74, 77, 92, 94, 96f., 196, 303
hexametric 138, 150f., 247
hexametric tradition 151
Hieron 49, 72, 86, 194, 267
hikesia 227
hiketeia 221, 224, 238
Hippodameia 329
historic, historical 6–8, 10, 19, 36, 43, 66, 73, 86, 108, 140, 183, 204, 213, 227f., 296, 354, 357, 369, 378
Homer 23, 36f., 57f., 61f., 119, 193, 249, 253, 270, 357
Homeric Hymn 311, 346, 348, 351, 353, 355, 357, 362f.
horizon of expectation 10, 66, 76
horse-riding imagery 142
hymenaios, hymeneal 13, 15, 119, 179, 229, 234, 236, 238, 243, 316, 319, 324, 327f., 331, 337–339, 367, 375
hymn, *hymnoi*, hymnic 3f., 6, 12, 14, 41, 45, 49, 51–53, 55, 59, 67, 81f., 136, 138–140, 143f., 146–154, 157–159, 161–163, 174, 189, 192, 207, 232, 235f., 261, 268, 271, 277, 281, 289, 298f., 321, 346, 348, 352, 355, 362f., 367, 373, 379
hyporchēma, hyporchematic 13f., 156, 160, 259, 265–279, 282–284, 287–289, 344, 367

Index of Proper Names and Subjects — 425

hypotext 241f., 249
Hypsipyle 359, 373

iambics, iambic trimeter 49, 161, 251, 285f.
iambo-trochaic 43, 46, 49, 52, 284, 369
Iapygia 228, 309
Ichneutae 15, 343, 345–350, 353, 357–360
Ida, Mount 254, 322f.
identity 1, 7, 12, 39, 69f., 77, 110, 164, 169, 171, 184, 197, 202f., 205, 207, 209, 218, 222, 227, 240, 260, 279, 297, 303, 328, 331, 347, 354f., 375f.
ideology 9, 66f., 71f., 83, 86, 110, 377
Iliad 53, 62, 88f., 151, 154, 166, 196, 205f., 248f., 270–272, 338
Iliou Persis (see also Stesichorus) 9, 49–51, 53f., 57f., 239, 242, 248f., 262
imagery 2, 5f., 11f., 40, 80f., 120f., 123–133, 136, 139, 172, 187f., 190, 192, 194–197, 201, 204, 207, 217, 237, 239f., 242f., 245, 259, 284f., 288, 305, 319, 329, 331, 333, 335f., 340, 356, 360, 364, 377, 380
imagery-pattern 121
immortality 68, 74, 83, 199f.
improvisation 137
in Aeschylus 31f., 40, 47, 50–52, 60f., 119, 166, 189, 221f., 245, 282f., 292, 310, 351
in Alcman 12, 80, 174f., 179, 300
in choral odes 241
in Sophocles 11, 76, 80, 151, 161, 205, 207, 241, 259, 265, 279, 343, 348, 352, 372
in Stesichorus 24f., 27–29, 31–34, 36, 49–51, 54, 56, 58, 61
Inachus 333, 348f., 363
incipit 11, 139, 141, 143, 148, 151, 154, 242, 246, 248
innovation 68, 82, 137, 205, 240, 247f., 250, 319f., 344–346, 359–361, 363, 365
institution 22, 76, 173, 234, 353, 368
instrument 140, 315, 318f., 322f., 327, 343, 347, 349–351, 353, 355, 357–359, 365
instrumental 42, 46, 53, 101, 250, 313, 321–324, 327, 336, 348, 365
integration 200

interaction 8, 10f., 41, 120, 187, 195, 202, 218, 233, 241, 246, 259, 312, 325f., 368
interpretation 11, 47, 50, 54, 57, 70, 75, 120, 136, 152, 188, 191, 199, 201, 204, 206, 209, 211, 224, 237, 249, 278, 297, 300–302, 304, 330, 356, 361
intertext 78, 82, 104, 108, 119
intertextual 10, 67, 140, 182–184, 241f., 249, 253, 256, 346, 377
intertextuality 120, 378
invocation 47, 122, 127, 140–142, 144, 146, 149, 152, 158f., 244, 247, 251, 257, 261, 378
Io 159, 173, 179f., 185, 221, 226f., 233, 236f.
Ion 1, 70, 98, 136, 151, 158, 225, 240, 296, 359, 363
Ionian 74, 93, 101f., 111, 294, 311
Iophon 344–5
Iphigenia 15, 28, 34–36, 52, 89, 280, 304, 315f., 318, 320–322, 326–332, 334–336, 338–341
Iphigenia among the Taurians 242, 254
Iphigenia at Aulis 15, 34, 280
irony 28, 58, 89, 145, 156, 188, 207, 209, 353, 376
Isthmian Games 197
Isthmiastai 345
Italy 19, 114, 147, 228, 309

Jocasta 23f., 29–31, 307f., 312
justice 120f., 123f., 129f., 133, 135f., 226, 233, 286, 368

καινότης 246f., 249, 262
kainotomia 247, 360
kallinikos 189, 195, 285
kephalaion 252f.
kerdos 212
kinship 70, 83, 221, 227f., 308, 312f.
kithara 45f., 271, 283, 311, 321f., 327, 336, 349f., 357–360, 363f.
kitharodes 256
kitharōidia (see also citharodic) 41, 46, 48, 345, 351, 359, 362, 364f.
Kleitias 325
kleos 12, 196f., 205, 212, 216, 374

knowledge   37, 75, 84 f., 127, 168, 185, 193, 211, 225, 312, 351, 356, 368, 373, 376 f.
kommos, kommoi   166, 371
kōmos   4, 357
kordax   273 f., 278
koryphaios (see also chorus leader)   140
krotala   327
kuklioi khoroi, κύκλιοι χοροί (see also circular chorus)   1

Labors of Heracles   191 f.
Laius   294
lament (see also dirge and kommos)   3, 47, 87–89, 107, 129, 179, 192, 242, 244 f., 248, 304, 336 f., 361, 371
leader   91, 103 f., 109 f., 132, 137, 140, 144, 155 f., 160, 198, 213, 222, 257 f., 270, 288, 304, 311
leap, leaping   90, 158, 271, 280–282, 284 f., 334 f.
Leitmotif   120, 375
libation   124 f., 128, 132 f., 322
light   12, 29, 66, 72, 79 f., 83, 86, 108, 121, 126 f., 138, 140 f., 150, 164–166, 174, 199, 201, 205, 213, 216, 218, 237, 250, 253, 266 f., 289, 297, 311, 313, 316, 338, 348, 379
lineage   191, 194, 196 f., 199, 204
Linos-song   47, 270
literary   8, 14, 36, 41, 43 f., 47, 53, 61, 71, 106, 119, 138, 140, 160, 162, 171, 183, 185, 210, 241, 244, 247, 249, 276, 374, 379
Loxias (see also Apollo)   33, 131, 294 f.
Lucian   268, 271 f., 282 f.
Lydian   176
lyre   3, 45, 53, 247, 270, 287, 313, 321, 323, 346–364
lyric   1–3, 5–15, 19 f., 22, 25 f., 35 f., 39, 41–44, 46, 48–50, 52 f., 60–63, 66 f., 86, 119 f., 123–125, 133, 136–140, 142, 144, 146, 148 f., 151 f., 154–157, 159, 161–163, 171 f., 174, 180, 182 f., 187, 239, 241 f., 246, 248–251, 254, 256 f., 261–263, 265, 267 f., 270, 272, 274–277, 282, 288, 291, 293, 301, 305, 315– 319, 325, 340, 347 f., 350, 353–355, 358–363, 367–369, 372–380
lyric-epic, definition of   8 f., 40, 49
lyric poetry   8, 10, 19, 22, 133, 139, 154, 171, 182, 184, 241, 271, 273, 282, 289, 379
Lysistrata   12, 88, 95, 103, 110 f., 115 f., 183

Maenads   198, 279, 351
Maia   150, 335, 347, 349, 354
maiden   4 f., 12, 99, 101, 147, 164 f., 169–173, 175 f., 178–182, 184, 229, 260, 270 f., 292, 296, 300, 304, 319, 327 f., 338 f.
maidenhood   172 f.
makarismos   328
male   125, 174, 181, 202, 234 f., 300
marker   121, 129, 169, 171, 233, 246, 324, 375
marriage   15, 20, 23, 29, 70, 99, 101, 172 f., 179 f., 185, 199, 208, 229, 232–238, 243, 288, 320–323, 325–328, 330, 332, 336–340, 372
Marsyas   241, 354
Melanippides   241, 275
Meleager   26
melopoiia, μελοποιία   6, 317, 319, 369
melos, μέλος, melic   45, 160, 179, 232, 244, 247–249, 251 f., 261, 269, 327, 362, 370
memory   79, 84, 94–96, 139, 253, 291, 312, 358, 378
Menoeceus   292
meta-musical features   15, 375
meta-performative features   15, 375
meta-poetic remarks   375
metre   9, 21 f., 41, 43, 46–53, 60, 139, 161, 261, 284, 369, 373
metrical pattern   50, 160, 254
military victory   119, 140
mimesis   275, 369
molpē   1, 243
monody   243, 246, 257 f., 262, 316, 327
moral stance   121
morality   39, 120, 181, 204
motif   3, 12, 33 f., 40, 58, 81, 120, 125, 129, 132–134, 138, 142, 152, 159, 162, 178, 187, 193, 198 f., 217, 226, 240 f., 243–

245, 254, 257f., 261f., 305, 307, 316, 319f., 328, 339, 341, 363–365
mousikē 7, 13, 15, 240–243, 245, 249, 258, 266, 272, 274, 315–325, 328f., 331–337, 340f., 343, 345, 351, 354, 358
movement 7, 13, 132, 135f., 146, 166f., 260, 266, 270, 273, 275, 277–281, 286f., 321, 324, 332, 335, 345, 354, 375
Mozart 348
murder 47, 52, 59, 61, 109f., 121, 125, 128, 130, 132, 193, 197f., 203, 234, 235, 237, 260, 266, 284, 335
muse, Muses 4, 20f., 148, 150, 154, 158, 185, 242, 244–247, 251, 268, 286, 323–332, 336, 351
music 5, 7, 13, 15, 40f., 43–48, 51, 56, 61, 104, 139, 156, 161, 240–242, 245, 248, 257, 260f., 265, 268–271, 274f., 278, 280, 283, 313, 315–317, 319f., 322, 326f., 332, 335–337, 343–349, 356, 358–360, 362–364, 369, 375
musical 1, 9, 14f., 40–43, 45, 47, 61f., 66, 121, 140, 152, 239–243, 245, 247f., 250f., 253f., 256f., 261–263, 267f., 274, 278, 300, 313, 315–320, 324, 326, 328, 331, 333f., 340, 343–346, 348, 350, 354–358, 360–365, 367f., 373, 376, 378
Mycenean 296
Mysian 156, 281
myth 9, 19, 22, 25–28, 30, 41, 67, 70–72, 74, 106f., 134, 138, 168, 173, 175, 188, 202, 209f., 227f., 234, 241, 249, 262, 291f., 296, 305–307, 309f., 312, 344, 374
mythos 317–319, 331, 333, 340

narrative 9, 11, 13f., 19, 26f., 40f., 45, 48, 51–53, 61f., 67, 71f., 74, 80, 114, 119f., 131, 133, 136, 143f., 146, 153f., 196, 200, 207, 221, 239f., 242f., 246, 248–251, 253–257, 259, 262f., 293, 302, 305f., 308, 313, 316, 318, 324–327, 332f., 335, 341, 343, 363
narrative technique 39–41, 51, 53f., 61, 253, 350

Nereids 88f., 101f., 287, 319, 324, 328f., 331f., 334, 340
New Music, New Musical 1, 13, 15, 241f., 248, 250, 261, 274, 318f., 340, 343, 345–347, 359–365
nikē 145f.
noise 41, 146, 165, 170, 173, 327, 347f., 351f., 354f., 358, 360–362
nomos 9, 14, 40–48, 50, 61, 240, 242, 246, 248, 253f., 262, 267f., 364
non-dramatic 1, 5f., 8, 13, 39, 137–139, 146, 164, 169, 171f., 175, 178, 180, 182, 184, 241, 261, 266, 369
norms 11, 119, 184
nostos 12, 80, 92, 133–135, 200f.

occasion 19, 39, 67, 70f., 81, 85, 126, 138, 140, 172, 179, 185, 228, 282, 292f., 302, 331, 374, 379
Oceanides 163, 167, 169, 172–174, 184
ode 1–3, 5f., 9, 12–15, 40, 48–50, 65–69, 72f., 75f., 80–84, 86f., 99, 120, 141, 143f., 148f., 154, 156f., 160, 187, 192, 195f., 199f., 210–212, 215, 218, 239, 241–246, 248–252, 254f., 259, 262, 266, 277–279, 283–285, 287, 289, 298, 316–318, 320f., 323, 325, 327–329, 331, 333–336, 338, 340, 367–370, 373f., 377, 379
Ode 17 10, 88, 99, 104, 111, 114
Ode 18 102, 104
Odyssey 36, 62, 80f., 202, 249, 270f., 331
Oedipus 29–31, 80–83, 151, 292, 295, 312, 374
Oedipus at Colonus 9f., 65f., 75, 82f., 86, 286, 377
Oedipus Tyrannus 152
offstage 349f.
oikos 166, 170, 173, 188, 190, 203, 215
Oligarchic Coup, 411 BC 82, 86
olive 67–81, 83, 85f., 97, 371
ololugē, ololugmos 126, 128–132
Olympia 9, 49, 65–75, 77, 79, 83, 86, 115, 128, 168, 211, 213, 295, 301, 303
Olympic victor, victory 68, 196, 213
opening 9, 14, 23, 45, 49–51, 80, 88, 101, 126, 138–140, 143, 146, 149–152, 154,

157, 160f., 164, 166, 193, 195, 241f.,
244–251, 253, 256f., 261f., 293, 298,
300, 303, 307f., 310, 321, 335f., 356
opera 315, 348f.
oral 39, 151
orchestra 137, 240, 260, 297, 348f., 353,
369–371
Oresteia 9, 11, 19–22, 27, 32, 35–37,
39–41, 45–51, 53, 61, 119–121, 123,
126, 133, 135f., 166, 284, 375
Orestes 9, 19, 32–34, 36, 121, 129–133,
135, 142, 153, 166, 189–191, 194, 196f.,
201, 203, 207–209, 266, 282–286,
288, 315, 324, 335
Orpheus 247, 351, 356
Orthios nomos 42

paean, *paian(es)* 3, 5, 47, 101, 140f., 143–
146, 149f., 158f., 191f., 227, 267f., 277,
279f., 289, 298–300, 304, 309–311,
327, 373
paeanic 2, 11, 47, 119–122, 124–132, 136,
140, 144, 146, 152, 159, 162, 373–375
paideia 353, 357, 361
Painted Stoa / *Stoa Poikile* 88, 104, 106–
110, 114, 377
Palamedes 12, 92, 188, 202, 210, 212, 218
Palinode 9, 27f., 36f., 49
Pan 154, 156–161, 246, 281
Panathenaia 44, 78, 344f.
Panhellenic 72, 74f., 136, 171
parabasis 371
paraclausithyron 347
parataxis 257
parodos 9, 11f., 39–44, 46–52, 54f., 58,
60–62, 87, 103, 121, 124, 132, 140f.,
143–146, 148f., 152, 155, 159, 161f.,
164, 166f., 169, 171, 174, 177f., 227,
236, 277, 287f., 293, 295f., 298–300,
306–308, 311, 331, 340, 358, 370f.,
373–375
parody 153, 214, 242, 315, 344f., 364, 379
parrhēsia 176
partheneion / *partheneia*, Parthenaic song
1, 8, 12, 95f., 98, 106, 108, 111, 138,
164, 171f., 174f., 177–182, 184f., 222,

234, 236, 238, 240, 259–262, 300, 319,
339, 367, 371
parthenoi 12, 171f., 182, 222, 234, 259f.,
262, 339
pathos 125, 248, 257
Pausanias 50, 58, 68–70, 82, 103–108
Pelasgos 223–227, 238
Peleus 15, 89, 190f., 194, 199f., 320f.,
323–328, 330, 332
performance 1f., 5–7, 11–15, 22, 39–41,
45, 53f., 66f., 70, 72, 74f., 83, 87, 102,
105, 108, 110, 115, 119, 123–125, 128,
132, 137, 140, 146, 154f., 160, 171–173,
176–178, 204, 206, 209, 211, 213f., 221,
227f., 233, 236, 240, 242–244, 246f.,
249f., 260, 266–268, 271, 274, 279,
283–289, 297, 299–302, 304f., 315–320,
322, 324f., 327f., 331, 336–341, 343,
345, 347, 357, 362f., 374f., 378–380
performance-cultur 7f.
performative 3, 7–9, 12, 14f., 40, 47, 54,
138, 152, 158, 161, 172, 223, 242, 247,
258, 261, 266, 343, 370, 375
performer 1, 3, 5, 42, 172, 175–177, 233,
271, 279, 287, 289, 299f., 316, 345, 362,
368, 376
peripeteia 364
Perithoos 329
Persians 69, 72, 88, 98, 111f., 114, 247,
253f., 256, 304
persona 53, 165, 167, 218, 292, 302, 305
Phaedo 226, 309
Phemius 355
Philoctetes 92, 161f., 166, 286
Phoebus (see also Apollo and Loxias) 3, 88,
150, 152, 294f., 297, 311, 332, 338, 373
Phoenician Women/*Phoenissae* 9, 14, 23f.,
29f., 37, 306, 375
Phrygian 21, 45, 88, 156, 240, 243, 248,
255, 258–261, 322f., 330, 335, 338, 346
Phrynis of Mytilene 345, 359
phthonos 134f.
physical movement 157, 266, 280, 289
physicality 165, 175, 182
Pindar 8–12, 33–35, 43, 49, 51f., 54, 58,
60f., 65–79, 81–86, 142, 148, 174, 177,
179, 181, 189, 193–196, 199, 207, 212,

216, 222, 227, 233, 240, 247f., 252, 260, 267, 269f., 281, 284f., 298–305, 309, 322f., 325, 330, 332, 339, 357f., 374, 376–378
Pindaric 3, 11f., 65–68, 75–78, 81–84, 134f., 141–143, 159, 174, 215, 267, 303f., 337, 367, 377
pipe, *lōtos* 4, 259f., 262, 275, 313, 318f., 321f., 328, 348–350, 352f., 358, 361
Plato 47, 213, 226, 261, 268, 274f., 277f., 309, 315, 322, 341, 361–363, 371, 374
Pleiades 287, 335
plot 7, 9, 12f., 19, 65, 89, 103, 108, 131, 173, 175, 182, 184, 187f., 190, 202–204, 208, 215, 217f., 223, 230, 238, 254, 291, 317, 335f., 343, 345f., 350, 369f., 372
Plutarch 32, 84, 107, 209, 213, 215, 228, 267–269, 303, 309, 378f.
poet 1, 5f., 8f., 11f., 19, 21–23, 25f., 29–32, 34–36, 40f., 43, 45f., 67f., 86, 104, 114, 120, 134–136, 139, 142, 145f., 151f., 154, 156, 159, 161f., 171, 173, 175, 178, 182–184, 189, 192, 200, 205f., 212, 248, 254, 256f., 268–270, 304, 317, 319f., 346, 351, 367f., 372–374, 376f., 379
poetic 2f., 6–8, 10f., 14f., 27, 31, 39, 48, 53, 61f., 67, 76, 80, 83–86, 136f., 139, 159, 162–164, 182, 199f., 233, 239–242, 244–253, 256, 261f., 275, 277, 313, 315, 317f., 340, 363–365, 369f., 372f., 378
Poetics 6, 137, 275, 277, 315, 317f., 340, 369f., 372f.
Polion 344f., 349, 359
polis 1, 52, 72, 74, 83, 86, 134, 136, 201, 226, 233
politics 71f., 74f., 114, 135, 209f., 215, 233, 315, 317, 344
Polynices 29f., 293, 298, 306
ponos 195
praise 2–5, 65, 72f., 76, 78, 80f., 83, 85f., 133–135, 146, 148, 152, 181, 188, 191f., 196, 198–200, 205, 207, 211, 217, 223, 232f., 235–237, 258, 267, 305, 323, 347, 357, 374
Pratinas 274–5, 280, 344

prayer 23, 121–123, 125f., 128, 139–143, 149, 151–154, 157, 159, 161f., 223, 232f., 237, 292, 298, 301–304
pre-dramatic poetry 12, 163, 185
Priam 13, 56, 107, 202–204, 207–209, 214, 217f., 256, 258, 330
priamel 153
prize 46, 70, 81, 198, 201f., 232, 358
procession 140, 213, 222f., 230, 235f., 277, 310, 325, 327, 330, 349
processional 14, 49, 131, 140f., 233, 235, 288, 349, 371
Proclus *Chrestomathia* 40, 48, 60, 92, 109, 205–6, 268,
proem 53, 148
professionalism 201
prooimion 242, 246f., 249, 251, 262
prosodion 50, 229, 233, 238, 268, 299, 310
protagonist 97, 165, 238, 287, 312, 339, 372
purification 131, 133
pyrrichē 255

quotation 12, 43, 53, 59, 88, 93–95, 101, 105, 110, 139, 222, 257, 267, 291, 303, 308, 321, 330

re-performance 48, 66, 76, 183, 374, 377
reception 11–13, 66, 82, 182–184, 189, 208f., 213, 224f., 240–242, 298, 301, 374
refrain 41, 43, 47, 61, 74, 82, 121f., 132, 140, 144, 152, 157–159, 233, 246, 257, 299, 338
reintegration 12, 189
relationship 8f., 13, 23, 26–29, 32, 37, 67, 119, 131, 135, 143, 150, 158, 165, 171, 182–184, 209, 211, 218, 222, 227f., 233, 253, 296, 307, 312, 316, 319, 346, 361, 369
religious 7, 61, 82, 126, 132, 136f., 140f., 144, 147, 152, 154, 162, 224, 250, 262, 268, 308, 310, 374
repertoire 1, 66, 162, 201, 274, 367, 376f.
Republic 322
resonance 12, 41, 48, 60, 85, 112, 121, 134, 164, 182, 224

retribution 61, 120
revenge 92, 122, 125, 195–197, 203f., 208
rhapsodic hymn 149, 153
rhetoric 73, 143, 149, 217, 221, 233, 238, 245, 247, 320
Rhodes 78
rhythm 6, 40–46, 50, 60f., 139, 236, 258, 275, 281, 284, 315, 369, 372, 375
ritual 1, 6, 12–14, 47, 68, 119, 121f., 125f., 131f., 137, 140, 144–146, 149, 151f., 157, 159, 162, 171, 175f., 188, 198, 221, 223–226, 230, 233, 235, 238, 241f., 244–246, 248, 257–259, 261f., 279, 288f., 297, 305, 336, 338, 367, 371, 375f.
rural 230

sacrifice 1, 9, 15, 27f., 34–36, 39, 47, 52, 54–56, 58–61, 70, 82, 109f., 121f., 124, 228, 271, 292, 296, 298f., 301, 321, 328, 336, 338f.
salvation 121, 126, 129, 132f., 190, 225, 233, 303
Sappho 178, 234, 235, 244, 323, 327, 338, 356
satyr drama, satyr play 13, 343f., 346, 351, 353, 356, 360
satyr(s) 198, 343–65
sea 10, 80, 88f., 98f., 101f., 104f., 109, 111, 114, 147–149, 153, 156–160, 169f., 229, 257, 281, 294, 311, 331, 333, 335
self-referential 102, 249, 258, 261, 283, 286, 298, 318, 343, 375
self-referentiality 13, 158, 173, 243, 251, 259f., 265, 279, 283, 300
Seven Against Thebes 31, 141, 276, 292, 306
sexuality 172, 229, 234, 237f.
shield of Achilles 270
ship 55f., 84, 90f., 96, 98f., 101, 106, 109, 114, 122, 160, 226, 253–255, 294, 309, 334, 379f.
Sicilian Expedition, the 84
Sicily 10, 25, 46, 67, 73f., 77, 81, 83–87, 114, 209, 286, 294, 311, 377
silence 124, 161, 223, 376
silence on the tragic chorus 6
Silenus 347f., 351, 353, 358, 360f.

Simonides 48, 58, 71, 183, 269, 302–3, 310, 376
skēnē 191, 286, 349f., 364
social 7, 11–13, 119, 173, 187, 202, 204, 206f., 209, 212, 221, 244, 288, 346, 353, 374f.
solo song 53, 364, 370
song 1–15, 19, 21f., 39, 41, 43, 45–49, 52f., 61, 65f., 87, 101f., 105f., 119f., 126, 129, 131, 134, 136–139, 142, 144–149, 151f., 154–157, 159–163, 171–173, 175, 178–185, 192, 200, 221, 223, 227, 229f., 232–241, 243–251, 257–261, 265–273, 275–287, 289, 291f., 294, 298–302, 305–310, 312f., 315–325, 327f., 330–335, 337–341, 343f., 346f., 351, 353–355, 357f., 361f., 364f., 367–380
song-culture 1f., 7, 289, 368
sophia 194
Sophocles 1, 26–8, 32–3, 59, 65–86, 137–62, 187, 196, 200, 203, 205, 207, 216, 241, 245, 259, 265, 279, 286, 318, 343–65, 372, 377
Sparta 57, 85, 95f., 99, 108–110, 113–116, 183, 194, 247, 262, 267f., 272, 304, 349
spectacle 166, 317, 353
spectators 5f., 9, 30, 66, 151, 162, 168, 207, 262, 350f.
speeches 54, 61, 215
Sphinx 253, 292, 313
stability 187, 201, 206, 209
stars 335
stasimon, stasima 2f., 5, 13–15, 65, 76, 78f., 81–83, 89, 97–99, 148, 151f., 154–158, 160f., 192, 227, 239–252, 254–256, 258–262, 265, 277f., 280f., 287, 292, 306–308, 312f., 316, 318, 320, 322f., 328, 331–333, 335f., 339–341, 369–371, 374, 380
stasimon, dithyrambic 242, 250–4
στάσις 222
statues 69, 223–225, 294, 296, 298
status 3, 12–14, 54, 134, 169, 171–173, 175, 182, 192–194, 197–199, 204–207, 209, 218, 222, 225f., 238, 256, 288, 293f., 350, 353, 368, 376

Stesichorus 19–64, 183, 242, 248
strophic 47f., 236, 251, 266, 283, 293, 296–298, 315, 334, 369
sungeneia (see also diplomacy, kinship) 227
supernatural nature 164f., 167
Suppliants 171, 183, 230
supplication (see also *hiketeia*) 193, 195, 224
survival 12, 66, 163, 182f., 201, 204, 218, 330, 377
symbolism 82, 101, 129
symposium 22, 47, 105, 125, 128, 214, 349, 380
synaulia 365
syrinx 320–323, 325f., 333, 336, 348f., 361, 363

Telestes 241, 257, 275–8, 363–4
Terpander 43–6, 50, 246–8, 301
tetrameter 138, 243
Thalassocracy 87
Thamyras 241, 345f., 348, 350f., 360
The Magic Flute 348
theatre 5, 7, 27, 112, 153, 167, 171, 287, 349, 351–353, 369, 371, 376, 378
theatre of Dionysus 39, 166, 350f., 357, 359, 378
theatrical 6, 20, 66, 138, 155, 160–162, 240, 292, 315, 343, 346, 349–352, 377
Thebais 23, 29–32, 54, 58–9, 148
Thebes 30f., 86, 113, 141–145, 147, 150, 191, 198, 279, 291–293, 306–308, 311–313, 378
Theocritus 174, 304
theōria 1, 224–228, 308–310
theoric hymn 367
theory 6, 138, 230, 242, 356
theoxeny 197, 202
Theseus 10, 28, 65, 81f., 87f., 91, 97, 99, 101–106, 111, 114, 198, 226, 228, 308f., 377
Thetis 15, 89, 92, 150, 199f., 320f., 323–330, 332, 334f.
thiasos 329, 336, 357f.
Thrace 71, 228

thrēnos, threnodic 2–3, 47, 65, 79–80, 129, 136, 241–50, 257, 262, 305
Thucydides 94–6, 112–13, 212
Timachidas 42–3, 46
Timotheus 242, 247, 253–8, 261–2, 359–64
Tiresias 24f., 30, 296, 312
Trachiniae 11, 190, 201, 207, 251, 260, 279f.
tragedian 1f., 9–11, 13f., 22, 26–29, 32–34, 36f., 40, 119, 136, 163, 265, 267, 315f., 320, 367, 372
tragedy 1, 5–8, 10, 12–15, 19f., 22f., 25–28, 31–37, 39–42, 46, 48f., 60, 62, 65–67, 75, 80–82, 86, 119, 128, 134, 137f., 144, 149, 156f., 162–167, 171–175, 178f., 182, 184f., 187–191, 198, 206, 210, 214, 217, 223, 233, 240f., 244f., 248–250, 265f., 272, 276–279, 281–283, 285, 288, 305, 307, 310, 312f., 315–320, 322, 328, 336–341, 343–345, 350, 359, 367–371, 373–376, 379
tragic 1–3, 5–8, 10–14, 22f., 25–28, 30–32, 34f., 37, 39, 42f., 46, 48, 50, 54, 61, 65, 67, 76, 86, 107, 119, 128, 134f., 137f., 142, 145, 150–152, 154–156, 163, 165, 170, 173, 179, 184, 187–192, 194, 196–201, 203f., 206, 208–210, 214, 217, 240f., 245, 250, 256, 259f., 262, 265–267, 273, 277–280, 282f., 287, 289, 292, 298, 315, 317–320, 341, 367–370, 373f., 376–380
trilogy (dramatic) 11f., 19, 40, 48f., 51, 53, 61f., 87, 108, 120–122, 125f., 129–132, 135f., 164, 180, 183, 185, 188, 202f., 207–212, 217f., 223, 230, 237f., 375
trimeters (see also iambics) 51, 58, 139, 151, 157, 160f., 243, 354, 367, 373
triumph 101, 104, 111, 114, 123, 128, 130, 133, 136, 145, 218
trochaic 43, 46, 48–51, 243, 370f.
Troilus 330
Trojan War 52, 330f.
Trojan Women/*Troades* 26–7, 87–116, 154–5, 217, 239–63, 373, 377–8
tropos 360

Troy 19, 23, 26, 28, 48, 52, 55f., 58, 88f., 92, 97, 102, 106f., 109, 111, 126, 128, 134, 154, 160, 187, 191, 196, 199, 201, 205f., 208, 213, 215, 217f., 239, 243f., 248–252, 255, 257, 260, 286, 321, 329–331, 333f., 339, 373
tsunami 94, 96
Tyre 293f., 307

ὕμνος, ὕμνοι 139

vengeance 36, 61, 96, 120–124, 127–132, 135
victor 3, 67f., 72, 77–79, 109, 133–135, 187–194, 196–205, 207–209, 213–215, 218, 361
victor 3, 67f., 72, 77–79, 109, 133–135, 187–194, 196–205, 207–209, 213–215, 218, 361
victory 3–5, 10, 65–68, 72, 74–76, 81–83, 96f., 106, 108, 111, 121, 123, 127, 134f., 140, 143–146, 191–193, 195f., 198, 200, 205, 207–209, 211–213, 215f., 218, 243, 255, 279, 284–286, 298, 301, 319, 346, 374–376
violence 11, 87f., 109–112, 120, 123f., 127–131, 136, 142, 189
virginity 229, 235f.

vocal 45, 321, 324, 327
voice 21, 87, 101, 124, 126, 161, 178, 180, 233f., 257, 270, 304, 311, 322, 331, 340, 354–357, 362, 364f.

war 20f., 28, 70–72, 78, 88, 92–95, 99, 103, 109–114, 116, 123–125, 127f., 132, 135, 144, 158, 216, 226, 232, 234f., 237, 275, 297, 312, 372, 376
wealth 73, 85, 92, 147, 190, 194, 211f., 350, 374
wedding (see also *hymenaios*) 12, 15, 21, 71, 89, 101, 119, 172, 174, 178–180, 182, 184f., 199, 208, 234f., 238, 256, 315f., 319–331, 333, 336, 338
wrestling 121, 123f., 127, 129f., 132f.

xenia 224
Xenophon 213
Xenophon of Corinth 300–2

Zephyr 294
Zeus 3f., 24, 47, 51f., 55, 57f., 76–78, 90f., 99, 106, 121–124, 128f., 131–133, 141, 145, 147, 150, 158, 160, 164, 166, 168, 172f., 179f., 185, 191–193, 225f., 232f., 237, 247, 260, 295, 322f., 327
Zeus Hikesios 227

Index Locorum

Acusilaus
– *FGrHist* 2 F30   70

Adespota melica
– fr. 867.3 *PMG* 159 n.77
  = *Pai.* 35.3 Käppel
– fr. 887.2 *PMG*   158 n.73
– fr. 887 *PMG*   158 n.70
– fr. 938e *PMG*   247
– fr. 933.1 *PMG* = *Pai.* 36a.37 – 39 Käppel
  159 n.77
– fr. 934.19 – 23 *PMG* = *Pai.* 37.19 – 23 Käppel   143 n.27

Adespota tragica
– fr. 286 *TrGF*²   207

Aelian   36
– *VH* 9.5   72

Aelius Aristides
– *Or.* 33.2   53

Aeschylus   1, 8f., 13, 25 – 27, 33 – 35, 37, 39 – 44, 46 – 51, 53 – 55, 58 – 62, 71, 109, 120, 128, 131, 133, 135, 139, 141, 163f., 167, 171f., 187, 200f., 210, 221 – 223, 233, 245, 292, 306, 310, 319, 344f., 376
Agamemnon
– *Ag.* 1   42f., 47, 49 – 52, 8 – 60, 63, 133, 251
– *Ag.* 22 – 9   126
– *Ag.* 40 – 54   40 n.6
– *Ag.* 56 – 62   40 n.6
– *Ag.* 60 – 7   40 n.6
– *Ag.* 98 – 9   126
– *Ag.* 104 – 7   251 n.49
– *Ag.* 105 – 59   251
– *Ag.* 106   1f., 2 n.5
– *Ag.* 108 – 24   40 n.6
– *Ag.* 121, 139, 159   132 n.29
– *Ag.* 123 – 59   56
– *Ag.* 146   47, 159 n.70
– *Ag.* 146 – 55   121 – 2

– *Ag.* 160 ff.   139 n.14
– *Ag.* 167 – 75   121
– *Ag.* 218 – 23   59
– *Ag.* 243 – 47   124
– *Ag.* 312 – 4   127
– *Ag.* 341 – 7   127
– *Ag.* 357 – 61   40 n.6
– *Ag.* 362 – 402   124 n.12
– *Ag.* 418   47 n.52
– *Ag.* 510 – 3   125
– *Ag.* 644 – 5   245 n.21
– *Ag.* 706   1 n.3
– *Ag.* 785 – 7   134
– *Ag.* 896 – 903   134
– *Ag.* 928 – 9   244 n.17
– *Ag.* 973   158 n.70
– *Ag.* 979   2 n.5
– *Ag.* 1141   47 n.52
– *Ag.* 1242 – 4   157 n.66
– *Ag.* 1385 – 7   128
– *Ag.* 1472   47 n.52
Atalanta   26
Bassarids   351
Choephori
– *Cho.* 10 – 3   166 n.5
– *Cho.* 24 – 5   177
– *Cho.* 164 – 204   33 n.67
– *Cho.* 167   282
– *Cho.* 236   132
– *Cho.* 244 – 5   132
– *Cho.* 246   158 n.70
– *Cho.* 339   133
– *Cho.* 410 – 1   282 n.55
– *Cho.* 523 – 53   32 n.64
– *Cho.* 578   132
– *Cho.* 719 – 29   160 n.81
– *Cho.* 730 – 82   33 n.68
– *Cho.* 942 – 5   129
– *Cho.* 1022 – 3   130
– *Cho.* 1068 – 76   132
Eumenides
– *Eum.* 9 – 14   310
– *Eum.* 34 – 59   168
– *Eum.* 60 – 3   131

- *Eum.* 179–84   34 n.72
- *Eum.* 307   279
- *Eum.* 328–33   245 n.21
- *Eum.* 329   1f., 2 n.5
- *Eum.* 342   2 n.5
- *Eum.* 589   133
- *Eum.* 759–60   133
- *Eum.* 1035   131
- *Eum.* 1038   131
- *Eum.* 1042   131
- *Eum.* 1043   1, 2 n.5
- *Eum.* 1046   2 n.5
- *Eum.* 1047   2 n.5, 131

Persae
- *Pers.* 447–64   158 n.72
- *Pers.* 448   158 n.73, 281 n.53
- *Pers.* 852–907 49 n.62
- *Pers.* 1038–77   47 n.53
- *Pers.* 1042   1 n.3
- *Pers.* 1056 177

Prometheus Vinctus
- *PV* 128–135   170
- *PV* 278–81   174 n.34
- *PV* 351ff.   183
- *PV* 399–401   177
- *PV* 526–60   49 n.62
- *PV* 555   1 n.3
- *PV* 555–60   179
- *PV* 848–52   173
- *PV* 887–906   49 n.62
- *PV* 894–9   179

Seven Against Thebes
- *Sept.* 90–1   141 n.19
- *Sept.* 391   362 n.63
- *Sept.* 835   2 n.5
- *Sept.* 866–70   245 n.21
- *Sept.* 951–4   47 n.52

Suppliant Women
- *Supp.* 11–13   222
- *Supp.* 11–18   171 n.171
- *Supp.* 12   222
- *Supp.* 16–18   227
- *Supp.* 21–6   128 n.21
- *Supp.* 40–93   49
- *Supp.* 41–55   227
- *Supp.* 57–65   223 n.7
- *Supp.* 57–72   47 n.53
- *Supp.* 69   47
- *Supp.* 69–71   223 n.7
- *Supp.* 70   178 n.43
- *Supp.* 115–6   223 n.7
- *Supp.* 141   227
- *Supp.* 141–3   236
- *Supp.* 151–3   236
- *Supp.* 168–74   227
- *Supp.* 209–21   224–5
- *Supp.* 218   225
- *Supp.* 234   223
- *Supp.* 241–3   224
- *Supp.* 258   79
- *Supp.* 271–85   49 n.62
- *Supp.* 291–315   227
- *Supp.* 340–53   225–6
- *Supp.* 369–75   226
- *Supp.* 455–67   238
- *Supp.* 531–89   227
- *Supp.* 567   282 n.55
- *Supp.* 625–9   223 n.7
- *Supp.* 656–8   223 n.7
- *Supp.* 785   282 n.55
- *Supp.* 808–10   223 n.7
- *Supp.* 996–1009   229
- *Supp.* 1018   232, 233
- *Supp.* 1018–21   236
- *Supp.* 1018–25   223 n.7
- *Supp.* 1018–73   230–31
- *Supp.* 1022   234 n.26
- *Supp.* 1022–9   236
- *Supp.* 1023   1 n.3
- *Supp.* 1023–5   236
- *Supp.* 1025   233
- *Supp.* 1028   233
- *Supp.* 1031f.   236
- *Supp.* 1043   234 n.26
- *Supp.* 1050   236
- *Supp.* 1052–3   236
- *Supp.* 1055   237
- *Supp.* 1062–4   237
- *Supp.* 1064–7   227
- *Supp.* 1067   237
- *Supp.* 1068   237
- *Supp.* 1069–70   237
- A1.30–32 *TrGF*^{3} 167 n.14
- T1.8–12 *TrGF*^{3} 46 n.44

– T88–92b *TrGF*³   46 n.44
– T100–14 *TrGF*³   41 n.11
– T155 *TrGF*³ = Tim. Rhod. fr. 11 Blinkenberg
~ fr. 26 Matijašić   42
– fr. 25a.2 *TrGF*³   25 n.26
– fr. 43 *TrGF*³   47 n.52
– fr. 55 *TrGF*³   128 n.21
– fr. 74 *TrGF*³   27 n.42
– fr. 84 *TrGF*³   42 n.13
– fr. 87 *TrGF*³   42 n.13
– fr. 132 *TrGF*³   42 n.13
– fr. 150 *TrGF*³   169
– fr. 236 *TrGF*³   42 n.13
– fr. 238 *TrGF*³   42 n.13, 43 n.17
– fr. 273 *TrGF*³   42 n.13, 52 n.72
– fr. 282 *TrGF*³   42 n.13
– fr. 387 *TrGF*³   157 n.66

Alcaeus   23, 330
– fr. 42.15–16 Campbell   330–31
– fr. 304.3 L.-P   143 n.26

Alcman   12, 41, 48–50, 80, 164, 173–178, 180–184, 240, 247, 376, 378
– TXIII Calame (p. 227)   48
= Sim. fr. 649 g *PMG*
– fr. 1 *PMGF*   45, 50
= fr. 3 Calame
– fr. 1.16–7 *PMGF*   180
– fr. 1.50 ff *PMGF*   173 n.27
– fr. 1.51–7 *PMGF*   175
– fr. 1.52 *PMGF*   173 n.28
– fr. 1.64–70 *PMGF*   176, 181
– fr. 1.78–9 *PMGF*   175
– fr. 1.85–7 *PMGF*   181
– fr. 1.101 *PMGF*   175
– fr. 3.9–10 *PMGF*   176
– fr. 3.64–70 *PMGF*   176
– fr. 3.71–2 *PMGF*   178
– fr. 10 *PMGF* 54 n.85
= fr. 18 Calame
– fr. 13a.5–7 *PMGF*   184 n.65
– fr. 14 *PMGF*   158 n.70
– fr. 14a *PMGF* 247
= fr. 4 Calame
– fr. 39 *PMGF* 49 n.61
= fr. 91 Calame

– fr. 98 *PMGF*   244 n.20
– fr. 126 *PMGF*   261 n.86
– fr. 241 Calame   49 n.61
= formerly Pind. *Dub.* fr. 345 S-M

Alexander Polyhistor
– *FGrHist* 273 F 77   46 n.43

Anacreon   54
– fr. 14.7 Gentili   142 n.21
= fr. 357.7 *PMG*

Andocides   210, 217
– 1.11–8   214 n.140
– 1.34–45   214 n.140
– 1.129   210 n.121
– 4.16   216 n.145, 217 n.150
– 4.22   210, 216 n.145, 217 n.150
– 4.24   214 n.141, 216 n.145
– 4.29–32   211 n.126

Androtion
– *FGrHist* 324 F 39   78

Apollodorus   92
– *Bibl.* 3.14.1   69
– *Bibl.* 3.14.1–2   70 n.12
– *Bibl.* 3.14.8   47 n.53
– *FGrHist* 244 F 147   78 n.39

Apollonius Rhodius
– *Argon.* 1.211–15   70 n.13
– *Argon.* 4.43   174 n.36

Archilochus   189
– fr. 120 *IEG*   53 n.76
– frr. 172–81 *IEG*   40 n.6
– fr. 177 *IEG*   158 n.70
– fr. 324 *IEG*   189 n.8

Ariphron   159
– *Hymn* to *Hygieia*   159
– fr. 813.2 *PMG*

Aristides Quintilianus   44
– 36.3   44

Aristophanes   9, 12, 20–23, 39, 41 f., 44, 88, 95 f., 103, 110, 116, 167, 183, 210, 230, 233, 242, 291, 315, 327, 371,376–378
– *Ach.* 16   43 f., 43 n.20
– *Ach.* 61–124   112
– *Ach.* 253–6   230
– *Ach.* 442–3   291
– *Ach.* 509–14   95
– *Ach.* 639–40   233 n.25
– *Av.* 212   47 n.53
– *Av.* 250 ff.   183
– *Av.* 851–8   233
– *Av.* 1280   371 n.60
– *Av.* 1372–1409   365 n.70
– *Av.* 1373–1409   242 n.12
– *Eccl.* 1154–7   378
– *Eq.* 8–10   43 n.21
– *Eq.* 504   371 n.6
– *Eq.* 1278–9   44 n.33
– *Lys.* 392–7   84
– *Lys.* 590   84
– *Lys.* 674–79   110
– *Lys.* 1122–35   115
– *Lys.* 1137–46   115
– *Lys.* 1296-end   183
– *Lys.* 1304   174 n.35
– *Nub.* 266   167 n.11
– *Nub.* 277–81   167 n.11
– *Nub.* 289–90   167 n.11
– *Nub.* 297   167 n.11
– *Nub.* 319   167 n.11
– *Nub.* 323   167 n.11
– *Nub.* 569   143 n.26
– *Nub.* 649–51   44 n.32
– *Nub.* 961–99   361 n.58
– *Nub.* 1357   376
– *Nub.* 1367   41 n.12
– *Pax* 735   371 n.6
– *Pax* 775–80   20, 39 n.2, 49 n.62
– *Plut.* 189–92   205 n.94
– *Plut.* 290   350 n.25
– *Ran.* 52–4   379
– *Ran.* 678–82   47 n.51
– *Ran.* 814–29   42 n.14
– *Ran.* 12764   42 n.13
– *Ran.* 1266   42 n.13
– *Ran.* 1273–4   42 n.13
– *Ran.* 1276   42 n.13
– *Ran.* 1281–2   9, 42 n.13
– *Ran.* 1284–5   42 n.13
– *Ran.* 1298–1363   315 n.2
– *Ran.* 1314   315 n.1
– *Ran.* 1425   210
– *Ran.* 1451   210
– *Thesm.* 315   143 n.26
– *Thesm.* 326   158 n.71
– *Thesm.* 953–1000   287 n.66
– *Vesp.* 220   378
– fr. 590 *PCG*[3.2]   183

Aristotle   6 f., 41, 71, 73, 78, 137 f., 207, 223, 228, 275, 277, 309, 315, 317–320, 340, 361, 367, 369–372, 378
– *Ath. Pol.* 60   70, 78
– *De Poet.* F21 Janko   6 n.20
– *Metaph.* 1.1.993b15   6 n.20
– *[Mir. ausc.]* 51.834a   71
– *Poet.* 1447a.14   6 n.20
– *Poet.* 1447a27   275
– *Poet.* 1448a.14–15   6 n.20
– *Poet.* 1448b.25–27   6 n.20
– *Poet.* 1449a9–18   367
– *Poet.* 1449a 10–15   137
– *Poet.* 1449a 15–17   6
– *Poet.* 1449b25–6   370
– *Poet.* 1449b28   369
– *Poet.* 1449b32–4   369
– *Poet.* 1449b33   6 n.20
– *Poet.* 1450a8-b20   317
– *Poet.* 1450a9–10   369
– *Poet.* 1450b15–6   369
– *Poet.* 1452b15–8   370
– *Poet.* 1452b16   6 n.20
– *Poet.* 1452b17–18   277 n.35
– *Poet.* 1452b20–1   371
– *Poet.* 1452b22–5   370
– *Poet.* 1454a30–31   6 n.20
– *Poet.* 1456a25–7   372
– *Poet.* 1456a25–31   317
– *Poet.* 1456a27–32   327
– *Poet.* 1456a28   327
– *Poet.* 1456a30–31   6 n.20
– *Poet.* 1456a36–56b1   372

– *Poet.* 1459a9   41 n.12
– *Poet.* 1462a2 – 4   378
– *Poet.* 1462a15   317 n.6
– *Poet.* 1462a15 – 6   317 n.8
– *Poet.* 1462b16 – 7   369
– *Pol.* 1254b16 – 1255a2   207
– *Pol.* 1339a11 – 1342b35   317 n.9
– *Pol.* 1339a-1342a   361 n.60
– *Pol.* 1339b-1342b   361 n.60
– *Pol.* 1341b24   6
– *Pol.* 1341b40   6 n.20, 317 n.9
– *Pol.* 1342a19 – 24   378
– *Pr.* 19.37 (920b)   42 f.
– *Pr.* 19.48 (922b)   48 n.55
– *Pr.* 19.48 922b26 – 7   372
– *Rh.* 1365a31 – 33   73
– *Rh.* 1400b5 – 8   6 n.20
– *Rh.* 1406b2   41 n.12, 361
– *Rh.* 1409a1 – 3   6 n.20
– *Rh.* 1411a2 – 4   73
– fr. 485 Rose   309
   = Plut. Mor.   298 f-299a

Aristoxenus   346
– fr. 79 Wehrli = *Vita Sophoclis* 23   156

Athenaeus   267 f., 270 – 278, 300, 344
– 1.15d   270, 274
– 1.20e   145 n.35, 278, 345 n.10
– 1.22a   277
– 5.180d-e   53 n.77
– 8.347e   62
– 13.573c-574b   300
– 14.616e   275
– 14.617b   274 f., 344
– 14.617b-f = fr. 708 *PMG*
– 14.618b-c   322 n.21
– 14.620c   1 n.2
– 14.628d   273
– 14.630c-d   273 f.
– 14.630e   278
– 14.631c   267, 273
– 14.631d   278
– 15.692 f-693c   128 n.21
– 15.696b-e   122

Athenagoras   70
– *Leg.* 17   70

Aulus Gellius   43
– *NA* 16.19.14   43 n.20

Bacchylides   8, 10, 49, 52, 54, 58, 87 f., 99,
   102 – 104, 106, 111, 114, 189, 240, 242,
   248, 250 – 252, 256, 260, 262, 267, 269,
   284 f., 309, 357, 377, 379
– 1.181 – 4   3 n.9
– 1.183 – 4   3 n.9
– 3.13 – 4   212 n.129
– 3.36 – 9   54 n.85
– 3.59   68 n.9
– 3.64 – 6   212 n.129
– 3.74 – 82   134 n.33
– 3.76 – 84   54 n.85
– 3.88 – 92   5 n.16
– 5.16 – 33   3 n.9
– 5.50 – 5   134 n.33
– 5.93 – 6   54 n.85
– 5.111 – 13   26 n.35
– 5.136 – 42   54 n.85
– 5.151 – 4   9 n.85
– 5.155 – 62   54 n.85
– 9.88 – 92   134 n.33
– 10.45 – 7   134 n.33
– 11.29   79
– 11.104 – 5   54 n.85
– 12.1 – 3   3 n.8
– 13.84 – 90   284
– 13.94 – 167   200 n.67
– 14.1 – 6   134 n.33
– 14.13   357
– 17   3, 6, 20 f., 23 f., 27, 29, 33, 35 f.,
   39 f., 42 f., 45, 47 – 49, 51 – 56, 58, 71, 76,
   82, 85 – 87, 99, 101, 103, 105, 123, 126,
   132, 134, 137 f., 145, 148, 150, 154, 156,
   160, 164, 167, 171 – 174, 176, 178 f., 181,
   187, 190 – 198, 204 f., 207, 212, 214, 222,
   226 f., 240, 242, 244 – 246, 248, 250 –
   253, 256, 261, 269, 288, 295 f., 299, 304,
   306, 309 f., 315, 317, 322, 327, 344, 346 –
   348, 351, 353 f., 356 f., 360 – 362, 372
– 17.89   250 n.45, 251 n.50
– 17.124 – 9   126 n.17

– 18.51–60   102–3
– 18.54–6   103
– 19.37   251 n.50
– fr. 14 Maehler   267 n.6

Bion
– 1.21   174

Callimachus   106, 174, 271
– *Hymn* 4.282   67
– *Hymn* 4.304–6   271 n.18
– *Hymn* 6.124   174 n.41
– fr. 112.9 Pfeiffer   53 n.80
– fr. 494 Pfeiffer   298 n.18

Catullus
– 62   234f., 331
– 64   331 n.49

CEG (= Hansen, P. A. *Carmina epigraphica graeca saeculorum VIII-V a. Chr. N.* Berlin 1983)   295f., 304
– 193 = 636 Lazzarini   295
– 194 = 679 Lazzarini   304
– 302.1 = 856.1 Lazzarini   295
– 302 = 856 Lazzarini   296
– 363 = 720 Lazzarini   295
– 414.1–2 = 803.1–2 Lazzarini   304
– 422 = 728b Lazzarini   295
– 429.1–2 = Lazzarini 688.1–2   304

Chamaeleon   300–304
– fr. 30 Martano 1 n.2, 45 n.35, 46 n.33
 = fr. 28 Wehrli
On Pindar
– fr. 35 Martano 300–304
 = fr. 31 Wehrli

Clement of Alexandria
– *Strom.* 1.3.24.3 344
 = *TrGF*¹ 22 F 1

Cornelius Nepos   213
– *Alc.* 6   213 n.136
– *Alc.* 6.3   213

Cratinus   5, 82, 183
– fr. 372 *PCG*⁴   5 n.18
– fr. 506 *PCG*⁴   82 n.50

Cypria   34, 55f., 60, 92, 205
– Arg. §8 *GEF*   34 n.74
– fr. 19 Davies   92

Damastes
– *FGrHist* 5 F 1   80

Diodorus Siculus   27, 85
– 4.8.4   27 n.41
– 11.24   72
– 13.75   86 n.60
– 13.81   73 n.23, 85
– 13.86   86

Dionysius of Halicarnassus   361
– *Comp.* 20   58 n.97
– *Dem.* 7   361
– *Dem.* 7.4   41 n.12
– *Dem.* 7.6   41 n.12
– *Imit.* 2.10,   58 n.97

Douris cup (anonymous writer)
– 938e *PMG* 247

Empedocles   181f.
– fr. 40 DK   182 n.55
– fr. 122 DK   181

Ephippus
– frr. 3–5 *PCG*   27 n.40

Epigoni   296
– fr. 3 Bernabé 296
 = 4 West

Eriphyle   9, 26, 49f., 54

Etymologicum Magnum
– 145.34-43 Gaisford   45

Eumelus   50
– 696 *PMG*   50

Eupolis   22, 135, 183, 351, 376–378
– fr. 148 *PCG*⁵   183, 376
– fr. 395 *PCG*⁵   22 n.16
– fr. 398 *PCG*⁵   135, 376, 376 n.16

Euripides   1f., 8–10, 12, 14f., 23f., 26–34, 37, 41f., 49, 59, 87–89, 92, 97, 99, 102–106, 108–112, 114–116, 139, 154, 166, 172, 187–191, 193f., 196, 200–206, 208–211, 213–218, 225, 239–243, 245, 247–250, 252–254, 256f., 260, 262f., 265f., 269, 279f., 283–289, 291f., 296, 300, 304, 306, 312f., 315f., 318–324, 327, 333, 337, 340f., 346, 351, 358–360, 372, 375–378
Alcestis
– *Alc. hypothesis* b.6–7   188 n.5
– *Alc.* 357   2 n.4
– *Alc.* 422–3   245 n.21
– *Alc.* 436–55   2 n.4
– *Alc.* 445–54   46
– *Alc.* 447   356
– *Alc.* 489   194 n.41
– *Alc.* 504   194 n.41
– *Alc.* 837–42   194 n.42
– *Alc.* 1025–35   202
– *Alc.* 1103   190 n.16
– *Alc.* 1136–9   191 n.20
– *Alc.* 1141   190 n.16
Alexandros
– *hypothesis* 15–7   204 n.90
– fr. 42d   204 n.88
– fr. 55 *TrGF*⁵·¹   212
– fr. 56 *TrGF*⁵·¹   216
– fr. 56.1 *TrGF*⁵·¹   216
– fr. 61b   191 n.21, 206 n.102
– fr. 61b.9–10   191, 206
– fr. 61b-c   207 n.106, 212
– fr. 61d.5   205 n.92
– fr. 61d.6–7   202
– fr. 62a.2–4   214–15
– fr. 62a.4   215
– fr. 62b   205, 212
– fr. 62b.30–1   205
– fr. 62b.31   205 n.94
– fr. 62b.33–4   205
– fr. 62c   203 n.82
– fr. 62c.5   203 n.82
– fr. 62d.12   190 n.17
– fr. 62d.22   210 n.19
– fr. 62d.27   202
– fr. 62d.27–8   213
– fr. 62d.50   213 n.134
– fr. **62 g   203, 209
Andromache
– *Andr.* 100–2   244 n.17
– *Andr.* 602–4   23 n.20
– *Andr.* 766–801   191, 195
– *Andr.* 789–801   191
– *Andr* 1173–96   49 n.62
– *Andr* 1231–32   89
– *Andr* 1231–73   200
– *Andr* 1253–8   89
– *Andr* 1259–62   200
– *Andr* 1266–8   89
Antiope
– fr. 179–227 *TGrF*⁵·¹   351
Autolycus
– fr. 282 *TGrF*⁵·¹   201
Bacchae
– *Bacch.* 23–54   197 n.53
– *Bacch.* 26–33   193 n.38
– *Bacch.* 160   322 n.21
– *Bacch.* 219–20   197 n.53
– *Bacch.* 221–5   198
– *Bacch.* 233–38   198
– *Bacch.* 248–54   198
– *Bacch.* 352–4   198
– *Bacch.* 370–1   158 n.70
– *Bacch.* 406   199
– *Bacch.* 453–59   198
– *Bacch.* 466–508   197 n.53
– *Bacch.* 487   198
– *Bacch.* 487–9   198 n.60
– *Bacch.* 584   158 n.70
– *Bacch.* 687   358
– *Bacch.* 857–61   197 n.53
– *Bacch.* 964   190 n.16, 197
– *Bacch.* 971   195 n.46
– *Bacch.* 974–5   197
– *Bacch.* 975   190 n.16
– *Bacch.* 1139–47   198
– *Bacch.* 1145–7   191 n.20
– *Bacch.* 1153–64   191 n.20

– *Bacch.* 1163   190 n.16, 197
– *Bacch.* 1169–71   197 n.57
– *Bacch.* 1172   198
– *Bacch.* 1173–5   197 n.57
– *Bacch.* 1179–84   197 n.57
– *Bacch.* 1195–6   197 n.57
– *Bacch.* 1233–43   198
– *Bacch.* 1234–43   197 n.57
– *Bacch.* 1340–8   197 n.53
– *Bacch.* 1350   200 n.69
– *Bacch.* 1363   200 n.69
– *Bacch.* 1377–8   197 n.53
Cyclops
– *Cycl.* 185–6   23 n.20
– *Cycl.* 443–4   358
Electra
– *El.* 112–66   2 n.4
– *El.* 130–6   190 n.14
– *El.* 167–212   287–8
– *El.* 174   288
– *El.* 178   288
– *El.* 178–9   304
– *El.* 367–90   201 n.74
– *El.* 388–9   201 n.74
– *El.* 388–90   201 n.74
– *El.* 432–41   333–4
– *El.* 432–86   287 n.68
– *El.* 435–6   334
– *El.* 437   334
– *El.* 452–86   334–5
– *El.* 465   335
– *El.* 467   335
– *El.* 476   252
– *El.* 479–86   335
– *El.* 509–29   33 n.67
– *El.* 566–76   59
– *El.* 585–95   190 n.14
– *El.* 614   208
– *El.* 695   190 n.16
– *El.* 699–746   333 n.55, 335 n.59
– *El.* 716   322 n.21
– *El.* 751   190 n.16
– *El.* 854   208 n.113
– *El.* 859–85   203
– *El.* 860–5   284–5
– *El.* 860–79   283–5
– *El.* 861   284

– *El.* 862   208 n.113
– *El.* 862–3   189 n.8
– *El.* 863   284
– *El.* 864–5   189 n.8
– *El.* 865   189 n.8, 287
– *El.* 866–72   285
– *El.* 866–89   191 n.20
– *El.* 870–1   285
– *El.* 872   208 n.113
– *El.* 874   286
– *El.* 874–8   286
– *El.* 875   286
– *El.* 880–2   196
– *El.* 883   201
– *El.* 883–5   196
– *El.* 884   190 n.16
– *El.* 899–915   33 n.67
– *El.* 1020–3   34 n.74
– *El.* 1041–5   28 n.46
– *El.* 1198–9   288 n.72
– *El.* 1280–3   28 n.48, 286 n.65
– *El.* 1334–41   200 n.69
Erectheus
– *Erecht.* fr. 369d *TrGF*$^{5.1}$ 248 n.40
– *Erecht.* fr. 370 *TrGF*$^{5.1}$ 322 n.21
– *Erecht.* fr. 370.5–10 *TrGF*$^{5.1}$ 2 n.5
Hercules Furens
– *HF* 49   188 n.7
– *HF* 116–7   189
– *HF* 145–6   189
– *HF* 153–4   197
– *HF* 180   188 n.7, 189
– *HF* 348–58   2
– *HF* 359–441   3 n.9
– *HF* 494–5   190 n.14
– *HF* 570   188 n.7
– *HF* 575–82   194
– *HF* 582   188 n.7
– *HF* 673–700   4, 191 n.20
– *HF* 676–9   2 n.5
– *HF* 681   188 n.7
– *HF* 683   356
– *HF* 687–700   192
– *HF* 696   191 n.21
– *HF* 761–4   279 n.44
– *HF* 761–821   259 n.81
– *HF* 763–97   279

- HF 772   47 n.48
- HF 789   188 n.7, 190
- HF 825–42   192
- HF 826   192
- HF 839   193
- HF 846–55   192
- HF 958–62   197
- HF 961   188 n.7
- HF 967–71   197 n.56
- HF 981–2   197 n.56
- HF 1046   188 n.7
- HF 1271–80   193
- HF 1308–10   192
- HF 1324–35   200
- HF 1346   2 n.4
- HF 1417–21   200 n.69

Hecuba
- Hec. 85–6   157 n.66

Helen
- Hel. 170–1   322 n.21
- Hel. 375–85   49 n.62
- Hel. 376   253 n.55
- Hel. 1107–11   152 n.50
- Hel. 1280–3   286 n.65
- Hel. 1317–9   250 n.45
- Hel. 1347–8   286 n.65
- Hel. 1362–3   324 n.28
- Hel. 1451–1511   240 n.6

Heraclidae
- Heracl. 609–28   49 n.62
- Heracl. 780   1 n.3
- Heracl. 782–3   260 n.85
- Heracl. 892   161, 322 n.21
- Heracl. 892–927   259 n.81

Hippolytus
- Hipp. 58   235 n.33
- Hipp. 245   177
- Hipp. 1016   190 n.17
- Hipp. 1391–3   166 n.9

Hypsiple
- Hyp. fr. 752f.9–10 $TrGF^{5.2}$ 373
- Hyp. fr. 752 g.9–10 $TrGF^{5.2}$ 248 n.40
- Hyp. fr. 752 h.5–9 $TrGF^{5.2}$ 245 n.22
- Hyp. fr. 752 h $TrGF^{5.2}$ 2 n.4
- Hyp. fr.757.102 $TrGF^{5.2}$ 190 n.17

Iphigeneia in Aulis
- IA 207–208   150 n.46
- IA 435–9   328
- IA 438   322 n.21
- IA 439   328
- IA 576–8   323 n.23, 348 n.18
- IA 676   304
- IA 695–713   329 n.45
- IA 1036   322 n.21
- IA 1036–57   89
- IA 1038   336
- IA 1040   323
- IA 1040–3   332
- IA 1042   174 n.37
- IA 1045   324
- IA 1049–53   323
- IA 1054   324
- IA 1055–7   324
- IA 1058   336
- IA 1058–62   329
- IA 1062–5   332
- IA 1064–5   332
- IA 1068–75   329–30
- IA 1071–2   330
- IA 1076–9   328, 332
- IA 1080   336
- IA 1080–1   336 n.61
- IA 1080–88   332–3
- IA 1085   336
- IA 1085–6   336 n.62
- IA 1201–2   28 n.46
- IA 1291–99   336 n.63
- IA 1466–1531   280
- IA 1477–9   336 n.61
- IA 1480–4   280

Ion
- Ion 125–7   158 n.70
- Ion 139   225 n.12
- Ion 141–3   158 n.70
- Ion 184–218   225
- Ion 310   296
- Ion 452–58   151 n.50
- Ion 1433–6   77 n.34

Iphigeneia in Tauris
- IT 178–85   248 n.40
- IT 407–12   254 n.60
- IT 410   254 n.60
- IT 422–6   254 n.60
- IT 439–46   254 n.60

– *IT* 1101   79
– *IT* 1103–4   324 n.28
– *IT* 1143   304 n.48
– *IT* 1234–83   154
Medea
– *Med.* 44–5   191 n.20
– *Med.* 45   195 n.47
– *Med.* 131 ff.   170 n.19
– *Med.* 235   190 n.16
– *Med.* 282–6   195
– *Med.* 292–302   194
– *Med.* 314–5   192
– *Med.* 366   190 n.16
– *Med.* 366–7   195 n.47
– *Med.* 403   190 n.16, 195 n.47
– *Med.* 404–6   197 n.57
– *Med.* 406   193, 199
– *Med.* 475–87   188
– *Med.* 539–41   194
– *Med.* 545–6   195
– *Med.* 546   215
– *Med.* 557   215
– *Med.* 677   194
– *Med.* 765   195 n.47
– *Med.* 765–6   191 n.20
– *Med.* 912–3   192
– *Med.* 1076–80   191
– *Med.* 1077   191
– *Med.* 1122–3   253 n.59, 254 n.60
– *Med.* 1181–2   204 n.86
– *Med.* 1214–7   204 n.86
– *Med.* 1245   195 n.47, 204 n.86
– *Med.* 1317–1414   195 n.44
Meleager   26
Orestes
– *Or.* 99   23 n.20
– *Or.* 268–9   33
– *Or.* 444   324 n.28
– *Or.* 658–9   28 n.46
– *Or.* 1305   23 n.18
– *Or.* 1305–6   23 n.19
Phaeton
– *Phaet.* 69   47
Phoenician Women
– *Phoen.* 3–5   142 n.23
– *Phoen.* 3–6   308
– *Phoen.* 66–74   30 n.55
– *Phoen.* 69–76   29 n.52
– *Phoen.* 84–5   24
– *Phoen.* 202–25   293
– *Phoen.* 203   294
– *Phoen.* 205   294
– *Phoen.* 208–11   311
– *Phoen.* 214   294
– *Phoen.* 215   294
– *Phoen.* 216   307
– *Phoen.* 216–9   308
– *Phoen.* 219   295
– *Phoen.* 220–1   294
– *Phoen.* 221   294
– *Phoen.* 223–4   294
– *Phoen.* 225   294
– *Phoen.* 226–38   296–7
– *Phoen.* 243–9   308
– *Phoen.* 261–637   29 n.51
– *Phoen.* 280–5 295
– *Phoen.* 291–2   308
– *Phoen.* 391–5   204 n.89
– *Phoen.* 638–42   307
– *Phoen.* 638–89   256, 333
– *Phoen.* 655–7   313
– *Phoen.* 784–817   49 n.62
– *Phoen.* 785   313
– *Phoen.* 786   297 n.15
– *Phoen.* 787   322 n.21
– *Phoen.* 793   253 n.55
– *Phoen.* 808   253 n.55
– *Phoen.* 819   308
– *Phoen.* 1028   313
– *Phoen.* 1033–8   313
– *Phoen.* 1185–6   324 n.28
– *Phoen.* 1302–3   248 n.40
– *Phoen.* 1480–4   312
– *Phoen.* 1703–7   82 n.52
Rhesus
– *Rh.* 924   345 n.7
Trojan Women
– *Tro.* 1–9   88
– *Tro.* 10   250 n.46
– *Tro.* 16–7   252
– *Tro.* 30–1   91
– *Tro.* 65–71   90
– *Tro.* 77–86   90, 92
– *Tro.* 87–97   91f.

- *Tro.* 98–121   246
- *Tro.* 105   246 n.27
- *Tro.* 112–9   246 n.27
- *Tro.* 120–1   245 n.23
- *Tro.* 122–8   257
- *Tro.* 122–52   257
- *Tro.* 128–9   257
- *Tro.* 130   257 n.74
- *Tro.* 138   257 n.74
- *Tro.* 142–5   257 n.74
- *Tro.* 146–52   258
- *Tro.* 151–2   258
- *Tro.* 153 ff.   170 n.19
- *Tro.* 208   104
- *Tro.* 220–3   84 n.56, 209 n.116
- *Tro.* 280   177
- *Tro.* 308–40   243 n.16
- *Tro.* 308–41   337–8
- *Tro.* 353–4   208
- *Tro.* 353–64   243 n.16
- *Tro.* 353–405   243 n.16
- *Tro.* 363   190 n.16
- *Tro.* 384–5   245 n.23
- *Tro.* 426–43   243 n.16
- *Tro.* 444–61   243 n.16
- *Tro.* 508–10   244
- *Tro.* 511   46, 155
- *Tro.* 511–3   244, 246
- *Tro.* 511–4   154
- *Tro.* 511–5   46, 46 n.45, 245 n.23, 248
- *Tro.* 511–67   89, 239, 241, 249, 251
- *Tro.* 513   250 n.44
- *Tro.* 513–4   242
- *Tro.* 515   160 n.81, 249, 251, 261
- *Tro.* 516   252, 253, 253 n.59, 256 n.69
- *Tro.* 516–7   252
- *Tro.* 516–21   251–2
- *Tro.* 517   256 n.69
- *Tro.* 519–21   252, 255
- *Tro.* 529–30   251 n.50
- *Tro.* 530   250 n.46
- *Tro.* 534   254, 254 n.61
- *Tro.* 536   256 n.69
- *Tro.* 537–8   254
- *Tro.* 542–44   240 n.5
- *Tro.* 545–7   258
- *Tro.* 551   251 n.50

- *Tro.* 551–61   256 n.71
- *Tro.* 553   260
- *Tro.* 554   260
- *Tro.* 555–7   256 n.70
- *Tro.* 562–7   255
- *Tro.* 565–6   252
- *Tro.* 577–607   246
- *Tro.* 595–608   49 n.62
- *Tro.* 608–9   245 n.23
- *Tro.* 799–803   97
- *Tro.* 802   79
- *Tro.* 840   158 n.70
- *Tro.* 1093–9   98
- *Tro.* 1100–17   98–9
- *Tro.* 1121   208
- *Tro.* 1209–13   208
- *Tro.* 1242–5   245 n.23

Dramatic Fragments
- fr. 42d   204 n.88

Lyric Fragments
- fr. 755.1 *PMG*   210 n.119
- fr. 755 *PMG*   211 n.124
- fr. 756 *PMG*   211 n.124
- frr. 755–756 *PMG*   187, 211

Eustathius   276 f.
- *ad Il.* 11.11, 13 van der Valk   43
- *ad Od.* 1.296   276 n.33
- *ad Od.* 5.64   5 n.18

FD (= Colin, M.G. *Inscription du tre'sor des Athe'niens*. Fouilles de Delphes. III.2. Paris 1909–1913)   299
192.45   299

Glaucus (epigrammatist)
- *AP* IX.341.5   158 n.70

Glaucus of Rhegium   44
- fr. 1 Gostoli/Lanata = fr. 2 *FHG*   45
- fr. 2 Gostoli/Lanata = fr. 3 *FHG*   44
- fr. 9 Gosotli = fr. 7 Lanata   45
- fr. 10 Gostoli   45 n.33

Hellanicus   80
- *FGrHist* 4 F 187a   80

Heraclides Ponticus
- fr. 109 Schütrumpf   43 n.21
  = fr. 157 Wehrli

Herodotus   10, 69–74, 77, 92, 94, 96 f., 196, 303
- 1.24   43 n.20
- 1.24.5   43 n.21
- 5.67   367
- 5.82   69
- 6.97–8   93
- 6.138   96
- 6.140   96
- 7.166   72
- 7.189   70–71
- 8.14   79
- 8.55   69, 70, 77, 98 n.25
- 8.76   158 n.72

Hesiod   57, 168
- *Catal.* fr. 1   148
- *Op.* 2–3   148
- *Op.* 167–73   68
- *Op.* 345   174
- *Op.* 503–4   74
- *Op.* 568   47
- *Theog.* 1–2   148
- *Theog.* 24–8   163
- *Theog.* 95   45
- *Theog.* 117   80
- *Theog.* 454   174
- *Theog.* 521–4   168
- fr. 1.1–2 M-W   53 n.76
- fr. 23a.17 M-W   61 n.108
- fr. 151.21 M-W   82 n.50
- fr. 278 M-W   56 n.88
- fr. 305.2 M-W   45 n.36
- fr. 357.3 M.-W   150

Hesychius   182, 246, 278
- α 3944 Latte   246 n.29
- α 7851 Latte   70
- θ 300 Latte   47
- τ 1343 Hansen-Cunningham   22 n.16
- *s.v.* ἀμφὶ ἄνακτα   246 n.29
- *s.v.* ἐρασμία   182 n.56

Himerius   25
- *Or.* 22.5 Colonna   45
- *Or.* 60.4 Colonna   43

Hippocrates
- *Aer.* 19   80

Homer   23, 36 f., 57 f., 61 f., 119, 193, 249, 253, 270, 357
- *Il.* 1.1–2   148 n.42
- *Il.* 1.69–105   56 n.89
- *Il.* 2.38–40   40 n.6
- *Il.* 2.299–330   56 n.89
- *Il.* 2.599–600   45 n.36
- *Il.* 4.169   160 n.80
- *Il.* 5.31   158 n.70
- *Il.* 5.485–9   40 n.6
- *Il.* 6.57–60   40 n.6
- *Il.* 6.156   207 n.111
- *Il.* 6.441–43   59 n.101
- *Il.* 6.459   301 n.36
- *Il.* 6.462   301 n.36
- *Il.* 7.87   301 n.36
- *Il.* 7.91   301 n.36
- *Il.* 8.124   160 n.80
- *Il.* 9.543–5   26 n.35
- *Il.* 11.10–11   44 n.25
- *Il.* 12.237–43   56 n.89
- *Il.* 12.322–8   60 n.104
- *Il.* 13.45–70   56 n.89
- *Il.* 13.731   45 n.36
- *Il.* 13.821–23   56 n.89
- *Il.* 14.170–4   166 n.8
- *Il.* 16.428–9   40 n.6
- *Il.* 16.431   40 n.6
- *Il.* 17.83   160 n.80
- *Il.* 18.39–49   182 n.54
- *Il.* 18.50–51   89 n.6
- *Il.* 18.569–72   270
- *Il.* 18.605   271
- *Il.* 20.308   60 n.104
- *Il.* 21.441–60   89
- *Il.* 22.87   150 n.46
- *Il.* 22.452   282 n.55
- *Il.* 23.10 = *Il.* 23.98   245 n.26
- *Il.* 23.653–99   206 n.100
- *Il.* 23.665   206 n.100

- *Il.* 23.733   123 n.10
- *Il.* 24.83–6   89 n.6
- *Il.* 24.324   253 n.59
- *Il.* 24.513   245 n.26
- *Od.* 1.1   148 n.42
- *Od.* 1.159   45 n.36
- *Od.* 2.158–9   58 n.96
- *Od.* 4.102   245 n.26
- *Od.* 4.277   255
- *Od.* 4.561–69   68 n.9
- *Od.* 4.832   53 n.76
- *Od.* 6.18   207 n.111
- *Od.* 6.42–6   68 n.9
- *Od.* 7.34   160 n.80
- *Od.* 8.159–64   212 n.130
- *Od.* 8.262–4   270
- *Od.* 8.263   270
- *Od.* 8.264   276
- *Od.* 8.457   207 n.111
- *Od.* 8.492   53 n.80
- *Od.* 8.515   255
- *Od.* 9.242   253 n.59
- *Od.* 11.212   245 n.26
- *Od.* 11.271–80   29 n.53
- *Od.* 11.604   174 n.37
- *Od.* 14.68–71   40 n.6
- *Od.* 15.165   56 n.89
- *Od.* 15.260–78   56
- *Od.* 16.216–19   40 n.6
- *Od.* 16.235   53 n.76
- *Od.* 17.160   56 n.89
- *Od.* 18.66–109   202
- *Od.* 18.274   160 n.80
- *Od.* 19.213   245 n.26
- *Od.* 19.251   245 n.26
- *Od.* 19.467–75   33 n.70
- *Od.* 19.513   245 n.26
- *Od.* 19.518   47 n.53
- *Od.* 21.57   245 n.26
- *Od.* 21.72–3   202 n.77
- *Od.* 21.106–7   202 n.77
- *Od.* 21.295–304   329 n.43
- *Od.* 21.320–9   206 n.101
- *Od.* 21.330–49   206 n.101
- *Od.* 21.406   45 n.36
- *Od.* 24.58–62   331
- *Od.* 24.60   163 n.1

Homeric Hymns   150–154, 246f., 299
- *Aesc.* 16.1–2   150
- *Ap.* 3.177–8   150 n.46
- *Ap.* 3.188   45 n.36
- *Ap.* 3.194–6   163 n.1
- *Ap.* 3.210   82 n.50
- *Ap.* 3.306–7   150 n.46
- *Ap.* 3.317   150 n.46
- *Ap.* 3.404–43   311
- *Bacch.* 7   246
- *Cer.* 2.216–17   59 n.103
- *Diosc.* 17.1   53 n.76
- *Diosc.* 33   246
- *Hel.* 31.1–3   150 n.46
- *Herc.* 15.1–3   150
- *Jun.* 12.1   150
- *Merc.* 4.1–3   150
- *Merc.* 4.3   150 n.46
- *Merc.* 4.32   363 n.63
- *Merc.* 4.40   363 n.63
- *Merc.* 4.52   363 n.63
- *Merc.* 4.57   174 n.37
- *Merc.* 18.1–3   150
- *Mus. et Ap.* 25.3   45 n.36
- *Pan.* 19   154, 246
- *Pan.* 19.22   158 n.73
- *Poseid.* 22   246
- *Ven.* 5.77   207 n.111
- *Ven.* 5.293   53 n.80
- *Vul.* 20.1   54 n.76

Hyginus
- *Fab.* 45   47 n.53

Ibycus   19, 45
- S151.48 *PMGF*   5 n.16

IG (*Inscriptiones Graecae*) 85, 158f., 299
- *IG* I³ 123 = M-L 92   84
- *IG* I³ 474–476   85 n.57
- *IG* IV² I 130   158 n.73
  = fr. 936.3, 10, 19 *PMG*
- *IG* IV⁴ 128   158 n.70

Ilias parva
- *Il. parv.* fr. 1   148 n.42
- *Il. parv.* fr. 28 Bernabé   248 n.37

Ion of Chios 356
- fr. 32 *IEG*   359 n.53, 363 n.64
- fr. 32.3 *IEG*   356

Iophon 344 f.
- *TrGF*¹ 22 F1   344

Isocrates 216
- 16.5   214, 216
- 16.6 – 7   214 n.140
- 16.25   214 n.141
- 16.25 – 8   211
- 16.28   212, 214 n.141
- 16.29 – 30   211, 216
- 16.32 – 5   211 n.126
- 16.38   216

Lasus of Hermione
- *Hymn. Dem.* 702 PMG   261 n.87

Limenius 310
- 13 – 21   311
- *Pai* 2.6   79 n.40
- *Pai.* 46.5 Käppel   150

Lucian 268, 271 f., 282 f.
- *Erotes* 38   59 n.103
- *Salt.* 16   268 n.7, 271, 282
- *Salt.* 26   274 n.22, 278 n.42
- Ps.-Luc. *Dem. Enc.* 27.8 – 11   145

Lysias 211
- 14.36 – 40   211
- 14.42   214 n.140

Maximus of Tyre
- *Or.* 17.5.15 – 22   43 n.22

Megasthenes
- *FGrHist* 715 F 27b   67 n.9

Nicander
- *Ther.* 680   79 n.40

Nicomachus
- 127 F 3 *TrGF*   27 n.40

Nonnus
- *Dion.* 5.407   174
- *Dion.* 22.72   79 n.40

Nostoi 9, 26 f., 40, 49 – 51, 53 f., 56, 92
- Argumen. §§1 – 5 *GEF*   40 n.6
- 18 – 19 Davies (p.67)   92

Oedipodea
- fr. 1 *GEF*   29 n.53

Orphic Hymns
- 61.5   59 n.103

Ovid
- *Met.* 6.424 – 674   47 n.53
- *Met.* 12.8 – 38   55 n.87

Papyri
- *P. Berol.* 6870 159 n.77
  = *Pai.* 48.1 Käppel
- *P.Mich. inv.* 3498 + 3250b verso and 3250c 254 n.61
- *P. Oxy.* 1174   347 n.15
- *P. Oxy.* 1174 + 2081a 347 n.15
  = fr. 314 *TrGF4*²
- *P. Oxy.* 1176 fr. 39 col. xxii   360 n.54
- *P. Oxy.* 1792   299 n.24
- *P. Oxy.* 2256 fr.3   223 n.6
- *P. Oxy.* 2360   23 n.17
- *P. Oxy.* 2506   32 n.62
- *P. Oxy.* 2635 = *SLG* 460   233
- *P. Oxy.* 2687 col.ii.3   44 n.28
- *P. Oxy.* 2687 col. iii.30-iv.1   44
- *P. Oxy.* 3876   25 n.28
- *P. Oxy.* 2081a   347 n.15

Pausanias   50, 58, 68 – 70, 82, 103 – 108
- 1.15.3   106
- 1.15.4   108
- 1.17.3   105
- 1.19.6   70
- 1.24.5   98 n.25
- 1.26.6   70
- 1.27.2   69, 70
- 1.28.2   103
- 1.30.2   78

– 1.30.4   82
– 4.4.1   50
– 4.33.2   50
– 5.5.7   69 n.10
– 5.7.7   68–69
– 5.14.3   71 n.18
– 5.15.3   69 n.10
– 10.26.3   107 n.46

Pherecrates
Chiron
– fr. 155.14–25 *PCG*   359

Pherecydes   29, 33, 71
– fr. 95 *EGM*   29 n.53
– fr. 134 *EGM*   33
– *FGrHist* 3 F 145   71 n.16

Philochorus   45, 78
– *FGrHist* 328 F 23   45 n.35
– *FGrHist* 328 F 67   70 n.12
– *FGrHist* 328 F 125   78

Philodemus
On Poems
– *De Poet.* 3 fr. 59 Janko   41 n.12
On Music
– *Mus.* 4.135 Delattre   298 n.18

Philostratus
– *VA* 3.17.13–15   145 n.35

Philostratus Junior
– *Im.* 13 145
– (p. 34.19 – p. 35.1–2 Schenkl – Reisch)

Phlegon   71, 79
– *FGrHist* 257 F 1.10–11   71 n.18
– *FGrHist* 257 F 36.442   79 n.40

Photius   5, 268
– α 505 Theodoridis   5 n.18
– α 1303 Theodoridis   44
– α 2835 Theodoridis   44
– *Bibl.* 319b-320a   268 n.9

Pindar   8–12, 33–35, 43, 49, 51f., 54, 58, 60f., 65–79, 81–86, 142, 148, 174, 177, 179, 181, 189, 193–196, 199, 207, 212, 216, 222, 227, 233, 240, 247f., 252, 260, 267, 269f., 281, 284f., 298–305, 309, 322f., 325, 330, 332, 339, 357f., 374, 376–378
Isthmians
– *Isthm.* 1.1–12   3 n.9
– *Isthm.* 1.12   189 n.8
– *Isthm.* 1.14–7   196
– *Isthm.* 1.29   143 n.24
– *Isthm.* 1.42   212 n.128
– *Isthm.* 1.67–8   212 n.130
– *Isthm.* 2.44   377 n.18
– *Isthm.* 3.1–6   134 n.33
– *Isthm.* 3.17–28   134 n.33
– *Isthm.* 4.33–7   134 n.33
– *Isthm.* 4.47   212 n.128
– *Isthm.* 4.55   193 n.37
– *Isthm.* 4.56–60   193 n.37
– *Isthm.* 4.73–8   199 n.62
– *Isthm.* 5.13–6   134 n.33
– *Isthm.* 5.27   322 n.22
– *Isthm.* 5.35–8   199 n.64
– *Isthm.* 5.54   189 n.8
– *Isthm.* 6.1–3   190 n.15
– *Isthm.* 6.10   212 n.128
– *Isthm.* 6.22–5   199 n.64
– *Isthm.* 6.25   199 n.62
– *Isthm.* 6.42–9   54 n.85
– *Isthm.* 6.52–4   54 n.85
– *Isthm.* 7.44–7   193 n.36
– *Isthm.* 8.1–4   213 n.135
– *Isthm.* 8.5–7   3 n.9
– *Isthm.* 8.14–6   134 n.33
– *Isthm.* 8.35a-45   54 n.85
Nemeans
– *Nem.* 1   52 n.71, 65
– *Nem.* 1.7   3 n.9
– *Nem.* 1.20   174
– *Nem.* 1.31–2   212 n.129
– *Nem.* 2.24   189 n.12
– *Nem.* 3   52 n.71, 84
– *Nem.* 3.9–17   3 n.9
– *Nem.* 3.19   189 n.8, 207 n.110
– *Nem.* 3.29   205 n.93

– *Nem.* 3.33–63   200
– *Nem.* 4   52 n.71
– *Nem.* 4.9–13   3 n.9
– *Nem.* 4.15   189 n.8
– *Nem.* 4.21–3   199
– *Nem.* 4.54–70   199
– *Nem.* 4.65–8   199 n.62
– *Nem.* 4.69   199
– *Nem.* 5   3, 284, 332
– *Nem.* 5.1–5   3 n.9
– *Nem.* 5.18–43   323
– *Nem.* 6.1–7   193
– *Nem.* 7.17–8   212 n.130
– *Nem.* 7.25–30   193 n.37
– *Nem.* 7.99   81 n.47
– *Nem.* 8.20–1   248 n.38
– *Nem.* 8.22–34   193 n.37
– *Nem.* 8.24   216
– *Nem.* 8.25   216
– *Nem.* 8.39   205 n.93
– *Nem.* 8.44–55 54 n.85
– *Nem.* 9   213 n.135
– *Nem.* 9.7   377 n.18
– *Nem.* 10.1–4   53 n.76
– *Nem.* 10. 19–22   3 n.9
– *Nem.* 10.23–9   194 n.40
– *Nem.* 10.34   357
– *Nem.* 10.76–9   54 n.85
– *Nem.* 10.80–8   54 n.85
– *Nem.* 11.26   189 n.12
Olympians
– *Ol.* 1.15–7   190 n.15
– *Ol.* 1.30–4   134 n.33
– *Ol.* 1.75–85   54 n.85
– *Ol.* 2.1–6   3 n.9
– *Ol.* 2.42–52   82
– *Ol.* 2.45   8
– *Ol.* 2.53–6   212 n.129
– *Ol.* 2.78   68 n.9, 199
– *Ol.* 3   67, 69, 72, 75, 81, 84
– *Ol.* 3.1–9   3 n.9
– *Ol.* 3.3–4   81
– *Ol.* 3.4–6   248 n.38
– *Ol.* 3.13   69 n.10, 79
– *Ol.* 3.23   68
– *Ol.* 3.31–2   67
– *Ol.* 3.32   68, 77

– *Ol.* 3.34   67 n.8, 74
– *Ol.* 3.37–38   81
– *Ol.* 3.39   82 n.50
– *Ol.* 3.59–62   180 n.49
– *Ol.* 4.1–5   3 n.9
– *Ol.* 4.9   163
– *Ol.* 4.18   191 n.19
– *Ol.* 4.24–7   54 n.85
– *Ol.* 5.1   84 n.56
– *Ol.* 5.8   84 n.56
– *Ol.* 5.15   212 n.128
– *Ol.* 6   3, 284
– *Ol.* 6.16–17, 62–63   54 n.85
– *Ol.* 6.33–6   58
– *Ol.* 6.45   79 n.40
– *Ol.* 7.1–10   3 n.9
– *Ol.* 7.12   322 n.22
– *Ol.* 8   52 n.71
– *Ol.* 8.1–2   191 n.19
– *Ol.* 8.19   207 n.110
– *Ol.* 8.37   79 n.40
– *Ol.* 8.42–6   54 n.85
– *Ol.* 8.47   82 n.50
– *Ol.* 8.69   215 n.143
– *Ol.* 9   52 n.71
– *Ol.* 9.1–4   189 n.8, 213 n.135
– *Ol.* 9.21–7   3 n.9
– *Ol.* 9.48–9   374
– *Ol.* 9.93–4   207 n.110
– *Ol.* 9.103   377 n.18
– *Ol.* 10.1–6   3 n.9
– *Ol.* 10.27–30   180 n.49
– *Ol.* 10.91   5 n.16
– *Ol.* 10.100–5   207 n.110
– *Ol.* 11.8–15   3 n.9
– *Ol.* 13   52 n.71, 301
– *Ol.* 13.11–2   3 n.9
– *Ol.* 13.67–9   54 n.85
– *Ol.* 13.68   81 n.47
– *Ol.* 13.85   81 n.47
– *Ol.* 13.91–2   193 n.36
– *Ol.* 13.100   202 n.79
– *Ol.* 14.1–5   148 n.43
Paeans
– *Pae.* 2.35b, 71, 107 47 n.48
   = D2.35b, 71, 107 Rutherford

– *Pae.* 2.73–75   54 n.85
  = D2.73–5 Rutherford
– *Pae.* 2.99–100   300
  = D2.99–100 Rutherford
– *Pae.* 3.1   126 n.15
– *Pae.* 3.5   126 n.15
– *Pae.* 4.31, 62   47 n.48
  = D4.31, 62 Rutherford
– *Pae.* 4.40–57   54 n.85
  = D4.40–57 Rutherford
– *Pae.* 4 = D4 Rutherford   227 n.17
– *Pae.* 5.1   159 n.77
  = fr. 52e S.-M. = D5 Rutherford
– *Pae.* 5.36–42   227–8
– *Pae.* 5 = D5 Rutherford   298
– *Pae.* 6.127–8   298 n.18
– *Pae.* 6.129   53 n.76
  = D6.129 Rutherford
– *Pae.* 6 = D6 Rutherford   298
– *Pae.* 7c(a).2   126 n.15
– *Pae.* 9.1–7   141
  = fr. 52k.1–7 S.-M. = A1.1–7 Rutherford
– *Pae.* 12.5–8   299
  = G1.5–8 Rutherford
– *Pae.* 12.15   126 n.15
Pythians
– *Pyth.* 1.1   53 n.77
– *Pyth.* 1.32   189 n.8
– *Pyth.* 1.32–3   202 n.79
– *Pyth.* 1.71–80   72 n.21
– *Pyth.* 1.85   194
– *Pyth.* 1.90   212 n.129
– *Pyth.* 1.92–4   3 n.9, 212 n.130
– *Pyth.* 2.1–6   3 n.9
– *Pyth.* 2.53–6   217 n.148
– *Pyth.* 2.127   267 n.7
– *Pyth.* 3.8   82 n.50
– *Pyth.* 3.16–9   339
– *Pyth.* 3.40–2   54 n.85
– *Pyth.* 3.80–3   134 n.33
– *Pyth.* 3.89–90   323
– *Pyth.* 3.92–5   199 n.62
– *Pyth.* 3.110–1   212 n.129
– *Pyth.* 4.2   82 n.50
– *Pyth.* 4.8   81 n.47
– *Pyth.* 4.11   59 n.99
– *Pyth.* 4.13–56   54 n.85

– *Pyth.* 4.87–92   54 n.85
– *Pyth.* 4.97–100   54 n.85
– *Pyth.* 4.102–119   54 n.85
– *Pyth.* 4.138–55   54 n.85
– *Pyth.* 4.156–67   54 n.85
– *Pyth.* 4.184   205 n.95
– *Pyth.* 4.201   58 n.98
– *Pyth.* 4.220–7   195
– *Pyth.* 4.229–31   54 n.85
– *Pyth.* 4.232–46   195
– *Pyth.* 4.249   79 n.40
– *Pyth.* 4.263–9   81 n.47
– *Pyth.* 5   52 n.71
– *Pyth.* 5.75–6   82 n.53
– *Pyth.* 5.106   189 n.8
– *Pyth.* 7.14–8   134 n.33
– *Pyth.* 8.44–55   54 n.85
– *Pyth.* 8.83   189 n.12
– *Pyth.* 8.83–7   215 n.43
– *Pyth.* 9.1–4   3 n.9
– *Pyth.* 9.30–7   54 n.85
– *Pyth.* 9.39–65   54 n.85
– *Pyth.* 9.75   205 n.96
– *Pyth.* 9.79–103   194 n.40
– *Pyth.* 9.92   377 n.18
– *Pyth.* 9.95–6   205 n.93
– *Pyth.* 10.4–7   3 n.9
– *Pyth.* 10.19–29   3 n.9, 134 n.33
– *Pyth.* 10.21–30   193 n.36
– *Pyth.* 10.55–60   207 n.110
– *Pyth.* 11.10–6   196
– *Pyth.* 11.17–8   33 n.69
– *Pyth.* 11.22–3   61 n.108
– *Pyth.* 11.46   189 n.8
– *Pyth.* 12   248
– *Pyth.* 12.19   322 n.22
Fragments
– fr. 6 S-M   174 n.37
– fr. 29 S-M   53 n.76
– fr. 43.1–5 S-M   54 n.85
– fr. 70b S-M   240 n.5
– fr. 76 S-M   81 n.47
– fr. 88 S-M   174 n.37
– fr. 94a.10 S-M   377 n.18
– fr. 94b.6–12 S-M   177
– fr. 94b.14   322 n.21
– fr. 94b.33–5 S-M   181

- fr. 94b 66–70 S-M   222–3
- fr. 94b.70 S-M   174 n.37, n.38
- fr. 95.1. S-M   158 n.70
- fr. 99 S-M   158 n.73, 281 n.53
- fr. 105ab S-M   267
- fr. 107ab S-M   267 n.6, 269, 269 n.13
- fr. 111 S-M   267
- fr. 121.4 S-M   377 n.18
- fr. 122.18–20 S-M   301
- fr. 125 S-M   358 n.49
- fr. 128c S-M   248 n.40
- fr. 166 S-M   329 n.43
- fr. 168b.1–7 S-M   54 n.85
- fr. 172 S-M   199 n.66
- fr. 345 S-M   49 n.61
  = Alcm. fr. 241 Calame

Plato   47, 213, 226, 261, 268, 274f., 277f., 309, 315, 322, 341, 361–363, 371, 374
Alcibiades
- Alc. I 119b5–10   209
Cratylus
- Cr. 417e   45
Gorgias
- Gorg. 501e-502c 361 n.60
Ion
- Ion 530a   2 n.2
- Ion 534c   265 n.1, 268
Laws
- Leg. 665a   173 n.26
- Leg. 669c-e   322 n.22
- Leg. 669c-d   315 n.2
- Leg. 669e   363
- Leg. 700d   315 n.2
- Leg. 700d-e   362 n.63
- Leg. 814e-816d   278
- Leg. 815c   274 n.26
Phaedo
- Phd. 58a-b   309
Phaedrus
- Phdr. 229b-e   70 n.13
- Phdr. 240c   59 n.103
- Phdr. 251a   157 n.67
Republic
- Resp. 397a   315 n.2
- Resp. 398c-d   41 n.10
- Resp. 399d 322 n.22

- Resp. 621d   213 n.134
Symposium
- Symp. 212c3–213b2   214

Pliny
- HN 4.89   67

Plutarch   32, 84, 107, 209, 213, 215, 228, 267–269, 303, 309, 378f.
- Alc. 2.1   215
- Alc. 17.3   84
- Alc. 22   214 n.140
- Alc. 23.3   210
- Alc. 23.3–9   209 n.118
- Alc. 32.3–4   213 n.136
- Cim. 4   107 n.44
- De Sera Num. Vin. 554f-55a   32 n.63
- Mor. 298f-299a   309
- Mor. 615b   128
- Mor. 871b   303
- Nic. 12.1   84
- Nic. 29.4   379
- Quaest. conv. 9.748a-b   269
- Quaest. Lac. 17.238c   46
- Them. 25.1   72
- Thes. 16.2–3 = 868 PMG   228

Pollux   43, 45, 278
- On. 4.65   43, 45
- On. 4.66   45
- On. 4.71   43 n.21, 44 n.25
- On. 4.77   45 n.40
- On. 4.99   278 n.42
- On. 4.103–5   269 n.12
- On. 9.17   70 n.12

Polycrates
- FGrHist 588 fr. 1   349 n.20

Pratinas   274, 280, 344
- fr. 708.6–7 PMG   41 n.10
- fr. 708 PMG   274
  = Ath. 14.617b-f = $TrGF^1$ 4 F3
- fr. 712a-b PMG   344 n.5

Pseudo-Plutarch
- De Mus. 1133c   246 n.30, 358 n.49

– *De Mus.* 1133 f   43 n.23
– *De Mus.* 1134b   267 n.7
– *De Mus.* 1134c-d   268 n.7, n.11
– *De Mus.* 1134d   43 n.21
– *De Mus.* 1140 f   43 f., 43 n.23, 301 n.34
– *De Mus.* 1143a-c   45 n.40

Quintus Smyrnaeus
– 6.61   55 n.87
– 8.475   55 n.87
– 12.1–103   56 n.88
– 12.11–20   57 n.91

Sappho   23, 178, 234 f., 244, 323, 327, 338, 356
– fr. 1.13–24 Voigt   54 n.85
– fr. 1.25 Voigt   142 n.21
– fr. 2.14 Voigt   323 n.25
– fr. 16.6–9 Voigt   23 n.20
– fr. 44   126, 143, 237, 327
– fr. 44.24–27 Campbell   327
– fr. 44.31–3 Voigt   126 n.17
– fr. 44.32–4 Voigt   47 n.46
– fr. 44 A.3 Voigt   143 n.26
– fr. 103 Voigt 178 n.46, 323 n.26
– fr. 103.7–9 Voigt   163 n.1
– fr. 103.13 Voigt   174 n.37
– fr. 104ab Voigt   178 n.46
– fr. 105ac Voigt   178 n.46
– fr. 107–117 Voigt   178 n.46
– fr. 111 Voigt   338
– fr. 118 Voigt   356 n.39
– fr. 135 Voigt   47 n.53
– fr. 144 Voigt   327 n.37
– fr. 150 Voigt   244

Scholia   20 f., 23, 42, 45, 47, 51, 68, 78, 280, 350
– Σ Ar. *Ach.* 16a Wilson   44 n.25
– Σ Ar. *Ach.* 443 Wilson   291
– Σ Ar. *Nub.* 540   278 n.42
– Σ Ar. *Nub.* 651c Holwerda   44 n.32
– Σ Ar. *Nub.* 971a   347 n.11
– Σ Ar. *Nub.* 1005 Holwerda   70
– Σ Ar. *Plut.* 586 Chantry   71 n.17
– Σ Ar. *Ran.* 66–7   316 n.4
– Σ Ar. *Ran.* 1282 Chantry   42 n.15

– Σ Ar. *Vesp.* 122a Koster   22 n.16
– Σ Aesch. *Ag.* 1142ab Smith   47 n.54
– Σ Aesch. *Eum.*1a   168 n.16
– Σ Aesch. *Pers.* 1055 248 n.40
Dähnhardt
– Σ Aesch. *Pers. Hypoth.* 1 45 n.33
Dähnhardt
– Σ Dem. 22.45 Dilts   70
– Σ Eur. *Hec.* 647   287 n.67
– Σ Eur. *Or.* 1384 Schwartz   45 n.39
– Σ Eur. *Phoen.* 202   278 n.40
– Σ Eur. *Phoen.* 1019 Schwartz   292
– Σ Eur. *Phoen.* 1053 Schawartz   292
– Σ Eur. *Tr.* 511 Schwartz   244 n.18
– Σ Pind. *Isth.* 1 *metro.* 51
Drachmann
– Σ Pind. *Isthm.* 6 (iii.251.24 Dr)   128 n.21
– Σ Pind. *Ol.* 3.33 Drachmann   69 n.10, 71 n.17
– Σ Pind. *Ol.* 3.60 Drachmann   68
– Σ Pind. *Ol.* 9.1 Drachmann   53 n.78
– Σ Pind. *Ol.* 12 *metro.* 51
Drachmann
– Σ Pind. *Ol.* 13 Drachmann   303
– Σ Soph. *Ant.* 133   145 n.34
– Σ Soph. *OC* 56 de Marco   78 n.39
– Σ Soph. *OC* 676 de Marco   81
– Σ Soph. *OC* 698 de Marco   78
– Σ Soph. *OC* 701 de Marco   78
– Σ Soph. *OC* 705 de Marco   78 n.39
– Σ Soph. *OC* 1248 de Marco   80
– Σ Soph. *Trach.* 216   280

Simonides   48, 58, 71, 183, 269, 302, 310, 376
– 14 Page = *FGE* 732–5   302
– 519 *PMG* fr. 35b.1–10   310
= fr. 100 Poltera
– 519 fr. 120(b) *PMG*   126 n.15
– 534 *PMG* (not in Poltera),   71 n.16
cf. Sim. 3 *IEG*
– fr. 271 Poltera = fr. 543 *PMG*   54 n.85
– fr. 273 Poltera = fr. 564 *PMG*   53 n.82
– fr. 649 g *PMG*   48 n.57
= Alcm. TXIII Calame (p. 227)

Solon
- fr. 13.32 *IEG*   60 n.104

Sophocles   1, 8–13, 15, 26–28, 32 f., 59, 66–68, 71, 75 f., 78–86, 137–140, 142 f., 145, 147, 149, 151 f., 154, 156–160, 162, 172 f., 187, 196, 200, 203, 205, 216, 245, 259, 265, 286, 318 f., 344–346, 348, 350 f., 354, 357 f., 360, 363 f., 372, 377
Ajax
- *Aj.* 172–93   49 n.61
- *Aj.* 364–372   161 n.84
- *Aj.* 596–599   148
- *Aj.* 600   148
- *Aj.* 641–645   160 n.82
- *Aj.* 693   279
- *Aj.* 693–705   259 n.81
- *Aj.* 693–708   155
- *Aj.* 693–719   265 n.2, 279, 281
- *Aj.* 701   158
- *Aj.* 702–703   143 n.24
- *Aj.* 705   159, 159 n.78
- *Aj.* 710   160 n.80
Antigone
- *Ant.* 100–5   141
- *Ant.* 100–161   140
- *Ant.* 101, 105, 109   143 n.25
- *Ant.* 106–7   141 n.19
- *Ant.* 112, 125, 130   146 n.139
- *Ant.* 131, 134, 139   146 n.39
- *Ant.* 132–3   145
- *Ant.* 136   144
- *Ant.* 141–7   145
- *Ant.* 148–9   143
- *Ant.* 148–54   279
- *Ant.* 152–4   158 n.74
- *Ant.* 153–4   144
- *Ant.* 412   166 n.7
- *Ant.* 530   177
- *Ant.* 582–92   80 n.42
- *Ant.* 588   80 n.42
- *Ant.* 781–2   158
- *Ant.* 781–6   147
- *Ant.* 783–4   178 n.43
- *Ant.* 785   158 n.71
- *Ant.* 997   157 n.66
- *Ant.* 1115–1123   147
- *Ant.* 1115–1154   279
- *Ant.* 1142–52   259 n.81
- *Ant.* 1149   142 n.21
- *Ant.* 1206   43 n.20
- *Ant.* 1307   157 n.66
Cerberus   26, 189
Electra
- *El.* 312–3   170 n.19
- *El.* 388   170 n.19
- *El.* 410–27   32 n.65
- *El.* 476   252
- *El.* 680–763   196
- *El.* 685–7   207 n.112
- *El.* 693–5   196
- *El.* 1407   157 n.66
Ichneutae
- *Ichneutae* 39–40   358 n.49
- *Ichneutae* 54   348
- *Ichneutae* 63   347
- *Ichneutae* 124–6   347
- *Ichneutae* 124–30   360
- *Ichneutae* 127–8   354
- *Ichneutae* 131   354
- *Ichneutae* 133   353
- *Ichneutae* 142–44   352
- *Ichneutae* 143   352
- *Ichneutae* 144   348, 354
- *Ichneutae* 159–60   360
- *Ichneutae* 160   348
- *Ichneutae* 173   353
- *Ichneutae* 176   353
- *Ichneutae* 203   353
- *Ichneutae* 204   348
- *Ichneutae* 217–9   347
- *Ichneutae* 217–20   354
- *Ichneutae* 221–42   354
- *Ichneutae* 222   347
- *Ichneutae* 223   360
- *Ichneutae* 229–30   354, 360
- *Ichneutae* 243–50   354
- *Ichneutae* 248–50   354
- *Ichneutae* 250   355
- *Ichneutae* 251–7   354
- *Ichneutae* 258–61   354
- *Ichneutae* 260   355
- *Ichneutae* 284   355, 359

- *Ichneutae* 289   349
- *Ichneutae* 297   355
- *Ichneutae* 299   349
- *Ichneutae* 300   355
- *Ichneutae* 324   355
- *Ichneutae* 325–8   364
- *Ichneutae* 325–31   362
- *Ichneutae* 327   363
- *Ichneutae* 328   355
- *Ichneutae* 329–31   356
- *Ichneutae* 329a   357 n.43
- *Ichneutae* 332   348
- *Ichneutae* 420   348
- *Ichneutae* 421–3   348
- *Ichneutae* 441–3   358
- *Ichneutae* 443–4   358
- *Ichneutae* 447   362
- *Ichneutae* 452   354
- *Ichneutae* 502   348

Inachus
- fr. 269c.7 *TrGF*⁴   348
- fr. 269c.22 *TrGF*⁴   348
- fr. 269c.27 *TrGF*⁴   348
- fr. 269c.39 *TrGF*⁴   348

Laocoon
- fr. 371 *TrGF*⁴   11, 147

Oedipus at Colonus
- *OC Argum.* II   83
- *OC* 59   82
- *OC* 312–13   81
- *OC* 668–719   65
- *OC* 675–8   79
- *OC* 694–706   76
- *OC* 696   77
- *OC* 697   77
- *OC* 701   77
- *OC* 707   65
- *OC* 707–19   82
- *OC* 720–21   65
- *OC* 888–9   82
- *OC* 1070–73   82
- *OC* 1239–48   79
- *OC* 1299   82
- *OC* 1434   82
- *OC* 1460–61   80
- *OC* 1463–7   80
- *OC* 1477–8   80

- *OC* 1502–4   80
- *OC* 1514–15   80
- *OC* 1556–78   162 n.85
- *OC* 1559   158 n.70
- *OC* 1658–60   80
- *OC* 1709–10   177

Oedipus Tyrannus
- *OT* 68–69   151 n.50
- *OT* 149–50   373
- *OT* 151–215   49 n.62, 162 n.85
- *OT* 153   282 n.55
- *OT* 154   144 n.31, 159 n.77, 373
- *OT* 203–15   144 n.31
- *OT* 275   159 n.78
- *OT* 896   158 n.74, 279 n.44
- *OT* 1086   156 n.64, 279 n.48
- *OT* 1086–1109   279
- *OT* 1096   159 n.77
- *OT* 1306   157 n..66
- *OT* 1524–30   244 n.17

Philoctetes
- *Phil.* 391–5   162 n.85
- *Phil.* 827–32   157 n.70
- *Phil.* 876   166 n.7
- *Phil.* 890–1   166 n.7

Thamyras
- fr. 236–45 *TrGF*⁴   345

Trachiniae
- *Trach.* 94–5   149
- *Trach.* 94–102   149
- *Trach.* 96–7   152
- *Trach.* 99   152
- *Trach.* 101   153
- *Trach.* 102   152
- *Trach.* 103   154
- *Trach.* 205–15   262 n.90
- *Trach.* 205–24   144 n.31
- *Trach.* 205–25   144, 279
- *Trach.* 205–21   259 n.81
- *Trach.* 216–20   158 n.74, 279
- *Trach.* 221   144 n.31
- *Trach.* 309   207 n.112
- *Trach.* 497–502 251 n.49
- *Trach.* 497–530 251
- *Trach.* 504   250 n.45
- *Trach.* 514–5   260 n.84
- *Trach.* 633–62   279

– *Trach.* 1044   157 n.66
Tympanistae
– fr. 636–645 *TrGF*⁴   156 n.65
Testimonia
– T 1.17–19 *TrGF*⁴ 145 n.35
  (*Vita Sophoclis* 3)
– T 1.95–7 *TrGF*⁴ 156 n.65
  (*Vita Sophoclis* 23)
– T 2.6–7 *TrGF*⁴   145 n.35
– T 28.3–4 *TrGF*⁴   145 n.35
– T 73a *TrGF*⁴   145 n.35
– T 73b *TrGF*⁴   145 n.35
– T 174.12–14 *TrGF*⁴   145 n.35
Fragmenta
– fr. 93 *TrGF*⁴   205 n.98
– fr. 242 *TrGF*⁴   46, 49
– fr. 305 *TrGF*⁴   34 n.74
– fr. 861 *TrGF*⁴   42 n.14
– fr. 1133** 51.2 *TrGF*⁴   82 n.50
– fr. 737(a) *PMG*   145 n.35
– fr. 737(b) *PMG*   145 n.35
  = *Pai.* 32 Käppel

Stesichorus   8 f., 19–37, 39–41, 44–49, 51, 53 f., 56–62, 183, 242, 248, 367, 375–377
– Tb1 Ercoles   53 n.82
– Tb2 Ercoles   25 n.30
– Tb3(a) Ercoles   53 n.82
– Tb11 Ercoles   50
– Tb17 Ercoles   49 f.
– Tb20 Ercoles   44 n.33
– Tb39 Ercoles   53 n.82
– Tb42 Ercoles   53 n.82, 58 n.94
– Tb47 Ercoles   58 n.94
Thebais (fr. 97 Finglass = 222b *PMGF*) 9, 23 n.22, 27, 29, 31, 36 f., 49 n.63, 54 n.84, 56, 58 f., 148
– fr. 97.225–30 Finglass 24
  = 222b.225–30 *PMGF*
– fr. 103 Finglass   54, 57 f.,
– fr. 103.30–49 Finglass 59
  = S88 col. ii.3–22 *PMGF*
– fr. 172 Finglass   20
  = 210 *PMGF*
– fr. 173.2 Finglass   45, 261 n.86
  = 212.2 *PMGF*

– fr. 173 Finglass   21
  = 212 *PMGF*
– fr. 174 Finglass   21, 47
  = 211 *PMGF*
– fr. 180 Finglass   54 n.85
  = 219 *PMGF*
– fr. 181ab Finglass   40 n.5
  = 217 *PMGF*
– fr. 181a.25–7 Finglass   34 n.74
  = 217.25–7 *PMGF*
– fr. 181a.11–13 Finglass   33 n.67
  = 217.11–13 *PMGF*
– fr. 181a.14–24 Finglass   33
  = 217.14–24 *PMGF*
– fr. 271 Finglass   244 n.20
  = 232 *PMGF*
– fr. 296 Finglass   53
  = 241 *PMGF*

Stobaeus
– 3.11.19   267 n.6

Strabo   67, 310
– 9.3.12   310
– 15.1.57 Radt   67 n.9

Suda   25, 44 f., 71, 78, 123, 145, 246, 267
– α 575 Adler   44 n.25
– α 1122 Adler   45 n.39
– α 1701 Adler   44 n.24
– σ 815 Adler   145 n.35
– τ 944 Adler 123 n.10
– *s.v.* ἀμφιανακτίζειν (α 1700) Adler   246 n.28
– *s.v.* ἐμμέλεια 278, 278 n.42
– *s.v.* κοτίνου στεφάνῳ (= κ 2161) Adler 71 n.17
– *s.v.* μορίαι (= μ 1248) Adler   78
– *s.v.* Πίνδαρος   267 n.6
– *s.v.* στάσιμον   278 n.40

Telestes   241 n.9, 257 n.75, 275–277, 363
– 805 *PMG*   241 n.9
– 805c *PMG*   363
– 806.3–4 *PMG*   363 n.66
– 808 *PMG*   363

Terpander 43, 46, 50, 246f., 301
- T27 Gostoli 46 n.43
  = Heracl. Pont. fr. 157.10–20 Wehrli
- T34 Gostoli 46 n.43
- T50 Gostoli 46 n.43
- fr. 2 Gostoli = fr. 697 *PMG* 154 n.60, 246, 248 n.29
- frr. 2–3 Gostoli = frr. 697–8 *PMG* 50

Thebais
- fr. 1 *PEG* 148 n.42

Theocritus 304
- *Id.* 1.123–124 158 n.70
- *Id.* 18.3 304
- *Id.* 18.50–53 158 n.70
- *Id.* 24.36 174 n.36

Theognis
- 11–14 58

Theophrastus 274
- *Char.* 6 274 n.22
- *Hist. Plant.* 4.3.3–4 322 n.21
- fr. 126 Wimmer 72

Thucydides 10, 94–96, 112f., 212
- 2.7.1–2 114
- 2.8.1–4 94
- 3.68.1–4 112
- 3.87.4 94
- 3.89.1 95
- 5.116.2–4 113
- 6.12.2 210 n.119, 212 n.127
- 6.15.2 212 n.127
- 6.15.3–4 214 n.141
- 6.16.1 211 n.125
- 6.16.2 211, 215
- 6.16.4 215
- 6.28.1 214 n.140
- 6.76–80 77 n.33
- 7.20.2 286
- 7.32.2 84
- 7.42.1 286
- 8.93–5 85

Timachidas 9, 42f., 46

- fr. 11 Blinkenberg = Aesch. T155 *TrGF^3* ~ fr. 26 Matijašić 42
- fr. 26 Matijašić ~ Aesch. T155 *TrGF^3* = fr. 11 Blinkenberg 42

Timomachus
- *FGrHist* 754 F 1 45 n.36

Timotheus 14, 242, 247, 253f., 256f., 262, 359f., 363f.
- *Pers.* fr. 103 Hord. = 791.103 *PMG* 245 n.26
- *Pers.* fr. 791.4–6 *PMG* 254 n.60
- *Pers.* fr. 791.7–13 *PMG* 254 n.60
- *Pers.* fr. 791.79–81 *PMG* 254 n.60
- *Pers.* fr. 791.126–31 *PMG* 254 n.60
- *Pers.* fr. 791.196–201 *PMG* 145 n.35
- *Pers.* fr. 791.211–2 *PMG* 247 n.35
- *Pers.* fr. 796 *PMG* 247
- *Pers.* fr. 1027 *PMG* 253 n.59

Triphiodorus
- Ἀλ. Ἰλ. 132–72 55 n.87
- Ἀλ. Ἰλ. 247–49 57 n.91

Tyrtaeus 201
- fr. 10.12 *IEG* 60 n.104
- fr. 12.30 *IEG* 60 n.104

Tzetzes 278
- *Trag. Poes.* 97 268 n.11

Vitae
- *Vita Sophoclis* 145 n.35
  / Life of Sophocles 3
- *Vita Sophoclis* 348 n.17
  / Life of Sophocles 4
- *Vita Sophoclis* 345 n.10
  / Life of Sophocles 5
- *Vita Sophoclis* 156 n.65, 346 n.12
  / Life of Sophocles 23

Xanthus 36, 40
- fr. 699–700 *PMG* 40 n.5
- fr. 700 *PMG* 36

Xenophanes 201
– 7 *IEG* 53 n.80

Xenophon 207, 213, 300–302
– *Hell.* 1.4.13 213

– *Mem.* 1.2.24 209 n.117
– *Oec.* 4.2–4 207 n.106
– *Oec.* 6.4–10 207 n.106
– *Symp.* 2.1 128

www.ingramcontent.com/pod-product-compliance
Lightning Source LLC
Chambersburg PA
CBHW071355300426
44114CB00016B/2066